DATE DUE

JUN 0 4 1996	
JUN 25 '01	
6/29/01	
FEB 27 '02	
MAR 20 '02	
GAYLORD	PRINTED IN U.S.A.

JUSTICE
Administration

JUSTICE Administration

Police, Courts, and Corrections Management

Kenneth J. Peak

Department of Criminal Justice
University of Nevada, Reno

Prentice Hall
Englewood Cliffs, New Jersey 07632

Library of Congress Cataloging-in-Publication Data

Peak, Ken, (date)
  Justice Administration : police, courts, and corrections
management / by Kenneth J. Peak.
    p.   cm.
  Includes bibliographical references and index.
  ISBN 0-13-189986-4
  1. Criminal justice, Administration of—United States.   2. Law
enforcement—United States.   3. Prison administration—United
States.   I. Title.
HV9950.P43 1995
364.973—dc20   94-13456
                                                      CIP

Editorial/Production Supervision, Interior Design,
    and Frontmatter Electronic Paging: **Kathryn Pavelec Kasturas**
Text Electronic Paging: **Stephen Hartner**
Cover Design: **Arminé Altiparmakian**
Production Coordinator: **Ed O'Dougherty**
Managing Editor: **Mary Carnis**
Director of Production: **Bruce Johnson**
Acquisitions Editor: **Robin Baliszewski**
Editorial Assistant: **Rose Mary Florio**
Marketing Manager: **Debbie Sunderland**
Text Line Illustrations: **Electra Graphics, Kingsport, Tenn.**
Printing/Binding: **R.R. Donnelley & Sons Co., Harrisonburg, Va.**

 ©1995 by **PRENTICE-HALL, INC.**
A Simon & Schuster Company
Englewood Cliffs, New Jersey 07632

Printed in the United States of America

10 9 8 7 6 5 4 3 2 1

ISBN 0-13-189986-4

Prentice Hall International (UK) Limited, *London*
Prentice Hall of Australia Pty. Limited, *Sydney*
Prentice Hall Canada Inc., *Toronto*
Prentice Hall Hispanoamericana, S.A., *Mexico*
Prentice Hall of India Private Limited, *New Delhi*
Prentice Hall of Japan, Inc., *Tokyo*
Simon & Schuster Asia Pte. Ltd., *Singapore*
Editora Prentice Hall do Brasil, Ltda., *Rio de Janeiro*

Contents

✦ PART III: THE COURTS

✦ PART IV: CORRECTIONS

✦ PART V   SPANNING THE SYSTEM: ADMINISTRATIVE PROBLEMS AND PRACTICES

✦ PART VI CHALLENGES OF THE FUTURE

Preface

The purpose and organization of this book are discussed in Chapter 1. However, I would like to add some prefatory comments here as well. First, it is my belief that while the criminal justice system is currently much maligned in many quarters in our society and may well continue to draw fire for many years to come, it is still the best system in the world. During my quarter-century in the business as a police and corrections practitioner, and administrator, planner, and educator, I have met hundreds of dedicated practitioners, both administrative and rank-and-file, and can still maintain in all sincerity to my students an abiding conviction that this occupation continues to be a special calling. To be sure, criminal justice administration is more challenging today than ever before.

This is a "people business," and this book reflects that fact as it looks at human foibles and some of the problems of personnel and policy in justice administration. However, thanks to many innovators in the field, there are a number of exciting innovations and positive activities that are highlighted in the "what works" sections throughout. The general goal of the book is to inform the reader of the primary *people, concepts,* and *terms* of justice administration; hopefully, the reader will feel that it served that purpose.

There may well be activities, policies, actions, and my own views with which the reader will disagree. That is good, because in the management of people and agencies there are no absolutes, only ideas and endeavors to make the system better. The case studies appearing at the end of each Part of the book are intended to allow the reader to experience some of the kinds of problems confronted daily by justice administrators; with a fundamental knowledge of the system, and a reading of the chapters in the respective book part, readers should be in a position to arrive at several feasible solutions to each problem presented.

I would like to thank several people who assisted in bringing this book to fruition. Robin Baliszewski (Senior Editor) and Kathryn Kasturas (Production Editor) at Prentice Hall, continued their thoroughly professional, helpful manner I have come to know and appreciate in the past. Michael Blankenship (University of Eastern Tennessee) and David Giacopassi (Memphis State University) provided key input during the early stages concerning organization and content.

The following reviewers contributed invaluable assistance to the final product (although any material found wanting is my responsibility alone): James D. Stinchcomb, Miami-Dade Community College; Gordon M. Armstrong; Hal Pepinsky, Indiana University; Roslyn Muraskin, C.W. Post campus, Long Island University; Lawrence F. Travis III, University of Cincinnati; and Eugene H. Czajkoski, Florida State Universtiy.

Case-study materials were contributed by the following educators and practitioners, all of whom I am proud to consider friends and thorough professionals (their titles and affiliations are listed in the text, following their respective case study): Ron Angelone, Ron Glensor, Ted Heim, Richard Kirkland, Matt Leone, Catherine Lowe, Dennis Metrick, Robert Payant, Linda Shepard, and Glen Whorton.

Others graciously rendered various kinds of input and/or materials, which are thoroughly appreciated: Clara Kelly and Marie Case, National Judicial College Law Library, Reno, Nevada; Kriss Winchester, National Center for State Courts, Williamsburg, Virginia; Jim Wenner, Reno, Nevada, Police Department; John Neill, Nevada Department of Prisons; Jim Myers, Chief, Washoe County (Reno), Nevada, Detention Facility; Carlos Concha, Director, and Dorla Salling, Nevada Department of Parole and Probation; and Jeffrey Washington, American Correctional Association. Several criminal justice students assisted with library research and deserve to be acknowledged: Nancy Flores, Nancy Genrich, Dixie Hallenburg, and Kelli Richards.

Finally, as always, I owe a huge debt of gratitude and apologies to my family—Pat, Tiffany, and Jason—for my preoccupation with writing this book. At times (i.e., all hours of the day and night), it surely became intrusive and, at other times, exclusive.

KENNETH J. PEAK
Department of Criminal Justice
University of Nevada, Reno

JUSTICE
Administration

Part I

Justice Administration: an Introduction

This part, consisting of three chapters, sets the stage for our analysis of criminal justice agencies and their successes and challenges in Parts II through V. In Chapter 1 we examine why we study justice administration and its scope. In Chapter 2 we discuss organization and administration in general, looking both at how organizations are managed and how people are motivated. In Chapter 3 we consider several major reformers in justice administration whose contributions and influence are still evident. Specific chapter content is provided within the introductory section of each chapter.

The Study
and Scope
of Justice
Administration

The ordinary administration of criminal and civil justice…contributes, more than any other circumstance, to impressing upon the minds of the people affection, esteem, and reverence towards the government.
—Alexander Hamilton,
The Federalist No. 17

If men were angels, no government would be necessary.
—James Madison,
Federalist No. 51

✦ WHY STUDY JUSTICE ADMINISTRATION?

This book is grounded on the assumption that the reader is an undergraduate or possibly even a graduate student, or an in-service practitioner, with a fundamental knowledge of the history and operations of the police, courts, and corrections subsystems. It is further assumed that whether or not you now possess, or seek to possess, the mantle of leadership, you will one day have thrust upon you greater administrative responsibilities within your organization. To coin a phrase, you may one day be "wearing the gold badge."

It is often difficult for all of us at an early stage in life to imagine ourselves assuming a leadership role. As one person quipped, we may have difficulty envisioning ourselves even becoming captain of our neighborhood block watch. But the fact is that organizations increasingly look to people with higher education and experience as prospective administrators. The college experience, in addition to the transmission of important and sought-after knowledge, is felt to make a person more tolerant and secure, less susceptible to debilitating stress and anxiety. Also, we assume that administration is a science that can be taught; it is not a talent that one must be born with. Unfortunately, administration is an endeavor that is often left to on-the-job training; many of us can attest to that fact by having suffered a poor boss.

✦ PURPOSE OF THE BOOK

The purpose of this book is not to attempt to transform the reader instantly into a bona fide expert in organizational behavior and administrative techniques. It alone cannot and will not prepare anyone to accept the reins of administration, supervision, or leadership; formal education, training, and experience are also necessary for those undertakings.

Many good, basic administration books exist which discuss general aspects of leadership, the use of power and authority, and a number of esoteric subjects that are beyond the reach of this book. Rather, here we simply consider some of the major theories, aspects, and issues of administration, laying the foundation for the reader's future study and experience.

Many textbooks have also been written on police administration; a few have been authored on administering courts and corrections agencies. And even fewer have analyzed justice administration from a *systems* perspective, considering all of the components of the justice system, their administration, issues, and practices. This book contributes to that demand. Further, most existing books on administration are immersed in "pure" administrative theory and esoteric concepts; in doing so, the *practical* criminal justice perspective is often lost on many college and university students. Conversely, many books dwell on minute concepts, thereby obscuring the administrative principles involved. This book, while necessarily delving into some theory and esoteric subject matter, is intended to focus on the practical aspects of justice administration.

This volume is not written as a guidebook for major, sweeping reform of the American justice system. Rather, its primary intent is to familiarize the student with the methods and challenges of criminal justice administrators. However, it also challenges the reader to consider where reform is desirable or even necessary, to be open-minded and able to visualize where changes might be implemented.

Although the terms "administrator," "executive," and "manager" are used synonymously throughout the book, it should be noted that *administration, management,* and *supervision* are unique concepts that occasionally overlap. Administration encompasses both management and supervision. Management is most closely associated with the day-to-day operations of the various elements within the organization. Supervision is direction provided on a one-to-one basis. Confusion may arise because a chief administrator may act in all three capacities. Perhaps the most useful and easiest description is to define top-level personnel as administrators, midlevel personnel as managers, and those who oversee the work as it is being done as supervisors.[1]

✧ ORGANIZATION OF THE BOOK

To understand the challenges of the administrators of justice organizations, we first need to place justice administration within the "big picture." Thus, in Part I, "Justice Administration: An Introduction," we generally discuss organization and administration and the nature of the U.S. justice system; the state of our country with respect to crime and government control; and the evolution of justice administration in all three components: police, courts, and corrections.

Parts II, III, and IV, covering contemporary police, courts, and corrections administration, respectively, all follow the same organization: The first chapter of each part deals with the organization and operation of the component, followed in the second chapter by an examination of the component's personnel roles and functions, and in the third chapter, a discussion of issues and practices; within each of the latter chapters is a section on "what works" within each component—programs and practices that have been attempted and appear to have been successful.

In Part V we look at administrative problems and factors that span and influence the entire system, including rights of criminal justice employees, labor relations, civil liability, AIDS, accountability, the future, and financial administration.

The book concludes with Part VI, a view of how administrators can predict the future and some of the changes and challenges that await them.

Parts II, III, and IV conclude with several case studies. As indicated in the Preface, these case studies are intended to allow the reader to encounter a few of the kinds of problems confronted daily by justice administrators. Several discussion questions follow each case study. With a fundamental knowledge of the system and a reading of the chapters in the respective book part, readers should be in a position to engage in some critical analysis—and even, hopefully, some spirited discussions—and arrive at several feasible solutions to the problems presented.

✦ CHAPTER INTRODUCTION

This chapter helps to set the stage for later discussions of the criminal justice system and its administration. We first consider whether the justice system composes a "process," a "network," a "nonsystem," or a true "system." Discussion then ensues about the legal and historical bases for justice and administration, followed by an examination of what some "great thinkers" have said about governance in general. The differences between public- and private-sector administration are reviewed next, and the chapter concludes with a discussion of policymaking in justice administration. Upon completing this chapter, the reader will have a better grasp of the structure, purpose, and foundation of our criminal justice system.

✦ A TRUE "SYSTEM" OF JUSTICE?

What is it that justice administrators—police, courts, and corrections administrators—actually *administer*? Obviously, these administrators do not provide leadership over a system that has succeeded in accomplishing its mission. But do individuals within the system work amiably and communicate well with one another? Do they all share the same goals? Do their efforts effectively result in crime reduction? We now turn to these questions, still taking a fundamental, yet expansive view of justice administration.

Succinctly, the American criminal justice system attempts to decrease criminal behavior through a wide variety of uncoordinated and sometimes uncomplementary efforts. Each system component—police, courts, and corrections—has varying degrees of responsibility and discretion for dealing with crime. However, there is a failure of each system component to engage in any coordinated planning effort; hence relations among and between these components are often characterized by friction, conflict, and deficient communication. Role conflicts also serve to ensure that planning and communication are stifled.

For example, the role of law enforcement is to arrest suspected offenders. They are not judged publicly on the quality of their arrests, but instead on the quantity. A common complaint voiced by prosecutors is the poor quality of case reports they receive from the police. The prosecutor, on the other hand, is partially judged by his or her success in obtaining convictions, while a public defender or defense attorney is judged by the success in getting suspected offenders' charges dropped. The courts are more independent in their operation, largely sentencing offenders as they see fit. Corrections agencies are torn between the philosophies of punishment and rehabilitation, and in the view of many, wind up performing neither function with any large degree of success. They are further burdened with overcrowded conditions, high caseloads, and antiquated facilities.[2] Unfortunately, this situation not only exists today, but has also existed for several decades.

This criticism of the justice system, or process—that it is fragmented and rife with role conflicts and other problems—is a common refrain. Following are several views toward the criminal justice system as it currently operates: the "process," "network," and "nonsystem" points of view. Following our discussion of those three viewpoints, we will consider whether or not criminal justice truly represents a "system."

✧ A CRIMINAL JUSTICE "PROCESS"?

What is readily seen in the foregoing discussion is that our criminal justice "system" may not be a system at all. Given its current operation and fragmentation, it might be better described as a *process*. As a process, it involves the decisions and actions taken by an institution, offender, victim, or society which influence the offender's movement into, through, or out of the justice system.[3] In its purest form, the criminal justice process occurs as shown in Figure 1.1. Note that the *horizontal* effects are a result of such factors as the amount of crime, the number of prosecutions, and the type of court disposition affecting the population in correctional facilities and rehabilitative programs. *Vertical* effects are exemplified by the primary system steps or procedures.[4]

At one end of this process are the police, who understandably view their primary role as getting lawbreakers off the street. At the other end of the continuum are the corrections officials, who may see their role as being primarily rehabilitative in nature. Somewhere in between are the courts, which try to ensure a fair application of the law to each case coming to the bar.

As a process, we assume that the justice system cannot reduce crime by itself, nor can any of the component parts afford to be insensitive to the needs and problems of the other parts. In criminal justice planning jargon, "You can't rock one end of the boat." In other words, for every action there is a reaction, especially in the justice process. If, say, a bond issue is passed in a community for funds that provide 10 percent more police officers on the streets, the additional arrests of those added police personnel will have a decided impact on the courts and corrections components as well. Obviously, although each component operates largely in a vacuum, the actions and reactions of each with respect to crime sends ripples throughout the process.

Much of the failure to deal effectively with crime may be attributed to organizational and administrative fragmentation of the justice process. There is fragmentation among the components of the process, within the individual components, among political jurisdictions, and between persons.

✦ A Criminal Justice "Network"?

Still others contend that U.S. justice systems comprise a network.[5] In the view of Steven Cox and John Wade, for example, the justice system functions much like a television or radio network, wherein the stations share many programs but in which each station also presents programs that are not aired by other stations in the network. The network appears as a three-dimensional model in which the public, legislators, police, prosecutor, judge, and correctional officials are involved in interactions with one another and with others who are outside the traditionally conceived criminal justice system.[6]

Furthermore, the justice system is said to be based on several key yet erroneous assumptions, including the following:

1. The components of the network cooperate and share similar goals.
2. The network operates according to a set of formal procedural rules to ensure uniform treatment of all persons, the outcome of which constitutes "justice."
3. Each person accused of a crime receives due process and is presumed innocent until proven guilty.

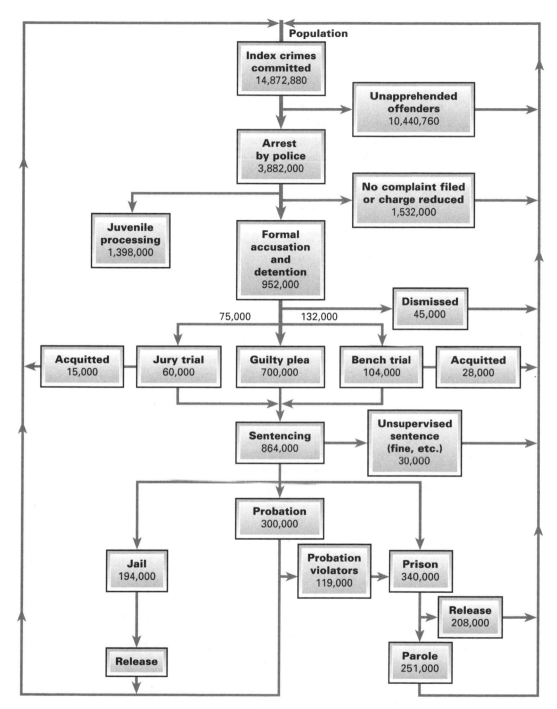

Figure 1-1 Criminal justice model. (*Source:* Adapted from the President's Commission on Law Enforcement and Administration of Justice. *The Challenge of Crime in a Free Society*, Washington, D.C.: U.S. Government Printing Office, 1967, pp. 262–263.)

4. Each person receives a speedy, public trial before an impartial jury of his or her peers, and is represented by competent legal counsel.[7]

Cox and Wade asserted that these key assumptions are erroneous because:

1. The three components have incompatible goals and are continually competing with one another for budgetary dollars.
2. Evidence indicates that blacks and whites, males and females, and middle- and lower-class citizens receive differential treatment in the criminal justice network.
3. Some persons are prosecuted, some are not; some are involved in plea bargaining, others are not; some are convicted and sent to prison, whereas others convicted of the same type of offense are not. A great deal of the plea negotiation remains largely invisible, such as that of "unofficial probation" with juveniles (described below). Also, they argue, there is considerable evidence pointing to the fact that criminal justice employees do not presume their clients or arrestees to be innocent.
4. Finally, these proponents for a "network" view of the justice process argue that the current tremendous backlog of cases ensures that a speedy trial is more fluff than substance, especially when a vast majority (at least 90 percent) of all arrestees plead guilty prior to trial.[8]

Taken together, the adherents to this position are compelled to believe that "justice" appears to be in the eyes of the beholder, that ours is probably not a "just" network in the eyes of the poor, the minority group, or the individual victim. Citizens, they further assert, may not know what to expect from the network. Some may feel that the network does not work at all and is not worth their support.[9]

✦ A Criminal Justice "Nonsystem"?

Many observers argue that the three components of the justice system actually comprise a "nonsystem". They maintain that the three segments of the system used in the United States to deal with criminal behavior do not always function in harmony, and that the system is neither efficient enough to create a credible fear of punishment nor fair enough to command respect for its values.

Indeed, these theorists are given considerable weight for their argument by the President's Commission on Law Enforcement and the Administration of Justice (commonly known as the Crime Commission), which made the following comment:

The system of criminal justice America uses to deal with those crimes it cannot prevent and those criminals it cannot deter is not a monolithic, or even a consistent, system. It was not designed or built in one piece at one time. Its philosophic core is that a person may be punished by the Government, if, and only if, it has been proven by an impartial and deliberate process that he has violated a specific law. Around that core, layer upon layer of institutions and procedures, some carefully constructed and some improvised, some inspired by principle and some by expediency, have accumulated. Parts of the system—magistrates, courts, trial by jury, bail—are of great antiquity. Other parts—juvenile courts, probation and parole, professional policemen—are relatively new. Every village, town, county, city and State has its own criminal justice system, and there is a Federal one as well. All of them operate somewhat alike, no two of them operate precisely alike.[10]

Alfred Cohn and Roy Udolf stated that criminal justice "is not a system, and it has little to do with justice as that term is ordinarily understood."[11] Also in this school of thought are Burton Wright and Vernon Fox, who asserted that "the criminal justice system...is frequently criticized because it is not a coordinated structure—not really a system. In many ways this is true."[12]

These writers would probably agree that little has changed since 1971, when Newsweek stated in a special report entitled "Justice on Trial" that

America's system of criminal justice is too swamped to deliver more than the roughest justice—and too ragged really to be called a system. "What we have," says one former government hand, "is a non-system in which the police don't catch criminals, the courts don't try them, and the prisons don't reform them. The system, in a word, is in trouble. The trouble has been neglect. The paralysis of the civil courts, where it takes five years to get a judgment in a damage suit...the courts—badly managed, woefully undermanned and so inundated with cases that they have to run fast just to stand still."[13]

Unfortunately, as will be demonstrated time and again throughout this book, those words still ring true in the 1990s. Clearly, the onus on modern-day justice administration is not to be innovators or reformers, but rather to simply "make do." As one law professor stated, "Oliver Wendell Holmes could not survive in our criminal court. How can you be an eminent jurist when you have to deal with this mess?"[14]

Those in this camp, holding that the justice system is in reality no system at all, can also point to the fact that many practitioners in the field (the police, judges, prosecutors, correctional workers, private attorneys), as well as academicians, also concede that the entire justice system is in crisis, even rapidly approaching a major breakdown. They can cite overcrowding everywhere—police calls for service, court dockets, prison populations—as well as riots (on the streets as well as within institutions). In short, they contend that the system is in a state of dysfunction, largely as a result of its fragmentation and lack of cohesion.[15]

System fragmentation is largely felt to affect directly the amount and type of crime that exists. The parts of the "system" are disunified. Contributing to this fragmentation are the wide discretionary powers possessed by actors of the justice system. For example, police officers (primarily those having the least experience, education, and training) have great discretion over whom they arrest and are effectively able to dictate policy as they go about performing their duties. Here again, the Crime Commission was moved to comment, realizing that how the police officer moves around his or her territory depends largely on this discretion:

> Crime does not look the same on the street as it does in a legislative chamber. How much noise or profanity makes conduct "disorderly" within the meaning of the law? When must a quarrel be treated as a criminal assault: at the first threat, or at the first shove, or at the first blow, or after blood is drawn, or when a serious injury is inflicted? How suspicious must conduct be before there is "probable cause," the constitutional basis for an arrest? Every [officer], however sketchy or incomplete his education, is an interpreter of the law.[16]

Judicial officers also possess great discretionary latitude. The state statutes require judges to provide deterrence, retribution, rehabilitation, and incapacitation—all in the same sentence. Well-publicized studies of the sentencing tendencies of judges—where participant-judges were given identical facts in cases and were to impose sentences based on the offender's violation of the law—have also demonstrated considerable discretion and unevenness in their sentences. This is felt by the "nonsystem" advocates to be further evidence that a basic inequality exists—an inequality in justice that is communicated to the offender. [17]

Finally, in corrections—the part of the criminal justice process that the American public sees the least of and knows the least about—fragmentation is also rampant in the mind of some people. Indeed, as the President's Commission noted, the federal government, all 50 states, the District of Columbia, and most of the country's 3047 counties now engage in correctional activities of some form or another. Each level of government acts independently of the others, and responsibility for the administration of corrections is divided within given jurisdictions as well.[18]

With this fragmentation comes polarity in identifying and establishing the primary goals of the system. The police, enforcing the laws, emphasize community protection; the courts weigh both sides of the issue—individual rights and community needs; and corrections works with the individual. These varied perceptions of the offender create goal conflict, wherein the goal of the police and prosecutor is to get the transgressor off the street, which is antithetical to the "caretaker" role of the corrections worker, who often wants to rehabilitate and return the offender to the community. The characteristics of the criminal justice process do not allow much in the way of alternative means of coping with offenders. Eventually, the "nonsystem" believer feels that the offender will become a mere statistic, more important on paper than as a human being.[19]

Because the justice process lacks sufficient program and procedural flexibility, these adherents argue, its workers can either circumvent policies, rules, and regulations, or they can adhere to organizational practices they know are, at times, dysfunctional. (As evidence, they can point to the many cases of *informal* treatment of criminal cases that occur, such as when a police officer "bends" someone's constitutional rights in order to return stolen property to its rightful owner; or the "unofficial probation" by a juvenile probation officer who, without a solid case but with strong suspicion, warns a youth that any further infractions will result in formal, court-involved proceedings.)

✧ OR TRUE CRIMINAL JUSTICE "SYSTEM"?

It is probably evident by now that all of the foregoing perspectives on the justice system are grounded in truth. In many ways, the police, courts, and corrections components work and interact such as to function like a "process," "network," or even a "nonsystem." But those factors, all of which include the disunity of the justice operation, may yet constitute a true system. As Willa Dawson stated, "Administration of justice can be regarded as a system by most standards. It may be a poorly functioning system but it does meet the criteria nonetheless. The systems approach is still in its infancy."[20] J. W. La Patra added, "I do believe that a criminal justice system does exist, but that it functions very poorly. The CJS is a loosely connected, nonharmonious, group of social entities."[21]

However, to be fair, perhaps this method of dealing with offenders is *best* after all; it may be that having a "well-oiled machine"—where all activities are coordinated, goals and objectives are unified, and communication between participants is maximized, all serving to grind out "justice" in a highly efficacious manner—may not be what we truly want or need in a democracy.

Hopefully, we have not belabored the subject; however, it is very important to establish early in this book the kind of system and components that you, as a potential criminal justice administrator of the future, may encounter. You can reconcile for yourself the differences of opinion described above. In this book, however, we adhere to the notion that even with all of its disunity and lack of fluidity, what criminal justice officials administer in the United States is a *system*. Nonetheless, it is good to look at its operation and shortcomings and, as stated earlier, force ourselves to confront the CJS problems and possible areas for improvement.

Now that we have a systemic view of what it is that criminal justice managers actually administer, it would be good to look briefly at how they may go about doing it. To begin in *tabula rasa* fashion, we first consider the legal and historical bases that provide for Americans to be regulated by a government and by a system of justice in our democracy; we include the consensus-conflict continuum, with the social contract on one end and maintaining the status quo/repression on the other. Then we examine what some noted writers of centuries past have offered as caveats concerning the desirable styles of leaders. Next we distinguish between administration and work in the public and private sectors, as the styles, incentives, and rewards of each are, by their very nature, quite different. This will provide the foundation for the final point of discussion, a brief look at the decision-making process in criminal justice agencies.

✦ THE FOUNDATIONS OF JUSTICE AND ADMINISTRATION: LEGAL AND HISTORICAL BASES

Given that our system of justice is founded on a bigger, more powerful system of government, the question that must be addressed is "Whence is that power derived? How can governments presume to maintain a system of laws that effectively serves to govern its people and, furthermore, a legal system that exists to punish persons who willfully suborn those laws?" We now consider the answers to those questions, which, on close examination, do indeed involve serious government powers.

✧ THE CONSENSUS VERSUS CONFLICT DEBATE

American society has innumerable lawbreakers. Most of them are easily handled by the police, and they do not challenge the legitimacy of the law while being arrested and incarcerated for violating it. Burglars do not argue that the crime for which they were arrested was unreasonable or morally wrong. Nor do they challenge the system of government that enacts the laws or the justice agencies that carry it out. The stability of our government for more than 200 years is a testimony to the existence of a fair degree of consensus as to its legitimacy. [22] Thomas Jefferson's statements in the Declaration of Independence hold as true today as the day when he wrote them, accepted as common sense: "We hold these truths to be self-evident, that all men are created equal, that they are endowed by their Creator with certain inalienable Rights, that among these are Life, Liberty and the pursuit of Happiness—That to secure these rights, Governments are instituted among Men, deriving their just powers from the consent of the governed. That whenever any Form of Government becomes destructive of these ends, it is the Right of the People to alter or abolish it."

The principles of the Declaration were almost a paraphrase of John Locke's *Second Treatise on Civil Government*, which justified the acts of government on the basis of his theory of *social contract*. In the state of nature, people, according to Locke, were created by God—free, equal, independent, and with inherent inalienable rights to life, liberty, and property. Each person had the right of self-protection against those who would infringe on those liberties. In Locke's view, although most people were good, some would be likely to prey on their fellows, who in turn would constantly have to be on guard against such evildoers. To avoid this brutish existence, people joined together, forming governments to which they surrendered their rights of self-protection. In return, they received governmental protection of their lives, property, and liberty. As in any "contract," there are benefits and considerations on both sides; people give up their rights to protect themselves and receive protection in return. Governments give protection and receive loyalty and obedience in return.[23]

Locke felt that the chief purpose of government was the protection of property, which people joined together to form the commonwealth. Once they do so, they cannot withdraw from it, nor can their lands be removed from it. But propertyholders within a commonwealth cannot be made members of that commonwealth; only their express consent can make them so. But they must accept that property only on the condition that they submit to the government of the commonwealth. This is Locke's famous theory of *tacit consent*: "...every Man...doth hereby give his *tacit Consent*, and is as far forth obliged to Obedience to the Laws of the Government."[24] Locke's theory essentially describes an association of landowners.[25]

Another theorist who is connected with the social contract theory is Thomas Hobbes, who argued that all people were essentially irrational and selfish. He maintained that people had just enough rationality to recognize their situation and to come together to form governments for self-protection, agreeing "amongst themselves to submit to some Man, or Assembly of men, voluntarily, on confidence to be protected by him against all others."[26] Therefore, they existed in a state of consensus with their governments, consenting to their existence.

Jean-Jacques Rousseau, however, a conflict theorist, differed substantively from both Hobbes and Locke, arguing that "Man is born free, but everywhere he is in chains."[27] Like Plato, Rousseau associated the loss of freedom and the creation of conflict in modern societies with the development of private property and the unequal distribution of resources. Rousseau described conflict between the ruling group and the other groups in society, where Locke had described consensus in the ruling group and the need to use force and other means to ensure the compliance of the other groups.[28]

Thus the primary difference between the consensus and conflict theorists, with respect to their view of government vis-à-vis the governed, concerns their evaluation of the legitimacy of the actions of ruling groups in contemporary societies. Locke saw those actions as consistent with natural law, describing societies as consensual and arguing that any conflict in them was "illegitimate," and as such could be repressed by force and other means. Rousseau evaluated the actions of ruling groups as irrational and selfish, creating conflicts among the various groups in society.[29]

This debate is important, as it plays out the competing views of humankind toward its ruling group; it also has relevance with respect to the kind of justice system (or process) we have. The systems model has been criticized for implying a greater level of organization and cooperation among the various agencies of justice than actually exists. The word "system" conjures up an idea of machinelike precision in which wasted effort, redundancy, and conflicting actions are nearly nonexistent; our current justice system does not possess such a level of perfection. As mentioned above, conflicts among and within agencies are rife, goals are not shared by its three components, and the system may move in different directions. Therefore, the systems approach is part of the *consensus model* point of view, which assumes that all parts of the system work toward a common goal.[30] The *conflict model*, holding that agency interests tend to make actors within the system self-serving, provides the other approach. Persons subscribing to this view point to the pressures for success, promotion, and general accountability which together result in fragmented efforts of the system as a whole, leading to a criminal justice nonsystem.[31]

This debate also has relevance for criminal justice administrators. Assume a consensus–conflict continuum, where we place social contract (the people totally allowing government to use its means to protect them) on one end and class repression on the other. It is of paramount importance that our administrators of criminal justice agencies *not* allow their agencies to "drift" too far to one end of the continuum or the other. Americans cannot allow the compliance or conflict that would result at either end; the safer point is more toward the middle of the continuum, where people are not totally dependent on their government for protection and maintain enough control to prevent totalitarianism.

✦ CRIME CONTROL THROUGH DUE PROCESS

Both the systems and nonsystems models of criminal justice provide a view of agency relationships. Another way to view American criminal justice is in terms of its goals. Two primary goals exist within this context: (1) the need to enforce the law and maintain social order, and (2) the need to protect people from injustice.[32] The first, often referred to as the crime control model, values the arrest and conviction of criminal offenders. The second, because of its emphasis on individual rights, is commonly known as the due process model. Due process—found in the Bill of Rights, particularly in the Fourteenth Amendment—is a central and necessary part of our system, requiring a careful and informed consideration of the facts of each individual case. It ensures that innocent people are not convicted of crimes.

It is often suggested that these dual goals of crime control and due process are in constant and unavoidable opposition to one another. Many critics of criminal justice, as it exists in the United States, argue that our attempt to achieve "justice" for offenders too often occurs at the expense of due process. Other, more conservative observers feel that our system is too lenient with its clients, coddling offenders rather than protecting the innocent.

We are never going to be in a position to avoid ideological conflicts such as these. However, some observers, such as Frank Schmalleger, believe it is realistic to think of the U.S. system of justice as representative of *crime control through due process*.[33] It is this model, of crime control infused with the recognition of individual rights, which provides the conceptual framework for this book.

✦ PUBLIC-VERSUS-PRIVATE SECTOR ADMINISTRATION

It has long been recognized that people experience positive personal consequences from their work.[34] Because work is such a vital part of our lives, an activity that carries tremendous meaning in terms of our personal identity and happiness, the right match of person to job has long been recognized as a determinant of job satisfaction.[35] Factors such as job importance, accomplishment, challenge, teamwork, management fairness, and rewards become very important.

People in both the public (i.e., government) and private (e.g., retail business) sectors derive positive personal consequences from their work. However, the means by which they arrive at those positive feelings, and are rewarded for their efforts, are often quite different. Basically, whereas private businesses and corporations can use a panoply of *extrinsic* rewards to motivate and reward their employees, people working in the public sector must achieve job satisfaction primarily through *intrinsic* rewards.

Extrinsic rewards include such perquisites as financial compensation, salary and benefits package, private office, a key to the executive washroom, bonuses, trips, a company car, awards (including such designations as the employee of the month or the insurance industry's "million-dollar roundtable"), expense account, membership to country clubs and organizations, and job title. The title assigned to a job can affect one's general perceptions of the job, independent of actual job content. For example, the role once known disparagingly as "grease monkey" in a gasoline service station has commonly become known as "lubrication technician"; garbage collectors have become "sanitation engineers"; and so on. Much of our society's "enhancement" of job titles is for the purpose of adding job satisfaction and extrinsic rewards to what may often be lackluster positions.

Corporations often devote tremendous sums of time and money to bestowing extrinsic rewards, incentives, and job titles to employees to enhance their job satisfaction. These rewards, of course, cannot and do not exist in the public sector nearly to the extent that they exist in the private sector.

As indicated earlier, public-sector workers must instead seek and obtain job satisfaction primarily from within—through intrinsic means. These workers, unable to become wealthy (in contrast to the Disney executive who in December 1992 cashed in $20 million in stock options!) and not being in a position that is fraught with "perks," instead need jobs that are gratifying and that intrinsically make them feel good about themselves and what they accomplish. Criminal justice work is often characterized by practitioners as intrinsically rewarding, providing a sense of worth in making the world a little better place in which to live. These employees also seek appreciation from their supervisors and co-workers and generally require challenges.

These views can easily be translated to individual views concerning the workplace. In other words, there are people who work primarily for a paycheck and other external rewards. For example, most police managers have probably supervised a few employees over the years who were merely putting in time on the job; they would probably have been glad to "patrol" around a flagpole all month if such was required to earn their pay.

This is an area where administration should attempt to understand the personalities, needs, and motivation of its employees, and attempt to meet those needs to the extent possible. The late Sam Walton, the multibillionaire founder of Wal-Mart Stores, served as a unique example in management philosophy. One night, Walton could not sleep. So he went to a nearby all-night bakery (in Bentonville, Arkansas), bought four dozen doughnuts, and took them to a distribution center where he chatted with graveyard-shift Wal-Mart employees. From that chat, he discovered that two more shower stalls were needed at that location.[36] Walton obviously solicited—and valued—employee input and was concerned about their morale and working conditions. Although Walton was known to be very unique in his business sense, these are elements of administration that can be applied by public administrators as well.

✦ POLICYMAKING IN JUSTICE ADMINISTRATION

Imagine the following scenario: Someone in a position having criminal justice operations within his or her purview (e.g., a city or county manager, or a municipal or criminal justice planner) is charged with the responsibility of formulating an omnibus policy with respect to crime reduction. He or she might begin by trying to list all related variables as they contribute to the crime problem: poverty; employment; demographics of people residing within the jurisdiction; environmental conditions (such as housing density and conditions and areas where living conditions are at their worst); mortality, morbidity, and suicide rates; educational levels of the populace; and so on.

Next, the administrator would request from each justice administrator within the jurisdiction more specific information to determine where problems might exist in the practitioners' view of the police, courts, and corrections subsystems. For example, a police executive would contribute information concerning calls for service, arrests, and crime data (including offender information and crime information—time of day, day of week, methods, locations, targets, and so on). The status of existing programs, such as community policing and problem-solving, would also be provided. From the courts, information would be sought concerning the sizes of court dockets (civil and criminal) and backlogs ("Justice delayed is justice denied"). Included in this report would be input from the prosecutor's office concerning the quality and quantity of police reports and arrests, as well as data on case dismissals and conviction rates at trial. From corrections administrators, he or she would be acutely interested in the average officer caseload and recidivism and revocation rates. Budgetary information would certainly be solicited from all subsystems, as well as miscellaneous data regarding their personnel levels, level of training, and so on. Finally, he or she would attempt to formulate a crime policy, setting forth goals and objectives needed for addressing the jurisdiction's needs.

In the alternative, the policymaker could approach policymaking in a far less complex manner, simply setting as a principal objective, either explicitly or without conscious thought, the relatively simple goal of "keeping crime down." This goal might be compromised or complicated by only a few other goals, such as a bullish economy. He or she could in fact disregard most of the other variables discussed above as being beyond the ken of his or her current needs and interest, and would for the time being not even attempt to consider them as being immediately relevant. The criminal justice practitioners would not be pressed to attempt to cull out these vast amounts of information and critical analyses. If pressed for time (as is often the case in these real-life scenarios), the planner would readily admit that these variables were being ignored.[37]

Because executives and planners of the second approach expect to achieve their goals only partially, they would expect to repeat endlessly the sequence just described, as conditions and aspirations changed and as accuracy of prediction improved. Realistically, however, the first of these two approaches assumes intellectual capacities and sources of information that people often do not possess; further, the time and money that can be allocated to a policy problem is limited. Public agencies are in effect usually too hamstrung to practice the first method; it is the second method that is practiced. Curiously, however, the literature on decision making, planning, policy formulation, and public administration formalizes and preaches the first approach.[38] The second method is much neglected in this literature.

In the United States, there is probably no part of government that attempts a comprehensive analysis and overview of policy on crime (the first method). Thus, making crime policy is at best a very rough process. For example, without a more comprehensive process, we cannot possibly understand how a variety of problems—education, housing, recreation, employment, race, and policing—might encourage or discourage juvenile delinquency. What we normally engage in is a comparative analysis of the results of similar past policy decisions. This explains why justice administrators often feel that outside experts or academics are not helpful to them—why it is safer to "fly by the seat of one's pants." Theorists often urge the administrator to go the long way to the solution of his or her problems, following the scientific method, when the administrator knows that the best available theory will not work. Theorists, for their part, do not realize that the administrator is often in fact practicing a systematic method.[39] So, what may appear to be mere "muddling through" is both highly praised as a sophisticated form of policy- and decision-making, and soundly denounced as no method at all. What society needs to bear in mind is that justice administrators possess an intimate knowledge of past consequences of actions that "outsiders" do not. While seemingly less effective and rational, this method, according to policymaking experts, has merit. Indeed, it is the method that is commonly used for personal problemsolving, where means and ends are often impossible to separate, aspirations or objectives undergo constant development, and drastic simplification of the complexity of the real world is urgent if problems are to be solved in reasonable periods of time.[40]

Summary

In this chapter we established the legal existence of governments, our laws, and the justice agencies that administer them. We also know that we live in a country rife with crime and that the general public has little faith that criminal justice organizations will be able to do anything about it in the foreseeable future. It was demonstrated that each of the three components of the justice system are independent, fragmented, and often working at odds with one another toward the accomplishment of the system's overall mission.

In the following chapter we look more closely at criminal justice agencies as organizations, how they are managed, and how the people within them are administered.

Questions for Review

1. Do the three justice components (police, courts, and corrections) constitute a true "system"? Or are they more appropriately described as a "process" or a true "nonsystem"? Defend your response.

2. Explain the legal and historical bases for a justice system and its administration in the United States. Why is the "conflict versus consensus" debate important?

3. What are some of the substantive ways in which public- and private-sector administration are similar? How are they dissimilar?

4. Which method—a rational process or one that some view as just "muddling through"—appears to be used in criminal-justice policy making today? Which method is probably best, given real-world realities?

For Further Reading

STEVEN M. COX and JOHN E. WADE, *The Criminal Justice Network: An Introduction* (2d ed.). Dubuque, Iowa: Wm. C. Brown, 1989.

VICTOR E. KAPPELER, MARK BLUMBERG, and GARY W. POTTER, *The Mythology of Crime and Criminal Justice*. Prospect Heights, Ill.: Waveland Press, 1993.

John KLOFAS, STAN STOJKOVIC, and DAVID KALINICH, *Criminal Justice Organizations: Administration and Management*. Pacific Grove, Calif.: Brooks/Cole, 1990.

FRANK SCHMALLEGER, *Criminal Justice Today* (2d ed.). Englewood Cliffs, N.J.: Regents/Prentice Hall, 1993.

SAMUEL WALKER, *Sense and Nonsense about Crime: A Policy Guide* (2d ed.). Pacific Grove, Calif.: Brooks/Cole, 199

Notes

1. For a more thorough explication of these terms and roles, particularly as applied in policing, see Richard N. Holden, *Modern Police Management* (Englewood Cliffs, N.J.: Prentice Hall, 1986).

2. Michael E. O'Neill, Ronald F. Bykowski, and Robert S. Blair, *Criminal Justice Planning: A Practical Approach* (San Jose, Calif.: Justice Systems Development, Inc., 1976), p. 5.

3. *Ibid.,* p. 12.

4. *Ibid.*

5. Steven M. Cox and John E. Wade, *The Criminal Justice Network: An Introduction* (2d ed.) (Dubuque, Iowa.: Wm. C. Brown, 1989), p. 1.

6. *Ibid.,* p. 4.

7. *Ibid.,* p. 12.

8. *Ibid.,* pp. 13-14.

9. Philip H. Ennis, "Crime, Victims, and the Police," *Trans-action* 4 (June 1967):36-44.

10. The President's Commission on Law Enforcement and the Administration of Justice, *The Challenge of Crime in a Free Society* (Washington, D.C.: U.S. Government Printing Office, 1967), p. 7.

11. Alfred Cohn and Roy Udolf, *The Criminal Justice System and Its Psychology* (New York: Van Nostrand Reinhold, 1979).

12. Burton Wright and Vernon Fox, *Criminal Justice and the Social Sciences* (Philadelphia: W. B. Saunders, 1978).

13. "Justice on Trial: A Special Report," *Newsweek* (March 8, 1971):16.

14. *Ibid.,* p. 18.

15. Alan R. Coffey and Edward Eldefonso, *Process and Impact of Justice* (Beverly Hills, Calif.: Glencoe Press, 1975), p. 32.

16. The President's Commission on Law Enforcement and the Administration of Justice, *The Challenge of Crime in a Free Society,* p. 5.

17. Alan R. Coffey and Edward Eldefonso, *Process and Impact of Justice,* p. 35.

18. *Ibid.,* p. 39.

19. *Ibid.,* p. 41.

20. Willa Dawson, "The Need for a System Approach to Criminal Justice," in Donald T. Shanahan (ed.), *The Administration of Justice System: An Introduction* (Boston: Holbrook, 1977).

21. J. W. La Patra, *Analyzing the Criminal Justice System* (Lexington, Mass.: Lexington Books, 1978).

22. Alexander B. Smith and Harriet Pollack, *Criminal Justice: An Overview* (New York: Holt, Rinehart and Winston, 1980), p. 9.

23. *Ibid.,* p. 10.

24. *Ibid.,* p. 366.

25. Thomas J. Bernard, *The Consensus–Conflict Debate: Form and Content in Social Theories* (New York: Columbia University Press, 1983), p. 78.

26. Thomas Hobbes, *Leviathan* (New York: E. P. Dutton, 1950), pp. 290–91.

27. Jean-Jacques Rousseau, "A Discourse on the Origin of Inequality," in G. D. H. Cole (ed.), *The Social Contract and Discourses* (New York: E.P. Dutton, 1946), p. 240.

28. Thomas J. Bernard, *The Consensus–Conflict Debate: Form and Content in Social Theories,* pp. 83, 85.

29. *Ibid.,* p. 86.

30. Frank Schmalleger, *Criminal Justice Today,* 2d ed. (Englewood Cliffs, N.J.: Regents/Prentice Hall, 1993), p. 15.

31. One of the first publications to express the nonsystems approach was the American Bar Association's *New Perspective on Urban Crime* (Washington, D.C.: ABA Special Committee on Crime Prevention and Control, 1972).

32. Frank Schmalleger, *Criminal Justice Today,* 2d ed., p. 16.

33. *Ibid.*

34. Fernando Bartolome and Paul H. Evans, "Professional Lives versus Private Lives: Shifting Patterns of Managerial Commitment," *Organizational Dynamics* 7 (1982):2–29; Ronald C. Kessler and James A. McRae, Jr., "The Effect of Wives' Employment on the Mental Health of Married Men and Women," *American Sociological Review* 47 (1979):216–27.

35. Robert V. Presthus, *The Organizational Society* (New York:Alfred A. Knopf, 1962).

36. Joseph A. Petrick and George E. Manning, "How to Manage Morale," *Personnel Journal* 69 (October 1990):87.

37. This scenario is modeled on that set out by Charles E. Lindblom, a Harvard economist, in "The Science of `Muddling Through,'" *Public Administration Review* 19 (Spring 1959): 79–89.

38. *Ibid.,* p. 80.

39. *Ibid.,* p. 87.

40. *Ibid.,* p. 88.

Organization and Administration: Principles and Practices

We are born in organizations, educated by organizations, and most of us spend much of our lives working for organizations. We spend much of our leisure time paying, playing, and praying in organizations. Most of us will die in an organization, and when the time comes for burial, the largest organization of all—the state—must grant official permission.

—Amitai Etzioni [1]

✦ INTRODUCTION

This chapter opens with a general discussion of organizations, focusing on their definition, theory and function, and structure. Included are several approaches to managing and communicating within them. We then focus on one of the most important aspects of leadership: personnel administration. Organizations are not inanimate; they are composed of *people*, who must be led and motivated to accomplish organizational goals. Included are discussions of different approaches to management (including analects of Confucius and Machiavelli concerning how to govern) and an examination of organizational leadership theories. We also review a chronology of management "fads" that have evolved over the last four decades. We conclude with a discussion of several motivational techniques that have been identified for use with employees, based on findings by major theorists in the field.

This chapter is necessarily replete with theories—a term which, unfortunately, often carries negative connotations. However, behind every good theory is a good *practical* foundation. Because organizations must get things done through people, especially in a labor-intensive field such as criminal justice, these tried-and-true theories tell us how administrators must conduct themselves and what they must know about their people for the organization to succeed.

✦ DEFINING ORGANIZATIONS

Like the terms "supervision" and "management," the word "organization" has a number of meanings and interpretations that have evolved over the years. We think of organizations as entities of two or more people who cooperate to accomplish an objective(s). In that sense, certainly the *concept* of organization is not new. Undoubtedly, the first organizations were primitive hunting parties. Organization and a high degree of coordination were required to bring down huge animals, as revealed in fossils from as early as 40,000 B.C.[2]

An organization may be formally defined as "a consciously coordinated social entity, with a relatively identifiable boundary, that functions on a relatively continuous basis to achieve a common goal or set of goals."[3] The term "consciously coordinated" implies management. "Social entity" refers to the fact that organizations are composed of people who interact with one another and with people in other organizations. "Relatively identifiable boundary" alludes to the organization's goals and the public served.[4]

Using this definition, many types of formal groups would qualify as full-blown organizations. Four different types of formal organizations have been identified by asking the question "Cui bono?", or "Who benefits?": (1) mutual benefit associations, such as police labor unions; (2) business concerns, such as General Motors; (3) service organizations, such as community mental health centers, where the client group is the prime beneficiary; and (4) commonweal organizations, such as the Department of Defense and criminal justice agencies, where the beneficiaries are the public at large.[5] Following is an analogy to assist toward understanding organizations.

> Organization corresponds to the bones which structure or give form to the body. Imagine that the fingers were a single mass of bone rather than four separate fingers and a thumb made up of bones joined by cartilage so that they are flexible. The mass of bones could not, because of its structure, play musical instruments, hold a pencil, or grip a baseball bat. A police department's organization is analogous. It must be structured properly if it is to be effective in fulfilling its many diverse goals. Organization may not be important in a police department consisting of three officers, but it is extremely important in [large] cities.[6]

It is important to note that no two organizations are exactly alike. Nor is there one best way to run an organization.

✦ ORGANIZATIONAL THEORY AND FUNCTION

✥ ELEMENTS OF AN ORGANIZATION

Max Weber (1864–1920), known as the "father of sociology," explored the organization structure in depth, as well as the dynamics related to bureaucracy. Weber argued that if a bureaucratic structure is to function efficiently, it must have the following elements:

1. *Rulification and routinization.* "A continuous organization of official functions bound by rules." Organizations stress continuity. Rules save effort by eliminating the need for deriving a new solution for every situation. They also facilitate standard and equal treatment of similar situations.
2. *Division of labor.* "A specific sphere of competence." This involves performing functions that have been marked off as part of a systematic division of labor and the provision of the necessary authority to carry out these functions.
3. *Hierarchy of authority.* "The organization of offices follows the principle of hierarchy; that is, each lower office is under the control and supervision of a higher one."
4. *Expertise.* "[S]pecialized training is necessary. It is thus normally true that only a person who has demonstrated an adequate technical training is qualified to be a member of the administrative staff...."
5. *Written rules.* "Administrative acts, decisions, and rules are formulated and recorded in writing."[7]

Bureaucracies often have several additional traits in common. Specialized tasks will be placed in separate compartments or "bureaus," with a hierarchical structure and division of labor between workers, first-line supervisors, and head supervisors. Career paths up the organization exist so that employees may progress in an orderly fashion.

Bureaucracies are often criticized on two grounds. First, they are said to be inflexible, inefficient, and unresponsive to changing needs and times. Second, bureaucracies are felt to stifle individual freedom, spontaneity, and self-realization of their employees.[8] James Q. Wilson referred to this widespread discontent with modern organizations as the "bureaucracy problem," where the key issue is "getting the frontline worker...to do 'the right thing.'"[9] In short, then, bureaucracies themselves can create problems.

✦ ORGANIZATIONAL INPUTS/OUTPUTS

Another way to view organizations is as systems that take *inputs*, process them, and thus produce *outputs*. These outputs are then sold in the marketplace or given free to citizens in the form of a service. A police agency, for example, "processes" reports of criminal activity and, like other systems, attempts to satisfy the "customer" (crime victim). Figure 2.1 demonstrates the input/output model for policing and private business. There are other types of inputs by police agencies; for example, a robbery problem might result in an input of newly created robbery surveillance teams, the processing would be their stakeouts, and the output would be the number of subsequent arrests by the team. Feedback would occur in the form of conviction rates at trial.

BUSINESS ORGANIZATION

Inputs	**Processes**	**Outputs**
Customer takes photos to shop to be developed.	Photos are developed and packaged for customer to pick up.	Customer picks up photos and pays for them.

Feedback
Analysis is made of expenses/revenues and customer satisfaction.

LAW ENFORCEMENT AGENCY

Inputs	**Processes**	**Outputs**
A crime prevention unit is initiated.	Citizens contact unit for advice.	Police provide spot checks and lectures.

Feedback
Target hardening results; property crimes decrease.

COURT

Inputs	**Processes**	**Outputs**
A house arrest program is initiated.	Certain people in pre- and post-trial status are screened and offered the option.	Decrease in number of people in jail, speeding up court process.

Feedback
Violation rates are analyzed for success; some offenders are mainstreamed back into the community more smoothly.

Figure 2.1   The organization as an input/output model.

PROBATION/PAROLE AGENCIES

Inputs	**Processes**	**Outputs**
Parole guidelines are changed to shorten length of incarceration and reduce overcrowding.	Qualified inmates are contacted by parole agency and given new parole dates.	A higher number of inmates are paroled into the community.

Feedback
Parole officer's caseload and revocation rates might increase; less time to devote per case.

Figure 2.1 (*continued*)

✦ ORGANIZATIONAL STRUCTURE

All organizations have an organization structure or table of organization, be it written or unwritten, very basic or highly complex. A trained manager uses this organization chart or table of organization as a blueprint for action. The size of the organization depends on the demand placed on it and the resources available to it. Growth precipitates the need for more people, greater division of labor, specialization, written rules, and other such elements.

In building the organization structure, the following principles should be kept in mind:

1. *Principle of the objective.* Every part of every organization must be an expression of the purpose of the undertaking concerned or it is meaningless and therefore redundant. You cannot organize in a vacuum; you must organize for something.
2. *Principle of specialization.* The activities of every member of any organized group should be confined, as far as possible, to the performance of a single function.
3. *Principle of coordination.* The purpose of organizing per se, as distinguished from the purpose of the undertaking, is to facilitate coordination and unity of effort.
4. *Principle of authority.* In every organized group the supreme authority must rest somewhere. There should be a clear line of authority to every person in the group.
5. *Principle of responsibility.* The responsibility of the superior for the acts of his or her subordinate is absolute.
6. *Principle of definition.* The content of each position, the duties involved, the authority and responsibility contemplated, and the rela-

tionships with other positions should be clearly defined in writing and published for the information of all concerned.

7. *Principle of correspondence.* In every position the responsibility and the authority should correspond.

8. *Span of control.* No person should supervise more than six direct subordinates whose work interlocks.

9. *Principle of balance.* It is essential that the various units of organization should be kept in balance.

10. *Principle of continuity.* Reorganization is a continuous process; in every undertaking specific provision should be made for it.[10]

The development of an organization should be done with careful evaluation, lest the agency be unable to respond efficiently to community needs. For example, the implementation of too many specialized units in a police department (e.g., community relations, crime analysis, media relations) may obligate too many personnel to these functions and result in too few patrol officers. As a rule of thumb, at least 55 percent of all sworn personnel should be assigned to patrol.[11]

A simple structure indicating the direct line of authority in a chain of command is shown in Figure 2.2. The classical pyramidal design is shown in Figure 2.3. The pyramidal structure has the following characteristics:

1. Nearly all contacts take the form of orders going *down* and reports of results going *up* the pyramid.

2. Each subordinate must receive instructions and orders from only one boss.

3. Important decisions are made at the top of the pyramid.

4. Superiors have a limited "span of control," supervising only a limited number of people.

5. Personnel at any level (except at the top and bottom) have contact only with their boss above them and their subordinates below them.[12]

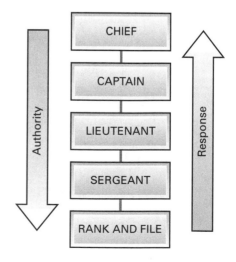

Figure 2.2 Chain of command.

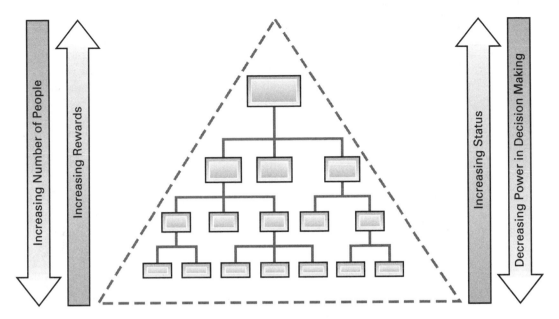

Figure 2.3 Organization pyramid. *(Source:* Adapted from L. R. Sayles and G. Strauss, *Human Behavior Organizations,* Englewood Cliffs, N.J.: Prentice Hall, 1966, p. 349.)

Some observers specializing in organization theory and management have been severely critical of organization charts, arguing that they create within the organization process excessive red tape and formality.[13] It has also been pointed out that such charts cannot possibly show all of the relationships that exist, especially in some of the more complex organizations.[14]

✦ MANAGING THE ORGANIZATION

The success of any organization normally depends on the quality of work life within the agency. Peter Drucker, one of the most influential management writers of modern times and often referred to as a "business guru",[15] observed that "nothing quenches motivation as quickly as a slovenly boss. People expect and demand that managers enable them to do a good job....People have...a right to expect a serious and competent superior."[16] Unfortunately, as Drucker was implying, there are both good leaders and bad, due to the fact that many people—untrained, uncaring, unfit, and/or unwilling to have the mantle of leadership thrust upon them—do not succeed (at least in the eyes of their subordinates).

We now look at leaders and what they can do to motivate their subordinates.

✦ What Is "Management"?

Probably since the dawn of time, when cave dwellers clustered into hunting groups and some particularly dominant person assumed a leadership role over the party, administrators have received from those around them, advice on how to do their jobs. Even today, manuals abound for managers, bosses, and upwardly mobile executives, offering quick studies in how to govern others. Although many have doubtless been profitable for their authors, most of these how-to primers on leading others enjoy only a brief, ephemeral existence.

To understand management (or leadership), we must first define the term. This is an important and fairly complex undertaking, however. Perhaps the simplest definition is to say that management is "getting things done through people." Ralph Stogdill, in a review of 3000 leadership studies, noted: "There are almost as many definitions of leadership as there are persons who have attempted to define the concept."[17] Among the most recent definitions are the following:

◊ "The process of influencing the activities of an individual or a group in efforts toward goal achievement in a given situation"[18]
◊ "Working with and through individuals and groups to accomplish organizational goals"[19]
◊ "The activity of influencing people to strive willingly for group objectives"[20]
◊ "The exercise of influence"[21]

Others have said the manager is viewed variously as a "team captain, parent, steward, battle commander, fountain of wisdom, poker player, group spokesperson, gatekeeper, minister, drill instructor, facilitator, initiator, mediator, navigator, candy-store keeper, linchpin, umbrella-holder and everything else between nurse and Attila-the-Hun."[22] In criminal justice organizations, leadership might best be defined as "the process of influencing organizational members to use their energies willingly and appropriately to facilitate the achievement of the [agency's] goals."[23]

Perhaps, though, a leader in the purest sense influences others by example. This characteristic of leadership was recognized in the sixth century B.C. by Lao-Tzu when he wrote:

> The superior leader gets things done
> With very little motion.
> He imparts instruction not through many words
> But through a few deeds.
> He keeps informed about everything
> But interferes hardly at all.
> He is a catalyst.

And although things wouldn't get done as well
If he weren't there.
When they succeed he takes no credit.
And because he takes no credit
Credit never leaves him.[24]

✦ ANALECTS OF CONFUCIUS AND MACHIAVELLI

The writings of two other major figures have stood the test of time. The analects (or brief passages) of both Confucius (551-479 B.C.) and Machiavelli (1469-1527 A.D.) are still quite popular today. Many graduate and undergraduate students in a variety of academic disciplines have been compelled to analyze the writings of both, especially Machiavelli's *The Prince*. Both men tend to agree on many points regarding the means of governance, as the following will demonstrate.

Confucius put great emphasis on moralism of leaders, writing that

> He who rules by moral force is like the pole-star, which remains in its place while all the lesser stars do homage to it. Govern the people by regulations, keep order among them by chastisements, and they will flee from you, and lose all self-respect. Govern them by moral force, keep order among them…, and they will…come to you of their own accord. If the ruler is upright, all will go well even though he does not give orders. But if he himself is not upright, even though he gives orders, they will not be obeyed.[25]

Confucius also felt that persons who the leader promotes is of no small importance: "Promote those who are worthy, train those who are incompetent; that is the best form of encouragement."[26] He also felt that leaders should learn from and emulate good administrators: "In the presence of a good man, think all the time how you may learn to equal him. In the presence of a bad man, turn your gaze within! Even when I am walking in a party of no more than three I can always be certain of learning from those I am with. There will be good qualities that I can select for imitation and bad ones that will teach me what requires correction in myself."[27]

Unlike Confucius, Machiavelli is often maligned for being cruel; the "ends justifies the means" philosophy imputed to him even today has cast a pall over his writings. However, although often as biting as the "point of a stiletto"[28] and seemingly ruthless at times ["Men ought either to be caressed or destroyed, since they will seek revenge for minor hurts but will not be able to revenge major ones,"[29] and "If you have to make a choice, to be feared is much safer than to be loved"[30], he, like Confucius, often spoke of the leader's need to possess character and compassion. For all of his blunt, management-oriented notions of administration, Machiavelli was prudent and pragmatic.

Like Confucius, Machiavelli felt that administrators would do well to follow examples set by other great leaders: "Men almost always prefer to walk in paths marked out by others and pattern their actions through imitation. A prudent man should always follow the footsteps of the great and imitate those who have been supreme. A prince should read history and reflect on the actions of great men."[31] Machiavelli's counsel also agreed with that of Confucius in the sense that leaders should surround themselves with persons both knowledgeable and devoted: "The first notion one gets of a prince's intelligence comes from the men around him."[32] But, again, like Confucius, Machiavelli believed that administrators should be careful of their subordinates' ambition and greed: "A new prince must always harm those over whom he assumes authority. You cannot stay friends with those who put you in power, because you can never satisfy them as they expected. The man who makes another powerful ruins himself. The reason is that he gets power either by shrewdness or by strength, and both qualities are suspect to the man who has been given the power."[33] On the need for developing and maintaining good relations with subordinates, he wrote:

> If...a prince...puts his trust in the people, knows how to command, is a man of courage and doesn't lose his head in adversity, and can rouse his people to action by his own example and orders, he will never find himself betrayed, and his foundations will prove to have been well laid. The best fortress of all consists in not being hated by your people. Every prince should prefer to be considered merciful rather than cruel. The prince must have people well disposed toward him; otherwise in times of adversity there's no hope.[34]

In this era of collective bargaining and a rapidly changing workforce, contemporary criminal justice administrators might do well to heed the analects of Confucius and Machiavelli.

✦ COMMUNICATION WITHIN THE ORGANIZATION

✧ COMMUNICATION DEFINED

Communication is one of the most important dynamics of an organization. Mark Twain once said that "The difference between the right word and the almost right word is the difference between lightning and lightning bug."[35]

Managers are in the communications business. It has been said that "Of all skills needed to be an effective manager/leader/supervisor, skill in communicating is *the* most vital. In fact, more than 50 percent of a [criminal justice] manager's time is spent communicating. First-line supervisors usually spend about 15 percent of their time with superiors, 50 percent of their time with subordinates, and 35 percent with other managers and duties. These estimates emphasize the importance of communications in everyday...operations."[36]

Communication is the complex process whereby information is transmitted from one person to another through common symbols. These symbols may be written or spoken words or signs and gestures. The communication process involves a message, a sender, a receiver, and an understanding of the idea that is transferred; in other words, successful communication does not occur if one is shouting while alone in the middle of a cow pasture or listening to someone speak in a completely foreign language.

We now communicate via facsimile machines, video camcorders, cellular telephones, satellite dishes, and on and on. We converse orally, in written letters and memos, through our body language, via television and radio programs, through newspapers and meetings. Even private thoughts—which take place four times faster than the spoken word—are communication. Every waking hour, our minds are full of ideas and thoughts. Psychologists say that nearly 100,000 thoughts pass through our minds every day, conveyed by a multitude of media.[37]

Communication within a bureaucratic organization may be *downward* (including directives from managers and supervisors, either verbal or written), *upward* (including requests from subordinates to their superiors, which may also be verbal or in the form of reports or memorandums), or *lateral* (which includes communication among managers or subordinates on the same level of the hierarchy).

✧ BARRIERS TO EFFECTIVE COMMUNICATION

Many barriers exist to effective communication. Some people, for example, are not good listeners. Unfortunately, listening is one of the most neglected and the least understood of the communication arts.[38] We allow other things to obstruct our communication, including time, inadequate or too great a volume of information, the tendency to say what we think others want to hear, failure to select the best word, prejudices, and strained sender-receiver relationships.[39]

In a criminal justice organization, communication becomes exceedingly important. Criminal justice communication is often sensitive in nature. Criminal justice practitioners, especially police officers, see people at their worst and when they are in their most embarrassing and compromising situations. To "communicate" what is known about these kinds of behaviors could be devastating to the parties concerned. A former Detroit police chief lamented several decades ago that "many police officers, without realizing they carry such authority, do pass on rumors. The average police officer doesn't stop to weigh what he says." Certainly the same holds true today, and includes courts and corrections personnel, especially in view of the very high-tech communications equipment now in use.

"Communication" also includes rumors, or the so-called "grapevine" or "rumor mill." Students of criminal justice administration should know that there is probably no type of organization in our society which has more grapevine "scuttlebutt" than that which exists in police agencies. Departments even establish "rumor control" centers during major riots. Compounding the usual barriers to communication is the fact that policing is a 24-hour, 7-day occupation, so that rumors are easily carried from one shift to the next. Most rumors are harmless, but some are malicious.

✦ HISTORICAL APPROACHES TO MANAGEMENT

According to Gerald Lynch,[40] the history of management can be divided into three approaches and time periods: (1) scientific management (1900–1940), (2) human relations management (1930–1970), and (3) systems management (1965–present).

✦ SCIENTIFIC MANAGEMENT

Frederick Winslow Taylor, who first emphasized time and motion studies, is known today as the "father of scientific management." Spending his early years in the steel mills of Pennsylvania, Taylor became chief engineer and later discovered a new method of making steel; this allowed him to retire at age 45 to write and lecture. He became interested in methods of getting greater productivity from workers, and was hired in 1898 by Bethlehem Steel, where he measured the time it took workers to shovel and carry pig iron. Taylor recommended giving workers hourly breaks and going to a piecework system, among other adjustments. Worker productivity soared; the total number of shovelers needed dropped from about 600 to 140, and worker daily earnings increasing from $1.15 to $1.88. The average cost of handling a long ton (2240 pounds) dropped from $0.072 to $0.033.[41]

Taylor, who was highly criticized by unions for his management-oriented views, nonetheless proved that administrators must know their employees. Taylor published a book on the subject in 1911, entitled *The Principles of Scientific Management.* This view caught on, and soon emphasis was placed entirely on the formal administrative structure; such terms as "authority," "chain of command," "span of control," and "division of labor" were generated.

In 1935, Luther Gulick formulated the often quoted POSDCORB, an acronym for planning, organizing, staffing, directing, controlling, reporting and budgeting [Figure 2.4]; this philosophy was emphasized in police management for many years. Gulick emphasized the technical and engineering side of management, virtually ignoring the human side.

Scientific management was heavily criticized as it applied to criminal justice agencies. First, it viewed employees as passive instruments whose feelings were completely disregarded. Further, employees were felt to be motivated by money alone.

✦ HUMAN RELATIONS MANAGEMENT

Beginning in 1930, people began to realize the negative effects of scientific management on the worker. In policing, there arose a view that management should instill pride and dignity in officers. The movement toward human relations management began with the famous studies conducted during the late 1920s through the mid-1930s by the Harvard Business School at the Hawthorne plant of the Western Electric Company.[42]

PLANNING: working out in broad outline what needs to be done and the methods for doing it to accomplish the purpose set for the enterprise;

ORGANIZING: the establishment of a formal structure of authority through which work subdivisions are arranged, defined, and coordinated for the defined objective;

STAFFING: the whole personnel function of bringing in and training the staff and maintaining favorable conditions of work;

DIRECTING: the continuous task of making decisions, embodying them in specific and general orders and instructions, and serving as the leader of the enterprise;

COORDINATING: the all-important duty of interrelating the various parts of the organization;

REPORTING: informing the executive and his assistants as to what is going on, through records, research, and inspection;

BUDGETING: all that is related to budgeting in the form of fiscal planning, accounting, and control.

Figure 2.4   Gulick's **POSDCORB**. *(Source:* Luther Gulick and Lyndall Urwick, *Papers on the Science of Administration* New York: Institute of Public Administration, 1937.)

These studies focused on finding ways to bring about production by changing working conditions, such as the number of hours, the number of work breaks per day, and the physical environment. A group of women who assembled telephone equipment were selected as subjects; they were located in a special room under close supervision. As researchers varied working conditions, they found that each major change brought a substantial increase in production. After the formal study ceased, the women were returned to their original, poorly lighted workbenches and were not given breaks or other benefits. Surprisingly, productivity rose again, to an even higher level than it had been under the experimental conditions. The major study findings, then, were that worker productivity is more closely related to *social* capacity than to physical capacity, that noneconomic rewards play a prominent part in motivating and satisfying employees, and that employees do not react to management and its rewards as individuals but as members of groups.[43] We will discuss the Hawthorne effect in more depth below.

In the 1940s and 1950s, police departments also began to recognize the strong effect of the informal structure on the organization; agencies began using such techniques as job enlargement and job enrichment to generate interest in policing as a career. Studies indicated that the supervisor who was "employee centered" was more effective than one who was "production centered." Democratic or participatory management began to appear in police agencies, and private industry began to move away from the pyramid-shaped organizational structure to a more flat type of structure. The human relations approach had its limitations, however.

With the emphasis being placed on the employee, the role of the organizational structure became secondary; the primary goal seemed to many to be social rewards, and little attention seemed to be given to task accomplishment. Many police managers saw this trend as unrealistic. Employees began to give less and expect more in return.[44]

✧ SYSTEMS MANAGEMENT APPROACH

In the mid-1960s, the features of the human relations and scientific management approaches were combined in the systems management approach. Designed to bring the individual and the organization together, it attempted to help managers use employees to reach desired production goals. The systems approach recognized that it was still necessary to have some hierarchical arrangement to bring about coordination, that authority and responsibility were essential, and that overall organization was required.

This approach combined the work of Maslow,[45] who developed his "hierarchy of needs," in which he classified the needs of people at different levels; McGregor,[46] who stressed the general theory of human motivation; and Blake and Mouton,[47] who developed the "managerial grid," which emphasized two concerns that managers must have: concerns for task and for people. (All of these theories are discussed in greater detail below.) In effect, the systems management approach holds that to be effective, the manager must have an interdependence with other individuals and groups and an ability to recognize and deal with conflict and change. More than mere technical skills are required; managers require knowledge of several major resources: people, money, time, and equipment.[48] Team cooperation is required to achieve organizational goals.

Several theories of leadership also evolved over the past several decades, the most common being trait theory, leadership styles, and situational approaches. Each is discussed briefly below.

✦ PRIMARY LEADERSHIP THEORIES

✧ TRAIT THEORY

The trait theory was very popular until around the 1950s. This theory was based on the contention that good leaders possessed certain character traits that poor leaders did not. Those who developed this theory, Stogdill and Goode, believed that a leader could be identified through a two-step process. First, leaders could be studied and compared to nonleaders to determine which traits were possessed solely by the leaders. Second, people would be sought who possessed these traits, and would be promoted into managerial positions.[49]

A study of 468 administrators in 13 companies found certain traits in successful administrators. They were more intelligent and better educated; had a stronger power need; preferred independent activity, intense thought, and some

Traits	Skills
Adaptable to situations	Clever (intelligent)
Alert to social environment	Conceptually skilled
Ambitious and achievement oriented	Creative
Assertive	Diplomatic and tactful
Cooperative	Fluent in speaking
Decisive	Knowledgeable about group task
Dependable	Organized (administrative ability)
Dominant (desire to influence others)	Persuasive
Energetic (high activity level)	Socially skilled
Persistent	
Self-confident	
Tolerant of stress	
Willing to assume responsibility	

Figure 2.5 Traits and skills commonly associated with leadership effectiveness. (*Source:* Gary Yuki, *Leadership in Organizations,* Englewood Cliffs, N.J.: Prentice Hall, 1981, pp. 70, 121–125.)

risk; enjoyed relationships with people; and disliked detail work more than did their subordinates.[50] Figure 2.5 shows traits and skills commonly associated with leader effectiveness, according to Yuki. Following this study, a review of the literature on trait theory revealed the traits most identified as being associated with leadership ability. Those traits were intelligence, initiative, extroversion, sense of humor, enthusiasm, fairness, sympathy, and self-confidence.[51]

Trait theory has lost much of its support since the 1950s, largely because of the basic assumption of the theory that leadership cannot be taught. A stronger reason, however, is simply the growth of new, more sophisticated approaches to the study of leadership. Trait theory had little quantifiable means to test its claims. What does it mean to say that a leader must be "intelligent"? By whose standards? As compared with persons within the organization or within society? How can such traits as sense of humor, enthusiasm, fairness, and the others listed above be measured or tested? The inability to measure these factors was the real flaw in, and reason for the decline of, this theory.

When the trait theorists could not empirically document characteristics found in leaders, researchers in the 1940s and 1950s began examining leaders and the situations in which leaders actually functioned.

✦ STYLE THEORY

A study at Michigan State University looked at how leaders motivated individuals or groups to achieve organizational goals. They determined that leaders must have a sense of the task to be accomplished as well as the environment in which the followers worked. Three principles of leadership behavior emerged from the Michigan study:

1. Leaders must assume the leadership role and give task direction to their followers.
2. Closeness of supervision directly affects employee production. High-producing units had less direct supervision; highly supervised units had lower production. Conclusion: Employees need some area of freedom to make choices. Given this, they produce at a higher rate.
3. Leaders must be employee oriented. It is the leader's responsibility to facilitate employees' accomplishment of goals.[52]

In the 1950s, Edwin Fleishman began studies of leadership at Ohio State University. After focusing on leader behavior rather than personality traits, Fleishman identified basic principles of leadership that could be taught, in two dimensions: "initiating structure" and "consideration" (Figure 2.6).[53] Initiating structure referred to supervisory behavior that focused on the achievement of organizational goals, and consideration was directed toward a supervisor's openness toward subordinates' ideas and respect for their feelings as persons. It was assumed that high consideration and moderate initiating structure yielded higher job satisfaction and productivity than did high initiating structure and low consideration.[54]

The major focus of this, the style theory, is the adoption of a single managerial style by a manager, based on his or her position in regard to initiating structure and consideration. Three pure leadership styles were thought to be the basis for all managers: autocratic, democratic, and laissez-faire.

Autocratic leaders are leader centered and have a high initiating structure. They are primarily authoritarian in nature and prefer to give orders rather than invite group participation. They have a tendency to be personal in their criticism. This style works best in emergency situations in which there is a need for strict control and rapid decision making. The problem with autocratic leadership is the inability of the organization to function when the leader is absent. It also stifles individual development and initiative, because subordinates are rarely allowed to make an independent decision.[55]

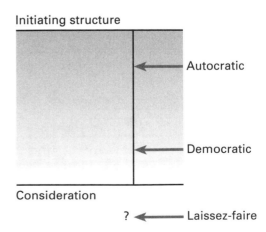

Figure 2.6 Style theory. *(Source: Richard N. Holden, Modern Police Management, Englewood Cliffs, N.J.: Prentice Hall, 1986, p. 40.)*

The *democratic*, or participative, leadership style tends to focus on working within the group and striving to attain cooperation from group members by eliciting their ideas and support. These managers tend to be viewed as consideration oriented and strive to attain mutual respect with subordinates. Democratic leaders operate within an atmosphere of trust and delegate much authority. This style is very useful in organizations where the course of action is uncertain and problems are relatively unstructured. The decision-making ability of subordinates is often tapped. However, in emergency situations requiring a highly structured response, democratic leadership may prove too time consuming and awkward to be effective. Thus, although the worker may appreciate the strengths of this style, its weaknesses must be recognized as well.[56]

The third leadership style, *laissez-faire*, is a hands-off approach where the leader is actually a nonleader. The organization in effect runs itself, with no input or control from the manager. This style has no positive aspects, as the entire organization is soon placed in jeopardy. In truth, this may not be a leadership style at all; instead, it may be an abdication of administrative duties.

✦ SITUATIONAL LEADERSHIP

Style theory assumes that each administrator will adopt one of the styles discussed above (autocratic, democratic, or laissez-faire) almost exclusively. Further, the style theory assumes that all administrators will select a style that they believe works and stay with it, due to managerial rigidity. This assumption has led many researchers to abandon its tenets for one that is more flexible: situational leadership (Figure 2.7).

Early work in situational leadership was conducted by Fred Fiedler. Fiedler held that personality characteristics relevant to leadership are stable over time and across situations. Some personality attributes are believed to contribute to effective leadership in other situations. Through some studies he conducted, Fiedler also concluded that leadership capacity is not likely to be improved

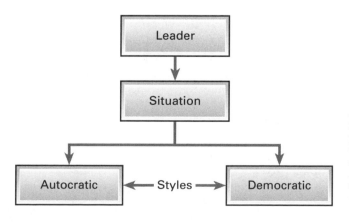

Figure 2.7 Stituational leadership. *(Source:* Richard N. Holden, *Modern Police Management,* Englewood Cliffs, N.J.: Prentice Hall, 1986, p. 40.)

through either training or experience.[57] Fiedler's work was known as contingency theory because he argued that there is no single best approach to leadership. He argued that the influence of the situation determined the appropriate leadership style.

◆ THE MANAGERIAL GRID

In 1964, Robert R. Blake and Jane S. Mouton developed their managerial grid from the studies done by Fleishman and others at Ohio State University. The Ohio team used two variables, focus on task (initiating structure) and focus on relationships (consideration), to develop a management quadrant describing leadership behavior.

The managerial grid includes five leadership styles, based on concern for output (production) and concern for people (Figure 2.8). Using a specially developed testing instrument, people can be assigned a numerical score depicting their concern for each variable. Numerical indications such as 9,1, 9,9, 1,1, and 5,5 are then plotted on the grid using the scales on the horizontal and vertical axes. The grid is read like a map, right and up. Each axis is numbered 1 to 9, with 1 indicating the minimum effort or concern and 9 the maximum. The vertical axis represents the concern for production and performance goals; the vertical axis represents the concern for human relations or empathy.

The points of orientation are related to styles of management. The lower-left-hand corner of the grid shows the 1,1 style (representing a minimal concern for task or service and a minimal concern for people). The lower-right-hand corner of the grid identifies the 9,1 style. This type of leader would have a primary concern for the task or output and a minimal concern for people. Here, people are seen as tools of production. The upper-left-hand corner represents the 1,9 style, often referred to as "country club management," with minimum effort given to output or task. The upper right, 9,9, indicates high concern for both people and production—a "we're all in this together," "common stake" approach of mutual respect and trust. In the center—a 5,5, "middle-of-the-road" style—the leader has a "give a little, be fair but firm" philosophy, providing a balance between output and people concerns.[58]

These five leadership styles can be summarized as follows:[59]

◊ Authority–compliance management (9,1)
◊ Country club management (1,9)
◊ Middle-of-the-road management (5,5)
◊ Impoverished management (1,1)
◊ Team management (9,9)

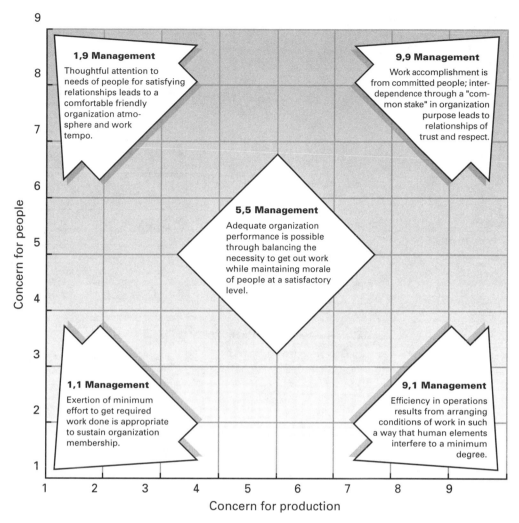

Figure 2.8 Managerial grid. (Reprinted by permission of *Harvard Business Review*. An exhibit from "Breakthrough in Organizational Development" by Robert R. Blake, Jane S. Mouton, Louis B. Barnes, and Larry E. Greiner Nov.–Dec. 1964. Copyright 1964 by the President and Fellows of Harvard College; all rights reserved.)

✦ TYPES OF LEADERSHIP SKILLS

In 1974, Robert Katz identified three essential skills that leaders should possess: technical, human, and conceptual (Figure 2.9). Katz defined a skill as the capacity to translate knowledge into action in such a way that a task is accomplished successfully.[60] Each of these skills (when performed effectively) results in the achievement of objectives and goals, which is the primary nature of management.

Supervisory Management

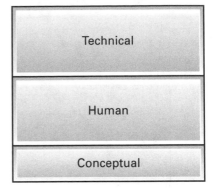

Middle Management

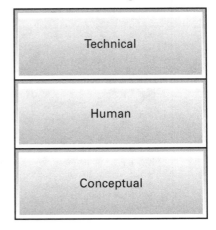

Executive Management

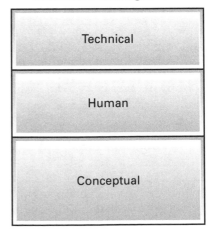

Figure 2.9 Managerial skills needed at different organizational levels. (Reprinted with permission of Macmillan College Publishing Company from *Behavioral Science Management*, by Harry W. More and W. Fred Wegener. Copyright 1992 by Macmillan College Publishing Company, Inc.)

Technical skills are those a manager needs to ensure that specific tasks are performed correctly. They are based on proven knowledge, procedures, or techniques. A police detective, a court administrator, and a probation officer have all developed technical skills directly related to the work they perform. Katz wrote that a technical skill "involves specialized knowledge, analytical ability within that specialty, and facility in the use of the tools and techniques of the specific discipline."[61] This is the skill most easily trained for.

A court administrator, for example, has to be knowledgeable in such areas as budgeting, caseload management, space utilization, public relations, personnel administration, and so on; a police detective must possess technical skills in interviewing, fingerprinting, surveillance techniques, and so on.[62]

Human skills involve working with people, including being thoroughly familiar with what motivates employees and how to utilize group processes. Katz visualized human skills as including "the executive's ability to work effectively as a group member and to build cooperative effort within the team he leads."[63] Katz added that the human relations skill involves (1) tolerance of ambiguity and (2) empathy. Tolerance of ambiguity means that the manager is able to handle problems where insufficient information precludes making a totally informed decision. Empathy is the ability to put oneself in another's place. An awareness of human skills allows a manager to provide the necessary leadership and direction, ensuring that tasks are accomplished in a timely fashion and with the least expenditure of resources.[64]

Conceptual skills, Katz said, involve "coordinating and integrating all the activities and interests of the organization toward a common objective."[65] Katz considered such skills to include "an ability to translate knowledge into action." For example, in a criminal justice setting, a court decision concerning the use of evidence would need to be examined in terms of how it affects detectives, court cases and evidence flow, the laboratory, the property room, and the work of the line officer.

Katz emphasized that these skills can be taught to actual and prospective administrators; thus good administrators are not simply born but can be trained in the classroom. Furthermore, as shown in Figure 2.9, all three of these skills are present in varying degrees for each management level. As one moves up the hierarchy, conceptual skills become more important and technical skills less important. The common denominator for all levels of management is *human* skills. In today's unionized, litigious environment, it is inconceivable that a manager could neglect the human skills.

Katz's conclusion should be read and reread countless times by anyone who has input in the selection or training of criminal justice executives:

> The administrator needs: (a) sufficient technical skill to accomplish the mechanics of the particular job for which he or she is responsible; (b) sufficient human skill in working with others to be an effective group member and to be able to build cooperative effort within the team that he or she leads; (c) sufficient conceptual skill to recognize the interrelationships of the various factors involved in the situation, which will lead [the administrator] to take that action which is likely to achieve the maximum good for the total organization.[66]

On the other hand, of course, there are people who, through no justification of their own, have managed to land themselves squarely in the "driver's seat"—the weak leaders. Solely through politics, guile, or for other irrational reason(s), they have ascended to a position of power within an organization.

✦ MANAGEMENT FADS

Paul Whisenand and Fred Ferguson [67] placed much of this theorizing into a chronology, the result being an interesting history of four decades of management "fads." This trend began in the 1950s when "seat of the pants" management was becoming outdated as a result of Frederick Taylor's insistence that running a company should be more a science than an art. Their four decades of fads are presented below.

The 1950s

1. *Computerization:* The first corporate mainframes were displayed as proud symbols of success.
2. *Theory X and Y:* Propounded by MIT professor Douglas McGregor, this theory held that workers are more productive if they have an influence in their work.
3. *Quantitative Management:* Trust the numbers; running a business is more like a science than an art.
4. *Diversification:* The problem of cyclical ups and downs could be countered by buying other businesses.
5. *Management by Objectives:* Peter Drucker popularized the process of setting an executive's goals through negotiation.

The 1960s

6. *T-Groups:* Encounter seminars were used to teach interpersonal sensitivity.
7. *Centralization, Decentralization:* This is a concern with whether headquarters or line managers should make decisions.
8. *Matrix Management:* Managers report to different superiors according to the task.
9. *Conglomeration:* Disparate businesses are placed under a single corporation umbrella.
10. *The Managerial Grid:* This is a process for determining whether a manager's chief concern is people or production.

The 1970s

11. *Zero-based Budgeting:* This year's budget is based on throwing out last year's numbers and starting from scratch.
12. *The Experience Curve:* This method uses past experience to generate profits by cutting prices, gaining market share, and boosting efficiency.

The 1980s

13. *Theory Z:* Japanese management techniques such as quality circles and job enrichment are adopted.

14. *Demassing:* Trimming the workforce and demoting managers leads to greater efficiency.

15. *Restructuring:* This technique involves sweeping out businesses that don't measure up, often while taking on considerable debt.

16. *Corporate Culture:* Attending to the values, goals, rituals and heroes that characterize a company's style is thought to improve overall performance.

17. *Management by Walking Around:* By leaving the office to visit the troops instead of relying on written reports, managers obtain more relevant information.

Why such a proliferation of fads? Whisenand and Ferguson speculated that it was because managers are under intense pressure to perform miracles, resulting in a mad scramble for instant solutions.[68]

The job of today's criminal justice manager appears to be one of applying the basics of management to existing and emerging trends. A return to the basics is now "in," with such values as integrity, innovation, quality, service, and a people orientation. These basics have been practiced for centuries and normally resulted in successful managers and organizations.[69]

Some authors now see a return to the authoritarian management style and the demise of the teamwork or participative management style begun in the 1950s. For example, evidence is accumulating that a number of quality circles, high-performance teams, and autonomous work groups are not living up to expectations. Newer theories of leadership focus on the power of the leader's personality to change workers' goals—to inspire them and provide a model they want to emulate—under the headings of *charismatic* or *transformational leadership.* The democratic movement ignored the fact that some workers simply are not interested in deriving personal growth and fulfillment from their jobs; for them, satisfaction comes from their personal lives, and the job merely finances that life.[70]

✦ MOTIVATING EMPLOYEES

One of the most fascinating subjects throughout the history of humankind is that of motivating people. Some have sought to do so through justice (Plato), others through psychoanalysis (Freud), some through conditioning (Pavlov), some through incentives (Frederick Taylor), and still others through fear (any number of dictators, czars, pharaohs and despots). Since the industrial revolution, managers have been trying to get a full day's work from their subordinates; today, this issue remains a primary concern in the workplace.

The 1992 flap caused by Japanese businessmen who stated that American workers were lazy certainly raised our collective ire; nonetheless, there are many American business people and managers who would probably agree that greater worker motivation is needed. As Donald Favreau and Joseph Gillespie [71] stated: "Getting people to work, the way you want them to work, when you want them to work, is indeed a challenge."

In recent years a debate has taken place between two groups of behavioral scientists: the behaviorists and the humanists. Behaviorist theory holds that human responses are conditioned by experience. Humanists argue that behavior modification leads to the manipulation of people—removing their free choice. Much of the controversy results from the writings of Harvard psychologist B. F. Skinner. Many other theories have attempted to explain motivation. Some of the best known were the Hawthorne studies and theories developed by Abraham Maslow, Douglas McGregor, and Frederick Herzberg, all of which are discussed below. The expectancy and contingency theories are also discussed.

✦ THE HAWTHORNE STUDIES

Discussed briefly above, one of the most important studies into worker motivation and behavior, launching intense interest and research in those areas, was Western Electric Company's study in the 1920s. In 1927, engineers at the Hawthorne Plant of Western Electric Company near Chicago conducted an experiment with several groups of workers to determine the effect of illumination on production. When illumination was increased in stages, the engineers found that production did increase. To verify their findings, they reduced illumination to its previous level; again, production increased! Confused by their findings, they contacted Elton Mayo and his colleague Fritz Roethlisberger from Harvard to investigate.[72]

First, the researchers selected several experienced women assemblers for an experiment. Management removed the women from their formal group and isolated them in a room. The women were compensated on the basis of the output of their group. Next, researchers began a series of environmental changes, each discussed with the women in advance of its implementation. For example, breaks were introduced and light refreshments were served. The normal 6-day week was reduced to 5 days and the workday was cut by one hour. *Each* of these changes resulted in increased output.[73] To verify these findings, researchers returned the women to their original working conditions; breaks were eliminated, the 6-day workweek was reinstituted, and all other work conditions were reinstated. The results were that production again increased!

A second study was then performed by Mayo and his team at the Hawthorne plant. A new group of 14 workers—all males who worked in simple, repetitive telephone coil winding duties—were given variations in rest periods and work weeks.[74] The men were also put on a reasonable piece rate; that is, the more they produced, the more money they would earn. The assumption was that the workers would strive to produce more since it was in their own economic interest.

The workers soon split into two informal groups on their own, each group setting its own standards of output and conduct. The workers' output did not increase. Neither too little nor too much production was permitted, and peers exerted pressure to keep members in line. The values of the informal group appeared to be more powerful than the allure of bigger incomes:

1. Don't be a "rate buster" and produce too much work.
2. If you turn out too little work, you are a "chiseler."
3. Don't be a "squealer" to supervisors.
4. Don't be officious; if you aren't a supervisor, don't act like one.[75]

Taken together, the Hawthorne studies revealed that people work for a variety of reasons, not just for money and subsistence. They seek satisfaction for more than their physical needs at work and from their co-workers. For the first time, clear evidence was gathered to support workers' social and esteem needs. As a result, this collision between the human relations school, begun in the Hawthorne studies, and traditional organizational theory sent researchers and theorists off in new and different directions. At least three major, new thrusts evolved: (1) inquiries into what motivates workers (leading to the work of Maslow and Herzberg), (2) leadership (discussed above), and (3) work on organizations as behavioral systems.

✧ MASLOW'S HIERARCHY OF NEEDS

Abraham H. Maslow (1908–1970), founder of the humanistic school of psychology, conducted research on human behavior at the Air University, Maxwell Air Force Base, Alabama, during the 1940s. Maslow's approach to motivation was unique, in that the behavior patterns analyzed were those of motivated, happy, and production-oriented people—achievers, not underachievers. He studied biographies of historical and public figures, including Lincoln, Einstein and Eleanor Roosevelt; he also observed and interviewed some of his contemporaries—all of whom possessed no psychological problems and had an absence of any signs of neurotic behavior.

Maslow hypothesized that if you could understand what made these people function, it would be possible to apply the same techniques to others, thus achieving a high state of motivation. His observations were coalesced into a "hierarchy of needs."[76]

Maslow concluded that since human beings are part of the animal kingdom, their basic and primary needs or drives would be physiological: air, food, water, sex, and shelter. These needs are related to survival. Next in order of prepotency are needs related to safety or security: protection against danger, murder, criminal assault, threat, deprivation, and tyranny. At the middle of the hierarchy is belonging, or social needs: being accepted by one's peers, and association with members of groups. The next level on the hierarchy are the needs or drives related to ego:

self-esteem, self-respect, power, prestige, recognition and status. Located at the top of the hierarchy is self-realization or actualization: self-fulfillment, creativity, becoming all that one is capable of becoming.[77] Figure 2.10 depicts this hierarchy.

Self-realization Needs	Job-related Satisfiers
Reaching Your Potential	Involvement in Planning Your Work
Independence	Freedom to Make Decisions Affecting Work
Creativity	Creative Work to Perform
Self-expression	Opportunities for Growth and Development

Esteem Needs	Job-related Satisfiers
Responsibility	Status Symbols
Self-respect	Merit Awards
Recognition	Challenging Work
Sense of Accomplishment	Sharing in Decisions
Sense of Competence	Opportunity for Advancement

Social Needs	Job-related Satisfiers
Companionship	Opportunities for Interaction with Others
Acceptance	Team Spirit
Love and Affection	Friendly Co-workers
Group Membership	

Safety Needs	Job-related Satisfiers
Security for Self and Possessions	Safe Working Conditions
Avoidance of Risks	Seniority
Avoidance of Harm	Fringe Benefits
Avoidance of Pain	Proper Supervision
	Sound Company Policies, Programs, and Practices

Physical Needs	Job-related Satisfiers
Food	Pleasant Working Conditions
Clothing	Adequate Wage or Salary
Shelter	Rest Periods
Comfort	Laborsaving Devices
Self-preservation	Efficient Work Methods

Figure 2.10 Maslow's hierarchy of human needs. (*Source:* A. H. Maslow, *Motivation and Personality*, 2nd ed. New York: Harper & Collins, 1970.)

Unlike the lower needs, the higher needs are rarely satisfied. Maslow suggested that to prevent frustration, the needs should be filled in sequential order. A satisfied need is no longer a motivator. Maslow's research also indicated that once a person reaches a high state of motivation (i.e., step 4 or 5), he or she will remain highly motivated, there will be a positive attitude toward the organization, and there will be a "pitch in and help" philosophy.

✦ McGregor's Theory X/Theory Y

Douglas McGregor (1906–1967), who served as president of Antioch College then on the faculty of the Massachusetts Institute of Technology, was one of the great advocates of humane and democratic management. At Antioch, McGregor tested his theories of democratic management. He noted that behind every managerial decision or action are assumptions about human behavior. He chose the simplest terms possible with which to express them, designating one set of assumptions as Theory X and the other Theory Y.[78]

Theory X managers hold the traditional views of direction and control, such as the following:

◊ The average human being has an inherent dislike of work and will avoid it if possible. This assumption has deep roots, beginning with the punishment of Adam and Eve—their banishment into a world where they had to work for a living. Management's use of negative reinforcement and the emphasis on "a fair day's work" reflect an underlying belief that management must counter an inherent dislike for work.[79]

◊ Because of this human characteristic of dislike of work, most people must be coerced, controlled, directed, or threatened with punishment to get them to put forth adequate effort toward the achievement of organizational objectives. The dislike of work is so strong that even the promise of rewards is not generally enough to overcome it. People will accept the rewards and demand greater ones. Only the threat of punishment will work.[80]

◊ The average human being prefers to be directed, wishes to avoid responsibility, has relatively little ambition, and wants security above all. This assumption of the "mediocrity of the masses" is rarely expressed so bluntly. Although much lip service is paid to the "sanctity" of the worker and human beings in general, many managers reflect this assumption in practice and policy.

(Note: Theory X managers would be autocratic and classified as a 9,1 on the managerial grid.)

Theory Y managers naturally take the opposite view of the worker:

◊ The expenditure of physical and mental effort in work is as natural as play or rest. The average human being does not inherently dislike work; it may even be a source of satisfaction, to be performed voluntarily.

◊ External control and the threat of punishment are not the only means for bringing about effort toward organizational objectives.

◊ Commitment to objectives is a function of the rewards associated with their achievement. The most significant of such rewards—satisfaction of ego and self-actualization needs—can be direct products of effort directed toward organizational objectives.

◊ Under proper conditions, the average human being learns not only to accept but to seek responsibility. Under this view, the avoidance of responsibility, lack of ambition, and the emphasis on security are general consequences of experience, not inherent human characteristics.

◊ The capacity to exercise a high degree of imagination, ingenuity, and creativity in the solution of organizational problems is widely, not narrowly, distributed in the population.

◊ Under the conditions of modern industrial life, the intellectual potentialities of the average human being are only partially utilized.

✧ HERZBERG'S MOTIVATION-HYGIENE THEORY

During the 1950s, Frederick Herzberg conducted a series of studies wherein he asked workers—primarily engineers—to describe the times when they felt particularly good and particularly bad about their jobs. The respondents identified several things that were sources of satisfaction and dissatisfaction in their work. Then, from these findings, Herzberg isolated two vital factors found in all jobs: (1) maintenance or hygiene factors, and (2) motivational factors.

Maintenance factors are those things in the work environment that meet an employee's hedonistic need to avoid pain. Hygiene factors include the necessities of any job (e.g., adequate pay, benefits, job security, decent working conditions, supervision, interpersonal relations, etc.). Hygiene factors do not satisfy or motivate; they set the stage for motivation. They are, however, the major source of dissatisfaction when they are inadequate.[81]

Motivational factors are those psychosocial factors in work that provide intrinsic satisfaction and serve as an incentive for people to invest more of their time, talent, energy, and expertise in productive behavior. Examples would include achievement, recognition, responsibility, the work itself, advancement, and potential for growth. The absence of motivators does not necessarily produce job dissatisfaction.[82]

Although these needs are obviously related, they represent totally different dimensions of satisfaction.

✧ EXPECTANCY AND CONTINGENCY THEORIES

In the 1960s, the *expectancy theory* was developed, holding that employees will do what their managers or organizations want them to do if the following are true:

1. The task appears to be possible (employees believe they possess the necessary competence).
2. The reward (outcome) offered is seen as desirable by the employees (intrinsic rewards come from the job itself; extrinsic rewards are supplied from others).
3. There is a perception in the mind of employees that performing the required behavior or task will bring the desired outcome.
4. There is a good chance that better performance will bring greater rewards.[83]

The expectancy theory will work for an organization that spells out, in specific terms, what behaviors it expects from people and what the rewards or outcomes will be for those who exhibit those behaviors. Rewards may be pay increases, time off, chances for advancement, a sense of achievement, or other benefits. Managers and organizations can find out what their employees want and see to it that they are provided with the rewards they seek.

Walter Newsom [84] said the reality of the expectancy theory can be summarized by the "nine C's": (1) capability (does a person have the capability to perform well?); (2) confidence (does a person believe that he or she can perform the job well?); (3) challenge (does a person have to work hard to perform the job well?); (4) criteria (does a person know the difference between good and poor performance?); (5) credibility (does a person believe the manager will deliver on promises?); (6) consistency (do subordinates believe that all employees receive similar preferred outcomes for good performance, and vice versa?); (7) compensation (do the outcomes associated with good performance reward the employee, with money and other types of rewards?); (8) cost (what does it cost a person, in effort and outcomes foregone, to perform well?).

Later, in the 1970s, Morse and Lorsch built upon McGregor's and Herzberg's theories with their theory of motivation called *contingency theory*. This theory sought to determine the fit between the organization's characteristics and its tasks, and the motivations of individuals. The basic components of the contingency theory are that (1) among people's needs is a central need to achieve a sense of competence; (2) the ways in which people fulfill this need will vary from person to person; (3) competence motivation is most likely to be fulfilled when there is a fit between task and organization; and (4) a sense of competence continues to motivate people even after competence is achieved. In essence, we all want to be competent in our work. Contingency theory contends that people performing highly structured and organized tasks perform better in Theory X organizations, and that those who perform unstructured and uncertain tasks perform better under a Theory Y approach. This theory tells managers to tailor jobs to fit people or to give people the skills, knowledge, and attitudes they will need to become competent.[85]

✧ EXTRINSIC AND INTRINSIC REWARDS

As discussed briefly in Chapter 1, people generally derive positive personal consequences from their work. However, different people seek different rewards from their work. Some tend to require mainly extrinsic rewards, including such perquisites as an office, a key to the executive washroom, bonuses, trips, a company car, awards, an expense account, membership to country clubs and organizations, a good salary and benefits package, and a job title. Corporations spend tremendous sums of money to provide extrinsic rewards to employees and thereby enhance their job satisfaction. These rewards, of course, are not found in the public sector to the extent that they are in the private sector.

Other workers attach less importance to extrinsic rewards, seeking instead satisfaction primarily from within themselves. These people need jobs that are gratifying, that intrinsically make them feel good about themselves and what they accomplish. Criminal justice work is often characterized by practitioners as intrinsically rewarding, particularly by people who work with juvenile offenders. They seek appreciation from their supervisors and co-workers and generally require challenges. This is yet another area where management should attempt to understand the personalities and motivation of its employees and meet those needs to the extent possible.

Summary—

Most young people entering the labor force would probably like to retain their individuality, feel free to express themselves, have a sense of being an important part of the "team," and realize both extrinsic and intrinsic rewards from their work. However, the reality is that a majority of people entering the job market will work within the structure of an organization and will not have all of their personal needs met.

We have seen that many organizations have a highly refined bureaucracy. Whether or not an organization will meet one's individual needs depends largely on the administrative philosophy within. Therefore, our discussions in this chapter covered the structure and function of organizations and, just as important, how administrators and subordinates function within them.

The point to be made above all else is that administrators must know their people. In addition to covering several prominent theories that have withstood the test of time, we pointed out some approaches that have not succeeded. One can learn much from a failed approach or even from a poor boss who failed to appreciate and understand subordinates and practiced improper or no motivational techniques.

In the following chapter we return to criminal justice administration per se, considering the careers of several reformers whose contributions helped to establish contemporary administrative models and justice system practices. Although the methods and philosophies of a few of these reformers are not practiced or even appreciated today, in their own way they contributed to our knowledge of how organizations should be managed.

Questions for Review

1. Define *organizations*, their function and structure.
2. Discuss the three historical approaches to management, distinguishing between the historical approach to management and the more "enlightened," contemporary view.
3. Highlight how people should be governed in the Confucian and Machiavellian views.
4. Delineate some of the skills that strong leaders will commonly possess (using the Katz model) and some of the common weaknesses in leadership.
5. Trace the major leadership "fads" that have arisen over the past decades, beginning with the 1950s.
6. Examine three major theories concerning the motivation of employees.
7. Define *communication*. Explain some of the major barriers to effective communication and why communication is particularly acute in criminal justice agencies.
8. Objectively assess what kind of leader you would be likely to be (if helpful, use the management grid). Is it an effective style? What are some of the possible advantages and disadvantages of that style (if any)?

For Further Reading

SAMUEL C. CERTO, *Principles of Modern Management: Functions and Systems* (4th ed.). Boston: Allyn and Bacon, 1989.

PETER F. DRUCKER, *The Effective Executive*. New York: Harper & Row, 1985.

AMITAI ETZIONI, *A Comparative Analysis of Complex Organizations*. Glencoe, Ill.: Free Press, 1961.

JUDITH R. GORDON, *Human Resource Management: A Practical Approach*. Boston: Allyn and Bacon, 1986.

Mariann Jelinek, Joseph A. Litterer, and Raymond E. Miles, *Organizations by Design: Theory and Practice* (2d ed.). Plano, Texas: Business Publications, 1986.

John Naisbitt, *Megatrends*. New York: Warner Books, 1984.

Notes

1. Amitai Etzioni, *Modern Organizations* (Englewood Cliffs, N.J.: Prentice Hall, 1964), p. 1.
2. David A. Tansik and James F. Elliott, *Managing Police Organizations* (Monterey, Calif.: Duxbury Press, 1981), p. 1.
3. Stephen P. Robbins, *Organizational Theory: Structure, Design and Applications* (Englewood Cliffs, N.J.: Prentice-Hall, 1987).
4. Larry K. Gaines, Mittie D. Southerland, and John E. Angell, *Police Administration* (New York: McGraw-Hill, 1991), p. 5.
5. Peter W. Blau and W. Richard Scott, *Formal Organizations* (Scranton, Pa.: Chandler, 1962), p. 43.
6. Larry K. Gaines, Mittie D. Southerland, and John E. Angell, *Police Administration*, p. 9.
7. Max Weber, *The Theory of Social and Economic Organization*, trans. A. M. Henderson and Talcott Parsons (New York: Oxford University Press, 1947), pp. 329–30.
8. James Q. Wilson, *Varieties of Police Behavior* (Cambridge, Mass.: Harvard University Press), pp. 2–3.
9. *Ibid.*, p. 3.
10. Lyndall F. Urwick, *Notes on the Theory of Organization* (New York: American Management Association, 1952).
11. Larry K. Gaines, Mittie D. Southerland, and John E. Angell, *Police Administration*, p. 9.
12. Leonard R. Sayles and George Strauss, *Human Behavior in Organizations* (Englewood Cliffs, N.J.: Prentice Hall, 1966), p. 349.
13. Robert Sheehan and Gary W. Cordner, *Introduction to Police Administration* (2d ed.) (Cincinnati, Ohio: Anderson, 1989), p. 30.
14. Ernest Dale, *Organization* (New York: American Management Association, 1967).
15. See, for example, Samuel C. Certo, *Principles of Modern Management: Functions and Systems* (4th ed.)(Boston: Allyn and Bacon, 1989), p. 103.
16. Quoted in Charles R. Swanson, Leonard Territo, and Robert W. Taylor, *Police Administration* (2d ed.)(New York: Macmillan, 1988), p. 127.
17. Quoted in Wayne W. Bennett and Karen Hess, *Management and Supervision in Law Enforcement* (St. Paul, Minn.: West, 1992), p. 61.
18. Paul Hersey and Kenneth H. Blanchard, *Management of Organizational Behavior* (3d ed.) (Englewood Cliffs, N.J.: Prentice Hall, 1977).
19. *Ibid.*
20. Quoted in Wayne W. Bennett and Karen Hess, *Management and Supervision in Law Enforcement*, p. 61.
21. *Ibid.*
22. Roger D. Evered and James C. Selman, "Coaching and the Art of Management," *Organizational Dynamics* (Autumn 1989):16.

23. Charles R. Swanson, Leonard Territo, and Robert W. Taylor, *Police Administration* (2d ed.), p. 61.

24. Wayne W. Bennett and Karen M. Hess, *Management and Supervision in Law Enforcement*, p. 61.

25. Arthur Waley (trans.), *The Analects of Confucius* (London: George Allen and Unwin, 1938), pp. 88, 173.

26. *Ibid.*, p. 92.

27. *Ibid.*, pp. 105, 127.

28. Robert M. Adams (trans.), *The Prince* (New York: W.W. Norton, 1992), p. xvii.

29. *Ibid.*, p. 7.

30. *Ibid.*, p. 46.

31. *Ibid.*, pp. 15, 41.

32. *Ibid.*, p. 63.

33. *Ibid.*, pp. 5, 11.

34. *Ibid.*, pp. 29, 60.

35. Quoted in Charles R. Swanson, Leonard Territo, and Robert W. Taylor, *Police Administration* (2d ed.), p. 161.

36. Wayne W. Bennett and Karen Hess, *Management and Supervision in Law Enforcement*, p. 85.

37. *Ibid.*, p. 86.

38. Robert L. Montgomery, "Are You a Good Listener?" *Nation's Business* (October 1981):65–68.

39. Wayne W. Bennett and Karen Hess, *Management and Supervision in Law Enforcement*, p. 101.

40. Ronald G. Lynch, *The Police Manager: Professional Leadership Skills*, (3d ed.) (New York: Random House, 1986), p. 4.

41. Samuel C. Certo, *Principles of Modern Management: Functions and Systems*, p. 35.

42. See Elton Mayo, *The Human Problems of an Industrial Civilianization* (New York: Macmillan, 1933).

43. Paul M. Whisenand and Fred Ferguson, *The Managing of Police Organizations* (3d ed.) (Englewood Cliffs, N.J.: Prentice Hall, 1989), pp. 218–19.

44. Ronald G. Lynch, *The Police Manager*, pp. 5–6.

45. Abraham H. Maslow, *Motivation and Personality* (New York: Harper & Row, 1954).

46. Douglas McGregor, *The Human Side of Enterprise* (New York: McGraw-Hill, 1960).

47. Robert R. Blake and Jane S. Mouton, *The Managerial Grid* (Houston: Gulf Publishing Company, 1964).

48. Ronald G. Lynch, *The Police Manager*, pp. 7–8.

49. Richard Holden, *Modern Police Management* (Englewood Cliffs, N.J.: Prentice Hall, 1986), p. 38.

50. Thomas A. Mahoney, Thomas H. Jerdee, and Alan N. Nash, "Predicting Managerial Effectiveness," *Personnel Psychology* (Summer 1960):147–63.

51. Joe Kelly, *Organizational Behavior: An Existential Systems Approach* (rev. ed.) (Homewood, Ill.: Richard D. Irwin, 1974), p. 363.

52. Wayne W. Bennett and Karen Hess, *Management and Supervision in Law Enforcement*, pp. 65–66.

53. Edwin Fleishman, "Leadership Climate, Human Relations Training and Supervisory Behavior," *Personnel Psychology* 6 (1953):208–22.

54. Stephen M. Sales, "Supervisory Style and Productivity: Review and Theory," in Larry Cummings and William E. Scott, (eds.), *Readings in Organizational Behavior and Human Performance* (Homewood, Ill.: Richard D. Irwin, 1969), p. 122.

55. Richard Holden, *Modern Police Management*, pp. 39–40.

56. *Ibid.*, pp. 41–42.

57. Fred Fiedler, *A Theory of Leadership Effectiveness* (New York: McGraw-Hill, 1967).

58. Donald F. Favreau and Joseph E. Gillespie, *Modern Police Administration* (Englewood Cliffs, N.J.: Prentice Hall, 1978), p. 80.

59. Wayne W. Bennett and Karen Hess, *Management and Supervision in Law Enforcement*, p. 66.

60. Robert L. Katz, "Skills of an Effective Administrator," *Harvard Business Review* 52 (1975):23.

61. *Ibid.*

62. Dan L. Costley and Ralph Todd, *Human Relations in Organizations* (St. Paul, Minn.: West, 1978).

63. *Ibid.*, p. 24.

64. James M. Higgins, *Human Relations: Concepts and Skills* (New York: Random House), 1982.

65. *Ibid.*, p. 27.

66. *Ibid.*, p. 33.

67. Paul M. Whisenand and Fred Ferguson, *The Managing of Police Organizations* (3d ed.), pp. 4–5.

68. *Ibid.*, p. 6.

69. *Ibid.*, pp. 7–8.

70. Robert D. Smither, "The Return of the Authoritarian Manager," *Training* 28 (November 1991):40–44.

71. Donald F. Favreau and Joseph E. Gillespie, *Modern Police Administration*, p. 85.

72. W. Richard Plunkett, *Supervision: The Direction of People at Work* (Dubuque, Iowa: Wm. C. Brown, 1983), p. 121.

73. Elton Mayo, *The Social Problems of an Industrial Civilization* (Boston: Division of Research, Graduate School of Business Administration, Harvard University, 1945), pp. 68–86.

74. Donald F. Favreau and Joseph E. Gillespie, *Modern Police Administration*, pp. 100–101.

75. Frederick J. Roethlisberger and William J. Dickson, *Management and the Worker* (Cambridge, Mass.: Harvard University Press, 1939), p. 522.

76. Donald F. Favreau and Joseph E. Gillespie, *Modern Police Administration*, p. 87.

77. *Ibid.*

78. *Ibid.*, p. 88.

79. *Ibid.*, p. 89.

80. *Ibid.*

81. Harry W. More and W. Fred Wegener, *Behavioral Police Management* (New York: Macmillan, 1992), pp. 163–64.

82. Frederick Herzberg, "One More Time: How Do You Motivate Employees?" in Walter E. Netemeyer (ed.), *Classics of Organizational Behavior* (Oak Park, Ill.: Moore, 1978).

83. Randall S. Schuler, *Personnel and Human Resources Management* (St. Paul, Minn.: West, 1981), pp. 41–43.

84. Walter B. Newsom, "Motivate, Now!" *Personnel Journal* (February 1990):51–55.

85. Warren Richard Plunkett, *Supervision: The Direction of People at Work*, pp. 131–32.

The Reformers: Evolution of Justice Administration

Man, when perfected, is the best of animals; but if he be isolated from law and justice he is the worst of all...

—Aristotle, *Politics*, Book I, and *Ethics*, Book X

✦ INTRODUCTION

Oliver Wendell Holmes reportedly said that to understand what is, we must understand what has been and what it tends to become. It is with that philosophy in mind that the views of several original and distinguished pioneers concerning police, courts, and corrections administration are highlighted. It will be instructive to see how they envisioned the administration of the justice agencies. It might also be helpful to look for patterns of thought contained in this overview.

✦ PROFESSIONAL POLICING COMES TO AMERICA

By the 1850s, American police departments had three major responsibilities: maintaining order, preventing and detecting crime, and regulating public morality. Mobs and gangs often controlled the streets of major cities, and gambling was easy to find. City councils decided how many police officers would be assigned and who the commander would be. Many cities used an independent board to oversee their police departments.

The New York law of 1853 providing for its board became the national model. By 1873 ten other major cities had established police boards, each wanting to keep police power limited and divided.[1] Corrupt persons found ways to circumvent the boards, however.[2] Eventually, most major cities dropped their independent boards; legislation such as that in New York in 1857 transferred control of the local police to state officials. In 1901, New York City began another trend, abolishing the state police board and substituting a single police commissioner. Soon other cities followed suit. By 1920, only 14 of 52 cities of more than 100,000 population, which at one time had boards, had retained them.[3]

Against this backdrop of confusion over how the police were to be administered and organized, several persons began exerting their influence in the early and middle twentieth century. This historical foundation will include some of the administrative views and accomplishments of Leonhard F. Fuld, August Vollmer, Raymond Fosdick, Bruce Smith, and O. W. Wilson.

✦ LEONHARD F. FULD

In 1909, Leonhard Fuld released his critical study of police organizations in the United States, entitled *Police Administration*.[4] He examined many topics in this book, ranging from the selection of police officers to police organization; he stressed that in all problems of administration the two factors of efficiency and humanity must be borne in mind.[5]

Fuld criticized the American system of choosing police chiefs and superintendents, noting that in Europe, especially in England and Germany, police administration was an honored and respected career that attracted university graduates and former army officers. Chief executives never came from the rank and file; administration was considered a demanding office that required a broader education and point of view than could not be found in a patrol officer.[6] Fuld wanted police heads to be strong professionals who could command the respect of the community and administer with integrity and impartiality. He was particularly critical of the nonprofessional heads of police departments (such as boards and commissions), and cynically pointed out that to become a chief of police, it was necessary for a person to have political influence, a good physical condition, the ability to pass the civil service examination, seniority, and in many cities, sufficient money to buy an appointment.[7]

Fuld also believed in the need for individual officers to uphold a higher code of conduct and morality than that demanded of other citizens.[8] He pointed out that patrol officers had a need for close supervision because "the authority with which they are invested, and the respect shown them by the citizens, create in them an inordinate desire to shirk their work."[9] Fuld was concerned with the selection and training of police officers, stating emphatically that all political considerations should be eliminated during the selection process.[10] He believed that the ideal police sergeant should be able to write and prepare reports, have a thorough knowledge of police business, be capable of being discrete and intelligent, and have a rudimentary knowledge of criminal law.[11]

Fuld also felt that the most important position within the American police system was that of captain, as the position had two broad and important duties: police and administrative. Police duties included maintaining public peace and the protection of life and property, while the administrative duties included clerical, janitorial, and supervisory functions.[12] He argued that the inspector was a primary position as well.

✦ AUGUST VOLLMER

August Vollmer's career of more than a quarter century in law enforcement was one of the most important periods in the development of police professionalism. Vollmer became a Berkeley, California, town marshal in 1905. Initially, he commanded a force of only three deputies, but Berkeley soon became one of the most progressive and best governed cities in the country.[13] Vollmer quickly expanded the size of his force, to form a day and night patrol. He soon formed a bicycle patrol (allowing officers to respond three times more quickly to calls than could officers on foot). Then he used $25,000 to purchase a system of red lights that hung at each street intersection, serving as an emergency notification system for police officers, the first such signal system in the country.[14]

In 1906, Vollmer began questioning the criminals he arrested, finding that nearly all of them used a particular method of operation, or *modus operandi*. He then contacted chiefs of police across the country, requesting information on criminals specializing in specific types of crimes. In 1907 he used a professor of biology at the University of California to assist in a criminal investigation, convincing Vollmer of the value of scientific knowledge in many cases. After reading several books, he developed a sound knowledge of the subject.[15]

Vollmer's most daring innovation came in 1908, when he created a preservice "police school" that covered a wide variety of subjects for police officers. This initial, formal training program for police officers drew on the expertise of university professors as well as veteran police officers. The school, later expanded to a three-year curriculum, included courses on police methods and procedures, fingerprinting, first aid, criminal law, anthropometry, photography, public health, and sanitation.[16]

Other innovations followed. By 1914 Vollmer had his entire patrol force operating out of automobiles—the first totally mobile patrol force in the country. In 1916 he persuaded a professor of pharmacology and bacteriology to become a full-time criminalist in charge of the department's criminal investigation laboratory.[17] In 1918, to improve the quality of police recruits in his department, he began to hire college students as part-time officers and to administer intelligence, psychiatric, and neurological tests to all applicants.[18] (Out of this group of "college cops" came several outstanding police leaders, including O. W. Wilson, discussed below.) In 1921, in addition to experimenting with the lie detector, Vollmer became interested in improving communications between officers on patrol. Officers soon had a crystal set and earphones in their Model-T touring cars, the first so equipped.

In 1923, Vollmer accepted a one-year appointment as chief of police of Los Angeles, where police corruption, gambling, and the illicit sale of liquor were major problems. He hired ex-offenders to gather intelligence information. He also promoted honest officers and required 3000 line officers to take an intelligence test. Using the test scores, Vollmer reassigned and promoted still more officers. Already unpopular with crooks and corrupt politicians, this last action made him very unpopular within the department as well. He returned to Berkeley in 1924, having made many enemies in the LAPD; his attempts at reform had met with too much opposition to have any lasting effect.[19]

In the late 1920s, Vollmer began reorganizing police departments in other cities. Like Fuld, Vollmer stressed the need for sufficient time and political support for police executives to improve a department; he argued that the single biggest drawback to good morale and effectiveness in American policing was the short and uncertain tenure of the chief administrator.[20]

Until his death in 1955, Vollmer argued for a liberal education for police officers: "Obviously, the officer on the beat need not be specially skilled in either the mental, biological or social sciences. But none of these can be overlooked in the training of police officers if they are to have a broad, cultural, scientific, and technical background requisite for the performance of the modern officer's duties."[21]

✧ RAYMOND B. FOSDICK

Raymond Fosdick completed in 1915 a comprehensive study of 72 American cities having populations in excess of 100,000. Fosdick shared many of Fuld's views, especially regarding the need for police chiefs to be well educated and politically independent, given tenure, and paid good salaries.

Fosdick identified numerous police problems, such as political control of the police, inadequate police leadership, limited tenure of office for chiefs of police, inadequate police techniques, organizational rigidity, and lack of supervision in investigative work.[22] He also found that American police departments had the same basic organization, generally including at least two principal branches: the uniformed force and the detective bureau. Most communities were divided into precincts and were in turn subdivided into beats for patrol purposes.

Fosdick stressed the need for a single police executive and felt that when there was more than one police executive, the duties were poorly defined and, consequently, many departments were top heavy with administrators.[23] He found most police departments primitive and crude, having developed without design and with little study given to the relationship between patrol duties and crime conditions.

There were, Fosdick felt, essentially three major problems with policing. First, many cities had poor organization, which in turn created local ordinances and methods of police operation that were unsuited to local needs. Second, legislatures had frustrated policing by the addition of extraneous and unrelated functions, such as issuing licenses for saloons and other business, inspecting steam boilers, supervising the dog pound, censorship, and collecting taxes.[24]

Finally, he found unskilled, unfit, and unprofessional police executives who had severely harmed their police organization.[25]

Fosdick felt that in addition to the patrol force, a corps of trained detectives and a crime prevention service were needed in all police departments. He contended that these three main police functions—patrol, investigation and crime prevention—were interrelated and that every police force involved these approaches.[26]

✦ BRUCE SMITH

In 1940, Bruce Smith released the first edition of *Police Systems in the United States*.[27] He wrote that administrative problems of police departments had often been neglected or ignored, recommending that the principles of organization commonly found in the industrial and military fields be applied to the structure of police forces.[28]

Smith found that the vast majority of American police agencies continued to function according to patterns laid down several generations before, and that the administrative structure had not kept pace with the growth of the departments and the creation of specialized units. This resulted in inadequate controls and the organizations failed to accomplish the ultimate purpose—unity of actions.[29]

Smith often used the term *span of control*—the concept that one supervisor can control only a limited number of subordinates. He pointed out that a determination of the actual span of control must rest upon each situation, although no doubt a span of control of five or six is proper in many instances.[30] He identified a broad classification of activities in police organizations: (1) patrol, (2) traffic regulation, (3) criminal investigation, (4) communication and records control, (5) property management, (6) personnel management, (7) crime prevention, and (8) morals regulation.[31]

Smith urged simplicity in the organization of the department as it reduced the number of responsible officers who the administrative head must control if policies were to be effective. He was also concerned about overspecialization in policing, acknowledging the increase in complexity in some areas of law enforcement and the need for specialization, but also emphasizing the importance of administrators to strive to maintain a flexible organization.[32]

✦ O. W. WILSON

In 1950, O. W. Wilson released his seminal work, *Police Administration*.[33] Soon becoming a much used and quoted text, it was very comprehensive and included such diverse topics as organization, control, the juvenile offender, public relations, and leadership. Subsequent editions were issued in 1963 and 1977 (in the latter editions he was co-author with Roy McLaren).

Wilson viewed the primary police objectives as (1) the prevention of the development of criminal and antisocial tendencies in individuals; (2) the repression of criminal activities; (3) the arrest of criminals, the recovery of stolen property, and the preparation of cases for presentation in court; and (4) the regulation of people and their noncriminal activities and the performance of a variety of nonregulatory services.[34]

He suggested that the following principles of police organization be kept in mind:

1. Tasks similar or related in purpose, process, or method are grouped together in one or more units under the control of a single person.

2. Lines of demarcation between the units are clearly drawn so that responsibility may be placed exactly.

3. Channels are established through which information flows up and down, and through which authority is delegated.

4. Each individual, unit, and situation must be under the immediate control of one, and only one, person, avoiding the friction that results from duplication of direction and supervision.

5. No more units or persons are placed under the direct control of one person than he or she is able to manage.

6. Each task is made the unmistakable duty of someone; responsibility for planning, execution, and control is definitely placed on designated persons.

7. Supervision is provided for each person at the level of execution regardless of the hour or place.

8. Each assignment of responsibility carries with it commensurate authority to fulfill the responsibility.

9. Persons to whom authority is delegated are invariably held accountable for its use.[35]

✦ DEVELOPMENT OF COURT ADMINISTRATION

As with police administration, several prominent individuals guided the evolution of formal administration of the courts. The primary difference between police and courts administration is in the time period of their development. Although police administration was shown above to have begun its development in the early 1900s (arguably in 1909, with the publication of Fuld's book on the subject), many point to a historic 1906 speech by Roscoe Pound in St. Paul at the annual meeting of the American Bar Association as the beginning of the formal discipline of court administration. Pound, a brash, young law professor from the plains of Nebraska, lashed out at his profession in his presentation, "The Causes of Popular Dissatisfaction with the Administration of Justice." This speech, later labeled "the spark that kindled the white flame of progress,"[36] has been reprinted many times since and is now considered a classic on the subject of court reform.

Yet little more would be done to move the courts toward an organized form of administration until 1940. Thus court administration is actually relatively young, at least in comparison with its cousins, the police and corrections components.

✧ ARTHUR T. VANDERBILT

Arthur Vanderbilt was born in 1888 in Newark, New Jersey, and attended Wesleyan University in Middletown, Connecticut. He earned his law degree from Columbia University and was admitted to the New Jersey State Bar. He later was dean at the New York University School of Law and chief justice of the New Jersey Supreme Court. A university law center, completed in 1951, is named in his honor. He established the Institute of Judicial Administration at New York University School of Law in 1952 (serving as its president from 1952 until his death in 1957).[37] This institute became known nationally and internationally for its services to the improvement of the administration of justice.[38]

During his nearly half-century-long law career, Vanderbilt wrote effusively on the subject of judicial administration. He felt that court reform—as initiated by Pound three decades earlier—was proceeding with the "imperceptible speed of a glacier."[39] He was also put off by the apathy of the legal profession and roadblocking of politicians. In 1947, with his guidance, New Jersey adopted a new constitutional article that proved to be the basis for a highly modern state court system.

Vanderbilt's most important writing on court reform was *Minimum Standards of Judicial Administration* [40] in 1949, which has been called an "arsenal of information;"[41] it provided the ammunition for the second powerful push for court reform (following that of Pound). Many phrases used in his introductory book have become part of the vocabulary of court administration. Vanderbilt was greatly concerned with the problem of delay and congestion in the courts as well as the cost of litigation, writing that these problems were "the most reprehensible phase of the disease" that had been allowed to become chronic, "while our judges and lawyers, who are professionally responsible for its cure, and our governors and legislators, a majority of whom are lawyers, sit idly by as if the disease were incurable."[42] He also chided lawyers for their indifference to the problems of court administration, writing that "It is a case of the shoemaker neglecting his barefoot children; lawyers are so preoccupied with the substantive problems of their clients that they have little time to devote to the great problems of ways and means in the law that we call judicial administration."[43]

Vanderbilt believed that the courts should be administered through the application of sound business principles; he bemoaned the "almost complete lack of administrative efficiency in most judicial systems," where courts "have become notorious for their reluctance to accept and put into practice even the most basic and simple principles of business administration."[44] He was quick to quote Chief Justice Taft, who said in 1921 that "each judge paddled his own canoe" under a "go-as-you-please system."[45]

In 1939, Congress passed the Administrative Office Act, described by Judge John J. Parker as "the most important piece of legislation affecting the judiciary since the Judiciary Act of 1789."[46] This view was not shared by all, however; one federal judge complained: "A word of warning is appropriate. It is inevitable that a director will come to feel that he has to direct something. As long as he confines his direction to the staff under him, he is performing his duty, but when he interferes with the work of the judges, he should be promptly and emphatically rebuffed."[47] Nonetheless, this act soon had a profound effect not only upon the administration of the federal courts. The Administrative Office of the United States Courts established an enviable reputation for efficient service, demonstrating to judges that the courts benefit from modern management methods. Most states were reluctant to follow the federal example, however. New Jersey took the lead, with a new state constitution passed in 1947 which designated the chief justice as "the administrative head of all of the courts in the states," and provided that the chief justice could appoint an administrative director of the courts to serve at the pleasure of the chief justice.[48] In the same year, at the urging of the Judicial Administration Section of the ABA, the National Commissioners on Uniform State Laws approved and published a model act to provide for an administrator for state courts.[49]

The examples set forth in the federal courts and New Jersey, and the support by the ABA—coupled with the growing national concern with rapidly growing volume and cost of litigation, delays, and congestion in the courts—provided the impetus for continued expansion of court administration. In 1951, North Carolina created the position of administrative assistant to the chief justice,[50] followed in 1951 by creation of an office of court administrator in Puerto Rico,[51] an administrative clerk to the presiding judge of the Superior Court in Rhode Island,[52] and an executive secretary of the Supreme Court in Virginia.[53] In 1953 Michigan established an office of court administration, [54] Oregon provided for an administrative assistant to the chief justice,[55] and Connecticut expanded the duties of its existing executive secretary to the judicial department.[56]

In 1954, Colorado created the position of deputy clerk of the Supreme Court to assist with administrative matters,[57] Kentucky provided for an administrative director of the courts,[58] Louisiana created the post of judicial administrator,[59] and an administrative assistant was furnished to the presiding judge of the federal district court for the District of Columbia.[60] In 1955, Iowa created the office of statistician of the judicial department,[61] a state administrator, and four deputy administrators (one for each department of the Appellate Division of the Supreme Court) were established in New York,[62] Maryland created an administrative office of the courts,[63] and Ohio initiated an office of administrative assistant to the Supreme Court.[64] Massachusetts followed suit in 1956, with its executive secretary of the Supreme Judicial Court.[65]

In 1957, Vanderbilt wrote with a considerable measure of pride:

> Thus today, twenty years after the creation of the Administrative Office of the United States Courts and ten years after the establishment of the first

state Administrative Office of the Courts in New Jersey, a total of fifteen states have given their courts some form of administrative assistance to help the courts manage their own business better. No longer is an administrative organization within the judicial establishment both rare and suspect...looked upon as novel experiments.[66]

In the early 1960s there were probably 30 people in the United States who really worked as court administrators. By 1970 there were some 60 to 70. By the 1980s there were between 2000 and 3000 court administrators in America, following a proliferation of people who were interested in the courts' activities in budgeting, planning, space management, designing information systems, personnel management, public relations, and so on. Some would argue that the pendulum has swung too far, given this influx of administrators into the court system; others argue that the massive caseloads and judicial duties warrant even more such positions. To further trace the evolution of court administration, following are discussions of three more persons who continued Vanderbilt's interest in court reform and management.

✧ A. Leo Levin

Another "innovator and reformer" was A. Leo Levin, born in New York City in 1919. After receiving his law degree from the University of Pennsylvania, Levin was admitted to the New York bar and became a law professor at the University of Pennsylvania. He served as director of the National Institute of Trial Advocacy, executive director for the Commission on Revision of Federal Court Appellate System, and director of the Federal Judicial Center (FJC). Levin kept Roscoe Pound's name in the limelight, being a key organizer of the 1976 conference on popular dissatisfaction with the administration of justice—known as the Pound Conference—and thus keeping the fires of court reform kindled.

Justice Holmes once said that "the business of a law school is...to teach law in the grand manner, and to make great lawyers."[67] According to Chief Justice William H. Rehnquist, Levin saw the FJC as "a place that pursued its educational and research programs 'in the grand manner,'" where his commitment was to a judiciary composed of "great judges."[68] Indeed, Levin's greatest contribution to court administration was in his support for research in the field. Like Vanderbilt, Levin's career of almost 50 years included many articles and books on the administration of justice, and he "commanded national recognition and respect as an outstanding teacher, scholar, and administrator."[69] He developed a judicial administration course for the University of Pennsylvania Law School. Upon leaving the law school in 1977 to become the director of the FJC, Levin began traveling to the various U.S. district and circuit courts, training judges how to judge, doing important research in a continuing effort to strengthen the federal court system, and constantly introducing new techniques for the courts to use. In 1987 he returned to the University of Pennsylvania Law School. He undertook the role as chairman of the task force created by the chief justice of

Pennsylvania, to make recommendations to the court for improvement of the judicial system.

As director of the FJC, Levin hired a committed cadre of researchers, educators, automation specialists, and support staff. Like Vanderbilt, Levin observed in his writings that neither law teachers nor attorneys "have rushed to embrace" the field of court administration; in 1979 he lamented the fact that the Directory of Law Teachers listed only three active professors who currently taught court administration.[70] Two factors, he felt, contributed to the profession's seeming lack of concern with court administration: "A rather narrow conception of the field and...a failure to appreciate the intellectual challenge, the value judgments, and the ultimate significance to litigants and to society inherent in resolving issues of 'mere administration.'"[71]

Levin used the definition of court administration policies as those "designed to enable courts to dispose—justly, expeditiously, and economically—of the disputes brought to them for resolution."[72] He asserted that court administration policies should guide the mechanics of budget administration; determine the number of personnel needed in a particular court; and define the scope of the rulemaking power, the use of staff attorneys to process appeals, the structure of a judicial system, and the processes of ensuring stability in the law of a court system. Levin felt strongly that the "crisis of volume" of case filings is not solved by "the simple expedient of adding resources; resources are too hard to come by."[73] Nor is the problem soluble, Levin argued, by adding more judges—that "in itself creates a new generation of problems."[74]

✦ EDWARD B. MCCONNELL

Ironically, the person in this group of people greatly influencing the development of court administration who is probably its foremost "futurist," once described himself as just the opposite: "I'm not a futurist and don't feel comfortable trying to 'peer over the rim' or to conjure up imaginary visions and scenarios of what might be. I do believe, however, that it is essential for judges, as the primary managers of the court, to plan how to deal effectively with the known."[75] Edward B. McConnell received his law degree from the University of Nebraska and a master's in business administration with distinction from Harvard. He later taught at the Rutgers University School of Business Administration, and became administrative assistant and law secretary to the chief justice of the New Jersey Supreme Court (and, thus, under Arthur T. Vanderbilt), president of the National Center for State Courts, and chairman of the National Conference of Court Administrative Officers.[76]

In a major article in 1984, "The Golden Future," McConnell observed that many of the problems confronting the courts for the past 25 years—especially that of delay—were still plaguing them. He predicted maximum delegation of authority and responsibility to judges and court administrators by state court systems, and that judges and court-support personnel will become increasingly professional.

McConnell also echoed Vanderbilt's view of applying business management techniques to the courts. He stated that something must be done to stem the flow of litigation, and that courts must become tougher in dealing with frivolous lawsuits. He also supported the televising of court trials to "take away the blindfold" that keeps the average person from understanding court operations.

McConnell saw the relationship of judges and court managers as a close one, not mutually exclusive. "The concept that judges should stick to judging and managers to managing is counterproductive," he wrote. "It fails to recognize the independent nature of court management."[77] He viewed it as a team approach, while conceding that the forging of an effective working relationship between judges and court managers—one that is not threatening to judges—is one of the major challenges facing the courts: "Judges have the organizational power but lack the operational knowledge, and the court managers have the knowledge but lack the power. The team approach merges these strengths."[78]

McConnell also felt that to be successful as court managers, judges must take the lead in planning; maintain good relations between the courts and the legislative and executive branches of government; better educate the public about the structure, role, and operation of the courts; monitor the performance and conduct of their judges and staff; and improve the quality of service to the public (by reducing the cost and delays, holding court at convenient times and places, and having personnel of the courts reflect the gender and racial composition of their community).[79]

✧ Ernest C. Friesen

Ernest C. Friesen, Jr., took his law degree from Columbia University and was then admitted to the New York bar. After stints in private practice and as a trial attorney for the Department of Justice, he taught law at the University of Cincinnati. He then served as an administrator for the ABA; dean of the National Judicial College (Reno, Nevada); assistant attorney general for the U.S. Department of Justice; director of the Administrative Office of United States Courts; director of the Institute for Court Management; and professor or dean of the law school at the University of Denver, Whittier College, and California Western.[80]

Friesen has possibly provided his greatest contributions to the field by assuming a "devil's advocate" role with court administration. Like those before him, Friesen focused on court delays, writing that neither Vanderbilt's application of Pound's court organization doctrines, nor later writings on the subject, though containing thoughtful analyses for court reform, had little practical effect on reducing court delay.

Friesen argued that opponents of the "controlled court management approach" to delay reduction usually argue from one of three premises: first, the problem is one of inadequate resources; second that control is a bad cure; and, third, that delay is not bad. He noted that one research project traced delay to the *addition* of law clerks to trial judges, who took more time to do tasks than did the judges.

✦ DEVELOPMENT OF CORRECTIONS ADMINISTRATION

Corrections administration has undergone several changes in philosophy, ranging from cruelty to inmates, to a more individualized treatment-oriented model, to the current punitive, "just desserts" philosophy. Those views and changes in governing philosophy did not occur by chance; they were driven by people who either had a personal vision of societal or inmate needs, or were compelled by their observations to take a stand. Following are discussions of five such persons: John Howard, Elam Lynds, Mary Belle Harris, Zebulon Brockway, and George Beto.

Some of these five individuals could be deemed harsh and even cruel; others were decidedly compassionate, even friendly with their charges. Surely their disparate methods were not always successful, by the usual standards of inmate behavior and recidivism. All, however, believed fervently in what they were doing and made a difference in the evolution of corrections administration. In reading of their careers, one might compare and contrast the means they used to accomplish their ends.

✧ JOHN HOWARD

Born in England in 1726, at age 16 John Howard inherited a considerable fortune and was deeply religious. He felt strongly about people's obligation to care for one another; some writers have even called him a fanatic.[81] Captured on a ship during hostilities with France, he spent several years as a prisoner of war—his first encounter with prisons. In 1773 he was appointed sheriff of Bedford, his primary duty being to visit the three local jails in town. He was shocked by their conditions, finding that debtors could be sent to prison by their creditors, inmates had to buy all amenities except a minimum amount of food, liquor was sold by brutal jailers, and orgies were prevalent in cells shared by men and women. Furthermore, prisoners were sometimes chained to walls, and disease was rampant.

Howard tried to convince the courts to force the county to pay for jail improvements; the judges were sympathetic, but ordered him to find a precedent in other counties. Thus began a career of sojourns to a number of European countries where he was allowed admission into many penal institutions and eventually became a renowned expert on existing conditions. In Gloucester he saw underground prisons and inmates who were half naked and almost dead of starvation; in Plymouth he found several men detained in excruciatingly small cells. After presenting his findings to the English House of Commons, he visited Europe, finding prisons in Paris and elsewhere (except the Bastille) reasonably satisfactory. He then went to Holland and Germany, finding in Mannheim that newly arrived prisoners were fastened by the neck, hands, and feet to a flogging machine and given "the great welcome"—20 to 30 lashes.[82]

On returning to England, Howard wrote and published *The State of the Prisons in England and Wales, with Preliminary Observations, and an Account of Some Foreign Prisons.* He recommended baths, adequate diet, and personal hygiene for prisoners; fire precautions in cells; segregation of women and young offenders; abandonment of solitary confinement and use of "trustee" guards; honest and well-paid jailers; prison infirmaries and doctors; and adequate diet for inmates. Making a third trip to France in 1778, he still found cruelty in prisons, but interest in reforming the judicial system was developing. He saw model prisons in Holland and Rome, and in 1784 set off on a tour that included Denmark, Sweden, and Russia. (It should be noted that these were all perilous trips; attacks by pirates were not uncommon, and indeed happened to him in 1786 on a voyage to Venice.) Howard constantly wrote of his observations and ideas for model prisons, and by the late 1780s much was being written about him. However, in 1790, in the course of making hospital visits to ascertain their conditions following the plague, Howard caught Asiatic fever in Russia and died. His gravestone at Kherson, Russia, bore the following inscription: "Whoever thou art, thou standeth at the tomb of thy friend." Perhaps this sums up his life and philosophy; one author stated that "no man did more to improve the treatment of prisoners than John Howard. He opened the eyes of his contemporaries to elementary human obligations."[83]

✧ ELAM LYNDS

In 1821, Elam Lynds was appointed warden of the Auburn prison system in New York. Lynds believed that the old congregate and solitary confinement systems, attempted earlier at the Walnut Street Jail (in Philadelphia) and with a preliminary design at Auburn, had failed. Lynds felt there was little hope of transforming older criminals into religious and law-abiding citizens, and felt that younger inmates could learn to work in prison and become good craftsmen. He put prisoners to work in small, strictly supervised units where complete silence was observed and a breach of rule was punished by flogging (which Lynds felt was the most effective and humane method, as it did not affect the offender's physical strength). Inmates were required to keep their eyes cast downward when walking. The "lock step" was used to move inmates in groups.[84] This "silent" system required that inmates spend their nights in solitary cells, with no other book than the Bible. No whisper was permitted while they reflected in silence on their errors.

Lynds also believed that prison wardens must be despised in order to rule with a firm hand.[85] Hearing that an inmate had sworn to murder him, Lynds summoned the offender to his bedroom and ordered him to dress and shave him. The prisoner dared not carry out his threat. Upon dismissing him, Lynds contemptuously said, "I knew you wanted to kill me. But you are too much of a coward...alone and unarmed, I am stronger than all of you together."[86]

Meanwhile, the population of New York and its criminality were growing rapidly. A new prison was needed and Lynds agreed to build one using Auburn inmates. In 1825, he put about 100 prisoners to work in strict silence, driving them to cut stone from the cliffs and build the first block of cells. A German observer reported that "within three years, these human beasts of burden had built cells for over five hundred prisoners and a chapel for nine hundred."[87]

The result of this toil was Sing Sing (an Indian phrase meaning "stone on stone"), built on Mount Pleasant but an ugly penal institution. The same inside cell plan was used as in the latest Auburn model. Inmates and guards moved about like ghosts, the latter wearing moccasins to muffle the sound of their footsteps. Two French authors wrote that Lynds's successor, Robert Wilste, felt also that "the best prison is the one prisoners consider the worst."[88]

✦ ZEBULON BROCKWAY

National discussions on penal problems were very lively during the late nineteenth century, with debate centering on the use of the separate system (prolonged solitary confinement), on the one hand, and the silent system (with inmates congregating) on the other. A new era in penal reform was ushered in by the first National Prison Congress, held in 1870 in Cincinnati, where a paper entitled "Declaration of Principles" called for reform based on the progressive Irish system. The Declaration was based on a paper written by Zebulon Reed Brockway, who had been employed in prisons as a young man and worked his way up to warden in Detroit. His speech at the congress catapulted him to the leadership of correctional administration.

Brockway believed that the central aim of the prison system was the protection of society against crime, not the punishment of criminals. Undoubtedly influenced by Cesare Lombroso's theories about the "born criminal," sentences, he felt, should not be determinate but indeterminate (Elmira became the "cradle" for this concept), and the true basis of classification for prisoners was *character*, not conduct. These views signaled the beginning of the reformatory movement in America.[89]

The crime rate and population were rising in New York and more prisons were needed. A prison modeled after Sing Sing was constructed near Elmira, and in 1876 Brockway was hired as warden. His first act was to build a solid wall around the entire facility. He then planned treatment programs, but all inmates coming to Elmira were to be young (16 to 30 years of age) first offenders (these conditions were never fully realized, however). He regarded vocational training as essential for inmates, along with military drill, occupational therapy, good nutrition, and active moral and religious influences. The institution, he felt, should work "with nature and not against it." He put prisoners to work at 34 major trades and began a prison newspaper, *The Summary*; by 1891 the prison library contained nearly 4000 volumes. Perhaps his most important innovation was the inmate wage system, where prisoners were compensated for their work but had to pay for everything they received except for their first meal and clothing issue upon arrival at Elmira.[90] It is estimated that by interviewing new arrivals and dealing with inmates in the evening, Brockway spoke to between 40 and 50 convicts per day,[91] serving at different times as "friend, minister, and prisonmaster."[92]

In later years of his life, after 20 years at Elmira dealing with inmates on an individual basis, Brockway sensed that his life's work had been destroyed by his successors (many of whom had a more punitive view) and through greater use of probation. He wrote in his autobiography that the result would inevitably be prisons that were less correctional institutions, and more scientific training centers for degenerate adults.[93]

✧ MARY BELLE HARRIS

One of the foremost proponents of the rehabilitative ideal was Mary Belle Harris, born in 1874 in Pennsylvania. She attended religious schools, earned a doctorate from the University of Chicago in 1900, then taught in schools in Kentucky and Chicago. She also worked at the famous Hull House, and soon became known for her high standards and creativity, later to become hallmarks of her administrative career.

Harris's entry into correctional administration was clearly unintended. A New York City commissioner of corrections who had befriended Harris earlier in Chicago took her on a tour of the workhouse on Blackwell Island, and later offered her a position as superintendent. Harris, then aged 39, accepted, but only temporarily, until "the right person" could be found for the job.[94]

Harris served in this capacity from July 1914 to January 1918. She later confessed that she was in a daze as the ferry took her to the workhouse, considered to be among the worst of the 12 New York institutions. In her 1942 book entitled *I Knew Them in Prison*, she wrote that "it was a depressingly grim place, and I shall never forget the feeling of utter desolation I had when…I left…there that evening to work out my own salvation, if I could."[95] Harris found the conditions "so unspeakable that abandonment and utter demolition seemed the evident course to recommend."[96] Chaos, in the form of fights, assaults, insubordination, and enforced idleness prevailed.

There she soon revealed her rehabilitative philosophy, all of which contrasted with conventional punitive approaches of the day: (1) crime is influenced by social factors; (2) individualized treatment is an appropriate social response for most deviant behavior; and (3) special emphasis should be placed on the person rather than the offense.[97] Over staff protests, Harris emphasized open lines of communication, provided regular table decorations, created outside exercise yards, and scheduled fresh air walks for every woman, along with flower gardening. She established a separate ward for the drug addicts, to enhance individualized treatment, and introduced Wassermann tests to help free the workhouse of venereal disease. She permitted inmates to play cards and appointed an inmate librarian. For the first time, the women had knives and forks, with meat served on plates instead of in bowls. She advocated inmate classification, individualization, and selective segregation, and believed that only a small percentage of all inmates required maximum security.[98]

Because of a change in political administration, Harris's tenure at the workhouse ended in 1917. Having grown accustomed to battling for correctional reform, she then sought another tough assignment, serving as superintendent of the state reformatory in Clinton, New Jersey, from February 1918 to April 1919. She began traveling to other correctional institutions, and soon observed considerable disparity between the facilities and programs established for men and women inmates. She began criticizing her female peers as often being too willing to "make things do" and too accepting of "left-overs." She was able to enhance many programs at Clinton, encouraging self-government in the cottages and discontinuing the stigmatizing practice of dressing runaways in red dresses and cutting their hair in "a disfiguring fashion."[99]

After a short stint as assistant director of the War Department's reformatory for women, Harris returned to New Jersey. From May 1919 to January 1925 she was superintendent of the State Home for Girls in Trenton, where she recruited several college students as aides in physical education, music, and domestic science. Escape attempts were common, and she reluctantly authorized the use of spankings of inmates. Later, she would describe this position as the lowest point in her career: "Although I should never wish to be quoted as condoning corporal punishment...I profited from this experience. It made me humble and less critical of others who are caught in a situation of a similar nature."[100]

Among other innovations at Trenton were (1) a "credit card" system whereby at the end of each day, a girl received her "pay" or "credit loss" on the basis of behavior; (2) annual "graduation" ceremonies, with parents and guest speakers, to honor each "class" of departing inmates; (3) a highly successful movie of the home, which became a public relations bonus; (4) tests for diphtheria and scarlet fever; and (5) special events, such as "Harvest Home," when the girls "ran" the institution and had an open house for family, friends, and the press.[101]

From March 1925 to March 1941, Harris served as the first superintendent of the Federal Industrial Institution for Women, Alderson, West Virginia. There she insisted on cottages rather than cells; discontinued heavily armed guards; enhanced the classification system; offered educational and vocational classes; implemented self-government and religious services; and provided a variety of entertainment, such as clubs, hobbies, special celebrations, contests, and dances. For some, Alderson was a model institution, for others, a fashionable girls' boarding school.[102]

Sanford Bates, the first director of the Federal Bureau of Prisons, summed up Harris's career by saying: "She belonged to that school which believed that there is basic goodness in everyone and if that can be reached and touched, then change will occur."[103]

✦ GEORGE BETO

There are a number of late-twentieth-century prison wardens who have realized acclaim by virtue of their experiences and methods, about whom we could write in this section, including W. J. Estelle and Raymond Procunier [both formerly of the Texas Department of Corrections (TDC)], Joseph Ragen (of Stateville Penitentiary in Illinois), and Paul Keve (Minnesota). Many prison wardens of this period, along with their inmate litigants, will live on and be remembered in criminal justice textbooks through the court cases filed against them. Some examples are *Ruiz v. Estelle*,[104] discussed below, which took 13 years and $1 billion to resolve; *Estelle v. Gamble* [105] (where inmate Gamble argued that prison administration showed "deliberate indifference" to his medical problems, which constituted cruel and unusual punishment); *Procunier v. Martinez* [106] (challenging mail censorship by the California Department of Corrections); and *Gideon v. Wainwright* [107] (where Louis Wainwright was sued as director of the Florida Department of Corrections by Clarence Gideon, who had been convicted and sentenced for commission of a felony without counsel present).

However, probably none of these wardens personified the essence of the control model of prison administration more than Dr. George Beto, a tall, lean Lutheran minister and college president turned prison director, known as "Walking George,"[108] who was himself a party in major inmate litigation.[109] Beto was director of the Texas Department of Corrections from 1962 to 1972. Two of the system's prisons were later named after him. Upon his hiring he promised to leave after 10 years, feeling that after a decade "You lose your courage. You come to know your subordinates too well. You learn too much about the legislature. Fresh ideas and energy fade with time."[110]

Beto's control model involved the strict enforcement of discipline and a daily routine; inmates had virtually no input. It has been suggested that to fully comprehend the philosophical lifeblood of the Texas control model, one should read Joseph Ragen's *Inside the World's Toughest Prison* (1962) and Martin Luther's *Secular Authority: To What Extent It Should Be Obeyed*, written in the first half of the sixteenth century.[111] (Luther was not a prison warden, of course; but the German Monk's ideas, set forth in his *Ninety Five Theses*, launched a theological and political revolution throughout Europe.) Beto's mentor, Ragen, firmly believed in the need to run a tight ship; Beto also believed that inmates had no right to challenge prison authority, following Martin Luther's writing that "if wrong is to be suffered, it is better to suffer it from rulers than that the rulers suffer it from their subjects."[112] Under Beto at TDC, all inmates wore regulation white uniforms and had short-cropped hair. All who were illiterate attended school at least one day a week. All worked in the fields the first six months, and addressed the officers as "boss" or "sir." All privileges had to be earned and could be taken away without a hearing.

Beto believed there existed a moral necessity for seeking and wielding worldly power to protect and guide those who were unable to do so for them-selves—to discipline those who behaved badly, educate them, and instill in them a respect for duly constituted authority. His style was unique; one officer recalled that "he could freeze a man—convict or boss—with a stare...like he was looking into your heart, finding evil, and putting you back to honesty." Another said "He was as tough as nails, but he had a big ol' bleeding heart."[113] Under Beto's leadership, prison industries developed (including everything from food to inmate clothing), and he forged legislation allowing the TDC to sell its industrial goods. He created a work-release program as well. As he walked the institution, any inmate could approach him with a problem or a letter containing information; Beto considered the latter "a source of useful intelligence and a barometer of conditions."[114]

Upon retirement from the prison in 1972 to enter academia, Beto hand-picked Estelle as his successor. Prison administration rapidly changed, and in 1985 Beto heard descriptions of the then-existing prison conditions in Texas: inmates killing one another and young or new inmates being gang raped; shakedowns of cells turning up hundreds of weapons and contraband; most staff members unable or unwilling to prevent violence; inmate classrooms and workplaces characterized by idleness. Beto had predicted the demise of the control model in 1983. Three factors helped bring its death to reality: the cessation of the building tender system (using trustee guards to help control inmates); a class action lawsuit, *Ruiz v. Estelle*,[115](where U.S. District Court Judge William W. Justice found that the TDC had violated the rights of inmates in the following areas: overcrowding, security, fire security, medical care, discipline, and access to the court); and changes in personnel and managerial philosophy, following *Ruiz*. The Beto era and the control model—for good or bad, depending on one's view of prison conditions—had passed.

✦ DEVELOPMENT OF PROBATION AND PAROLE

✧ JOHN AUGUSTUS

Although contemporary probation has roots dating back to biblical times, its history in the United States dates back to the nineteenth century. "Judicial reprieve" was used in English courts to serve as a temporary suspension of sentence to allow the defendant to appeal to the Crown for a pardon. In the United States the suspended sentence was used as early as 1830 in Boston and became widespread in American courts, even though there was no statutory provision for it. By the mid-nineteenth century, though, many courts were using a judicial reprieve to suspend sentences.[116] This posed a legal question: Could judges suspend sentences wholesale, after trials that were scrupulously fair, simply to give the defendant a second chance? [117]

In 1916 the U.S. Supreme Court, in a decision affecting only the federal courts, held that judges did not have the discretionary authority to suspend sentences. However, the Court ruled that Congress could authorize the temporary or indefinite suspension of sentences; this led to the development of probation statutes.[118]

The term *probation* was utilized by John Augustus, a Boston shoemaker who began taking people to his home from court in the mid-1800s, most of whom were charged with being drunkards. He later wrote that "I was in court one morning…in which the man was charged with being a common drunkard. He told me that if he could be saved from the House of Correction, he never again would taste intoxicating liquors; I bailed him, by permission of the court."[119] During his first year of service as an unpaid, volunteer probation officer, Augustus assisted 10 drunkards; eventually, he helped other types of offenders, and of 2000 cases he handled over an 18-year period, only 10 persons jumped bail or probation. Augustus's work was not viewed favorably, however, by prosecutors (who felt that he clogged court calendars) or by the police and court clerks (who received a fee for each case resulting in a commitment to the infamous House of Correction). [120]

Augustus performed several tasks that are reminiscent of modern probation. He investigated each case—inquiring into his or her character, age, and influences—and kept careful records of each person's progress. His probation work soon caused him to fall into financial difficulties, however, requiring his friends' monetary assistance. Augustus died in 1859.

✦ ALEXANDER MACONOCHIE

The word *parole* stems from the French *parol*, or "word of honor," which was a means of releasing prisoners of war who promised not to resume arms in a current conflict.[121] One writer cited the year 1840 as one in which "one of the most remarkable experiments in the history of penology was initiated...."[122] In that year, Alexander Maconochie (1787-1860) became superintendent of the British penal colony on Norfolk Island, about 930 miles northeast of Sidney, Australia. He began a philosophy of punishment based on reforming offenders: The convict was to be punished for the past while being trained for the future. Maconochie advocated open-ended ("indeterminate") sentences. His system worked, although it was harshly ridiculed by some Australians as "coddling criminals."

Returning to England in 1844, Maconochie began writing and speaking of his experiment. One of those impressed by Maconochie was Walter Crofton, who in 1854 became director of the renowned Irish System of penal management. Crofton implemented, among many other things, a "ticket of leave" system, allowing inmates to be conditionally released from prison, to be supervised by the police. Crofton recommended a similar system for the United States.

In 1876, when Zebulon Brockway was appointed superintendent of the Elmira Reformatory in New York, he drafted a statute providing for indeterminate sentences. Continued good behavior by inmates resulted in early release—America's first parole system. Paroled inmates remained under the jurisdiction of reformatory authorities for an additional six months, during which the parolee was required to report on the first day of every month to his appointed guardian and provide an account of his or her conduct and situation. This system was copied by other states; it was further expanded by the Great Depression, which abolished economic exploitation of convict labor.[123]

Summary

The foregoing overview of several people who had a profound influence on the development of justice administration served a major purpose: it demonstrated that change and creativity are possible in criminal justice. It is easy for administrators to become so enmeshed with problems of the day-to-day variety that they forget to consider other, more progressive or beneficial way of accomplishing tasks.

Each person discussed in this chapter felt that he or she had something better to offer than the system inherited. In hindsight, some of their methods were not better or more popular, but nonetheless were attempts to improve the current situation. Some pioneers, such as Vollmer, Vanderbilt, and Harris, worked from a "clean slate" and thus had the luxury of experimenting with completely new methods.

We now shift to an examination of the contemporary problems and practices of police, courts, and corrections administration—disciplines that are often criticized for being too bound up in tradition. Hopefully, the potential for innovation and new directions projected by the people described in this chapter will be borne in mind.

Questions for Review

1. What significant contributions to police administration were made by nineteenth-century police pioneers? What patterns of agreement exist among the views of these early contributors? Which contributors, if any, appear to have provided the greatest impact on modern police administration?

2. Clearly, Arthur T. Vanderbilt was a tremendous force on early court administration. What were some of his major contributions? What did each of his followers contribute?

3. Each of the prison reformers discussed varied in his or her philosophies and approaches to administration; some were even quite harsh in their view toward offenders. Briefly discuss each person's contributions, focusing on the impact today.

4. How did probation and parole evolve? Who were the major actors in their development?

For Further Reading

Howard Abadinsky, *Probation and Parole: Theory and Practice* (3d ed.). Englewood Cliffs, N.J.: Prentice Hall, 1987.

GENE E. CARTE and ELAINE H. CARTE, *Police Reform in the United States: The Era of August Vollmer, 1905–1932.* Berkeley, Calif.: University of California Press, 1975.

TORSTEN ERIKSSON, *The Reformers: An Historical Survey of Pioneer Experiments in the Treatment of Criminals.* New York: Elsevier, 1976.

EDWARD C. FRIESEN, JR., EDWARD C. GALLAS, and NESTA M. GALLAS, *Managing the Courts.* Indianapolis, Ind.: Bobbs-Merrill Company, 1971.

HERBERT A. JOHNSON, *History of Criminal Justice.* Cincinnati, Ohio: Anderson, 1988.

CARL B. KLOCKARS, *Thinking about Police: Contemporary Readings.* New York: McGraw-Hill, 1983.

JAMES F. RICHARDSON, *Urban Police in the United States.* Port Washington, N.Y.: Kennikat Press, 1974.

RUSSELL R. WHEELER and HOWARD R. WHITCOMB, *Judicial Administration: Text and Readings.* Englewood Cliffs, N.J.: Prentice Hall, 1977.

Notes

1. James F. Richardson, *Urban Police in the United States* (Port Washington, N.Y.: Kennikat Press, 1974), pp. 35–37.
2. *Ibid.*, pp. 37–38.
3. Raymond Fosdick, *American Police Systems* (New York: Century Books, 1920), pp. 108–109.
4. Leonhard F. Fuld, Police Administration (New York: G. P. Putnam, 1909).
5. *Ibid.*, p 304.
6. James F. Richardson, *Urban Police in the United States*, p. 70.
7. Leonhard F. Fuld, *Police Administration* p. 41.
8. *Ibid.*, p. 112.
9. *Ibid.*, p. 49.
10. *Ibid.*, p. 153.
11. *Ibid.*, p. 56.
12. *Ibid.*, pp. 59-60.
13. Alfred E. Parker, *Crime Fighter: August Vollmer* (New York: Macmillan, 1961).
14. Nathan Douthit, "August Vollmer," in Carl B. Klockars (ed.), *Thinking about Police: Contemporary Readings* (New York: McGraw-Hill, 1983), p. 102.
15. *Ibid.*.
16. *Ibid.*
17. *Ibid.*
18. Ibid., p. 103.
19. Paul Jacobs, *Prelude to Riot: A View of Urban America from the Bottom* (New York: Random House, 1966), pp. 13-60.
20. James F. Richardson, *Urban Police in the United States*, p. 83.
21. Nathan Douthit, "August Vollmer," p. 108.
22. Raymond B. Fosdick, *American Police Systems* (Montclair, N.J.: Patterson Smith, 1969), pp. 382–383.

23. *Ibid.*, pp. 189–190.

24. *Ibid.*, p. 213.

25. *Ibid.*, p. 215.

26. *Ibid.*, pp. 268–270.

27. Bruce Smith, *Police Systems in the United States* (New York: Harper and Brothers, 1960).

28. *Ibid.*, p. 208.

29. *Ibid.*, p. 209.

30. *Ibid.*, p. 218.

31. *Ibid.*, pp. 219–220.

32. *Ibid.*, p. 241.

33. O. W. Wilson, *Police Administration* (New York: McGraw-Hill, 1950).

34. *Ibid.*, p. 9.

35. *Ibid.*, p. 17.

36. See *Journal of the American Judicature Society* 20 (1937):176.

37. Fannie J. Klein and Joel S. Lee (eds.), *Selected Writings of Arthur T. Vanderbilt* (Vol. I) (Dobbs Ferry, N.Y.: Oceana Publications, 1965), p. xv.

38. *Ibid.*, p. xiv–xvi.

39. Fannie J. Klein and Joel S. Lee (eds.), *Selected Writings of Arthur T. Vanderbilt* (Vol. II) (Dobbs Ferry, N.Y.: Oceana Publications, 1965), p. 37.

40. Arthur T. Vanderbilt, *Minimum Standards of Judicial Administration* (New York: National Conference of Judicial Councils, 1949).

41. *Ibid*, p. 38.

42. See 39 Mass.L.Q. 9 (1954); 22 J.B.A.D.C. 618 (1955).

43. Arthur T. Vanderbilt, *Minimum Standards of Judicial Administration*, pp. 41–42.

44. *Ibid.*, p. 68.

45. *Journal of the American Judicature Society* 37 (1921).

46. John J. Parker, "The Federal Judiciary," 22 Tul. L. Rev. 569, 575 (1948).

47. Quoted in Edward B. McConnell, "What Does the Future Hold for Judges?" *Judges Journal* 30 (Summer 1991):8.

48. New Jersey Constitutional article VI, Section VIII, paragraph 1.

49. 9 Uniform Laws 75 (Cum. Supp. 1956).

50. N. Car. Gen. Stat. Sec. 7-29.1 (1953).

51. P.R. Laws Ann. Tit. 4, Secs. 331–334 (1954).

52. R.I. Gen. Laws c. 3030 (1952).

53. Va. Code Ann. Secs. 17-111.1, 17-111.2 (Supp. 1950).

54. Mich. Stat. Ann. Secs. 27.15(1)–27.15(7) (Supp. 1953).

55. Ore. Rev. Stat. Secs. 2.310–2.340, 8.260 (1953).

56. Conn. Gen. Stat. Sec. 7661 (1949); Conn. Practice Book 371-73 (1951).

57. Colo. Rev. Stat. Ann. Secs. 37-10-1 to 37-10-3 (1953).

58. Ky. Rev. Stat. Ann. Sec. 21.220 (Baldwin 1955).

59. La. Sup. Ct. Rev. Rule XXI (1952).

60. No enabling legislation or rule was required.

61. Iowa Code Sec. 685.6 (1955).

62. Laws of 1955 (N.Y.) Ch. 869.

63. Laws of 1955 (Md.) Ch. 343.

64. Ohio Rev. Code Sec. 2503.05; 126 Ohio Laws 51 (1955).

65. Laws of 1956 (Mass.) Ch. 707.

66. See Arthur T. Vanderbilt, *Improving the Administration of Justice: Two Decades of Development* (Cincinnati, Ohio: College of Law, University of Cincinnati, 1957); 26 Cin. L. Rev. 155 (1957).

67. O. W. Holmes, "The Use of Law Schools," in *Collected Legal Papers* 35, 37 (1920) (oration before the Harvard Law School Association, November 5, 1886).

68. William H. Rehnquist, in "Tribute to Leo Levin," 138 Penn. L. Rev. 317-318 (1989).

69. See *American Law Schools, Directory of Law Teachers, 1979-80* (St. Paul, Minn.: West, 1979), p. 945.

70. A. Leo Levin, "Research in Judicial Administration: The Federal Experience," 26 N.Y.L. Rev. 237 (Winter 1981).

71. Russell Wheeler, "Judicial Reform: Basic Issues and References," *Policy Studies Journal* 8 (1979), 134, 135.

72. *Ibid.*

73. A. Leo Levin, "Research in Judicial Administration: The Federal Experience," p. 239.

74. Quoting Judge Harold Levanthal, in A. Leo Levin and R. Wheeler (eds.), *The Pound Conference: Perspectives on Justice in the Future* (1979), p. 224.

75. Edward B. McConnell, "What Does the Future Hold for Judges?" *Judges Journal* 30 (Summer 1991):13.

76. *Who's Who in American Law* (7th ed.) (Chicago: Marquis Who's Who, 1991), p. 603.

77. *Ibid.*, p. 11.

78. *Ibid.*.

79. *Ibid.*, pp. 39–40.

80. *Who's Who in American Law, 1992–93* (7th ed.) (Chicago: Marquis Who's Who, 1991), p. 336.

81. Torsten Eriksson, *The Reformers: An Historical Survey of Pioneer Experiments in the Treatment of Criminals* (New York: Elsevier, 1976), p. 32.

82. *Ibid.*, p. 36.

83. *Ibid.*, p. 42.

84. *Ibid.*, p. 50.

85. G. de Beaumont and Alexis de Tocqueville, *Du Système pénitentiaire aux État-Unis, et de son Application en France, suivis d'un Appendice sur les colonies pénales et de Notes statistiques* (Paris: Fournier, 1833), pp. 281–285.

86. Quoted in Torsten Eriksson, *The Reformers: An Historical Survey of Pioneer Experiments in the Treatment of Criminals*, pp. 50–51.

87. Nicolaus Heinrich Julius, *Nord Americas Sittliche Zustande nach eigenen Anschauugen in den Jähren* (Leipzig: F.A. Brockhaus, 1839), pp. 470–471.

88. Frederick A. Demetz and Abel Blouet, *Rapports à M. le Comte de Montalivet sur les Pénitenciers des États-Unis* (Paris: Imprimerie Royale, 1837), pp. 10–14.

89. Torsten Eriksson, *The Reformers: An Historical Survey of Pioneer Experiments in the Treatment of Criminals*, pp. 98–99.

90. *Ibid.*, p. 102.

91. Herbert A. Johnson, *History of Criminal Justice* (Cincinnati, Ohio: Anderson, 1988), p. 223.

92. Alexander Winter, *The New York State Reformatory at Elmira* (London: Swan Sonnenschein & Co., 1891), p. 37.

93. Zebulon R. Brockway, "The Ideal of a True Prison System for a State," in *Transactions of the National Congress on Penitentiary and Reformatory Discipline*, Cincinnati, Ohio, October 12–18, 1870, E. C. Wines (ed.) (Albany, N.Y., 1871), pp. 38–65.

94. Joseph W. Rogers, "Mary Belle Harris: Warden and Rehabilitation Pioneer," *Criminal Justice Research Bulletin* (Huntsville, Texas: Sam Houston State University) 3 (1988): p. 2.

95. Mary B. Harris, *I Knew Them in Prison* (New York: Viking, 1942), pp. 6–7.

96. *Ibid.*, p. 8.

97. Joseph W. Rogers, "Mary Belle Harris: Warden and Rehabilitation Pioneer," pp. 1–2.

98. *Ibid.*, p. 3.

99. *Ibid.*, p. 5.

100. Mary B. Harris, *I Knew Them in Prison*, p. 42.

101. Joseph W. Rogers, "Mary Belle Harris: Warden and Rehabilitation Pioneer," p. 6.

102. *Ibid.*, p. 7.

103. H.G. Moeller, *Federal Prison System: Fiftieth Anniversary, 1930–1980* (Springfield, Mo.: U.S. Department of Justice, 1980), p. 7.

104. 503 F. Supp. 1265 (S.D. Tex. 1980).

105. 97 S.Ct. 285 (1976).

106. 416 U.S. 396 (1974).

107. 372 U.S. 335 (1963).

108. John J. DiIulio, Jr., *Governing Prisons* (New York: Free Press, 1987), p. 195.

109. See *Cruz v. Beto*, 405 U.S. 319 (1972), where inmate-plaintiff, a Buddhist, argued that he was not allowed to use the prison chapel and was placed in punitive segregation for two weeks for distributing religious literature.

110. Quoted in John J. DiIulio, Jr., *Governing Prisons*, p. 203.

111. *Ibid.*, p. 175.

112. Cited in Duncan B. Forrester, "Martin Luther and John Calvin," in Leo Strauss and Joseph Cropsey (eds.), *History of Political Philosophy* (2d ed.) (Chicago: University of Chicago Press, 1981), p. 311.

113. Quoted in John J. DiIulio, Jr., *Governing Prisons*, p. 199.

114. *Ibid.*, p. 202.

115. 503 F. Supp. 1265 (S.D. Tex. 1980)

116. Howard Abadinsky, *Probation and Parole: Theory and Practice* (3d ed.) (Englewood Cliffs, N.J.: Prentice Hall, 1987), p. 18.

117. Lawrence M. Friedman, *A History of American Law* (New York: Simon and Schuster, 1973), p. 518.

118. Paul F. Cromwell, Jr., George C. Killinger, Hazel B. Kerper, and Charles Walker, *Probation and Parole in the Criminal Justice System* (2d ed.)(St. Paul, Minn.: West, 1985).

119. John Augustus, *John Augustus, First Probation Officer* (Montclair, N.J.: Patterson Smith, 1972), pp. 4–5.

120. Howard Abadinsky, *Probation and Parole: Theory and Practice* (3d ed.), p. 19.

121. *Ibid.*, p. 143.

122. Torsten Eriksson, *The Reformers: An Historical Survey of Pioneer Experiments in the Treatment of Criminals*, p. 81.

123. Howard Abadinsky, *Probation and Parole: Theory and Practice* (3d ed.), p. 146–147.

Part II

The Police

This part consists of three chapters. In Chapter 4 we examine police organization and operation, Chapter 5 covers personnel roles and functions, and in Chapter 6 we discuss police issues and practices. Specific chapter content is provided in the introductory section of each chapter.

Organization and Operation

Blessed are the peacemakers.

—Matthew 5:8

✦ INTRODUCTION

To perform smoothly (as smoothly as society, resources, politics, and other influences will permit), police agencies are "organized" in such a way as to enhance the potential accomplishment of their basic mission and goals. In this chapter we consider first how police agencies are defined and operate as bona fide organizations. The contemporary organization of police departments is then presented, to include an overview of the bureaucratic model that has evolved and recent challenges to it.

The need for developing appropriate policies, procedures, rules, and regulations is then discussed. Then we examine the influence recent research has had on contemporary policing functions, to learn "what works" and what myths of police practices are largely debunked today. Finally, we explore a "back-to-the-basics" concept that is being resurrected across the country: community-oriented and problem-solving policing. We define the meaning of the two terms and consider the differences between this form of policing and the professional, reactive, incident-driven method. Essentially, the goal of this chapter is to "set the stage" for our analyses to follow, of personnel and problems that exist within the field.

The terms *police* and *law enforcement* are generally used interchangeably. *Administration* is a process whereby a group of people are organized and directed toward achievement of the group's objective.[1] The exact nature of the organization will vary among the various types and sizes of police agencies, but the general principles used and the form of administration are similar. Administration focuses on the overall organization, its mission and its relationship with other organizations and groups external to it. *Management*, which is a part of administration, is more involved in the day-to-day operations of the various units within the organization. Finally, *supervision* involves the direction of staff members in their day-to-day activities.[2] While we tend to think of the chief executive as the administrator, the bureau chiefs or commanders as management, and the sergeants as supervisors, it is important to note that often all three of these tasks are required of one administrator.

✦ POLICE AGENCIES AS ORGANIZATIONS

✧ MISSIONS AND GOALS

An *organization* is a group of people working together to accomplish a desired goal.[3] Certainly, police agencies fit the description of an organization. First, these agencies are managed by being organized into a number of specialized units (e.g., patrol, traffic, investigation, records). Administrators, middle managers, and supervisors exist to ensure that these units work together toward a common goal; for each unit to work independently would lead to fragmentation, conflict, and competition and subvert the entire organization's goals and purposes. Second, police agencies consist of people who interact within the organization and with external organizations (in policing, there are both line and staff personnel, discussed later in this chapter), and they exist to serve the public.

Police administrators, through a mission statement, policies and procedures, a proper management style, and a number of other means, attempt to ensure that the organization maintains its overall goals of crime suppression and investigation and that it works amiably with similar organizations. As the organization becomes larger, the need becomes greater for people to cooperate to achieve the organizational goals. Formal organizational charts, also discussed later in this chapter, assist in this endeavor, spelling out areas of responsibility, lines of communication, and the chain of command.

Police administrators modify or design the structure of their organization to fulfill their mission. An organizational chart reflects the formal structure of task and authority relationships determined to be most suited to accomplishing the police mission. The major concerns in organizing are: (1) identifying what jobs need to be done, such as conducting the initial investigation, performing the latent or followup investigation, and providing for the custody of evidence seized at crime scenes; (2) determining how to group the jobs, such as those responsible for patrol, investigation, and the operation of the property room; (3) forming grades of authority, such as officer, detective, corporal, sergeant, lieutenant, and captain; and (4) equalizing responsibility, illustrated by the example that if a sergeant has the responsibility to supervise seven detectives, that sergeant must have sufficient authority to discharge that responsibility properly or he or she cannot be held accountable for any results.[4]

✦ SPECIALIZATION IN POLICE AGENCIES

As shown later in Figure 4.2, the larger the agency, the greater the need for specialization and the more vertical the organizational chart will become. Some 2300 years ago, Plato observed that "each thing becomes...easier when one man, exempt from other tasks, does one thing."[5] Specialization or the division of labor is also one of the basic features of traditional organizational theory.[6] Specialization produces different groups of functional responsibilities and the jobs allocated to meet those different responsibilities are staffed with people who are believed to be especially well qualified to perform those jobs. Thus specialization is crucial to effectiveness and efficiency in large organizations.[7]

However, specialization makes the organization more complex by complicating communication, by increasing the units from which cooperation must be obtained, and by creating conflict among different units. Also, a greater need for coordination is created, and therefore additional hierarchy, which can lead to the creation of narrow jobs that stifle the creativity and energy of their incumbents. Police departments are aware of these potential shortcomings of specialization, however, and attempt through various means to inspire their employees to the extent possible. Personnel can be rotated to various jobs and given additional responsibilities that challenge them. For example, in a medium-sized department serving a community of 100,000 or more in population, it would be possible for a police officer with 10 years of police experience to have been a dog handler, a motorcycle officer, a detective, and/or a traffic officer, while simultaneously holding a slot on the special weapons or hostage negotiation teams. Officers can be "empowered" through a community-policing and problem-solving strategy (discussed below) or involved in organizational decision making as in "total quality management" (discussed in Chapter 17).

In sum, the advantages to specialization in large police departments include the following:

◊ *Placement of Responsibility:* The responsibility for the performance of given tasks can be placed on specific units or individuals. For example, the traffic division investigates all accidents and the patrol division handles all calls for service.

◊ *Development of Expertise:* Occupants of specialized responsibilities receive specialized training. Homicide investigators, for example, can be sent to forensic pathology classes; special weapons and tactics teams train regularly to deal with terrorists or hostage situations.

◊ *Group Esprit de Corps:* Groups of specially trained persons share a camaraderie and depend on one another for success; this leads to cohesion and high morale.

◊ *Increased Efficiency and Effectiveness:* Specialized units have a high degree of proficiency in job task responsibility. For example, a white-collar crime unit will normally be more successful with complex fraud cases than will a general detective division.[8]

✦ CONTEMPORARY POLICE ORGANIZATION

✧ THE TRADITIONAL BUREAUCRATIC MODEL

By the 1950s some police chiefs began to demonstrate that good administration could make a difference in the efficiency of police organizations. They would not allow their departments to be footballs for local politicians.[9] These administrators stressed the military organization; for them, police reform meant close supervision and strong internal discipline. This movement improved police service and probably appealed to most police officers, since most of them were military veterans. Given the backgrounds of police recruits and the demands being made by communities at the time, the move from political patronage to the military model was probably the wisest change possible.[10]

Frederick Taylor's scientific management theory was in vogue, but its task-oriented approach to worker productivity was not universally popular. Ronald Lynch [11] argued that the major criticisms of the scientific management theory as it relates to policing were that:

1. Officers were considered passive instruments; their personal feelings were completely disregarded. Any differences, especially regarding motivation, were ignored; all officers were treated basically alike.

2. The employee was considered to be an "economic man" who could be motivated through wage incentives or fear of job loss.

3. The focus was on technical efficiency, not the effectiveness of the organization.

4. The efficiency of operation was to be obtained only through division of labor (breaking the job down into small parts), specialization of police activities, rigid structure of line and staff departments, and the use of a span of control whereby supervisors had only a few subordinates.

The scientific management theory, as many police officers know, is alive and well in some agencies today, where employees are still motivated by fear and administrators practice a "do as I say and not as I do" philosophy.

Police organizations in the United States are "bureaucracies," as are virtually all large organizations in modern society, such as the military, universities, and private corporations. To a large extent, police agencies are similar in their structure and management process. The major differences between agencies exist between the large and the very small departments; the former will be more complex, with much more specialization, hierarchical structure and a greater degree of authoritarian style of command.

The administration of most police organizations is based on the traditional, pyramidal, quasimilitary organizational structure containing to one extent or another the elements of a bureaucracy noted above. According to Thomas Johnson, Gordon Misner, and Lee Brown (former chief of police in New York City), this pyramidal organizational environment is undergoing increasing challenges, especially by large numbers of college-educated police personnel; indeed, these writers express surprise at the large numbers of people who are disillusioned with it.[12] The reasons for this disillusionment are several and include the quasimilitary discipline of police organizations; the lack of opportunity of management to match talent and positions; the organizational restrictions on personal freedom of expression, association, and dress; communication blockage in the tall structure; the organizational clinging to outmoded methods of operation; the lack of management flexibility and real challenge of the job; and the narrowness of job descriptions in the lower ranks of police organizations.

✦ ATTEMPTS TO REFORM THE TRADITIONAL MODEL

Attempts to reform the traditional, tall pyramid structure of police organizations and its inherent rank structure have been described as "attempts to bend granite."[13] Since the rank structure controls the incentives of pay, status, and power, it seriously hinders attempts to provide counterincentives for the officer on the street. Some attempts have been made to replace the traditional structure, however, including the following:

1. Expanded pay scales or salary incentives for the patrol officer (with step or ladder increases).
2. The "Master Police Officer" designation—recommended in 1967 by the President's Crime Commission, this would afford patrol officers pay and status while working on the street.
3. Skill attainment plans—this would provide incentive pay for the patrol officer rank on the basis of longevity, certification in a skill, an academic degree, or a job assignment requiring a particular skill.
4. Separation of autonomy from rank—designed to overcome the problem of patrol officers with college backgrounds being overruled by less knowledgeable superiors. Here the patrol officer with the most knowledge would be in charge of a situation. An example is an evidence technician with the rank of patrol officer having authority over ranking officers at a crime scene.

5. Career development—this rare system includes formal job rotation, special assignment into positions that have career value, leaves of absence to pursue education or experience in other agencies, and exchange programs with other departments.[14]

In the 1940s and 1950s, some police departments began to recognize the strong effect of the informal structure on the organization; agencies began using such techniques as job enlargement and job enrichment to generate interest in policing as a career. Studies indicated that the supervisor who was "employee centered" was more effective than one who was "production centered." Democratic or participatory management began to appear in police agencies, and private industry began to move away from the pyramid-shaped organizational structure to a more flat type of structure.

The human relations approach had its limitations, however. With the emphasis being placed on the employee, the role of the organizational structure became secondary; the primary goal seemed to many to be social rewards, and little attention seemed to be given to task accomplishment. Many police managers saw this trend as unrealistic. Employees began to give less and expect more in return.[15]

A number of agencies have experimented with other approaches, and the results have been mixed.[16] Indeed, where police agencies have attempted to flatten the organizational structure and replace paramilitary police uniforms with blazers, they have most often returned to the traditional style. In the late 1960s the military model was replaced by one that leaned more toward bureaucratic accountability than toward military command. In the 1970s experts on police organization, such as Egon Bittner, were contending that the military-bureaucratic organization of the police was a serious handicap, creating obstacles to the development of a truly professional police system.[17] Paul Whisenand listed four reasons why bureaucratic organization is beginning to disappear in modern society: (1) it is too rigid to adapt to change; (2) it is incapable of meeting the demands of sustained growth; (3) it cannot integrate the greater diversity of contemporary society; and (4) bureaucracy is not designed to accommodate "new concepts of man, power, and human values."[18]

Michel Crozier [19] described a "vicious circle" that develops in bureaucracies, which has four parts: (1) bureaucracies require impersonal rules; (2) centralization of decision making limits supervisors in the field (they cannot adjust to problems, as they must go by the book); (3) very often one level of the organization is not aware of what is happening at another level; and (4) unofficial power relationships control areas of uncertainty (areas not covered by rules).

The alternative is to keep a few features of the military model (police officers taking orders from superiors during critical incidents), a few features of the bureaucratic model, and go beyond these to create a reasonably professional organization.[20] Until that occurs, large law enforcement agencies will probably continue to experience the lethargy described by a Pennsylvania state trooper as "being herd-bound." [21]

There may be disenchantment with the traditional bureaucratic structure of police organizations, but that structure continues to prevail; for many administrators, it is still the best structure when rapid leadership and division of labor are required in times of crises. The traditional school of thought, that each police supervisor can effectively supervise only seven employees, is part of the reason for this "tall" organizational structure. This simple statement actually causes a chain reaction in policing: narrow spans of control make police departments taller, and taller organizations are complex and may react slowly during crisis situations, as effective communication is hampered by the number of different levels present within the chain of command. Successful tall departments, therefore, must develop policies and procedures to overcome this complexity. Many police departments have redesigned their organizations to reflect larger spans of control or management and hence flatter organizational structures.[22]

✦ A BASIC LAW ENFORCEMENT STRUCTURE

There has evolved a special organizational structure to help carry out the many complex responsibilities of policing. But the highly decentralized nature and the varying size of police departments in the United States compels police agencies to vary in organization. The police must take into account such demographic information as population density, ethnicity, income, and education in determining how the department will be organized. It is possible, however, to combine the traits of most departments and make certain general statements about all to obtain an idea of a "typical" police organization.

As mentioned earlier, the police have traditionally been organized along military lines—being "quasimilitary," with a rank structure that normally includes the patrol officer, sergeant, lieutenant, captain, and chief. Many departments, particularly larger ones, employ additional ranks, such as corporal and major, but there is a legitimate concern with becoming too top-heavy. The rank hierarchy allows the organization to designate authority and responsibility at each level and to maintain a chain of command. The military model also allows the organization to emphasize supervisor-subordinate relationships, and for discipline and control to be maintained. More will be said about the military model later.

Every police agency, irrespective of size, has a basic plan of organization. Further, every such agency, no matter how large or small, has an organizational chart. A visitor to the police station or sheriff's office may even see the organizational chart displayed prominently on a wall. But even if not on paper, such a chart exists. A basic organizational chart for a small agency is shown in Figure 4.1.[23]

Line elements are engaged in active policing functions in the field. They may be subdivided into primary and secondary line elements. The patrol function—often called the "backbone" of policing—is the primary line element because of its major responsibility for law enforcement within the police organization. Most small police agencies, in fact, can be described as patrol agen-

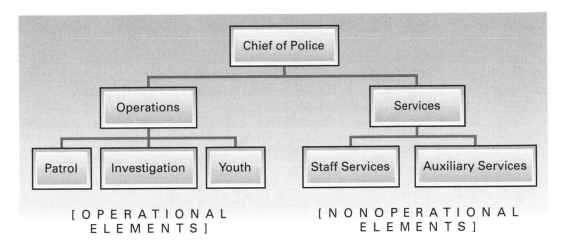

Figure 4.1 Basic police organization structure.

cies where the patrol forces are responsible for all line activities.[24] They provide routine patrol, conduct investigations of criminal and traffic nature, make arrests, and are basically generalists. In a city marshal community that has only one employee, the marshal obviously must perform all the functions displayed above—the organizational chart in that police agency will exist, but will simply be very horizontal, with little or no specialization.

The investigative and youth functions are the secondary line elements. There would be no need for these functions if the police were totally successful in their patrol and crime prevention efforts—an obviously impossible goal. Time and area restrictions on the patrol officers, as well as the need for specialized training and experience, require that some "spin-off" from the patrol component take place.

The nonline functions and activities can become quite numerous, especially in a large community. The nonline functions fall within two broad categories: staff services and auxiliary services. Other terms may be used to describe these functions; for example, staff services are sometimes called administrative services and auxiliary services may be known as technical services. The *staff services* are usually oriented to people and include such matters as recruitment, training, promotion, planning and research, community relations, and public information services. *Auxiliary services* are the types of functions that a nonpolice or civilian person rarely sees. They include jail management, property and evidence, crime laboratory services, communications (dispatch), and records and identification. There are many career opportunities for persons interested in police-related work who, for some reason, cannot or do not want to be a field officer.

The Chicago Police Department's organization structure (Figure 4.2) demonstrates the extent to which specialization exists in a large police department (discussed more fully below), and depicts the horizontal chain of command in a large organization. This organizational structure is designed to fulfill

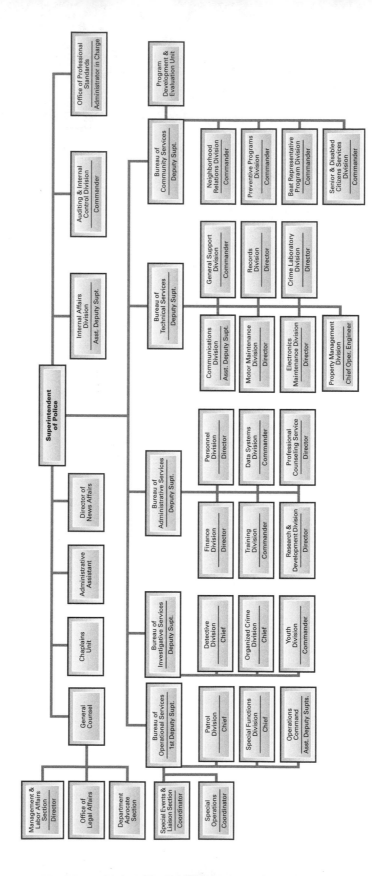

Figure 4.2 Organization for command. (*Source*: Chicago Police Department. Used with permission.)

five functions: (1) it apportions the workload among members and units according to a logical plan; (2) it ensures that lines of authority and responsibility are as definite and direct as possible; (3) it specifies a unity of command throughout, so there is no question as to which orders should be followed; (4) it places responsibility and authority, and if responsibility is delegated, the delegator is held responsible; and (5) it coordinates the efforts of members so that all will work harmoniously to accomplish the mission.[25] In sum, this structure establishes the so-called "chain of command" and determines lines of communication and responsibility.

In addition to these generally well-known and visible areas of specialization, there are a number of other branches in policing; crime prevention, drug education, juvenile delinquency, and child abuse units are the most commonplace.

✦ POLICIES, PROCEDURES, RULES, AND REGULATIONS IN POLICING

In policing, policies, procedures, rules, and regulations are very important for defining role expectations for all officers. The police officer is granted authority that is unusually powerful in a democratic society; because they possess this extraordinary power, the police pose a potential threat to individual freedom. Thus because police agencies are intended to be service-oriented in nature, they must work within well-defined, specific guidelines designed to ensure that all officers conform consistently to behavior that will enhance public protection.[26]

Related to this need for policies, procedures, rules and regulations is the fact that police officers possess a broad spectrum of discretionary authority in performing their duties. This, coupled with the danger posed by their work and their opportunities for settling problems informally, work against having narrow, inflexible job requirements.

Thus the task for the chief executive is to find the "middle ground" between unlimited discretion and total standardization. The police role is much too ambiguous to become totally standardized, but it is also much too serious and important to be left completely to the total discretion of the patrol officer. As Robert Sheehan and Gary Cordner put it, the idea is for the chief executive to "harness, but not choke, their employees."[27]

Organizational *policies* are more general than procedures, rules, or regulations. Policies are basically guides to thinking, rather than action. They reflect the purpose and philosophy of the organization and help interpret those elements to the officers.[28] Policies should be committed to writing, then controlled, adjusted, and deleted according to the changing times and circumstances of the department and community.

Procedures are more specific than policies; they serve as "guides to action." According to Wilson and McLaren, a procedure is "more specific than a policy but less restrictive than a rule or regulation. It describes a method of operation while still allowing some flexibility within limits."[29]

Most organizations are awash in procedures. Police organizations have procedures that cover investigation, patrol, booking, radio, filing, roll-call, arrest, sick leave, evidence handling, promotion, and many more job elements. These procedures are not totally inflexible, but they do describe in rather detailed terms the preferred methods for carrying out policy.

Some procedures are mandated by the U.S. Supreme Court. A good example is the Court's 1985 decision in *Tennessee v. Garner*, which basically mandated new policy concerning when officers could use deadly force. Essentially, since *Garner*, police officers may only use deadly force when a "suspect threatens the officer with a weapon or there is probable cause to believe that [the suspect] has committed a crime involving the infliction or threatened infliction of serious physical harm."[30]

Some police executives have attempted to run their departments via flurries of temporal memos containing new procedures or rules and regulations. This path is often fraught with difficulty. As Loen [31] observed, an abundance of standardized procedures can stifle initiative and imagination, as well as complicate jobs. On the positive side, procedures can decrease the time wasted in figuring out how to accomplish tasks and thereby increase productivity.[32] As with policies, chief executives must seek the middle ground in drafting procedures and remember that it is next to impossible to have procedures that cover all possible exigencies.

Rules and *regulations* are specific managerial guidelines that leave little or no latitude for individual discretion; they require action (or in some cases, inaction). Some examples are requirements that police officers not smoke in public, wear their hats when outside their patrol vehicle, check the patrol vehicle's oil and emergency lights before going on patrol, not consume alcoholic beverages within 4 hours of going on duty, arrive in court 30 minutes before sessions open or at roll call 15 minutes before scheduled duty time. These rules and regulations are not always popular, especially if perceived as unfair or unrelated to the job (such as having to lock/unlock municipal parking lots, pick up receipts from golf courses or swimming pools, or deliver meeting agendas and other materials to the homes of the city or county commissioners on a daily basis). Nonetheless, they contribute to the total police mission of community service.

Rules and regulations should obviously be kept to a minimum because of their coercive nature. If they accumulate over time, the message received by the rank and file is that management feels that it cannot trust subordinates to act responsibly on their own. Once again, the middle range is the best. As Thomas Reddin, former Los Angeles police chief, stated: "Certainly we must have rules, regulations and procedures, and they should be followed. But they are no substitutes for initiative and intelligence. The more a [person] is given an opportunity to make decisions and, in the process, to learn, the more rules and regulations will be followed."[33]

✦ THE INFLUENCE OF RESEARCH ON POLICE FUNCTIONS

✧ THE MID-1970s: CRISES STIMULATE PROGRESS

There was very little research concerning police functions and methods until 1964.[34] In fact, there was actually very little substantive research examining police methods until the mid-1970s. The reasons for this lack of inquiry into "what works" (or, more appropriately, what does not work) in policing are twofold. First, there was a tendency on the part of the police to resist outside scrutiny. Functioning in a bureaucratic environment, they, like other bureaucracies, were sensitive to outside research. Many police administrators perceived a threat to personal careers and the image of the organization, as well as a concern as to the legitimacy of the research itself. There was a natural reluctance to invite trouble. Given these obstacles, sociologists were often reluctant to attempt to penetrate the walls of what appeared to be a closed fortress.

Second, few police administrators perceived a need to challenge traditional methods of operation. The "if it ain't broke, don't fix it" attitude prevailed, particularly among old-school administrators. Some ideas were etched in stone, such as more police personnel and vehicles equaled more patrolling and therefore less crime, a quicker response rate, and a happier private citizen. And the more officers riding in the patrol car, the better. The methods and effectiveness of detectives and their investigative techniques were not even open to debate. The old myths of good policing were well entrenched.

Then, however, as Herman Goldstein stated: "Crises stimulate progress. The police came under enormous pressure in the late 1960s and early 1970s, confronted with concern about crime, civil rights demonstrations, racial conflicts, riots and political protests."[35] Five national studies looked into police practices, each with a different focus: the President's Commission on Law Enforcement and the Administration of Justice (1967), the National Advisory Commission on Civil Disorders (1968), the National Advisory Commission on the Causes and Prevention of Violence (1969), the President's Commission on Campus Unrest (1970), and the National Advisory Commission on Criminal Justice Standards and Goals (1973). Another problem consisted of limits or cuts in police budgets in the 1970s and 1980s. A 1985 national survey found that 44 percent of police and sheriff's departments had the same number or fewer personnel than they had five years earlier.[36] As a result, police administrators came under increasing pressure to use personnel and equipment in the most efficient fashion—to do more with less. This pressure may explain why police administrators became more willing to challenge traditional assumptions and beliefs and to open the door to researchers. That willingness to allow researchers to examine traditional methods led to the growth and development of two important policing research organizations: the Police Foundation and the Police Executive Research Forum (PERF). The results have been significant. As Joan Petersilia of the Rand Corporation observed, "although systematic research on policing began [only recently], it is already influencing major changes in the way police departments operate and in public perceptions of policing."[37]

The first major research effort was in the early 1970s and examined the effectiveness of patrol. Patrol operations consume a larger percentage of most police departments' resources than does any other activity. And since the early period of policing there have been several assumptions about patrolling: that random patrolling of city streets prevented crime and made citizens feel safe, that the police should respond immediately to all service calls, and that a quick response to all calls prevented harm to citizens and improved the chances for arresting suspects.

The best-known study of patrol efficiency was in Kansas City, Missouri, in 1973, by George Kelling and a research team at the Police Foundation. The researchers divided the city into 15 beats, which were then categorized into five groups of three matched beats each. Each group comprised neighborhoods that were similar in terms of population, crime characteristics, and calls for police services. Patrolling techniques used in the three beats varied; there was no preventive patrolling in one (police responded only to calls for service), there was increased patrol activity in another (two or three times the usual amount of patrolling), and there was the usual level of service in the third beat. Citizens were interviewed and crime rates measured while the "Kansas City Preventive Patrol Experiment" was conducted for one year. The results showed no significant differences in the crime rates or citizen perceptions of safety as a result of the type of preventive patrol an area received. Similar results occurred in studies in St. Louis and Minneapolis. Another finding from these studies was that the police can stop routinely patrolling their beats for up to a year without necessarily being missed by the residents and without a rise in crime rates in the patrol area.[38]

Police response time has also been analyzed. The long-standing assumption was that as police response time increased, the ability to arrest perpetrators decreased proportionately. Thus, conventional wisdom held, more police are needed on patrol, in rapid vehicles, so as to get to the crime scene more quickly and catch the crook(s). In 1977 the National Institute of Justice (NIJ) awarded a grant to analyze the effect of response time on the outcome of police services (arrests, citizen injury, witness availability, and citizen satisfaction). Again the site of the research was Kansas City, Missouri. Over a two-year period, the police department collected information on Part I crimes in 56 of their 207 beats; observers rode with police officers and collected travel-time data. The results indicated that police response time was unrelated to the probability of making an arrest or locating a witness, and neither dispatch nor travel time was strongly associated with citizen satisfaction. The time it takes to report a crime, the study found, is the major determining factor of whether an on-scene arrest takes place and whether witnesses are located.[39]

✧ RETHINKING "SACRED COW" TRADITIONS

On the basis of these two major studies of patrol methods and effectiveness, many police executives are rethinking the "sacred cow" traditions that have kept the old myths in a protective shroud. For example, one chief of police stated that

> Evidence from the Kansas City study, and others since then, has definitely impacted the way in which I allocate resources. The research findings certainly got me focused on looking at the effectiveness of my own policies and made me do some evaluations of my own. Also, once I understood that preventive patrol does not necessarily reduce crime, I became more flexible in using that manpower in other ways. The Kansas City experiment really opened up the doors for researchers, previously thought to be mostly academic, done for other academics.[40]

Another sacred cow to be examined by researchers was the methods and effectiveness of criminal investigations by police. Police departments have always ranked criminal investigation—attempting to link a crime with a suspect—as one of their most critical functions. A kind of mystique historically surrounded the area of investigation, largely perpetuated by fictional movies, that most crimes can be solved, most cases involving unknown criminals are solved through good detective work, and all but the most minor criminal cases should be assigned for follow-up investigation.[41]

As a result of this detective mystique, countless present and former police officers can attest to the elitism and aloofness often displayed by detectives. The author learned by personal observation as a patrol officer in the early 1970s that a kind of invisible "leash" was attached to the necks of patrol officers, to be jerked by the investigators when a patrol officer unilaterally took an investigation too far. Indeed, when a patrol officer, trained in criminal investigation, made a felony arrest as the result of good police work, he or she was likely to incur the wrath of the detectives, even being totally ostracized by them. To those of us who incurred that wrath, the recent research on the detective function, and the patrol function, has been especially rewarding.

But until recently the criminal investigation function had itself never been investigated. In 1975 a National Institute of Justice grant began to penetrate the mystique of "sleuthing." The Rand Corporation undertook a national study of the criminal investigation process, surveying 150 large police agencies and interviewing and observing investigators in more than 25 police departments. At about the same time, another study of investigations was being performed by the Stanford Research Institute (SRI), which found that in Alameda County, California, in more than 50 percent of the burglaries in which the burglar was arrested, the arrest was made within 48 hours of the report of the burglary. This study, and the one by Rand, implied that detectives actually played a relatively minor role in the solving of burglaries, that the information provided by patrol officers from their preliminary investigations was a very important determining factor in whether or not a follow-up investigation would result in an arrest.[42]

As a result of these findings, NIJ funded more studies of the investigation process in the late 1970s, in Santa Monica, California; Cincinnati, Ohio; and Rochester and Syracuse, New York. These grants were specifically to test the investigative reforms suggested in the earlier studies. Again, several consistent findings emerged: Many serious crimes are not solved; patrol officers are responsible, directly or indirectly, for most arrests (either arresting the suspect at the scene or obtaining helpful descriptions from victims or witnesses); and only a small percentage of all arrests for Part I offenses result from detectives with specialized training and skill.[43] In 1983, PERF published the results of its own look at the investigative function, saying that "Changes have occurred in investigative management as a result of the earlier studies; all of them had a profound influence on investigative management today. For instance, there has been a greater emphasis on case screening and on improving the role of patrol officers in investigations—policy changes that were recommended by many of the earlier studies."[44] These studies proved that if not all cases can be solved, then not all cases should be pursued as vigorously as others. The SRI research produced "predictors of case closure"—an index to be used by the police for estimating the solvability of burglaries. Included are such elements as the estimated range of time when the crime occurred, whether a witness reported the offense and an eyewitness was present, if usable fingerprints were retrieved, and if a suspect was described or named. Using this yardstick, police can better manage the burglary caseload and determine which burglaries have little or no chance of being solved. Obviously, this predictor and its "solvability factors" can save tremendous amounts of time and resources from being expended on dead end investigations.

✧ OTHER MAJOR FINDINGS

Other major research findings have shaken the foundations of old assumptions about policing. The following points are now accepted in most quarters as part of the "common wisdom" of the police:

1. The police do much more than deal with crime; they deal with many forms of behavior that are not defined as criminal.
2. Too much dependence in the past has been placed on the criminal law in order to get the police job done; arrest and prosecution are simply not an effective way to handle much of what constitutes police business.
3. Police use a wide range of methods—formal and informal—in getting their job done. "Law enforcement" is only one method among many.
4. The police (contrary to the desires of earlier advocates of the "professional" model, such as Fuld, Fosdick, Vollmer and Wilson) are not autonomous. The sensitive function they perform requires that they be accountable, through the political process, to the community.
5. Individual police officers exercise a great deal of discretion in deciding how to handle the tremendous variety of circumstances they confront.[45]

It is also known that two-person patrol cars are no more effective than one-person cars in reducing crime or catching criminals. Furthermore, injuries to police officers are not more likely to occur in one-person cars. And, as mentioned earlier, most officers on patrol do not stumble across felony crimes in progress—only "Dirty Harry" does so.[46]

Although these studies should not be viewed as conclusive—different results could be obtained in different communities—they do demonstrate that old police methods should be viewed very cautiously. The "we've always done it this way" mentality, still pervading policing to a large extent, may not only be an ineffective means of organizing and administering a police agency, but may also be a costly squandering of valuable human and financial resources.

There are several types of "research" that can be performed within a police agency, provided that it has the desire and personnel. For example, many city beats are configured without having any rational basis; beat boundaries are often determined by a conveniently located major street or river in town. It would be far better if the geographical boundaries for beats were drawn after an analysis of where most crimes were committed and with a view toward distributing the workload among available officers. In the same vein, it would be a better use of resources to assign personnel by the time of day and day of week when most crimes and calls for service occur—not to attempt to reduce response time, but rather, to distribute workload more evenly. Other types of in-house research that can be accomplished are comparisons of arrests to convictions, personnel hours worked to incidents handled, vehicles to personnel, and error rate to reports.[47] Additional quantitative information that can be generated for practical advantage are the numbers of crimes cleared by arrest, the jurisdiction's number of officers per 1000 population, types of crimes committed and value of items taken, and crime projections.

✦ INNOVATION AND VALUES IN POLICE ORGANIZATIONS

Research has shown that neither agency size, technological approach to policing, population variables, nor type of local government act as substantial constraints on police organizational structure. In other words, none of these factors determines, to any substantial degree, how agencies are structured.[48] This finding is important, because it means that innovative police leadership can shape police organizations far more effectively than might have been expected on the basis of traditional theory. While changing police organizations may sometimes appear, as mentioned earlier, like "bending granite,"[49] it appears that even this task can be accomplished by a leader with vision and the skills to articulate and implement that vision.

Indeed, innovative police departments in six cities examined by Jerome Skolnick and David Bayley—Santa Ana, Newark, Oakland, Denver, Houston, and Detroit—were some with earlier reputations for corruption, insensitivity to citizens' needs, gross inefficiency, and even repression and brutality. Yet as

Skolnick and Bayley showed in their book, *The New Blue Line*, innovative administrators kindled the hope that these agencies, despite their bureaucracies, can be transformed into more responsive servants of their communities.

Skolnick and Bayley undertook this study in part because of the "almost unrelievedly negative findings" about policing methods in America.[50] The innovations they observed incorporated "community-oriented policing" (discussed below). Additionally, successful innovation was associated with four critical ingredients: (1) the chief executive's active commitment to policing that is oriented toward crime prevention, (2) the chief's motivation of personnel to "enlist in the cause" of these new norms, (3) the leadership's commitment to protect the integrity of the innovations and not allow their quality to decline due to everyday demands, and (4) the support and patience of the public.[51]

Also during the course of this examination, Skolnick and Bayley identified six obstacles to police innovation: (1) tradition and bureaucratic inertia, (2) public resistance to change and support for traditional police services, (3) resistance by labor unions, (4) the costs of innovation, (5) a lack of vision by police executives, and (6) the inadequate capacity of police departments to evaluate their own effectiveness.[52]

A related subject is that of values in police organizations. All organizations have values. Values are the beliefs that guide an organization and the behavior of its employees. They provide the organization a reason for existing.[53] Police departments are powerfully influenced by their values. Policing styles reflect a department's values. Sometimes the values of police organizations are stated publicly. As an example, the value statements for the Houston Police Department under former chief Lee Brown included that the department:

◊ Will involve the community in all policing activities that directly affect their quality of community life.

◊ Believes that policing strategies must preserve and advance democratic values.

◊ Believes that it must structure service delivery in a way that will reinforce the strengths of neighborhoods.

◊ Believes that the public should have input into the development of policies that directly affect the quality of life.

◊ Will seek the input of employees into matters that affect their job satisfaction and effectiveness.[54]

The growing emphasis on community policing has generated a substantial amount of discussion about values because, by definition, community policing reflects a set of values, rather than a technical orientation toward the police function. There is a service orientation, where citizens are to be treated with respect at all times. When riding in patrol vehicles, supervisors and managers must listen for the "talk of the department" to see if values expressed by officers reflect those of the department.

The values of community policing are different from those of previous eras in police history. Also, values are no longer hidden, but serve as the basis for citizen understanding of the police function, judgments of police success, and employee understanding of what the police agency seeks to achieve.[55]

✦ COMMUNITY-ORIENTED POLICING AND PROBLEM-SOLVING

✧ WHY RETURN TO OLD METHODS?

Today the uniformed patrol officer remains largely unchanged, the personification of policing in the United States. To many people, uniformed officers are the criminal justice system, the government, the establishment. People who do not feel they are in a position to talk to a prosecutor, judge, or other politician often seek out the police with their problems, fears, and wrath.

But with the research findings and insights summarized above, many police administrators and academicians view this as a new era in policing. Many in the police field are unaware of or refuse to accept the collective meaning of these studies: that the traditional, professional methods of patrolling are open to serious challenge, and that it is time to ask new questions and try new approaches. Herman Goldstein [56] identified five concerns that have most strongly influenced the development of new patrol strategies: (1) the police field is preoccupied with management, internal procedures, and efficiency to the exclusion of concern for effectiveness in dealing with serious problems; (2) the police devote most of their resources to responding to calls from citizens, reserving too small a percentage of their time and energy for acting on their own initiative to prevent or reduce community problems; (3) the community is a major resource with an enormous potential, largely untapped, for reducing the number and magnitude of problems that otherwise become the business of the police; (4) police also have available the rank-and-file officers—another huge resource whose time and talent have not been used effectively; and (5) efforts to improve policing have often failed because they have not been adequately related to the overall policies and structure of the police organization.

✧ DEFINING THE CONCEPTS

As a result of these concerns and the current state of policing, Goldstein proposed what he termed *problem-oriented policing*. The fundamental elements of this proposal are not difficult to grasp. The first step in problem-oriented policing is to move beyond just handling incidents. It calls for recognizing that incidents are often merely overt symptoms of problems. This pushes the police in two directions: it requires that they recognize the relationships between incidents (similarities of persons, behavior, locations involved) and that officers take a more in-depth interest in incidents by acquainting themselves with some of the conditions and factors that cause them. Under this model, there are five possible degrees of impact that the police might have on a community problem: totally eliminating it, reducing the number of incidents it creates, reducing the seriousness of the incidents, designing methods for better handling the incidents, and removing the problem from police consideration.[57]

Although the dividing line is blurred, a related, yet separate concept (as they are presently viewed) is that of "community-oriented policing and problem solving" (COPPS). This concept goes much further than being a mere police-community relations program [58] and is intended to be more comprehensive than problem-oriented policing in attempting to improve crime control through a working partnership with the community. Here, community institutions such as families, school, and neighborhood and merchants' associations are seen as key partners with the police in the creation of safe, secure communities. The community's views have greater status under community policing.[59] The major points where community policing is intended to depart from traditional policing are shown in Figure 4.3.

In the past decade more than 200 communities have implemented the COPPS concept, with several of them carefully monitoring and documenting

	Traditional	Community Policing
Question: *Who are the police?*	A government agency principally responsible for law enforcement.	Police are the public and the public are the police: the police officers are those who are paid to give full-time attention to the duties of every citizen.
Question: *What is the relationship of the police force to other public service departments?*	Priorities often conflict.	The police are one department among many responsible for improving the quality of life.
Question: *What is the role of the police?*	Focusing on solving crimes.	A broader problem-solving approach.
Question: *How is police efficiency measured?*	By detection and arrest rates.	By the absence of crime and disorder.
Question: *What are the highest priorities?*	Crimes that are high value (e.g., bank robberies) and those involving violence.	Whatever problems disturb the community most.
Question: *What, specifically, do police deal with?*	Incidents.	Citizens' problems and concerns.
Question: *What determines the effectiveness of police?*	Response times.	Public cooperation.

Figure 4.3 Traditional vs. community policing: questions and answers.
(*Source:* Malcolm K. Sparrow, *Implementing Community Policing*, U.S. Department of Justice, National Institute of Justice. Washington, D.C.: U.S. Government Printing Office, November 1988, pp. 8–9.)

the effects. Flint, Michigan, began its foot patrol experiment in 1979. The project dealt with the problems the community identified, and the patrol officer developed into a neighborhood problem solver. Officers were encouraged to work problems through from beginning to end. Local support for this project has been declining since 1987, with changes in local officials. Newport News, Virginia, entered community-oriented policing in 1983, with a grant from the National Institute of Justice. This experiment proved successfully that a problem-solving operation can be introduced to an entire agency; that management and line officers can be engaged in the process successfully; and that problem solving can be applied to a wide range of problems, with impressive results and with a more positive, productive atmosphere in the agency.

New York City began its Community Patrol Officer Program (CPOP) in 1984 (see the case study below). CPOP was later expanded to cover all of the city's 75 precincts. Designated community patrol officers (CPOs) provide a full range of services within their beats and work with residents to identify and hopefully solve local problems. Houston began rapid change with the appointment of Chief Lee Brown in 1982, including the commitment to fashion a partnership with each neighborhood (including changes in beats so as to conform more closely to "natural" neighborhoods), opening storefronts, and conducting an experiment in

	Traditional	**Community Policing**
Question: What view do police take of service calls?	Deal with them only if there is no real police work to do.	Vital function and great opportunity.
Question: What is police professionalism?	Swift effective response to serious crime.	Keeping close to the community.
Question: What kind of intelligence is most important?	Crime intelligence (study of particular crimes or series of crimes).	Criminal intelligence (information about the activities of individuals or groups).
Question: What is the essential nature of police accountability?	Highly centralized; governed by rules, regulations, and policy directives; accountable to the law.	Emphasis on local accountability to community needs.
Question: What is the role of headquarters?	To provide the necessary rules and policy directives.	To preach organizational values.
Question: What is the role of the press liaison department?	To keep the "heat" off operational officers so they can get on with the job.	To coordinate an essential channel of communication with the community.
Question: How do the police regard prosecutions?	As an important goal.	As one tool among many.

Figure 4.3   *(continued)*

Chapter 4 ✦ *Organization and Operation*

citizen fear reduction. Brown, later appointed chief of police in New York City (resigning in 1993), also implemented a new COPPS strategy there.

The traditional means of evaluating police productivity—response time, felony arrests, crimes cleared by arrest, and so on—are not emphasized in these efforts. The COPPS philosophy is vastly different from the traditional, "professional" school of police patrol work, which is reactive and incident driven; it may be compared to the bus line that bankrupted itself by speeding past crowds of customers at bus stops, the company saying "it is impossible for the drivers to keep their timetables if they have to stop for passengers."[60] Like this bus line, the reactive, incident-driven system sometimes forgets what policing is all about: helping citizens by solving their problems. COPPS recognizes that the community and the rank-and-file officers have large amounts of information that can be shared toward that endeavor.

We already know from several studies that most of what a patrol officer does is not crime related; indeed, much of what they do now is order maintenance in nature. Studies also show that the typical officer's tour of duty does not involve an arrest. The COPPS approach to policing subscribes to the "broken windows" theory of James Q. Wilson and George Kelling, which states in effect that signs of deterioration in a neighborhood—broken windows, rubbish, weeds, empty and rundown homes, and buildings in disarray—will, if uncorrected, lead citizens to reduce their efforts to maintain the neighborhood and send a signal to others that "no one cares"; soon, vandalism and crime begin to occur.[61]

A novel approach to the "broken windows" problem is being attempted in Columbia, South Carolina. In early 1992, the city unveiled a program whereby Columbia police officers—with no money down or closing costs and with a 4 percent loan—could purchase and renovate former "crack houses" in rundown neighborhoods of the city. Several officers took advantage of the offer.

✧ THE "DEVIL'S ADVOCATE": CONCERNS WITH THE CONCEPT

There are legitimate concerns about COPPS, however. Lawrence Sherman [62] provided thought-provoking insights about the COPPS concept, indicating concerns about

> the tendency all too often to talk about community policing with a serene image of a peaceful English village in which everybody's friendly and gets along with each other and they have a 100 percent consensus about what kind of peace and order they want. The fact is that in big cities, where you have different ethnic groups, age groups and income groups living right on top of one another, you don't have a community. You have diverse, competing and conflicting communities in the same space, putting diverse pressures on the police, and the police have to make some choices. Where that conflict is great, it can lead to violence about the choices they make, and yet it's still "community" policing because they are responding to an issue at a community level. I think we've raised expectations way too high about being able to police all of the community all of the time. We can have a variety of programs, storefront efforts or community outreach

meetings without really changing the nature of a police officer's day and how the officer spends his or her time. Talk about community policing is sweeping the country, but I don't think actually doing community policing, in the sense of doing anything other than what we've been doing the last 20 years, is sweeping the country. If it does, it will probably be in the form of problem-oriented policing...trying to identify priorities for certain groups in a local community. That's very different from being an Officer Friendly or doing foot patrol or a lot of other things that get associated with community policing. Ironically, problem-oriented policing can be done very effectively in ways that please the community, without taking one minute of the community's time.

Another concern, one held by many police executives, is with the increased use of discretionary authority of patrol officers under this concept; greater intimacy with the public may threaten officer accountability (i.e., lead to graft). Police managers are also worried that the concept will require too many police officers, where resources are already spread too thin (it can require more personnel, especially where foot patrol and storefront police stations are involved).[63] To address the latter problem, several departments are increasingly using civilians as police assistants, performing a variety of jobs once performed by more costly, sworn personnel.

In sum, this "innovative" approach to policing—actually borrowing from wisdoms of policing of the last century—carries tremendous risk, because it may be dismissed as a public relations gimmick. Americans in general react very much like the working-class English boy in grade school, as recounted by Jerome Skolnick and David Bayley. The teacher asked the class to write a one-sentence description of the police, and the boy wrote, "The police are bastards." The teacher decided something had to be done about such an attitude, so she arranged for the class to visit with the police station, the kids being able to climb in and out of the patrol car and meet the officers over tea. Again assigning the class a one-sentence description of the police, she found this time the boy had written, "The police are clever bastards."[64]

Summary

Today, Robert Peel would be amazed. His persistent efforts in the mid-1800s to organize and deploy a full-time police force have resulted in a proliferation of police around the globe. We explored the contemporary organization of law enforcement in general; the policies, procedures, rules, and regulations that guide them; and how a vast amount of recent research has shed new light on policing methods. Hopefully, this recent surge of police research will continue so as to provide greater, ongoing adaptation to our shifting society.

Contemporary police organization was also discussed. This is probably an area that presently bears close observation, being highly prone to research and change. With the clear spreading of COPPS and its subsequent impact on the traditional organization of police agencies, it would not be unlikely for the traditional bureaucratic model of policing to change as well.

Questions For Review

1. Delineate the distinctions among *policy, procedure*, and *rules and regulations*. Why are they necessary in law enforcement agencies? What is their relationship and role vis-a-vis police discretion?
2. How do police agencies constitute bureaucracies? Can such a form of organization ever be eliminated?
3. Express the basic police organizational structure. Then draft an organizational chart with most of the specialization you might find in your city or county police agency.
4. What are some of the major recent findings by researchers in policing? How have they made an impact on the field?
5. What role do innovation and values play in police organizations?
6. Explain what is meant by *community-oriented policing and problem-solving*. How does this concept differ from past policing methods, and what improvements does it offer? Will it last or simply fade away? What are some concerns with the concept?

For Further Reading

LARRY K. GAINES, MITTIE D. SOUTHERLAND, and JOHN E. ANGELL, *Police Administration*. New York: McGraw-Hill, 1991.

RICHARD HOLDEN, *Modern Police Management*. Englewood Cliffs, N.J.: Prentice Hall, 1986.

RONALD G. LYNCH, *The Police Manager: Professional Leadership Skills* (3d ed.). New York: Random House, 1986.

ROBERT SHEEHAN and GARY W. CORDNER, *Introduction to Police Administration* (2d ed.). Cincinnati, Ohio: Anderson, 1989.

CHARLES R. SWANSON, LEONARD TERRITO, and ROBERT W. TAYLOR, *Police Administration* (3d ed.). New York: Macmillan, 1993.

Notes

1. Richard Holden, *Modern Police Management* (Englewood Cliffs, N.J.: Prentice Hall, 1986), p. 2.

2. Geoffrey P. Alpert and Roger G. Dunham, *Policing Urban America* (2d ed.) (Prospect Heights, Ill.: Waveland Press, 1992), p. 79.

3. Larry K. Gaines, Mittie D. Southerland, and John E. Angell, *Police Administration* (New York: McGraw-Hill, 1991), pp. 5–6.

4. Stephen P. Robbins, *The Administration Process* (Englewood Cliffs, N.J.: Prentice Hall, 1976).

5. *The Republic of Plato*, trans. Allen Bloom (New York: Basic Books, 1968), p. 7.

6. See Luther Gulick and L. Urwick, eds., *Papers on the Science of Administration* (New York: Augustus M. Kelley, 1969).

7. Charles R. Swanson, Leonard Territo, and Robert W. Taylor, *Police Administration* (3d ed.) (New York: Macmillan, 1993), p. 134.

8. Orlando W. Wilson and Roy C. McLaren, *Police Administration* (3d ed.) (New York: McGraw-Hill, 1972), p. 79.

9. Egon Bittner, *The Functions of the Police in a Modern Society*, Public Health Service Publication 2059 (Washington, D.C.: U.S. Government Printing Office, 1970), p. 53.

10. John J. Broderick, *Police in a Time of Change* (Prospect Heights, Ill.: Waveland Press, 1987), p. 231.

11. Ronald G. Lynch, *The Police Manager: Professional Leadership Skills* (3d ed.) (New York: Random House, 1986), p. 4.

12. Thomas A. Johnson, Gordon E. Misner, and Lee P. Brown, *The Police and Society: An Environment for Collaboration and Confrontation* (Englewood Cliffs, N.J.: Prentice Hall, 1981), p. 53.

13. Dorothy Guyot, "Bending Granite: Attempts to Change the Rank Structure of American Police Departments," *Journal of Police Science and Administration* 7 (1979):253–284.

14. Ibid., pp. 273–274.

15. Ronald G. Lynch, *The Police Manager*, pp. 5–6.

16. Geoffrey P. Alpert and Roger G. Dunham, *Policing Urban America* (Prospect Heights, Ill.: Waveland Press, 1988), p. 71.

17. Egon Bittner, *The Functions of the Police in a Modern Society*, p. 51.

18. Paul M. Whisenand and Fred Ferguson, *The Managing of Police Organizations* (Englewood Cliffs, N.J.: Prentice Hall, 1973), p. 9.

19. Michel Crozier, *The Bureaucratic Phenomenon* (Chicago: University of Chicago Press, 1964), p. 190.

20. John J. Broderick, *Police in a Time of Change* (2d ed.), p. 233.

21. In Ray Graham and Jeffrey R. Cameron, "The Integrated Approach to Career Development," *The Police Chief* (June 1985):26–30.

22. Charles R. Swanson, Leonard Territo, and Robert W. Taylor, *Police Administration* (3d ed.), p. 142.

23. George D. Eastman and Esther M. Eastman (eds.), *Municipal Police Administration* (7th ed.) (Washington, D.C.: International City Management Association, 1971), p. 17.

24. *Ibid.*, p. 18.

25. President's Commission on Law Enforcement and Administration of Justice, *Task Force Report: The Police* (Washington, D.C.: U.S. Government Printing Office, 1967), p. 46.

26. Robert Sheehan and Gary W. Cordner, *Introduction to Police Administration* (2d ed.) (Cincinnati, Ohio: Anderson, 1989), pp. 446-447.

27. *Ibid.*, p. 449.

28. *Ibid.*, p. 449.

29. Orlando W. Wilson and Roy C. McLaren, *Police Administration* (3rd ed.), p. 130.

30. 471 U.S. 1 (1985).

31. Raymond O. Loen, *Manage More by Doing Less* (New York: McGraw-Hill, 1971), pp. 86–89.

32. Robert Sheehan and Gary W. Cordner, *Introduction to Police Administration* (2d ed.), p. 453.

33. Thomas Reddin, "Are You Oriented to Hold Them? A Searching Look at Police Management," *The Police Chief* (March 1966): 17.

34. Peter K. Manning, "The Researcher: An Alien in the Police World," in Arthur Niederhoffer and Abraham S. Blumberg (eds.), *The Ambivalent Force: Perspectives on the Police* (2d ed.) (Hinsdale, Ill: Dryden Press, 1976), pp. 103–121.

35. Herman Goldstein, *Problem-Oriented Policing* (New York: McGraw-Hill, 1990), p. 9.

36. Joan Petersilia, "The Influence of Research on Policing," in Roger C. Dunham and Geoffrey P. Alpert (eds.), *Critical Issues in Policing: Contemporary Readings* (Prospect Heights, Ill.: Waveland Press, 1989), p. 230.

37. *Ibid.*

38. *Ibid.*, pp. 231-232.

39. *Ibid.*, p. 235.

40. *Ibid.*, p. 236.

41. *Ibid.*, p. 237.

42. *Ibid.*, p. 237.

43. *Ibid.*, p. 238.

44. John E. Eck, *Solving Crimes: The Investigation of Burglary and Robbery* (Washington, D.C.: Police Executive Research Forum, National Institute of Justice, 1983), p. xxiii.

45. Herman Goldstein, *Problem-Oriented Policing*, pp. 8–11.

46. Jerome H. Skolnick and David H. Bayley, *The New Blue Line, Police Innovation in Six American Cities* (New York: Free Press, 1986), p. 4.

47. Larry K. Gaines, Mittie D. Southerland, and John E. Angell, *Police Administration*, p. 349.

48. Robert H. Langworthy, *The Structure of Police Organizations* (New York: Praeger, 1986).

49. Dorothy Guyot, "Bending Granite: Attempts to Change the Rank Structure of American Police Departments," pp. 253–284.

50. Jerome H. Skolnick and David H. Bayley, *The New Blue Line*, p. 4.

51. *Ibid.*, pp. 220–224.

52. *Ibid.*, pp. 225–227.

53. Thomas J. Peters and Robert H. Waterman, Jr., *In Search of Excellence* (New York: Harper & Row, 1983), p. 15.

54. Robert Wasserman and Mark H. Moore, *Values in Policing* (Washington, D.C.: U.S. Department of Justice, National Institute of Justice, November 1988), p. 4.

55. *Ibid.*, pp. 6–7.

56. Herman Goldstein, *Problem-Oriented Policing*, pp. 18–19.

57. *Ibid.*, p. 33, 36.

58. For a comparison of the concepts, see Robert C. Trojanowicz, "Community Policing Is Not Police-Community Relations," *FBI Law Enforcement Bulletin* (October 1990):6–11.

59. Mark Moore and Robert Trojanowicz, "Corporate Strategies for Policing," U.S. Department of Justice, National Institute of Justice (Washington, D.C.: U.S. Government Printing Office, 1988), pp. 8–9.

60. Philip Ryan, "Get Rid of the People, and the System Runs Fine," *Smithsonian* (September 1977):140.

61. James Q. Wilson and George L. Kelling, "Broken Windows: The Police and Neighborhood Safety," *The Atlantic Monthly* (March 1982):29–38.

62. See Marie Simonetti Rosen, "Law Enforcement News Interview: Lawrence Sherman," *Law Enforcement News* (March 31, 1990):9–12.

63. George L. Kelling, Robert Wasserman, and Hubert Williams, *Police Accountability and Community Policing* (Washington, D.C.: National Institute of Justice, 1988).

64. Jerome H. Skolnick and David H. Bayley, *The New Blue Line*, p. 85.

Personnel Roles and Functions

The police are the public and the public are the police.

—Robert Peel

✦ INTRODUCTION

It is probably accurate to say that one of the most important and challenging positions one can hold in our society, or any democratic society, is that of a police administrator, manager or supervisor. Given the weight of decisions in contemporary times, and the omnipresent threat of liability in the event of failure to make proper decisions all of the time, this administrative role takes on a much greater level of importance than in past decades.

Changing times have required a higher caliber of leader, for reasons that are as much related to internal aspects of the police organization as they are to external matters. The requirements that officers march and salute militarily and refrain from expressing opinions about politics, religion, or police matters—rules found in many departments as late as the 1970s and 1980s—are clearly outmoded today. The Theory X, "do as I say and not as I do" philosophy of the past engendered many officer complaints and brought about the creation of many police unions; thus the difficult nature of today's police administration is in large part due to the iron hand rule of the past. But it is also very directly a result of a changing, more difficult and litigious society. (Unionism, liability, and other contemporary issues will be discussed more thoroughly in Chapter 15.)

In this chapter we examine today's police executives. We begin by identifying the various roles they fulfill. This is accomplished by adapting Mintzberg's model of chief executive officers; included in this section are considerations of whether or not there is a "dominant" style among police managers, and the agreed upon observable skills of good police managers. Police chiefs and sheriffs are highlighted in this section; we explore the assessment center, a means used for hiring and promoting people into the position of police chief, undersheriff, captain, lieutenant, and so on. Several appropriate methods of assessing chief executive performance are described as well.

Then we look at roles and functions of some other very important people in the rank-ordered nature of policing: the middle managers (captains and lieutenants) and the primary supervisory officers (sergeants). We conclude this chapter with an examination of methods and considerations that surround the deployment of police personnel.

✦ ROLES OF THE POLICE EXECUTIVE: A MODEL

✧ APPLYING THE MINTZBERG MODEL OF CEOS

A police chief executive has many roles. Some openly endorse and subscribe to the philosophy of Henry Mintzberg,[1] who described a set of behaviors and tasks of chief executive officers in any organization. Following is an overview of the role of the chief executive officer (CEO)—that is, the chief of police or sheriff—as adapted to policing, using the Mintzberg model as an analytical framework.

✧ THE INTERPERSONAL ROLE

First is the *interpersonal* role, which includes (1) figurehead, (2) leadership, and (3) liaison duties. As a *figurehead*, the CEO performs various ceremonial functions. Examples include riding in parades and attending other civic events; speaking before school and university classes and civic organizations; meeting with visiting officials and dignitaries; attending academy graduation and swearing-in ceremonies, and certain weddings and funerals; and visiting injured officers in the hospital. Like the mayor who cuts ribbons and kisses babies, these are duties the police CEO performs simply because of his or her title and position within the organization; they come with being a figurehead, and although a chief or sheriff can certainly not be expected to attend every grand opening of retail or commercial businesses and such events to which they are invited, they are certainly obligated from a professional standpoint to perform most of the duties described above.

The *leadership* function requires the CEO to motivate and coordinate workers while having to resolve different goals and needs within the department and the community. Also, a chief or sheriff may have to urge the governing board to enact a code or ordinance that, whether popular or not, is in the best interest of the jurisdiction. For example, a Western chief recently led a drive to pass an ordinance that prohibited parking by university students in residential neighborhoods surrounding the campus. This was a highly unpopular undertaking, but the chief was so prompted because of the hardships suffered and complaints by the area residents. The CEO also provides leadership in such things as bond issues (for more officers or new buildings) and advises the governing body on the effects of proposed ordinances.

The role as *liaison* occurs when the CEO of a police organization interacts with other organizations and coordinates work flows. It is not uncommon for police executives from a geographical area—the police chief, sheriff, ranking officer of the local highway patrol office, district attorney, campus police chief, and so on—to meet informally each month to discuss common problems and strategies. Also, the chief executives serve as liaison between their agencies and others in forming regional law enforcement councils, narcotics units, crime labs, dispatching centers, and so on. They also meet with representatives of the courts, juvenile system, and other criminal justice agencies.

✧ THE INFORMATIONAL ROLE

The second major category under the Mintzberg model is the informational role. Here, the CEO engages in tasks relating to (1) monitoring/inspecting, (2) dissemination, and (3) spokesperson duties. In the *monitoring/inspecting* function, the CEO constantly looks at the workings of the department to ensure that things are operating smoothly (or, as smoothly as a police agency can be expected to run). This function is often referred to as "roaming the ship," and many CEOs who isolated themselves from their personnel and the daily operations of the agency can speak from sad experience of the need to be alert and make a presence. As an example, a Midwestern sheriff in a small county was voted out of office in part because it was revealed that two deputies on graveyard shift were engaged in a "Batman and Robin" style of police work which included the use of an M-16 automatic rifle and a police dog. The sheriff, in the dark about departmental operations and preferring the "ostrich" method of administration, failed to realize that these "midnight cowboys" and other activities were causing ripples until it had turned into a tidal wave of opposition. Daily staff meetings are used by many police executives to acquire information about the jurisdiction, crime, and other goings-on during the previous 24 hours that affect the department.

The *dissemination* tasks involve getting information to members of the department. This may be in the form of memoranda, special orders, general orders, and policies and procedures described in Chapter 4. The *spokesperson* function is related, but is more focused toward getting information to the news media. This is another very difficult task for the chief executive; news organizations, especially the television and print media, are in an especially competitive business where getting the most news in the fastest time often translates to wider viewership and therefore greater advertising. On the one hand, the media must appreciate that there are many occasions when a criminal investigation can be seriously affected by premature or overblown coverage. But the other side of the argument is that there is a legitimate right for the public to know what is occurring in their community—especially matters of crime. Therefore, the prudent police executive would do well to keep the door open to the media and attempt to have an open and professional relationship where each side knows and understands its responsibilities. The chief executive would also do well to remember the power of the pen and not alienate the media; a wise person once said, "Never argue with someone who buys his ink by the barrel." Again, many police executives (a good number who involuntarily left office) can speak of the results of such arguments.

✦ THE DECISION-MAKER ROLE

Finally, as a decision-maker, the CEO of a police organization serves as (1) an entrepreneur, (2) a disturbance-handler, (3) a resource-allocator, and (4) a negotiator. In the capacity of *entrepreneur*, the CEO must *sell* ideas to the governing board or the department. This might include a new computer or communications system, a policing strategy, different work methods, and the like, all of which are intended to improve the organization. Sometimes there is a blending of roles, as when several police executives band together (in a liaison function) and go to the state attorney general and the legislature to lobby (in an entrepreneurial capacity) for new crime-fighting laws. As a *disturbance-handler* the executive's tasks range from the minor (such a disputes between staff members, or a problem with vehicle maintenance resulting in too few vehicles available for patrol) to the major (such as riots, muggings in a local park, or cleaning up the downtown area of undesirable people). Sometimes the intradepartmental disputes can reach major proportions, however, as when the patrol commander tells street officers to arrest more public drunks, therefore causing a severe strain on the jail division commander's resources; this can cause enmity between the two commanders and a need for the chief executive to intervene.

In a word, the CEO as a *resource-allocator* must be able to say "no" to subordinates. However, subordinates should not be faulted for trying reasonably to obtain more money, personnel, or equipment for their operation and attempting to improve it as best they can. Nonetheless, the CEO must have a clear idea of the budget status and where priorities exist. Also, in a position as resource allocator the police executive must listen to citizen complaints and act accordingly. For example, ongoing complaints of speeding motorists in a specific area may soon result in a shifting of patrol resources to that area or neighborhood.

As a *negotiator*, the police manager resolves employee grievances and sits as a member of the negotiating team for labor relations. A recent survey by PERF found that presently 7 out of 10 municipal police departments of more than 75 employees have some form of union representation. This puts the CEO in a difficult position where the police agency has collective bargaining; as a member of management, the CEO is often compelled to argue against salaries and benefits that would assist the rank and file. However, as mentioned above, as long as there is a limited supply of funds available to the jurisdiction, managers will have to draw the line at some point and say "no" to subordinates. Again, the collective bargaining unit and individual officers cannot be severely faulted for trying to better themselves and their working conditions to the maximum extent possible, but at times such associations overstep the line of reasonableness and even reach an impasse or deadlock in contract negotiations with management. These situations can become very uncomfortable and even disastrous, leading to a work stoppage, speedup, slowdown, or other recourse by the rank-and-file.

✦ IS THERE A DOMINANT STYLE?

Several studies have attempted to determine the leadership styles of police managers. An interesting study by Jack Kuykendall and Peter Unsinger [2] involved 155 police managers in California and Arizona, ranging in size from 3 to over 1700 personnel; about half of the managers were from agencies with over 100 personnel. The basic purpose of the study was to determine whether the manager put emphasis on accomplishing the task (therefore using primarily one-way communication with subordinates) or having positive relationships with people (with the leader engaging in a lot of two-way communication with subordinates).

Managers' styles were measured with a survey instrument to determine if they fit into one or more of the following four categories: (1) the "telling" style—a high-task, low-people orientation where the leader is characterized by one-way communication, telling followers what, when, where, and how to do various tasks; (2) the "selling" style places high emphasis on both task accomplishment and people relationships, using two-way communication and emotional support to get workers to "buy into" decisions that have to be made; (3) the "participating" style emphasizes relationships and has low task orientation; it involves two-way communication and encourages shared decision making; and (4) the "delegating" style has low task and people orientations, basically letting people "run their own show."[3]

Kuykendall and Unsinger found that police managers had no dominant style; rather, there tended to be a style flexibility. None of the managers used all four styles, however. The style used least often was the delegating style. Data showed that about 80 percent of the managers tended to be effective, shifting to a particular style that suited a situation. It was common to find police managers using two styles with great frequency; more than three-fourths (78 percent) of the police managers tended to emphasize participating-selling or telling-selling combinations. What was apparent in this study was that police managers did tend to use the selling style more frequently than other styles.

✦ OBSERVABLE SKILLS OF GOOD MANAGERS

According to Robert Katz, as discussed in Chapter 2, there are certain basic skills that the police executive must develop. First is *technical* skill, which involves specialized knowledge, analytical ability, and facility in the use of tools and techniques of the specific discipline. This is the skill most easily trained for. Examples in policing might include budgeting, computer usage, and fundamental knowledge of some specialized equipment, such as radar or breathalyzer machines. Second is the *human* skill, which is the executive's ability to work effectively as a group member and build cooperation; this includes being sensitive to the needs and feelings of others, tolerating ambiguity, being able to empathize with different views and cultures. Finally, there are *conceptual* skills, which involve coordinating and integrating all the activities and interests of the organization into a common objective: in other words, being able to translate knowledge into action.[4]

These skills can be taught just as other skills can. Thus good administrators are not simply born but can be trained in the classroom and by practicing the skills on the job.

✦ POLICE EXECUTIVES

Prior to examining the role and functions of contemporary police executives, we digress a bit and consider how persons in these positions are selected for them. Given the obvious weight of responsibility put on persons occupying these positions, the means employed to test for hiring or promoting people into them becomes equally important.

✧ PROMOTING AND HIRING THE BEST: THE ASSESSMENT CENTER

It should be noted that because a person has been functioning effectively at one level in the organization, there is no guarantee that he or she will perform effectively at a higher level. For several reasons, many excellent "street cops" failed upon being promoted. Perhaps they wanted to remain "one of the troops" and could not maintain the personal distance, perspective, or disciplinary authority needed at times. Or perhaps they could not see the "big picture," still identifying most strongly with one of their former pet assignments (for example, one who worked in, and strongly identified with the investigative division, now promoted to deputy chief or undersheriff and wanting to provide disproportionate resources to the detectives). For these reasons, every reasonable means must be utilized to select the best person for the job while weeding out those who do not have the ability, temperament, or desire for it.

To obtain the most capable people for executive positions in policing—and to avoid personnel, liability, and other kinds of problems that can arise from poor personnel choices—the assessment center method has surfaced as a more elaborate yet efficacious means of hiring and promoting personnel. This method, which originated in Germany in World War I and is now used increasingly for securing people of all management or supervisory ranks, may include interviews; psychological tests; in-basket exercises; management tasks; group discussions; simulations of interviews with subordinates, the public, and news media; fact-finding exercises; oral presentation exercises; and written communications exercises.[5]

First, behaviors are identified that are important to successful job performance of the person holding the position. Clearly stated responsibilities and skills should exist for all executive, midmanagement, and supervisory positions (such as chief, captain, lieutenant, sergeant, and so on). Then several of the foregoing techniques are used to evaluate each candidate in those dimensions. (Note: Unlike local police chiefs, sheriffs are normally elected, not hired or promoted into their position; thus there is little use of the assessment center with that position.)

A lot of individual and group role-playing provides a "hands-on" atmosphere during the process. For example, candidates may be required to perform in simulated police-community problems (such as having candidates conduct a "meeting" to hear concerns of local minority groups); a major incident (candidates explain what they will do, and order done, in a simulated shooting or riot situation); a news briefing; or other such exercises. They may be given an in-basket situation where they are the new chief or captain who receives an abundance of paperwork, policies, and problems to be prioritized and dealt with in a prescribed amount of time. Writing abilities may also be evaluated. For example, candidates may be given 30 minutes to develop a use-of-force policy for a hypothetical or real police agency; this kind of exercise not only illustrates the candidate's written communications skills and understanding of the technical side of police work, but also shows how he or she thinks cognitively and can build a case.

During each exercise, several assessors analyze candidates' behavior, perform some kind of evaluation of each candidate, and at the end of the assessment center turn over their individual rating information to the person making the hiring or promotional decision. Typically selected by virtue of their having held the position for which candidates are now vying, assessors must not only know the types of problems and duties that are incumbent upon persons in the position, but should be keen observers of human behavior as well.

Although assessment centers are obviously more costly than conventional testing procedures, they are well worth the extra investment. As with other occupations, in policing "what goes around, comes around." Monies invested at the early stages of a hiring or promotional process, to avoid selecting the wrong person, can save untold dollars and problems for many years to come. Good executives, midmanagers, and supervisors make fewer mistakes and are probably sued less often. They better know the law of personnel administration. They simply perform better.

✧ Today's Police Manager

Today, the management process in a police setting is affected by the management style of the administrator, the people being managed, and the situation. Therefore, one's management style must obviously be flexible. The style used by a commander at the scene of a hostage situation would be much different from that used by a supervisor at a shoplifting scene. A less experienced employee will require a more authoritarian style of management than a more experienced employee. Management style is always contingent on the situation and the people being managed.[6] Management occurs throughout the organization. As mentioned earlier, management levels include administrators (chief, assistant chiefs, and majors), commanders or midlevel managers (captains and lieutenants), and supervisors (sergeants). Figure 5.1 shows the hierarchy of managers within the typical police organization and the inverse relationship between rank and numbers of personnel; in other words, as rank increases, the number of persons in the hierarchical ranks decreases.

What does a contemporary police manager really *do?* Ronald Lynch stated their primary tasks simply yet directly, saying that police managers "listen, talk, write, confer, think, decide—about men, money, materials, methods, facilities—in order to plan, organize, direct, coordinate, and control their research service, production, public relations, employee relations, and all other activities so that they may more effectively serve the citizens to whom they are responsible."[7] Contemporary police management is certainly not without its problems. One western police administrator saw his primary duties as involving internal personnel matters, telling the author "I'm really a personnel manager who happens to wear a uniform. I couldn't tell you how to process a DUI arrest, but I *can* tell you how to investigate and discipline an officer. That's how [police management] has changed." Another administrator saw civil liability as overshadowing other

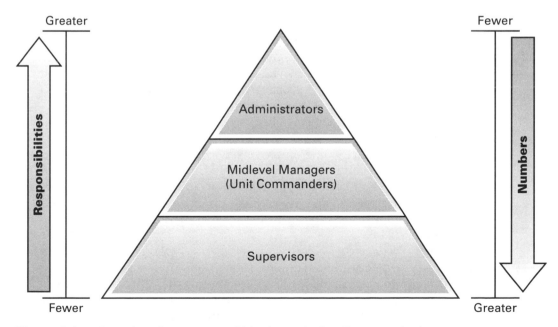

Figure 5.1 Hierarchy of managers within the typical police organization. (*Source:* Larry K. Gaines, Mittie D. Southerland, and John E. Angell, *Police Administration* New York: McGraw-Hill, 1991, p. 11.)

functions, saying, "The decisionmaking process is not directed by the question, 'Is it right or wrong,' but rather, 'How much will it cost us if we're sued?'"

Chiefs or sheriffs in a 10-person agency are faced with the same problems and expectations as their big-city counterparts. The differences between managing large and small departments are a matter of scale. Executives of large departments are faced with a larger volume of many of the same problems than executives of small departments face. Yet the leader of a small department not only must deal with all these managerial concerns, but in many cases must also perform the duties of a working officer.

Next we focus specifically on the two primary law-enforcement executive positions: the chief of police (also known as commissioner or superintendent) and the sheriff. We consider their qualifications and functions, and later discuss some appropriate means for evaluating the performance of each.

✦ CHIEFS OF POLICE

✧ POLITICAL AND COMMUNITY EXPECTATIONS

The chief of police is generally considered to be one of the most influential and prestigious persons in local government. Indeed, in earlier times they often amassed great power and were able to influence the level of crime in a community. However, participatory management, the advent of city managers and public safety directors, the attrition rate of police chiefs, the increased power of local personnel departments, and the influence of police unions have all served to erode much of this traditional power in recent times. Furthermore, mayors, city managers and administrators, members of the agency, citizens, special-interest groups, and the media all have differing role expectations of the chief of police. These are often conflicting in nature.

The mayor or city manager is likely to feel that the chief of police should be an "enlightened" administrator whose responsibility is to promote departmental efficiency, reduce crime, improve service, and so on. Other mayors and managers will appreciate the chief who simply "keeps the lid on" and manages to keep the morale high and citizens' complaints low. All too many mayors and managers view the police chief in much the same way as the owners of professional football teams view their coaches—as scapegoats for conditions beyond the chief's control.[8]

However, the mayor or city manager may properly expect the chief to communicate with city management about police-related issues and to be part of the city management team; to communicate city management's policies to police personnel; to establish agency policies, goals, and objectives, and put them in writing; to develop an administrative system of managing people, equipment, and the budget in a professional and businesslike manner; to set a good example, both personally and professionally; to administer disciplinary action consistently and fairly when required; and to select personnel who are going to perform the organizational objectives ably and professionally.

Police chiefs also have differing points of view from mayors, managers, judges, and legislators on a variety of issues, such as police use of force, minimum entry-level educational requirements and incentive pay, the use of civilian review boards, increased civilianization of police as opposed to the use of sworn officers, legalization of certain behaviors, one-person versus two-person patrol cars, off-duty employment of officers, and gun control.[9]

Members of the agency also have expectations of the chief executive; these expectations may differ in important aspects from those of the mayor or manager. The rank and file may be less concerned with the city's wish for efficiency and cost-effectiveness and more concerned with good salaries, benefits, and equipment. The officers expect the chief to be their advocate, "backing them up" when necessary and representing the agency well in dealings with judges and prosecutors who may be indifferent or hostile to their interests. Citizens also tend to expect the chief of police to provide efficient and cost-effective police services while keeping crime and tax rates down (this is often an area of built-in conflict) and corruption and illegal use of force nonexistent.

Special interest groups include a number of individuals and groups who expect the chief to advocate desirable policy positions; these include neighborhood or community associations that can have high expectations of the chief executive. For example, the Mothers Against Drunk Driving (MADD) group would insist on strong anti-DUI measures (e.g., patrols and arrests) by the police and would oppose any movement to reduce such expenditure of resources and enforcement. Finally, the media (discussed more fully below) expect the chief to cooperate fully with their efforts to obtain fast and complete crime information; some media organizations (in the author's personal experience and observation) have also demonstrated that they are capable of participating in a human version of a "feeding frenzy" at times, embroiling the chief in a lively or controversial news story when the opportunity presents itself.

There are several pressures attached to the chief's position; it is a "fishbowl" environment and lifestyle, where even the mere *appearance* of improper behavior can be devastating to one's career. Their personal appearance and demeanor must be above reproach, so as to set a good example to the subordinates and present the proper public image. There is also a certain amount of social distance that must be maintained, from both the public and the lower-ranking officers. The families of police chiefs (and other officers, for that matter) often pay a price for this social distance, but it is important that the chief not get too "chummy" with the public or too socially close to subordinates. Regarding social distance with subordinates, the chief must remember that it is difficult if not impossible to be objective when having to discipline personal friends, and that possibility always exists. The weight of responsibility is also great, as it is "lonely at the top." Telephone calls come day and night, and they often carry extremely sad news.

✦ QUALIFICATIONS, SELECTION AND TENURE

Qualifications for the position of police chief vary widely, depending on the size of agency and the region of the country. Smaller agencies, especially those in rural areas, may not have any minimum educational requirement for the job. The National Advisory Commission on Criminal Justice Standards and Goals surveyed police chiefs and their superiors to determine qualities that were felt essential for the job. Figure 5.2 shows a rating of the importance of 11 factors in the selection of police chief executives. All factors except age and military experience received positive responses from more than 80 percent of both groups. Law enforcement experience received the highest positive response of "very important" from both groups.

Education is also shown in Figure 5.2 to be an important consideration. However, the common requirement is high school graduation, plus several years of experience as a police supervisor. In large agencies it is common to find a requirement for college education, plus several years of progressively responsible police management experience.[10] In 1985, Don Witham surveyed 493 police chiefs in agencies of more than 75 employees.[11] He found that the "typical" police chief was 49 years old, had 24 years of law enforcement experience (17.7 of which were with their present department), and worked 56.6 hours per week; about 57 percent had earned a baccalaureate degree and 25

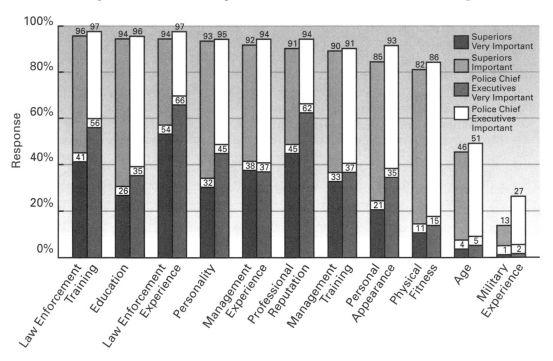

Figure 5.2 Factors in the selection of police chief executives. (*Source:* National Advisory Commission on Criminal Justice Standards and Goals, *Police Chief Executive* Washington, D.C.: U.S. Government Printing Office, 1975, p. 21.)

percent had a graduate degree (this compares with a 1985 survey of campus police chiefs by the author which found that 48 percent had a baccalaureate degree and 24 percent had graduate degrees.[12]

There are also several areas of important management skills that are needed in police chief executives. The National Advisory Commission asked police chiefs and their superiors to rate, on a scale of 1 to 10, the importance of 14 desirable management skills. Figure 5.3 shows the results, with the ability to motivate and control personnel and relate to the community having overall greater importance. A similar survey today would probably yield similar results. In fact, when PERF recently asked almost 500 police chiefs to list the areas in which they needed more training for better decision making, they listed the executive's role in management, legal problems and issues, personnel management, computers, and strategic planning as their training priorities.[13]

Although it is certainly cheaper to select a police chief from within the organization, the question is often raised as to whether or not it is better to do so. That debate will probably not be resolved soon, and there are obvious advantages and disadvantages to both. But a recent study of police chiefs promoted from within and hired from outside in the west found significant differences in only one area: educational attainment. The outsiders were more highly educated, but the two groups did not differ in other areas, including back-

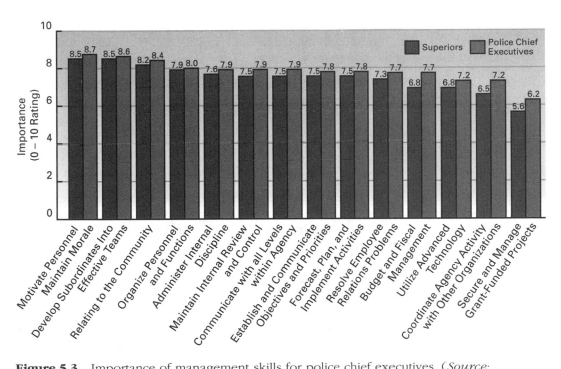

Figure 5.3 Importance of management skills for police chief executives. (*Source:* National Advisory Commission on Criminal Justice Standards and Goals, *Police Chief Executive* Washington, D.C.: U.S. Government Printing Office, 1975, p. 22.)

ground, attitudes, salary, tenure in current position or in law enforcement, or size of agency, community, and current budget.[14]

Job security of police chiefs ranges from full civil service protection in a small percentage of agencies to appointment and removal at the discretion of the mayor or city manager. There is a growing trend for a fixed term of office, such as a 4- or 5-year contract. Traditionally, however, the tenure of police chiefs has been low. A federal study found in the mid-1970s that the average length of office by chiefs of police was 5.4 years.[15] Another PERF study in the mid-1980s found the average to be practically unchanged, 5.5 years. Those who are appointed from within the agency tend to have longer tenure than those appointed from outside.

This lack of police-chief job tenure has several negative consequences, including the lack of long-range planning that is done, the effect on the organization in frequently having new policies and administrative styles, the inability of the short-term chief to develop a political power base and local influence, and the time and expense in hiring a new chief. These problems in job security and tenure have been seen in recent years. Former New York City Police Commissioner, Patrick V. Murphy, commented in 1977 that "even the leaders of our biggest, most consequential police departments continue to run things as though all of America were still a small town, and Matt Dillon an appropriate role model for a metropolitan police chief."[16] Murphy also felt that "the police chief—behind a big oak desk in a private office, insulated from the outside world by hordes of officious aides and layers of bureaucracy—must, by all means, focus the entire institutional effort around one job: that of the police officer closest to the community."[17]

✧ THE DEPARTURE OF SOME REFORM-MINDED CHIEFS

The 1991 Rodney King incident, and the 1992 rioting that followed the acquittal of the officers involved, heightened local dissension against the Los Angeles Police Department and fomented a movement to oust Chief Daryl Gates. Further, Los Angeles citizens voted to amend the Los Angeles city charter to end the system that kept Gates in office for 14 years. This attempt at reform may appear rational under the circumstances, but it will never erase the chronic tension among the city, its politicians, and its police. And the central problem will remain: there is no way to take the police out of politics.

Across the country, police executives are in the "eye of the storm." Rising crime, limited budgets, unionization, and conflicting public demands have caused many American police executives to be heavily scrutinized and inspected in all they do. The toll has been great. From mid-1991 to mid-1992, eight of the 15 largest city police departments faced turmoil or turnover at the top. The tenure of a metropolitan police chief has fallen from 5 1/2 years to somewhere between 3 1/2 and 4 1/2 years.[18]

Yet it is because of historical political influence and control over police executives that city charters across the country were amended decades ago to insulate chiefs from politicians. Now the mood and temper of the public has changed. "There has to be civilian control of the police," asserted Patrick V. Murphy, director of the U.S. Conference of Mayors police policy board.[19]

However, in many cities, this need for civilian control leaves the police chief vulnerable to the whims of the mayor, city council, or city manager. The problem lies in how to balance the civilian control with some protection from local politics; and many cities have not mastered that balance. For example, in Boston a special commission appointed by the mayor concluded in January 1992 that the police department was grossly mismanaged and that the commissioner should be replaced; but the mayor, a lifelong friend of the chief's, reappointed him in May. A former chief in Houston, nationally recognized for her community policing efforts, lost her job in 1992 after a new mayor was elected during a crime wave. In Dallas, a police chief who struggled to improve minority relations there was indicted on a misdemeanor perjury charge that some believe was the work of a vengeful old guard; he was then fired in late 1990, but a jury later found him innocent.[20] Tulsa's chief, who won wide praise for emphasizing community relations and crime prevention, resigned in late 1991 after union members gave him a no-confidence vote and two city council members accused him of being too soft on crime. San Francisco's chief was fired after only 45 days on the job because of accusations that he had officers confiscate newspapers displaying an unflattering likeness of him. Similar situations have occurred in St. Petersburg, Florida, and other cities across the nation.[21]

The various community constituencies will battle more viciously when chiefs attempt to implement major change, like community policing. Unions often resist, and civil-service rules prevent many chiefs from naming even their own commanders. But political pressures to improve with the times remain. The message being sent from chiefs is that, without some job protection, do not expect too much real reform—or many long-tenured chiefs.[22]

✦ THE SHERIFF

✧ CONTEMPORARY NATURE AND FUNCTIONS

Unfortunately, because of television and movie portrayals, much of the public perceives the county sheriff as stupid, cruel, overweight, corrupt, and wearing a Stetson hat and sunglasses while talking with a Southern drawl (see, e.g., "Smoky and the Bandit," "Mississippi Burning," "The Dukes of Hazzard," "Walking Tall," and many others). This image is not only unfair but also highly inaccurate; county sheriffs and their offices are dedicated to order maintenance while providing valuable services to unincorporated areas, maintaining detention facilities, performing important civil-process functions, and other duties as delineated below.

The position of sheriff has a long tradition. Sheriffs tend to be elected; thus most candidates are aligned with a political party. Therefore, it is possible that the only qualification a person brings to the office is the ability to get votes. (Indeed, the author once met a sheriff who was approximately 60 years old and attending a course at the state police academy, whose only "qualification" for being elected was his popularity—he had owned and operated a beer hall in his home town practically all his life.) In some areas of the country, the sheriff's term of office is limited to 2 years and the sheriff is prohibited from serving successive terms (thus the office has been known to be "rotated" between the sheriff and undersheriff). In most counties, however, the sheriff has a 4-year term of office and can be reelected. They enjoy no guarantee to tenure in office, although a federal study found that sheriffs (averaging 6.7 years in office) had longer tenure in office than chiefs of police (5.4 years).[23] This politicization of the office of sheriff can obviously result in high turnover rates of personnel not having civil service protection and a lack of long-range (strategic) planning.

Also, largely due to the political nature of the office, sheriffs tend to be older, less likely to be promoted through the ranks of the agency, have less specialized training, and are less likely to be college graduates than police chiefs. Research has also found that sheriffs in small agencies have more difficulty with organizational problems (field activities, budget management), while sheriffs in large agencies find dealing with local officials and planning and evaluation to be more troublesome. Because of the diversity of sheriff's offices throughout the country, it is difficult to describe a "typical" sheriff's department; those offices run the gamut from the traditional, highly political, limited-service office to the modern, fairly nonpolitical, full-service police organization.[24] However, it is possible to list functions commonly associated with the sheriff's office.

1. Service of civil processes (divorce papers, liens, evictions, garnishments and attachments, and other civil duties, such as extradition and transportation of prisoners.
2. Collection of certain taxes and the conduct of real estate sales (usually for nonpayment of taxes) for the county.
3. Performing routine order-maintenance duties by enforcing state statutes and county ordinances; arresting offenders and performing traffic and criminal investigations.
4. Serving as bailiff of the courts.
5. Maintenance and operation of the county correctional institutions.

Other general duties will, of course, be found from one region to another.

Sheriffs often see themselves as police officials and regard their jail administration duties as a liability. They are frequently untrained and uninterested in corrections management, yet that is one of their primary functions. This lack of training and interest has resulted in some major scandals and problems in jail administration in this country. However, a few sheriffs tolerate the jail function because of its financial opportunities. One sheriff, allowed a certain amount of money per day to feed each prisoner, told the author that he fed cheap "TV dinners" and pocketed the savings—a very handsome annual profit.

Overcrowding is a national jail problem, as is the problem of what to do with prisoners who are released from jail. One sheriff was unfairly criticized because released inmates bothered area residents by begging money and transportation and shoplifting at nearby quick-stop establishments; however, had the sheriff proposed mandatory transportation of prisoners to another area, it is certain that civil rights suits would have followed.

✧ REGIONAL ROLE DIFFERENCES

Some researchers have examined the current operations of sheriff's offices in four regions of the country: the east, south, midwest and west.[25] Their findings were interesting. In the east, most sheriff's departments lie at the traditional/political/limited-service end of the continuum. In most areas of that region, the sheriff has lost all police authority and has been reduced to functions of court security, civil process serving, and such duties. Even the traditional jail management function is being diminished; an increasing number of counties in the east are establishing independent jail management boards.

At the same time, there are an increasing number of state police agencies (meaning essentially that they have full police powers everywhere in the state—considerably greater authority than just being empowered to patrol state highways). Some county police departments have replaced sheriffs. The eastern sheriff's office, therefore, is often quite small, with a tight budget. The office has become increasingly political, and legislation is regularly introduced to abolish the office altogether. The future of the office is shaky, and many people believe that it may soon be extinct altogether in this region.[26]

In total contrast, the sheriff in the south continues to be a strong law enforcement figure; larger agencies provide a full range of law enforcement services, and therefore they have prevented the need of state police forces to be created. These sheriffs have also maintained enough political clout to survive challenges to their existence and authority, and have developed strong formal lobbying efforts and sheriffs' associations. The political power of southern sheriffs has led to abuse and corruption; nonetheless, these sheriff's offices tend to be efficient, effective, and secure.[27]

Midwestern sheriffs' offices can be categorized into two types: one similar to the eastern model, and one similar to the southern model. Vast geographical distances, relatively low population density, and a general lack of demand for law enforcement services have created a unique situation. While being a full-service agency, the office is also required to perform a wide range of civil functions while deemphasizing proactive crime prevention and patrolling. Therefore, in many areas staffing is usually fairly small, with little specialization.

Although politically significant, these sheriffs no longer carry the clout of their southern counterparts. They provide services to unincorporated areas of the county, operate jails, and generally provide all the civil processes as found in the east. Midwestern sheriffs tend to have more professional status, more basic qualifications, and receive a somewhat higher salary than those in the other two regions. The office is secure, with few attempts to overcome the authority of the office.

The western sheriff still carries many of the vestiges of the Wild West, with vast, wide open territories of responsibility. In many respects these sheriffs resemble midwestern sheriffs; in the Great Plains region and Rocky Mountain West, the modern, political, full-service (yet limited-activity type) sheriff's office is the most common, primarily because of geographical conditions, low population density, relatively low crime rates and limited resources bases. As in the urbanized midwest, the western sheriff remains the chief law enforcement officer in the county.

✦ RATING CHIEF EXECUTIVE PERFORMANCE

How good is your police chief or sheriff (hereafter referred to as the chief executive officer, or CEO)? The answer probably depends on the person you ask. To some, the CEO is the best thing that ever happened to the community or county; to others, he or she is a gift from hell. The CEO's job is very complex; there are several potential "traps" in rating effectiveness. Also, CEOs are human; they err, but are often wronged by citizen perceptions of them and their performance. Therefore, it is difficult to assess accurately how the person occupying the position is performing; there is not a litmus test or a simple "fill in the boxes" exercise. However, there are broad, general guidelines that can be applied to these unique positions.

✧ USE OF INAPPROPRIATE CRITERIA

As pointed out by Jerald Vaughn, former police chief and author in a report for the Police Executive Research Forum (PERF),[28] some of the "traps" in evaluating the local CEOs, were as follows:

1. *Personal popularity.* The longer the tenure of a CEO, the greater the chance that people within and without the department will have complaints about something the CEO did or did not do; furthermore, a conscientious chief often does the proper thing, while knowing it is not going to be the most popular course of action.

2. *Morale in the department.* Morale is a fragile thing. It is more of an individual than a collective effort. Peter Drucker wrote that "morale" does not mean that "people get along together"; the test is performance, not conformance. [29] Like soldiers and other workers in bureaucratic organizations, some police officers can become chronic and notorious complainers; the "grapevine" normally keeps people stirred up, and a certain amount of griping will occur even when things are running smoothly. Thus, like the polygraph operator who must first measure the

subject's anxiety level before asking pointed questions, it is important to assume a certain level of superficial malcontent with police officers.

3. *Controversy surrounding the CEO.* Few chief executives are controversial; however, some may have controversy thrust upon them as a result of local issues. Controversy and conflict can even be productive, causing people to challenge old ideas and methods. CEOs are highly visible and influential; they should speak out and provide leadership on matters of public safety.

4. *A rising crime rate.* As Madison, Wisconsin's former chief, David Couper, observed, social and economic factors have a large influence on community crime levels.[30] As the saying goes, "There is a lot of crime prevention in a T-bone steak." The police are severely restricted in their ability to control crime. To blame the chief executive is to miss the point. However, where there is a serious crime rate or public concern about crime, the chief executive should be developing programs and strategies for combatting it, rather than merely watching crime statistics soar and engaging in mere "bean counting."

5. *Single issues: "Run the bum out of town."* Occasionally, a single, critical event or issue arises that can mushroom into a call for the CEO's ouster (such as the Rodney King incident in Los Angeles in 1991). Sometimes the chief executive will survive the incident if an objective review of his total performance is made. On other occasions, years of dedicated service may be lost to the passion of the moment. Indeed, in some incidents the chief may deserve to be relieved of his command; however, more often a multidimensional review of the chief's total performance should be made. Further, the ouster of the chief does not ensure that the basic problem causing the upheaval will be eliminated.

✧ APPROPRIATE MEASURES AND TRAITS

In rating a police executive, then, it is important to consider the qualities, characteristics, and behavior that guide performance on the job. After honesty and integrity, probably the most important quality is the leadership effectiveness of the chief. The direction of the department, its commitment to professional and ethical standards, and its basic values emanate from the chief's leadership role. To be effective, the chief must be able to persuade and move people without shoving them, inspiring people both inside and outside the department. Any assessment of the chief executive must begin with his or her leadership effectiveness. An effective chief, as a subordinate to the mayor and city manager/council, must also be a good follower. It is important to know where the lines are drawn, when it is time to quit leading and start following. On occasion, he or she must also know when, in the best interest of the organization, it is time to leave it.

The National Advisory Commission on Criminal Justice Standards and Goals surveyed police chief executives and their superiors to determine the personal-

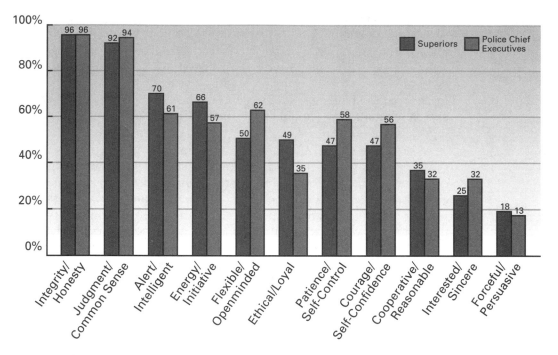

Figure 5.4 Importance of traits for police chief executives. (*Source:* National Advisory Commission on Criminal Justice Standards and Goals, *Police Chief Executive*, Washington, D.C.: U.S. Government Printing Office, 1975, p. 23.)

ity traits deemed most important. Figure 5.4 shows those traits, with the overwhelming selections being integrity/honesty and judgment/common sense. All options may be viewed as relatively positive.

CEOs must also manage a significant amount of resources—human and financial resources, equipment, and physical facilities—in a professional manner. Their ability to do so reflects the amount of return the taxpayers receive on their investment in police services. They must make timely and responsible decisions as well, realizing the impact and legal ramifications of those decisions. It is also important that the chief executive delegate authority and decision making to others; taking on too much himself will often result in a sluggish operation. Finally, a chief must be innovative and creative in thinking. Policing can seldom afford to continue doing things the way they were done in the past. Further, traditional thinking about police work is being challenged. Today's chief executive must be willing to keep up with those challenges and move the agency into a new era of research, experimentation, and risk-taking.[31]

Thus there are several general measures of a chief executive's performance. First are the values of the department; is it a high-quality police organization, committed to the rights of individuals and its employees? Values are the foundation of a top-quality police organization. A related consideration is the department's view toward the use of force—an area that must be managed carefully and aggressively to ensure that the public is not subjected to unlawful or unwarranted physical force by police. Next are "rules of the game"; does the agency have clear policies, rules, and procedures for guiding employees? This written directive system is another key part of the foundation of the organization. Of course, those directives must be constantly updated and enforced fairly and consistently. The recent interest by police departments in accreditation is reflective of this desire to have professional standards. Crime strategies, mentioned above, are also important. The question can legitimately be asked of the chief: "What crime-specific strategies have you developed to make your community safer?"

The labor climate of the organization is also a valid criterion of the chief's performance. The ability of the organization to combat crime is undermined seriously in agencies that have serious labor-management strife. A police strike ("blue flu") is the extreme example of a breakdown in the relationship between labor and management. Labor relations is also an area where taxpayers are the biggest losers. This is a very difficult area for today's police executive; civil service, unions, appeal boards, the courts, and the changing profile of today's police officer have made managing labor relations a constant challenge.[32]

Finally, the skilled CEO will have a good idea of where the department stands with the community, as well as the major concerns of the public. Knowing community perceptions—toward their police agencies, crime, willingness to provide financial resources, and so on—should be a paramount concern of the chief executive. No other sector of government in our society has more frequent and direct contact with the public than the police. As Darlene Walker and Richard Richardson [33] observed, "Whatever the citizen thinks of the police, they can hardly be ignored. Whereas other police bureaucrats are often lost from the public's view, locked in rooms filled with typewriters and anonymity, police officers are out in the world—on the sidewalks and in the streets and shopping malls, cruising, strolling, watching, as both state protectors and state repressors." Public opinion surveys provide vital information and feedback to the police executive concerning public perception of officer performance and the department's standing and communication with the public. The mood of the public should be a vital consideration when making public policy decisions.[34]

✦ MIDDLE MANAGEMENT: CAPTAINS AND LIEUTENANTS

Few police administration books contain information about the middle-management members of a police department—the captains and lieutenants. This is unfortunate, because they are too numerous and too powerful within police organizations to ignore. Opinions vary toward these midmanagement personnel, however, as will be seen below.

One of the early progressive police administration contributors, Leonhard Fuld, said in 1909 that the captain is one of the most important officers in the organization. Fuld felt the position had two broad duties—police and administrative. The police duties held the captain responsible for the preservation of the public peace and the protection of life and property within the precinct. Fuld defined the captain's administrative duties as being of three kinds: clerical, janitorial, and supervisory.[35]

Normally, captains and lieutenants are commissioned officers, with the position of captain second in rank to the executive managers. Captains have authority over all officers of the agency below the chief or sheriff and are responsible only to them. Lieutenants are in charge of sergeants and all officers within assigned responsibility, and report to captains. Captains and lieutenants may perform the following functions:[36]

◊ Inspecting assigned operations
◊ Reviewing and making recommendations on reports
◊ Helping develop plans
◊ Preparing work schedules
◊ Overseeing records and equipment
◊ Overseeing recovered or confiscated property
◊ Enforcing all laws and orders

One of the problems of police organizations is that they tend to become too top-heavy. Such organizations—having too many leaders and not enough followers—often do not function well, as such a structure can generate autocracy in its worst form, stifle creative thought or suggestions from the lower ranks, frustrate communication, and pose a hindrance to accomplishing goals and objectives. The people who make the key decisions, top administrators, must be close to the point at which the job is accomplished. Middle management—including captains and lieutenants—often becomes a major barrier between the administrator and the officer in the field.

Too often, middle managers become glorified paper pushers, especially in the present climate of myriad reports, budgets, grants, and so on. The agency should take a hard look at what managerial services are essential and whether or not lieutenants are needed to perform such services. Recently, some communities, such as Kansas City, Missouri, eliminated the rank of lieutenant, finding that this move had no negative consequences and some positive effects.[37]

Obviously, when a multilayered bureaucracy is created, a feudal kingdom and several fiefdoms will occupy the building. However, as Richard Holden observed, "If feudalism was so practical, it would not have died out in the Middle Ages."[38] It is important to remember that the two crucial elements to organizational effectiveness include (1) top administrators, and (2) operational personnel. Middle management can pose a threat to the agency by acting as a barrier between these two primary elements. As has often been noted, the Roman Catholic Church serves many millions and employs many thousands of people with only five levels in the hierarchy.[39] Research has shown an inverse relationship between the size of the hierarchy in an organization and its effectiveness.[40] Normally, the closer the administrator is to the operations, the more effective the agency.

✦ THE ROLE OF PATROL SERGEANT

✧ SEEKING THE "GOLD BADGE"

Sometime during the career of a patrol officer (provided that he or she acquires the minimal years of experience), the opportunity is presented for career advancement—to a three-striped sergeant. This is a very difficult position to occupy, with sergeants as midlevel administrators being caught between upper management and the rank-and-file officers; people who can successfully work with, yet command people are in short supply and long demand.

Because most rank-and-file officers will retire with the same rank at which they entered the occupation—patrol officer—the initial promotional opportunity to attain the rank of sergeant is normally an attractive one. There is practically no lateral entry from agency to agency at the lower ranks; therefore, patrol officers are not able to transfer to another police agency with a promotion. Their promotional opportunities are therefore limited to their present agency, and the waiting period for sergeant's vacancies to arise through retirement or otherwise—especially in smaller agencies—can seem interminable.

Intracity and departmental politics certainly influence the promotional process; mayors, city managers, and police administrators have been known to predetermine who will be promoted even before testing and interviewing begin. Another administrative consideration that filters in is the knowledge that good patrol officers do not automatically become good midlevel supervisors. Many good patrol officers promoted to the rank of sergeant cannot divorce themselves from being "one of the troops" and are unable to flex their supervisory muscles when necessary. In short, a good sergeant must wear two hats, that of a people-oriented, democratic leader with concern for subordinates, but one who is task oriented and authoritarian when that style is called for. Unfortunately, many supervisors (within policing as well as without) today feel that their subordinates are motivated more by money than anything else; over the years a number of studies have shown that intrinsic rewards—such as full appreciation, sympathetic help and being made to feel a part of the organization—take precedence over income. Research results such as the Hawthorne effect (productivity increases when management shows labor it cares) have also demonstrated this aspect of the rank-and-file.

Fuld argued in 1909 that when considering the first-line supervisor, the ideal sergeant needed to possess four qualifications: the ability to write and prepare reports, a thorough knowledge of police business, a capacity for being discrete and intelligent, and a rudimentary knowledge of criminal law.[41]

✧ GETTING THAT FIRST PROMOTION

It is not uncommon for 60 to 65 percent or more of those who are eligible to take the test; and it is common for more than half of all persons promoted to sergeant in an agency to be persons working outside the patrol division at the time. Senior administrators feel that this is better than bringing the "patrol officer's mentality" to the sergeant role. Exams change over time, and with it go the officer's sense of knowing where he or she stands on the promotional market. Competition for sergeant in most departments is obviously quite keen, but the material rewards are actually quite slight. Those who are promoted lose opportunities for overtime and court that are available to patrol officers. Conventional wisdom among many officers is that their immediate supervisors take home less money than they do. Still, the opportunity to test for sergeant normally draws a crowd. Many officers test simply for the experience, because of pressure from peers, through curiosity, or just to get off the streets for a short while.

Becoming a sergeant in a good-sized American police agency is governed by departmental and civil service procedures, intended to guarantee legitimacy and impartiality for the process. As mentioned above, there is still room for sponsorship or "political pull" to work, although it may not be the blatant "hook" or "rabbi" systems of past decades.[42] Officers are often told it is best to rotate into different assignments before testing for sergeant, to gain exposure to a variety of police functions and supervisors. The promotional system, then, favors not only those officers who are skilled at test-taking, but also those skilled at cultivating relationships outside the patrol division.[43]

Sergeants are chosen from a final, rank-ordered list of names, often based on scores from written and oral tests as well as factors such as years of experience, minority status, supervisory ratings, military experience, and departmental commendations. Often, the testing process is regarded by officers as a gauntlet, being capricious, testing inappropriate skills and knowledge, giving unfair advantage to certain groups (e.g., women, minorities, college graduates, veterans) and emphasizing "trick" or subtle questions. The test is also seen as mildly embarrassing, a process that dishonors more than it honors. As Van Maanen observed, however, "One could hardly expect a favorable impression of a testing procedure that screens out over 95 percent of its takers."[44]

✧ ASSUMING THE ROLE

After becoming a sergeant, there are several dynamics at work that make the transition difficult. The new sergeant confronts a solitary process; there is little, if any, formal training about the new position; thus advice and counsel must be sought out. New sergeants are often given the unpopular and relief assignments, therefore having few officers assigned that the sergeant knows, no officers permanently assigned to him, and little loyalty from subordinates.

The new sergeant eventually adapts to the new role, developing individual characteristics that become quite well known to officers supervised.

✦ DISTRIBUTION AND DEPLOYMENT OF PATROL FORCES

✧ EVALUATING NUMBERS OF OFFICERS NEEDED

Once the police officers are hired, the next question becomes how to deploy them in the best, most advantageous manner. Every modern police department has a patrol unit; even in large specialized departments, patrol officers constitute up to two-thirds of all sworn officers. In small communities, police operations are not specialized, and the patrol division—full of generalists who perform a wide range of duties—is the department.

Roughly four and a half police officers are required to provide one officer around the clock, 7 days per week, 365 days per year. This is due to days off, sick leave, holidays, and so on. Thus it typically costs more than $150,000 to deploy one patrol officer on the street permanently. Another consideration is the actual availability of the officer. For example, an officer working 8-hour shifts, 5 days on duty and 2 days off per week, will be available only about 1760 hours or 220 shifts per year—or 60 percent of the time, after subtracting days off, vacation, training, holidays, and all the other forms of leave.

Given the expense and limited resources available for policing the crime and drug problems in the United States today, it would seem logical that every possible consideration would be given to proper deployment of personnel. Police agencies need more hard data on what is being done on patrol; then that data should be used to maximum benefit for patrol officer deployment. Unfortunately, as will be seen below, such an approach is often not followed.

Essentially, there are three ways to determine the "appropriate" number of police personnel that a department needs. First is the *intuitive approach*, which is basically an educated guess. This method, probably used with considerable frequency in the United States and in most small jurisdictions, is obviously not based on any rational scheme. Often, conveniently intersecting streets or highways are used to create permanent "beat" sectors, without regard to an analytical consideration of the when, where, or how of crime occurrences.

The *workload approach* is rarely used for an entire department because it requires an elaborate information system, standards of expected performance, and prioritization of police activities. The last approach, the *comparative* method, is becoming more widespread and involves comparing one or more communities, using the ratio of police officers per 1,000 population as a standard; this method is used to attempt to justify additional personnel.[45]

According to the FBI *Uniform Crime Reports*, presently the national average is 2.2 full-time sworn officers for every 1000 inhabitants; the range was 1.7 for cities with populations of 25,000 to 99,999, to 2.8 in cities with 250,000 or more inhabitants. Geographically, the highest rate of officers to population was recorded in the northeastern and southern states, where there were 2.4 officers per 1000 inhabitants. It is important to note that intercity comparisons should be done with extreme caution. For example, one community with 100,000 population may have adequate police protection with 200 officers, while another 24-hour city (as in a gambling or tourism state) may not be sufficiently covered with 350 officers.

The two most important variables in allocating police personnel, as alluded to earlier, are location and time. Knowing the *location* of problems assists the police in dividing a community into geographic beats or sectors of approximately equal workload. *Time of occurrence* is important because it determines how personnel will be grouped into working time periods or shifts. *Mobility* is also an important consideration; police officers travel by several means; therefore, speed, density, visibility, and community consequences need to be taken into account.[46]

Summary

Clearly, the task of police management now carries tremendous responsibility. Our initial foray into the roles and functions of police managers provided a glimpse into the awesome trust and challenges of this assignment. How should I lead? How do I best perform all of my roles? Should I aggressively recruit and hire more women and minority officers? What is my standing with the governing board? With the rank and file? How is it best to deploy and evaluate the officers? These are some of the questions and issues daily facing contemporary police managers.

Although there are doubtless thousands of capable, dedicated police administrators in this country, it is obvious from occasional news accounts that some administrators, managers, and supervisors attained their level of leadership responsibility by having been good subordinates or through political favoritism. For example, many good street cops became lackluster or even ineffective administrators. This promoting of unqualified personnel to positions of leadership has been one of the major reasons for the major growth of employee labor unions and lawsuits for improper supervision of personnel. Historically, it has also led to graft and corruption.

In conclusion, to be an effective administrator, a person must first learn all that he or she can about our most valuable asset—people. Upon acquiring these human skills, the technical, conceptual, and other necessary skills of the job will probably follow, assuming that the person has moderate ability and appropriate levels of education and training. This formalized process is surely preferred over simply marching the new leader off the plank, to either sink or swim in the ocean of alligators.

In this chapter we have presented a fairly broad analysis of police managers and their problems. In the following chapter we provide more specific kinds of problems and issues they encounter, some of which pose grave concerns, indeed, for those wearing the bars and stripes.

Questions for Review

1. What are some of the primary roles of police executives? (Use the three major categories under the Mintzberg model of chief executive officers in developing your response.)

2. Is there a dominant management style of police executives? If so, is it the best style? Defend your responses.

3. What are some elements of the police chief's position that make it attractive or unattractive? Are contemporary hiring requirements adequate?

4. How do chiefs and sheriffs differ in role and background?

5. How is the performance of chiefs and sheriffs being evaluated? Are there other, better criteria that could be used? What personal traits are most important for persons occupying or seeking these offices?

6. How do the role and function of sergeant differ from those of upper or middle management?

7. What criteria should be used to determine the distribution and performance evaluation of street officers?

For Further Reading

WAYNE K. BENNETT and KAREN M. HESS, *Management and Supervision in Law Enforcement*. St. Paul, Minn.: West, 1992.

NATHAN F. IANNONE, *Supervision of Police Personnel* (4th ed.). Englewood Cliffs, N.J.: Prentice Hall, 1987.

ROY R. ROBERG and JACK KUYKENDALL, *Police Organization and Management: Behavior, Theory, and Processes*. Pacific Grove, Calif.: Brooks/Cole, 1990.

EDWARD A. THIBAULT, LAWRENCE M. LYNCH, and R. BRUCE MCBRIDE, *Proactive Police Management* (2d ed.). Englewood Cliffs, N.J.: Prentice Hall, 1990.

PAUL M. WHISENAND and GEORGE E. RUSH, *Supervising Police Personnel: Back to the Basics*. Englewood Cliffs, N.J.: Prentice Hall, 1988.

Notes

1. Henry Mintzberg, "The Manager's Job: Folklore and Fact," *Harvard Business Review* 53 (July/August 1975):49–61.

2. Jack Kuykendall and Peter C. Unsinger, "The Leadership Styles of Police Managers," *Journal of Criminal Justice* 10 (1982):311–322.

3. Paul Hershey and Kenneth H. Blanchard, *Management of Organizational Behavior* (Englewood Cliffs, N.J.: Prentice Hall, 1977), pp. 161–172.

4. Robert Katz, "Skills of an Effective Administrator," *Harvard Business Review* (January/February 1955):33–41.

5. R. J. Filer, "Assessment Centers in Police Selection," in C.D. Spielberger and H.C. Spaulding (eds.), *Proceedings of the National Working Conference on the Selection of Law Enforcement Officers* (Tampa, Fla.: University of South Florida, March 1977), p. 103.

6. Larry K. Gaines, Mittie D. Southerland, and John E. Angell, *Police Administration* (New York: McGraw-Hill, 1991), pp. 10–11.

7. Ronald G. Lynch, *The Police Manager* (3d ed.) (New York: Random House, 1986), p. 1.

8. Clemens Bartollas, Stuart J. Miller, and Paul B. Wice, *Participants in American Criminal Justice: The Promise and the Performance* (Englewood Cliffs, N.J.: Prentice Hall, 1983), p. 35.

9. *Ibid.*, pp. 39–40.

10. *Ibid.*, p. 42.

11. Donald C. Witham, *The American Law Enforcement Executive: A Management Profile* (Washington, D.C.: Police Executive Research Forum, 1985).

12. Ken Peak, "Campus Policing in America: The State of the Art," *The Police Chief* 54 (June 1987):22–24.

13. Donald C. Witham, *The American Law Enforcement Chief Executive: A Management Profile*, p. xii.

14. Janice K. Penegor and Ken Peak, "Police Chief Acquisitions: A Comparison of Internal and External Selections," *American Journal of Police*, 11 (1992): 17–32.

15. National Advisory Commission on Criminal Justice Standards and Goals, *Police Chief Executive* (Washington, D.C.: U.S. Government Printing Office, 1976), p. 7.

16. Patrick V. Murphy, *Commissioner: A View from the Top of American Law Enforcement* (New York: Simon and Schuster, 1977), p. 217.

17. *Ibid.*, p. 270.

18. Gordon Witkin, "Police Chiefs at War," *U.S. News and World Report* (June 8, 1992), p. 33.

19. *Ibid.*

20. *Ibid.*, p. 34.

21. *Ibid.*

22. *Ibid.*

23. National Advisory Commission on Criminal Justice Standards and Goals, *Police Chief Executive*, p. 7.

24. Clemens Bartollas, Stuart J. Miller, and Paul B. Wice, *Participants in American Criminal Justice: The Promise and the Performance*, pp. 51–52.

25. *Ibid.*, pp. 53–59.

26. *Ibid.* pp. 53, 55.

27. *Ibid.*, pp. 55–56.

28. Jerald R. Vaughn, *How to Rate Your Police Chief* (Washington, D.C.: Police Executive Research Forum, 1987), pp. 7–14.

29. Peter Drucker, *Management, Tasks, Responsibilities, and Practices* (New York: Harper & Row, 1974).

30. David C. Couper, *How to Rate Your Local Police* (Washington, D.C.: Police Executive Research Forum, 1973).

31. Jerald R. Vaughn, *How to Rate Your Police Chief*, pp. 15–20.

32. *Ibid.*, pp. 23–29.

33. N. Darlene Walker and Richard J. Richardson, *Public Attitudes toward the Police* (Chapel Hill, N.C.: Institute for Research in Social Science, 1974), p. 1.

34. Mervin F. White and Ben A. Menke, "On Assessing the Mood of the Public Toward the Police: Some Conceptual Issues," *Journal of Criminal Justice* 10 (1982):211–230.

35. Leonhard F. Fuld, *Police Administration* (New York: G.P. Putnam's Sons, 1909), pp. 59–60.

36. Wayne K. Bennett and Karen M. Hess, *Management and Supervision in Law Enforcement* (St. Paul, Minn.: West, 1992), pp. 44–45.

37. Richard N. Holden, *Modern Police Management* (Englewood Cliffs, N.J.: Prentice Hall, 1986), pp. 294–295.

38. *Ibid.*, p. 295.

39. *Ibid.*, p. 117.

40. Thomas J. Peters and Robert H. Waterman, Jr., *In Search of Excellence* (New York: Warner Books, 1982), pp. 306–317.

41. Leonhard F. Fuld, *Police Administration*, p. 56.

42. Arthur Niederhoffer, *Behind the Shield* (New York: Doubleday, 1967), p. 79.

43. John Van Maanen, "Making Rank: Becoming an American Police Sergeant," in Roger G. Dunham and Geoffrey P. Alpert (eds.), *Critical Issues in Policing: Contemporary Readings*, (Prospect Heights, Ill.: Waveland Press, 1989), pp. 146–161.

44. *Ibid.*, p. 151.

45. Roy R. Roberg and Jack Kuykendall, *Police Organization and Management: Behavior, Theory, and Processes* (Pacific Grove, Calif.: Brooks/Cole, 1990), p. 284.

46. *Ibid.*

6

Issues
and Practices

*Since this is a time of increasing crime,
increasing social unrest and increasing
public sensitivity to both, it is a time when
police work is peculiarly important, complicated, conspicuous, and delicate.*
—The President's Commission on Law
Enforcement and Administration
of Justice, 1967

✦ INTRODUCTION

It has been stated that in the infancy of policing, "a size 3 hat and a size 43
jacket" were the only qualifications for one to enter police work. Given the
weight and breadth of the nature and responsibilities of the job, that metaphor
certainly does not apply today.

We begin with an overview of some very positive activities recently undertaken by the police across the country, most of which are connected with formal community policing programs (described in Chapter 4). We also examine
supervision and policy development for the use of force (including warning
shots, weapons, pursuits, and special weapons and tactics) and special operations (including crowd control, hostage negotiation, and disasters). Next we
discuss a growing trend to issue a "grade card" evaluation of police agencies:
national accreditation. The changing nature of police technology is then
explored, including video camcorders, forensic tools, and ongoing research
with new nonlethal weapons. After discussing options administrators may
employ for measuring officer productivity and the increasingly important
administrative function of providing adequate training for officers, we

conclude with a brief look at administrative approaches to coping with police stress and burnout.

In this chapter, unlike the two chapters preceding it, we address administrative matters that are literally life and death in nature, again underscoring the extremely challenging nature of contemporary police administration. Grave issues such as those listed above require policies and procedures that are well thought out, written, explained, and implemented.

✦ "WHAT WORKS": COMMUNITY POLICING AND PROBLEM SOLVING IN ACTION

The concept that is sweeping the country—community policing and problem solving (COPPS)—applies to communities of all sizes. Below is a sampling of but a few success stories where a "return to the basics"—taking police officers out of their patrol vehicles and placing them in closer contact with their communities to unite for solving problems—has paid huge dividends.

Monroe County, Florida, is a tourist haven located near Stock Island, a community of 5000 that had become a retreat for drug dealers and prostitutes and, literally, a garbage dump. The sheriff's office spearheaded the formation of a neighborhood improvement committee, held meetings, and went door to door to explain to residents how to handle everything from animal complaints to zoning problems. They were also educated on fire safety and medical services as well as garbage disposal. A one-day cleanup by some 100 volunteers resulted in the removal of 102 tons of waste, 15 tons of discarded major appliances, and many abandoned vehicles. Deputies arrested 19 drug dealers in one day. Landowners were told to evict drug dealers or run the risk of their property being seized. Today, the crime rate has dropped and citizens have become committed to keeping the island clean.[1]

Provincetown, Massachusetts, the site of the Mayflower Compact signing, has over time become a popular artists' and writers' colony which is almost totally dependent upon summer tourism. More than 30,000 people populate its less than 3 square miles in the summertime, taxing its force of 17 sworn officers. Hate crimes and summer unrest broke out in the 1980s—with 20 of 25 hate crimes on Cape Cod occurring in Provincetown—and soon marches and protests against such crimes were held and near-riot situations ensued. Police developed and implemented policies to investigate and prosecute hate incidents and to establish protocol for referring victims to providers of assistance. Diversity training was provided routinely, and supervisors provided quality control and evaluation. The city, working with police and other human services agencies, also developed a "Plan to Overcome Hate Incidents" and a number of other policies. Reported hate incidents dropped 30 percent, but data still revealed that one-third of the remaining incidents occurred within one block of city hall. Thus a police substation was opened next door to the town hall.[2]

In *Aurora, Colorado*, on the eastern edge of Denver, a popular bar catering to hordes of young people was hit with a rash of purse thefts from customers' cars. COPPS police officers working with the bar owner and patrons determined that young women left their purses in their cars because they liked to dance and feared their purses would be stolen off tables while they danced. Police got the bar owner to install lockers where women could lock their purses; the incidents went from hundreds per month to virtually none.[3]

Police in *Newport News, Virginia*, received calls of concern in quiet neighborhoods that had suddenly experienced large groups of rowdy teenagers on weekends. Police response to calls accomplished little, and an area officer was assigned to look for a better solution. The officer found that a roller skating rink was trying to increase business by offering reduced rates and transportation home for teenagers on weekends. However, the one bus used for transportation could not handle the volume of kids needing rides home—hence the rowdiness in the once-quiet neighborhoods. Police informed the rink owner of the size of the problem; the owner agreed to lease more buses, no kids had to walk home, and in the course of one week and four hours of an officer's time, there were fewer citizen calls, happier kids, and satisfied homeowners.[4]

The *Los Angeles* Police Department's community police program's "Operation Cul-de-Sac" selected one of the highest Part I crime areas as an experimental site—an inner-city area known as the "Newton Division RD 1345." The department had difficulty identifying the residents of the particular "community," let alone their specific needs. Therefore, the first step was to create a community by placing physical barriers (in the form of iron gates) on the streets to mark the outer boundaries of the Operation Cul-de-Sac area. Sixty LAPD officers worked full-time for two weeks patrolling the area on foot, bicycle, and horseback. Then six officers were assigned permanently to the area, meeting with community groups, sponsoring picnics and graffiti cleanups, and initiating neighborhood watch programs. Citizens who had feared to leave their homes began starting to communicate with one another and using public parks and streets. Part I crimes decreased 20 percent, and drive-by shootings dropped by 70 percent. Evaluations determined that the greatest improvements in police/citizen partnerships occurred following face-to-face contact with officers, citizens' seeing an officer at least daily, citizens' interacting with police officers in their homes, and when officers projected an appearance of caring for citizens as persons.[5]

Farmington Hills, Michigan, police developed a special program to combat a problem that haunts many elderly citizens—loneliness. Working with a city project, the Police and Seniors Together (PAST) program matches police volunteers with elderly residents to promote strong personal bonds. Officers interact frequently with senior citizens, including on- and off-duty visits and telephone calls. During these visits, officers strive to make the seniors feel more secure and connected to their community. As the relationships grow, the visits become more routine, and the senior citizens come to view the officers' presence as a normal and positive aspect of their lives.[6]

Reno, Nevada, is surrounded by high desert country. Citizens complained about abandoned vehicles in the desert for years. Following meetings with the area Neighborhood Advisory Group (NAG), an officer secured donated towing equipment, and more than 100 such vehicles were towed. A convenience store was a popular hangout for drug dealers who used the pay telephones to transact business with other dealers and users. The NAG and RPD personnel sought the assistance of the local telephone company, which programmed the phones to receive no incoming calls. This solution obviously displaced the problem to another area, but it was removed from an area heavily frequented by the public, including many children. A small neighborhood park in a low-income area had become unfit for public use, being transformed into a hangout for drug dealers and gang members. Area residents, police, and local ministries brainstormed about possible solutions. As a result, patrols and arrests were increased, the problems dissipated, and the community staged a "We Took Back the Park" parade and picnic to celebrate their success. The RPD surveys 700 to 800 citizens twice each year, using university students and other volunteers. A side benefit of COPPS was that citizens passed a bond issue for 88 new police officers, primarily a result of publicity concerning the above and other positive police activities.[7]

Gainseville, Florida, was hit with a rash of convenience store robberies. Suspect descriptions determined that many different offenders were responsible. Word had spread that convenience stores were easy targets. Officers researched the matter and learned that most targeted stores had posted large advertisements in their front windows, the checkout stand could not be seen by passersby, many stores failed to light their parking lots and kept large sums of money in the register, and some provided only one inexperienced clerk during late hours. Police also arranged for a psychiatrist to interview 65 offenders who were imprisoned for convenience store robberies, confirming that many simply took advantage of the opportunities described above. Findings were presented to a local merchants' association, but the members refused to participate in crime prevention techniques, preferring more patrols instead. Thus police approached the city commission with a proposed ordinance that would require store owners to address the problems that lured would-be robbers. After the ordinance went into effect and the stores had crime-prevention methods in place for a full year, robberies had dropped 65 percent overall, 75 percent at nighttime. Store owners now admit that the police department's citywide approach solved a difficult problem.[8]

Note that all of the foregoing case studies had a common core theme: working with the community to identify and address problems. In all cases, the police were responsive to community needs and took advantage of opportunities for collaboration. The once-widening gap between citizens' expectations of the police and the results they actually received is greatly narrowed. Police and government must address the problems of social deterioration that threaten to strangle their communities and forever destroy the quality of life they once enjoyed.

✦ SUPERVISING THE LEGITIMATE USE OF FORCE

✧ VIOLENCE IN OUR SOCIETY

The beating of Rodney King by several Los Angeles police officers occurred on March 3, 1991. That event, which has been described as a "landmark in the recent history of law enforcement,"[9] was later witnessed by the world in an 82-second videotape by citizen George Holliday. The tumult following the Simi Valley acquittals of officers criminally charged for that beating now belongs to the ages. Many observers believe that someday the history of policing will be delineated in "pre-Rodney King" and "post-Rodney King" terms.

If any good came from the King incident, perhaps it was that the public and police leadership realized that they must be cognizant of the potential for excessive force by officers. The riot and the police response to it also provided police administrators across the country with a crowd-control guide. Many people believe that this knowledge—another lesson from Los Angeles—may soon be necessary, because the potential for conflict remains in Los Angeles and in other major cities across the country.

The United States, especially from the point of view of its police officers, is a mean and dangerous place. As William A. Westley wrote in 1969 in *Violence and the Police*, "The policeman's world is spawned of degradation, corruption and insecurity. He sees man as ill-willed, exploitative, mean and dirty; himself a victim of injustice...he walks alone, a pedestrian in Hell."[10] For many American police officers, their job is like a daily foray into a combat zone. Indeed, the inner-city streets have been deemed a "domestic Vietnam,"[11] However, instead of facing Viet Cong or some other foreign enemy, their foes include the gangs, the homicidal killers, and the drug addicts. Facing such stress and human misery daily, some officers become burned out to the point that they are referred to as "crispy critters." Police adversaries are more heavily armed and more arrogant than ever. Being a cop today has been described as a "stop-and-go nightmare."[12] About 80 police officers are killed each year in the line of duty. All of this is occurring while the United States is becoming even more heavily armed.

✧ LEVELS OF FORCE

There are three unique aspects of police work in the United States, elements of an officer's job that no one else is allowed to perform: (1) the use of deadly force, (2) the ability to restrain the freedom of others, and (3) the capability to engage in high-speed pursuits.

The exercise of force by police can take several forms. Its escalation ranges from a simple verbal command, to a light touch on the arm to encourage someone to move along or comply with an order, to the use of the baton or Mace to control someone, to the use of the lateral-vascular neck restraint (the so-called "chokehold" or "sleeper hold" that has come under fire following several deaths from its application); to the use of lethal or deadly force. These levels of legitimate force are especially important in policymaking and on the street; as stated in police circles, "You don't bring a baton to a knife fight, and you don't bring a knife to a gunfight."

The use of lethal force is a tragedy not only for the victim but also for the victim's family, the officer, and in many cases, for the officer's family. For this reason, deadly force has become one of the major sources of tension between the police and minority communities. Only recently has any meaningful attempt been made to examine or control the use of deadly force by police officers. Prior to the 1970s, police officers had tremendous discretion regarding their use of firearms; police departments often had poorly defined or nonexistent policies regarding this issue. Investigations into police shootings were sometimes conducted in a half-hearted manner, and police agencies did not always keep records of all firearm discharges by officers.[13]

In 1985, the U.S. Supreme Court ruled that shootings of any unarmed, nonviolent fleeing felony suspect violated the Fourth Amendment to the Constitution.[14] Almost all major urban police departments enacted restrictive policies regarding deadly force. The Supreme Court also made it easier for a private citizen to sue and collect damages as a result of a questionable police shooting.[15]

A study of 57 cities concerning justifiable homicides by the police, conducted by the International Association of Chiefs of Police (IACP), was instructive. Regarding use of force, the study showed the following variables to be associated with high justifiable homicide rates: the awarding of incentives for firearms marksmanship; in-service officer survival training; the issuance of on-duty weapons larger than .38 caliber; the issuance of shotguns; a high supervisory/officer ratio; the use of semiautomatic handguns by SWAT units; in-service SWAT training; the absence of policy for the management of stakeout and decoy units; and exertion-type pre- and in-service firearms training.[16] What these variables appear to demonstrate is that homicides by police occur with more frequency where there is organizational and peer support—a "hardware milieu"—for firearms use and training. Certainly, police administrators need to take these findings into account when developing policy for the carrying, caliber, training, and rewarding of use of the weapons that officers carry and must employ occasionally.

✦ WARNING SHOTS, WEAPONS, AND PURSUITS: POLICY AND PROCEDURE

We now consider several specific types of uses of force, and whether policy is needed to provide instruction and uniformity in their use.

◊ Should a department policy exist for high-speed pursuits? Definitely. This is a commonly overlooked form of force used by the police, one that many observers believe will soon be controlled by a Supreme Court decision similar to *Tennessee v. Garner.* Many people believe that the propelling of a 5000-pound vehicle down a public street at 80 miles per hour to attempt to catch a misdemeanant is tantamount to overkill and requires legal parameters. Such pursuits present a tremendous danger to the public and have already resulted in numerous lawsuits and settlements.

◊ Should warning shots be fired in the line of duty? Most police department policies prohibit them, because "what goes up must come down." However, there are situations when the use of a warning round—into a tree or the dirt—may be necessary to halt a serious brawl or disturbance.

◊ Should police policy state that officers must shoot to wound an assailant or other persons they must fire upon? The answer from an administrative standpoint is a resounding "never." Only Roy Rogers and his peers always managed to "wing" their adversaries. However, normally the police technically do not shoot to kill, either. Rather, policy requires that they direct their fire with the expressed purpose of stopping aggressive behavior—normally into an assailant's "center of mass." Only snipers, normally operating at a considerable distance from their targets, must actually shoot to kill.

◊ Should department policy mandate that all officers be qualified with their off-duty weapons? Absolutely. Furthermore, experts suggest that the same policy prohibit the carrying, off-duty, of low-caliber weapons, which are often ineffective and cause more problems than they cure.

◊ Should department policy allow officers to carry and use lead-filled "slappers" and blackjacks? No. The problem is, these "tools" have historically been intended for use as head weapons and can inflict considerable damage. It is therefore extremely difficult, if not impossible, to find an "expert" to train officers who will testify that an officer is certified in their use.

◊ Should department policy cover accidental discharges of police weapons? Yes. There are very few truly "accidental" discharges of weapons. Most are the result of officer negligence. The problem with such discharges is that no one knows where the bullet is going. A policy is needed that provides for disciplinary action when such "accidents" occur. When existing and enforced, such policies normally have the effect of greatly reducing such occurrences.

To develop policy and procedures for the use of force by police officers, administrators should consider the information contained in Figure 6.1. There are police activities and behaviors, such as those within the upper-left quadrant of the figure, which occur with a considerable degree of frequency (the HI, or "high incident" variety), along with a high liability factor (HL), which combine to produce a much greater probability of legal problems for the individual officer, the supervisor, the department, and employing jurisdiction. Such activities or behaviors include such activities as high-speed pursuits, lateral-vascular neck restraint, drug raids, and the execution of felony warrants.[17]

In these cases, police administrators must take special care to develop, review, and update their policies each year to see if new court decisions

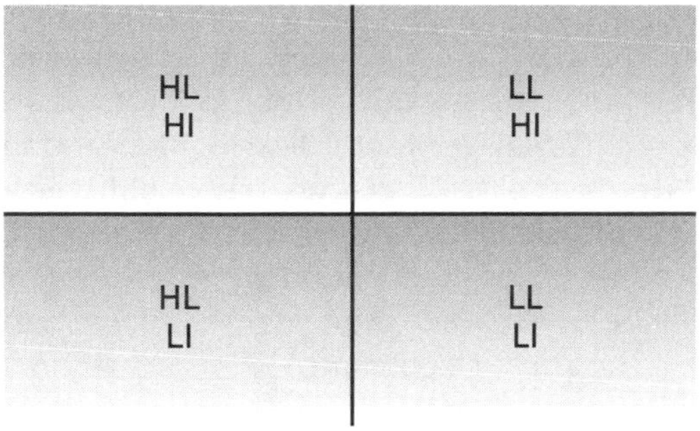

"HL" = high liability
"HI" = high incident of occurrence
"LL" = low liability
"LI" = low incident of occurrence

Figure 6.1 Guidelines for developing use-of-force policies.

require further policy modification. These types of activities are also those which civil attorneys will focus on.

Another policy action that police administrators should consider is the creation of a "Red Flag Warning System" when an officer receives three citizen complaints within a one-year period. This system would cue the administration to engage in a close review of the officer's personnel file and, possibly, initiate counseling or other measures. There are other indicators of the need for inquiry and intervention. For example, if an officer books a lot of citizens into jail following a routine stop for traffic violations, there is the possibility of a problem.

✦ MANAGING SPECIAL OPERATIONS: STRATEGIES AND TACTICS

There are several unique types of incidents that tend to "test the mettle" of police administrators. Some examples of such problems include crowd and riot control, hostage situations, major disasters, and undercover work. In these types of occurrences, one's ability to analyze and react rapidly are thoroughly challenged. In both the police and military realms, leadership qualities are often measured by a person's reaction under duress. In fact, a number of people quickly blamed a precinct lieutenant for the delayed police response to rioting in Los Angeles following the Rodney King verdict. In this section we consider briefly these types of situations, and some of the important elements of each, from the administrative perspective.

✧ CROWD AND RIOT CONTROL

One of the reasons there was no explosion of violence and rioting following the second Rodney King-related trial (the civil action against four police officers) was that the Los Angeles Police Department under Chief Willie Williams was extremely well prepared for the verdict—and everyone knew the department had made ready for it. One young man, a veteran of the first riot, was asked by a reporter why he failed to engage in civil disorder following the second verdict. He remarked metaphorically: "Hey, we play *black-top* basketball here; we're not going to go downtown to play against the *Lakers*."[18] The message is clear: the police must be ready for such occurrences, and the public must realize they are prepared. "Manmade disasters" like those in Los Angeles, Miami, and other cities serve as constant reminders that the power keg can blow at any time; all that is often needed is something to kindle the flame.

Forming officers in a line and doing the "stomp-and-drag" maneuver, also known in police circles as the "hat and bat" routine, worked well in the 1960s and 1970s and is still appropriate for some types of problems. However, such formations present a larger target for snipers, and officers must quickly disperse if fired upon. Today's "field force plan" calls for greater use of small-unit tactics, with a sergeant commanding only five or six officers. Spotters are placed high on building tops to observe citizen activities. The teams take control of, and occupy, areas of the city as they move. Meanwhile, some officers must be kept in reserve for other duties, as it is not uncommon for a police agency's calls for service ("I want to see an officer" types of communications) to triple during a major disturbance.

When such incidents occur, the first step toward mobilization of personnel is to discontinue all nonessential police tasks, such as routine patrolling, and response to miscellaneous calls for service. Off-duty and reserve officers may need to be called to duty quickly. Many jurisdictions also have mutual aid agreements and compacts that allow for officers from contiguous jurisdictions to respond and assist, and military and federal law enforcement personnel may also be needed. Normally, the decision to involve military personnel is a grave one; our system of government eschews a military state. Thus requests for the imposition of martial rule must come from the chief executive of the local government or from some other official source, such as a magistrate or sheriff. The governor may also make the decision independently.[19] This course of action is one of last resort; local policing has long been recognized as the primary law enforcement body in the country, and laws have been passed with that concept in mind.

✧ HOSTAGE NEGOTIATION

Of all the situations confronted by the police, few are as emotionally charged or psychologically complex as incidents in which hostages have been taken. Hostages are pawns in a deadly game; the barricade-and-hostage incident presents a no-win situation in which police strategies, procedures, and competence will be highly scrutinized by the media and the public.[20] B. Grant Stitt defined a hostage situation as "when one or more persons seize another person(s) by force and hold them captive against their will for the purpose of bargaining to have certain demands met by authorities."[21] Hostage takers may be divided into four categories: (1) traditional (or criminal trapped at the scene of a crime or while escaping from a crime scene, (2) terrorists, (3) prisoners, and (4) the mentally disturbed.

The police have several available options when facing hostage situations. They can assault or attack without making any attempt to negotiate, or they can neither attack nor assault but instead, attempt to wait out the hostage takers. Other options are to negotiate but make no concessions to demands, or they can negotiate and give in to demands. Finally, the police can negotiate and lie about giving in to demands.[22]

The job of the specially trained hostage negotiator is to seek peaceful resolution of a dangerous situation by talking and listening. The negotiator attempts to engage in a dialogue with the hostage taker, barricaded suspect, or person threatening suicide. The purpose of the dialogue is to calm the person, become a sympathetic listener, determine the person's motivation and negotiate a peaceful solution.[23] The negotiator must obviously be a patient person who can ferret out any relevant information about hostages, weapons, and conditions that can be passed on to the SWAT team in the event that negotiations fail.

The success rate of skillful hostage negotiators is high. Negotiations often take hours and sometimes days, but eventually most hostage takers and barricaded subjects are convinced to surrender. The negotiator's patience and skills are thus rewarded.

✦ SPECIAL WEAPONS AND TACTICS

Since the 1970s, a large number of police departments have developed a special weapons and tactics (SWAT) team to cope with a variety of special problems that arise. Several departments have gone to a softer, more expansive title for their team, such as special operations and response team (SORT). According to a report by the Los Angeles Police Department (LAPD), the SWAT concept was initiated there in late 1967 [24] in response to the increased incidence of urban violence, including snipers, political assassins, and urban guerrilla warfare. LAPD's SWAT team was activated almost 200 times from 1967 to 1974.[25]

Special weapons teams are trained to protect police officers during crowd control from sniper attack, provide high ground and perimeter security for visiting dignitaries, rescuing hostages, providing for the nonviolent apprehension of desperate barricaded suspects, providing control assault firepower in certain nonriot situations, rescuing officers or citizens endangered by gunfire, and neutralizing guerrilla or terrorist operations directed against government personnel or general public.

The special weapons team often wears distinctive clothing (black overalls and baseball caps), and members are well equipped with automatic rifles, shotguns, "flash bang" grenades, gas masks and canisters, smoke devices, ropes, pry bars, and walkie-talkies. Teams often have several position designations, such as leader, scout, marksman or sniper, observer, and rear guard. In larger cities, they are accompanied by a mobile command post that carries communications systems, armored vests, steel helmets, ballistic shields, extra ammunition, battering rams, and other provisions (including robots equipped with cameras).[26]

There are heavy responsibilities and concerns with this concept. Given the tremendous firepower and aggressive behavior of these assault teams, their operations must be supervised with great care. As former police chief and author Anthony Bouza said: "Operations that use dynamite, 'thunderflash stun grenades,' and aggressive SWAT teams can experience spectacular failures. There are the thumpers and Rambos who must be controlled, especially in such popular operations as drug raids, where they like to think they've been granted *carte blanche*."[27]

✧ DISASTER PLANNING

Almost every citizen of United States, irrespective of geographical area of residence, lives under threat of some act of nature: a tornado, flood, earthquake, hurricane, a fire of holocaust proportions. In addition, there are humanmade disasters, such as plane/train crashes, chemical spills, power plant explosions, structure collapse, and major auto accidents (such as the major pileups that occur on the coasts in fog). Many police officers may never encounter such disasters personally during their career, but all must be prepared for whatever occurrences can befall in their jurisdiction. Because such events occur so infrequently, it is not uncommon for the police to be caught unprepared when they do take place.

As always, the responsibility lies at the door of the administrator to ensure that an adequate disaster plan is developed and kept current as needs dictate. Many jurisdictions have mock disasters to keep their personnel sharp in coping with them; these mock exercises also provide experience in establishing a command post and communications networks, first-aid techniques, interagency coordination, logistics, and mobilization.

✧ UNITY OF COMMAND

In chapter 5 we discussed a major principle of hierarchy of authority—span of control. A second principle of hierarchy of authority is unity of command, which refers to placing one and only one superior officer in command or in control of every situation and employee. When a situation occurs such as those described above, it is imperative that someone be responsible and in command of the situation. The unity of command principle ensures that multiple and/or conflicting orders are not issued to the same police officers by several superior officers.[28]

Using a barricaded subject as an example, a patrol sergeant may arrive, deploy personnel, and give all appropriate orders, only to have a shift lieutenant or captain come to the scene and countermand the sergeant's orders with his or her own orders. This type of situation would obviously be counter-productive for all concerned. However, due to the vast geographic and frequently overlapping jurisdictional nature of law enforcement, it is not impossible for such confusion to arise.

It is also important that all officers know and follow the chain of command at such incidents. Every person in the organization should report to one and only one superior officer. A problem could arise if a patrol lieutenant gives a patrol officer orders without advising or conferring with the patrol officer's sergeant. This type of activity, in addition to giving rise to confusion, also causes friction between co-workers. When the unity of command principle is followed, everyone involved is aware of the actions initiated by superiors and subordinates.[29]

Occasionally, however, there are instances where the normal chain of command is circumvented in police work. For example, a crime scene technician's or detective's orders may supersede those of a ranking person at a major crime scene. Again, to ensure smoothness and uniformity, the unity of command principle, through departmental policy and procedures, should dictate how and when these situations will be handled.[30]

✦ SANCTIONING AND ENHANCING POLICE METHODS

Police executives have long been criticized as resistant to outside examination and generally reluctant to change. However, in this section we see that this is not necessarily the case, at least in recent times. We review police accreditation, a movement that has begun sweeping the country, as well as recent technological innovations which are serving to extend the "long arm of the law" and help address forensic problems in the laboratory.

✧ AN AGENCY "REPORT CARD": ACCREDITATION

The Commission on Accreditation for Law Enforcement Agencies (CALEA) is a private, nonprofit organization located in Fairfax, Virginia. It was formed in 1979 by the four major national law enforcement associations: the International Association of Chiefs of Police (IACP), the National Sheriffs Association (NSA), the Police Executive Research Forum (PERF), and the National Organization of Black Law Enforcement Executives (NOBLE). CALEA has developed over 900 law enforcement standards for all types and sizes of state and local agencies.

For two reasons, many law enforcement agencies have felt impelled to devote personnel and financial resources toward seeking accreditation during the last decade. First, most of the standards identify topics and issues that must be covered by written policies and procedures. Therefore, successful accreditation provides a "liability shield" against successful litigation.[31] Second, the process provides a nationwide system for change.[32] One of the most important parts of the accreditation process is self-assessment. Agencies undergo a critical self-evaluation and are later assessed by an on-site team of law enforcement professionals to determine whether they have complied with the applicable standards for a department of their type and size.[33]

Accreditation may be viewed as a direct outcome of the reform era to professionalize the police. The accreditation process is voluntary for all agencies (although in this era of greater police accountability, many believe the time is coming when the public will demand that their local agency be accredited, or want to know why their agency is *not* accredited).

Table 6.1 presents a sample of a CALEA standard, the example being of the use of force. The standards are applied to six agency-size categories, by the total number of personnel employed: 1–9, 10–24, 25–49, 50–199, 200–999, and 1000 or more, respectively. The six letters at the end of each standard indicate whether the standard is mandatory ("M") or optional ("O") for each respective agency by size. (Note that all standards shown in Table 6.1 are serious enough to be mandatory in nature.)

CALEA enjoys wide support from police executives and community leaders. For example, when a city manager seeks to hire a police executive from another jurisdiction, a candidate's experience with the accreditation process is a definite plus. However, the concept does have its critics. Some see it as "window dressing...long on show and short on substance"—a reference to the notion that some departments develop the necessary policies to meet the standards and then fail to follow them. Some city managers are reluctant to authorize their police departments to enter a process that takes an average of 21 months to complete at an average cost of $73,708. This cost includes a modest CALEA accreditation fee, ranging from $3800 for a department of up to nine full-time employees, to $14,700 for agencies with 3000 or more full-time employees.[34] Included in the cost, however, are purchases needed to meet standards (such as putting first-aid kits in all patrol vehicles, or buying body armor for SWAT teams) and modifications to facilities and capabilities (e.g., upgrading the evidence storage area and radio communication), and indirect costs, such as the cost of personnel to do the work necessary to write policies and procedures.[35]

Overall, however, accreditation carries an important national influence. Even business people seeking to relocate evaluate local government agencies in terms of their professionalism and ability to provide services. In one instance a well-managed community of 300,000 lost a major prospective employer to another city solely because its police department was not accredited. As soon as this fact became known, the mayor directed the police chief to pursue accreditation by CALEA as a "top priority."[36]

✧ TECHNOLOGICAL DEVELOPMENTS: THE CAMCORDER ERA

Use by the Public. Videotape technology has had a major impact on policing and its administration since the Rodney King incident; "video vigilantes" now abound. A woman in Fort Worth, Texas, taped a police officer striking a

Table 6.1 EXAMPLE OF A CALEA STANDARD ON THE USE OF FORCE

1.3   Use of Force

1.3.1   A written directive states personnel will use only the force necessary to effect lawful objectives.

Commentary: The directive should encompass the use of all types and kinds of force (whether deadly or nondeadly) and all types and kinds of weapons. The directive may be issued in the form of a policy, rule, or order. (M M M M M M)

1.3.2   A written directive that states that an officer may use deadly force only when the officer reasonably believes that the action is in defense of human life, including the officer's own life, or in defense of any person in immediate danger of serious physical injury.

Commentary: The purpose of this standard is to provide officers with guidance in the use of force in life-and-death situations and to prevent unnecessary loss of life. Definitions of "reasonable belief" and "serious physical injury" should be included in the directive. (M M M M M M)

1.3.3   A written directive specifies that use of deadly force against a "fleeing felon" must meet the conditions required by Standard 1.3.2.

Commentary: A "fleeing felon" should not be presumed to pose an immediate threat to life in the absence of actions that would lead one to believe such is the case, such as a previously demonstrated threat to or wanton disregard for human life. (M M M M M M)

1.3.4   A written directive requires that all sworn personnel be issued copies of and be instructed in the policies described in standards 1.3.1 through 1.3.3 before being authorized to carry a firearm.

Commentary: Because of the importance of standards 1.3.1, 1.3.2, and 1.3.3, the agency should disseminate the directives to all sworn personnel. (M M M M M M)

1.3.5   A written directive governs the discharge of "warning shots."

Commentary: Warning shots pose a danger to officers and citizens alike and should not be used. (M M M M M M)

1.3.6   A written directive governs the carrying of side arms and ammunition while off duty.

Commentary: The policy should specify the circumstances under which an officer may or may not carry a sidearm and ammunition while off duty. (M M M M)

1.3.7   A written directive governs the use of nonlethal weapons by agency personnel.

Commentary: Agency personnel usually have numerous nonlethal weapons at their disposal. The intent of this standard is to ensure the proper use of agency-authorized weapons. (M M M M M)

1.3.8   A written directive establishes criteria for authorizing the carrying of nonissued, personal firearms.

Commentary: The intent of this standard is to ensure that poor quality or inherently dangerous firearms are not used by officers. The directive should address caliber, barrel length, type of weapon, on- and off-duty use. (M M M M M)

handcuffed auto theft suspect 24 times with a baton. A gay man in California taped his own beating by a neighbor; doctors in Houston hid a camera in the room of a 7-month-old girl and recorded her mother attempting to smother the child to death.

Many of America's 14 million video-camcorder owners are now taping their own medical surgeries, wills, and prenuptial agreements. AIDS activists routinely take video cameras to demonstrations to record possible confrontations with police.[37]

Use by the Police. The spread of videotaping by the general public, and the benefits of utilizing camcorders as tools for police activities, have not gone unnoticed by police administrators. Some administrators have equipped patrol vehicles with videocameras; many now have personnel videotape all their press conferences. Police videos have been particularly useful in drunk-driving arrests and at crime-scene and traffic accident investigations. Videocameras are used to record eyewitness testimony and in-progress events, such as robberies and building checks. And, with little investment in money or personnel, in-house tapes can be made for police roll-call training and for public relations, to use in such programs as drinking and driving.

A recent study found that one-third of all police and sheriff's departments serving populations of 50,000 or larger in the United States are videotaping at least some interrogations. [38] Tragically, a constable in Nacogdoches County, Texas, turned on his camera as he stopped a weaving car and ended up filming his own murder by two subjects. Being especially beneficial during interrogations, the likelihood of interrogation videotaping increases as the severity of the felony increases. Thus agencies are more likely to videotape interrogations or confessions in homicide, rape, and armed robbery cases. The reasons for videotaping in these cases are several: to avoid defense attorneys' challenges of the accuracy of audiotapes; to jog detectives' memories when testifying; and to counter allegations of "nice guy" or "softening up" techniques for interrogating suspects.[39]

Clearly, the videotaping of America has changed the face of police administration. This high-tech boom has raised some troubling questions. For example, is everything that occurs anywhere, anytime, fair game for someone with a camcorder? Presently, the police and other Americans have no legal protection against being pursued by videotape vigilantes. In general, anything that occurs in public, or can be seen from a public place, is fair game. Oddly, one's voice enjoys greater protection than one's picture—federal law requires a warrant for secret wiretaps but is silent on videotaping. And what appears to be occurring on tape may not be what is actually happening at all (e.g., money changing hands may appear to be a bribe).

The law is lagging behind the technology with respect to these and other legal and ethical issues.[40] Police administrators may need to consider policy decisions and legislative lobbying where these problems are concerned, for protection of their officers.

✦ OTHER TECHNOLOGICAL PROGRESS

Technological opportunities are rapidly developing for police practitioners. Cutting-edge technological research is now under way in the following areas: computer profiling to identify and track serial killers; DNA testing of crime scene evidence to link criminal suspects to crimes; the use of hair analysis to improve detection of drug use; and computerized age progression, facial imaging, and other technologies to aid in the search for and recovery of missing children.

Tests are also being performed of oleoresin capsicum, or "pepper spray," for use as a nonlethal weapon. Laptop computers are in more and more patrol vehicles, serving as a "voiceless dispatcher" to assist in crime-related activities. Laser-disc projectors enable officers in firearms training to confront situations like those on the street by confronting lifelike images and firing shots that show up as red dots on a light-sensitive screen. Police are also more likely to capture bank robbers with the aid of a computer chip that can be secreted inside the stolen bills, later triggering a signal to the police.

Fingerprints, still the most frequently used tool for identifying criminal suspects, are also undergoing major technological advances. Chief among these advances is the use of laser technology for highlighting prints previously unrecognized on smooth and other difficult surfaces. Forensic scientists have also developed a process for applying "superglue" to certain surfaces, thereby sealing the fingerprint and permitting highlighting for lifting. Computer technology and digitization of photographs on computer screens made the Automated Fingerprints Identification System (AFIS) possible. Police agencies across the country have adopted this system.

✦ EVALUATING PATROL OFFICER PERFORMANCE

Because of the varying nature of the work done by shifts, individual officers, and a variety of other factors, any attempt to evaluate the performance of officers—especially using a quantitative instrument—is very difficult. Should the officers be judged on numbers of felony arrests or traffic citations issued, the graveyard shift would suffer; if finding open doors and windows of businesses is a criterion, the day shift is disadvantaged. What criteria, if any, should administrators use to fairly assess the productivity of police officers? Should there be a quota system at all?

Attempts to measure the efforts of subordinates are not new. The first recorded efficiency report of personnel may be found in the records of the War Department, 1813, when Lewis Case presented his unadorned impressions of infantry soldiers to a new commanding officer (Table 6.2). Today, there are more sophisticated methods for evaluating performance of the police. Once an administrator decides to measure police productivity (in the traditional, as opposed to community policing model), it must be decided which types of data

Table 6.2

Lower Seneca Town
August 15, 1813

Sir:

I forward a list of the officers of the 27th Regt. of Infty. arranged according to rank. Annexed thereto you will find all the observations I deem necessary to make.

Respectfully
I am, Sir
Your obedient servant,
/s/Lewis Case.

27th Regt., Infantry

Alex, Deniston - Lieut. Col., Comdg. - A good natured man.
Clarkson, Crolins - First Major - A good man but no officer.
Jesse D. Wadsworth - 2nd Major - An excellent officer.
Captain Shotwell - A knave of whom all unite in speaking ill, a
                man despised by all.
"   Thomas Earle - Indifferent, but promises well.
"   Allen Reynolds - An officer of capacity, but impudent and
                a man of violent passions.
"   Porter - Stranger but little known in the regiment.
1st Lieut. Thos. Darling)   Merely good, nothing promising.
"   "   Wm. Perrin   )   Low vulgar men with exception of Perrin,
"   "   Danl. Scott   )   Irish and from the meanest walks of life
"   "   Jas. I. Ryan   )   and possessing nothing of the character
                         of officers and gentlemen.
"   "   Robt. P. Ross   Willing enough - has much to learn with
                         little capacity.
2nd Lieut. Nicholas G. Carmer - A good officer but drinks hard and
                         disgraces the service and himself.
"   "   Seward Elder - An ignorant unoffending Irishman.
"   "   McConkey - Raised from the ranks, ignorant, vulgar, and
                         incompetent.
"   "   James Garrey - A stranger in the regiment.
"   "   Darrow - Just joined the regiment - of fine appearance.
"   "   Piercy   )   Raised from the ranks but all behave
"   "   Thos. G.   well and promise to make excellent
          Spicey   )   officers.
"   "   Oliver Vance   All Irish, promoted from the ranks,
"   "   Royal Geer   )   low vulgar men, without any one quali-
"   "   Mars   )   fication to recommend them, more fit
"   "   Clifford   )   to carry the hod than the epaulettes.
"   "   McKeen   )   Promoted from the ranks, behave well
"   "   John G.   and will make good officers.
         Scholtz   )
Ensign Mehan - The very dreg of the earth. Unfit for anything under
           heaven. God only knows how the poor thing got an
           appointment.
"   "   John Brown) - Promoted from the ranks - men of no
"   "   Bryon   )   manner and no promise.

First Recorded Efficiency Report in Files of the War Department must be collected, whose productivity will be measured, and how. Some police officers are more productive than others. For example, William Walsh, in a study of patrol officer felony arrests, found that approximately 10 percent of the officers made approximately 57 percent of the felony arrests.[41] However, these differences may be due to the characteristics of the work situation (officer assigned to high-crime-activity area), or it may be due to characteristics of the officers. A commander may wish to examine the number of felony and misdemeanor arrests made and the number of citations issued. This is not to say that disciplinary action should be taken against those officers falling short of the averages, but it may serve as an indicator of where corrective action should be taken. These quantitative indicators are in some respects better than subjective, abstract, and qualitative measures, such as "dependability," "decision making," and "cooperation."

According to Larry Gaines, Mittie Southerland, and John Angell,[42] other more accurate productivity measures for patrol officers would include the following:

1. *Time spent at work.* This measure involves looking to see if an officer takes a high amount of sick leave, which might indicate job dissatisfaction, poor working conditions, or the need for additional training.

2. *Arrest rates and citations issued.* Although commonly used, the police manager should use caution when using these measures, as mentioned above. Officers working different shifts and jurisdictions will have different arrests rates, due to variations in workloads and calls for service.

3. *Percentage of arrests that lead to convictions.* An important measure that commanders will want to measure is the percentage of so-called "good arrests." If a particular officer has a low conviction rate, it may indicate the need for skills development in the area of investigation or court presentation.

4. *Citizen complaints against officers.* This measure evaluates the public's acceptance of a particular officer. Valid complaints indicate a gruff manner or worse; officers should be counseled. However, it should be realized that officers who handle large numbers of disturbance or fight calls will probably receive more complaints than will other officers.

Gaines, Southerland, and Angell also state that the most effective way to develop and retain information on the productivity of individual officers is through a standardized reporting system.[43] Figure 6.2 is an example of an officer's daily report as used by the Englewood, Colorado, police department. Note that it contains a compilation of the officer's activity for the day, and that the form contains a weighting system whereby each category of activity is given a certain number of points (e.g., DUI arrests are given 5 points, etc.). The Englewood police manager examines an officer's total points. The Kentucky State Police use a similar scheme, but it is based on the average time it takes an officer to accomplish a given task; the manager there examines the percentage of an officer's time working in relation to patrol time.

DAILY FIELD ACTIVITY REPORT

Englewood, Colorado, Police Department

1. OFFICER'S NAME, RADIO NUMBER	2. DATE	3. DAY	4. VEHICLE	5. TTL HRS	6. REMARKS
KING R.R. 202	11-14-78	TUE	6876	11	NO SPARE TIRE — VEHICLE NOT SERVICED

	7. TIME REC.	8. TIME CLEAR	9. MIN USED	10. SRC	11. LOCATION	12. TYPE OF ACTIVITY	NAME	OR SUMMONS
A		1700	15		GCPD	ROLL CALL / VEHICLE INSPECTION		
B	1710	1750	40	DIS	411 S. BANNOCK	PRIOR BURGLARY OFFENSE REPORT	JONES	OR 791 316472
C	1803	1812	09	OFF	TABOR AND CHEROKEE	TRAFFIC STOP / COLO LIC # PP6171 IMPROPER TURN SUMMONS	KESSLER	TS T1001
D	1825	1840	15		LAMPLIGHTER	CODE 7 COFFEE		
E	1908	1920	12	OFF	3500 S. DELAWARE	SUSPICIOUS SUBJECT F.I. CARD	BARNES	I F.I.
F	1935	2010	45	DIS	701 W. KANSAS KING 500PERS	ADULT SHOPLIFTER O.R. PENAL SUMMONS MISDM ARREST	WALLACE	22631 79-31650
G	2025	2137	70	F	GCPD JAIL	BOOKING PRISONER	WALLACE	
H	2230	2245	15	DIS	ST. CATHERINES HOSPITAL E.R.	DISTURBANCE ASSIST UNIT 201		ASSIST 791 31680
I	2250	0010	80	DIS	4219 S. 4TH	DISTURBANCE – MENTAL CASE STOOD BY FOR AREA MENTAL HEALTH WORKER – INCIDENT RPT	SHERWOOD	I.R. 79-31681B
J	0015	0025	10	I	MENTAL HEALTH CENTER	TRANSPORT SUBJECT TO MENTAL HEALTH CENTER	SHERWOOD	
K	0105	0115	10	SPV	STEVENS PARK	MEET SGT. JONES / CK REPORTS 2 - O.R. 1 - I.R. 1 - P.S. 1 - T.S. 1 - F.I. 1 - M.A.	JONES Jones	
L	0120	0200	40	DIS	MAIN AND PINE	PROPERTY DAMAGE ACCIDENT (SPU ASSISTED) DUI ARREST – ACCIDENT REPORT-SUMMONS	WELLS	572632 79-31695
M	0200	0205	5	L	TO G.C.P.D.	TRANSPORT PRISONER	WELLS	
N	0205	0400	175	L	G.C.P.D.– JAIL	BOOKING AND PROCESSING PRISONER	WELLS	
O		0400				END OF WATCH		
P								

	SOP	WT	TTL
13. OFFENSE RPT	2	5	10
14. INCIDENT RPT	1	3	3
15. H&R ACCIDENT RPT	0	5	
16. P.P. ACCIDENT RPT	0	3	3
17. ACCIDENT RPT	1	4	4
18. ACCIDENT SUMMONS	0	4	
19. RADAR SUMMONS	0	3	
20. TRAFFIC SUMMONS	1	4	4
21. PENAL SUMMONS	1	3	3
22. PARKING SUMMONS	0	1	
23. WARNING SUMMONS	0	1	
24. WARRANT ARREST	0	5	
25. FELONY ARREST	0	20	
26. MISDMR ARREST	1	4	4
27. PETTY ARREST	0	3	
28. D.U.I. ARREST	1	5	5
29. DETOX	0	4	
30. MISC. DETENTION	0	4	
31. F.I.	1	2	2
32. DEF VEHICLE	0	2	2
33. TOTAL			35
34. ASSIGNED CALLS	4	1	4
35. ASSIGNED ASSISTS	1	1	1
36. OFF. INITIATED	2	3	6
SPV. NAME	Sgt. Jones		

R.R. King

Figure 6.2

The advantages of these types of productivity monitoring include the fact that they cause officers and supervisors to focus on the complete range of police work, they allow managers to exert a degree of control over officers via the examination of periodic summaries (they can identify activity which is much lower or higher than that of other officers), and they cause officers to be more goal-directed by informing them of management's expectations.

✦ A NOT-TO-BE-OVERLOOKED STAPLE: TRAINING

Since the King incident and rioting in Los Angeles, and other incidents evoking questions concerning police use of force, the surge of liability, the growth of community-oriented and problem-solving policing, the rise of new police technology, and other developments, police training has come under the spotlight. In this section we examine how police administrators may be deemed negligent for failure to train their officers adequately, and how training generally has become a prominent function of contemporary police administrators and supervisors.

✧ LIABILITY AND NEGLIGENCE

The gravity of the training function is perhaps best demonstrated by a very unfortunate incident in Colorado, which points out how negligence can be found in the supervision and training of personnel. In *Sager v. City of Woodlawn Park*,[44] a police officer accidentally killed a person when the shotgun he was pointing at the head of the prisoner discharged; the officer was attempting to handcuff the prisoner with his other hand. At trial, the officer stated that he had seen the technique in a police training film. The training officer, however, testified that the film was intended to show how *not* to handcuff a prisoner; unfortunately, no member of the training staff made that important distinction to the training class. The court ruled that improper training resulted in the prisoner's death.

Another case involving training negligence is *Popow v. City of Margate*,[45] where an innocent bystander was killed on his front porch at nighttime by a police officer in foot pursuit. The court held the city negligent because the officer had had no training on night firing, shooting at moving targets, or use of firearms in a residential area. In *Beverly v. Morris*,[46] a police chief was held liable for improper training and supervision of his officers following the blackjack beating of a citizen by a subordinate officer.

These cases are but a sampling of the body of legal precedent that now exists because of inadequate police training. The need for officers to secure adequate training is evident, to safeguard both the officers and the public.

✧ CONTRIBUTIONS OF THE RECRUIT ACADEMY

Much of the development and later performance of the police officer turns on his or her experiences at the recruit academy. For many police agencies, academy training provides the bulk of the formal training that the officer will acquire for an entire career. The academy also shapes the officer's attitudes and is the beginning point for the occupational socialization of the officer.

It is here, at the academy, that recruits adopt a new identity. Through formal instruction and informal discussions, the recruits begin to form a collective understanding of policing and how they are supposed to function, and gradually develop a common language and demeanor. This is the beginning of the officer's "working personality." The police personality is being formed.[47] In addition to fundamental subjects (such as law, report writing, physical defense, and accident investigation), they receive human relations training and are encouraged not to be prejudicial in their actions or speech.

There are in-house police academies, where the department is authorized by some certifying body to train its own officers, and there are state and regional academies. Some of these academies are operated by community colleges and universities using instructors from the area. In a relatively new concept, civilians attend police academies at their own cost, hoping to gain employment as a "free agent" with a police agency upon graduating and becoming formally certified. This "preservice" model is becoming more and more popular; police administrators are realizing tremendous savings by not paying salaries, registration fees, and other costs normally accrued while their already employed officers attend academies.

Once the recruits leave the academy, they will often be assigned to one or more veteran officers for initial field instruction and observation. This veteran will often be known as a "field training officer" (FTO). The field training program provides rookies an opportunity to bridge the protected environment of the academy and the isolated, dangerous environment of the streets, while still under the protective arm of a veteran officer.

Police officers also receive ongoing, in-service training throughout their careers. News items, court decisions, and other relevant information can be covered daily at roll-call prior to the beginning of each shift. Short courses are available for the in-service officers, ranging from a few hours to several weeks' duration. Computer-assisted training modules, videotapes, and even laser-disc training formats are now available. Some states require a minimal number of hours of in-service training for their police officers; many police departments exceed the minimum requirement.

The technology and various means exist for ensuring that both new and veteran police officers receive adequate training. Although not all agencies have the luxury of high-tech training, abundant in-house training, or an in-house legal advisor to instruct officers on criminal law and procedure, administrators nonetheless are responsible for obtaining adequate training for their personnel. As we saw above, the cost of failure can be quite high in both human and financial terms.

✦ ADMINISTRATIVE RESPONSES TO STRESS AND BURNOUT

Much has been written about the causes and management of stress in criminal justice, particularly in policing.[48] However, what has been addressed to a far less extent is how administrators can assist by understanding, recognizing, and assisting their subordinates in dealing with this ominous problem.

Stress and burnout are often related to problems *within* the organization. Therefore, the administrator's management style can have a direct impact on the stress problem. For example, it is well known that the lack of opportunity to participate in the decision-making processes that affect one's job is a major source of stress and eventual burnout.[49]

Police officers have comparatively high levels of stress and burnout; for these individuals, many of whom often deal with people who are at their worst, there is no retreat or "fight/flight" choice available. They are on firing line, so to speak, and need to understand the causes of stress, paying particular heed to the emotional and physical signals they receive, and understanding what they can do to manage stress.

✧ TREATMENT FOR POLICE OFFICERS

Traditionally, many police administrators have been reluctant to acknowledge that their employees (and themselves) were suffering from personal problems. If an officer had marital problems, drank too much, or was getting abusive on the job, a cloak of secrecy was pulled over the matter; if the officer did not shape up, he or she was either buried at a desk job or fired. Police officers, after all, were supposed to help others, not succumb to such problems themselves. In fact, a police chaplain's first attempt at creating a police stress program, in New York in 1958, failed to materialize. It was not until 1966, after eight years of persistent efforts, that the police bureaucracy finally allowed Monsignor Joseph Dunne to initiate an alcohol program for police. In 1966, a more sympathetic police administration allowed Dunne to counsel problem drinkers; during the next decade the program would treat more than 2000 officers with alcohol problems.[50]

The traditional view began changing in the late 1970s, for a number of reasons: officers were being better trained, particularly in human relations; the investment in personnel had risen; and along came the recognition that the life-and-death decisions and danger of the job were not the sole causes of police stress. Studies showed that the police hierarchy, rotating shift work, and anger and frustration with the public and other criminal justice agencies were contributing factors as well.

The Los Angeles Police Department became the first to provide free, voluntary psychological counseling services under the direction of Martin Reiser, the nation's first police psychologist. These early programs became prototypes for other cities.[51]

Today nearly one in five police agencies has a stress management program.[52] This may be a liberal estimate; however, the number of formal, systematic programs has unquestionably increased in the past decade. Police psychologists recommend that systematic programs to combat stress minimally include the following features: (1) a behavioral profile of each officer, to indicate different reactions or patterns—"red flags"; (2) the ability to respond to those red flags as they appear—training supervisors to recognize early warning signs (e.g., withdrawal, accidents, drinking, depression) and intervene; (3) a flexible counseling program for groups as well as for families and individuals (utilizing the peer counseling method); (4) training in biofeedback, relaxation and other methods of handling stress; and (5) encouragement of the police organization to reduce department-induced stress (through the use of objective performance criteria, decreased busywork, and other stressors).[53]

Summary

This chapter opened with a discussion of the growing trend of police administrators to implement community-policing and problem-solving strategies and to proactively improve the quality of life in their communities. Readers should "stay tuned" as this concept continues to expand across the nation.

Also demonstrated was the gravity of the work performed by administrators and the rank and file. Compared with the types of decisions made daily by the rest of us, surely no other occupation carries such responsibility and, at times, substantive decision making. What was implied was the importance of *readiness*—from the standpoint of policymaking and being physically and mentally prepared for civil unrest; for the occasion to use force and handle special operations; for confronting "video vigilantes"; being accredited; receiving adequate training; and the debilitating effects of stress.

Shakespeare's observation that "uneasy lies the head that wears the crown" becomes clear upon viewing the contents of this chapter. It is probably a tribute to the professionalism and restraint of police officers of all ranks that more have not succumbed to the effects of stress.

Questions for Review

1. What types of issues involving the use of force should be addressed in the form of policy? What are some essential considerations for each policy?
2. What are some of the major ramifications of the current high-tech era? What might police administrators do to prepare for it.
3. Why are police accreditation and training important and worth the time and money invested?

4. What appear to be sound methods for evaluating police productivity?

5. Why is the issue of police training particularly important at present? Give examples of problems and consequences if training is inadequate.

6. What can police administrators do to recognize and treat officer stress?

For Further Reading

THOMAS F. ADAMS, *Police Field Operations.* Englewood Cliffs, N.J.: Prentice Hall, 1985.

DONALD F. FAVREAU and JOSEPH E. GILLESPIE, *Modern Police Administration.* Englewood Cliffs, N.J.: Prentice Hall, 1978.

LARRY K. GAINES, MITTIE D. SOUTHERLAND, and JOHN E. ANGELL, *Police Administration.* New York: McGraw-Hill, 1991.

NATHAN F. IANNONE, *Supervision of Police Personnel* (4th ed.). Englewood Cliffs, N.J.: Prentice Hall, 1987.

JOHN KLOFAS, STAN STOJKOVIC, and DAVID KALINICH, *Criminal Justice Organizations: Administration and Management.* Pacific Grove, Calif.: Brooks/Cole, 1990.

ROBERT SHEEHAN and GARY W. CORDNER, *Introduction to Police Administration* (2d ed.). Cincinnati, Ohio: Anderson, 1989.

PAUL M. WHISENAND and GEORGE E. RUSH, *Supervising Police Personnel: Back to the Basics.* Englewood Cliffs, N.J.: Prentice Hall, 1988.

Notes

1. Ordway P. Burden, "The Key to Community Policing," *Law Enforcement News* (March 31, 1993):5.

2. International City Management Association, MIS Report, *Responsive Service Delivery: A Community Orientation for Problem Solving* (Washington, D.C.: Author, May 1993), pp. 5–6.

3. "Community Policing: Cops Head for the Neighborhoods," *San Francisco Chronicle* (November 20, 1992):A10.

4. William Spelman and John E. Eck, "Sitting Ducks, Ravenous Wolves, and Helping Hands: New Approaches to Urban Policing," *Comment* 35 (Winter 1989):6.

5. Robert L. Vernon and James R. Lasley, "Police/Citizen Partnerships in the Inner City," *FBI Law Enforcement Bulletin* 61 (May 1992):18–22.

6. William J. Dwyer, "Building Bridges: Police and Seniors Together," *FBI Law Enforcement Bulletin* 62 (May 1993):6–8.

7. See Ken Peak, Robert V. Bradshaw, and Ronald W. Glensor, "Improving Citizen Perceptions of the Police: 'Back to the Basics' with a Community Policing Strategy," *Journal of Criminal Justice* 20 (1992):25–40.

8. William Spelman and John E. Eck, "Sitting Ducks, Ravenous Wolves, and Helping Hands: New Approaches to Urban Policing," pp. 5–6.

9. Independent Commission on the Los Angeles Police Department, *Report of the Independent Commission on the Los Angeles Police Department* (Los Angeles: Author, 1991), p. i.

10. William A. Westley, *Violence and the Police: A Sociological Study of Law, Custom, and Morality* (Cambridge, Mass.: MIT Press, 1970).

11. Gordon Witkin, Ted Gest, and Dorian Friedman, "Cops under Fire," *U.S. News and World Report* (December 3, 1990):32– 44.

12. *Ibid.*, p. 34.

13. Mark Blumberg, "Controlling Police Use of Deadly Force: Assessing Two Decades of Progress," in Roger G. Dunham and Geoffrey P. Alpert (eds.), *Critical Issues in Policing: Contemporary Readings* (Prospect Heights, Ill.: Waveland Press, 1989), pp. 442–464.

14. In *Tennessee v. Garner*, 471 U.S. 1, 105 S.Ct. 1694, 85 L.Ed.2d 1 (1985).

15. *Monell v. Department of Social Services*, 436 U.S. 658, 98 S.Ct. 2018 (1978).

16. International Association of Chiefs of Police, *A Balance of Forces: A Study of Justifiable Homicide by the Police* (Gaithersburg, Md.: Author, 1981).

17. John Sullivan, personal communication, May 20, 1993.

18. David Kieckbush, personal communication, May 19, 1993.

19. Thomas F. Adams, *Police Field Operations* (Englewood Cliffs, N.J.: Prentice Hall, 1985), pp. 310–311.

20. B. Grant Stitt, "Ethical and Practical Aspects of Police Response to Hostage Situations," in Roslyn Muraskin (ed.) *Issues in Justice: Exploring Policy Issues in the Criminal Justice System* (Bristol, Ind.: Wyndham Hall Press, 1990), pp. 20–45.

21. *Ibid.*, p. 21.

22. Joseph Betz, "Moral Considerations Concerning the Police Response to Hostage Takers," in Frederick Elliston and Norman Bowie (eds.), *Ethics, Public Policy and Criminal Justice* (Cambridge, Mass.: Oelgeschlager, Gunn & Hain, 1982), pp. 110–132.

23. Robert Sheehan and Gary W. Cordner, *Introduction to Police Administration* (2d ed.) (Cincinnati, Ohio: Anderson, 1989), p. 387.

24. Los Angeles Police Department, *Special Weapons and Tactics* (Los Angeles: Author, 1974), p. 101.

25. Center for Research on Criminal Justice, *The Iron Fist and the Velvet Glove: An Analysis of the U.S. Police* (Berkeley, Calif.: Author, 1975), p. 49.

26. Ibid., pp. 48–49.

27. Anthony V. Bouza, *The Police Mystique* (New York: Plenum Press, 1990), p. 277.

28. Larry K. Gaines, Mittie D. Southerland, and John E. Angell, *Police Administration* (New York: McGraw-Hill, 1991), p. 84.

29. *Ibid.*, p. 85.

30. *Ibid.*.

31. Gary W. Cordner, "Written Rules and Regulations: Are They Necessary?" *FBI Law Enforcement Bulletin* 58 (1988):18.

32. Russell Maas, "Written Rules and Regulations: Are They Necessary?" *Law and Order* (May 1990):36.

33. Charles R. Swanson, Leonard Territo, and Robert W. Taylor, *Police Administration* (3d ed.) (New York: Macmillan, 1993), p. 51.

34. Gerald Williams, *Making the Grade: The Benefits of Law Enforcement Accreditation* (Washington, D.C.: Police Executive Research Forum, 1989), pp. xv and xvii.

35. *Ibid.*, pp. xvii and xviii.

36. Charles R. Swanson, Leonard Territo, and Robert W. Taylor, *Police Administration* (3d ed.), p. 52.

37. Melinda Beck, "Video Vigilantes," *Newsweek* (July 22, 1991): 42–47.

38. U.S. Department of Justice, National Institute of Justice Research in Brief, *Videotaping Interrogations and Confessions* (Washington, D.C.: Author, March 1993), p. 2.

39. *Ibid.*, p. 3.

40. Melinda Beck, "Video Vigilantes," p. 45.

41. William W. Walsh, "Patrol Officer Arrest Rates: A Study of the Social Organization of Police Work," *Justice Quarterly* 2 (1985):273–290.

42. Larry K. Gaines, Mittie D. Southerland, and John E. Angell, *Police Administration*, pp. 421–422.

43. *Ibid.*, p. 423.

44. 543 F.Supp. 282 (D. Colo. 1982).

45. 476 F.Supp. 1237 (1979).

46. 470 F.2d 1356 (5th Cir. 1972).

47. Geoffrey P. Alpert and Roger G. Dunham, *Policing Urban America* (Prospect Heights, Ill.: Waveland Press, 1988), p. 50.

48. See Kenneth J. Peak, *Policing America: Methods, Issues, Challenges* (Englewood Cliffs, N.J.: Regents/Prentice Hall, 1993), Chapter 11; W. Clinton Terry III, *Policing Society: An Occupational View* (New York: Wiley, 1985), Part 7; Roger G. Dunham and Geoffrey P. Alpert, *Critical Issues in Policing: Contemporary Readings*, Section VIII; Harry W. More, Jr., *Critical Issues in Law Enforcement* (Cincinnati, Ohio: Anderson, 1985), Chapter 8.

49. Paul W. Brown, "Probation Officer Burnout: An Organizational Disease/An Organizational Cure," *Federal Probation* 50 (1986):4–7; Cary Cherniss, *Professional Burnout in Human Services Organizations* (New York: Praeger, 1980).

50. John Blackmore, "Are the Police Allowed to Have Problems of Their Own?" *Police Magazine* (July 1978):51.

51. Ibid., p. 47.

52. Joseph L. Victor, "Police Stress: Is Anybody Out There Listening?" *New York Law Enforcement Journal* (June 1986):19–20.

53. Ben Daviss, "Burnout," *Police Magazine* (May 1982):58.

Case Studies

Intruding Ima and the Falsified Report*

An eight-year employee of your police agency, Officer Ima Goodenough, is a patrol officer who often serves as a field training officer. Goodenough is generally capable and experienced in both the patrol and detective divisions. She takes pride in being of the "old school" and has developed a clique of approximately 10 people that she gets along with, while generally shunning other officers.

As an officer of the old school, she typically handles calls for service without requesting cover units or backup. She has had six complaints of brutality lodged against her during the past three years. For Ima and her peers, officers who call for backup are "wimps." She has recently been involved in two high-speed pursuits where her vehicle was damaged when she attempted to run the offender off the road.

Ima will notify a supervisor only when dealing with a major situation. She is borderline insubordinate when dealing with new supervisors. She feels that, generally speaking, the administration exists only to "screw around with us"—the field officers. You, her shift commander, have been fed up with her deteriorating attitude and lackadaisical performance for some time and have been wondering if you will soon have occasion to take some form of disciplinary action against her.

You have also learned that Ima has a reputation among her supervisors as being a "hot dog." Some of her past and present supervisors have even commented that she is a "walking time bomb" that is unpredictable and could "blow" at any time.

One day while bored on patrol, Ima decides to go outside her jurisdiction, responding to a shooting call that is just across the city limit and in the county. She radios the dispatcher that she is out "assisting," then walks into the home where paramedics are frantically working on a man lying on the floor with a head wound. Nearby on the floor is a large, foreign-made revolver; Ima holds and waves the revolver in the air, examining it. A paramedic yells at her, "Hey! Put that down, this may be an attempted homicide case!" Ima puts the revolver back on the floor. Meanwhile, you have been attempting to contact Ima via radio to get her back into her jurisdiction. Later, when the sheriff's office complains to you about her actions at their crime scene, you require that she write a report of her actions. She completes a report describing her observations at the scene, but denies touching or picking up anything.

---

*Contributed by Chief Richard C. Kirkland and Sgt. Linda Shepard, Reno, Nevada, Police Department.

Looking at Ima's personnel file, you determine that her performance evaluations for the past eight years are "standard"—average to above average. She has never received a suspension from duty for her actions. While verbally expressing their unhappiness with her for many years with her, it appears that Ima's supervisors have not expressed that disdain in writing.

Questions for Discussion

1. What are the primary issues involved in this situation?
2. Do you believe that there are sufficient grounds for bringing disciplinary action against Goodenough? If so, what would be specific charges? What is the appropriate punishment?
3. Do you believe that this is a good opportunity, and do grounds exist, for termination?
4. Does the fact that her supervisors have rated her as standard have any bearing on this matter or create difficulties in bringing a case for termination?

"Racin' Ray," the Graveyard-Shift Gadabout*

Members of the Hooterville County sheriff's department have been involved in several vehicle pursuits within the past year. One such incident resulted in the death of a 14-year-old juvenile who crashed during a pursuit in which he was joyriding in his parents' vehicle. This tragedy sparked a massive public outcry and criticism of the police department for using excessive force. A lawsuit against the department and individual officers involved in the pursuit is pending.

The sheriff immediately changed the department's policy regarding pursuits. The policy now requires that a supervisor cancel any pursuit that does not involve a violent felony crime or other circumstances that would justify the danger and potential liability. All officers have been trained in the new policy. A separate policy prohibits the firing of warning shots unless "circumstances warrant."

Last night at 1:00 a.m., Deputy Raymond "Racin' Ray" Roadhog was patrolling an industrial park in his sector. Deputy Roadhog, freshly graduated from the state police academy and field training, engages in pursuits at every opportunity; also, unbeknown to the sheriff and other supervisors, he occasionally takes along his personal German Shepherd dog for use in building checks and has an M-16 automatic rifle in his trunk. He was providing extra patrol due to reports of vandalism and theft of building materials in that area of the county.

---

*Contributed by Chief Richard C. Kirkland and Sgt. Linda Shepard, Reno, Nevada, Police Department.

Generally, after 6:00 p.m., no one should have any reason to be in any construction area. A parked vehicle attracts his attention because private vehicles are not normally parked in the area at this time.

As Roadhog approaches the vehicle with his cruiser's lights off and spotlight on, he notices the brake lights on the vehicle flash on and off. Roadhog, immediately getting out of his vehicle for a better view, calls dispatch for back-up assistance in the event that a burglary or theft is in progress.

At this point, the vehicle takes off at a high rate of speed, in Roadhog's direction. Roadhog, being out of his vehicle and seeing the vehicle is coming at him from about 30 yards, fires a warning shot into the ground. When about 15 yards away, the vehicle veers away from him, then leaves at a high rate of speed. As the escaping vehicle crosses the path of his spotlight, Roadhog sees that there are two young people inside, a man driving and a woman in the passenger's seat. Roadhog yells for the driver to halt, then lets loose another warning shot, this time into a nearby fire hydrant. He then takes off in pursuit of the vehicle.

The officer radios dispatch to inform him of his observations and of his present pursuit. You, the shift commander—a patrol lieutenant—hear this radio transmission.

Questions for Discussion

1. What are the central issues involved?
2. Is the deputy in compliance with the use-of-force policy?
3. Are you going to "shut down" Roadhog's pursuit? Explain.
4. Should the deputy have fired warning shots?
5. Assuming that all of the information above comes to light, will the sheriff be likely to begin disciplinary action against Roadhog?
6. Do the policies appear to be sound as written? Are additional policies needed?

Dismal City P.D.'s Command to "Do More With Less"*

Dismal City, USA, is a rapidly growing community of 50,000 residents located in the southern part of the state along the ocean. The city gains a population of 10,000 to 20,000 visitors a day during the summer months, when ocean recreation is a popular activity.

---

*Contributed by Deputy Chief Ronald W. Glensor, Reno, Nevada, Police Department.

The city's demographics are changing rapidly. Its Hispanic and Asian populations are growing at a tremendous rate. However, most of these new residents work outside the city. The downtown area has slowly degenerated over the past few years resulting in increased crime and disorder.

A property tax cap has resulted in reduced revenues to local jurisdictions, and the recent recession has also taken a substantial toll on the city's budget. The result has been significant reductions in staffing. The city's two attempts to have voters approve bond issues for increased taxes and police officers have failed. The police department has experienced its share of budget cuts and reduced staffing levels. The chief recently retired due to continued problems with the city council, the budget, and low morale in the agency. As a result of these matters, relations between the community and the department have been tense at best.

The police department has experienced a continued reduction in staffing over the past five years. It is not expected to continue, but increases are also not expected. The morale of the department is at its worst and is fueled by the increase in workload and what is perceived as an uncaring chief. The increase in violent crime only aggravates the problems, as officers believe that their safety is in jeopardy as a result of the lower staffing levels. Furthermore, the increase in Hispanic and Asian residents creates an additional burden as the department consists largely of white male officers. The department has no bilingual officers.

You have been hired as the new chief and will begin work in two weeks. The city manager and council have asked for a meeting with you to discuss the future of the department. At this meeting they explain the situation to you and request a staff report within one month of your reporting to work. The manager and several council persons recently attended a conference that presented several workshops on the implementation of community policing. They are convinced that this trend, now apparently sweeping the nation, would result in a more efficient police department.

The manager and governing board enthusiastically seek your views on community policing, its potential for Dismal City, and how you might approach its implementation. They inform you that the police officers' union has heard rumors of this idea and have made it clear that they probably would not want anything to do with changing the organization at a time when resources are strained.

Questions for Discussion

1. In your report, how will you respond concerning whether or not community policing is the panacea for the city's financial and demographic woes? Will it help the department?

2. Do you envision any problems with "traditional-thinking" supervisors and community policing? If so, how do you handle their concerns?

3. What would you do to mend the poor relations between labor and management?

4. Would the community need to be involved in the program's design and implementation? If so, how?

5. How might community policing provide more effective delivery of services?

6. Would you anticipate that the officers' workload would be reduced or increased under this program?

7. What types of information would you use to evaluate the progress of your program for city hall?

Part

The Courts

III

This part consists of three chapters, all of which focus on the courts. In Chapter 7 we examine court organization and operation; Chapter 8 covers personnel roles and functions; and in Chapter 9 we discuss court issues and practices. Specific chapter content is provided in the introductory section of each chapter.

Organization and Operation

The place of justice is a hallowed place.
—Francis Bacon

Courts and camps are the only places to learn the world in.
—Earl of Chesterfield

✦ INTRODUCTION

Courts have existed in some form for hundreds of years. Indeed, as early as the fourteenth century in England, either common law judges or the lord chancellor would dispose of legal problems as they arose. Since then, the court system has survived the dark era of the Inquisition and the Star Chamber; it assisted in the settling of the colonies; developed rapidly after the Revolution, and attended the establishment of law and justice on the western frontier. The court system has survived around the globe, and contemporary courts are compelled frequently to reckon with matters of a very grave and dangerous nature, such as offenses involving drug cartels and organized crime.

Federal, state, and local courts in the United States employ about 204,000 full-time personnel (excluding prosecution and defense employees); the annual payroll for these workers is about $6.6 billion. The largest percentage of these employment and payroll expenditures is at the local level (57.0 percent and 46.5 percent, respectively).[1] We will examine these courts from several perspectives.

First we address the questions of whether courts represent "organizations" in the usual sense of the term, with a bureaucratic structure and function, and courtroom decor and decorum. We then turn to a discussion of whether the adversary system and other procedural mechanisms of our courts maintain serious impediments to finding the "truth," and a discussion of courts in general as policymaking bodies. A sidebar problem is then pondered: our adversarial society in which we have little compunction about suing our neighbors—often clogging the courts with frivolous matters—and the cost of this litigious predilection. In considering this problem we are obliged to confront what is currently being foisted upon the courts: a veritable avalanche of suits, petitions, writs, briefs, and motions. A relatively new and promising concept is then examined that has developed to counter the escalating court dockets: alternative dispute resolution. Finally, we look at the citizen or "consumer" relationship with our court system, and a subject that serves as a "bridge" to the following chapter: court administration and reform.

✦ COURTS AS ORGANIZATIONS

Scholars refer to courts as organizations in very different and seemingly unrelated ways. In the view of Edward Clynch and David Neubauer, part of the problem stems from the fact that many academics have made erroneous characterizations of courts as bureaucracies.[2] A bureaucracy has differentiated and separate divisions tied together by a distinctive authority structure (hierarchy). It also has well-defined organizational rules governing the disposition of particular cases and individually defined specialized tasks.[3]

Trial courts are relatively autonomous single work units that do not function in this manner. A trial court as an entity does not report to a single authority figure in a chain of command. Formal rules often are ignored in favor of shared decision making among judges, prosecutors, and defense attorneys. [4] Rather than being bureaucracies, trial courts are informal workgroups where interaction among members occurs on a continuing basis. Court actors have discretion in carrying out their tasks; the employees have mutual interdependence as well as the ability to modify formal rules and procedures so that people can complete their assignments successfully. A common professional bond exists because most actors are lawyers. A professionally dominated organization, bureaucratic management styles are inappropriate for courts. In fact, the more a judge insists on being treated with great deference, the more that work group cohesion is lessened. And more important, the roles are interchangeable: defense attorneys may become prosecutors or judges, and so on. [5]

Formal authority is modified in trial courts in many ways. For example, while the judge has the authority to make the major decisions—setting bail, determining guilt, and imposing sentence—he or she often relies on input from others. Also, because they know more about cases coming to court, the judges' subordinates (prosecutors and defense attorneys) can influence his or her decisions by selective information flow.[6]

For these informal work groups to be effective, group norms must be enforced. Group members must comply with the norms of behavior; if they do, they are rewarded, and if not, they are subject to being sanctioned. Defense attorneys who do not file unnecessary motions or avoid pushing for "unreasonable" plea bargains may be rewarded by receiving greater amounts of information, such as being allowed to read the police reports of their cases. Prosecutors may receive more time to talk with witnesses or defense counsel. Conversely, sanctions for defense attorneys who violate group norms may include less access to case information, not being appointed to represent indigents in future cases, or their clients being punished with harsher sentences. Furthermore, prosecutors may not receive requested continuances (most requests for continuances come from the district attorney's office).[7] In sum, it is important to remember that "courts are not an occasional assemblage of strangers who resolve a particular conflict and then dissolve, never to work together again."[8]

Turning now to the *functional* organization of the courts, Figure 7.1 shows an organization structure for a county district court serving a population of 300,000. Note the variety of functions and programs that exist and which are in addition to the basic court role of hearing trials and rendering dispositions.

Perhaps the best example of how courts should be organized statewide is by looking at a system that has become "unified" on a statewide basis. Overall, however, court organization has "demonstrated little logic or planning, because adding certain new courts serves various political goals."[9] In states without a unified court system, there is often a confusing maze of overlapping courts and jurisdictions, which can cause considerable confusion for litigants. Kansas (which unified in 1977) serves as a good example of how a change in court organization results in success.

Kansas has a supreme court (seven justices; exclusive appellate and original jurisdiction); an intermediate court of appeals (seven justices; hears appeals from district courts); district courts (70 district, 64 associate district, and 76 district magistrate judges; general original jurisdiction in all civil and criminal matters, hearing appeals from lower courts); and municipal courts (384 judges; handle city ordinance violation, with no jury trials).[10]

This may seem a bit confusing, but it is actually about as simple as court unification can be. Witness the Kansas court system *prior to* unification in 1977: a supreme court; district courts (29 such courts; note that there was no intermediate court of appeals); county courts (93; civil cases involving less than $1000, felony preliminaries, misdemeanors, traffic cases of less than $2500, jury trials); city courts (8; civil matters of less than $3000, felony preliminaries, misdemeanors, traffic cases of less than $2500, jury trials); magistrate courts (5; civil cases under $3000, felony preliminaries, misdemeanors, traffic cases under $2500); probate courts (109); juvenile courts (109); common pleas courts (4; civil cases involving less than $3000, felony preliminaries, misdemeanors, traffic cases involving less than $2500); and municipal courts (384; city ordinance violations, including traffic, of less than one-year imprisonment).[11]

Note in the pre-1977 Kansas system the several different titles and types of courts, having similar yet different roles and jurisdiction. Imagine the confusion, redundancy, and fragmentation that is found in a nonunified state having much greater population and geographic area. It is obvious that the earlier Kansas

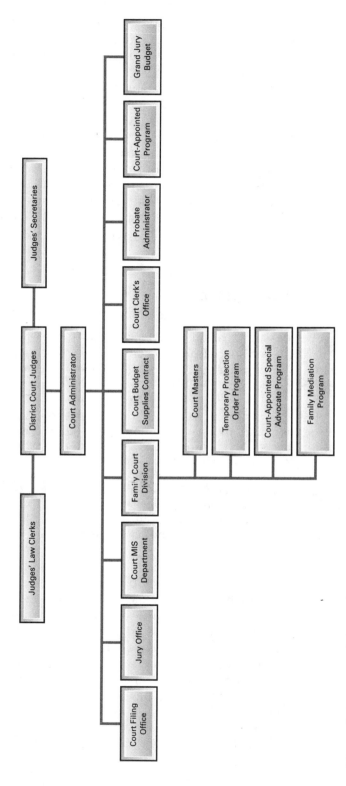

Figure 7.1 Organization structure for a district court serving a population of 300,000.

system's fragmentation, duplication, and confusion were discontinued by the creation of a statewide, unified system. No matter where in the state a citizen resides, he or she is able to understand what the local "district" court does.

Court unification contains three components: (1) a simplified state trial court structure; (2) judicial system policy- and rule-making authority vested in the supreme court or judicial council, with overall system governance vested in the state supreme court chief justice; and (3) state funding of all or a substantial portion of judicial system, with the budget prepared by the administrative office of the courts. The American Bar Association endorses such a unified court structure, which characteristically has uniform jurisdiction, uniform standards of justice (such as rules of procedure, management systems, education and training, etc.), clearly vested policymaking authority (preferably in the state supreme court), and clearly established administrative authority (normally by the chief justice as the administrative head of the state court system).[12]

✦ COURT DECOR AND DECORUM

Practically everything one sees and hears in an American courtroom is intended to convey the meaning that it is a special place. Even Alexis de Tocqueville, in his study of the United States more than a century ago, observed the extent to which our legal system permeates our very lives:

> Scarcely any political question arises in the United States that is not resolved, sooner or later, into a judicial question. Hence all parties are obliged to borrow, in their daily controversies, the ideas, and even the language, peculiar to judicial proceedings. The jury extends this habit to all classes. The language of the law thus becomes, in some measure, a vulgar tongue; the spirit of the law, which is produced in the schools and courts of justice, gradually penetrates beyond their walls into the bosom of society, where it descends to the lowest classes, so that at last the whole people contract the habits and the tastes of the judicial magistrate.[13]

The physical trappings and demeanor one finds in the courts convey this sense of importance. Normally, citizens are struck by the unique decor commonly found in the courtroom: high ceilings, ornate marble walls, expensive furnishings. (Of course, there are exceptions, and two midwestern instances that the author has witnessed make the point: A judge allowed a dog to run loose during a trial where the pet's owner had been charged for permitting the animal to run at large; and another court had long suffered a broken skylight, permitting rain and pigeons to invade the courtroom at will, forcing persons on the premises to stride carefully around the droppings.)

Citizens who observe court proceedings will also note the traditional decorum that is accorded this institution. All must rise when the judge enters the courtroom; permission must be granted before one can approach the elevated bench; and a general air of deference is granted the judge—the same vitriol that could lawfully be directed to the President of the United States will result in the utterer's being jailed for contempt of court when directed toward a judge.

The design of the courtroom, although dignified and intended to convey a message of singularity, is also to provide a safe, functional space that is conducive to efficient and effective court proceedings. The formal arrangement of the participants and furnishings reflect society's view of the appropriate relationships between the defendant and judicial authority. The courtroom must also accommodate judges, court reporters, clerks, bailiffs, witnesses, plaintiffs, defendants, attorneys, juries, and spectators. From time to time it must also include police officers, social workers, probation officers, guardians ad litem, interpreters, and the press. Space must also be allotted for evidence, exhibits, recording equipment, and computers.[14]

The trend the past 20 years has been toward building smaller, more specialized courtrooms; however, in recent years, several large and complex civil cases have highlighted the need for extremely large courtrooms to accommodate as many as 250 participating attorneys and to seat several judges. Criminal trials have burgeoned in size as well. For example, a drug-conspiracy trial in Nevada, involving a dozen co-defendants and their attorneys, required the installation of an elaborate communications system as well as extreme security measures.

Judges and court staff now also require audiovisual equipment and computer terminals to access automated information systems; such systems are becoming increasingly important to trials and caseload management. Provision must also be made for the projection of slides, movies, x-rays, and overhead materials. Also, a computer is often placed on the bench and at the court clerk's station for note taking, equipped with a keyboard tray and a silent printer. A telephone and silent alarm are almost indispensable for emergency communications.

✦ JUSTICE PROCESSORS OR "SEEKERS OF TRUTH"?

Ralph Waldo Emerson stated that "Every violation of truth…is a stab at the health of human society."[15] Certainly most people would probably agree that the traditional, primary purpose of our courts is to provide a forum for seeking—and through the adversarial process, obtaining—the truth. Indeed, the U.S. Supreme Court declared that fact in 1966 in *Tehan v. United States ex rel. Shott,* [16] stating that "the basic purpose of a trial is the determination of truth."

Today, however, many people possess a growing perception of our court system, in the words of a state supreme court justice, as a "domain of fiddlers preoccupied with dissonance while citizens' houses are threatened by fire."[17] More and more Americans are under the impression that truth is being compromised and even violated with regularity in the trial, plea bargaining, and appellate apparatus of our justice system—thereby, in the words of Emerson, stabbing at the health of human society.

These observers see many impediments to truth that should be eliminated in the judicial process. High on their list of impediments is the adversary system itself. Under this system, the courtroom becomes a battleground where participants often have little regard for guilt or innocence; rather, concern centers on whether or not the state is able to prove guilt beyond a reasonable doubt. To many people, this philosophy flies in the face of what courts were intended to accomplish; according to former Chief Justice Warren Burger, "the responsibility of an ethical lawyer, as an officer of the court and a key component of a system of justice, dedicated to a search for truth, is essentially the same whether the client announces an intention to bribe or threaten witnesses or jurors or to commit or procure perjury. No system of justice worthy of the name can tolerate a lesser standard."[18]

In the adversary system, the incentive to win can become overpowering. As one state supreme court justice put it, prosecutors "are proud of the notches on their gun."[19] Defense counsel equally enjoy winning. Attention shifts from the goal of finding truth to the effectiveness of the game's players. Who will foster change in the adversary system? Prosecutors? Defense attorneys? That is an important and difficult question. As one law professor observed: "Although the adversary system may need a watchman, the task need not be assigned to the watched. Lawyers are simply not appropriate to correct the defects of our adversary system. Their hearts will never be in it, and more importantly, it is unfair to both their clients and themselves to require them to serve two masters."[20]

Other impediments to truth finding must be rooted out of the system. Judge-made law that impedes the system's truth-seeking processes should be overruled. Other impediments often cited for elimination are the Fourth and Fifth Amendments, both of which have been given expansive application by the U.S. Supreme Court. Both, it has been argued, should be restrained so as to assist the courts in getting the truth. Rules of discovery should be modified as no longer to be a "lawyer's favorite weapon in jousting for a position of trial advantage."[21] Discovery should be a vehicle for revealing truth and should minimize "trial by ambush." The battle between expert witnesses that often develops into a circus atmosphere must be revamped as well. Unfortunately, there are those "experts" who are not really expert at all or will bend their testimony in the direction of those who are paying them. And in many instances, trial results depend more on who wins the race to the best expert and the most competent lawyer.

Unfortunately, as noted earlier, the third branch of government remains aloof and unresponsive to society's alarm over our truth-retarding system. But, in the words of one jurist, "The public ox will not be gored indefinitely. The criminal justice system as we know it today is simply too costly, too cumbersome, too protracted, and most importantly, too compassed with truth retardants. If we are willing to acknowledge the truth as the paramount trial value and work to eliminate truth impediments, then the stage exists for changing attitudes and maintaining a healthy zeal among lawyers. The predominant master must be the truth…"[22]

✦ THE INFLUENCE OF COURTS IN POLICYMAKING

It is the responsibility of the judicial branch to determine what the law is and to provide a public forum—the courts—for resolving disputes. This is accomplished by determining the facts of each case and their legal significance. If the court determines the legal significance of the facts by applying an existing rule of law, it is engaging in pure dispute resolution.[23] "But if to resolve the dispute the court must create a new rule or modify an old one, that is law creation."[24]

Each of these activities involves the courts in policymaking. Policy can be defined as choosing among alternative choices of action, particularly in the allocation of limited resources "where the chosen action affects the behavior and well-being of others who are subject to the policymaker's authority."[25] The policy decisions of the courts affect virtually all of us in our daily living. And in recent decades the courts have been asked to deal with issues that previously were within the purview of the legislative and judicial branches. Because many of the Constitution's limitations on government are couched in vague language, the judicial branch must eventually deal with potentially volatile social issues, such as those involving the prisons, abortion, and the schools.[26]

The U.S. Supreme Court has dramatically changed race relations, overhauled the juvenile court, increased the rights of the accused, prohibited prayer and segregation in public schools, legalized abortion, and allowed for destruction of the American flag. State and federal courts have together overturned minimum-residency requirements for welfare recipients, established standards for prison life, equalized school expenditures, and prevented road and highway construction from damaging the environment. They have eliminated the requirement of a high school diploma for a firefighter's job and ordered increased property taxes to desegregate public schools.[27] The only area that has not witnessed judicial policymaking since the Civil War is foreign affairs.[28]

Cases in which courts make policy determinations usually involve government, the Fourteenth Amendment, and the use of equity—the remedy most often used against governmental violations of law. Recent policymaking decisions by the judicial branch have not been based on the Constitution, but rather, on federal statutes concerning the rights of the disadvantaged, consumers, and the environment.[29]

The courts have become particularly involved in administrative policy, because of public-interest-group litigation. For example, legislation was enacted allowing citizen lawsuits when certain federal regulatory agencies, such as the Environmental Protection Agency (EPA), failed to perform certain duties as required by statute. Thus a citizens' environmental group was allowed to sue the EPA. This form of entry of the judicial branch into the policy arena has not been without severe criticism. For example, Jeremy Rabkin decried the courts' assuming their role as overseers of policy: "Courts are not entirely equipped to act as ongoing, freestanding guardians of administrative performance. Our entire judicial system has developed on the assumption that courts will simply be deciding cases about property rights or personal rights, in the traditional sense."[30]

It may appear that the courts are overbroad in their review of issues. However, it should be remembered that judges "cannot impose their views...until someone brings a case to court, often as a last resort after complaints to unresponsive legislators and executives."[31] And plaintiffs must be truly aggrieved, or have *standing*. The independence of the judicial branch, particularly at the federal court level, where judges enjoy lifetime appointments, allows the courts to champion the causes of those who are the underclass: those with fewer financial resources, votes, or a positive public profile.[32] It is also important to note that the judiciary is the "least dangerous branch," having no enforcement powers. And the decisions of the courts can be overturned by legislative action. Even decisions based on the Constitution can be overruled by subsequent constitutional amendment. Thus the judicial branch is dependent on a perception of legitimacy surrounding its decision.[33]

In addition, judicial decisions are not self-implementing. For example, the 1954 *Brown v. Board of Education* desegregation decision did not receive immediate and full compliance, and the 1963 decision prohibiting prayer in public schools was implemented to varying degrees across the country. In some cases it has been necessary for judges to retain jurisdiction long after legal issues have been settled. As examples, federal judges had to continue monitoring and enforcing their decisions in prison cases in Arkansas (in the 1960s) and Texas (in the 1980s).

✦ A DIVERSION: OUR NEW NATIONAL PASTIME— "HAIR-TRIGGER SUING"

✧ AN OVERWHELMED LEGAL SYSTEM

Before looking at some of the types of lawsuits that appear in and clog today's courts, we need to examine the size of our legal system, specifically the number of people who are the "prime beneficiaries" from it and derive their living from it, and why many believe that this system is breaking down. Today, there are about 780,000 lawyers in the United States, one for every 307 people (the highest ratio in the world). This ratio has tripled since 1971, and the ranks of lawyers is expected to continue to swell to 1 million by the year 2000. The number of civil suits in federal courts has soared 300 percent since 1960, and in the state courts, by more than 4 million. In 1990 there were 18.4 million lawsuits filed in state courts alone. Former vice president Dan Quayle, noticeably critical of lawyers and their litigious mentality during his term of office, estimated that Americans spend more than $80 million per year on direct litigation costs and higher insurance premiums. Indirect costs, he added, reach $300 billion annually, about 1.8 percent of the nation's gross domestic product. The fear of being sued has become almost endemic to our society, changing the way we interact and do business. One American company sells spinal implants for back problems virtually all over the world, except at home. The reason: "We don't feel confident in the U.S. with such a product. Our legal system is totally out of control."[34]

✦ OUR FRIVOLOUS TENDENCIES

Many Americans are exceedingly greedy. Egged on by similarly greedy attorneys and the prospect of a hugh financial windfall, we are suing one another with unprecedented frequency. Many of today's cases would have been laughed out of court not long ago. But the number and type of lawsuits faced by the courts today is no laughing matter. Following are some of the types of actions that have been taken to the doors of our courts by people seeking to obtain "justice":[35]

- ◊ A former student sought $853,000 in damages from a university, in part for the "mental anguish" he said he suffered after being given a "D" grade rather than the "A" he expected in an advanced German course.
- ◊ Two fans of the Washington Redskins filed a suit to overturn a loss by the team, contending that a crucial call by a referee violated the rules and robbed them of their "right" to see a victory.
- ◊ A young Colorado man sued his parents for $350,000, charging that they gave him inhumane and inadequate care as a child, making it impossible for him to fit into society as an adult.
- ◊ A 41-year-old California man, upset at being stood up on a date, sued his would-be companion for $38 to compensate him for getting dressed up and driving 40 miles for nothing.
- ◊ A convicted Utah killer sued the state prison for $2 million, claiming that it "allowed" him to escape with two other convicts, and that he was forced to swim several irrigation ditches, a "raging" Jordan River, and expose himself to innumerable bites by many insects.
- ◊ A young Portland man (the plaintiff), employed as a checkout clerk in a grocery store, sued another young man for $100,000; the suit charged that the defendant "continually and repeatedly" sought out the plaintiff on the premises of the grocery store, and after locating him, directed his "gas" toward plaintiff, humiliating plaintiff and inflicting severe mental stress upon him.

We who think of ourselves as rational can only hope that few or none of these litigants prevailed at the bar. However, lawsuits of this ilk—smacking of blatant frivolity—do not always fail. Following are some examples of jury awards of this nature.

- ◊ A jury awarded $200,000 to a Chicago couple who were "bumped" from a flight to Florida, causing the "humiliation, indignity, and outrage" of missing the birth of a horse.

- An award of $425,000 was granted to a Long Island woman who bit into a squirming beetle while eating a cup of yogurt.
- $280,000 was awarded to a pair of neighbors who were injured while attempting to trim their common hedge with a lawn mower.
- A 36-year-old Philadelphia real estate manager who spent 11 years as a student and teacher in transcendental meditation groups sued because he was never able to achieve the "perfect state of life" they promised. He alleged that he had been told he would learn to "fly" through self-levitation, but he learned only to "hop with the legs folded in the lotus position." A jury awarded him nearly $138,000 in damages.
- In New Hampshire, the parents of a 9-year-old won $30,200 from their 88-year-old neighbor who refused to return their son's ball after it rolled into her yard.[36]

We can hope that at least some of these verdicts were overturned or reduced on appeal. Nonetheless, jurors today are often sympathetic with "aggrieved" individuals, especially when the defendant is a large corporation with "deep pockets." In 1962 there was just one personal-injury verdict of more than $1 million; in 1989 there were 588 such verdicts.[37]

✧ EFFECTS ON BUSINESS AND THE ECONOMY

In addition to causing justice to bog down—the average lawsuit filed in court now languishes for 19 months—this litigious nature is very costly. Americans now pay more than $22 billion in attorney's fees.[38] Business executives fear that the U.S. legal system is crippling our ability to compete in the global marketplace, and for good reason. Dow Chemical, which is now hit with about 2000 new product-liability suits a year (with only about 20 such claims against it in the rest of the world), now spends more than $100 million a year on legal services and liability insurance; it costs Dow an average of $250,000 just to get a case to trial. Many other companies are fed up with watching their legal bills erode profits. But they often settle even frivolous suits just to avoid legal fees and unpredictable juries with their often exorbitant punitive-damages awards, which averaged an estimated $1.5 million per case paid in 1991.[39]

Contrast this with Japan, which has just 14,336 *bengoshis*, or lawyers, while having half the population of the United States. The Japanese have a distaste for confrontation; their legal system therefore discourages litigation, and litigious persons are not held in high esteem. Imagine its shock upon being sued by IBM in 1982 when Hitachi discovered that the first bill from its U.S. law firm exceeded its total payments for legal services in Japan since the company was founded in 1920.

Barriers exist to litigation in Japan. For example, to become a lawyer, one must win a spot in the Legal Training and Research Institute, which accepts only 2 percent of its applicants each year. Thus only 400 lawyers are added annually. There is no discovery, and plaintiffs must also have deep pockets: they are compelled to pay an up-front fee of up to 8 percent of the damages sought in liability suits. Japan also bars class-action suits and contingency-fee arrangements.[40]

✧ POSSIBLE SOLUTIONS

A number of means are now being proposed to stem the tide of lawsuits in this country. Caps could be placed on punitive damages; such awards could be limited to the amount of compensatory awards, with only the judge being allowed to levy them. Losers could be forced to pay the winners' legal fees. This proposal draws the most ire, as many legitimately aggrieved persons would not sue because of the risk involved.

The process of discovery wastes a lot of time and money during the pretrial search through the other side's records. This process could also be revamped, requiring both sides to disclose core information in discovery. As a response to the explosion of "junk science"—where trials become contests between well-paid "experts"—a proposal would require that expert testimony be based on "widely accepted" theories and would ban payouts to experts based on whether their side wins.[41]

Another proposal that is already in relatively widespread use is "alternative dispute resolution." Realizing that the exploding backlog of both criminal and civil cases pushes business cases to the back of the queue, many private corporations are attempting to avoid courts and lawyers, looking instead to alternative means of resolving their legal conflicts. Such innovative techniques include "rent-a-judge" services and minitrials. One utility company even pays for its opponents to sit down with a mediator. Some corporations have even opted out of litigation altogether; about 600 top corporations have signed pledges with other companies to consider negotiation and other forms of alternative dispute resolution (ADR) prior to suing other corporate signers. It is estimated that in 1990, 142 such pledged corporations saved more than $100 million in legal costs.[42]

The leading ADR firm is Judicial Arbitration & Mediation Services, Inc. (JAMS), based in Orange, California. Started in 1979, it now hears 14,000 cases per year, has 18 offices, employs a panel of 175 former judges, and grosses more than $30 million per year. Washington-based Endispute, Inc., and the Philadelphia-based Judicate, Inc., are rapidly growing in the field as well. These private arbitration and mediation firms charge $300 to $350 per hour, a huge savings from the $300 an hour that a battery of lawyers might each charge litigants.[43]

Given the burgeoning number of lawsuits in this country, it appears that ADR is the wave of the future. In fact, a federal court in northern California now sends up to 300 cases a year to mediation through a settlement program known as "early neutral evaluation." In that program, parties meet with a voluntary attorney who sizes up the case, gives an opinion, and then asks whether the parties want to work out a deal. Up to 40 percent of these cases are settled on the spot. Such programs are redefining the role of the courts; as one law professor noted, "in the future, instead of walking into a building called a courthouse, you might walk into the Dispute Resolution Center."[44]

✦ CITIZENS IN COURT

Contemporary society has separated the citizen from the courts. In fact, one survey found that far more Americans knew Judge Wapner (of the former television program, "People's Court") than could identify the chief justice of the U.S. Supreme Court. Nonetheless, judges occupy the public's bench of justice. Judges implement the public's sense of justice by interpreting and enforcing laws. We expect our courts to "do justice."

However, whether justice is done depends on the interests or viewpoints of the affected or interested parties. A victim may not agree with a jury's verdict; a "winner" in a civil case may not feel that he or she received an adequate sum of money for the suffering or damages involved. Thus in light of the fact that "justice" is not always agreed upon, we must make another distinction and also say that the courts must *appear* to do justice. The court's responsibility is to provide a fair hearing, with rights accorded to all parties to speak or not to speak, to have the assistance of counsel, to cross-examine the other side, to produce witnesses and relevant documents, and to argue their viewpoint. This process, embodied in the due process clause, must appear to do justice.[45]

Low public esteem for the courts diminishes the cooperation required from the public in reporting crime and in testifying as witnesses. Certainly, many people in today's society do not believe that courts provide an unwavering appearance of justice; they are fed up with accounts of corrupt judges, what they perceive as coddling of offenders, and the ravages of the "law's delay," which often allows convicted murderers to spend more than a decade awaiting final judgment. People tell their neighbors of long waits at the courthouse, waiting to take care of business or having been summoned for jury service. They hear victims and witnesses talk of having been treated badly at the hands of the justice system, leading one attorney to comment that "the only worse thing than being a victim or witness at trial is having terminal syphilis."

Citizens' groups have undertaken to study the courts. Leading this court-watching effort have been such organizations as the Mothers Against Drunk Drivers, the League of Women Voters, and the National Council of Jewish Women. They observe court hearings, examine state juvenile codes, tour correctional institutions, interview justice personnel, and publish their findings. Many times these groups have probably had unrealistic expectations, as courts do not prevent crime or enact legislation and only see a small fraction of offenders (see the discussion of the "crime control model" in Chapter 1). They may also have an insufficient understanding of the problems or operations of the courts.

Conversely, other "consumers" take a very positive view of the courts. For example, law professor Shirley Abrahamson maintained that "this country has one of the best judicial systems in the world. If I had to be in a court anywhere in the world, as litigant, lawyer, or judge, I would choose to be in a court in the United States."[46] However, Abrahamson conceded that there are problems. She has found through informal surveys that most people in her own field would not go to court to resolve a dispute if they could avoid it. Second, she learned that an overwhelming majority of people in the legal field would not like having a randomly selected judge preside over their case. Americans are concerned about inappropriate judicial conduct and judges' conflict of interest.[47]

Americans are also seeking to demystify their courts; they complain about trial delays, high costs, and even unjust decisions. They want to know what judges are doing about these problems. Americans are saying to themselves, "The people are talking in China, in the [former] Soviet Union, in Eastern Europe. Do we have enough people power in this country? Or have the public officials, including judges, stopped listening to the people?"[48] Americans will increasingly judge their judges. They are going to want the courts to circulate questionnaires and listen to local groups. Succinctly, according to Abrahamson, judges must begin looking at judging from the perspective of the consumer.[49]

✦ COURT ADMINISTRATION AND REFORM

In this country, the judicial branch is characterized by a lack of specialization. Judges with private practices in civil law are found on benches in criminal courts. A criminal lawyer is found hearing juvenile court matters. And all judges are responsible for the administration of their courts, usually with little or no formal training on the subject. In addition to this lack of training, they seldom have an interest in such mundane matters as providing adequate utilities, sanitary rest rooms, and other such amenities of courtrooms. In addition, they must confront problems involving case management, assignment of judges to cases, court security, and the proper maintenance and storage of files and records. Judges prefer to remain independent, often eschewing a chain of command and formal types of interaction with other judges. In short, they resist bureaucratization.

A fact that compounds these problems is that no two court systems are exactly alike. There is no ministry of justice, as is found in many foreign countries. Managerial control of the federal courts is distributed throughout the federal judiciary. The Supreme Court promulgates rules for the lower courts, but its control over budgetary matters and policymaking is minimal. The chief justice appoints the administrator for the Administrative Office of the United States Courts, which is now appropriated about $44.7 million per year for its operations, but the administrator's responsibilities are limited to collecting statistics and other data to assist the work of the judicial branch. Each federal circuit has a circuit judicial council, and in each of the federal districts there is a chief judge who has administrative responsibilities. But the chief judge's ability to carry out policies is based more on the level of cooperation in a district than any real powers that he or she possesses; each judge is independent and appointed for life. One observer found that in each district there were "great differences in the scope of court-wide policy on administrative matters and case management, and in the extent to which court-wide policy was enforced."[50]

The Judicial Conference, established in 1922, is the primary administrative policymaking body of the federal judiciary. Chaired by the chief justice of the U.S. Supreme Court, the conference consists of the chief judges of the courts of appeals, a district judge from each circuit except Washington, D.C., and the chief judge of the Court of International Trade. The conference meets twice a year. Specialized committees conduct much of the work: enacting rules of evidence and procedure, determining numbers of new judges to handle the workload, ethical standards for judges, qualifications of other court personnel, and the budget for the entire federal judiciary. Then the Judicial Conference as a whole votes on committee recommendations, and later makes recommendations to Congress for legislation.[51] In 1970, the 26-member Conference voted against a recommendation by Chief Justice Rehnquist to permit states to speed the pace of death penalty cases. Later, in 1971, Congress passed the Circuit Executive Act, establishing an executive for each federal circuit to provide managerial expertise in budgeting, information systems, personnel and training, facilities, furnishing, supplies, research, and public relations.[52]

Unfortunately, notwithstanding these measures at the federal level, concern remains with the overall administration of U.S. courts. The manner in which courts are administered can affect the level of justice dispensed; yet according to legal-system expert Howard Abadinsky, "judicial management has typically been the most primitive of governmental services."[53] Abadinsky noted that the judicial branch was the last to take advantage of the revolution in information management that resulted from the use of computers. David Saari added that the courthouse has a natural aversion to change; the lawyers who frequent the courthouse "are not interested in working in a typical executive type of bureaucratically dominated, centralized atmosphere, which they will resist by keeping courts locally controlled to suit their own professional interest. This antibureaucratic strain of courts seems to explain many local examples and variations where the public and courts have rejected reform aimed toward centralized control."[54] Judges must be open to change and new methods for conducting the court's business. Justice is affected not only by how the judges decide their cases, but also by how the courts process their cases. Case backlog and trial delay are additional problems that affect many of the nation's courts. The magnitude of the backlog and the length of the delay vary greatly from court to court.

In the United States in the late 1960s, systematic attention began to be directed toward court management and judicial administration. These matters, including the reduction of court delay, the various other functions involved in the day-to-day operations of the courts, who should be overseeing the performance of those functions, and how it should be done, constitute the subject of the next chapter, which deals specifically with judicial administration.

Summary

In this chapter we have underscored the distinctive nature of the courts, which are in many ways set apart from police and corrections organizations. Certainly, the independence enjoyed by, and functions of the courts are dissimilar. Courts have thus far resisted attempts to be "bureaucratized," having comparatively little formalized, hierarchical structure or chain of command; consisting of informal work groups; and being largely autonomous in their environment (however, as will be seen in Chapter 15, the courts are unable to be completely independent or escape political influence, being very dependent on legislatures and the political process for their funding).

Several areas of growing concern were highlighted as well. One increasing concern, even among jurists, is whether several elements of "due process" afforded the accused, the adversary system generally, and the omnipresent will to win by some court actors combine to overshadow the courts' historical search for truth. Another growing dilemma, because of the lawsuit mentality permeating our country, concerns how long our courts will be able to cope with the burgeoning civil and criminal litigation. A final concern was that of consumer involvement with, and knowledge of, court operations. The mystique surrounding the courts and the fear of being involved with court processes that has been engendered, the public's perception of "justice delayed," and the perception of poor treatment of victims and witnesses combine to indicate a need for improved community relations. Together, these areas of court functions bode potentially serious problems for the future.

Next we look at the personnel involved in the management of the courts' business: judges and court administrators, including clerks. Courts do not operate in a vacuum; furthermore, their operations, including such functions as budgeting and management of personnel, cases, juries, and witnesses, are inert without trained persons to perform them. We examine this group's methods and problems in its attempts to manage the court's case flow and thereby avoid the "mother of all sanctions" under the Sixth Amendment's provision of a speedy trial.

Questions for Review

1. Discuss how the courts differ from police agencies and other traditional bureaucracies in their organization. How and why do courts shun the usual characteristics found in a bureaucracy?

2. What are the effects of society's litigious nature on court administration, and what possible solutions hold promise for reducing the avalanche of lawsuits?

3. How do the courts' clientele—the public—view their courts today? What specific areas need improvement?

For Further Reading

HOWARD ABADINSKY, *Law and Justice: An Introduction to the American Legal System* (2d ed.). Chicago: Nelson-Hall, 1991.

JOHN J. DIIULIO, JR. (ed.), *Courts, Corrections, and the Constitution.* New York: Oxford University Press, 1990.

WILLIAM E. HEWITT, GEOFF GALLAS, and BARRY MAHONEY, *Courts That Succeed.* Williamsburg, Va.: National Center for State Courts, 1990.

RICHARD NEELY, *Why Courts Won't Work.* New York: McGraw-Hill, 1983.

DAVID W. NEUBAUER, *America's Courts and the Criminal Justice System* (3d ed.). Pacific Grove, Calif.: Brooks/Cole, 1988.

Notes

1. Kathleen Maguire, Ann L. Pastore, and Timothy J. Flanagan (eds.), *Sourcebook of Criminal Justice Statistics* 1992. U.S. Department of Justice, Bureau of Justice Statistics (Washington, D.C.: U.S. Government Printing Office, 1993), p. 23.

2. Edward J. Clynch and David W. Neubauer, "Trial Courts as Organizations: A Critique and Synthesis," in Stan Stojkovic, John Klofas, and David Kalinich (eds.), *The Administration and Management of Criminal Justice Organizations: A Book of Readings* (Prospect Heights, Ill.: Waveland Press, 1990), pp. 43–61.

3. Peter M. Blau and Marshall W. Meyer, *Bureaucracy in Modern Society* (New York: Random House, 1971), Chapter 2.

4. Edward J. Clynch and David W. Neubauer, "Trial Courts as Organizations: A Critique and Synthesis," p. 43.

5. *Ibid.*, pp. 46–48.

6. *Ibid.*, pp. 49–50.

7. *Ibid.*, pp. 51–52.

8. James Eisenstein and Herbert Jacob, *Felony Justice* (Boston: Little, Brown, 1977), p. 20.

9. Henry R. Glick, *Courts, Politics, and Justice* (New York: McGraw-Hill, 1983), p. 41.

10. William E. Hewitt, Geoff Gallas, and Barry Mahoney, *Courts That Succeed* (Williamsburg, Va.: National Center for State Courts, 1990), p. vii.

11. *Ibid.*, p. vii.

12. American Bar Association, Judicial Administration Division, *Standards Relating to Court Organization*, Vol. 1 (Minneapolis, Minn.: American Bar Association, 1990), pp. 6–7.

13. Alexis de Tocqueville, *Democracy in America* Vol. 1 (H. Reeve, trans.), 1875, pp. 283–84.

14. Don Hardenbergh, "Planning and Design Consideration for Trial Courtrooms," *State Court Journal* 14 (Fall 1990):32–38.

15. Stephen Whicher and R. Spiller (eds.), *The Early Lectures of Ralph Waldo Emerson* (Philadelphia: University of Pennsylvania Press, 1953).

16. 382 U.S. 406 (1966), at 416.

17. Thomas L. Steffen, "Truth as Second Fiddle: Reevaluating the Place of Truth in the Adversarial Trial Ensemble," *Utah Law Review* 4 (1988):799.

18. In *Nix v. Whiteside*, 475 U.S. 157 (1986), at 174.

19. Thomas L. Steffen, "Truth as Second Fiddle," p. 821.

20. W. Alschuler, "The Preservation of a Client's Confidences: One Value among Many or a Categorical Imperative?" 52 U.Colo.L.Rev. 349 (1981), at 354.

21. *Ibid.*, p. 835.

22. Ibid., pp. 842–843.

23. Howard Abadinsky, *Law and Justice: An Introduction to the American Legal System* (2d ed.)(Chicago: Nelson-Hall, 1991), p. 123.

24. Richard A. Posner, *The Federal Courts: Crisis and Reform* (Cambridge, Mass.: Harvard University Press, 1985), p. 3.

25. Harold J. Spaeth, *Supreme Court Policy Making: Explanation and Prediction* (San Francisco: W. H. Freeman, 1979), p. 19.

26. Jethro K. Lieberman, "What Courts Do and Do Not Do Effectively," in Sheldman Goldman and Austin Sarat (eds.), *American Court Systems: Readings in Judicial Process and Behavior* (New York: Longman, 1989), pp. 18–32.

27. Howard Abadinsky, *Law and Justice: An Introduction to the American Legal System* (2d ed.), p. 124.

28. Harold J. Spaeth, *Supreme Court Policy Making: Explanation and Prediction.*

29. Howard Abadinsky, *Law and Justice: An Introduction to the American Legal System* (2d ed.), p. 125.

30. Jeremy Rabkin, *Judicial Compulsions: How Public Law Distorts Public Policy* (New York: Basic Books, 1989), p. 20.

31. Stephen L. Wasby, *The Supreme Court in the Federal System* (3d ed.)(Chicago: Nelson-Hall, 1989), p. 5.

32. Howard Abadinsky, *Law and Justice: An Introduction to the American Legal System* (2d ed.), p. 126.

33. *Ibid.*, p. 131.

34. Michele Galen, Alice Cuneo, and David Greising, "Guilty!" *Business Week* (April 13, 1992): 62.

35. David F. Pike, "Why Everybody Is Suing Everybody," *U.S. News and World Report* (December 4, 1978):50–54.

36. Bob Cohn, "The Lawsuit Cha-Cha," *Newsweek*, August 26, 1991: 58.

37. *Ibid.*

38. *Ibid.*

39. Michele Galen, Alice Cuneo, and David Greising, "Guilty!" pp. 62, 64.

40. *Ibid.*, p. 64.

41. Bob Cohn, "The Lawsuit Cha-Cha," p. 59.

42. Michele Galen, Alice Cuneo, and David Greising, "Guilty!", p. 63.

43. *Ibid.*

44. *Ibid.*, p. 64.

45. H. Ted Rubin, *The Courts: Fulcrum of the Justice System* (Santa Monica, Calif.: Goodyear, 1976):3.

46. Shirley S. Abrahamson, "The Consumer and the Courts," *Judicature* 74 (August/September 1990):93–95.

47. *Ibid.*, p. 94.

48. *Ibid.*

49. *Ibid.*

50. Steven Flanders, *Case Management in the United States District Courts* (Washington, D.C.: U.S. Government Printing Office, 1977), p. 8.

51. Stephen L. Wasby, *The Supreme Court in the Federal System* (3d ed.).

52. Howard Abadinsky, *Law and Justice: An Introduction to the American Legal System* (2d ed.), p. 161.

53. *Ibid.*, p. 162.

54. David J. Saari, *American Court Management: Theories and Practice* (Westport, Conn.: Quorum Books, 1985), pp. 32–33.

Personnel Roles and Functions

The justice or injustice of the cause is to be decided by the judge.

—Samuel Johnson

✦ INTRODUCTION

The administration of the judicial process is probably the least known and understood area of justice administration. Therefore, in this chapter we delineate the role of judges and other court staff members toward ensuring that cases are processed in a timely and fair manner.

We base this discussion on the general observation, supported by the relevant literature,[1] that judges and lawyers are normally not well trained in handling the administrative tasks of their courts, nor do they often have the time required to accomplish them. Furthermore, few judges today would probably "like to spend all day or most of the day handling union grievances or making sure that employees know what their benefits are."[2]

A major function of the courtroom work group is to assure that there is a smooth flow of cases through the courts. It being an underlying purpose of judicial administrators, case management is strongly implicated in this chapter.[3]

We begin by considering the need for judicial independence and the relationship of that long-standing doctrine to the courts. We define and distinguish the terms *judicial administration* and *court administration*, then discuss the historically important role of court clerks—the original administrators of the court process. Following is the "heart and soul" of this chapter: the relatively new position of the specially trained court administrator. We then review some criteria that judges can employ to determine whether their court administrators are functioning effectively and efficiently. We close the chapter with a program of court administration and a view of courts that fail and succeed.

✦ DEFINING JUDICIAL AND COURT ADMINISTRATION

The purpose of judicial independence is to mitigate arbitrariness in judging. But what is the purpose of judicial administration? That is more difficult to define. Consequently, as Russell Wheeler noted, "many court administrators today find themselves under the inevitable strain of not knowing for certain what their purpose is."[4]

Most works on judicial administration point to Roscoe Pound as the chief thinker in the field of judicial administration as a result of his 1906 essay, "The Causes of Popular Dissatisfaction with Administration of Justice" (discussed in Chapter 3). However, the field should properly regard a major essay by Woodrow Wilson 19 years earlier (in 1887), entitled "The Study of Administration," as just as much a founding document as the noted address by Dean Pound.

Wilson stressed that the vocation of administration was a noble calling, not a task for which every person was competent. [5] He emphasized that policy and administration are two different matters and, in extremely foresighted fashion, wrote that judges were responsible for judging and "establishing fundamental court policy," and that a third task was for a "trained executive officer, working under the chief judge or presiding judge," to "relieve judges generally" of "the function of handling the numerous business and administrative affairs of the courts."[6] Courts have *not* always regarded administration as a noble calling, but they have always been a bastion in defense of the distinction Wilson drew between policy and administration.[7]

Wilson's essay certainly gave intellectual respectability to the field of administration. However, it also poses two troubling aspects. First, although it is accurate in the abstract to state that a wall exists between administration and policy, almost every administrator and policymaker knows, as Wheeler phrased it, that "the wall is full of many gaps and is easily scaled."[8] Policy decisions inevitably intertwine with administrative decisions. Second, trying to honor this policy–administration dichotomy would leave the administrator adrift when confronted with inevitable policy decisions.

The difficulty of defining judicial administration became obvious during the 1970s, when it became vocationally attractive. Various people and commissions tried to define it, but still seemed capable of only listing the duties of the office. For example, the National Advisory Commission on Criminal Justice Standards and Goals stated in 1973 that "the basic purpose of court administration is to relieve judges of some administrative chores and to help them perform those they retain."[9] Furthermore, in 1974 the American Bar Association specified a variety of functions for the court administrator to perform "under the authority of the judicial council and the supervision of the chief justice."[10]

The problem of definition continued into the 1980s; one law professor who had done a large amount of research in the field felt in 1986 that the safest approach was "not...to attempt a definition" but simply "to accept that it is a sub-branch of administration—more precisely of public administration."[11]

To assist in this dilemma and provide more clarity, a very good working definition of judicial administration is that advanced by Russell Wheeler and Howard Whitcomb; this definition allows an analysis from a variety of perspectives: "The direction of and influences on the activities of those who are expected to contribute to just and efficient case processing—except legal doctrinal considerations, insofar as they dispose of the particular factual and legal claims presented in a case."[12] This definition also nicely separates the judicial and nonjudicial functions of the court and implies that there is a *set* of people who share a role norm and that judicial administration constitutes *all* of the factors that direct and influence those people.[13]

Notably, however, the term *court administration* might be conceived of loosely as the specific activities of those persons who are organizationally responsible for manipulating these various judicial administration directions and influences.[14] This term is that which is more commonly used in this chapter, as we focus on the development of the role and functions of the *individual trial court administrator*. This will become clearer as the chapter unfolds and the judge's and court administrator's relationship is discussed.

✦ JUDGES AS ADMINISTRATORS

Since the origin of our Constitution, the judiciary was intended to play a key role in its application; the overriding duty of judges is to protect the individual from the state. Our courts were created to provide the final defense of freedom: to be, in the words of James Madison, "an impenetrable bulwark against every assumption of power in the legislative or executive."[15] For this reason, as noted in Chapter 7, for the most part our society accords its jurists a high level of esteem. However, many people take a more temperate, rational view of those occupying the bench, agreeing with the eminent Judge Learned Hand: "Here I am, an old man in a long nightgown making muffled noises at people who may be no worse than I am."[16] Another famous jurist, Marvin Frankel, offered that "self-criticism, uncertainty, and a resultant disposition toward restraint are useful qualities in judges....They are not, however, in oversupply."[17]

✧ SOCIALIZATION OF JUDGES

What makes judges behave and decide matters as they do? What elements of their education and experience might affect their views toward judicial administration? There is a considerable body of literature concerning forces that shape the attitudes of judges prior to their appointment.[18] For example, most judges were recruited from the locality in which they serve, bringing with them to the bench certain biases, values, and perceptions peculiar to their own locality.[19] However, a judge's socialization process *after* his or her appointment may also have a significant bearing on the decisionmaking process, including both sentencing and judicial administration.

Research has shown that when one is appointed to a judgeship, he or she knows relatively little about the duties that come with the job. However, as a judge, he or she must become an expert in *all* aspects of law, be it federal or state in nature. Ignorance of criminal law is a common problem, as most judges (especially those in federal courts) did not specialize in criminal practice.[20]

The judgeship also requires that the holder be a competent administrator, a fact of judicial life that comes as a surprise to many new judges. One survey of 30 federal judges found that 23 (77 percent) acknowledged having major administrative difficulties upon first assuming the bench. Half complained of heavy caseloads, stating that their judgeship had accumulated backlogs and that other adverse conditions compounded the problem. One federal judge maintained that it takes about four years to "get a full feel of a docket."[21]

Most trial judges experience psychological discomfort upon assuming the role as well. Seventy-seven percent of new federal judges acknowledged having psychological problems in at least one of five areas: maintaining a judicial bearing both on and off the bench, the loneliness of the judicial office, sentencing criminals, forgetting the adversary role, and local pressure. One aspect of the judicial role is that of assuming a proper mien, or "learning to act like a judge." One judge remembered his first day in court: "I'll never forget going into my courtroom for the first time with the robes and all, and the crier tells everyone to rise. You sit down and realize that it's all different, that everyone is looking at you and you're supposed to do something."[22]

Like a common complaint of police officers and probation and parole workers, judges "can't go to the places you used to. You always have to be careful about what you talk about. When you go to a party, you have to be careful not to drink too much so you won't make a fool of yourself."[23] And the position can be a lonely one: "After you become a…judge some people tend to avoid you. For instance, you lose all your lawyer friends and generally have to begin to make new friends. I guess the lawyers are afraid that they will some day have a case before you and it would be awkward for them if they were on too close terms with you."[24]

Sentencing criminals is frequently described by judges as their most difficult psychological problem. A federal judge felt that "sentencing criminals is another problem which often troubles me. I have often said to the other judges that this is the hardest part of being a judge. You see so many pathetic people and you're never sure of what is a right or a fair sentence."[25]

Judges often meet together on a regular basis, and, in matters involving sentencing criminals, the new judge may frequently be guided by the experience of an older colleague. However, in most jurisdictions there is almost no exchange of information between the novice trial judge and appellate judges. Novice trial judges typically feel that there may be an impropriety in discussing a judicial problem with an appellate judge; furthermore, trial judges often presume that there is nothing appellate judges can do to help them with their day-to-day problems.[26]

Consequently, many new judges rely on their court staff—particularly their court administrators—to assist them with the difficult early months of their judgeship. Another major source of socialization for novice judges is local lawyers. When the case subject matter is new to them, judges frequently ask opposing lawyers for information about "what the law says." Or, when they have a new or difficult case with which they need help, they occasionally contact a local attorney who specializes in the subject matter of the case at bar. Bench books and seminars are also helpful in socializing and training the judge after appointment or election to the bench.[27]

✧ Judges As Court Managers

Federal courts have the Administrative Office of the United States Courts to coordinate and administer their operations. At the state level, there are basically three types of administrative levels assumed by judges: statewide jurisdiction, as that found with state supreme court chief justices; that which merely involves a local trial judge's being responsible for administering the operations of his or her individual court; and that of a "presiding" or "chief" judge's position, wherein the judge supervises several courts within a judicial district.

The position of a judge presiding over several courts within a district developed duties as early as 1940, when Dean Roscoe Pound recommended that a chief or presiding judge of a district or a region be responsible for and have the authority for case and judge assignment.[28] Today, these judges assume "general administrative duties over the court and its divisions" and are typically granted authority over all judicial personnel and court officials.[29] The duties of the presiding judge are numerous and include personnel and docket management and case and judge assignments; coordinating the development of all judicial budgets; convening *en banc* court meetings; coordination of judicial schedules; creation and use of appropriate court committees (to investigate problems, handle court business, etc.); dealing with outside agencies and the media; drafting local court rules and policies; maintaining the courts' facilities; and issuing orders for keeping, destruction, and transfer of records.[30]

However, a basic flaw in this system is that the chief or presiding judge is actually a "first among equals" with his or her peers. The title of chief judge is often assigned by seniority; therefore, there is no guarantee that the chief judge will have the interest, temperament, or skills needed to manage a large court system. And where the chief judge is elected, there is always the possibility that a popular person will be elected, one who is not willing to "rock the boat."[31]

From a court administrator's standpoint, the office of and person serving as presiding judge are of utmost importance. As one judge put it, "the single most determinative factor of the extent of the administrator's role, aside from his personal attributes, is probably the rate of turnover in the office of the presiding judge."[32] As we will see later, the method of selection of judges is also an important process and consideration.

As mentioned above, although judges are ultimately responsible for court administration, they have historically been ineffective managers overall. Judges are often confronted with issues about which they have little knowledge or experience. As one author stated: "Until recently, judges typically proceeded without the advice of professional managers or the benefit of modern techniques of careful research, planning, evaluation and training. Even today, with court administrators having served for over ten years in many courts, judges are often slow to heed their advice and continue to rely on intuitions and predilections born of legal training and disposition to follow precedents."[33]

Much of this lack of knowledge of behind-the-scenes court processes can be explained by the environment in which courts function. Judges primarily exist to hear cases; furthermore, they are often not given the necessary authority to govern all court operations. Moreover, they typically are not trained in court management. Lawyers learn early in law school training to treat each case individually; then, when becoming a judge, they are unaccustomed to having to handle a large number of cases or analyzing caseloads or patterns of dispositions. However, as will be seen in Chapter 9, case management is a primary duty of the judge.

✦ HOLDING JUDGES ACCOUNTABLE

Ideally, our judges are flawless, not allowing emotion or personal biases to creep into their work, treating all cases and individual litigants with an even hand and "justice tempered with mercy." The perfect judge would be like that described by the eminent Italian legal philosopher, Pierro Calamandrei: "The good judge takes equal pains with every case no matter how humble; he knows that important cases and unimportant cases do not exist, for injustice is not one of those poisons which…when taken in small doses may produce a salutary effect. Injustice is a dangerous poison even in doses of homeopathic proportions."[34]

However, not all judges are cut from this cloth. Recognizing this fact, nearly 800 years ago King John met with his barons on the field of Runnymede and, in the Magna Carta, promised that henceforth he would not "make men justices…unless they are such as know the law of the realm and are minded to observe it rightly."[35] Unfortunately, not all judges "observe it rightly." Therefore, we require some means of dealing with judicial misconduct and disability. For that reason, judicial conduct commissions exist in nearly all states and the District of Columbia. Most were created by statute or constitutional amendment, with a mandate to receive, investigate, and dispose of complaints regarding judicial misconduct. They handle complaints such as judicial prejudice or bias, slow processing of orders, procedural or administrative irregularity, courtroom demeanor, and conflict of interest.[36]

Life tenure and the difficulty in removing judges from office were supposed to shield judicial decision making from hostile, popular, or legislative majorities. However, there are some authors who feel that the judiciary over time has lost sight of its proper constitutional role. Others believe that judicial misconduct and disability are at unacceptable levels and that it is much too difficult to remove an errant judge from the bench. Today, the House may impeach and the Senate remove federal jurists, but the process is cumbersome (Thomas Jefferson stated that "[impeachment is] a bungling way of removing judges—an impractical thing—a mere scarecrow)"[37] and rarely used.

There are probably very few truly corrupt judges in this country. Nonetheless, the conduct of judges must be above suspicion. The test is not whether the judge acted in good faith but whether his or her conduct is prejudicial to the judicial office. As the Pennsylvania Supreme Court put it: "For generations…it has been taught that a judge must possess the confidence of the community; that he must not only be independent and honest, *but equally important, believed by* all men to be independent and honest.…Without the appearance as well as the fact of justice, respect for the law vanishes in a democracy."[38]

Many court administrators would agree that the manner by which one gets to the bench will significantly affect his or her administrative style and overall efficiency and effectiveness. [39] The bottom line is whether one ascended to the position through political appointment or by a process involving *merit*, which takes into account the candidate's qualifications and temperament. One popular method of selecting judges is the so-called "Missouri Plan," whereby the governor appoints new judges from a list of nominees selected by a nonpartisan nominating commission. In fact, as of mid-1993, 20 states (40 percent) and the District of Columbia employed the nominating-commission method to select their highest appellate court judges, and 15 states (30 percent) and the District of Columbia used this method to select judges in general jurisdiction courts.[40]

✦ COURT CLERKS

Not to be overlooked in the administration of the courts is the clerk, also referred to as prothonotaries, registrar of deeds, circuit clerk, registers of probate, and even auditor. Most courts have de facto court administrators in these clerks, irrespective of whether or not they have appointed administrators. These are key individuals in the administration of local court systems. They docket cases, collect fees and costs, oversee jury selection, and maintain court records. These local officials, elected in all but six states, can amass tremendous power.[41]

From the inception of British North America, court clerks were vital members of society. The early "clerks of writs" or "clerks of the assize" existed in early Massachusetts, where people were litigious primarily because of land boundaries. There was a hostility toward lawyers carried over from England, and the clerk was the intermediary between the litigants and the justice of the peace. Their list of fees was twopence for summonses, threepence for attachment and replevin, and fourpence to take bond in order to prosecute a suit. During the late seventeenth century, American courts became more structured and formalized. Books were available that superimposed English court usage in the colonies, and clerks, judges, and attorneys were provided proper forms that had to be used. In fact, the forms used by clerks 200 years ago are very close to those in use today.[42]

The clerk's office was one of considerable power and dignity during colonial and post-Revolutionary times. Duties included summoning the grand jury, recording bills of indictment, providing for the security and comfort of the jury, and the smooth conduct of the court's business during arraignments. The clerk also swore in the jury and ensured the smooth flow of the criminal trial. After the trial concluded, the clerk polled the jury, then summoned the gaoler to take the prisoner into custody. In cases where women accused of a capital offense were granted special consideration due to pregnancy (in order that the court would not have innocent blood on its hands), the clerk called upon the sheriff to bring together 12 women to examine the defendant to determine whether she was in fact pregnant; if so, she would not be put to death until after she had given birth.[43]

Clerks have traditionally competed with judges for control over local judicial administration. In fact, one study found that the majority (58.9 percent) of elected clerks perceived themselves as colleagues, thus being coequal with the judges.[44] However, court clerks have not as a rule been identified with effective management. The reasons have been summarized as follows: "Generally they are conservative in nature and reflect the attitudes and culture of the community. Their parochial backgrounds coupled with their conservative orientation, in part accounts for this resistance to change. This resistance often compels judicial systems to retain archaic procedures and managerial techniques."[45] Much of America is rural in nature; although not suggesting that all clerks' offices are "parochial" and "archaic," there are many observers who believe that rural clerks are not adequately trained to manage courts as required for modern times.

✦ COURT ADMINISTRATORS

✧ DEVELOPMENT AND TRAINING

One of the most recent and innovative approaches to solving the courts' management problems has been the creation of the position of court administrator. This relatively new criminal-justice position began to develop in earnest during the 1960s; since that time, the number of practicing trial court administrators has increased tenfold and continues to expand. Actually, this concept has its roots in early England where, historically, judges have abstained from any involvement in court administration. This fact has not been lost on contemporary court administrators and proponents of this occupation: "It seems to be a very valuable characteristic of the English system that the judges expect to *judge* when they are in the courthouse…it does not allow time for administrative distractions."[46]

However, the development of the position of court administrator has been sporadic. In the early 1960s there were probably 30 people in the United States who really worked as court administrators. By 1970 there were still fewer than 50 such specially trained employees.[47] Estimates differ concerning the expansion of the administrator's role during the 1980s. While one expert maintained that by 1982 there were probably between 2000 and 3000 people in the ranks of court managers,[48] another argued that there were only about 500.[49] At any rate, most estimators agree that more than twice as many of these positions were created between 1970 and 1980 than in the preceding six decades.[50]

We also know that by the 1980s every state had established a statewide court administrator, normally reporting to the state supreme court or the chief justice of the state supreme court. State court administrators' primary functions may be consolidated into three categories: preparing annual reports summarizing caseload data, preparing budgets, and troubleshooting.[51]

Today few, if any, metropolitan areas are without full-time court administrators [52] (the court organization chart shown in Chapter 7 demonstrates the breadth of responsibilities held by court administrators). An underlying premise and justification for this role is that by having a trained person performing the tasks of court management, judges are left free to do what they do best: decide cases. Indeed, since the first trial court administrative positions began to appear, "there was little doubt or confusion about their exact purpose."[53]

As court reformers have called for better trained specialists (as opposed to politically appointed persons) for administering court processes, the qualifications that are required for these persons has come under debate. The creation of the Institute for Court Management in 1970 was a landmark in the training for this role, legitimizing their standing in the legal profession. However, many judges still feel that a law degree is essential, whereas others prefer a background in business administration. There will probably never be total agreement concerning the skills and background necessary for this position, but the kind of specialized training that is offered by the institute and a few graduate programs in judicial administration across the country would seem ideal.

This group is trained specifically for this task, providing the courts with the expertise and talent they have historically lacked. This point was powerfully made by Bernadine Meyer:

> Management—like law—is a profession today. Few judges or lawyers with severe chest pains would attempt to treat themselves. There would be slight hesitation about consulting the medical profession. Congested dockets and long delays are symptoms that court systems need the help of professionals. Those professionals are managers. If court administration is to be effective, judicial recognition that managerial skill and knowledge are necessary to efficient performance is vital.[54]

✧ GENERAL DUTIES

Turning to individual trial court administrators, a recent survey of these practitioners revealed that they actually perform six major duties:

1. *Reports:* Eighty percent of all trial court administrators reported primary responsibility for the preparation and submission to the judges periodic reports of the activities and state of business of the court.

2. *Personnel administration:* Seventy-nine percent of all court administrators have as a primary duty serving as personnel officer for court's nonjudicial personnel.

3. *Research and evaluation:* These duties were performed by 78 percent of all respondents, to improve court business methods.

4. *Equipment management:* Three-fourths of all administrators are engaged in procurement, allocation, inventory control, and replacement of furniture and equipment.

5. *Preparation of court budget:* This major task is done by 74 percent of all administrators.

6. *Training coordinator:* About 73 percent of trial court administrators surveyed provide training for nonjudicial personnel.[55]

Other duties that are assumed by the trained court administrator include jury management (reported as a primary duty by 42 percent of trial courts administrators), case-flow or calendar management (42 percent), public information (56 percent), and management of automated data processing (59 percent).[56]

A few critics of this branch of the judicial reform movement feel that trial court administrators have in fact made little difference in the courts' efforts to function more effectively and dispense a higher quality of justice. However, another reform segment perceives a different, more subtle problem: a growing judicial uneasiness over the evolution of bureaucratic structures in trial courts. The addition of the professional manager/technocrat to the court's administrative staff could appear to many judges to be yet another step toward the creation of an unresponsive bureaucracy. Reformers fear that this judicial concern is producing a heightened reluctance to all trial court administrators to evolve into true court managers with broad responsibilities for implementing policy. If this truly be the case, it raises questions of whether trial court administrators will ever realize the potential that is seen by so many people in the court administration community.[57]

✧ SUCCESSFUL OR MERELY SURVIVING?

Although in its fourth decade of active existence, the field of court administration still appears unsettled. Beginning in the 1980s a debate began to enlarge concerning whether or not the field was successful or "merely surviving." The debate appears to rage on, centering on its function and place in the courts, criminal justice, and society.

In the early 1980s a debate took place between Ernest C. Friesen (profiled in Chapter 3), and Robert C. Harrall, a Rhode Island court administrator and national consultant in the field. Friesen was the antagonist. First, he maintained that court administration had gone through three stages: the stage of intrusion (when a few people began to be accepted as working in the courthouse as assistants or secretaries), the stage of experimentation (when judicial administrators began exploring different roles, and during which time the Institute of Court Management was created), and the phase of survival (Friesen referred to this as a "bad mode" since it had no goal except itself). He argued that if court administration was indeed in a survival mode, it could not evolve into the next phase—trust—in which administrators could be treated as peers in the justice system.[58]

Friesen also felt that court administrators should not wear the label of "professionals," as they are generalists in the court system, and they have no perceived or defined role. Although court administrators had proliferated, Friesen was of the opinion that they had not necessarily succeeded in assisting the courts to "do justice." While the ranks of administrators had swollen, he said, from 30 to 3000, the average time from filing to trial for a civil case had probably increased from two to four and a half years from 1972 through 1982. After 10 years of "heavy court management work," court administration had obviously not solved the problem of case delay. Friesen added that "Court administrators have put their heads in the sand and said, `Well, I'm taking very good care of all these other things. The judges and other people ought to do that.' After 10 years of having a manager in every one of our major courts…it is apparent that those managers did not get involved in these issues. They were surviving, but not being efficient and not moving the court in the direction it needed to be moved."[59]

Friesen also chided court administrators for not taking unpopular positions or risks; he felt it was not right to allow America's lawyers to run the court calendars or secretly agree to postpone and continue cases. Administrators, he felt, need to be more efficient and effective, and not be afraid to protect individuals from the arbitrary use of government power. In short, as Friesen put it, "you may have to get between the dog and the lamppost occasionally."[60] Friesen asserted that if court administrators did not possess such information as how long it took judges to dispose of cases, how many cases were pending, or generally did not do "this kind of work," they were merely surviving, not managing.

Following Friesen's barrage, Harrall made a gallant attempt to defend court administration. He laid the blame for the reproach of the field at the door of academics, who, he asserted, tended "to reject out of hand the things that are not done to their standards." He derided academics who were critical of the work of court managers but who had "studied" the courts but had never worked in the field. "They really do not know of what they write."[61]

Harrall offered what he felt were major accomplishments of the field: technical assistance in areas such as personnel, finance, records and jury management, management, and case and data processing. "I would argue that it is in these areas that court managers have been the most effective, for the application of technology…certainly upgrades the fairness of the system."[62] Court managers, he added, have also served as "transfer vehicles" for techniques and ideas coming into the courts. "Prior to their existence there was no one who would try in *X* what works over there in *Y*." Managers, he claimed, provided continuity to the courts as well. "Judges change, but managers generally do not change as frequently." Also, managers have brought evaluation to the courts. "Evaluation is increasingly a major component. The manager who does not evaluate on a routine basis loses his credibility and possibly his position."[63]

Harrall also took serious issue with Friesen's contention that managers would not take chances. "The relatively high rate of turnover in certain court positions in this country shows that they are doing just that (`getting between the dog and the lamppost'). Very often administrators do serve as spokespersons for unpopular views, and many have paid a price for doing so."[64] Managers, he added, have also learned to deal with new constituencies: unionized courts, minority bar groups, and court watchers; they have also forged professional organizations that contribute to the education and technical assistance of "the profession." He concluded with a clear swipe at Friesen:

> To those who say we have accomplished very little in the last 10 years, I say that you have forgotten from whence we came…if you visited any jurisdiction in which court managers have been at work you would find virtually no one who wished to return to the "good old days.…" Finally, to those who say we have neither developed perceived and defined functions nor brought efficiency and fairness to the courts, I say that your position is only tenable if you misconceive our role.[65]

✦ CONFLICT BETWEEN JUDICIAL ADMINISTRATORS

✧ A DIFFICULT DICHOTOMY

The nature of the administrative relationship between the judge and the court administrator, as well as the court administrator and the clerk, has also been troubling. Of particular concern is where the line should be drawn with respect to the supervisory powers possessed by each employee. Where clerks are employed, the relatively new position of court administrator is often viewed as a threat; clerks may even resent the intrusion. Clerks, therefore, have assumed a central role in resisting the creation of a court executive's position. Yet to manage a court's operations, the court administrator is often dependent on receiving the kind of information that only the clerk can provide.[66]

Tension and conflict may arise between the judge and the court administrator because some judges are reluctant to delegate responsibility over major aspects of court operations: budgeting and case scheduling, for example. In fact, some studies have shown that because of conflicts with clerks and judges, court administrators have not been given full responsibility over court duties of a nonjudicial nature; they are often allowed to perform only minor tasks.[67] In many courts, however, the court administrator has been given full responsibility, including the latitude to be extremely innovative. Unfortunately, however, substantial confusion still exists over the proper role of the court administrator.[68] And in practice, the line separating the administrative and the adjudicatory functions of the courts has not been well established.

The rift that can exist between judges and court managers is also related to the fact that judges and courts resist bureaucracy; Thomas Leitko stated the problem in general terms: "The integration of professionals into a professional bureaucracy has always been problematic. Because professionals identify more with their occupations than with their organizations, because they often control their own certification and performance standards, and because they have separate sources of legitimacy within their organizations, they often have functioned somewhat autonomously from and at odds with administrators."[69] Judges resist measures of performance; their productivity is an intensely personal and private matter to them. The ultimate, and perhaps only test of judicial performance is when the voters are asked to retain or reject them or during the appointment process. Not even other judges serve as performance evaluators. There are no merit salary programs or incentive or performance appraisal systems. Judges need autonomy and discretion. Conversely, for the court administrator, accountability is the bottom line. Measures of performance are external to the individual administrator; supervisors evaluate their subordinates and people are hired, fired, and promoted with accountability in mind.[70]

Nonetheless, the two roles must support and cooperate with one another, even mesh together. The concept that judges should stick to judging and administrators to managing is counterproductive. There must be a mutual commitment to three fundamental values: the importance of joint policy formulation, respect for individual expertise, and mutual trust and support for achievement.[71]

In an ideal situation, the administrative and judicial activities operating within a court would be coordinated and equally balanced between the judge and the administrator. There would be activities that are clearly administrator centered, those that are judge centered, and those that involve joint decision making or information sharing—a "shared role" in the latter instance. Figure 8.1 depicts on a continuum how all court administration activities would be distributed and performed, and where collaboration between judge and administrator would be required.

Unfortunately, the relationship between court administrators and judges can involve a "clash between two cultures." Judges and administrators not only differ typically in background, education, and training, but also approach their job roles from very different perspectives. Judges have the organizational power but lack the operational knowledge to perform all of the courts' operations, and the court managers have the knowledge of court operations but lack the power. Obviously, if judges and court administrators can develop a team approach, they will merge these two strengths.[72]

Administration		Adjudication
Administrator makes the decisions without consulting the judge	Joint decision-making or information-sharing; "a shared role."	Judge makes the decisions without consulting the administrator

Examples of Activities

Budgeting	Agency relationships	Case decisions
Training for non-judicial personnel	Legislative relationships	Directing meetings of judges
Purchasing	Public information	Assigning judges
Accounting	Planning committees	Training for judges
Statistics	Research on rules and procedures	Selecting law-trained support personnel
Report preparation	Probation	Supervising screening and instructing of jurors
Systems analysis and research	Case processing	Record creation
Record keeping	Financial policy	
	Personnel rules	

Figure 8.1 Continuum of administrative-judicial activities. (*Source:* E. Keith Stott, Jr., "The Judicial Executive: Toward Greater Congruence in an Emerging Profession," *The Justice System Journal* 7(2) (1982); pp. 152–179.)

✧ SOURCES OF DISAGREEMENT

Larry Mays and William Taggart examined court administrators' perceptions of the sources of conflict in managing the courts. First, they asked respondents to indicate who had primary responsibility—a court administrator or a judge—for performing four administrative functions: budgeting, personnel, case scheduling, and jury management. Table 8.1 demonstrates that at least half of the managers reported having the primary responsibility for each of these four functions. Note, however, that the degree of managerial control was not uniform across functions. The most prevalent function assigned to court administrators concerned the budget, for which nearly 9 of 10 respondents claimed responsibility. Less than two-thirds claimed primary responsibility for jury management and case scheduling.

The major source of conflict for both elected and appointed court managers was case-flow management (also known as calendar management), one of the crucial elements in any court's administrative scheme. Respondents commented on postponement of cases, judges rescheduling the calendar, docketing, judicial assignments, and backlogs.[73] This finding generally concurred with other researchers, that (1) case-flow management was one of the 10 least-delegated duties of presiding judges; and (2) case-flow management ranked last in a list of the 10 administrative duties most often mentioned in conjunction with court administration.[74] One explanation for this finding is that case-flow management has been felt to be one function that "judges would be reluctant to dele-

TABLE 8.1   ADMINISTRATIVE RESPONSIBILITY FOR FOUR FUNCTIONS

| | Primary Responsibility for: | | | | | | | |
| | Budget | | Personnel | | Jury Management | | Case Scheduling | |
	No.	%	No.	%	No.	%	No.	%
Manager	325	88.8	319	86.9	215	65.7	202	54.6
Judge	14	3.8	28	7.6	99	30.3	149	40.3
Both	23	6.3	18	4.9	9	2.8	15	4.1
Someone else	4	1.1	2	0.5	4	1.2	4	1.1
Total	366	100.0	367	99.9	327	100.0	370	100.1
Missing cases	11		10		50		7	

Reprinted from the *Journal of Criminal Justice*, Vol. 14, G. Larry Mays and William A. Taggart, "Court Clerks, Court Administrators, and Judges: Conflict in Managing the Courts," pp.1–7. Copyright 1986, with permission from Pergamon Press, Ltd., Headington Hill Hall, Oxford, England. OX3 OBW, UK.

gate," as it is a duty that "might be considered judicial in nature."[75] At the same time, however, Mays and Taggart found that case-flow management ranks high among the areas giving court administrators the greatest problems. Thus it seems ironic that although case-flow management is described by many authors [76] as one of the primary functions of court managers, it is also one that is grudgingly delegated by judges and is a leading source of conflict within the courtroom work group.

Other sources of judge–administrator conflict in court management found by Mays and Taggart revolved around financial issues and personnel matters, two of the five major sources of conflict. Financial issues included accounting problems and methods, unbudgeted expenditures, procurement policies, and budget cutbacks. Among the personnel issues most often cited by respondents were employee evaluations, salary disputes, lack of adequate staffing, and the competency of staff.[77]

Courts do not operate in a vacuum; they are not to any large extent masters of their own fates. Court administrators must live by rules not of their own making. There are internal court procedures and policies allowing judges and others to hire, fire, direct, and compensate the manager's own employees. Additionally, as mentioned above, there may also exist within a court two administrative infrastructures: one for the elected court clerk and one for an appointed administrator. Both internal and external sources of conflict are evident in the areas of budgeting and personnel. Mays and Taggart learned that court administrators appear to feel constrained by legislative control, by the state administrative offices of the courts, and by the wielding of power—often perceived as interference—by judges.[78]

Finally, other sources of conflict between judges, court administrators, and clerks were policy and planning issues and what may be called "authority to administer." Court administrators have cited poor planning and the lack of goal setting, standardization of procedures, policy consistency, and reorganization as sources of conflict. Regarding authority to administer, court administrators mentioned such issues as authority not being clearly established, delegation of responsibility without authority, lack of major policymaking authority, and changes that must be initiated by the judge(s). The latter concern is understandable. Appointed administrators do not enjoy constitutional status (as do elected clerks in the majority of the states), and 82 percent of the respondents in the Mays-Taggart study were appointed to their positions by a judge or a panel of judges and served at the pleasure of their appointer(s). Thus their authority is derived, or an extension of the judge's (or judges'). This "reflected glory" can leave an appointed administrator unsure of his or her power base and direction.[79] They must constantly "check with judges" to determine their wants and needs.[80] In fact, only 37.1 percent of court administrators perceived themselves as colleagues with the judges.[81]

Several court administrators have expressed that their judges either failed to provide support or leadership or, at worst, questioned the need for a court administrator position. Many administrators sense that their relationship is tenuous; nearly four in ten (41.4 percent) consider their position as that of a court employee.[82] Other researchers have concluded that judges view their court administrators as administrative aides [83]—an attitude that could easily result in the discontinuation of such positions in tight fiscal times.

It is perhaps ironic that the more court managers attempt to control the administrative processes, the wider the gap may become between themselves and judges and lawyers. These two groups can have widely divergent perspectives on *what* is to be done and *how* it is to be accomplished.[84]

✦ HOW JUDGES EVALUATE ADMINISTRATORS

Like other mortals, judges and court administrators often see the world through "rose-colored glasses." As one Arizona judge observed:

> Judges and court administrators are not likely to view themselves in a negative light. As part of an organization that creates a certain amount of respect and awe for itself, it is not surprising that the [judge] and the court administrator may believe that they are better than they actually are. Distance, pomp, ceremony, privileges, and ornate surroundings are all used to create awe. As a result, their top members frequently believe that the awe displayed toward them is intrinsic to their person, and not to the office….[85]

The common problem of "rose-colored glasses" is a pervasive impediment to objective assessment and clear decision making. With the court administrators' position being relatively new, all trial courts may not have any establish work performance criteria for assessing their output. The judge needs to be able to determine whether his or her court administrator is performing competently and effectively.

First, we need to establish that there is a "middle ground" in court administration and in evaluation of their work; administrators should not be given too little or too much responsibility. For example, we must acknowledge that in some courts the judge usurps the administrator's role and makes most management decisions unilaterally. That defeats the purpose of having an administrator. Clearly, the judge needs to delegate sufficient responsibility to the administrator that the former is getting his or her money's worth and the latter is doing what he or she was trained to do and is providing the level of assistance that is the overall intent of the position. In short, they were hired to allow judges to do what they do best: judging. On the other hand, judges sometimes totally abdicate their responsibilities, delegating too much of the court's work to the administrator and exercising virtually no oversight of the latter's performance. Abdication is particularly present when judges and administrators are in separate buildings or cities. In this instance, the court administrator will in effect be supervised.[86]

According to John Greacen,[87] there are basically five strategies for judges to follow in determining the quality of work performed by their administrators:

1. *Look for the indications of good management.* A well-managed organization will have a number of plans and procedures in place, including personnel policies, recruitment and selection procedures, an orientation program for new employees, performance evaluation procedures, a discipline and grievance process, case management policies, financial controls, and other administrative policies (such as facilities and records management).

2. *The judge should be getting regular information.* Critically important reports and data on the court's performance, plans, activities, and accomplishments should be provided the judge on a routine basis. The judge should be notified of the numbers of case filings and terminations, pending cases, financial information, staff performance, long- and short-range plans, and other statistical data.

3. *Judges should be watching carefully.* Judges observe a lot of the staff's activities. They alone can make an assessment of their administrator's strengths and weaknesses. How does the administrator respond to problems and crises? Does he or she show initiative?

4. *Judges must often ask others about the performance of the administrator.* This includes soliciting input from lawyers, other judges, and other court staff members.

5. *The judge would be well advised to watch for danger signs.* Some people are basically retired in place, "putting in their time." If communication, energy, and new ideas seem to have dwindled or discontinued, there may be problems ahead.

✦ COURT ADMINISTRATION REFORM: A MODEL PROGRAM

Imagine that you are in a crowded main lobby of a courthouse; it is packed, with sweltering heat. Tempers of others are short, lines are long, and people appear frustrated; some are even angry. Many have been waiting several hours simply to pay a traffic-violation fine.

Unknown to you is that behind the wall of the lobby and inside the courtrooms, matters are little better. Cases are dismissed for want of a speedy trial because records are lost; continuances abound for the same reason. The calendar is in a shambles. In the office areas the same condition prevails. Large sums of money frequently disappear; boxes of money orders, checks, and even cash are piled up because no one knows what they are intended to pay or where they go. There are also huge piles of case files in 20 or more locations around the courthouse; dozens of cubic feet of warrants are stacked in boxes in bathrooms and closets because they cannot be matched to case files. The data-entry section is at least 5000 cases behind and getting deeper. There is a large backlog of criminal cases. There are no written procedures; no forms management program; no employee performance reviews. Turnover is 50 percent and absenteeism is rampant. There is no training program. Public relations is a disaster, and complaints to the mayor and city council abound. This court does not work.[88]

Imagine that you return to the same court on a sweltering summer day three years later. Now, inside the lobby there is a cool, white tile floor and ceiling fans, citizens cool off during an average 15-minute wait until being served by well-trained, motivated court staff members (citizens give them a 90 percent favorable rating). An express box now allows many to pay fines without waiting. In the courtrooms, action is fast paced but smooth flowing. The calendar is prompt and accurate; missing files now average less than 1 in 1000. Dismissals due to speedy trial violations are now rare, and continuances are under control. No funds have disappeared from court offices in years, and cash security is tight. All payments are deposited within 24 hours; computer case records are updated within 48 hours. Loose paperwork is no problem, and each section has written procedures, lines of authority, flowcharts, and job standards. Comprehensive training is now provided to employees, who leave at an annual rate of only 4.5 percent and have comparatively little absenteeism. The public, attorneys, and media recently gave the court high marks for efficiency, and complaints to the politicians are nominal. The court now works very well.[89]

How does a total program of court administration turn itself around to such an extent? Some courts and their administrators, such as that in Tucson, Arizona, and administrator Ron Zimmerman, have done so; they have provided useful information for others to follow as a model. First, there must be an atmosphere of trust and confidence between the administration and the judiciary. The presiding judge must delegate authority to the court administrator sufficient to get the job of reform going. In turn, the court administrator must respect the ultimate authority of the presiding judge. Second, the leadership must recognize that the currency of case filing is *the* priority for a high-volume court. All case files acted upon today must be processed (computer update, manual logging, mailing distribution, calendaring) and filed tomorrow.[90]

Third, all judicial administrators and staff must understand the fundamentals of court productivity. First, the clerk/judge ratio is of compelling importance. Zimmerman observed that "it makes no difference how many competent, hardworking judges a court may have if it does not have enough clerks to process the cases arriving daily from the bench." Zimmerman further noted that nine support staff for each full-time judge seems appropriate. The daily productivity of judges must be quantified according to the types of cases handled; then the average time to complete the case must be measured to determine how many hours of clerical time are involved in the actual actions received daily. With this information, the number of clerk positions needed may be calculated. Another factor contributing to court productivity is the ratio of total filings (complaints) per operations clerk. Zimmerman determined that a clerk can be expected to handle no more than 3000 case filings per year. Thus, if each judge is found to handle all work derived from 15,000 complaints, each judge needs 4.66 clerical staff members to handle his or her work output.[91]

Court operations may need to be totally reorganized as well. In Tucson this meant revamping a large, open bay of desks and pandemonium into three operating divisions and a support branch:

◊ Court services (including calendaring, motions, records, and domestic violence)
◊ Public services (counter transactions, mail and insurance, public telephones, and case initiation)
◊ Case management (warrant team, misdemeanor team, traffic team, arraignment team)
◊ Administrative support branch (bonds, restitution, enforcement team, fiscal-audit, and appeals).[92]

Where supervision of court staff had been, to paraphrase Abe Lincoln, "thinner than soup made from the shadow of a starved chicken," more people were elevated to supervisory positions, allowing for greater decentralized decision making.

Following the inception of this structure, Tucson courts reduced their case-processing backlogs from 25,000 to 40,000 cases to zero; the number of dismissals for lack of a speedy trial became statistically insignificant; and judicial backlogs were reduced from several thousand to zero. Furthermore, the average time to service persons at the counter dropped from more than 10 minutes to 2.5 minutes each. The court calendar was also reformatted for easier readability and maintenance. A new case-tracking and management system was installed, including automatic reporting to the state motor vehicle division, automatic surcharge calculation, revenue distribution, and court scheduling.[93]

This changeover and its results required more than four years to accomplish, and the job is still undone. However, many years of failure to plan can require such an elongated effort; the benefits of changing from chaos to excellence are obvious. The message provided by a program of reform is to plan and, perhaps just as important, *simplify*.[94]

Summary

The evolution of judicial administration is not simply the history of the court administrator's office. Conversely, the appointment of the first court administrator did not establish the beginning of judicial administration. Today, the court administrator's functions are something quite different from the "housekeeping chores" seen in its earlier times, involving policymaking as well. Judicial administration possesses a basic body of practical knowledge, a rudimentary theoretical perspective, and a concern for professional ethics.

In evolving, court administration has surpassed the expectations of their earlier supporters, who thought administration would merely carry out judge-made policy. Administrators have created another source of power within the courts. In the view of many, they have allayed earlier fears that they posed a threat to judicial independence.[95]

However, this chapter has shown that several obstacles still exist in the total acceptance of court administration as an integral part of the judiciary. First, some judges are still wary that these new employees will slowly but inevitably transform their courts into a bureaucracy. The extent of actual and potential areas of conflict between judges and administrators were seen as a major source of problems. Rifts can also develop easily between court clerks and administrators.

Although administrators strive to be viewed as doing more than the mere "housekeeping chores" of the court, perhaps, in the short run that will be their best and strongest *raison d'être*. Nonetheless, no one can deny that court administration is a rapidly developing field. While it still has its detractors who feel that the field is merely "surviving," many feel that it has succeeded and has evolved into a full-blown profession.

Questions for Review

1. Explain why the term *judicial administration* is multifaceted. Provide a good working definition for this term.
2. Discuss why judges need, and acquire, others to assist in keeping the courts' processes flowing smoothly. Include in your response a consideration of the socialization of judges and their accountability.
3. How have court clerks traditionally assumed and performed the role of court administrator?

4. Examine why there is still a debate concerning the efficacy of court administrators. Discuss whether, given their history and relationships with judges, they have been completely successful or still have areas that need improvement.

5. What are some common areas of conflict between judges and court administrators? What criteria may judges employ to evaluate the effectiveness of their administrators?

For Further Reading ————————————————

HOWARD ABADINSKY, *Law and Justice: An Introduction to the American Legal System* (2d ed.). Chicago: Nelson-Hall, 1991.

WILLIAM E. HEWITT, GEOFF GALLAS, and BARRY MAHONEY, *Courts That Succeed*. Williamsburg, Va.: National Center for State Courts, 1990.

CHARLES R. SWANSON and SUSETTE M. TALARICO (eds.), *Court Administration: Issues and Responses*. Athens, Ga.: University of Georgia, 1987.

RUSSELL WHEELER, *Judicial Administration: Its Relation to Judicial Independence*. Williamsburg, Va.: National Center for State Courts, 1988.

RUSSELL R. WHEELER and HOWARD R. WHITCOMB, *Judicial Administration: Text and Readings*. Englewood Cliffs, N.J.: Prentice Hall, 1977. This book provides an excellent history of the development of judicial administration.

Notes ————————————————

1. See, for example, Edward B. McConnell, "What Does the Future Hold for Judges?" *Judges Journal* 30 (Summer 1991):11; Russell R. Wheeler and Howard R. Whitcomb, *Judicial Administration: Text and Readings* (Englewood Cliffs, N.J.: Prentice Hall, 1977), p. xiii.; and Edward C. Friesen, Jr., Edward C. Gallas, and Nesta M. Gallas, *Managing the Courts* (Indianapolis, Ind.: Bobbs-Merrill, 1971), p. 13.

2. Robert C. Harrall, "In Defense of Court Managers: The Critics Misconceive Our Role," *Court Management Journal* 14 (1982):52.

3. James Eisenstein and Herbert Jacob, *Felony Justice: An Organizational Analysis of Criminal Courts* (Boston: Little, Brown, 1977).

4. Russell Wheeler, *Judicial Administration: Its Relation to Judicial Independence* (Williamsburg, Va.: National Center for State Courts, 1988), p. 19.

5. Woodrow Wilson, "The Study of Administration," *Political Science Quarterly* 2 (1887):197; reprinted in *Political Science Quarterly* 56 (1941):481.

6. Quoted in Paul Nejelski and Russell Wheeler, *Wingspread Conference on Contemporary and Future Issues in the Field of Court Management* 4 (1980).

7. Russell Wheeler, *Judicial Administration: Its Relation to Judicial Independence*, p. 21.

8. *Ibid.*, p. 22.

9. National Advisory Commission on Criminal Justice Standards and Goals, *Courts* (Washington, D.C.: U.S. Government Printing Office, 1973), p. 171.

10. American Bar Association, *Standards on Court Organization*, Standard 1.41 (1974).

11. Ian R. Scott, "Procedural Law and Judicial Administration," *Justice System Journal* 12 (1987):67–68.

12. Russell R. Wheeler and Howard R. Whitcomb, *Judicial Administration: Text and Readings*, p. 8.

13. *Ibid.*

14. *Ibid.*, p. 9.

15. Quoted in Doug Bandow, "Making Judges Accountable," *USA Today Magazine* (January 1988):55–57.

16. Quoted in Marvin E. Frankel, "Judicial Arrogance and Restraint," in John R. Snortum and Ilana Hader (eds.), *Criminal Justice: Allies and Adversaries* (Pacific Palisades, Calif.: Palisades Publishers, 1978), pp. 109–116.

17. *Ibid.*, p. 111.

18. See, for example, Joel B. Grossman, "Social Backgrounds and Judicial Decision-Making," 79 Harv.L.Rev. 1551 (1966); Walter F. Murphy and Joseph Tanenhaus, *The Study of Public Law* (New York: Random House, 1972), Chapter IV.

19. Robert Carp and Russell Wheeler, "Sink or Swim: The Socialization of a Federal District Judge," *Journal of Public Law* 21 (1972):359–393.

20. *Ibid.*, p. 362–363, 368.

21. *Ibid.*, p. 370 (direct quote from the original).

22. *Ibid.*, p. 372.

23. *Ibid.*

24. *Ibid.*

25. *Ibid.*, p. 373.

26. *Ibid.*, p. 378.

27. *Ibid.*, pp. 382–383.

28. Roscoe Pound, "Principles and Outlines of a Modern Unified Court Organization," *Journal of the American Judicature Society* 23 (April 1940):229.

29. See, for example, the Missouri Constitution, Article V. Sec. 15, paragraph 3.

30. Forest Hanna, "Delineating the Role of the Presiding Judge," *State Court Journal* 10 (Spring 1986):17–22.

31. David W. Neubauer, *America's Courts and the Criminal Justice System* (3d ed.) (Pacific Grove, Calif.: Brooks/Cole, 1988), p. 434.

32. Robert A. Wenke, "The Administrator in the Court," *Court Management Journal* 14 (1982):17–18, 29.

33. Mark W. Cannon, "Innovation in the Administration of Justice, 1969–1981: An Overview," in Philip L. Dubois (ed.), *The Politics of Judicial Reform* (Lexington, Mass.: D.C. Heath, 1982), pp. 35–48.

34. Quoted in Frank Greenberg, "The Task of Judging the Judges," *Judicature* 59 (May 1976):464.

35. *Ibid.*, p. 460 (direct quote from the original).

36. The Center for Judicial Conduct Organizations, *Judicial Conduct Reporter* (Fall 1981):2.

37. Quoted in Frank Greenberg, "The Task of Judging the Judges," p. 460.

38. *In re Greenberg*, 442 Pa. 411; 280 A.2d 370 (1971).

39. See Bradley Canon, "The Impact of Formal Selection Processes on the Characteristics of Judges: Reconsidered," *Law and Society Review* 6 (May 1972):579–594.

40. Kathleen Maguire, Ann L. Pastore, and Timothy J. Flanagan (eds.), *Sourcebook of Criminal Justice Statistics 1992*. U.S. Department of Justice, Bureau of Justice Statistics (Washington, D.C.: U.S. Government Printing Office), 1993, pp. 84, 87–88.

41. Marc Gertz, "Influence in the Court Systems: The Clerk as Interface," *Justice System Journal* 2 (1977):30–37.

42. Robert B. Revere, "The Court Clerk in Early American History," *Court Management Journal* 10 (1978):12–13.

43. *Ibid.*, p. 13.

44. G. Larry Mays and William Taggart, "Court Clerks, Court Administrators, and Judges: Conflict in Managing the Courts," *Journal of Criminal Justice* 14 (1986):1–7.

45. Larry Berkson, "Delay and Congestion in State Systems: An Overview," in Larry Berkson, Steven Hays, and Susan Carbon (eds.), *Managing the State Courts: Text and Readings* (St. Paul, Minn.: West, 1977), p. 164.

46. Ernest C. Friesen and I.R. Scott, *English Criminal Justice* (Birmingham, England: University of Birmingham Institute of Judicial Administration, 1977).

47. Harvey E. Solomon, "The Training of Court Managers," in Charles R. Swanson and Susette M. Talarico (eds.), *Court Administration: Issues and Responses* (Athens, Ga.: University of Georgia, 1987), pp. 15–20.

48. Ernest C. Friesen, "Court Managers: Magnificently Successful or Merely Surviving?" *Court Management Journal* 14 (1982):21.

49. Harvey E. Solomon, "The Training of Court Managers," p. 16.

50. Robert C. Harrall, "In Defense of Court Managers: The Critics Misconceive Our Role," p. 51.

51. David W. Neubauer, *America's Courts and the Criminal Justice System* (3d ed.), p. 435.

52. *Ibid.*

53. Geoffrey A. Mort and Michael D. Hall, "The Trial Court Administrator: Court Executive or Administrative Aide?" *Court Management Journal* 12 (1980):12–16, 30.

54. Bernadine Meyer, "Court Administration: The Newest Profession," *Duquesne Law Review* 10 (Winter 1971):220–235.

55. Geoffrey A. Mort and Michael D. Hall, "The Trial Court Administrator: Court Executive or Administrative Aide?" p. 15.

56. *Ibid.*

57. *Ibid.*, p. 12.

58. Ernest C. Friesen, "Court Managers: Magnificently Successful or Merely Surviving?" p. 20.

59. *Ibid.*, pp. 48–49.

60. *Ibid.*, p. 49.

61. Robert C. Harrall, "In Defense of Court Managers: The Critics Misconceive Our Role," pp. 22, 23, 51.

62. *Ibid.*, p. 52.

63. *Ibid.*

64. *Ibid.*

65. *Ibid.*

66. David W. Neubauer, *America's Courts and the Criminal Justice System* (3d ed.), p. 436.

67. Larry Berkson, "Delay and Congestion in State Systems: An Overview."

68. E. Keith Stott, "The Judicial Executive: Toward Greater Congruence in an Emerging Profession," *Justice System Journal* 7 (1982):152–179.

69. Quoted in R. Dale Lefever, "Judge-Court Manager Relationships: The Integration of Two Cultures," *The Court Manager* 5 (Summer 1990):8–11.

70. *Ibid.*, p. 10.

71. *Ibid.*

72. *Ibid.*, p. 9.

73. G. Larry Mays and William Taggart, "Court Clerks, Court Administrators, and Judges," p. 3.

74. Burton W. Butler, "Presiding Judges' Perceptions of Trial Court Administrators," *Justice System Journal* 3 (1977):181.

75. Geoffrey A. Mort and Michael D. Hall, "The Trial Court Administrator: Court Executive or Administrative Aide?" p. 14.

76. See W. LeBar, "The Modernization of Court Functions: A Review of Court Management and Computer Technology," *Journal of Computers and Law* 5 (1975):97–119; Burton W. Butler, "Presiding Judges' Perceptions of Trial Court Administrators;" J. M. Scheb, "Florida Conference Examines Education of Court Administrators," *Judicature* (1981):465–468; David Saari, *American Court Management: Theories and Practice* (Westport, Conn.: Quorum Books, 1982).

77. G. Larry Mays and William Taggart," Court Clerks, Court Administrators, and Judges," p. 4.

78. *Ibid.*

79. *Ibid.*, p. 5.

80. David Saari, *American Court Management: Theories and Practice*, p. 62.

81. G. Larry Mays and William Taggart, "Court Clerks, Court Administrators, and Judges," p. 6.

82. *Ibid.*

83. For example, Geoffrey A. Mort and Michael D. Hall, "The Trial Court Administrator: Court Executive or Administrative Aide?"

84. G. Larry Mays and William Taggart,"Court Clerks, Court Administrators, and Judges," p. 7.

85. James Duke Cameron, Isaiah M. Zimmerman, and Mary Susan Downing, "The Chief Justice and the Court Administrator: The Evolving Relationship," 113 *Federal Rules Decisions* 443 (1987).

86. John M. Greacen, "Has Your Court Administrator Retired? Without Telling You?" National Association for Court Management, Conference Papers from the Second National Conference on Court Management, *Managing Courts in Changing Times*, Phoenix, Ariz., September 9–14, 1990, pp. 1–20.

87. *Ibid.*, pp. 5–20.

88. Adapted from Ron Zimmerman, "From Chaos to Excellence: Four Tough Years," *State Court Journal* 12 (Summer 1988):13–18.

89. *Ibid.*

90. *Ibid.*, pp. 14–15.

91. *Ibid.*, p. 15.

92. *Ibid.*, pp. 15–16.

93. *Ibid.*, p. 16.

94. *Ibid.*, p. 18.

95. See Burton W. Butler, "Presiding Judges' Perceptions of Trial Court Administrators," p. 181.

Issues and Practices

Justice is such a fine thing that we cannot pay too dearly for it.

—Alain Rene LeSage

There is no such thing as justice—in or out of court.

—Clarence Darrow

✦ INTRODUCTION

Having looked at courts as organizations and explored the roles and functions of their personnel, we next examine their contemporary issues and practices. First, however, we highlight some traits of courts that "succeed," considering why they have been dubbed as thriving and effective in this era of previously discussed courts' burdens.

We have touched on the central issue of case delay; however, we discuss it again in this chapter in more detail, looking at the means by which caseloads are managed, the practical effects of delay, and the potentially exacerbating problems of records and paperwork. Next we address a matter that the courts have had to reckon with probably since their inception but which is becoming more difficult and commonplace: the management of "notorious" cases, followed by a review of the legal basis for, and recent growth in, the use of interpreters in the courtroom.

The rural courts—a forgotten majority in the United States—are then considered. A unique milieu, we will see that the philosophy and methods of the "rurals" are vastly dissimilar from those of their urban counterparts. We then examine some of the courts' "struggles," discussing some additional issues they confront: gender bias, the struggle with the "boom" in complex scientific court-room testimony, and the practical effect of delay. The chapter concludes with a brief discussion of stress on the bench.

✦ COURT INNOVATIONS THAT SUCCEED

✧ PROGRAMS INVOLVING NEW TECHNOLOGY

One of the most exciting occurrences in America's courts presently centers on technology. Rapid advances in computer technology, particularly in available software, have allowed some courts to be more effective, efficient, and customer oriented. For example, some states now have "electronic kiosks" installed in public places and shopping malls. This is an interactive screen that allows citizens to pay traffic fines with their ATM card and obtain information on contesting traffic citations, attending traffic school, or setting court dates. Some electronic kiosks are used to provide citizens information on small-claims court (in the Spanish and English languages). These devices are obviously convenient for consumers, comparatively cheap to operate, and free court clerks to handle more serious problems and inquiries.

Other "successful" applications of computer software are as follows:[1]

◊ The Los Angeles Municipal Court has developed a Traffic Records Imaging System to support traffic citation processing. Approximately 90 percent of all manual tasks involved in handling a traffic citation have been eliminated, resulting in significant savings in labor and improvements in customer service.

◊ A Florida court's Criminal Justice Information System unites courts and criminal justice agencies in six counties with common hardware, software, procedures, and terminology, making transactions between agencies easier and more efficient. Another Florida court developed the Automated Telephone Calendaring System, which diverts hundreds of calls per month from clerks. Attorneys interact directly with the scheduling computer by telephone to schedule hearings.

◊ In Oregon trial courts, the Financial Information and Accounting System tracks all financial transactions of a case statewide; it segregates trust and revenue accounts and integrates financial and case management.

◊ Ventura County, California, Municipal Court's Information System and Automated Citation Device is an interactive case record, tracking, and management system with special features, including automatic lookup of driver histories at the motor vehicles office. The citation device provided California Highway Patrol officers with hand-held computers to issue and file citations electronically.

◊ The Arkansas Supreme Court uses CaseBase, a CD-ROM legal research database for access to state court cases and statutes on computer disk; it saves time and increases the effectiveness of legal research in the appellate courts.

✧ OTHER NOTABLE PROGRAMS

Additional court programs warrant mention. One innovative program was begun when a justice of the Massachusetts Superior Court (a part of the trial court system) observed:

> I had become accustomed to scanning the courtroom in the midst of a particularly gruesome piece of testimony, only to discover, to my horror, a child (or several) seated in the courtroom, nestled into the corner of its mother's arm, listening in rapt attention as a trembling, weeping victim described the excruciating details of a rape or a beating, or both. "Why is this child here?" I would ask myself with annoyance, "And what on earth can she be thinking of all of this?"[2]

As a result, over the course of four years of planning, pleading for money, and convincing skeptics it was needed and would work, Massachusetts' trial courts developed a child care center for court employees and members of the public bringing children to court; CourtCare now serves more than a thousand families each year.

The National Center for State Courts also performed a feasibility study of facsimile transmission of court documents, surveying all 50 states to determine what benefits, if any, could be derived. Fax machines have indeed been a welcomed addition to the courts, especially the smaller courts, for use in transmitting all kinds of court documents, pleadings, search and arrest warrants, orders, and correspondence. Although the courts present a special circumstance where the use of facsimile is concerned and some basic issues have to be addressed, it has proved to be used effectively by judges, lawyers, clerks, and staff.[3]

Courts have many other innovative programs, such as those dealing with alternative dispute resolution (examined in Chapter 7) and domestic violence; a number of pilot programs are experimenting with ways to reduce case delay.

✧ COURT PERFORMANCE STANDARDS

Another innovative project has been undertaken nationally by the National Center for State Courts. The center, in conjunction with the U.S. Department of Justice, set out in 1987 to develop a set of standards that would define effective court performance. The purpose was to focus not on the structures and machinery of the courts, but on their performance (what courts actually accomplish with the means at their disposal).[4]

There are 22 standards in five broad areas: access to justice; expedition and timeliness; equality, fairness, and integrity; independence and accountability; and public trust and confidence. The standards provide guiding principles, not rigid rules. These standards are also different in that they also have a set of measures and methods of data collection that accompany them. The standards—endorsed by all of the major judicial organizations in the country—are now being field tested in 12 courts across the nation.

✦ CONTRIBUTING ELEMENTS OF COURT ORGANIZATION

An underdeveloped area of inquiry in the courts is the effect of a court's organization on its efficacy. A federally funded study by the National Center for State Courts profiled six courts that succeeded, finding that these courts held ten elements in common—a "synergistic relationship": leadership, goals, judicial responsibility and commitment, case-flow management procedures, administrative staff involvement, mechanisms for accountability, communications, backlog reduction/inventory control, staff education, and staff training.[5] Figure 9.1 depicts the interrelationships among these elements.

With regard to *leadership*, a court may have several levels of effective leadership, such as the supreme court, the state's administrative judges, and a presiding judge. And where they exist, the court administrators and clerks provide additional leadership. *Goals* come into play at several points in court functions, but perhaps one of the most important goals is that of disposition time goals for reducing court delay. In a related vein, *case-flow management procedures* are

Figure 9.1 Common elements of successful courts: A synergistic relationship. (*Source:* William E. Hewitt, Geoff Gallas, and Barry Mahoney, *Courts That Succeed: Six Profiles of Successful Courts* (Williamsburg, Va.: National Center for State Courts, 1990). p. viii. Used with permission.)

important, and can include and revolve around early discovery, a full-time discovery judge, firm trial dates, and a policy against granting continuances. *Management information* entails a court's possessing an information system that provides accurate and complete case-flow management information; this system is an integral part of the court's overall function. Judges and staff in these exemplary court systems used computers to *communicate* with each other. Judges can identify who is available for trial and make themselves available for trials by leaving messages on the computer. Staff also communicated via computer mail.

Another essential aspect of the exemplary courts was *judicial responsibility and commitment*; judges must be committed to maintaining an atmosphere of dignity and making cases flow through the court efficiently. Also, rules of procedure, discovery, and pretrial conferences must be revised often. To keep the cases flowing smoothly, *administrative staff* are engaged in monitoring motions, cases going to a pretrial conference, and cases that get assigned to judges; compiling discovery schedules and handling discovery orders; and obtaining estimates on the length of future jury trials. A large proportion of employees in these six exemplary courts have received *education and training* in case management; the judges in some courts also attend yearly training courses. *Mechanisms for accountability* are found in the successful court's case management system, affecting their ability to meet scheduled dates. Judges feel accountable to themselves and the public. The court and its administrative judge may even be supervised by a member of the state's supreme court having administrative responsibility for the region. Reports are submitted to the state with frequency (e.g., monthly). Meanwhile, the successful court pays attention to *current issues and concerns*. It recognizes problems that exist, and gaps that must be closed. In sum, the successful court is aware of concerns that must be addressed soon.

✦ THE DILEMMA OF DELAY

The principle that "justice delayed is justice denied" says much about the longstanding goal of processing court cases with due dispatch. Charles Dickens condemned the practice of slow litigation in nineteenth-century England, and Shakespeare mentioned "the law's delay" in *Hamlet*. More recently, delay in processing cases remains one of the most visible problems of America's courts. The public often hears of cases that have languished on court dockets for years. Public commissions have criticized the effect of delay on justice, especially as it negates much of the deterrent effect desired of punishment.

Over half of all persons polled rated the efficiency of the courts as a "serious" or "very serious" social problem. Two specific findings from this survey underscored the public's dissatisfaction with court efficiency. First, persons with direct court experience were more likely to rate their inefficiency as a problem than were those with no experience. Second, the general public was more likely to perceive delay as a major problem than were judges and lawyers.[6]

Case backlog and trial delay affect many of our country's courts. The magnitude of the backlog and the length of the delay vary greatly, however, depending on the court involved. This was the conclusion of a comprehensive survey by the National Center for State Courts, which found that the typical criminal case in Detroit, Portland, and Phoenix reached disposition rather rapidly—within about two months. But in other courts, the processing time was much more extensive. In Newark the median disposition time was over eight months.[7]

It is best to view delay not as a problem but as a symptom of a problem.[8] Generally, the term *delay* suggests abnormal or unacceptable time lapses in the processing of cases. Yet some time is needed to prepare a case. What is a concern is *unnecessary* delay. The total time that a case is on the court's docket may consist of an acceptable or normal amount of time as well as an unacceptable or abnormal amount of time. Therefore, according to David Neubauer, it is better to employ a neutral term, such as *case-processing time.*[9] Neubauer also observed that our present difficulties in defining what delay is help explain why there is no consensus about how long is *too* long. Past commissions have provided yardsticks ranging from six months to two years;[10] most recently, a special committee of the Conference of State Court Administrators proposed a maximum of 180 days from arrest to trial in felony cases and 90 days in misdemeanors.[11]

An important question is which time periods to measure. The Law Enforcement Assistance Administration's criteria divided total case processing time into three segments: lower court time, upper court time, and sentencing time. Courts do not control all case processing time. For example, time spent by probation departments in preparing presentence investigations is seldom controllable by the courts. Furthermore, if the lower courts are slow in processing their cases, trial courts can do little to speed up these dispositions.

A companion question is how to measure case processing time. Statistical averages or means or commonly used; however, they are often inappropriate because a handful of unusually long cases can skew the estimates. A better measure is the median: half of the cases took more time and half took less than the median amount of time. Even medians, though, provide a limited picture of what is often a complicated matter.[12]

✦ CONSEQUENCES OF DELAY AND POSSIBLE SOLUTIONS

The costs of consequences of delay can be severe. Not only can the values and guarantees of the justice system be jeopardized, but there are also costs to the defendant, society, the citizen, and to system resources. The defendant suffers from delay because his or her Sixth Amendment rights to a speedy trial are compromised. Defendants may languish in jail for an inordinate amount of time before their case is adjudicated. They also have an interest in moving the case to trial because their witnesses may move or die, or their memories may fade. It has also been suggested that lengthy pretrial incarceration pressures a defendant into pleading guilty.[13]

Society needs a speedy trial because it needs speedy convictions. Delay can also strengthen a defendant's bargaining position; prosecutors are more apt to accept a plea of guilty when their dockets are crowded and cases are growing stale. And, when delay occurs for defendants out on bond, the public is concerned about additional criminal activity. General public confidence is eroded through delay; the swiftness of punishment is undermined, and victims and witnesses must make futile trips to the courthouse. Finally, pretrial detainees clog the jails, police officers must appear in court on numerous occasions, and attorneys expend unproductive time appearing on the same case.[14]

One of the problems with managing court delay is that there is little incentive to attempt to process cases speedily. The U.S. Supreme Court has refused to give the rather vague concept of a "speedy trial" any precise time frame.[15] Similarly, while speedy trial statutes exist in all 50 states and 35 states provide for a speedy trial in their constitutions, the latter provisions apply only when the delay has been "extensive." The best known piece of legislation addressing speedy trials is the Speedy Trial Act of 1974, enacted by Congress and amended in 1979, which provides firm time limits. Thirty days is allowed from the point of arrest to indictment, and 70 days may pass from indictment to trial. Thus federal prosecutors have a total of 100 days to bring the time of arrest until trial.

The problem with time frames, however, is twofold: first, some cases that are more complex will legitimately take longer to prepare; second, these time limits may be waived. A prosecutor cannot be expected to bring a case to the courtroom when the court's own docket is so crowded that bringing the matter to trial was a physical and scheduling impossibility. In sum, there is no legally binding mechanism that works.

This is obviously a complex problem; we have merely scratched the surface. However, the problem becomes more severe when one considers that in at least 10 states, if one's right to a speedy trial is denied, the case must be dismissed and the defendant released. Other states permit dismissal but allow reprosecution. The latter approach can undermine the effectiveness of speedy trial provisions by subjecting defendants to a series of reprosecutions.[16]

Thus, overall, speedy trial laws have had only a limited impact in speeding up the flow of cases through the criminal courts.[17] Unfortunately, as Neubauer noted, "state laws have failed to provide the courts with adequate and effective enforcement mechanisms."[18]

In addition to some internal methods that can be employed by administrators to streamline case flow (discussed below), over the years a number of proposals have emerged to help alleviate the courts' logjam, ranging from judicial jury selection and limits on criminal appeals, to six-person juries. The latter was actually suggested more than two decades ago as a means of relieving congestion of court calendars and reducing court costs for jurors.[19] Thirty-three states have specifically authorized juries of fewer than 12, but most allow smaller juries only in misdemeanor cases. In federal courts, defendants are entitled to a 12-person jury unless the parties agree in writing to a small jury.[20]

✦ CASE SCHEDULING

Waiting is a courthouse activity that everyone finds repugnant but almost everyone engages in; many people must come together in order to "pull off" a trial, and waiting for a defense attorney or prosecutor, a vital witness, the court reporter, the judge, or some other party is almost standard procedure. Many of these people have cases in other courtrooms that last longer than anticipated, or they must appear in several courts on a single day. The court administrator learns early in his or her career that the courts are extremely complex institutions from the standpoint of scheduling.

The problem of scheduling people for trials is exacerbated by other forces outside the administrator's control: slow or inaccurate mail delivery, notices of court appearances arriving on the day after the scheduled hearing, an illegible address preventing a key witness or defendant from ever being contacted about a hearing or trial, a jailer's inadvertent failure to include a defendant on a list for transportation. If just one key person is late, all others must wait. If one of the key players fails to appear altogether, the entire matter must be rescheduled. To compound matters, judges have limited ability to control other agencies; the court is therefore often unable to control the actions of personnel from law enforcement, probation, or court reporter's offices. And in fairness to them, the latter agencies have scheduling problems of their own.[21]

A major study of the courts found that most of the best-run federal courts hold regular meetings of top officials of the various organizations to iron out administrative problems. In less well-run courts, the study found that agency heads were critical of operating procedures of the others for causing delay and inconvenience. However, they never did meet to work out a coordinated plan.[22]

A key part of court administration is the ability to set a certain date for trial. One study found that courts with low backlogs and little delay were those that set a date for trial early in the history of a case.[23] Lawyers knew they had to be prepared by that date. If the judge sets a date that is uncertain, and if lawyers know that court dates are fluid and easily continued, they do not prepare.

There are two primary methods by which cases are scheduled by the courts: the individual and master calendars.

✧ INDIVIDUAL CALENDAR SYSTEM

The simplest procedure for scheduling cases is the individual calendar. A case is assigned to a single judge, who must see all aspects of it through: arraignment, pretrial motions, and trial. The primary advantage is continuity; all parties to the case know that a single judge is responsible for its conclusion. There are other important advantages as well. Judge shopping is minimal, and administrative responsibility for each case is fixed. Also, it is easier to pinpoint delays, because one can easily compare judges' dockets to determine where cases are moving along and where they are not.

Under this system, however, there are often major differences in "case stacking," because some judges are fast, others are slow. Also, if a judge draws a difficult case, others must wait. Because most cases will be pleaded, however, case stacking is not normally a major problem unless a judge schedules too many cases for adjudication on a given day. Conversely, if a judge is too conservative and stacks too few cases for hearing or adjudication each day, delay will also result. If all cases settle, the judge has dead time, with a large backlog and nothing to do all day.

✦ MASTER CALENDAR SYSTEM

The master calendar is a more recent development. Here judges specialize (usually on a rotating basis) on given stages of a case: preliminary hearings, arraignments, motions, bargaining, and trials. A judge is assigned a case from a central or master pool; once he or she has completed that phase of it, the case is returned to the pool. The primary advantage with this system is that judges who are good in one particular aspect of litigation (such as preliminary hearings) can be assigned to the job they do best. The disadvantage is that it is more difficult to pinpoint the location of or responsibility for delays. Judges also have less incentive to keep their docket current because when they dispose of one case, another appears. Also, the distribution of work can be quite uneven. If, for example, three judges are responsible for preliminary hearings and one is much slower than the others, an unequal shifting of the workload will ensue; in other words, the two harder-working judges will be penalized by having to work more cases.

✦ WHICH SYSTEM IS BEST?

A running debate has developed over which of the calendaring systems described above is best. One can see from the foregoing descriptions that each has advantages and disadvantages. The answer to which is best probably depends on the nature of the court. Small courts, such as the U.S. district courts, use the individual calendar system more successfully. But due largely to their complex dockets, metropolitan and state courts almost uniformly use the master calendar system. Research also indicates that courts using the master calendar experience the greatest difficulty. Typical problems include the following: (1) some judges refuse to take their fair share of cases; (2) the administrative burden on the chief judge is often great; and (3) as a result of the above, a significant backlog of cases may develop. In those courts where the master calendar system was discontinued in favor of the individual system, major reductions in delay were realized.[24]

✦ MANAGING NOTORIOUS CASES

✧ A HISTORICAL PHENOMENON

"Murder and mystery, society, sex and suspense were combined in this case in such a manner as to intrigue and captivate the public fancy to a degree perhaps unparalleled in recent annals. Throughout...the nine-week trial, circulation-conscious editors catered to the insatiable interest of the American public in the bizarre. In this atmosphere of a `Roman Holiday' for the news media, Sam Sheppard stood trial for his life." Thus stated the U.S. Supreme Court in *Sheppard v. Maxwell,*[25] 1966.

The existence of notorious cases has always been a part of, and caused problems in the courtrooms. The Salem witch trials, the trial of Aaron Burr, the Scopes trial, the Lindbergh kidnapping trial, the Sacco and Vanzetti trials, and those involving the Chicago 7, the Manson "family," and Alger Hiss point up the historical nature of trials that remain in our collective memories long after their conclusion. More recently, the trials of Mike Tyson, William Kennedy Smith, Oliver North, Marion Barry, Bernhard Goetz, Imelda Marcos, John Gotti, Manuel Noriega, and the police officers who were tried for assaulting Rodney King were clearly "notorious." Some trials, like those of Amy Fisher, gained nationwide notoriety through media depictions even after the actual trial was ended. In addition to the national and local news and the print media, such television programs as "Current Affair" and "Inside Edition" bring details of such cases into our homes as well. (As this book goes to press, O.J. Simpson has pled not guilty to charges of brutally murdering his ex-wife, Nicole, and her friend, Ronald Goldman. This case, of course, could become one of the most notorious cases of this generation.)

How do the courts handle such celebrated cases? Must the courts behave differently in the process and make adjustments for these cases, or is it important to maintain a "business as usual" mien? If adjustments are necessary, what is the role of court administrators in this arena? And are other cases on the courts' calendar heard concurrently or delayed indefinitely? These important questions are addressed below.

✧ ADMINISTRATIVE PROBLEMS

The first problem in handling a notorious case is that of selecting the judge; this decision will ultimately determine the ease and efficiency with which the case will be handled. In these cases it is particularly important that the judge be experienced and have good legal skills, possess a good reputation in the legal community, be temperate and in command in the courtroom, and be seen as fair and unbiased. He or she should also possess good health and the ability to deal with the media. In short, notorious-case trial judges should be individually handpicked by presiding judges for this assignment, and only after the judges' concurrence; random selection is dangerous. A workable alternative is to develop a small pool of judges who have the above qualifications, from which the trial judge is selected; this method avoids some of the criticism that may be leveled against individual selection, that a certain judge was handpicked.[26]

In addition to the trial judge, court administrators and other court staff members will also find notorious cases demanding. They must devote considerable thought and planning efforts to these cases, with the goal of all being to maintain an air of normal operations. They must anticipate all possible problems and concerns that might arise, including media requests; courtroom and courthouse logistics for handling crowds, the media, and security; managing the jury; and managing the court's docket of other existing cases. The judge must take firm control, communicating to staff the court's policies and procedures as they relate to each of these issues. In short, the judge must control not only the trial, but also the immediate environmental surroundings in which it will be conducted. Staff must be kept apprised of the status of the case, then allowed to do their jobs without close supervision.

A notorious trial may require that a larger courtroom be used in order that larger than usual numbers of people from the press and the public, as well as defendants and attorneys, may be accommodated. If so, planning is essential for providing adequate space for judge's chambers, jury rooms, witness rooms, clerk's office, security personnel, parking, and lunchroom facilities.[27] In all such cases, the care, comfort, and safety of the prospective and actual jurors must be provided for. Jurors in these cases also typically want to be kept informed of all case details relating to their task and time frames relating to the proceedings. Another major decision by the judge is whether the jury needs to be sequestered; if it is, and the sequestration may last for a considerable length of time, there are a number of logistical matters involving security (such as outside interference, conjugal visits, room searches, and transportation) and personal needs (meals, entertainment, medical supplies) that will fall to the court administrator and staff.[28] Another issue, of course, is the cost for these arrangements and amenities.

The adequate number of security personnel must also be determined (an especially critical decision in drug-trafficking or organized crime cases, when defendants may become disruptive or the environment dangerous). Will identification and press passes be needed? Are entry screening devices necessary? What seating arrangements will the case require? Should court observers be allowed to exit and reenter at will? Do purses, briefcases, and other such items need to be searched by hand? Is it necessary that all mail and telephone calls coming to the courthouse be monitored? Is a special command center desirable for coordination and communication?[29]

In addition to potential problems from the outside, the impact of a notorious case on people within the system—court staff—also cannot be underestimated. One California court administrator's office was used by Cary Grant during his divorce case. The administrator's office was overwhelmed for weeks by staff visitors wanting to see "the chair that Cary Grant sat in."

Administrative problems can also arise when a change of venue is ordered. Although motions for changes of venues are rarely granted today, some cases definitely should not be tried in their original venue because of a poisoned atmosphere and the extreme difficulty or impossibility of sitting an unbiased jury. Some states, like California, provide that when a change of venue has been ordered, the case will be tried in the court receiving the case by a judge from the court in which the case originated. Reimbursement of expenses incurred at the new site can become an issue and may therefore add an additional burden for the court administrator.

The judge and court administrator should attempt to follow normal case-flow-management principles with notorious cases, continuously managing the time and events that take place. The judge should insist on timely preparation by attorneys, adhere to dates set for court processes, and avoid granting continuances unless absolutely necessary. Regardless of whether the court uses a master calendar assignment system or the individual case assignment system, there will be filings of new cases and other calendars while the notorious case is pending. Judges seldom have the luxury of dropping all other court business to hear a high-profile case. The consensus of judicial personnel, as determined in a survey by Timothy Murphy, Genevra Loveland, and Thomas Munsterman, is that once a notorious case begins, the active trial and motion responsibilities of the trial judge should be transferred to another judge(s). The judge presiding over a notorious judge must avoid distractions and disruptions, taking care not to overlook any of the several important matters that accompany such a trial. Other matters should be transferred to other judges or deferred until the notorious case is completed.[30]

Perhaps the most important task in managing notorious cases and avoiding and resolving problems is communication with the media. Some judges have established an open-door policy in dealing with the media, setting aside a certain time when reporters may discuss the case. This method will go a long way toward ensuring that the media are receiving accurate information rather than their having to rely on rumor and other sources of inaccurate information. The judge may designate a liaison with the media, but it is important that the media understand that the person in the liaison represents the court and is not a reporter on behalf of the media, reporting everything within his or her sight and hearing.[31]

✧ CHANGES WROUGHT BY NOTORIOUS CASES

Changes in the courts, and indeed the entire legal system, often stem from notorious cases. The acquittal of John Hinckley in the early 1980s for shooting President Reagan led to major curbs in the insanity defense. More recently, even before the King trial, the American Bar Association began overhauling its national standards for criminal cases. Judges will be urged to instruct jurors as many as three times. Nine states have taken steps to translate arcane legal instructions into plain English. And the Simi Valley, California, "King I" jury's acquittal of the officers involved could prove to be another watershed, leading to changes in the way juries do their job. West Coast judges are delaying or moving cases involving bias charges. A Florida court recently shifted a Miami police brutality case to Orlando. California and New Jersey legislators introduced proposals to ensure that racially tinged cases that must be moved at least go to sites with similar ethnic populations. Other reformers argue that juries would also be more representative if judges cracked down on those who shirk trial duty—more than half of those summoned in some courts.[32]

Jury watchers are profiting from sophisticated analyses by marketing their services to trial lawyers who handle notorious cases. More than 200 trial lawyers now belong to the American Society of Trial Consultants. In Miami, William Kennedy Smith paid $200,000 for consulting aid to help pick the jury that eventually acquitted him of rape. Research indicates that juries in such cases are far from being wild and unpredictable; overall, they make reasonable and rational decisions.[33]

✦ INTERPRETERS IN THE COURTROOM

✦ THE LEGAL BASIS

The Sixth Amendment allows criminal defendants to confront witnesses who testify against them. Furthermore, the Fifth and Fourteenth Amendments guarantee due process—the right not to be deprived of life, liberty, or property without due process of law—"fundamental fairness." A relatively recent development has changed the nature and complexity of court proceedings and required additional responsibilities of court administrators. Since the late 1960s there has been a veritable explosion in the use of foreign-language interpreting in America's courtrooms. However, one major event engendered the current trend toward greater use of interpreters in the courts: passage of Public Law 95-539, the federal Court Interpreters Act of 1978. This was the first federal statute granting the accused the right to a court interpreter. The act provides for court-appointed interpreter services:

> In any criminal or civil action initiated by the United States in a United States District Court...if the presiding judicial officer determines on such officer's own motion or on the motion of a party that such party...(1) speaks only or primarily a language other than the English language; or (2) suffers from a hearing impairment...so as to inhibit such party's comprehension of the proceedings or communication with counsel or the presiding judicial officer, or...such witness' comprehension of questions and the presentation of such testimony.

Note that the guarantee covers civil as well as criminal matters, and that the judge determines whether a given defendant or witness is in need of an interpreter's services.

Although specifically applicable to federal courts, this legislation has served to stimulate measures in state and municipal courts as well. Many states provide for courtroom interpreters by administrative or judicial regulations or by statute. Courts of lower jurisdiction are increasingly assigning foreign-language interpreters to non-English-speaking or hearing-impaired defendants, witnesses, and litigants.[34]

✧ THE COURT ADMINISTRATOR'S ROLE

The need for interpreting arises in a multitude of languages, ranging from the commonplace such as Spanish (in 96.6 percent of all interpreter appearances), Italian, and German, to the "exotic" languages, such as the languages of Asia, Africa, and the Middle East. Court interpreters are commonly found on duty at criminal trials for initial appearances, bail hearings, preliminary hearings, pretrial and in-trial motions, pleas and changes of plea, sentencing, trials, and probation department recommendation. For the most part, interpreting services at the state level are reserved for criminal actions, not civil; however, some experts feel strongly that such services are more sorely needed at the civil level because it is there that persons most often tell their version of an incident directly to a judge.[35] At trial, court interpreters must be sworn in, swearing an oath that they will interpret to the best of their ability, and as accurately as possible, the proceeding at hand. They may be required to be sworn several times a day. They are quickly called to the attention of others in the courtroom during jury selection, with the judge formally introducing the lawyers and the interpreter to the pool of jury candidates.[36]

Interpreting is a highly complicated process, involving much more than a "machine" to convert the English speech of attorneys, judges, and witnesses. The interpretation of that speech is in no way perfect, and at worst, it can become a gross distortion of what has been said. For this reason, at the federal level court interpreters must be certified by a court administrator, the director of the Administrative Office of the U.S. Courts. In addition to being responsible for a certification program for interpreters, the director is responsible for ensuring that every district court maintains a list of certified interpreters in its district and determines the fee rate for interpreting services. The test is quite rigorous; in 1986 only 4 percent of those taking the exam passed it in its entirety.[37]

✧ APPEALS DUE TO ERROR

Appeals based on errors in interpreting or translating have increased dramatically in recent years. This trend became particularly evident beginning in 1977, prior to the enactment of the Court Interpreters Act one year later.[38] Judges generally uphold the rulings of lower courts, rejecting claims by defendants that their trial was unfairly conducted. Because foreign-language testimony is not entered into the court record, there is no way that alleged errors of interpretation can be directly verified or discounted on appeal.[39]

Several appeals have been successful, however, primarily when it was shown that interpreters were unqualified (as in *People v. Starling*, 1974).[40] In *People v. Medrano*,[41] where the defendant's wife served as his interpreter at a change of plea hearing, the issue on appeal was whether or not Medrano had "knowingly, voluntarily, and intelligently" waived his right to trial by jury by pleading guilty. The appellate court held that Medrano's wife should not have been used as an interpreter since there was no assurance that her interpretation was accurate or that her husband had knowingly and intelligently given up his constitutional rights.

State v. Mitjans[42] was a Minnesota case where a police officer began interpreting for the defendant but did not swear an oath stating that he would interpret accurately (as required by Minnesota statute). The appellate court, using language that should be heeded by all police administrators and policymakers, held that "Interpreters should be neutral and objective if at all possible. [The interpreting officer] had a built-in conflict of interest. He and the others had actively focused on appellant as a serious suspect in a murder and felony assault and were working to gather evidence against appellant. The police at that point should have invested time and work in attempting to find someone outside the department to translate."

✦ RURAL COURTS: THE FORGOTTEN MAJORITY

✧ A WORLD APART FROM URBAN COUNTERPARTS

The American legal system is grounded in county government, and the heritage of our culture is largely fashioned from the values and lore of rural life. There are approximately 2450 general jurisdiction and 14,100 limited jurisdiction courts in this country;[43] nearly four-fifths of these courts exist in rural counties. A *rural court* is any trial court of general jurisdiction having fewer than two full-time judges authorized.[44] The difference between what is meant by *court administration* in urban courts and rural courts, and the nature of duties and management philosophies encompassed in that term, is enormous.

There are approximately 2500 rural courts in America, about 80 percent of all trial courts. About 46 million people live in jurisdictions served by rural courts. The small scale of rural courts has two implications for court management. First, there are a small number of people in the community, and an even smaller number of people involved in the legal system. Second, rural areas have few resources available with which to conduct the business of the court. Another major difference is with the type of person seeking a career in court administration. While urban courts pay higher salaries to obtain specially trained and educated court administrators (who tend to be upwardly mobile), a rural court clerk is often a former police officer, typically grew up in his or her community and intends to remain in the community forever.[45]

Kathryn Fahnestock and Maurice Geiger spent more than two years interviewing rural court clerks in 25 counties across the United States. They learned that the rural court is best exemplified by a special type of comity—courtesy among court actors. To earn a living, a small number of attorneys must deal with each other year after year, so accommodation becomes a way of life. Continuances are stipulated and defendants go untried until the lawyers are paid.

Judges find probable cause in cases where no probable cause is apparent. The prosecutor overcharges to make the defense attorney look good when charges are reduced. Police make arrests rather than offend an "upstanding" citizen complainant. Defendants from "nice" families may have their cases set before a more lenient judge. Prosecutors often proceed with inappropriate cases rather than offend police officials on whom they must rely. The judge, who once practiced or prosecuted in the community, avoids challenging the prosecution because he or she needs the prosecutor's cooperation in order to dispose of cases. The clerk, highly visible and known by practically everyone in town, is the intermediary and does all that is possible to ensure that everyone is happy.[46]

In rural courts, clerks must attend to both administrative and record-keeping duties. Although the essence of court administration in urban courts is calendar control, in rural courts the clerks, while ultimately accountable for that process, actually have little power to control the calendar. In most rural courts, lawyers actually review the proposed calendar before it is final. The prevailing view is that "People are more important than procedures." Rural courts find other facets of their role challenging as well, such as the custody and transportation of prisoners. If the county cannot or will not provide detention facilities, the clerk must persuade enforcement or correctional officers to transport the prisoner to and from court. Rural probation officers often cover several courts and several hundred miles; presentence investigations therefore often require extensive time and travel. Similarly, a single court reporter may be responsible for courtroom work in a large area. No local crime laboratory exists. Expert witnesses must often be brought in from outside. And the trial judge may be available only a few days each month. Because resources are so scarce or distant, thrift is a widely held value; funds are guarded zealously.

✦ MORE THAN A "JOB AT THE COURTHOUSE"

To rural court clerks, occupying the position in these environs is more than "having a job at the courthouse" or "managing the court." They possess significant community memories, insights, and knowledge; they are keepers of tradition and maintain important office rituals of the generations past. In their care are the land grants of the town ancestors, the naturalization records of the people who broke the sod, and the records of births, deaths, marriages and divorces of the community. It is a position of importance in the community, and the clerks as well as the other court actors are very "community rooted." The town troublemaker is assumed guilty. Bail is often used punitively or protectively. The largest percentage of criminals may be people writing bad checks to local merchants. Destruction-of-property offenses are common, but prosecution of white-collar crimes, environmental violations, or abuse of law-enforcement authority is virtually nonexistent. The application of community values is frequently illustrated. A farmer may be released on his own recognizance because "a man with cows won't go anywhere," while his co-defendant who owns no cows may be required to post bail.[47]

Fahnestock and Geiger determined that most (60 percent) of rural court clerks feel that they do not get enough attention from the state court administrative office. These clerks see their big-city counterparts as "getting it all" and able to spend more time lobbying for money, writing grants, and engaging in public-relations activities. Management information reports are viewed by nearly all rural clerks (95 percent) as of *no* use in managing their courts (thus one wonders about the accuracy of statistical information rural clerks provide to the state, and, consequently, the validity of statewide court information that state offices generate).

Notwithstanding their administrative flaws and not being as "modern" as some people would like them to be, to others the rural clerks provide their greatest service in maintaining the history and tradition of their cities and counties. They eschew being transformed into technocrats, instead clutching to methods similar to those practiced centuries ago and values that have largely vanished in urban areas. They would agree with the words of Wendell Berry: "[F]or better or worse I like this place. The world's curse is a man Who'd rather be someplace else."[4])

✦ COURTS' STRUGGLES

Massive caseloads; delays; notorious cases; administrative and personnel matters; politics; public relations—these and other problems discussed above and in other chapters exist to some degree within the court system. Unfortunately, the list has not been exhausted. We examine in this section three additional concerns: accusations of gender bias, the use of complex scientific testimony, and the practical effect of court delay.

Are the courts in trouble? Has society and our entire legal system thrust them into a quagmire? We attempt to determine the answers to those questions after examining these additional issues that are now pressing the courts.

✦ GENDER BIAS

What is gender bias in the courts? It has been described as "a problem with several aspects."[49] The term includes society's perception of the relative worth of women and men, what is perceived as women's and men's work, and myths and misconceptions about the economic and social realities of women's and men's lives."[50]

More specifically, gender bias in the courts can take the following forms:

1. In juvenile law, the American Bar Association has found that although the "crimes" that females are accused of are categorized as less serious and harmful to society than those of males, girls are often held in detention for longer periods and are less likely to be placed in community programs than are boys.[51]

2. Early studies noted the casual response of the legal profession and the judiciary to the plight of battered women. Some researchers interpreted this finding as evidence of faint echoes of the common-law view of a wife as her husband's property, lingering in the minds of some judges and attorneys.

3. There is extensive literature created by the antirape movement showing that judicial myths regarding the nature of male and female sexuality and attitudes toward the "proper" roles of women served to punish rape victims by defining rape and spousal abuse as "victim-precipitated" crimes.

4. The looming "disaster" in family law that most disturbs those interested in equal justice is the underclass of women and children being created through inadequate child support and alimony awards. Social scientists studying the consequences of no-fault divorce in California uncovered the unwitting contribution that courts were making to the "feminization of poverty."[52]

In courtrooms across the country, women still find themselves judged on the basis of factors that trial researchers and feminists consider antiquated and prejudicial. Bias and stereotyped images, they say, influence jury selection, the treatment of female witnesses, and attitudes toward women attorneys and judges. The New York Task Force on Women in the Courts in 1986 termed gender bias "pervasive" because of the tendency of some judges and attorneys to accord less credibility to the claims and testimony of women. These findings were nearly identical to those of a New Jersey study in 1983. These and other studies consistently turn up stereotypes that women jurors are more likely than male jurors to acquit in criminal cases (except in cases involving a child or threat to family); female jurors are less likely to favor female defendants or plaintiffs; and in civil cases, female jurors are more likely than males to vote in favor of the plaintiff, but vote for smaller awards than men do.[53]

The need to educate judges about the findings of researchers and the concerns of women lawyers was first articulated in 1969 by Sylvia Roberts, a pioneer Title VII litigator from Louisiana. Still, progress has been slow in coming. A visit to a law library in 1980 yielded only one article on the subject of gender bias in the mainstream legal and judicial literature. By 1989, however, there were dozens of articles on the topic. Also, courses and workshops are now included in numerous judicial education programs for state and federal court judges. Special task forces across the country are investigating the problem as well.[54] In fact, as of 1990 some 27 task forces had taken on the task of documenting incidents of gender bias in the courts.[55]

Roberts said women should adopt the Taoist philosophy of the Chinese ancients and "think of ourselves as water on stone."[56] Although the stone is hard and the water is merely splashing around it, the stone eventually wears away and the landscape is transformed. They will continue to act as water on stone; perhaps through their consistent efforts the stone will eventually give way.

✧ THE STRUGGLE WITH SCIENTIFIC TESTIMONY

Another problem facing courts today is that of complex testimony rendered by experts who speak in esoteric language and often disagree with each other in their findings. "Exhibit C" in today's courtroom might be a brain scan from a neuroscientist's laboratory instead of a murder weapon. The demand for expert testimony has tripled in the past decade; scientists now make approximately 400,000 appearances per year to give depositions, attend briefings, and testify in court. Scientific evidence is used in nearly 30 percent of all court cases, and outcomes now often turn on the ability of judges and jurors with little or no scientific background to comprehend the complexities of such specialized subjects as physics, toxicology, and organic chemistry.[57]

Many persons now question whether courts and juries can properly digest the material and produce accurate decisions. Scientists shudder when a rapist is released by a jury despite a 99 percent probability that semen in evidence was the defendant's; they recoil when a judge fails to understand that animal studies can have strong implications for human beings and will not admit such research into evidence. Attorneys and clients are befuddled and outraged when two cases with identical scientific evidence yield opposite verdicts. Growing concern over such inconsistencies has led scientific societies, legal scholars, and even the U.S. Justice Department to call for changes to improve the quality of science-based verdicts.[58]

The most publicized dilemma for the courts is how to guarantee the quality and credibility of scientific testimony. Because lawyers seek the experts most likely to help win a case, many scientists regard courtroom testimony as suspect and simply refuse to participate. One federal judge observed that "an expert can be found to testify to the truth of almost any factual theory, no matter how frivolous."[59]

One solution is the court-appointed witness, chosen by a judge to act as a neutral voice in the midst of scientific disputes. The American Association for the Advancement of Science has pledged to aid judges in their quest for court experts by screening scientists and providing lists of suitable candidates. A Federal Judicial Center study revealed that although 80 percent of judges think appointing neutral experts can be useful, only 20 percent have ever done so. Most judges express concerns about affecting the outcome of a trial and worry that they lack the scientific expertise to choose an expert.[60]

The Justice Department is considering offering seminars to help judges better understand scientific methods, but with 400 cases on the average federal judge's calendar, attending such seminars may be difficult if not impossible. An alternative plan is for other groups to prepare primers on subjects like DNA evidence and statistical methodology to guide judges through the relevant issues and debates. Pretrial crash courses for jurors and juror notebooks are also possibilities.[61]

Notwithstanding these efforts, studies suggest that judges and jurors base their decisions on a wide range of human impulses other than scientific rationality: sympathy, dread, the desire for revenge, and so on.[62] In the end, a verdict may not turn on their perception of scientific evidence, but instead, on their gut feelings of guilt and innocence.

✧ THE PRACTICAL EFFECTS OF DELAY

The overload in our bloated court system has been building for years, especially in heavily populated areas. The crisis has had some unusual consequences, such as those in Vermont, where a case-load increase and budget cut have caused an unprecedented suspension of civil trials; unable to pay jurors' fees of $700,000, the state supreme court recently halted jury trials for five months.[63]

The most immediate source of pressure for the courts is the intensifying drug war. As police make increasing numbers of drug arrests and new prosecutors are hired to bring the cases to court, backlogs are growing. Although drug cases comprise about one-fourth of the federal criminal docket, they account for 42 percent of criminal trials [64] and 56 percent of all criminal appeals.[65] Because speedy-trial laws require federal courts to give priority to criminal cases, nearly 1 in 10 civil suits has been on the calendar for more than three years.[66]

Courts are hurting primarily because they get short shrift when compared with law enforcement and prisons—12.5 percent of the total justice system budget (excluding prosecution and defense activities) of about $74.2 billion; this compares with law enforcement's share of about 43 percent and corrections' 34 percent).[67] Anticrime grants tend to favor "glitzier" programs such as boot camps for drug offenders rather than those aimed at processing cases more rapidly. Judges, typically suffering in silence, have begun to organize and voice their frustrations; in 1990, jurists from the nine most populous states began devising ways for their courts to process the crush of drug cases more effectively.[68]

Meanwhile, horror stories continue. In New York City, felony filings jumped by 76 percent from 1986 to 1990; it now requires about 200 days after arraignment before a trial verdict is reached in a misdemeanor case. Across the country, more criminals are committing new offenses while out on bail awaiting trial. A panel of legal experts declared that the Philadelphia criminal justice system stood "at the edge of a precipice." With nearly 13,000 pending felony charges, sheriff's deputies there are so busy transporting prisoners to court appearances that they have stopped serving papers on defendants in civil suits, bringing case processing to a halt. It is not unusual to see rats scurry through antiquated courtrooms, and a temporary holding room designed for 50 people regularly holds 250 suspects.[69]

Without more funds, the criminal docket of our courts will not only bring civil cases to a virtual halt but less-serious criminal crimes will be jeopardized as well. Unfortunately, judges at both the state and federal levels cannot simply order the crisis to go away.[70]

Some reform-minded persons concerned with delays tell us unequivocally that the courts' greatest need is for better management and efficiency. All too often, they say, poor management prevents actors in the system from focusing on priorities, which at times results in criminals falling between the cracks. But others ask, "Efficiency for whose benefit?"[71] Court reforms can make the process harsher. This was the conclusion of a study of the effects of the "no-plea bargaining" policy in Alaska; the strongest negative impact was on middle-class defendants charged with property crimes.[72]

In considering how the courts may function better, we must bear in mind that justice must be served; and perhaps more important, the *appearance* of justice must be present. Where justice ends and expediency begins can be a difficult distinction to comprehend. Courthouse officials are to both "do justice" and move cases. It is the job of the court work group—some members of whom are actually the courts' greatest foes of efficiency—to assist the courts in performing both functions.

✧ COURTS "ON THE PRECIPICE"

In summary, we might consider the words of a former state supreme court justice, who wrote a book pointedly addressing the courts' poor state of affairs entitled *Why Courts Don't Work*.[73] In the book we are urged to view the courts as "the most terrifying governmental force in the United States" and to remember that "courts are to be avoided at all costs."[74] (Perhaps this judge had to confront many of the issues discussed in this and previous chapters. Unfortunately, our litany of issues is still incomplete; in Chapter 15 we view courts and politics, unionism, and allegations of racism.)

Taken together, we are forced to conclude that our courts are indeed "on the precipice"; we must admit that the state of the courts is not one of good health. They need relief from their rigors, and soon; judicial administrators will play an increasingly important role in trying to convince the legislative branch of this need to be extricated from the "morass." As we have seen, both the actual delivery of justice and the mere appearance of justice will probably continue to suffer in the meantime.

✦ STRESS ON THE BENCH

Very little has been written concerning stress and burnout among members of the judiciary or other actors of the court. However, they are not immune to their causes and effects. And when psychological problems develop for those on the bench, it can have grave consequences for all concerned. Such a case was that which recently unfolded in New York, and a strange one it was indeed. It demonstrates how vulnerable even placid, seemingly in-control professionals are to psychological problems and irrational behavior.

For several weeks in late 1992, a wealthy Manhattan divorcée had listened to menacing telephone calls that demanded payment for some supposedly compromising photos and tapes. With the caller's voice electronically disguised, the woman had no inkling of the caller's identity. When the FBI unmasked the caller, after tailing him for more than a month, even scandal-hardened New York was stunned. The accused blackmailer was a guardian of the law, the chief judge of New York's supreme court. He was later arraigned on charges of attempting to extort money from the woman and threatening her 14-year-old daughter (it was later determined that the judge had been having an affair with the woman, who had recently ended the relationship). The judge was ingloriously shackled to a psychiatric-ward bed for nearly three days before being placed under house arrest with an electronic monitoring bracelet. Hours later he resigned from the bench, with an apology, from the court he had served with distinction for two decades.[75]

Although this is an isolated case, psychiatrists and psychologists say it is not uncommon for professionals to crumble at or near the pinnacle of their careers, especially after a business failure or sexual setback. One stated that "when their sense of power is pierced, these individuals often try to recapture it through very inappropriate means." Another added, "when a judge has his jurist's robes on, that may compensate for the inadequacy in other parts of his life."[76]

Although on-the-job stress may not be the sole contributing factor in this or similar cases, it may well be a major precipitating element in such behavior. Often, job-related stress can lead to problems in other areas in one's life, including interpersonal relationships and low self-esteem.

Summary

In this chapter and the two preceding ones we have laid bare several major problems and issues confronting the courts, generated from both internal and external means. The core problem is that of case management, for all else revolves around that key function. It was seen that the provision for interpreters is a burgeoning matter that like the speedy-trial rule, has constitutional underpinnings. The management of notorious cases, although a long-standing duty of judicial administrators, appears to be more commonplace and one which, because of the generally dangerous nature of our society, requires more attention to planning.

We emphasized in this chapter that the courts are in a precarious situation, a veritable morass. It has become clear in the preceding three chapters that the courts are struggling with a bevy of problems. Certainly, legislators and policymakers must become more aware of the externally caused difficulties posed to the courts, and be prepared to provide additional resources for meeting the increasing caseloads. On the other hand, as experts are noting, court personnel must also be more open to change and prepared to approach it in an organized fashion.

Questions for Review

1. What are some common elements of innovative court programs that succeed? What role has technology played in their success?
2. Describe the two primary methods of case scheduling employed by the courts. Which of the two methods is used most frequently in the United States? What are its advantages and disadvantages?
3. What is a "notorious" court case? What are some of the administrative problems that accompany the trying of such cases, and how they have wrought changes in court operations?
4. Explain the court administrator's role in dealing with non-English-speaking defendants. Why is this a potentially serious matter?
5. How do rural courts differ in philosophy, operation, and administration from their urban counterparts? What are some advantages and disadvantages of both?
6. Discuss how the courts may be viewed as "on the precipice" of gridlock. Include in your response considerations of delay and workload.

For Further Reading

SUSAN BERK-SELIGSON, *The Bilingual Courtroom: Court Interpreters in the Judicial Process*. Chicago: University of Chicago Press, 1990.

MALCOLM FEELEY, *Court Reform on Trial: Why Simple Solutions Fail*. New York: Basic Books, 1983.

JOHN GOERDT, CHRIS LOMVARDIAS, GEOFF GALLAS, and BARRY MAHONEY, *Examining Court Delay*. Williamsburg, Va.: National Center for State Courts, 1989.

TIMOTHY K. MURPHY, GENEVRA KAY LOVELAND, and G. THOMAS MUNSTERMAN, *A Manual for Managing Notorious Cases*. Williamsburg, Va.: National Center for State Courts, 1992.

DAVID W. NEUBAUER, *America's Courts and the Criminal Justice System* (3d ed.). Pacific Grove, Calif.: Brooks/Cole, 1988.

CHARLES R. SWANSON and SUSETTE M. TALARICO (eds.), *Court Administration: Issues and Responses*. Athens, Ga.: University of Georgia, 1987.

Notes

1. National Center for State Courts, *Court Technology Reports: Vol. 4, 1991* (Williamsburg, Va.: Author, 1992), pp. iii–iv.

2. Massachusetts Trial Court Child Care Project, *CourtCare: Policy Guidelines and an Operating Plan for Child Care in the Courts* (Boston: Author, October 1992), Foreword.

3. Monica R. Lee, *Facsimile Transmission of Court Documents: A Feasibility Study* (Williamsburg, Va.: National Center for State Courts, August 1990), pp. 1, 76.

4. National Center for State Courts, *Trial Court Performance Standards with Commentary* (Williamsburg, Va.: Author, 1990), p. 1.

5. William E. Hewitt, Geoff Gallas, and Barry Mahoney, *Courts That Succeed* (Williamsburg, Va.: National Center for State Courts, 1990), p. vii.

6. David W. Neubauer, *America's Courts and the Criminal Justice System* (3d ed.) (Pacific Grove, Calif.: Brooks/Cole, 1988), p. 422.

7. *Ibid.*, p. 423.

8. David W. Neubauer, Maria Lipetz, Mary Luskin, and John Paul Ryan, *Managing the Pace of Justice: An Evaluation of LEAA's Court Delay Reduction Programs* (Washington, D.C.: U.S. Government Printing Office, 1981).

9. David W. Neubauer, "Improving the Analysis and Presentation of Data on Case Processing Time," *Journal of Criminal Law and Criminology* 74 (1983):1589.

10. American Bar Association Commission on Minimum Standards for Criminal Justice, *Standards Relating to Speedy Trial* (Chicago: Author, 1968); President's Commission on Law Enforcement and Administration of Justice, *Task Force Report: The Courts* (Washington, D.C.: U.S. Government Printing Office, 1967); National Advisory Commission on Criminal Justice Standards and Goals, *Courts* (Washington, D.C.: U.S. Government Printing Office, 1973).

11. J. Denis Moran, "Stating the Case for Timely Standards," *State Court Journal* 8 (1984):23–25.

12. David W. Neubauer, "Improving the Analysis and Presentation of Data on Case Processing Time," p. 1589.

13. Jonathan Casper, *American Criminal Justice: The Defendant's Perspective* (Englewood Cliffs, N.J.: Prentice Hall, 1972).

14. David W. Neubauer, *America's Courts and the Criminal Justice System* (3d ed.), pp. 424–425.

15. See *Barker v. Wingo*, 407 U.S. 514 (1972).

16. David W. Neubauer, *America's Courts and the Criminal Justice System* (3d ed.), p. 438.

17. Raymond Nimmer, *The Nature of System Change: Reform Impact in the Criminal Courts* (Chicago: American Bar Foundation, 1978).

18. David W. Neubauer, *America's Courts and the Criminal Justice System* (3d ed.), p. 439.

19. National Advisory Commission on Criminal Justice Standards and Goals, *Courts*.

20. David Neubauer, *America's Courts and the Criminal Justice System* (3d ed.), p. 306.

21. *Ibid.*, pp. 429–430.

22. Steven Flanders, *Case Management and Court Management in the United States District Courts* (Washington, D.C.: Federal Judicial Center, 1977).

23. *Ibid.*

24. David W. Neubauer, Maria Lipetz, Mary Luskin, and John Paul Ryan, *Managing the Pace of Justice: An Evaluation of LEAA's Court Delay Reduction Programs.*

25. 86 S.Ct. 1507, 1519 (1966).

26. Timothy R. Murphy, Genevra Kay Loveland, and G. Thomas Munsterman, *A Manual for Managing Notorious Cases* (Washington, D.C.: National Center for State Courts, 1992), pp. 4–6.

27. *Ibid.*, p. 23.

28. *Ibid.*, p. 53, 73.

29. *Ibid.*, pp. 89–94.

30. *Ibid.*, p. 22.

31. *Ibid.*, pp. 27–30.

32. Ted Gest and Constance Johnson, "The Justice System: Getting a Fair Trial," *U.S. News and World Report* (May 25, 1992):36, 38.

33. *Ibid.*

34. Susan Berk-Seligson, *The Bilingual Courtroom: Court Interpreters in the Judicial Process* (Chicago: University of Chicago Press, 1990), p. 1.

35. *Ibid.*, pp. 3–4, 8–9.

36. *Ibid.*, pp. 55, 57.

37. J. Leeth, *The Court Interpreter Examination* (Washington, D.C.: National Resource Center for Translation and Interpretation, Georgetown University, no date).

38. Susan Berk-Seligson, *The Bilingual Courtroom: Court Interpreters in the Judicial Process*, pp. 199–200.

39. *Ibid.*, p. 200.

40. 315 N.E.2d 163 (1974).

41. *People v. Medrano*, N.Y.S.2d 375 (1986).

42. 394 N.W.2d 221 (Minn. App. 1986).

43. Kathryn L. Fahnestock and Maurice D. Geiger, "Rural Courts: The Neglected Majority," *Court Management Journal* 14 (1982):4–10.

44. *Ibid.*, p. 6.

45. *Ibid.*, pp. 6, 8.

46. *Ibid.*, p. 7.

47. *Ibid.*, p. 8.

48. *Ibid.*, p. 8 (direct quote from the original).

49. Lynn Hecht Shafran, in Marilyn Roberts, "National Conference on Gender Bias in the Courts," *State Court Journal* 13 (Summer 1989):12.

50. *Ibid.*

51. American Bar Association, *Little Sisters and the Law* (Washington, D.C.: Author, 1977).

52. Norma J. Wikler, "Water to Stone: A Perspective on the Movement to Eliminate Gender Bias in the Courts," *State Court Journal* 13 (Summer 1989):13–18.

53. Kathleen Mulvihill, "Female Stereotypes Persist in U.S. Courts, Recent Studies Show," *The Christian Science Monitor* (July 27, 1987):7.

54. *Ibid.*, p. 14.

55. Marilyn Roberts, "National Conference on Gender Bias in the Courts," *State Court Journal* 13 (Summer 1989):12.

56. *Ibid.*, p. 18 (direct quote from the original).

57. Joannie M. Schrof, "Courtroom Conundrum," *U.S. News and World Report* (October 26, 1992):67–69.

58. *Ibid.*

59. *Ibid.*, p. 68 (direct quote from the original).

60. *Ibid.*, p. 69.

61. *Ibid.*

62. *Ibid.*

63. Ted Gest and Scott Minerbrook, "Little Hope for Justice," *U.S. News and World Report* (April 9, 1990):24–27.

64. Kathleen Maguire, Ann L. Pastore, and Timothy J. Flanagan (eds.), *Sourcebook of Criminal Justice Statistics 1992*, U.S. Department of Justice, Bureau of Justice Statistics (Washington, D.C.: U.S. Government Printing Office, 1993), pp. 476, 485.

65. *Ibid.*, p. 57.

66. Ted Gest and Scott Minerbrook, "Little Hope for Justice," p. 24.

67. Kathleen Maguire, Ann L. Pastore, and Timothy J. Flanagan (eds.), *Sourcebook of Criminal Justice Statistics 1992*, p. 2.

68. Ted Gest and Scott Minerbrook, "Little Hope for Justice," p. 25.

69. *Ibid.*, p. 26.

70. *Ibid.*, p. 27.

71. David W. Neubauer, *America's Courts and the Criminal Justice System* (3d ed.), p. 447.

72. Michael Rubinstein and Teresa White, "Plea Bargaining: Can Alaska Live without It?" *Judicature* 62 (1979):270.

73. Richard Neely, *Why Courts Don't Work* (New York: McGraw-Hill, 1983).

74. *Ibid.*, pp. 9, 243.

75. David Gelman, Susan Miller, and Bob Cohn, "The Strange Case of Judge Wachtler," *Newsweek* (November 23, 1992):34–35.

76. *Ibid.*, pp. 34, 35.

Case Studies

The Court Administrator
and the Prudent Police Chief*

You are the court administrator in a system that has the following procedure for handling traffic matters:

1. All persons who are given a traffic citation are required to appear in court at 9:00 A.M. on either Monday or Wednesday within two weeks of their arrest. They are given a specific date to appear.

2. At the initial appearance the arresting agency is represented by a court officer who has previously filed copies of all the citations with the clerk of the court.

3. The clerk, prior to the return date on the citation, prepared a file for each citation.

4. The clerk calls each case, and those persons appearing are requested by the court to enter a plea; if the plea is "not guilty," the matter is set for trial at a future date.

5. One case is scheduled per each hour. On the trial date, the prosecutor and arresting officer are required to appear, ready for trial.

6. Those persons who fail to appear either at the return date or at trial are not required to appear, but have the option of staying home and simply forfeiting their bond, which has been posted in advance of their initial appearance.

7. Statistics show that 75 percent of those persons pleading not guilty in this jurisdiction fail to appear for trial.

The chief of police in the court's jurisdiction is very concerned about overtime for officers. He communicates with you, the court administrator, about this concern and explains that all police officers who appear in court for trial are entitled to the minimum two hours of overtime when they are not appearing during their regular shift. He views this as a tremendous and unnecessary expense to the city, in view of the fact that most of the officers are not needed because the defendants do not appear. He recognizes that defendants have a right to post bond under the law and simply forfeit it at the initial appearance

---

*Contributed by Hon. Burton A. Scott, Associate Dean of the National Judicial College, Reno, Nevada.

or on the trial date. He is interested, however, in devising some system to save the city the tremendous cost for all the officers' overtime. He explains that other municipalities are faced with similar problems.

Questions for Discussion

1. What kind of a system would you propose to address the problem, and how would you go about accomplishing this end? In creating a modified system, you are to work within the existing law, with no changes in statutes or ordinances.

2. After you have completed designing a system and explaining how you would go about obtaining the cooperation of the judges, prosecutors, clerk's office, and other law enforcement agencies as well as that of the defense bar, discuss any proposed changes in the law you think might improve the system further.

3. How would you go about accomplishing other *significant* changes for improvement in the procedures and operation of this system? Consider the creation of an ongoing mechanism or committee that would propose, discuss, adopt, and carry out changes for the benefit of the system as a whole.

Chief Judge Cortez's Embattled Court[*]

You have just been hired as the new court administrator for a medium-sized court with approximately 90 employees. Once on the job, you discover that you have been preceded by two heavy-handed court administrators who together lasted less than a year on the job, due to their inability to handle employee conflicts and to achieve a minimal level of productivity. They were more or less forced to resign because of a lack of employee cooperation and increasing talk of unionization.

There is general turmoil and distrust throughout the organization. Employees do not trust each other, and as a group, they do not trust management. The courthouse runs on gossip and inertia. There is very little official communication throughout the organization. Prior court administrators made no attempt to solicit employee opinions or ideas.

The judges are all aware of the problem, but they have formed no clear consensus as to how to respond to it. In fact, there is turmoil and conflict among the judges themselves. They engage in "turf protection" with operating

---

[*]Contributed by Dennis Metrick, Management Analyst, Court Services Department, Administrative Office of the Courts, Phoenix, Arizona.

funds and the court's cases, and often take sides in office squabbles. As a result, they are unable to come to any clear consensus or to provide the court administrator with any guidance.

The chief judge, Dolores Cortez, has served in that capacity for 10 years and is known to be exceedingly fair, compassionate, and competent; however, she is approaching retirement (in six months) and appears unwilling to take a firm stand on, or a strong interest in, addressing intraoffice disputes and difficulties. In fact, she is not altogether convinced that there is a problem. Furthermore, in past years she has been quite reluctant to intervene in arguments between individual judges.

Questions for Discussion

1. As the "new kid on the block," how would you respond to this organization problem? What is the first problem you would address, and how would you address it? What additional problems require your attention?

2. As court administrator, how would you respond to the inability of the judges to develop a consensus? How could the decision-making process be improved?

3. What techniques could be employed to improve communication through the organization, lessen tension and strife, and generally create a more harmonious work environment?

4. What would be your general approach to Judge Cortez? To her successor?

An Unmanageable
Case-Management Quandary*

You are court administrator for a court of 50 employees. This court, which used to dispose of about 700 cases per month, now hears an average of 100 criminal and 400 civil cases per month. Case filings have doubled in the past seven years.

The present "hybrid" case-management system has evolved over a long period of time through tradition and expediency. However, a growing caseload and increasing difficulties in avoiding a backlog has prompted the judges to rethink their present system. Criminal cases that used to reach final disposition in a month now require two to three months. The situation shows no signs of improving in the foreseeable future.

---

*Contributed by Dennis Metrick, Management Analyst, Court Services Department, Administrative Office of the Courts, Phoenix, Arizona.

Again, the court has a mixed calendar system. Two judges are assigned to hear criminal cases and motions for a one-month period, while the remaining four judges hear all manner of civil matters on a random basis upon the filing of the civil complaint. The judges are responsible for the management of these cases until final disposition.

At the end of the one-month period, the two judges hearing criminal cases return to the civil division and two other judges rotate onto the criminal bench; any pending criminal cases or motions are then heard by these two incoming criminal judges.

One of the judges hears all juvenile-related matters in addition to any assignment in the criminal and civil divisions. The court collects statistics on the number of court filings and motions filed in each division on a month-to-month basis.

Questions for Discussion

1. In a general way, discuss both the merits and difficulties posed by this case management approach. Relate your response to the general advantages and disadvantages of both the individual and the master calendar systems.

2. What specific problems could arise in the criminal division? Why?

3. What specific problems could be created by the permanent assignment of a judge to the juvenile division? Advantages?

4. What comments would you make with regard to the court's statistical report? Are other data needed for management purposes? If so, what kind?

Part

Corrections

IV

This part consists of four chapters, all of which focus on corrections administration. In Chapter 10 we examine corrections organization and operation, including prisons and jails; in Chapter 11 we cover personnel roles and functions; in Chapter 12 we discuss the administration of community corrections through probation and parole; and in Chapter 13 we review corrections issues and practices. Specific chapter content is provided in the introductory section of each chapter.

Organization and Operation

Prisons are built with stones of Law.
— William Blake

The founders of a new colony...recognized it among their earliest practical necessities to allot a portion of the virgin soil as a cemetery, and another portion as the site of a prison.
— Nathaniel Hawthorne

✦ INTRODUCTION

The subculture of prisons and jails has comprised much of America's television and movie fare for several decades. *The Big House* (1930), *White Heat* (1949), *Inside the Walls of Folsom Prison* (1951), *Birdman of Alcatraz* (1962), *Cool Hand Luke* (1967), and *Chain Gang Women* (1971) are but a few. Most of these movie dramas about prison life have portrayed prison administrators and their personnel and organizations as cruel, bigoted, corrupt, and morally base. Furthermore, such prison literature as Jack Henry Abbott's *In the Belly of the Beast*, Eldridge Cleaver's *Soul on Ice*, George Jackson's *Soledad Brother*, and Malcolm Braly's *On the Yard*, among others, have presented similar views. These movies and books reflect the public's interest in, and often their lack of knowledge about, our correctional institutions. As we show below, corrections has become a boom industry and promises to continue being so well into the twenty-first century. Indeed, it is selected by most futurists to be the most rapidly growing criminal-justice career area for the future as well.[1]

In this chapter we do not trace the history of correctional institutions in detail; rather, we focus generally on their organization and operation. We look at the primary roles of correctional institutions as organizations. Specifically, we look at the unique aspects of corrections organizations; the prison crowding and its causes and effects, as well as some approaches available to, and limitations for, institutional administrators to attempt to help the incarcerated, who often bring serious emotional and behavioral problems to the institution: narcotics addiction, sexual deviance, a violent personality, and/or alcoholism.

We also look at local jails, including a demographic profile, crowding, programs, and a relatively new jail design and philosophy, the "new generation" jail. We conclude the chapter by looking at obstacles to correctional research and recent findings concerning the emotional and physical effects of incarceration, including solitary confinement and death row, and some implications for correctional administrators and society at large.

✦ CORRECTIONAL ORGANIZATIONS

✧ UNIQUE FEATURES

The correctional organization is a complex, hybrid organization that utilizes two distinct, yet related management subsystems to achieve its goals: one that is concerned primarily with the management of correctional employees, the other concerned primarily with the delivery of correctional services to a designated offender population. The correctional organization, therefore, employs one group of people—correctional personnel—to work with and control another group—offenders.[2]

Another unique feature of the correctional organization is that every correctional employee who exercises legal authority over offenders is a *supervisor*, even if the person is the lowest-ranking member in the agency or institution. Therefore, there are two distinct, yet related supervisory roles. One supervisory role involves the supervision of employees, referred to as "first-level supervision," while the other involves the role of offender supervision, or *line* or *field supervision*. Furthermore, in most organizations, line personnel normally represent labor that is converted into products or units of production. In correctional organizations, the product is the type of correctional service being delivered to the correctional client, be the client an inmate, probationer, or parolee. The unit of production is the pattern of supervisory interaction between the line employee and the offender.[3]

Another unique feature of the correctional organization is that everything a correctional supervisor does may have civil or criminal ramifications, both for the supervisor and for the agency or institution. Therefore, the extent of both legal and ethical responsibility is greater for the correctional supervisor than it is for supervisors in other types of organizations.

Finally, in correctional organizations there are two ideologically competing suborganizational structures: (1) the *custodial* organization, with its emphasis on control and surveillance of offender activities; and (2) the *treatment* organization, emphasizing the goals and methods of treatment and rehabilitation. This arena contains potential conflict between treatment and custody personnel which must be managed at the supervisory level.[4]

✦ OPEN SYSTEMS

Traditionally, many correctional organizations have been, like Erving Goffman's "closed social institutions," a closed system view in the administration of the correctional organization. This view holds that the organization's responsibility is limited only to the structural boundaries of the official organization.[5] These institutions experience a degree of difficulty in communicating with the outside world and are often loathe to provide information to the outside world concerning their activities and methods.[6] Historically, this closed perspective contributed to the problem of political alienation and fragmentation of correctional services.[7]

Today, however, most correctional administrators and policy makers recognize that their organizations are intricate components of larger government systems and of society itself. This open systems view recognizes that problems and solutions are generated by forces outside the organization, and that these forces and resources must be managed. For example, a decision to close a state prison in a small community, where the local economy is dependent on the prison, may create significant political pressure not to close the prison. Local pressure can also hinder locating a prerelease center in an established residential area.[8]

In short, the contemporary correctional organization is an intricate part of the social, political, and economic setting in which the organization functions. Therefore, the organization must be administered as an open system.

✦ LEVELS OF CORRECTIONAL ADMINISTRATION

According to Vernon Fox, correctional administration is "the organization and management of the delivery system that brings the basic necessities and treatment programs of the correctional institutions or agencies to the correctional client."[9] William and Betty Archambeault add that correctional administration refers to the processes of managing the social, political, and economic forces, pressures, and influences "which are EXTERNAL to the correctional organization, yet which IMPINGE ON or AFFECT the INTERNAL OPERATIONS of the organization, as the process of managing the organization's INTERNAL SYSTEM for DELIVERING CORRECTIONAL SERVICES AND FOR GOALS, OBJECTIVES, and POLICIES" [emphasis theirs].[10]

Correctional administration and management are both concerned with internal organizational issues, such as personnel, budgets, and programs. However, administration is concerned with obtaining personnel, securing funds, and interfacing programs with other agencies, whereas management is concerned primarily with making use of available manpower and resources to implement programs. Most of an administrator's time and energy are expended on activities outside the organization, while most of management's time is spent on activities within the organization.[11]

Correctional administrators are responsible for developing policy; managers are responsible primarily for implementing policy. Therefore, administration is concerned with long-range planning that affects the entire organization, while management is responsible for day-to-day planning. Finally, correctional administration is highly political, whereas management positions tend to be less so.[12]

Figure 10.1 shows the levels of correctional organizations, including top administration, executive management, middle-management, supervisory manager, and line correctional supervisor. In the figure, top administration refers to the "person in charge" of an agency, institution, or unit of government. They

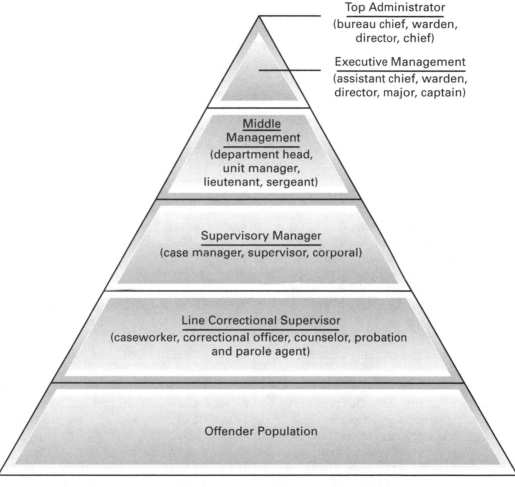

Figure 10.1 Levels of correctional organization (*Source:* William G. Archambeault and Betty J. Archambeault, *Correctional Supervisory Management: Principles of Organization, Policy, and Law* (Englewood Cliffs, N.J. Prentice Hall, 1982), p. 53. Used with permission.)

may be a bureau chief or commander, warden, executive director, or person with a similar title. This person is responsible for the entire operation of the organization and is more often than not a politically appointee.

The line between the levels of top administration and executive management is blurred in many organizations. Most top-level decisions are made at this level, with top administration often approving recommendations made by executive management. Titles are often similar to those of top administration, with the addition of the prefix "assistant" or "deputy" or "vice" (e.g., deputy or assistant warden, assistant commander, and so on). Executive managers normally develop and review long-range plans; evaluate key management personnel; develop policies, rules, regulations, and standards for the organization; and perform other functions set by top administrators.[13]

Middle-management in correctional administration may refer to a variety of positions and to a number of levels within the organizational structure of an organization or institution. Middle-management positions may be called a department head, captain, lieutenant, sergeant, team leader, manager, program head, coordinator, shift commander, and so on. This level is normally concerned with managing the delivery of one or more services, which may be organized into departments or divisions. Examples include custody, treatment, food services, maintenance, prison industries, personnel, research, and education. Each division is ultimately responsible to an executive manager (such as an assistant warden for custody or treatment). A major function of middle managers is the development of intermediate plans. They also implement rules and regulations, maintain records, supervise subordinate supervisors, periodically evaluate personnel, account for unit resources (funds, property, equipment), process grievances, and so on.[14]

The lowest level of correctional administration is that of the first-level supervisor of employees, often titled unit manager, supervisor, corporal, team leader, or section leader. They are responsible for the day-to-day operations of specific areas within organizational units. They make first-level job assignments; maintain close contact with operational employees; make detailed and short-range operating plans; provide counseling, motivation, control, and training to employees; and implement agency policies, rules, and regulations at the employee level. In short, the first-level supervisor translates organizational policy, goals, and objectives into action.[15]

The line or field correctional supervisors are not normally designated as part of administration and management; however, they exercise legal supervisory authority over members of an offender population. They must bring to their job the skillful application of basic supervisory techniques and the ability to influence the offender. This position—be it that of probation and parole officer, correctional officer, counselor, or other—must carry out all of the administrators' wishes: interpreting and applying institutional policy; planning, organizing, and supervising inmate activities and work functions; ensuring maintenance of the physical plant and equipment; avoiding circumstances that might lead to litigation; engaging in decision making; and so on. These workers are the "point of delivery" for all correctional services within the organization; the effectiveness of the organization is closely linked to their performance.[16]

✦ PRISONS AS ORGANIZATIONS

Until the beginning of the twentieth century, prisons were administered by state boards of charities, boards comprised of citizens, boards of inspectors, state prison commissions, or individual prison keepers. Most prisons were like individual provinces; wardens, who were given absolute control over their domain, were appointed by governors through a system of political patronage.

Today, every state has some form of centralized department of corrections that is empowered to set and carry out policies for all correctional institutions within the jurisdiction. At the top of this department of corrections is the secretary or commissioner of corrections, who works directly under the governor to establish policy and institutional procedures, and negotiates operating budgets for the various institutions and make major personnel decisions. (However, it has been stated that "it is almost a cliché today to assert that there are no...prison policies in the United States.")[17]

The aforementioned "spoils system" of past decades led to the warden's office having a questionable reputation, as the position carried many fringe benefits such as a lavish residence, unlimited inmate servants, food and supplies from institutional farms and warehouses, furnishings, and a personal automobile. Indeed, control over inmates tended to be quite autocratic. Today, the head of each prison, generally appointed by the commissioner of corrections, is a warden, director, or superintendent. The more common title for the head of a prison today is superintendent; the title of "warden" still carries negative connotations from the past.[18] However, because most wardens (or superintendents) are now civil service employees who have earned their position through seniority and merit, their reputations are greatly enhanced from that of earlier times.[19] Figure 10.2 shows an organization structure for a state prison system serving a population of about 2 million and an inmate population of about 5000.

Because the traditional prison was autocratic, with the central purpose of maintaining custody of inmates, the organization was highly stratified and rigid, organized along military lines, with authority and status related to rank. Decision making was focused at the top. The past few decades have witnessed the reorganization of many correctional institutions and the addition of another layer of hierarchy, commonly referred to as the noncustodial personnel. These personnel are the *professional* staff of the prison, which includes the psychiatrists, psychologists, medical personnel, chaplains, teachers, counselors, and dieticians.

Thus today's warden or superintendent may be assisted by one or more associate deputy wardens: normally, one in charge of custody, including discipline, security, inmate movement, and control, and a second deputy who may be in charge of business matters, programs, records, library services, mail and visitation, recreation, and release procedures. An industries manager will be in charge of prison industries, farms, production, and supplies. A medical supervisor is in charge of prison health services and sanitation.[20] There may also be directors of honor camps. This reorganization has produced a more vertical type of organization, forcing the actual making of decisions downward within

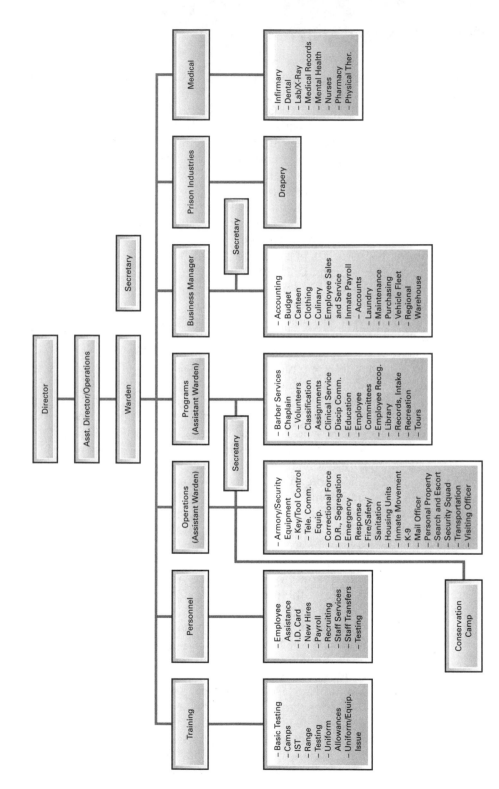

Figure 10.2 Organizational structure for a maximum security prison.

the organization, among deputies and their personnel. Today, organizing and managing a prison is obviously a major task, one that rivals many large industries and businesses.

Although we have discussed the general organization of prisons, again it is difficult to describe a "typical" organizational structure for them. There are many kinds of adult institutions, and their organizational attributes for providing custody and treatment have become so complicated that separate chapters are devoted to discussing the personnel, methods, and problems that revolve around these two basic functions.

✦ MANAGING THE PRISON BOOM BUST

Barry Nidorf has asserted that 1989 will surely be remembered as the year when the public first became fully aware of the crowding crisis in the nation's prisons and jails. The steady flow of news stories that year highlighted what prison administrators and justice system professionals had known for nearly a decade.

◊ During just a single week in May 1989, two major news magazines carried articles on prison overcrowding, and a nationally syndicated radio commentator told listeners about a criminal who was pursued for months by Massachusetts police only to be released, because of crowding, just two days after his arrest.

◊ In April, a Texas prison inmate, interviewed on the nightly news, told how crowding was working to his benefit. He explained that with several dozen new inmates arriving at his facility every day, his term would have to be cut to make room for them. He wanted to look serious as he talked, but he had to try hard to keep from smiling at his good fortune.

◊ A just-released Los Angeles County jail inmate did not even try to refrain from smiling. In February he posed, smiling and happy, for press photographers outside the jail where he had just served a 14-day sentence in 14 hours, a rate of 2 1/2 minutes per hour.[21]

Many reasons have been offered for America's rapidly rising prison and jail populations. Some commonly cited factors are violence on television in the movies (indeed, a Pennsylvania State University study reported in mid-1993 that the more television they watch, the more violent and disobedient schoolchildren become),[22] as well as a general deterioration of morals and of the family. Drug abuse is perhaps a symptom of other fundamental social problems; nearly one-third of all state prison inmates were drug offenders.[23]

A related development contributes to crowding: an ideological restatement across the United States. In response to the criticisms and failures of rehabilitative philosophy and policies, the prevailing ideology of incapacitation, punishment, and deterrence has resulted in get-tough sentencing practices (including mandatory sentencing laws) which contribute to rising prison populations. The word *rehabilitation* was essentially removed from the penal code by legislators and a scheme of fixed sentences begun, quadrupling the number of prisoners and requiring $4.5 billion for new lockups.[24] This shift to "just deserts" focuses on the fact that offenders make "free will" decisions to commit crime, and therefore they no longer deserve compassion and correction. This ideology has wrought an "exclusionary" era of repressive social control, which attempts to banish, expel, and stigmatize the criminal deviant.[25]

Unfortunately, this philosophy and the addition of more prisons—and more prisoners—have not brought about less crime. Violent crime began rising again in 1990 after reaching a plateau for several years. The shortcomings of the tougher philosophy and lock-em-up strategy have resulted in record numbers of inmates. As succinctly put by Malcolm Feeley, "there is no evidence of imprisonment's deterrent effect."[26]

According to Ted Gest, the logic of the "lock-em-up campaign" is defeated by a combination of demography and justice-system inefficiency. Each year, a new crop of youths in their upper teens constitute the majority of those arrested for serious crimes. As "seasoned" offenders are arrested and removed from the crime domain, this new crop replaces them. "The justice system is eating its young. It imprisons them, paroles them, and rearrests them with no rehabilitation in between," according to Dale Secrest.[27] Law enforcement seems to be little deterrent; even California's aggressive law enforcement—40,000 felons enter its state prisons each year—deals with only a small fraction of those who commit a million serious crimes annually in the state.[28]

There is no question that large-scale, long-term imprisonment does keep truly serious offenders behind bars longer, preventing them from committing more crimes. One estimate is that the most predatory street criminals commit an average of 15 or more crimes per year. But the benefit-to-cost ratio declines with short-term incarcerations, which cost taxpayers large sums without preventing much crime. It is the incarceration of this class of offenders that is creating the greatest need for more prison space. The percentage of incoming prisoners convicted of violent crimes has dropped from 56 to 41 since 1986. However, as an example, it now costs California taxpayers $43,000 to house and monitor a typical convict, who serves a 14-month term, then is paroled, rearrested, and returned to prison for six months.[29]

As of mid-year 1991, 37 states and the District of Columbia had adult and/or juvenile institutions under court order to monitor or reduce crowding.

✦ ADMINISTRATIVE APPROACHES TO THE "KEPT"

It is clear that "offenders enter prison with a variety of deficits. Some are socially or morally inept; others are intellectually or vocationally handicapped; some have emotional hangups that stem from...psychological problems; still others have of mixture of varying proportions of some or even all of these."[30]

These characteristics obviously do not bode well for the success of correctional administration and institutional treatment in general. The prison culture makes the environment inhospitable to programs designed to rehabilitate or reform. High recidivism rates indicate that existing correctional strategies have not been successful, and that these strategies cannot operate in a vacuum. But as will be seen below and in chapters to follow, the prison director's philosophy and practice with respect to inmate treatment and programs may in large measure have an impact on that success rate.

Somewhat ironically, a recent survey found that about half (48 percent) of all Americans feel it is more important to try to rehabilitate prisoners than merely to punish them (38 percent).[31] However, that finding flies in the face of all "conventional wisdom" concerning how to administer prison programs. Robert Martinson's well-publicized finding that "almost nothing works" in correctional treatment programs served to "ignite a firestorm of debate that has lasted" nearly two decades.[32] Martinson's assessment clearly had a major impact on corrections administration, either through the unwillingness of the latter to fund treatment programs from dwindling budgets, or through the claims of academicians and policymakers that the medical model of correctional treatment programs failed to accomplish their ends. Paul Louis and Jerry Sparger concluded that "perhaps the most lasting effect of the `nothing works' philosophy is the spread of cynicism and hopelessness" among prison administrators and staff members.[33]

With the demise of the rehabilitative philosophy and the national call for "just deserts" in the 1970s, the 1980s witnessed an even greater widening of the gap between the two perspectives. Ted Palmer [34] identified these modified positions as the "skeptical" and "sanguine" camps. The skeptical viewpoint is that relatively few prison programs work, and that those that are successful account only for negligible reductions in recidivism. Furthermore, due to either design flaws or poor implementation, rehabilitation programs have not been given an adequate chance in correctional settings. The sanguine perspective is that while the existing rehabilitation programs have not been very effective to date, there is evidence that many programs provide positive treatment for selected portions of the offender population.

However, a recent reassessment of Martinson's "nothing works" statement by such researchers as Palmer has given new hope to the rehabilitation ethic. Palmer rejected Martinson's indictment of correctional treatment modalities and demonstrated that many of the programs initially reviewed by Martinson were actually quite successful.[35] Other research has supported Palmer's position.[36]

There is also evidence of contemporary success in correctional settings with respect to *narcotics addiction, sexual offenses, violent offenders,* and *alcoholism.* More than a third (36 percent) of all male state prison inmates used illegal drugs daily in the month before their offense, and 31% were under the influence of drugs at the time of their current offense.[37] Drug-addicted offenders are currently subjected to one of three types of treatment: punitive, medical, or communal approaches. The punitive modality, the most widely used model since the early 1920s, consists largely of withdrawal and is based on the premise that drug addition is a crime that requires punishment and is not a disease. However, the view of drug addiction as a medical problem consists of detoxification, rebuilding of physical health, counseling, and social services. Several studies of such programs indicate success. The communal approach, using group encounters and seminars conducted by ex-addicts, who serve as positive role models, has been used by various penal facilities. [38]

A recent survey of correctional administrators revealed that there were approximately 85,650 sexual offenders in federal and state prisons. All 48 states participating in the survey, as well as the Federal Bureau of Prisons and the District of Columbia, reported that they provided individual and/or group counseling for these offenders.[39] The treatment of sexual offenders is premised on the idea that intervention should be focused on the offender as a total person, not just on the offender's deviant behavior.[40] The offender is encouraged to articulate fears, anxieties, wishes, fantasies, and ambitions to relieve mental and emotional distress. Rapists, voyeurs, and exhibitionists may benefit through group therapy, in which touching and close physical contact are stressed. Child molesters or pedophiles may be similarly treated as whole personalities; however, treatment efforts in prison are unlikely to produce positive outcomes because of the nature of the environment.[41] Research has shown that the main concern, regardless of the sexual offender's specific problem, is to individualize treatment.[42]

There is no uniform, simple treatment modality for the wide range of violent offenders. All types of personalities may resort to violent acts. However, these offenders are diagnosed as having "antisocial personality disorders," and those inmates are not often amenable to psychotherapeutic intervention.[43] A complicating factor is that alcoholism is prevalent among those offenders;[44] therefore, each case requires formulation of an individual treatment plan. Research has indicated that if the violent offender appears to possess the values of a "subculture of violence," peer influences seem to work best in treatment; however, if deep-seated psychological factors appear to be present, a one-to-one relationship, in which the therapist is supportive, kind, and permissive but firm, may be utilized.[45] Alcoholism is generally acknowledged as being a disease with medical, social, and psychological dimensions.[46] Psychological treatment varies with the personality of the offender. The regimen used by Alcoholics Anonymous is frequently employed in the institutional setting.[47]

In sum, the idea that "nothing works" presently overrides most serious attempts to rehabilitate offenders. That philosophy is not expected to subside in the foreseeable future. However, it is good to remember the attempts that were made to salvage such people in earlier times; there may one day be a return to that era. Regarding the future of rehabilitation, Palmer made three points: (1) rehabilitation need not be married to a medical model, (2) rehabilitation need not be linked to indeterminate sentencing, and (3) rehabilitation or correctional intervention need not demean its participants or interfere with extant reform movements.[48]

✦ JAILS AS ORGANIZATIONS

✧ A PROFILE

Across the United States, there are an estimated 3316 locally administered jails, with approximately 137,000 individual housing units.[49] As with prisons, there is no "typical" organizational structure for jails; their organization and levels of programming and specialization will obviously be determined by several factors: size, budget, level of crowding, local views toward punishment and treatment, and even the levels of training and education of the jail administrator. There are some common characteristics, however; an organizational structure for a jail serving a population of about 250,000 is presented in Figure 10.3.

The administration of jails is frequently one of the major tasks of county sheriffs. In fact, 81 percent of the 3100 sheriff's departments in the United States are responsible for jail operation,[50] compared with only 5 percent of the nation's 12,288 local police departments (primarily in larger cities). Right or wrong, several writers have concluded that sheriff and police personnel typically see themselves as law enforcers first, and view the responsibility of organizing and operating the jail as a millstone.[51] Therefore, their approach is often said to be at odds with advanced corrections philosophy and trends. Although burdened by community apathy and a meager budget, the sheriff and his or her staff are nevertheless charged with the care and custody of a large number of relatively short-term prisoners. In 1973, the National Advisory Commission on Criminal Justice Standards and Goals recommended that by 1982 localized jail operations be merged into a state-controlled system.[52] Although this plan might have some merit (as in state-mandated training and program development), it has understandably met with considerable resistance at the local level. The problem remains that many consider jails and detention facilities "by far the most neglected area of the criminal justice system."[53]

✧ POPULATION DENSITIES IN U.S. JAILS

Between 1983 and 1988, the average number of square feet per inmate declined from 54.3 to 50.9 square feet. The average number of inmates per unit, the measure of social density, changed only negligibly, from 2.4 inmates in 1983 to 2.5 in 1988. Jails confined inmates to housing units an average of 13.5 hours per day. Nationally, local jails held about one-fourth of all inmates alone in a cell, which had an average floor space of 68 square feet. Inmates held in two-person units had the smallest average space per person, 39.2 square feet. The smallest jails, those with an average daily population of fewer than 50 inmates, provided the most space per person, 60.6 square feet in 1988. The largest jails, confining a daily average population of more than 1000 inmates, provided the least space, 45.7 square feet per person. The smallest jails had the lowest average number of persons per housing unit (1.9), and the largest jails,

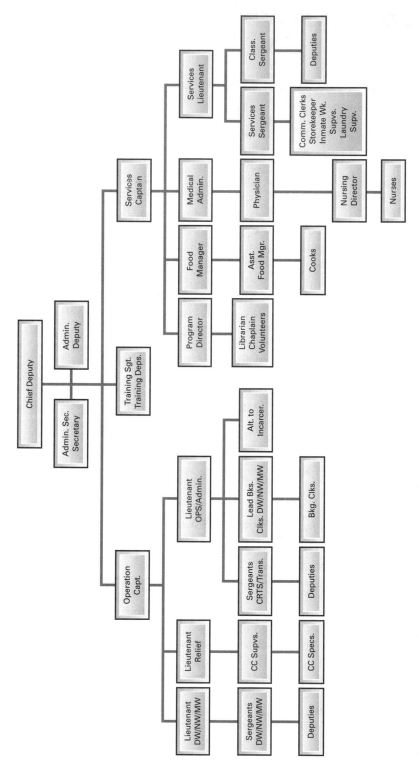

Figure 10.3 Organizational structure for a jail serving a county of 250,000 population.

the highest number (3.4 persons). However, inmates confined in the largest facilities spent an average of one hour less in their housing unit per day than did inmates in smaller jails.[54]

✧ SPATIAL AND SOCIAL DENSITIES

Organizing and managing jails becomes more difficult when more inmates are living in high-density situations. Maintaining high population densities can affect routine activities such as food service, visitation, recreation, medical care and sick call, inmate property management, and inmates' movements to and from court or consultations with attorneys. High-spatial-density facilities are identified as those in which over 40 percent of the inmates have less than the American Correctional Association standard of 60 square feet per person in housing where they are confined for 10 hours or more.[55] Among jails in 1988, 28.1 percent operated with a population in the highest-spatial-density category.

The standard in the "highest social density" residence category is an average of five or more persons per housing unit. By that definition, 27.6 percent of all jails, housing 61.1 percent of all jail inmates nationwide, were high-social-density facilities. Higher population densities are more common in larger jails, with an average daily population between 500 and 999 inmates; of those, 43.8 percent had at least 40 percent of their inmates residing in less than 60 square feet for more than 10 hours per day. The smallest jails, housing fewer than 50 inmates daily, were less likely to report high-density conditions.[56]

Inmate suicide rates are higher in small jails and highest in small jails with lower population densities.[57] Seventy percent of all jail suicides occurred in facilities with average daily populations of fewer than 250 inmates.[58] These facilities account for 37 percent of all jail inmates,[59] and 52 percent of all jail admissions nationwide.[60]

✧ A SHIFT IN DESIGN AND PHILOSOPHY: THE "NEW GENERATION" JAIL

In the mid-1960s, the federal courts began to abandon their traditional "hands-off" philosophy toward prison and jail administration. This change in viewpoint was largely in response to the deplorable conditions and treatment of inmates in the past. The courts became more willing to hear inmate allegations of constitutional violations, ranging from inadequate heating, lighting, and ventilation to the censorship of mail. The number of inmate petitions increased from 218 in 1966 to 16,741 in 1981. [61] One of every five cases filed in federal courts was on behalf of prisoners[62] and 20 percent of all jails were a party in a pending lawsuit.[63]

In response to this deluge of lawsuits and to improve conditions, many local jurisdictions constructed new jail facilities. These new buildings did not totally vanquish the old philosophies, architecture, and practices prevalent in the old jails, but for a small number of local officials, the court-ordered pressures to improve jail conditions afforded an opportunity to explore new ideas and designs. During the mid-1960s, the federal government undertook construction of the first federally operated detention facilities for federal prisoners. The Bureau of Prisons, although inexperienced with administering pretrial facilities, set out to study the issues and problems of short-term detention. From this research emerged a set of principles that were incorporated into its new Metropolitan Correctional Centers.[64]

First, these new facilities had to provide safe and secure detention. Corrections officers were to observe all areas, and "blind spots" were to be minimized. They were also designed for the purpose of detainment rather than punishment. To the extent possible, "symbols of incarceration" would be removed. No bars were to be used in the living units, windows were to be provided in every prisoner's room, and carpets, padded and movable furniture, and colorful wall coverings were to be used to reduce the institutional atmosphere of the facility. Third, inmates were to be divided into small groups of approximately 40 to 50 for housing purposes. Officers would interact with inmates rather than remain inside an office or behind a desk. Finally, interior features of the facility were to be designed to reduce the "trauma" of incarceration.[65]

The single most important feature of these facilities, as required by the Bureau of Prisons, were single cells for inmates, direct staff supervision, and "functional inmate living units." Functional units were to place all "sleeping, food, and hygiene facilities...in one self-contained, multi-level space."[66] A corrections officer was to be assigned to each unit to ensure direct and continuous supervision.

By 1977, functional units existed in 23 federal correctional institutions. Although several minor design problems were found in some facilities, they still met the goals of the bureau: there was little violence, tension, or vandalism, and officers seemed more satisfied with their jobs.[67]

This concept was not instantly accepted in other jurisdictions, however. Many local jail administrators felt their inmates to be too hardened for this approach. Despite this reluctance, the first local facility designed in the new style opened in the 1970s in Contra Costa County, California. This facility quickly became a success, deemed cost-effective to build and safer for inmates and staff. Contra Costa's facility marked the birth of the "new generation" philosophy. This term was coined to characterize a style of architecture and inmate management totally new and unique to local detention facilities, and a new generation in correctional thought.[68]

Even the infamous New York City jail, "The Tombs," was gutted and renovated in accordance with the new generation design in 1983. At about the same time, the concept was endorsed by the American Correctional Association and the Advisory Board of the National Institute of Corrections. W. Walter Menninger, Director of Law and Psychiatry at the Menninger Foundation in Topeka, Kansas, observed that "Careful studies of these new generation facilities have found significant benefits for inmates, staff and society at large. There are fewer untoward incidents and assaults, [a] greater level of personal safety for both staff and inmates, greater staff satisfaction, more orderly and relaxed inmate housing areas, a better maintained physical plant. Finally, these facilities are cost effective to construct and to operate."[69]

✧ MAKING JAILS PRODUCTIVE

In 1981, then Chief Justice Warren Burger challenged correctional administrators to create "factories with fences." The 1984 Justice Assistance Act removed some of the long-standing restrictions on interstate commerce of prisoner-made goods. By 1987, private-sector work programs were under way in 14 state correctional institutions and two county jails.[70] Today, many inmates in American jails are getting into productive work. Some are simply earning privileges, while others earn wages that are applied toward their custodial costs and compensation to crime victims. Some are honing new job skills, improving their chances for success following release.

In 1987, the National Institute of Justice (NIJ) and the National Institute of Corrections (NIC) developed the first certified private-sector jail industry program in Strafford County, New Jersey. NIJ helped the county win federal certification and provided support in developing policies and procedures, an accounting system, and internal scheduling. An NIC grant provided seed money to employ and industries developer and sponsored trips to visit other inmate work programs.

Convinced of the tremendous potential for the nation's 3300 jails to make their inmates more productive, in 1988 NIJ studied 15 counties and cities operating inmate work programs. By definition, a "jail industry" is one that uses inmate labor to create a product or provide a service of value to the client, for which the inmate receives compensation in the form of pay, privileges, or other benefits. At one end of the continuum is the trusty who mows the grass in front of the jail and thereby earns privileges for doing so; at the other end would be those jail inmates working for private industry for real dollars.[71]

It should also be noted that many jails provide drug treatment services for their inmates. Generally, the larger the jail, the greater the likelihood of such services being available to inmates. Many jails also provide training in drug abuse and AIDS screening for correctional officers. In addition to treatment programs, some jails have undertaken training programs for their wards, following the recommendations of the American Jail Association. For example, the state-of-the-art facility in Washoe County (Reno), Nevada, trains inmates to operate a plastic-sign engraving machine, and there are plans to teach dog grooming at the local animal control center. The engraving equipment, as well as the facility's 24 computers for inmates, cost taxpayers nothing; they were purchased through commissary funds. Inmates can also earn a GED. The facility is also considering auto detailing, food service, book mending, mailing service, painting, printing, carpet installation, and upholstering.

✦ RESEARCH IN CORRECTIONAL INSTITUTIONS

✧ OBSTACLES TO CORRECTIONAL RESEARCH

In Chapter 4 we examined how research findings had changed police functions rather dramatically, forcing administrators in that domain to rethink many old "sacred cow" traditions. Given the current prison "boom" and its cost (discussed above), the preceding debate over "what works" with regard to prison programs, and the rehabilitation versus punishment rift in general, perhaps it is in the corrections area that research is now even more important (and timely). As we will see, attempts to engage in correctional research have not always been successful.

In his classic work, *Asylums*,[72] Erving Goffman defined a *total institution* as "a place of residence and work where a large number of like-situated individuals, cut off from the wider society for an appreciable period of time, together lead an enclosed, formally administered round of life."[73] Unquestionably, many (including Goffman) would include prisons within that definition. In fact, Richard McGee acknowledged as much, stating that prisons were "the most closed communities yet devised."[74]

The need for research in corrections cannot be overstated. Even Robert Martinson, the author of the "nothing works" idea discussed above, acknowledged in an often overlooked caveat that "it is just possible that some of our treatment programs are working to some extent, but that our research is so bad that it is incapable of telling."[75] The President's Commission on Law Enforcement and Administration of Justice spoke to the point, saying "the greatest need is the need to know. Criminal justice agencies *must open their doors and reveal their secrets.*"[76] A special report for the governor of New York added that

> the single most important need in the post-adjudicatory treatment system is the development of a body of knowledge…through an organized program of research. Unless administrators come to look upon research as an indispensable part of the decision making, policy planning and treatment processes, there will continue to be no way of telling whether anything we are doing is achieving the objective of the system and whether any new plan is worth acceptance.[77]

Daniel Glaser was moved to refer to correctional research as "an elusive paradise."[78]

Some authors have indicated that academics should share part of the blame for the relative scarcity of corrections research.[79] The outside researcher may seek entree into prisons with briefcase, questionnaires, notepads, tape recorders, and seek to evaluate, inspect files, ask questions, and generally want to know what's going on.[80] Prison administrators may feel threatened or put off by their approach and/or demeanor and methods. Furthermore, a corrections practitioner is "likely to be a warm, outgoing personality,"[81] concerned with the here and now and believing in what he or she is doing; this person may see research as a diversion, consuming scarce resources, and feel forced to bear the brunt of unflattering research conclusions.

There are doubtless many correctional administrators who are open to research. Nonetheless, some researchers have met considerable obstacles to using self-administered surveys in prisons and have found high levels of paranoia among staff members within.[82] The U.S. Supreme Court held in *Wolff v. McDonnell*,[83] in 1974 that "there is no Iron Curtain drawn between the Constitution and the prisons of this country." No "iron curtain," politics, red tape, or reticence should impede research in an area where knowledge is so badly needed. What *is* needed, according to Philip Zimbardo in testimony before Congress on prison reform, is for correctional administrators to "remove the cloak of secrecy."[84] What is not needed is "political rhetoric [that] has thrived on the resulting diet of fragmentary information, half-truths, and dramatic anecdotes."[85]

We will see in the following section, however, that a number of correctional administrators have indeed opened their doors and gates to academic researchers in an ongoing attempt to learn "what works."

✦ RECENT RESEARCH FINDINGS

Many writers have painted a horrible landscape of prisons, describing them as being devoid of even the most basic elements of humanity,[86] detrimental to the humanity of the offender,[87] and generally issuing a scathing indictment of prisons.[88] However, according to James Bonta and Paul Gendreau, "Careful empirical evaluations have failed to uncover these pervasive negative effects of incarceration that so many have assumed. Even Goffman did not collect data directly from prisons."[89] The following research findings should establish who is more correct in their assessment, because prisons, although appearing similar on the outside, have been proven via research to vary widely in terms of their security, programming, and living conditions.

Prison and Jail Crowding. Crowding is seen by many correctional administrators as *the* major barrier to humane housing of offenders. As mentioned earlier, this problem has wrought court intervention in 37 states. Researchers have viewed it as a complex phenomenon, with most agreeing that crowding is a psychological response to high population density which is often viewed as stressful.[90] Bonta and Gendreau, after a review of the literature, stated that they could *not* conclude that high population density is always associated with aggressive behavior. They found that other variables, such as age of the inmates, played important moderating roles, and that the relationship between misconduct and population density was more pronounced in institutions housing young offenders.[91] They also found evidence that factors other than prison variables may influence aggressive behavior; for example, crowded prisons may be poorly managed.[92] Furthermore, the chronicity, or increased length of exposure to overcrowded conditions also seems to increase the risk of inmate misconduct.[93]

In summary, crowded prisons and jails may cause physiological and psychological stress among many inmates, However, more disruptive effects depend on moderating personal variables such as age, institutional parameters (such as sudden shifts in the inmate membership), and the chronicity of the situation.[94]

Health Risks from Incarceration. Given that crowding can cause stress for inmates, does incarceration threaten the health of the confined? Correctional administrators have also assisted in determining the response to that question. First, while it is widely believed that the risk of homicide is greater within prison than in the community at large, the findings are mixed.

In Canadian penitentiaries, the homicide rates have been about 20 times that of similar-aged males in society.[95] But in the United States, deaths due to homicide are actually less likely within prison.[96] Regarding self-injurious behavior, the results are more consistent, with the finding that inmate suicides for a 20-year period in the United States occurred at a rate of 17.5 per 100,000 inmates, compared with 11 per 100,000 people in the general population.[97] Self-mutilations are at an even higher rate.[98] A number of other researchers have failed to find negative effects on inmate health.[99] Two studies have even found a significantly lower incidence of hypertension among inmates than in the general population.[100]

Indeed, the evidence indicates that many prisons may actually be conducive to good health. In a number of cases, complaints have either decreased with time served [101] or remained unchanged.[102] Interestingly, we may conclude that because most prisons afford regular and nutritious diets, access to recreational exercise, and opportunity to sleep, along with available medical care, the offender may receive a fortuitous benefit in isolation from a highly risky lifestyle in the community.[103]

Effects of Long-Term Incarceration. What happens to people who serve lengthy prison terms? In late 1992, there were nearly 68,000 men and women serving life sentences in the state and federal prisons (the range was from 3 in Hawaii to 11,767 in California).[104] Of course, few of them will probably spend an entire lifetime in prison, but with the advent of mandatory sentencing laws, increases in violent crimes, decreasing early paroles, and new crimes being committed while in prison, inmates nonetheless have considerable opportunity for long-term incarceration.

Using cognitive tests, these inmates have demonstrated no differences in intellectual performance from that of short-term inmates. However, long-termers showed increased hostility and social introversion [105] and decreased self-evaluation and evaluation of work and father.[106] Other studies have found no evidence of psychological deterioration; in fact, verbal intelligence improved over time and hostility decreased.[107]

Timothy Flanagan compared misconduct rates of short- and long-term inmates, finding that even after controlling for age, the misconduct rate among the long-term inmates was approximately half that of the short-term offenders.[108] Additional studies assessing lifers found no deterioration in health, psychiatric symptoms, or intellect.[109] Even long-termers themselves have reported that the earlier portion of their sentences was more stressful and that with time they learned to cope effectively. [110] Similar findings have occurred with respect to female offenders; in fact, long-term women inmates were more bothered by boredom and lack of activity than by anxiety.[111]

In summary, the evidence indicates little support for the notion that long-term imprisonment has detrimental effects. As a caution, however, Flanagan suggested that lifers may change in areas that are as yet unmeasured,[112] such as family separation issues and vocational skill training needs.[113]

Effects of Solitary Confinement. Solitary confinement, also referred to as punitive segregation, has been described as "the most individually destructive, psychologically crippling, and socially alienating experience that could conceivably exist within the borders of the country."[114] Is this scathing denouncement an accurate depiction? Is it per se "cruel and unusual"? There exists an extensive body of literature on the effects of placing people (usually college students) in solitary confinement or under conditions of sensory deprivation. Considerable research has also been performed with inmates themselves.

Studies using volunteers have found few detrimental effects for subjects placed in solitary confinement for periods of up to 10 days. Perceptual and motor abilities were not impaired, physiological levels of stress were lower than for control groups, and various attitudes toward the experience and the self did not worsen.[115] Studies using prison inmates have also found no detrimental effects. In general, inmates found the first 72 hours the most difficult but after that they adjusted quite well. Researchers concluded that there was "no support for the claim that solitary confinement...is overwhelmingly aversive, stressful, or damaging to the inmates."[116] Note, however, that two studies found indications of pathology for inmates incarcerated for periods up to a year (but no control groups were used).[117]

Effects of Death Row. As of mid-1993, there were 2737 prisoners under sentence of death in 36 states, by the federal government (4), and the military (6). This is an increase from 1050 in 1982, or 161 percent.[118] The growing numbers have led to crowded conditions on some death rows; in one incident, two condemned prisoners took hostages apparently as a sign of protest against crowded conditions.[119]

There is very little research available concerning how inmates adjust to death row. The first such study was probably done in 1962, of 19 inmates awaiting execution in Sing Sing. Expecting to find intense anxiety and depression, researchers found none.[120]. Another study which tested eight men awaiting execution found that five men showed no observable deterioration, while three displayed symptoms ranging from paranoia to insomnia.[121] A larger study of 34 death row inmates showed increased feelings of depression and hopelessness; severe disturbances (psychosis) was not observed.[122]

Robert Johnson interviewed 35 men on death row and found them concerned over their powerlessness, fearful of surroundings, and feeling emotionally drained. Younger inmates were more susceptible to these concerns.[123] Similar studies using unstructured interviews found that most inmates exhibited well-intact defenses regarding their alleged guilt [124] and that all slept well and felt relatively good about themselves.[125]

Although limited in number, these studies demonstrate a lack of evidence of severe psychological reactions to a tragic fate. In fact, there are indications that the family and friends of condemned inmates suffer the most.[126]

Implications for Correctional Administrators. All of the foregoing research findings have implications for correctional administrators, some of which are quite pointed and others being less clear. Of particular note was the finding that if emotional distress is reported by inmates, it is more often early in their incarceration. It is at this point that they may be more receptive to treatment; the implication for the timing of institutional treatment programs is obvious.

However, in view of several factors—the contemporary tough law-and-order stance toward offenders, levels of violent crimes, jail and prison crowding, recidivism, new construction costs, and the paucity of programming for inmates—we are forced to contemplate what message society is sending correctional administrators. If the primary purpose of incarceration is *custody* and incapacitation for a set period, we have clearly succeeded. However, recalling that nearly half of all Americans support rehabilitative efforts, if society really wishes to *rehabilitate* them, the data indicate that we are failing.

We now know that the "free market" system of programming for inmates has not reduced or deterred crime, and that the specter of imprisonment appears to do little to prevent crime. Most offenders today come from communities where conditions fall below the living standards that most Americans would recognize.[127] We must wonder whether, for many members of our society, the threat of incarceration really holds any deterrent benefit.

John DiIulio complained that those who know the most about what prisons do have rarely taken part in the debates over what prisons are for. People who have actually spent their lives working with prisoners have ideas on the subject, but more attention is given, he said, to outside researchers whose focus is on the inmates rather than the overall organization.[128] Should correctional administrators crusade for greater latitude in punishing and treating their charges? Have the courts and society at large played too large a role in this traditionally "laissez-faire" area? Are correctional administrators even in a position to make a difference in criminality? Do they know what works better than those of us in the outside world? These are pressing and important questions, given the data and history of correctional administration.

Summary

At the beginning of this chapter we considered whether or not the free-market approach to correctional programming is working. We must conclude that it has not, and that taking the responsibility of punishing and treating offenders out of the hands of correctional administrators has, in light of all available data, and the physical, emotional, and economic toll of crime, accomplished little. Although this is by no means a call for a return to the cruel bygone era of imprisonment, it is to signal that what we have done with our sentenced offenders, particularly short-term offenders, has not succeeded; perhaps it is time once again to rethink our methods and philosophy. It would seem that we need either to give correctional administrators more resources for programming, or divorce ourselves completely from the notion that the free-market allocation of resources is a proper use of them.

We also presented an overview of correctional organization and the treatment and custody operations. Increases in violent crime, and the general finding that institutionalization can be more of a positive than negative experience, led us to two general conclusions: (1) serious offenders neither accept nor abide by society's norms; and (2) most offenders today come from communities where conditions fall below the living standards that most Americans would recognize. We must question whether or not, for many persons in our society, the threat of incarceration holds any deterrent value whatsoever.

Questions for Review—————————————

1. Describe the typical organization of the modern prison.
2. In what ways are correctional organizations unique? Why is it important that they adhere to the open system of management?
3. What factors are presently contributing to America's prison "boom"? What is the "new generation" jail, and how might it help reduce the effects of overcrowding and the quality of life in institutions?
4. What options are available to administrators for attempting to work with emotional or behavioral problems of inmates? Should administrators even attempt to "rehabilitate" offenders? Why or why not?
5. In what major ways do jails differ from prisons? (Include in your response the types of offenders housed in each.) How are prisons and jails *similar* (incorporate a discussion of programs offered in each)?
6. Delineate some major recent findings in corrections research regarding offenders and the effects of incarceration and death row. Enumerate the implications for correctional administrators.

For Further Reading—————————————

HARRY E. ALLEN and CLIFFORD E. SIMONSEN, *Corrections in America* (5th ed.). New York: Macmillan, 1989.

JOHN J. DIIULIO, JR., *Governing Prisons: A Comparative Study of Correctional Management.* New York: Free Press, 1988.

JOHN J. DIIULIO, JR., *Principled Agents: Leadership, Administration, and Culture in a Federal Bureaucracy.* New York: Oxford University Press, forthcoming.

ROBERT JOHNSON and HANS TOCH (eds.), *The Pains of Imprisonment.* Beverly Hills, Calif.: Sage Publications, 1982.

J. M. MOYNAHAN and EARLE K. STEWART, *The American Jail: Its Development and Growth.* Chicago: Nelson-Hall, 1980.

JOHN W. MURPHY and JACK E. DISON (eds.), *Are Prisons Any Better? Twenty Years of Correctional Reform.* Newbury Park, Calif.: Sage Publications, 1990.

ALEXANDER B. SMITH and LOUIS BERLIN, *Treating the Criminal Offender.* New York: Plenum, 1988.

Notes —————————————————————————

1. George F. Cole, personal communication, April 18, 1991.
2. William G. Archambeault and Betty J. Archambeault, *Correctional Supervisory Management: Principles of Organization, Policy, and Law* (Englewood Cliffs, N.J.: Prentice Hall), 1982, p. 5.
3. *Ibid.*
4. *Ibid.*, p. 6.
5. Jim L. Munro, "Towards a Theory of Criminal Justice Administration: A General Systems Perspective," *Public Administration Review* (November/December 1977):621–631.
6. See Ken Peak, "Correctional Theory in Theory and Praxis," *Criminal Justice Review* 10 (1985).
7. Richter H. Moore, Jr., "The Criminal Justice Non-system," in R. Moore, T. Marks, and R. Barrow (eds.), *Readings in Criminal Justice* (Indianapolis, Ind.: Bobbs-Merrill, 1976), pp. 5–13.
8. William G. Archambeault and Betty J. Archambeault, *Correctional Supervisory Management: Principles of Organization, Policy, and Law*, pp. 44–45.
9. Vernon Fox, *Introduction to Corrections* (2d ed.) (Englewood Cliffs, N.J.: Prentice Hall, 1977), p. 406.
10. William G. Archambeault and Betty J. Archambeault, *Correctional Supervisory Management: Principles of Organization, Policy, and Law*, p. 47.
11. *Ibid.*, p. 48.
12. *Ibid.*, p. 49.
13. *Ibid.*, p. 54.
14. *Ibid.*, p. 55.
15. *Ibid.*, p. 56.
16. *Ibid.*, p. 59.
17. T. Paul Louis and Jerry R. Sparger, "Treatment Modalities Within Prison," in John W. Murphy and Jack E. Dison (eds.), *Are Prisons Any Better? Twenty Years of Correctional Reform* (Newbury Park, Calif.: Sage Publications, 1990), p. 166.
18. Harry E. Allen and Clifford E. Simonsen, *Corrections in America* (5th ed.) (New York: Macmillan, 1989), p. 469.

19. James A. Inciardi, *Criminal Justice* (3d ed.) (San Diego, Calif.: Harcourt Brace Jovanovich, 1990), p. 576.

20. *Ibid.*

21. Barry J. Nidorf, "Community Corrections: Turning the Crowding Crisis into Opportunities," *Corrections Today* (October 1989):82–88.

22. Marilyn Elias, "Study Links TV Violence, Behavior," *USA Today* (May 23, 1993).

23. U.S. Department of Justice, Bureau of Justice Statistics Bulletin, *Prisoners in 1991* (Washington, D.C.: Author, May 1993), p. 7.

24. Ted Gest, "The Prison Boom Bust," *Newsweek* (May 4, 1992): 28–31.

25. John P. Conrad, "The Redefinition of Probation: Drastic Proposals to Solve an Urgent Problem," in Patrick D. McAnany, Doug Thomson, and David Fogel (eds.), *Probation and Justice: Reconsideration of Mission* (Cambridge, Mass.: Oelgeschlager, Gunn, and Hain, 1984), p. 258.

26. Ted Gest, "The Prison Boom Bust," p. 29.

27. *Ibid.*

28. *Ibid.*

29. *Ibid.*, p. 31.

30. Robert Levinson, "Try Softer," in Robert Johnson and Hans Toch (eds.), *The Pains of Imprisonment* (Beverly Hills, Calif.: Sage Publications, 1982), p. 246.

31. Kathleen Maguire, Ann L. Pastore, and Timothy J. Flanagan (eds.), *Sourcebook of Criminal Justice Statistics 1992* (U.S. Department of Justice, Bureau of Justice Statistics. (Washington, D.C.: U.S. Government Printing Office, 1993), p. 210.

32. T. Paul Louis and Jerry R. Sparger, "Treatment Modalities Within Prison," in John W. Murphy and Jack E. Dison (eds.), *Are Prisons Any Better? Twenty Years of Correctional Reform*, pp. 147–162.

33. *Ibid.*, p. 149.

34. Ted Palmer, "The `Effectiveness' Issue Today: An Overview," *Federal Probation* 42 (1983):3–10.

35. Paul Gendreau and Robert R. Ross, "Correctional Treatment: Some Recommendations for Effective Intervention," *Juvenile and Family Court Journal* 34 (1984):31–39.

36. See D. A. Andrews, "Program Structure and Effective Correctional Practices: A Summary of the CAVIC Research," in Robert R. Ross and Paul Gendreau (eds.), *Effective Correctional Treatment* (Toronto, Ontario, Canada: Butterworth, 1980)); R. Peters, *Deviant Behavioral Contracting with Conduct Problem Youth* (Kingston, Ontario, Canada: Queen's University, 1981).

37. Kathleen Maguire, Ann L. Pastore, and Timothy J. Flanagan, (eds.), *Sourcebook of Criminal Justice Statistics 1992*, p. 626.

38. T. Paul Louis and Jerry R. Sparger, "Treatment Modalities within Prison," pp. 152–153.

39. CEGA Publishing, *Corrections Compendium* (Lincoln, Neb.: Author, July 1991), pp. 10–15.

40. Alexander B. Smith and Louis Berlin, *Treating the Criminal Offender* (New York: Plenum Press, 1988).

41. T. Paul Louis and Jerry R. Sparger, "Treatment Modalities within Prison," p. 155.

42. Murray L. Cohen, Theohans Seghorn, and Wilfred Calmas, "Sociometric Study of the Sex Offender," *Journal of Abnormal Psychology* 74 (1971):249–255.

43. Stanley L. Brodsky (ed.), *Psychologists in the Criminal Justice System* (Urbana, Ill.: University of Illinois Press, 1973); Fritz A. Henn, Marijan Herjanic, and Robert H. Vanderpearl, "Forensic Psychiatry: Profiles of Two Types of Sex Offenders," *American Journal of Psychiatry* 133 (1976):654–696.

44. Samuel B. Guze, *Criminality and Psychiatric Disorders* (New York: Oxford University Press, 1976).

45. T. Paul Louis and Jerry R. Sparger, "Treatment Modalities within Prison," p. 154.

46. See, for example, U.S. Department of Justice, Bureau of Justice Statistics, *Report to the Nation on Crime and Justice: The Data* (Rockville, Md.: National Criminal Justice Reference Service, 1983); C. R. Bartol and A. M. Bartol, *Criminal Behavior: A Psychosocial Approach* (Englewood Cliffs, N.J.: Prentice Hall, 1986); Marvin Wolfgang, *Patterns in Criminal Homicide* (Philadelphia: University of Pennsylvania Press, 1958).

47. T. Paul Louis and Jerry R. Sparger, "Treatment Modalities within Prison," p. 157.

48. *Ibid.*

49. U.S. Department of Justice, Bureau of Justice Statistics Special Report, *Population Density in Local Jails: 1988* (Washington, D.C.: Author, 1990), p. 1.

50. U.S. Department of Justice, Bureau of Justice Statistics Bulletin, *Sheriff's Departments: 1990* (Washington, D.C.: Author, 1992), p. 5.

51. For example, see James M. Moynahan and Earle K. Stewart, *The American Jail: Its Development and Growth* (Chicago: Nelson-Hall, 1980), p. 100; Clemens Bartollas, Stuart J. Miller, and Paul B. Wice, *Participants in American Criminal Justice: The Promise and the Performance* (Englewood Cliffs, N.J.: Prentice Hall, 1983), p. 59.

52. National Advisory Commission on Criminal Justice Standards and Goals, *Corrections* (Washington, D.C.: U.S. Government Printing Office, 1973), p. 292.

53. See Larry Mays and Joel Thompson, "Mayberry Revisited: The Characteristics and Operations of America's Small Jails," paper presented at the Annual Meeting of the Academy of Criminal Justice Sciences, St. Louis, Mo., March 17, 1987.

54. U.S. Department of Justice, Bureau of Justice Statistics Special Report, *Population Density in Local Jails*, 1988, p. 4.

55. See *Manual of Standards for Adult Correctional Institutions*, (College Park, Md.: American Correctional Association, August 1977), and *Federal Standards for Correction* (Washington, D.C.: U.S. Department of Justice, 1980).

56. U.S. Department of Justice, Bureau of Justice Statistics Special Report, *Population Density in Local Jails: 1988*, pp. 2, 7.

57. *Ibid.*, p. 9.

58. *Ibid.*

59. *Ibid.*

60. *Ibid.*

61. A. E. D. Howard, "The States and the Supreme Court," 31 *Catholic University Law Review* 375 (1982), at 379.

62. J. Moore, "Prison Litigation and the States: A Case Law Review," *State Legislative Report* 8 (1981):1.

63. National Sheriffs' Association, *The State of Our Nation's Jails, 1982* (Washington, D.C.: Author, 1982), p. 55.

64. Linda L. Zupan, *Jails: Reform and the New Generation Philosophy* (Cincinnati, Ohio: Anderson, 1991), p. 66.

65. Ibid., p. 67.

66. R. Wener and R. Olson, *User Based Assessments of the Federal Metropolitan Correctional Centers: Final Report* (Washington, D.C.: U.S. Bureau of Prisons, 1978), p. 4.

67. S. H. Gettinger, *New Generation Jails: An Innovative Approach to an Age-Old Problem* (Washington, D.C.: National Institute of Corrections, 1984), p. 11.

68. Linda L. Zupan, *Jails: Reform and the New Generation Philosophy*, p. 71.

69. Quoted in William R. Nelson and M. O'Toole, *New Generation Jails* (Boulder, Colo.: Library Information Specialists, Inc., 1983), pp. 35–36.

70. U.S. Department of Justice, National Institute of Justice Research in Brief, *Making Jails Productive* (Washington, D.C.: Author, 1987), p. 1.

71. *Ibid.*, p. 16.

72. Erving Goffman, *Asylums* (Garden City, N.Y.: Anchor Books, 1961).

73. *Ibid.*, p. xiii.

74. Richard McGee, *Prisons and Politics* (Lexington, Mass.: Lexington Books, 1981).

75. Robert Martinson, "What Works? Questions and Answers about Prison Reform," *The Public Interest* 35 (1974):48–49.

76. President's Commission on Law Enforcement and Administration of Justice, *The Challenge of Crime in a Free Society* (Washington, D.C.: U.S. Government Printing Office, 1967), p. 273 (emphasis added).

77. State of New York, *Preliminary Report of the Governor's Special Committee on Criminal Offenders* (New York: Author, 1968), pp. 316–318.

78. Daniel Glaser, "Correctional Research: An Elusive Paradise," *Journal of Research in Crime and Delinquency* 11 (1965):1–11.

79. Gordon P. Waldo, "The Dilemma of Correctional Research," *American Journal of Correction* 31 (1969):6–7.

80. Ken Peak, "Correctional Theory in Theory and Praxis," pp. 27–31.

81. Carol Weiss, *Evaluation Research* (Englewood Cliffs, N.J.: Prentice Hall, 1972).

82. See, for example, Ken Peak, "Correctional Theory in Theory and Praxis," pp. 27–31.

83. 418 U.S. 539 (1974).

84. See Philip Zimbardo, "The Psychological Power and Pathology of Imprisonment," in John Snortum and Ilana Hadar (eds.), *Criminal Justice: Allies and Adversaries* (Pacific Palisades, Calif.: Palisades Publishers, 1973), pp. 202–210.

85. Richard McGee, *Prisons and Politics* (Lexington, Mass.: Lexington Books, 1981).

86. Cf. Gresham Sykes, *The Society of Captives: A Study of a Maximum Security Prison* (Princeton, N.J.: Princeton University Press, 1958).

87. Milton G. Rector, "Prisons and Crime," *Crime and Delinquency* 28 (1982):505–507.

88. Jessica Mitford, *Kind and Unusual Punishment* (New York: Alfred A. Knopf, 1973).

89. James Bonta and Paul Gendreau, "Reexamining the Cruel and Unusual Punishment of Prison Life," *Law and Human Behavior* 14 (1990):347–372.

90. Irwin Altman, "Crowding: Historical and Contemporary Trends in Crowding Research," in A. Baum and M. Y. M. Epstein (eds.), *Human Response to Crowding* (Hillsdale, N.J.: Lawrence Erlbaum, 1978), pp. 3–29.

91. James Bonta and Paul Gendreau, "Reexamining the Cruel and Unusual Punishment of Prison Life," p. 353.

92. See Gerald G. Gaes, "The Effects of Overcrowding in Prison," in Michael Tonry and Norval Morris (eds.), *Crime and Justice*, Vol. 6 (Chicago: University of Chicago Press, 1985), pp. 95–146.

93. James Bonta and Geoff Nanckivell, "Institutional Misconduct and Anxiety Levels among Jailed Inmates," *Criminal Justice and Behavior* 7 (1980):203–214; Peter L. Nacci, Hugh E. Teitelbaum, and Jerry Prather, "Population Density and Inmate Misconduct Rates in the Federal Prison System," *Federal Probation* 41 (1977):26–31.

94. James Bonta and Paul Gendreau, "Reexamining the Cruel and Unusual Punishment of Prison Life," p. 355.

95. F. J. Porporino and J. P. Martin, *Strategies for Reducing Prison Violence* (Ottawa, Ontario, Canada: Solicitor General Canada, 1983).

96. R. Barry Ruback and Christopher A. Innes, "The Relevance and Irrelevance of Psychological Research: The Example of Prison Crowding," *American Psychologist* 43 (1988):683–693.

97. W. T. Austin and Charles M. Unkovic, "Prison Suicide," *Criminal Justice Review* 2 (1977):103–106.

98. Robert R. Ross and H. B. McKay, *Self Mutilation* (Lexington, Mass.: Lexington Books, 1979).

99. See Seth B. Goldsmith, "Jailhouse Medicine: Travesty or Justice?" *Health Services Report* 87 (1972):767–774; R. A. Derro, "Administrative Health Evaluation of Inmates of a City-County Workhouse," *Minnesota Medicine* 61 (1978):333–337.

100. See L. Culpepper and J. Floom, "Incarceration and Blood Pressure," *Social Services and Medicine* 14 (1980):571–574; Lloyd F. Novick, Richard Della-Penna, Melvin S. Schwartz, Elaine Remlinger, and Regina Lowenstein, "Health Status of the New York City Prison Population," *Medical Care* 15 (1977):205–216.

101. Doris L. MacKenzie and Lynne Goodstein, "Long-Term Incarceration Impacts and Characteristics of Long-Term Offenders: An Empirical Analysis," *Criminal Justice and Behavior* 13 (1985):395–414.

102. J. S. Wormith, "The Effects of Incarceration: Myth-Busting in Criminal Justice," paper presented at the 94th Annual Conference of the American Psychological Association. Washington, D.C., August 1986.

103. James Bonta and Paul Gendreau, "Reexamining the Cruel and Unusual Punishment of Prison Life," p. 357.

104. Kathleen Maguire, Ann L. Pastore, and Timothy J. Flanagan (eds.), *Sourcebook of Criminal Justice Statistics* 1992, p. 633.

105. K. J. Heskin, F. V. Smith, P. A. Banister, and N. Bolton, "Psychological Correlates of Long-Term Imprisonment:II. Personality Variables," *British Journal of Criminology* 13 (1973):323–330.

106. K. J. Heskin, F. V. Smith, P. A. Banister, and N. Bolton, "Psychological Correlates of Long-Term Imprisonment:III. Attitudinal Variables," *British Journal of Criminology* 14 (1974):150–157.

107. N. Bolton, F. V. Smith, K. J. Heskin, and P. A. Banister, "Psychological Correlates of Long-Term Imprisonment:IV. A Longitudinal Analysis," *British Journal of Criminology* 16 (1976):36–47.

108. Timothy J. Flanagan, "Time Served and Institutional Misconduct: Patterns of Involvement in Disciplinary Infractions among Long-Term and Short-Term Inmates," *Journal of Criminal Justice* 8 (1980):357–367.

109. W. Rasch, "The Effects of Indeterminate Sentencing: A Study of Men Sentenced to Life Imprisonment," *International Journal of Law and Psychiatry* 4 (1981):417–431.

110. Doris L. MacKenzie and Lynn Goodstein, "Long-Term Incarceration Impacts and Characteristics of Long-Term Offenders: An Empirical Analysis," p. 414.

111. Doris L. MacKenzie, James W. Robinson, and C. S. Campbell, "Long-term Incarceration of Female Offenders: Prison Adjustment and Coping," *Criminal Justice and Behavior* 16 (1989):223–238.

112. Timothy J. Flanagan, "Lifers and Long-Termers: Doing Big Time," in Robert Johnson and Hans Toch (eds.), *The Pains of Imprisonment*, pp. 115–128.

113. Deborah G. Wilson and Gennaro F. Vito, "Long-Term Inmates: Special Needs and Management Considerations," *Federal Probation* 52 (1988):21–26.

114. M. Jackson, *Prisons of Isolation: Solitary Confinement in Canada* (Toronto, Ontario, Canada: University of Toronto Press, 1983), p. 243.

115. James Bonta and Paul Gendreau, "Reexamining the Cruel and Unusual Punishment of Prison Life," p. 360.

116. P. Suedfeld, C. Ramirez, J. Deaton, and G. Baker-Brown, "Reactions and Attributes of Prisoners in Solitary Confinement," *Criminal Justice and Behavior* 9 (1982):303–340.

117. B. M. Cormier and P. J. Williams, "Excessive Deprivation of Liberty as a Form of Punishment," paper presented at the meeting of the Canadian Psychiatric Association, Edmonton, Alberta, Canada 1966; Stuart Grassian, "Psychopathological Effects of Solitary Confinement," *American Journal of Psychiatry* 140 (1983):1450–1454.

118. Kathleen Maguire, Ann L. Pastore, and Timothy J. Flanagan (eds.), *Sourcebook of Criminal Justice Statistics* 1992, pp. 670, 673.

119. "Killers Release Hostages after Death Row Siege," *The Citizen* (March 18, 1986).

120. Harvey Bluestone and Carl L. McGahee, "Reacting to Extreme Stress: Impending Death by Execution," *American Journal of Psychiatry* 119 (1962):393–396.

121. Johnnie L. Gallemore and James H. Panton, "Inmate Responses to Lengthy Death Row Confinement," *American Journal of Psychiatry* 129 (1972):81–86.

122. James H. Panton, "Personality Characteristics of Death Row Prison Inmates," *Journal of Clinical Psychology* 32 (1976):306–309.

123. Robert Johnson, "Life under Sentence of Death," in Robert Johnson and Hans Toch (eds.), *The Pains of Imprisonment*, pp. 129–145.

124. Charles E. Smith and Richard Reid Felix, "Beyond Deterrence: A Study of Defenses on Death Row," *Federal Probation* 50 (1986):55–59.

125. Julius Debro, Komanduri Murty, Julian Roebuck, and Claude McCann, "Death Row Inmates: A Comparison of Georgia and Florida Profiles," *Criminal Justice Review* 12 (1987):41–46.

126. John O. Smykla, "The Human Impact of Capital Punishment: Interviews of Families of Persons on Death Row," *Journal of Criminal Justice* 15 (1987):331–347.

127. Joan Petersilia, "When Probation Becomes More Dreaded Than Prison," *Federal Probation* 54 (March 1990):23–27.

128. John J. DiIulio, Jr., *Governing Prisons: A Comparative Study of Correctional Management* (New York: Free Press, 1987) p. 165.

Personnel Roles and Functions

The mood and temper of the public in regard to the treatment of crime and criminals is one of the most unfailing tests of the civilization of any country.

—Winston Churchill

The vilest weeds like poison-weeds Bloom well in prison-air.

—Oscar Wilde

✦ INTRODUCTION

In this chapter we focus on the administrative methods and problems of correctional organizations. First, we analyze several facets and challenges of prison administration (including how to govern prisons, carry out death sentences, deal with crowding, and use confidential information and inmate self-help groups). We then turn to the front-line personnel in prisons: the correctional officers, including a view of their stereotyped roles and function, and professional orientation. Finally, we examine the "cousin" of prisons, the jails. In this section we highlight how jail staff, inmates, and facilities are in reality quite different from those of prisons.

Two basic principles constitute the philosophy of the "keepers": first, whatever the reasons for sending a person to prison, the prisoner is not to suffer pains beyond the deprivation of liberty—confinement itself is the punishment; second, regardless of the crime, the prisoner will be treated humanely and in accordance with his or her behavior; even the most heinous offender is to be treated with respect and dignity and given privileges if institutional behavior warrants it.[1] Our analysis of institutional management is predicated on those two principles.

✦ PRISON ADMINISTRATION FOR THE 1990S

✧ WARDENS AND THE "NEW OLD PENOLOGY"

The key to the conditions and general climate of any prison is the warden (or superintendent). As we discussed in Chapter 10, the role of warden has changed over the past few decades, from one of being a czar over his dominion, to that of a well-trained manager. Like police administration, however, it is probably accurate to say that the "old ways" of many wardens—riding roughshod over staff and inmates alike—probably fostered the growth of unionism among correctional officers (unionism is discussed in more detail in Chapter 15). As prison employees have gained power to confront wardens through their unions, some wardens have sought to rely more on inmates to control the prison. For example, a warden at Walla Walla, Washington, sought to manipulate inmate clubs to control both inmates and disgruntled officers, allowing a bikers' club and similar organizations within the walls. This ploy did not work, and the result was more inmate strikes and riots, along with heightened guard upheaval.[2]

Another nuance has come with the "new penology": women administrators and staff members in prisons. Today women are employed at all levels in prisons. In fact, a recent survey found that 12 percent (2627 of 21,498) of all supervisory officers in adult correctional institutions were women.[3] Until recently, however, women have not worked in all-male institutions. Research in three areas of early concern—fitness for correctional work, disruptive influence of women, and issues of inmate privacy—has determined that these are seldom problematical for female employees and, when they are, they are easily overcome.[4]

✧ GOVERNING PRISONS

Throughout the nineteenth and the early part of the twentieth centuries, studies of prisons generally focused on the administrators rather than on the inmates. Beginning in the 1940s, however, there was an ideological shift from sympathy for the work of prison administrators to sympathy for the inmates and social order of the cell blocks. The central theme seems to be that these institutions were poorly run—what prison researcher John J. DiIulio, Jr. referred to as the "ineffective prisons" view.[5] Many writers expressed grave doubts about the efficacy of correctional administrators and went so far as to express the idea that prison managers could do nothing to improve conditions behind bars. The rise of a younger, more aggressive, and politicized breed of inmates in the 1960s, with obstreperous leaders, wrought a situation that was about to go out of control.

It is not surprising that when contemporary researchers attempt to relate prison management practices to the quality of life behind bars, the results are normally quite negative: Prisons that are managed in a tight, authoritarian fashion are seen as plagued with disorder and inadequate programs, and those that are managed in a loose, participative fashion are equally troubled; and those with a mixture of these two styles are not seen as doing any better.[6]

In a three-year study of prison management in Texas, Michigan, and California, DiIulio did not find that levels of order (rates of individual and collective violence, and other forms of misconduct), amenity (availability of clean cells, decent food, etc.), and service (availability of work opportunities, educational programs, etc.) varied with any of the following factors: a "better class" of inmates; greater per capita spending; lower levels of crowding; lower inmate-to-staff ratios; greater officer training; more modern plant and equipment; and more routine use of repressive measures. DiIulio concluded that "all roads, it seemed, led to the conclusion that the quality of prison life depended mainly on the quality of prison management."[7]

DiIulio also found that prisons led by a stable team of like-minded executives, structured in a paramilitary, security-driven, bureaucratic fashion, had higher levels of order, amenity, and service than those managed in other ways, *even when* the former institutions were more crowded, spent less per capita, had higher inmate/staff ratios, and so on. *"The only findings of this study that, to me at least, seem indispensable, is that…prison management matters"* [emphasis his].[8]

Other recent studies have addressed what constitutes the "well-governed prison." One analysis of major prison riots from 1971 and 1986 found that riots were due primarily to a breakdown in security procedures—the daily routine of numbering, counting, frisking, locking, contraband control, and cell searches—that are the heart of administration in most prisons.[9] Problems in areas such as crowding, underfunding, festering inmate-staff relations, and racial animosities may make a riot more *likely*, but poor security management will make riots *inevitable*.[10]

DiIulio offered six general principles of good prison leadership:

1. Successful leaders focus, and inspire their subordinates to focus, on results rather than process, on performance rather than procedures, on ends rather than means. In short, managers are judged on results, not on excuses.

2. Organizational culture is custodial at core. Even professional staff members, DiIulio emphasized—such as doctors, psychiatrists, accountants, nurses, and other nonuniformed staff—are trained to think of themselves as correctional officers first, and all receive some basic training. As an example, in a recent disturbance at a federal penitentiary, middle-aged secretaries in skirts toted guns on the perimeter.

3. Leaders of successful institutions follow the MBWA principle: management by walking around. ("Walking George" Beto, discussed in Chapter 3, was a prime example of this approach to management.) These managers are not strangers to the cellblocks and are always on the scene when trouble erupts.

4. Successful leaders make close alliances with key politicians, judges, journalists, reformers, and other outsiders. (The need to practice openness is discussed below.)

5. Successful leaders rarely innovate, but their innovations are far-reaching and the reasons for them are made known to staff and inmates well in advance. Line staff are notoriously sensitive to what administrators do "for inmates" versus "what they do for us." Thus leaders must be careful not to upset the balance and erode staff loyalty.

6. Successful leaders are in office long enough to understand and, as necessary, modify the organization's internal operations and external relations. DiIulio classified leaders' terms of office as "flies," "fatalists," "foot soldiers," and "founders". The flies come and go unnoticed and are inconsequential. Fatalists serve brief terms as well, always complaining about the futility of incarceration and the hopelessness of correctional reform. The foot soldiers served long terms, often inheriting their job from a fly or fatalist, making consequential improvements whenever they could. Founders either created an agency or reorganized it in a major and positive way.[11]

To summarize, to old penologists, prison administrators were admirable public servants, inmates were to be restricted, and any form of self-government was eschewed. To new penologists, prison administrators are loathsome and evil, while inmates are responsible victims, and complete self-government is the ideal. DiIulio calls for a "new old penology," or a shift of attention from the society of captives to the government of keepers. He asserted that tight administrative control is more conducive to decent prison conditions than loose administrative control. This approach, he added, will "push administrators back to the bar of attention," treating them at least as well as their charges.[12]

✧ OTHER CONTEMPORARY CHALLENGES

Today's corrections administrator is faced with a fascinating array of challenges, including the siting of correctional facilities; design and building of facilities (cheaper and quicker); health care cost containment; managing overcrowding; developing alternatives; addressing issues of gangs, AIDS, and staff safety and training; continuing to satisfy old court orders and consent decrees (while avoiding new court oversight due to burgeoning institution populations); and enhancing security and programs while facing a reduction in resources.[13]

Ten to 20 years ago the correctional administrator who was a solid manager could survive quite well; today, he or she must spend large amounts of time in the public policymaking arena. The "tough on crime" stance adopted by the political process has required administrators to enter the political domain more than ever before, projecting resources that will be required and shaping a course of public policy within available resources.

Many of the economic pressures found in the communities are also found in corrections: rising food, construction, and health care costs (the latter exacerbated by individuals whose health has deteriorated through alcoholism, drug use, hepatitis, AIDS, and other abuses) and personnel expectations with regard to salary and benefits (with greater union activism in those areas). Society's litigious nature has also permeated the prison walls. The cost in time and money to defend against inmate lawsuits is sharply felt by today's correctional administrators. Inmates sue not only for traditional alleged conditions of confinement abuses, but over tattoos, pornography, voting rights, accessibility to lottery tickets, too little dessert, clothing style, air quality, and so on. Death penalty cases are on appeal indefinitely, negligent supervision suits abound, and employees are increasingly seeking assistance from the courts in resolving their differences.[14]

Meanwhile, the corrections field suffers from a lack of information. The field is almost devoid of strong research (see Chapter 10) and, therefore, new methodologies to use in either controlling or changing the behavior of the inmates. Therefore, correctional administrators today mimic or develop programs that are generally advertised as "cheaper" and therefore inevitably hold "political charm." Also, correctional administrators of the 1990s must deal with the "Willie Horton" legacy: On any given day an offender may escape or reoffend, causing public and political winds to change completely within a jurisdiction. Politicians have all learned the lesson of Willie Horton well, and perceive that the "tough on crime" stance is a political cornerstone.[15]

Many people working in correctional administration feel that the public image of the field is bad. A corrections consultant wrote that the low level of public esteem does not lie with the media: "The public view of corrections in this country is, frankly, horrible. People are inundated with stories about explosions in offender populations, monopoly-money costs for new prison and jail construction, and vexatious prison and jail litigation. The big stories that reach the public about corrections are almost universally negative."[16] Also attacked were correctional administrators' "deafening silence" when prison furloughs were attacked in a presidential campaign (the 1988 Willie Horton case) and the concurrent implication that long, inflexible sentences were the only acceptable alternative; because awards for exemplary performance are only presented in the obscurity of professional meetings; and because professionalism in the field has remained in the shadows. Correctional administrators have also been chastised for not being politically adept, and taking a "no news is good news" attitude in working with politicos.

It is also argued that a "fortress corrections" mentality has become a philosophy within the field; too many staff, from the top to the bottom, do not understand the public's right to know, and paranoia about the media is rampant. Most often, prison-media relations involve the institution "that has had a suicide in the middle of the night," or they "approach the next morning hoping that the newspapers and TV will not get the story. The myth persists that if one holds onto negative information tightly enough, one will be able to hide in plain sight."[17]

The field has also been reproached by its own for the manner in which it communicates:

> There are no widely-read professional journals in the field. The lack of serious research efforts is criminal considering the magnitude of public pol-

icy questions arising from corrections. There is good research, but most of that is never published. Thus, we re-create each other's mistakes too often. That picture does not connote professionalism. We have a very poor self-image. We don't like ourselves a lot and we don't think well of ourselves. I defy [anyone] to identify an occupation in which such a high percentage of people acknowledge going into the field "by accident."[18]

✦ "DEATH WORK": CARRYING OUT EXECUTIONS

One of the major duties of prison administrators, at least in a majority of the states, is to carry out the wishes of the people and see that condemned persons are executed in a manner that is professional and does not "shock the conscience." The discharge of the death penalty requires a number of people who are trained in individual tasks. Robert Johnson, who has referred to this entire undertaking as "death work,"[19] has studied and witnessed the process personally. Although there is no "typical" process of bringing executions to fruition, following is a general description of the key events.

Death work gains momentum when an execution date draws near and the prisoner is moved to the death house, a short walk from the death chamber. As the date draws near, the process culminates in the so-called "death watch," a 24-hour period that ends when the prisoner has been executed. This final period is generally undertaken by the execution team, who report directly to the warden or superintendent of the institution. The warden or a representative by law presides over the execution. In many states it is a member of the death watch or execution team, acting under the warden's authority, who in fact plays the formal role of executioner.[20]

Although the public image of the executioner is often one of a sinister, solitary figure who wears a black hood and likes to "walk in the misty rain," today that impression is largely inaccurate and misleading. Although there are still a few states that publicly advertise for a "state executioner" as needed, today most executions are carried out by a highly trained team. One prison administrator described the team thus: "An execution is something that needs to be done and good people, dedicated people who believe in the American system, should do it. When they have to hang tough, they can do it and they can do it right. And it's just the right thing to do."[21] "Do it right" in this context means that the execution should be accomplished professionally. Again, in the words of an administrator, "We had to be sure that we did it properly, professionally, and that we gave as much dignity to the person as we possibly could in the process.... If you've gotta do it, it might just as well be done the way it's supposed to be done—without any sensation."[22] Here "proper" means that procedures are performed smoothly; "professional" means without personal feelings that intrude on the procedures in any way.

Johnson found, surprisingly enough, that few personnel on the execution team actually supported the death penalty without reservation. Nonetheless, they are committed to doing it right, "by the book." To minimize the possibility of error, the death watch team is carefully drilled in the mechanics of execution. The process has been broken down into distinct tasks and practiced repeatedly. Division of labor allows each team member to become a specialist, and practice allows them to become confident and, later, accurate under pressure.

During the actual death watch, an officer is with the prisoner at any given time. Officers sit and keep the inmate calm, serving his or her immediate needs. At this stage, they view the condemned as people with explosive personalities, so surveillance is constant and quite intense. During the last five or six hours, two officers are assigned to guard the prisoner. They attempt to maintain a conversation, keeping tabs on the prisoner's state of mind and trying to avoid subjects that might cause depression or anger. As the execution moves closer, the mood normally becomes more somber and subdued. There is a last meal (they normally eat little or nothing at all), then the prisoners box all of their worldly goods, which are inventoried by staff, for delivery to family or friends.[23]

The prisoner then showers, dons a fresh set of clothes, and is placed in an empty tomblike cell, the death cell. All that is left is the wait. At this point there is normally a numb resignation; they wait peacefully to be escorted to their deaths. The warden and the remainder of the death watch team then come, the former then reading the court order, or "death warrant." Meanwhile, official witnesses are preparing themselves for their role. Normally, from 6 to 12 disinterested citizens in good standing serve as witnesses to the execution.[24]

The steps that are taken from this point, with regard to the actual execution, will of course depend on the actual method that is used. For example, 22 states employ lethal injection, 12 use electrocution, 7 utilize gas, 3 use hanging, and 2 employ a firing squad (18 authorize a choice between two methods of execution).[25]

✧ STAFF–INMATE RELATIONSHIPS

A common misconception by the public is that prison administrators, through their correctional officers, have complete control over inmates. Until the 1960s, prisoners were expected to do as they were told. We saw in Chapter 3 that even the courts deferred to the heavy-handed methods of wardens, stating that they did not have the expertise or the jurisdiction to determine how the prison should be managed.[26]

Today, however, inmates do have power. Without the consent and cooperation of the inmates, the modern correctional institution could not function. According to Victor Lofgreen, today's "mega-prison" has changed from a correctional facility with programs and activities aimed at rehabilitating offenders to a racially segregated, gang-controlled warehouse for convicts to do their time. By depending on inmate labor and leadership in order to function, the prisons give power to the inmate groups. In addition, correctional officers are under constant scrutiny by administrators and subject to litigation by inmates. In sum, "the modern prison has become a combat zone."[27]

Lofgreen described a model of the life cycle of the power relationship between the staff and inmates in an adult prison (Figure 11.1); the model

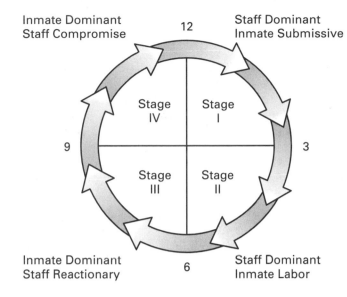

Inmate Dominant
Staff Compromise

Staff Dominant
Inmate Submissive

12

Stage IV | Stage I

9 | | 3

Stage III | Stage II

Inmate Dominant
Staff Reactionary

6

Staff Dominant
Inmate Labor

Figure 11.1 Model of the life cycle of the inmate–staff power relationship in an adult prison (*Source:* Victor D. Lofgreen, "A Model of the Dynamic Power Relationship between Staff and Inmates in a Secure Correctional Facility," paper presented at the Annual Meeting of the Academy of Criminal Justice Sciences, 1991, Reno, Nevada, Used with permission.)

demonstrates the change in the balance of power in the prison from staff to inmates over time, from total staff domination to total inmate domination. Stage I, that of "staff dominant—inmate submissive" begins with administration and staff being in clear, visible, and total control of the institution, with inmates in a lockdown status, usually following a rebellion or major shakedown. However, a correctional facility of today cannot operate very long under these circumstances. The institution depends on inmate labor to function, such as cooking, laundry, cleaning, and so on. Therefore, to provide enough personnel for these tasks, the institution moves into stage II—the "staff dominated–inmate labor" stage. As soon as possible following a disturbance, staff begin to classify inmates and identify those who can be trusted to work. Over time other inmates are released from lockdown and returned to their work assignments. The institution regains its equilibrium and inmates are given more autonomy, freedom of movement, and privileges. A balance of power is created between the two groups, with each side cooperating with the other (although the inmates know they could take control of the prison whenever they wished).[28]

However, after reaching this state of equilibrium, a phenomenon occurs whereby each time a privilege is extended to the inmates by the administration, it becomes locked into the expectations of the inmate subculture. Any attempt by administration to withdraw privileges is met with extreme inmate resistance. Eventually, if administration and staff continue to award new privileges in order to motivate inmates, the latter will have the most power. Inmates may expect to be catered to, even pressuring officers to participate in activities that violate institutional rules or law. A prison in this stage of development, known as the "inmate dominant–staff reactionary" stage, or stage III, has its inmates in a position of superiority over the administration and staff.[29]

The institution becomes more and more unstable. Certain inmates are protected, while others are punished unfairly. At some point, the lack of consistent treatment and favoritism toward certain inmates causes a major loss of credibility in prison administration. Inmates and officers are confused, not knowing what to expect. This is stage IV, "inmate dominant–staff compromise." The tension and anxiety lead to a major disturbance. When the disturbance occurs, the institution is again thrown into an emergency lockdown status (stage I). Order is restored and the process begins again. It can take an institution 2 or 20 years to proceed through this developmental cycle, depending upon how long it takes the inmate subculture to compromise administration and staff. The goal of the administrator is to develop an institutional culture that creates a balance between the power of the staff and the inmates.[30]

By managing change in a deliberate manner, it is possible for the correctional administrator to keep the balance of power between stages II and III for an extended period of time. Lofgreen recommended that administration occasionally "move inmates to a periodic scheduled lockdown to prevent the accumulation of contraband and maintain staff power over the inmates."[31]

✦ POSSIBLE APPROACHES TO CROWDING

As discussed in Chapter 10, crowding may well be the primary problem affecting prisons and jails today. However, according to some observers, a bigger problem may be that corrections has admitted defeat in the battle against crowding. The heart of the problem, it is argued, lies in the fact that density and crowding, although related, are not the same. "The major factors responsible for crowding effects lies within the dynamic properties of social interactions" rather than in density per se.[32]

In other words, the real "pains" of crowding come not from inmate density, but from the fact that prisoners feel crowded and suffer its ill effects; it interferes with their preferred ways of living. Social interactions, marked by poor coping behavior, cause various difficulties. Therefore, improving the quality of prison life should be the first order of reform "business." Some authors maintain that other reforms, such as building new prisons and using alternative forms of punishment (such as those discussed, in Chapter 12), are important but play a secondary role in reducing prison crowding. These strategies should be pursued *after* the crowding problem has been fought where it exists—on the yards and in the cell blocks of our prisons.[33]

Inmates feel crowded when they live under conditions of high density (many bodies), low resources (little to do), and limited control over their lives (few if any ways to escape unpleasant encounters). These conditions magnify the pressures of prison life. The key, it is argued, is to provide more resources and to expand the inmates' capacity to choose how resources are deployed. Prisoners will thus be treated as bona fide "consumers of correctional services."[34] Administrators could conduct "consumer" surveys to determine their perceptions of their needs and the means to meet those needs. Services that inmates do not want or use could be modified or discarded; others could be retained for program development.[35] Prisoners themselves might even find sources, through a variety of existing self-help organizations (described below).

Administration and inmates, Robert Johnson asserted, can work together to develop decent prisons. More areas of stable private space can be developed for prisoners in densely populated, close-custody institutions. Functional units offer a means for doing so. They subdivide larger prisons into smaller "institutions" or "mini-prisons." Cubicles can be used in dormitories, shops, and classrooms. "Small prisons with private spaces for inmates are very desirable for the physical and psychological welfare of the inmates as well as from a prison management perspective."[36] These functional units "rearrange the distribution of currently available resources with the likely result that if we are not doing more with less, at least we are doing it for the same costs."[37]

No new space is needed to house functional units; only existing space is needed. These, Johnson added, are eminently practical means to convert a crowded prison from an interpersonal wasteland to a civilized social environment.[38]

✧ DEALING WITH PRISON RULE VIOLATORS

Institutional administrators must develop, implement, and enforce rules and procedures for their organizations. These rules regulate inmate conduct to assure orderly operation of the institution and to protect all who live and work there; they help to manage confined populations that outnumber staff by 3 to 1. Prisons respond to the more serious violations through administrative hearings and consider the merits of the charges and appropriate penalties.

A recent national survey of state prison inmates found that over half (53 percent) had been charged with violating prison rules at least once since entering prison on their current sentence.[39] This finding is consistent with that of a similar survey in 1979. Among the findings from the study were that prison-rule violators were somewhat more likely than those never charged with a rule violation during their current sentence to be young, unmarried, and currently incarcerated for a property offense or a robbery. They were also more likely than other inmates to be recidivists, to have been arrested for the first time at an early age, to have used drugs regularly, and to have completed less than 12 years of formal education. Furthermore, inmates housed in larger prisons or maximum-security prisons had higher percentages of rule violations than did prisoners in other types of facilities.[40]

A slightly higher percentage of male inmates (53 percent) than female inmates (47 percent) were charged with rule breaking. Marital status seemed to influence violations: about 60 percent of inmates who had never married were charged with violating prison rules, compared with about 41 percent of married inmates. Age was the prisoner characteristic that related most directly to prison rule violation—the younger the age category, the larger the percentage of inmates charged with rule violations. About 60 percent of the inmates aged 18 to 24 were charged with infractions. White and black rule violators reported nearly identical distributions of punishments received for rule violations. The most common penalties were solitary confinement or segregation and loss of good-time credits.[41]

✦ Use of the Snitch System and Confidential Information

Accurate information is necessary for the orderly and effective operation of every organization and its administration. Correctional institutions are certainly no exception; prison and jail administrators and staff members need to observe conditions, listen to complaints, and monitor the results of their actions. However, the unique nature of these organizations creates a need for information unlike that of normal business. Timely information is crucial for staff and administration to avert riots, escape plots, or other threats to security. It is also essential that criminal acts that occur often in such institutions be prosecuted successfully.[42]

One obvious source of information is the inmates themselves. However, one of the strongest taboos in the inmate subculture is "thou shalt not snitch on other inmates or cooperate with the man." That philosophy militates against obtaining needed information. Inmate informants can become targets of death threats, and protecting them can become a serious problem for the administration.

There are three situations that involve inmate informants: the "snitch system," the innocent witness or victim, and co-conspirators. The idea of using snitches—trusted inmates who provide a regular flow of information—is attractive. However, this system often causes more problems than it solves. Inmates soon learn of its existence and who is reporting on them. The snitch system can also become undependable—some clever informants take great delight in working as double agents.[43] The negative side of this system was ingloriously demonstrated at the 1980 New Mexico Penitentiary riot, where 33 inmates were murdered, some after being mutilated with blowtorches. Many inmates were also raped repeatedly. Among the first to be dragged from their cells and murdered were, of course, known snitches.

In place of a formal snitch system, information can be sought from inmates during the investigation of crimes, serious rule violations, or in response to threats to safety and security in the prison. Although many inmates will report that "I didn't see anything," many serious crimes and incidents in prison have been solved through cooperation from inmates. Co-conspirators present special problems. Many serious crimes would never be solved without inside information from co-conspirators wishing to "save their own hides." However, correctional administrators need to consider that the co-conspirator may actually be the principal offender, willing to sacrifice partners with a minor role for personal immunity. Unless the information is corroborated by conclusive evidence, it may be difficult to determine whether inmates are innocent witnesses or co-conspirators.[44]

Legal problems arise when confidential information is to be presented to a disciplinary committee. Correctional administrators need a basic working knowledge of the law surrounding the use of confidential information as evidence, to ensure that inmate due process is upheld and to avoid lawsuits based on disciplinary actions. Information used to punish an inmate must meet at least some minimal standard of reliability. First, the committee must be shown that the informant had firsthand knowledge. Second, the committee should receive information to help it determine the informant's reliability. *Mendoza v. Miller* [45] explained three ways in which an informant's reliability can be established. First, the investigator can swear an oath that the investigative report is true and then appear before the discipline committee to answer questions; second, the informant's information can be corroborated by other evidence (this is possible when there is more than one informant); and third, the committee can verify firsthand knowledge of the informant based on the past record.[46]

✧ ADMINISTRATIVE USE OF THE INMATE SELF-HELP MOVEMENT

The Seventh Step Program at Kansas State Prison in Lansing, 1963—a spinoff of Alcoholics Anonymous—was the original prisoner self-help organization. Like many free-world groups, it was based on the personal experiences of its founder, Bill Sands. Designed to help long-term, hard-core recidivists to return to the mainstream of life, Sands' philosophy was simple: "Such classes should be conducted by ex-convicts rather than correctional authorities. For two good reasons. One, because such a man knows what must be done, knows what it feels like to be out in the world, branded with a felony record; and two, because the men inside prisons refuse, for the most part, to take moral lessons from the so-called do-gooders."[47]

According to Mark Hamm, inmates have demonstrated a strong and sustained interest in self-help organizations during the past two decades. He asserted that this "movement" has captured the attention of correctional administrators concerned with the plight of special offender populations. From the familiar Alcoholics Anonymous to the little-known Schizophrenics Anonymous; from Taking Pounds Off Sensibly to Women Who Love Too Much, Partners Without Partners, Mended-Hearts, Widow-to-Widow, Tough Love, and support groups for stutterers and diabetics; from Hell's Angels seeking spiritual enlightenment to groups of transsexuals coping with their transitions, the self-help movement involves activities that reach into many areas of our social world. The American Veterans in Prison, Vietnam Veterans of America, and the Disabled American Veterans organizations also provide help for inmates.[48]

Hamm also believes that this interest in self-help groups reflects inmate dissatisfaction with traditional approaches to rehabilitation. Historically, correctional treatment focused on past problems and errors and attempted to build a better tomorrow; however, several authors have observed that too often the immediate struggle for survival in prison distracts an inmate's attention from these "official" treatment programs.[49] As a result, inmates have increasingly turned to gangs, religious fellowships, and self-help organizations as alternatives to state-sanctioned programming.[50]

The prisoner self-help movement suggests certain opportunities for both administrators and inmates. First, they may relieve the "pains of imprisonment" for inmates. These groups provide a support system that meets certain social and/or cultural needs of prisoners.[51] Some groups also provide training in leadership, prisoner-administration politics, and organizational development and management. They also hold the promise of relieving administration of some of the burden they carry for providing rehabilitative sanctions. Unlike gangs, these groups are of little threat to the administration of corrections.[52]

A number of ethnic self-help groups have also sprung up, including Black Awareness for Community Development, Chicanos Organizados Pinton Aztlan, Afro-American Coalition, Affirmative Action Latin Group, and the Native American Brotherhood. These groups seek strong ties with minority communities on the outside and try to elicit support from religious and university communities. Because group leaders have tended to provoke and challenge them, correctional administrators have often taken a dim view of ethnic self-help groups.[53]

Overall, however, Hamm suggested that inmate self-help groups can work in concert with administrators to improve conditions of confinement. For the future, the challenge for administrators will be to understand the potential of these groups, how they may contribute to institutional stability, and to what extent they might facilitate community integration. Hamm cautioned, however, that administrators will not tolerate threats from these groups, regardless of their noble intentions.[54]

✦ "THY BROTHER'S KEEPER": CORRECTIONAL OFFICERS

✧ STEREOTYPES AND DUTIES OF THE JOB

Between the institutional director and the sentenced trusties are the correctional staff—those who, in the words of Gordon Hawkins, are "the other prisoners."[55] Their role and nature is particularly important, given that they are on the front line in supervising and controlling inmates and because it is from this level that correctional administrators may be promoted.

Correctional officers, in close association with inmates, know that brute force and the system of rewards and punishments (especially in light of recent court decisions) are inadequate as control mechanisms. The officers cannot withdraw physically and are given little respect by their charges. Thus officers can achieve a smooth-running tour of duty "not with the stick but with the carrot."[56] The officers know that there may eventually be a day of reckoning, when all IOUs come due, when they may become hostages to the inmates, and the decision as to whether the officers live or die may turn on their treatment of, and their reputation among, the inmate population. Thus, to be successful, officers may feel compelled to engage in *quid pro quos*—"trades" or "deals"— overlooking small infractions by inmates, in return receiving general compliance with rules and orders. Sykes noted that "it is apparent, then, that the power of custodians is defective...the ruled are rebellious...the rulers are reluctant." He also asserted that "it is a paradox that they [the officers] can insure their dominance only by allowing it to be corrupted."[57]

One guard stated: "We're all doing time, some of us are just doin' it in eight-hour shifts."[58] Richard Hawkins and Geoffrey Alpert compared officers and inmates: Both groups are likely to be drawn from lower- and working-class backgrounds; both are likely to be in their present roles because of lack of employment opportunities; each group is largely invisible; both are closely watched and experience some depersonalization (e.g., they wear uniforms and are subject to psychological testing and probing into their past); both develop feelings of powerlessness; and both groups are fighting for their individual rights (conditions of incarceration and employment, respectively).[59]

Most applicants for correctional officer positions probably had little knowledge of the job when they applied. A job description for the position might read something like this:

> [They] must prevent rape among two hundred convicts enraged by their powerlessness and sexual deprivation...prevent violence among the convicts...shake down all cells for contraband...know what is going on in the convicts' head and report it to their supervisors...account for all material entering or leaving each cellblock...maintain sanitation in each cell...give individual attention to all...convicts... [and] prevent the suicide or running amok of the raped, the depressed, and the terrified...and look out for their own physical and psychological survival.[60]

In most assignments, correctional officers will experience stimulus overload, assailed with the sounds of "doors clanging, inmates talking or shouting, radios and televisions playing, and food trays banging...(and odors) representing an institutional blend of food, urine, paint, disinfectant, and sweat."[61]

Since the demise of the treatment model in the 1970s (discussed in Chapter 10), correctional officers have essentially been stripped of their mandate to do informal counseling or aid in the rehabilitative effort. Due process rights for prisoners have made the job even more difficult.[62] Therein lies what Hawkins and Alpert referred to as "the big bitch" of correctional officers: they are losing power and influence, while inmates, accorded more and more due process rights, are gaining in power and influence.[63] This frustration can be vented in physical ways. Although certainly not frequent today, beatings and even sexual attacks by some officers have been documented.[64]

✧ WHAT MAKES AN "EFFECTIVE" CORRECTIONAL OFFICER?

The issue of what specific skills and level of education are needed to do the work of a correctional officer has rarely been raised. One of the Department of Labor's issues of *Dictionary of Occupational Titles* [65] reported that correctional officers required the same skill complexity level as road construction flagmen, school bus monitors, and morgue attendants!

Several federal commissions have issued strong recommendations for higher educational standards among correctional officers, although none of them provided evidence that better educated persons necessarily made better officers.[66] The question of whether or not higher education is required for correctional officers is an important one. Education has a tendency to raise a person's aspirations and expectations. As one person put it, "better educated people expect to do better."[67]

There is considerable evidence that higher education is not beneficial for correctional officers and that it may, indeed, lower job satisfaction. One observer noted that "except for the somewhat disappointing finding that COs with more education are less satisfied with their jobs, the overall picture shows that education is not related to any attitudinal variable examined thus far."[68] Other researchers have commented that "more highly educated officers were significantly less satisfied with their jobs,"[69] A recent study determined that as officers' educational levels increased, so did their desire to become administrators; the less likely that he or she was to feel a sense of accomplishment working as a correctional officer or to want to make a career of corrections; the more likely an officer was to express dissatisfaction with the pace of career advancement; and the more interest that he or she had in counseling.[70]

Two Canadian researchers studied the behavioral skills making effective correctional officers, comparing the correctional officers', supervisors', and offenders' perceptions of the correctional officers' tasks.[71] Correctional officers and supervisors attributed more importance to the "responsibility/leadership" skills than the inmates. These job skills were perceived by staff members as their *primary* task, while inmates were obviously less concerned with those skills, which include report writing; enforcement of rules and regulations; working independently without excessive supervision; working effectively with others; providing inmates with appropriate information on different aspects of their incarceration; and providing clear direction to inmates on how to improve unacceptable behavior before applying negative consequences.[72]

✦ PROFESSIONAL ORIENTATION

Individual Characteristics. Recent studies indicate a consensus that while a few correctional officers may live up to the old stereotypes,[73] "many officers see correctional work as an intrinsically worthwhile endeavor."[74] One study even found that the attitudes of correctional officers toward inmates were very similar to those held by college students and by community residents.[75]

Several individual characteristics of correctional officers have been examined regarding their attitudes toward and interaction with inmates, including race, gender, education, chronological age, and age of entry into correctional work. Regarding race, studies have not found any significant relationship between race and punitive attitudes toward inmates.[76] However, one study of New York officer recruits from four maximum-security prisons established a significantly higher likelihood that nonwhite officers would prefer more social distance from inmates.[77] More recently, however, one study uncovered no differences in officers' professional orientation by race or by region (rural or urban).[78] Conversely, however, another researcher determined that nonwhite officers expressed a more optimistic orientation toward inmates.[79] Finally, while one researcher found no significant racial differences regarding support for custody, black officers reported significantly greater support for rehabilitation.[80]

No studies have reported that officer gender was a significant source of attitudes toward inmates.[81] A significant negative relationship was found in one study between education and custody orientation, however.[82] Although chronological age was not found to be related to punitive attitude, a significant relationship between being older and support for a counseling orientation was discovered.[83] Similarly, older officers have been found significantly more optimistic regarding inmates,[84] and officers who entered corrections at a later age were significantly more likely to express support for rehabilitation.[85]

In summary, there are conflicting studies on individual characteristics of corrections officers regarding the impact of race and age, a consensus that gender is not a significant variable, and an indication that education may be of some importance.[86]

Organizational Conditions. In addition to individual characteristics, a number of organizational conditions have been examined, including institutional security classification, frequency of inmate contact, shift, correctional seniority, role conflict, job stress, perceptions of danger, and supervisory support. Regarding institutional security classification, one study detected a significantly greater punitiveness among officers in minimum-security units,[87] but another found significantly more optimism toward inmates in minimum-security units.[88] A study inquiring into whether or not frequency of inmate contact affected officers' attitudes did not uncover a significant relationship in the degree of optimism regarding inmates.[89]

Not surprisingly, officers assigned to the night or "graveyard" shift, when inmates are normally "locked down," have reported a significantly more custodial and less rehabilitative orientation.[90] Although correctional seniority has not been significantly related to attitudes toward inmates,[91] one study determined that seniority was significantly negatively related to beliefs in inmates' rehabilitation potential (as seniority increased, their belief decreased).[92] Similarly, other studies found a significant positive relationship between seniority and custody orientation,[93] and that as seniority increased, optimism toward inmates decreased.[94]

✦ JAIL ADMINISTRATION

✧ PRISONERS AND PHILOSOPHY

Because they are also "incarcerated" with the misfits of society for much of the day, most if not all of the research findings on prison administrators and staff members described above can probably be extended to workers in jails and detention facilities. However, jails are uniquely different from prisons. Although many more people pass through the nation's 3300 jails (more than 10 million per year, about 15 times as many people as are housed in state and federal prisons),[95] social scientists like the general public have shown little interest in the administration and operation of jails. But in a legal sense, the jail is the point of entry into the criminal justice system. It is where arrested persons are booked and are held for their court appearances if they cannot arrange bail. Also, sentences for misdemeanors are served, for up to one year.

One author, John Irwin, a noted penal expert and author who served time in several jails and prisons, had some interesting views on jails and those who live and work in them. He wrote that jail inmates share two essential characteristics: detachment and disrepute. They are detached because they are not well integrated into conventional society, having few ties to social networks, and carrying unconventional values and beliefs. They are disreputable because they are perceived as irksome, offensive, threatening, and capable of arousal.[96]

Irwin referred to jail prisoners as "rabble," meaning the "disorganized" and "disorderly"—the "lowest class of people." He also referred to jail administration as "managing rabble."[97] Certain significant physical characteristics and management processes of jail, he wrote, reflect the fact that they are intended to hold only the rabble. First, because not many of the rabble are expected to appear in court or even to stay in jail, security has been the fundamental concern in the construction of jails. The result has been massive buildings, complicated locking systems, and elaborate surveillance techniques. Second, Irwin maintained that because the rabble cannot be expected to behave themselves in jails, they must be controlled.[98] Hans Mattick agreed, but felt that

> ...some jail administrators go overboard when it comes to the smaller details of jail security. Instead of relying on good peripheral security and the rational internal deployment of staff, they deplete the time and energies of their limited staffs by harassing the inmates in the details of daily living by frequent head counts, strip searches, cell "shakedowns," and the censorship of prisoner mail. In general, this is a wasteful use of scarce personnel. There is also a general tendency to treat *all* prisoners, except "trusties," as maximum security cases.[99]

Irwin felt that these security-oriented measures resulted in jail prisoners generally experiencing more punishment per day than a convict in a state prison. Jailed persons, he said, suffered sudden interruption of their affairs, abrupt initiation into the jail, restriction of activities to a very small area, virtually no opportunities for recreation and expression, and a reduced health regimen that can lead to physical deterioration and occasionally to serious illness.[100] (*Note:* These several characteristics do indeed indicate a harsher incarceration for those in jails as compared with prisons, especially with regard to health-related issues; see the discussion of research on prison inmates in Chapter 10.)

Although there are, no doubt, a large number of U.S. jails that approach those described by Irwin and Mattick, there are also a number of "state of the art" jail facilities that are progressive, treatment-oriented to the extent possible, and generally "softer" than those described above.

✧ CAREER PATHS AND TRAINING

Because no single jail administrator is responsible for statewide jail management, there may be vastly different perceptions and philosophies concerning how a jail should be staffed and operated. Most detention officers (or "jailers") are under the supervision of a sheriff's office, where career advancement may be quite limited. In cases where they are separate units of local government with their own director, they seem to attract better job candidates with greater career commitments. These careerists do not aspire to patrol duty because it is not an option and they are truly "correctional officers."

However, in some facilities, individuals may transfer to patrol on the basis of seniority. Many of these officers, after receiving their basic training, want to do "real police work" and go out on patrol; they eschew the confined, nonpolice duties of detention that many agencies first require of new personnel. Many good officers, unwilling to serve a period of several years working in detention, resign. Consequently, a major need of jail administration today is to develop a separate, jail-related career path for correctional workers.

Those officers who stay, however, may eventually be promoted, which brings about a separate set of concerns. For example, an exemplary person in detention is promoted to sergeant, but an opening is in the patrol division; upon transferring, he or she may have limited knowledge of the personnel or methods in the patrol field. The opposite can also occur, with a sergeant's vacancy in detention being won by a patrol officer who has little awareness of the jail functions and processes. The challenge for police administrators is to create two separate career paths, one for patrol and one in detention, where those persons beginning in one path can remain and eventually be promoted and hopefully retire therein.

Another problem of jail administration is seeing that their personnel are thoroughly trained in all aspects of their job. Writers have been particularly unkind on this subject, often having the opinion that for the most part, jail workers are "untrained and apathetic," although many of course are highly effective and dedicated. One observer wrote that "Personnel is still the number one problem of jails. Start paying decent salaries and developing decent training and you can start to attract bright young people to jobs in jails. If you don't do this, you'll continue to see the issue of personnel as the number one problem for the next 100 years."[101] Possible training topics include the booking process, inmate management and security, liability issues generally, AIDS policies, dealing specifically with inmates who are alcohol and substance abusers, communication and security technology, suicide, mental health problems, and medication of mentally ill inmates.

✧ Administrative Strategies to Alleviate Jail Crowding

As with prisons, justice administrators across the country have identified jail crowding as the most serious problem facing criminal justice today.[102] With nearly a third of the nation's jails under court order to limit their populations or improve conditions, this problem assumes a greater level of seriousness. For the local sheriff or jail administrator, crowding increases staff and inmate tensions and wear and tear on facility and equipment; creates overtime budgetary problems; and foments an inability to meet program and service standards. Judges, prosecutors, probation and parole, and other officials often find jail crowding a severe constraint where jailing offenders seems necessary but space is unavailable. Finally, court functions suffer overall when crowding affects the movement of inmates to and from scheduled appearances.[103]

Justice administrators and policymakers can affect jail crowding, however. As one judge said, they can use "a lot of little ways" to halt or reverse jail population increases without releasing serious offenders.[104] *Police administrators* can invoke policies concerning arrest practices—whether to arrest, transport to jail, book or detain for bail setting—which are critical determinants of jail population size. Stationhouse release before booking, field citations, and court-authorized bail schedules also eliminate unnecessary confinement.

Jail administrators can reduce crowding by assuring ready access for pretrial release screening and bail review. Prosecutors can engage in early case screening to reduce unnecessary length of confinement by eliminating or downgrading weak cases as soon as possible. *Prosecutors* can also use "vertical case screening," where the same attorney or team of attorneys prosecute a case from start to finish. (Reassigning cases from one assistant prosecutor to another while the matter is before the court—"horizontal case screening"—may cause stagnation in case flow.) *Judges* make more decisions affecting jail population than anyone else; they can issue summonses instead of arrest warrants; provide guidelines authorizing direct release by police, jail, and pretrial staff; and provide bail setting outside normal court hours. Courts may defer service of jail sentences when the jail is at capacity. *Defense attorneys* can perform early screening for indigency, defender appointment, and defendant contact can decrease length of confinement and yield substantial savings of jail space. *Probation and parole agencies* can provide nonjail alternatives for sentencing and enhance case-processing efficiency by streamlining presentence investigation (PSI) procedures and expediting revocation decisions.[105] In addition, state legislation, court rules, executive orders, and other "external factors" can affect jail populations.

Summary

Certainly, the pressures now put on prison and jail administrators are, by the standards for most of us, substantial. They must maintain custody, offer some degree of treatment, and create an atmosphere of openness with the public and the political process, while protecting inmates against themselves and others. At the same time, they are to avoid decisions and behaviors that might lead to costly liability, while doing something to avoid or remedy court-ordered overcrowding.

Undoubtedly, for most of us, the prospect of having to face these kinds of pressures around the clock each day seems highly onerous and undesirable. The work of corrections officers was shown to be as challenging and stressful as that of the administration. Probably the best tribute to their work is the relative calm, lack of escapes, and success in the foregoing areas that society has come to take for granted.

Unfortunately, the administrative and line challenges discussed in this chapter are not the sum total of those faced daily by people working inside the walls of correction. In the following chapter we continue this litany of administrative challenges, with additional issues involving sex and violence, civil litigation, gangs, and stress among corrections employees.

Questions for Review

1. What is meant by the term *new old penology?*
2. What are some of the major elements of "well-governed" prisons? Enumerate the major principles of good prison governance.
3. Describe the life cycle of the inmate–staff power relationship in an adult prison. Why is it so rare for a prison to pass through all phases of the cycle?
4. What can prison administrators do to alleviate crowding? How can inmates be provided relief from crowding without adding new space?
5. Discuss some problems and methods of correctional administrators for dealing with prison rule violators and snitches.
6. What are some tradition-bound stereotypes of correctional officers? Are they currently accurate?
7. What makes an effective correctional officer? Given research findings concerning their attitudes toward offenders, do these officers approach their work with rehabilitation in mind?
8. How does jail administration differ from prison administration? (Consider the duties and approaches of each in framing your answer.)

For Further Reading

Leo Carroll, *Hacks, Blacks, and Cons: Race Relations in a Maximum Security Prison*. Prospect Heights, Ill.: Waveland Press, 1974.

JOHN J. DiIULIO, JR., *Governing Prisons: A Comparative Study of Correctional Management*. New York: Free Press, 1987.

JOHN J. DiIULIO, JR., *No Escape: The Future of American Corrections*. New York: Basic Books, 1991.

RICHARD HAWKINS and GEOFFREY P. ALPERT, *American Prison Systems: Punishment and Justice*. Englewood Cliffs, N.J.: Prentice Hall, 1989.

ROBERT JOHNSON, *Hard Time: Understanding and Reforming the Prison*. Monterey, Calif.: Brooks/Cole, 1987.

Notes

1. John J. DiIulio, Jr., *Governing Prisons: A Comparative Study of Correctional Management* (New York: Free Press, 1987), p. 167.

2. Charles Stastny and Gabrielle Tyrnauer, *Who Rules the Joint* (Lexington, Mass.: D. C. Heath, 1982).

3. Kathleen Maguire, Ann L. Pastore, and Timothy J. Flanagan (eds.), *Sourcebook of Criminal Justice Statistics 1992* (U.S. Department of Justice, Bureau of Justice Statistics. (Washington, D.C.: U.S. Government Printing Office, 1993), p. 98

4. Richard Hawkins and Geoffrey P. Alpert, *American Prison Systems: Punishment and Justice* (Englewood Cliffs, N.J.: Prentice Hall, 1989) p. 359.

5. In George F. Cole (ed.), *Criminal Justice: Law and Politics* (6th ed.) (Belmont, Calif.: Wadsworth, 1993) pp. 438–446.

6. *Ibid.*, p. 439.

7. John J. DiIulio, Jr., *Governing Prisons: A Comparative Study of Correctional Management*, p. 256.

8. *Ibid.*

9. Bert Useem, *States of Siege: U.S. Prison Riots, 1971–1986* (New York: Oxford University Press, 1988).

10. John J. DiIulio, Jr., "Well Governed Prisons Are Possible," in George F. Cole (ed.), *Criminal Justice: Law and Politics* (6th ed.) (Belmont, Calif.: Wadsworth, 1993), p. 440.

11. John J. DiIulio, Jr., *No Escape: The Future of American Corrections* (New York: Basic Books, 1991), Chapter 1.

12. John J. DiIulio, Jr., "Well Governed Prisons Are Possible," p. 445.

13. Chase Riveland, "Being a Director of Corrections in the 1990s," *Federal Probation* 55 (June 1991):10–11.

14. *Ibid.* p. 10.

15. *Ibid.*, p. 11.

16. Jeffrey A. Schwartz, "Fortress Corrections," *Corrections Today* 51 (August 1989):216–223.

17. *Ibid.*, p. 222.

18. *Ibid.*, pp. 222–223.

19. See Robert Johnson, *Death Work: A Study of the Modern Execution Process* (Pacific Grove, Calif.: Brooks/Cole, 1990).

20. Robert Johnson, "This Man Has Expired," *Commonweal* (January 13, 1989):9–15.

21. *Ibid.*

22. *Ibid.*

23. *Ibid.*

24. *Ibid.*

25. U.S. Department of Justice, Bureau of Justice Statistics Bulletin, *Capital Punishment 1991* (Washington, D.C.: Author, December 31, 1991).

26. See *Banning v. Looney,* 213 F.2d 711 (10th. Cir., 1954.

27. Victor D. Lofgreen, "A Model of the Dynamic Power Relationship Between Staff and Inmates in a Secure Correctional Facility," paper presented at the Annual Meeting of the Western Social Science Association, Reno, Nev., 1991, p. 6.

28. *Ibid.*, pp. 8–10.

29. *Ibid.*, pp. 12–14.

30. *Ibid.*, pp. 14–16.

31. *Ibid.*, p. 18.

32. Verne C. Cox, Paul B. Paulus, and Garvin McCain, "Prison Crowding Research: The Relevance for Prison Housing Standards and a General Approach Regarding Crowding Phenomena," *American Psychologist* 39 (October 1984):1148–1160.

33. Robert Johnson, "Crowding and the Quality of Prison Life: A Preliminary Reform Agenda," in Clayton A. Hartjen and Edward E. Rhine (eds.), *Correctional Theory and Practice* (Chicago: Nelson-Hall, 1992), pp. 139–145.

34. See Robert Johnson, *Hard Time: Understanding and Reforming the Prison* (Monterey, Calif.: Brooks/Cole, 1987).

35. Robert Johnson, "Crowding and the Quality of Prison Life: A Preliminary Reform Agenda," p. 142.

36. Verne C. Cox, Paul B. Paulus, and Garvin McCain, "Prison Crowding Research: The Relevance for Prison Housing Standards and a General Approach Regarding Crowding Phenomena," p. 1156.

37. Robert B. Levinson, "Try Softer," in Robert Johnson and Hans Toch (eds.), *The Pains of Imprisonment* (Prospect Heights, Ill.: Waveland Press, 1988), pp. 241–256.

38. Robert Johnson, Hard Time, p. 170.

39. U.S. Department of Justice, Bureau of Justice Statistics Special Report, *Prison Rule Violators* (Washington, D.C.: Author, 1989), p. 1.

40. *Ibid.*, p. 2.

41. *Ibid.*, pp. 1–2.

42. Perry Johnson, "The Snitch System: How Informants Affect Prison Security," *Corrections Today* (July 1989):26, 28, 72.

43. *Ibid.*, p. 28.

44. *Ibid.*, p. 72.

45. *Mendoza v. Miller* (7th Cir. 1985).

46. Van Vandivier, "Do You Want to Know a Secret? Guidelines for Using Confidential Information," *Corrections Today* (July 1989):30, 32, 73.

47. Bill Sands, *My Shadow Runs Fast* (Englewood Cliffs, N.J.: Prentice Hall, 1964).

48. Mark S. Hamm, "Current Perspectives on the Prisoner Self-Help Movement," *Federal Probation* 52 (June 1988):49–56.

49. John Irwin, "Adaptation to Being Corrected," in Daniel Glaser (ed.), *Handbook of Criminology* (Chicago: Rand McNally, 1974); Robert Johnson, *Hard Time*, 1987; G.G. Kassebaum, D.A. Ward, and D.M. Wilner, *The Effectiveness of a Prison and Parole System* (Indianapolis, Ind.: Bobbs-Merrill, 1971).

50. E. M. Abdul-Mu'Min, "Prisoner Power and Survival," in Robert M. Carter, Leslie T. Wilkins, and Daniel Glaser (eds.), *Correctional Institutions* (New York: Harper and Row, 1985; John Irwin, *Prisons in Turmoil* (Boston: Little, Brown, 1980).

51. *Ibid.*

52. Mark S. Hamm, "Current Perspectives on the Prisoner Self-Help Movement," p. 50.

53. Milton Burdman, "Ethnic Self-Help Groups in Prison and on Parole," *Crime and Delinquency* (April 1974); Patrick D. McAnany and Edward Tromanhauser, "Organizing the Convict: Self-Help for Prisoners and Ex-cons," *Crime and Delinquency* (January 1977).

54. Mark S. Hamm, "Current Perspectives on the Prisoner Self-Help Movement," p. 55.

55. Gordon Hawkins, *The Prison* (Chicago: University of Chicago Press, 1976).

56. Gresham Sykes, "The Defects of Total Power," in John R. Snortum and Ilana Hader (eds.), *Criminal Justice: Allies and Adversaries* (Pacific Palisades, Calif.: Palisades Publishers, 1978), pp. 195–202.

57. *Ibid.*, p. 201.

58. Cited in Eric D. Poole and Robert M. Regoli, "Alienation in Prison: An Examination of the Work Relations of Prison Guards," *Criminology* 19 (1981):251–270.

59. Richard Hawkins and Geoffrey P. Alpert, *American Prison Systems: Punishment and Justice*, p. 338.

60. Adapted from Carl Weiss and David James Friar, *Terror in the Prisons* (Indianapolis, Ind.: Bobbs-Merrill, 1974), p. 209.

61. Ben M. Crouch, *The Keepers: Prison Guards and Contemporary Corrections* (Springfield, Ill.: Charles C. Thomas, 1980), p. 73.

62. Richard Hawkins and Geoffrey P. Alpert, *American Prison Systems: Punishment and Justice*, p. 340.

63. Richard Hawkins and Geoffrey P. Alpert, *American Prison Systems: Punishment and Justice*, p. 345.

64. See Lee H. Bowker, *Prison Victimization* (New York: Elsevier, 1980), Chapter 7.

65. United States Department of Labor, *Dictionary of Occupational Titles* (4th ed.) (Washington, D.C.: U.S. Government Printing Office, 1977).

66. Robert Rogers, "The Effects of Educational Level on Correctional Officer Job Satisfaction," *Journal of Criminal Justice* 19 (1991):123–137.

67. Ivan Berg, *Education and Jobs: The Great Training Robbery* (New York: Praeger, 1970), p. 128.

68. Susan Philliber, "Thy Brother's Keeper: A Review of the Literature on Correctional Officers," *Justice Quarterly* 4 (1987):9–37.

69. Nancy Jurik and Michael C. Musheno, "The Internal Crisis of Corrections: Professionalization and the Work Environment," *Justice Quarterly* 3 (1986):457–481.

70. Robert Rogers, "The Effects of Educational Level on Correctional Officer Job Satisfaction," p. 134.

71. Cindy Wahler and Paul Gendreau, "Perceived Characteristics of Effective Correctional Officers by Officers, Supervisors, and Inmates across Three Different Types of Institutions," *Canadian Journal of Criminology* (April 1990):265–277.

72. *Ibid.*, pp. 268–269.

73. James W. Marquart, "Prison Guards and the Use of Physical Coercion as a Mechanism of Prisoner Control," *Criminology* 24 (1986):347–366.

74. Robert Johnson, *Hard Time*, p. 138.

75. Kenneth B. Melvin, Lorraine K. Gramling, and William M. Gardner, "A Scale to Measure Attitudes toward Prisoners," *Criminal Justice and Behavior* 12 (1985):241–253.

76. James B. Jacobs and Lawrence Kraft, "Integrating the Keepers: A Comparison of Black and White Prison Guards," *Social Problems* 25 (1978):304–318; Ben M. Crouch and Geoffrey P. Alpert, "Sex and Occupational Socialization among Prison Guards: A Longitudinal Study," *Criminal Justice and Behavior* 9 (June 1982):159–176.

77. Hans Toch and John Klofas, "Alienation and Desire for Job Enrichment among Correction Officers," *Federal Probation* 46 (1982):35–44.

78. John Klofas, "Discretion among Correctional Officers: The Influence of Urbanization, Age and Race," *International Journal of Offender Therapy and Comparative Criminology* 30 (1986):111–124.

79. Nancy C. Jurik, "Individual and Organizational Determinants of Correctional Officer Attitudes toward Inmates," *Criminology* 23 (August 1985):523–539.

80. Francis T. Cullen, Faith E. Lutze, Bruce G. Link, and Nancy T. Wolfe, "The Correctional Orientation of Prison Guards: Do Officers Support Rehabilitation?" *Federal Probation* 53 (March 1989):33–42.

81. Nancy C. Jurik, "Individual and Organizational Determinants of Correctional Officer Attitudes toward Inmates;" Francis T. Cullen, Faith E. Lutze, Bruce G. Link, and Nancy T. Wolfe, "The Correctional Orientation of Prison Guards: Do Officers Support Rehabilitation?"

82. Eric D. Poole and Robert M. Regoli, "Role Stress, Custody Orientation, and Disciplinary Actions: A Study of Prison Guards," *Criminology* 18 (August 1980):215–226.

83. Hans Toch and John Klofas, "Alienation and Desire for Job Enrichment among Correction Officers."

84. Nancy C. Jurik, "Individual and Organizational Determinants of Correctional Officer Attitudes toward Inmates."

85. Francis T. Cullen, Faith E. Lutze, Bruce G. Link, and Nancy T. Wolfe, "The Correctional Orientation of Prison Guards: Do Officers Support Rehabilitation?"

86. John T. Whitehead and Charles A. Lindquist, "Determinants of Correctional Officers' Professional Orientation," *Justice Quarterly* 6 (March 1989):69–87.

87. Carol F. W. Smith and John R. Hepburn, "Alienation in Prison Organizations," *Criminology* (August 1979):251–262.

88. Nancy C. Jurik, "Individual and Organizational Determinants of Correctional Officer Attitudes toward Inmates."

89. *Ibid.*

90. Francis T. Cullen, Faith E. Lutze, Bruce G. Link, and Nancy T. Wolfe, "The Correctional Orientation of Prison Guards: Do Officers Support Rehabilitation?"

91. James B. Jacobs and Lawrence Kraft, "Integrating the Keepers: A Comparison of Black and White Prison Guards;" Francis T. Cullen, Faith E. Lutze, Bruce G. Link, and Nancy T. Wolfe, "The Correctional Orientation of Prison Guards: Do Officers Support Rehabilitation?"

92. Boaz Shamir and Amos Drory, "Some Correlates of Prison Guards' Beliefs," *Criminal Justice and Behavior* 8 (June 1981):233–249.

93. Eric D. Poole and Robert M. Regoli, "Role Stress, Custody Orientation, and Disciplinary Actions: A Study of Prison Guards."

94. Nancy C. Jurik, "Individual and Organizational Determinants of Correctional Officer Attitudes toward Inmates."

95. Kathleen Maguire, Ann L. Pastore, and Timothy J. Flanagan, eds., *Sourcebook of Criminal Justice Statistics 1992*, p. 594.

96. John Irwin, *The Jail: Managing the Underclass in American Society* (Berkeley, Calif.: University of California Press, 1985), p. 2.

97. *Ibid.*, p. 8.

98. *Ibid.*, p. 43.

99. Hans Mattick, "The Contemporary Jails of the United States: An Unknown and Neglected Areas of Justice," in Daniel Glaser (ed.), *Handbook of Criminology* (Chicago: Rand McNally, 1974).

100. John Irwin, *The Jail: Managing the Underclass in American Society*, pp. 45–46.

101. Quoted in Advisory Commission on Intergovernmental Relations, *Jails: Intergovernmental Dimensions of a Local Problem* (Washington, D.C.: Author, 1984), p. 1.

102. U.S. Department of Justice, National Institute of Justice Research in Brief, *Systemwide Strategies to Alleviate Jail Crowding* (Washington, D.C.: Author, 1987), p. 1.

103. *Ibid.*, p. 2.

104. *Ibid.*

105. *Ibid.*, pp. 2–4.

Administering Community Corrections: Probation and Parole

Even I
Regained my freedom with a sigh.
—Lord Byron

✦ INTRODUCTION

We examined the development of the two primary forms of community corrections—probation and parole—in Chapter 3. We now view their contemporary role and functions. Community corrections, it has been stated, is "the last bastion of discretion in the criminal justice system."[1] Only a few decades ago, community-based corrections was enthusiastically viewed as a humane, logical, and effective approach for working with and changing criminal offenders. The President's Task Force endorsed this model in 1967, saying that it "includes building or rebuilding solid ties between the offender and the community, integrating the offender into community life-restoring family ties, obtaining employment and education, securing in the large sense a place for the offender in the routine functioning of society. This requires...efforts directed towards changing the individual offender (and) mobilization and change of the community and its institutions."[2]

Changes in national ideological thought and other matters have combined to cause difficulties for these lofty ideals, as well as for probation and parole organizations. These factors have also compelled us increasingly to use incarceration instead.

We begin with what is perhaps the core of this chapter: a call for national consideration of tough alternatives to imprisonment. Then we examine the types of administrative systems and issues that are related to the administration of probation and parole. Next, after considering the training of probation and parole administrators, we specifically analyze the relatively new alternatives to incarceration and conventional probation and parole, known as intermediate sanctions: intensively supervised probation, electronic monitoring (or home detention), and shock probation.

✦ "MAKING A CASE" FOR ALTERNATIVES TO IMPRISONMENT

Sanctions for offenders are most likely to deter if they meet two conditions: "the social standing is injured by the punishment," and "the individual feels a danger of being excluded from the group."[3] This country bases assumptions about "what punishes" on the norms and living standards of society at large. This view overlooks too very important facts: first, most serious offenders neither accept nor abide by those norms; and second, most of the incarcerated people today come from communities where conditions fall far below the living standards that most Americans would accept.[4] The grim fact—and national shame —is that for most people who go to prison, the conditions inside are not all that different from the conditions outside. Social isolation is another presumably punitive aspect of imprisonment. However, when a person goes to prison, he or she is not "among aliens." The newly admitted inmate may find friends, if not family, already there.[5]

Furthermore, it seems plausible to believe that prison terms, on average, are not perceived as being as severe as they once were. Inmates' actions speak loudly in this respect: More than 50 percent of today's inmates have served a prior prison term. Knowing what prison is like, these inmates evidently still believe the "benefits" of committing a new crime outweigh the "costs" of being in prison.[6] We must wonder how punitive the prison experience is for these offenders.

Finally, possessing a prison record is not as stigmatizing as in the past, because so many of the offenders' peers and family members also have "done time." One survey found that 40 percent of youths in state training schools have parents who have also been incarcerated.[7] Imprisonment also confers status in some neighborhoods. Gang members have repeatedly stated that incarceration was not a threat because they knew their sentence would be minimal. Also, to many people, imprisonment is a "badge of courage" that also provides food, clothing, shelter, and something to brag about upon returning to the community.[8]

We have thus begun our discussion of community sanctions with these unfortunate caveats about society's views toward punishment, particularly the use of prison. In doing so, the question begged of society at large is whether the time has come to consider seriously alternatives to incarceration; and probation and parole administrators might question whether conventional probation and parole are effective in all cases, or whether other alternatives—such as intensive supervision programs—should or must be implemented.

✦ CASELOADS

We must first recognize that the quality of service that a probation or parole officer can provide to his or her caseload is quite likely proportional to the individual officer's caseload. *Caseload* refers to the average number of nonincarcerated offenders on probation and parole who are supervised by an officer. As John Conrad observed:

> There is much that a good probation/parole officer can do for the people on his or her caseload. A parole officer who makes it clear that, "fellow, if you don't watch your step I'm gonna run your ass right back to the joint," is not in a position to be helpful as a counselor or facilitator. With the best intentions, a[n] officer struggling with the standard unwieldy caseload of 100 or more will deal with emergencies only, and sometime will not be able to do that very well.[9]

Although ideal caseloads for probation officers range from 25 to 50, many probation officers actually have caseloads of 200 or more. Since the quality of their contact with probationers is affected directly by the officers' ability to have face-to-face contact with these probationers regularly, probation is often judged unfairly as being ineffective as a deterrent to crime. Probation departments are often the last in line for additional funding to create new positions to handle larger numbers of offenders. Few agencies or courts consider the negative implications of giving understaffed and underfunded probation departments increasing numbers of persons to supervise.[10]

Regarding parole caseloads, the American Correctional Association recently determined that there were 10,670 parole officers to supervise 362,192 parolees in the United States.[11] This means that, on average, parole officer caseloads are about 31 offenders per officer. However, it is well known that in some jurisdictions, the parolee/parole officer ratio is as high as 300 to 1.

What can probation and parole administrators do about excessively high caseloads? Probably very little. Being at the end of the justice-system process, they have little control over the number of people that the police arrest, prosecutors formally charge, juries convict, or judges sentence to prison.

✦ PROBATION ADMINISTRATION

✧ ADMINISTRATIVE SYSTEMS: TYPES AND RELATED ISSUES

Figure 12.1 depicts an organization structure for a regional probation and parole organization. Probation is the most frequently used sanction of all; it costs offenders their privacy and self-determination, and usually includes some element of the other sanctions: jail time, fines, restitution, or community service.[12] Probation in the United States is administered by more than 2000 agencies.

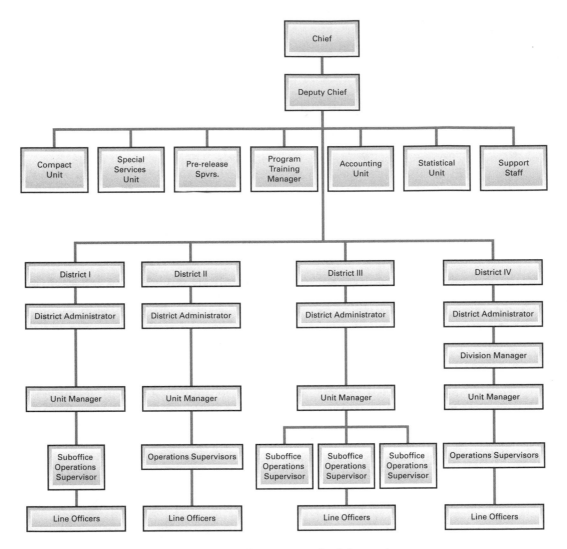

Figure 12.1 Organizational structure for a regional adult parole and probation agency.

Organizationally, it is a patchwork that defies simple explanation. Texas alone has more than 100 county adult probation departments, while in about three-fourths of the states, adult probation is located in the executive branch of state government. By contrast, more than half of the agencies providing juvenile probation services are administered on the local level.[13]

Furthermore, according to Howard Abadinsky, a former senior parole officer in New York, the administration of probation systems can be separated into six categories:

1. *Juvenile.* Separate probation services for juveniles are administered on a county or municipal level or on a statewide basis.

2. *Municipal.* Independent probation units are administered by the lower courts under state laws and guidelines.
3. *County.* Under laws and guidelines established by the state, a county operates its own probation agency; this is similar to the municipal system.
4. *State.* One agency administers a central probation system, which provides services throughout the state.
5. *State combined.* Probation and parole services are administered on a statewide basis by one agency.
6. *Federal.* Probation is administered as an arm of the courts.[14]

In view of this situation, two central organizational issues have been posed which are involved in the administration of probation services: First, should probation be part of the judicial or the executive branch of government? Second, does the lack of uniformity in administering probation make justice less equitable statewide?[15] These are important issues in probation administration and organization, being considered over a quarter century ago by the President's Task Force on Corrections.[16] Regarding the first issue, those who support placement of probation services within the judicial branch contend that:

1. Probation is more responsive to the courts, when it is administered by the judiciary.
2. The relationship of probation staff to the courts creates an automatic feedback mechanism concerning the effectiveness of various dispositions.
3. Courts have greater awareness of the resources needed by the probation agency.
4. Judges will have greater confidence in an agency for which they are responsible and thus will allow probation staff more discretion than they would allow members of an outside agency.
5. If probation is administered on a statewide basis, it is usually incorporated into a department of corrections, where probation servers might be assigned a lower priority than they would as part of the court.[17]

But some authors have also raised compelling arguments against the placement of probation in the purview of the courts:

1. Judges, trained in law and not administration (as discussed in Chapter 3), are generally not equipped to administer probation services.
2. Under judicial control, services to persons on probation may receive a lower priority than services to the judge (such as presentence investigations).
3. Probation staff may be assigned duties unrelated to probation.
4. The courts are adjudicatory, not service oriented in nature.[18]

Placement in the executive branch also has a number of positive features:

1. All other human services agencies and corrections subsystems are within the executive branch.
2. There would be better coordination of program budgeting and ability to negotiate in the resource allocation process.
3. Such placement facilitates a coordinated continuum of services to offenders and better utilization of probation personnel.[19]

In light of the above, Kim Nelson and colleagues concluded that when compared, these arguments tend to support placing probation in the executive branch. A state administered probation system has decided advantages over local administration. A total system planning approach to probation as a subsystem of corrections is needed. Such planning requires state leadership.[20]

Probation services that are within the executive branch are part of state government under the office of the governor. Probation may be part of a larger department of corrections, or part of an independent probation and parole agency. Probation services that are part of the judicial branch of government are usually under the judges of the county.[21]

Abadinsky argued that probation administered by the judiciary on a *county* level promotes *diversity*.

> Innovative programming can be implemented more easily in a county agency since it has a shorter line of bureaucratic control than would a statewide agency. A county agency can more easily adapt to change, and the successful programs of one agency can more easily be adopted by other probation departments...and unsuccessful programs avoided. Although the judiciary is nominally responsible for administering probation, the day-to-day operations are in the hands of a professional administrator—the chief probation officer.[22]

One problem with the county-level administration of probation services, however, is that of increased dissimilarity in operations. The officer/client ratios may differ in large measure from one county to another, as would probably not be the case if monitored by a statewide agency, where personnel can easily be shifted from one county to another. There will thus be a wide range of officer caseloads from county to county.

This brings us to the second issue stated above, concerning whether or not this lack of uniformity in providing probation services makes justice less equitable statewide. Abadinsky noted that this issue has led states with county-based probation systems to create statewide bodies for better coordination and uniformity of services.

✦ NEEDS, PROBLEMS, AND CONCERNS

As early as 1924, a probation executive wrote "without a consistent, orderly, and practical plan of organization, and without adequate, competent and sensible methods of supervising the staff, a probation department cannot function properly."[23] As will be seen, studies indicate that those problems still exist. "What are my resources? How can I use them to maximize our supervision and services?" These are questions that constantly challenge the probation administrator. Yet, according to Patricia L. Hardyman, who recently performed a major study of probation administration, they are seldom addressed directly, although the answers to those questions would enable the probation administrator to better control limited resources, select supervision strategies, and pursue attainable outcomes.[24] As indicated above, each year millions of dollars are invested in building and acquiring the capital investment needed to house and facilitate the tasks of probation departments. This does not include the human resources invested by community volunteers and the families of probationers. Yet little is known about how these resources are translated into activities or the outcomes and impacts of these activities.[25]

As with the administration of a police, court, or prison organization, the probation department administrator's goal may affect the services provided to the client, which in turn may have an impact on the client's request for services. This systematic interaction between an organization's resources, structure, and community has been referred to as its "sociotechnical environment,"[26] the systems principles that are organized to execute the basic production technologies of the organization. What each probation administrator needs to recognize, then, is that their organization is a system of inputs, processes, and outputs. This understanding of probation, using systems theory, provides a means for learning how probation departments function and interact with their environment, and an examination of the resources, activities, and outcomes in a way that will identify the goals, describe the day-to-day activities, and link the department's activities to resources and outcomes.

Using systems theory, probation may be conceptualized as a network of interwoven resources, activities, and outcomes.[27] According to Hardyman, *resources* include the probation department's funding level, goals, policies and procedures, organizational structure and caseloads; the probation staff's characteristics; the services available to probationers; and the rates of unemployment, poverty, and crime in the county. *Activities* would be supervision techniques, rewards, leadership style, contacts, and direct/indirect services provided by the probation department. *Outcomes* according to systems theory would be the number of probationers who were arrested, incarcerated, and/or received a technical violation during the follow-up period, and the needs of probationers and the community that were considered.[28]

Hardyman's study of probation administrators focused on their management style—the fundamental determinant of the nature of the probation organization—and was quite instructive in terms of the impact of their style on the department's operation. Few departments, even with most having the hierarchical organizational structure, had a pure management style; administrators vacillated among a variety of styles, including laissez-faire, democratic, and authoritarian. Administrators varied particularly in the degree to which they included the probation officers in the decision-making process and communicated with officers. The *authoritarian* administrator created emotional and physical distance between the officers and themselves. Officers reported feeling that they had little control over their cases—that policies and procedures were developed and enforced by those persons who were unconcerned with their plight [29].

Surprisingly, the most common management style used by probation administrators was *laissez-faire*. Hardyman found that many probation administrators simply did not participate in the day-to-day activities and supervision strategies of the staff. They remained remote but made final decisions on critical policies and procedures.[30]

Hardyman found that few probation administrators across the country operated with the *democratic* style. Those who did, of course, listened more to the concerns and suggestions of the line supervisors and officers. Final decisions were still made by the administrator, but information was generally sought from the line staff and their opinions addressed. Officers working under this style obviously had a greater sense that their opinions mattered and that the administrator valued their input. An additional benefit of the democratic style was that the administrators had power both by virtue of their position and of their charisma. They also had strong personal power, inspiring teamwork and task accomplishment.[31]

Hardyman found several negative aspects of probation administration in her study as well. Crisis management was related to management style. Chaos was extremely high in urban, laissez-faire probation departments. She observed shouting matches between staff members, and officers reported conflicting departmental policies and standards of supervision. There was lack of communication between the administrator and the staff and an inability to create and finish projects; changes were viewed as imposed from above and were therefore resisted, and officers were convinced that their administrators would not listen. Even in democratic probation departments with an open and friendly environment, projects were abandoned because of current crises, and there were frequent disagreements between line staff and administrators. None of the probation departments studied was proactive.[32]

✦ PAROLE ADMINISTRATION

✧ MODELS FOR PROVIDING SERVICES

The administration of parole is much less complex than probation; consequently, there is less information and fewer studies are available concerning its needs, problems, and practices. (It should also be noted that in about 20 states, probation officers also serve as parole officers; thus much of the information presented in the foregoing section applies to parole as well.) One agency per state administers the parole function on a statewide basis. Even with parole, however, there is a slight deviation: In a number of states, persons paroled from a local jail come under the supervision of a *county* probation and parole department.[33]

Three basic services can be provided by a parole agency: parole release, parole supervision, and executive clemency. In a number of states that have abolished parole release (such as California), parole officers continue to supervise offenders released, not by a parole board, but on "good time." The National Advisory Commission on Criminal Justice Standards and Goals delineated two basic models for administering parole services:

1. *The independent model.* A parole board is responsible for making release (parole) determinations as well as the supervision of persons released on parole (or good time). It is independent of any other state agency and reports directly to the governor.
2. *The consolidated model.* The parole board is a semiautonomous agency within a larger department that also administers correctional institutions. Supervision of persons released on parole (or good time) is under the direction of the commissioner of corrections, not the parole board.[34]

In both models, probation services are sometimes combined with parole services in a single statewide agency.

The President's Task Force on Corrections summarized the arguments for the independent model:

1. The parole board is in the best position to promote the idea of parole and to generate public support and acceptance. Since the board is accountable for parole failures, it should be responsible for supervising parolees.
2. The parole board in direct control of administering parole services can evaluate and adjust the system more effectively.
3. Supervision by the parole board and its officers properly divorces parole release and parolees from the correctional institution.
4. An independent parole board in charge of its own services is in the best position to present its own budget request to the legislature.[35]

The President's Task Force also summarized the arguments for including both parole services and institutions in a single department of corrections:

1. The correctional process is a continuum; all staff, both institutional and parole, should be under a single administration rather than be divided, with the resultant competition for public funds and friction in policies.
2. A consolidated correctional department has consistent administration, including staff selection and supervision.
3. Parole boards are ineffective in performing administrative functions; their major focus should be on case decision, not on day-to-day field operations.
4. Community-based programs partway between institutions and parole, such as work release, can best be handled by a single centralized administration.[36]

Critics contend that the independent model tends to be indifferent or insensitive to institutional programs and that the parole board, in this model, places undue emphasis on variables outside the institution. Conversely, critics of the consolidated model contend that the parole board will be under pressure to emphasize institutional factors in making parole decisions.[37] Clearly, the trend in this country, beginning in the late 1960s, was in the direction of consolidation.

In the past, there has also been some controversy concerning whether institution staff or independent agencies, such as those described above, should make the parole decision. The arguments for staff deciding when inmates will be released included the following: staff know the inmates better, independent agencies and parole boards are too far removed from institutions to know what goes on within them, and giving this responsibility to independent boards downgrades the professional competence of staff and is unnecessarily complicated. These arguments are countered by those contending that independent agencies granting paroles will eliminate irrational decision making by staff, that staff often lengthen stays for the violation of trivial and meaningless rules, and that staff may be secretive about the criteria for release and hold release over the heads of inmates.[38]

✧ THE DEMISE OF FEDERAL PAROLE

The U.S. Sentencing Commission was created and established a new set of sentencing guidelines that were officially instituted on November 1, 1987. In addition to that major legislation, parole was abolished for federal prisoners. Supervised release from prison was *not* discontinued entirely, however; in effect, something equivalent to parole is still in place, but the sentencing court is now the controlling authority over the inmate rather than a federal parole commission. The court has the authority to impose sanctions on released prisoners if they violate conditions of their release.

It is too soon to tell what impact the demise of federal parole—and the new federal sentencing guidelines—will have. Many, if not most, prisoners sentenced under the new guidelines are still in prison (and have attempted a substantial amount of litigation attacking the new sentencing guidelines, most of which has been rejected by the courts). Prison wardens have undoubtedly experienced a higher inmate population that is serving longer terms because of this legislation; as a result, they must expend greater effort toward seeking alternatives to incarceration.

✦ TRAINING FOR PROBATION AND PAROLE ADMINISTRATORS

To ensure that probation and parole departments operate with greater effectiveness and efficiency, management and leadership training should be provided for all supervisors and administrators.[39] Generally speaking, probation and parole managers attained their supervisory positions by being good line officers, working their way up through the ranks of the department. As we have learned by observing the police, however, there is no guarantee that persons who were good line officers will automatically become good managers. And again, as with policing, few probation administrators were hired from outside their agencies. Their training and experience generally has been parochial in nature, and promotions were based on civil service examination scores and seniority. Their personnel evaluations were based on case management skills, not on leadership and negotiation skills.

Thus the need is clear for mandatory, formal orientation as well as ongoing in-service training for these community corrections administrators. They need exposure to what other agencies are doing, including what works and does not work, and to national trends. Such training should not be limited to in-house staff meetings but should include national seminars on management issues and leadership theories and practices. Probation administrators should also encourage their line officers to participate in training sessions and see that such sessions are provided on a routine, professional basis.

Such in-service training for line officers has been identified as a major problem for probation departments, with several barriers being present. First, such training is often perceived by line officers as unwarranted interference and as attempts to dominate local probation departments. Second, there is a perceived lack of time for them to participate in training. (This is probably a very legitimate concern, given that caseloads are often as high as 200 to 300 cases.) Finally, such training is seldom provided locally; officers are often required to travel considerable distances to a state capital to receive training. Unfortunately, Hardyman found that many local probation administrators did little to alleviate these barriers. They were very protective of their departments against perceived interference. They provided only minimal support for initial and in-service training, possibly a product of their own lack of training and experience.[40]

✦ INTERMEDIATE SANCTIONS

✧ A BURDENED CORRECTIONS SUBSYSTEM

As can readily be seen in this and preceding chapters, the state of corrections is not altogether healthy. The criminal justice community, including probation, is said to be involved in "guerrilla warfare," where the highest-risk probationers are out of control, and they generally reside in "out-of-control communities."[41] As one author observed, offenders may be smiling because "revolving door justice" has become an all-too-frequent fact of prison and jail life.[42] Institutional and community systems are being utilized beyond capacity. America is not soft on crime. Since prisons are not in a position to effect great change,[43] the search for solutions must involve change for corrections in the community.

The demand for space has created a reactivity throughout corrections. New construction has become characteristic of many state systems; however, these reactive efforts have raised further financial, legal, and administrative issues.[44] With the cost of prison construction now at more than $50,000 per bed (going as high as $150,000 in maximum security institutions), cost-saving alternatives are becoming more attractive if not necessary. Opening the gates of jails and prisons and liberating inmates is, of course, one solution to the overcrowding problem. But it is not a serious alternative. A real alternative to incarceration has three elements to be effective: It has to incapacitate offenders enough so that it is possible to interfere with their lives and activities, such that committing a new offense becomes extremely difficult; it must be unpleasant enough to deter offenders from wanting to commit new crimes; and it has to provide real and credible protection for the community.[45]

As mentioned in Chapter 10, in addition to overcrowding, two interrelated developments characterize the state of corrections today and reflect major correctional problems: ideological restatement and, as a result, intermediate initiatives. In response to the criticisms and failures of rehabilitative philosophy and policies, the prevailing ideology of incapacitation, punishment, and deterrence has resulted in get-tough sentencing practices that contribute to rising prison populations. This shift to "just desserts" focuses on the fact that offenders make "free will" decisions to commit crime, and therefore they no longer deserve compassion and correction. This ideology has wrought an "exclusionary" era of repressive social control, which attempts to banish, expel, and stigmatize the criminal deviant.[46]

✦ THE SEARCH FOR ALTERNATIVE METHODS

Probation and parole do not operate in a vacuum; their operations are affected in large measure by what occurs in the rest of the justice system and actions of other justice administrators. As the number of crimes continues to increase, the availability of incarceration decreases. This vicious circle is not lost on offenders; if they commit more crimes, they cause more overcrowding, spend less time in an institution, and are quickly released to commit a new round of offenses.[47]

Much of what has been done by way of experimentation with community-based alternatives to imprisonment reflects, of course, the current crisis in our prisons. The tension between the "get tough" philosophy and the realities of prison overcrowding has led to a "search for intermediate punishments...an attempt to find mid-range solutions."[48] This in turn has brought about the emergence of a "new" generation of techniques, making community-based corrections, according to Barry Nidorf, a "strong, full partner in the fight against crime and a leader in confronting the crowding crisis. It is no longer considered a weak stepchild of the justice system."[49] Economic reality dictates that cost-effective measures be developed, and this is motivating the development of intermediate sanctions.[50] The growing interest in these sanctions is based not only on the need to develop cheaper alternatives to prisons; but the economic realities cannot be overlooked.[51] Today's probation and parole administrators must have an arsenal of risk-control tools at their disposal. Following is an overview of programs that illustrate what community corrections agencies are doing to combat these problems:

◊ *Intensive supervision:* a part of community corrections for a long time, but its latest form is quite different; "intrusive supervision" might be a better term to describe this close, near-constant surveillance of probationers and parolees. Intensive supervision is discussed more fully below.

◊ *Electronic surveillance:* popularly known as "house arrest," this is one of the most promising programs for toughening community corrections and, at the same time, relieving institutional crowding. This program is also discussed in more detail later in the chapter.

◊ *Probation/police cooperative action:* a program where probation officers work closely with local police, sharing information about offenders under supervision in the community. In effect, these probationers are under the surveillance of two agencies. May initially add to jail populations as violators are rapidly returned to custody.

◊ *Probation/prosecution cooperative action:* probation departments and local prosecutors work closely to get dangerous offenders out of the community and into prison immediately if they recidivate. Instead of going through long court hearings and trials, felons are sent immediately to prison, getting repeat offenders out of the community.

◊ *Narcotics and drug deterrence programs:* community corrections has developed drug testing programs to detect and deter drug use among probationers and parolees, making it possible for thousands of drug-abusing offenders to be supervised effectively in the community instead of being housed in jail.[52]

Other administrative programs include probationer violation and restitution residential centers, work furloughs, day reporting centers, urine analysis, and curfews, to name a few. Intensive supervision and electronic monitoring/house arrest are discussed more fully below.

Using these tools, other community-based diversionary programs have met with success across the country. Following are examples for a recent fiscal-year period:

◊ Tennessee diverted 504 offenders from prison in one recent year, at a cost of $7600 per offender compared to the state average of about $20,000 to incarcerate an inmate. In addition, offenders paid $59,000 in restitution to victims and performed 76,000 hours of community service. Total savings to the state was $6.1 million.

◊ Virginia diverted 699 felons from prisons and jails, saving more than $8 million; offenders performed 230,000 hours of community service and paid $77,000 in restitution.

◊ Florida's house arrest program, a nationally recognized model, cost the state $2650 per year per offender—80 percent less than the cost for imprisonment.

◊ Illinois' intensive probation supervision (IPS) program cost $2367 per year; from 1984 to 1989, the state collected $1 million in restitution, taxes, fines, and court costs. IPS participants performed 145,349 hours of community service valued at about $500,000; the state saved about $8 million total through the program.

◊ Georgia's restitution centers can house 2600 offenders annually. The state collected more than $250,000 in restitution, over $600,000 in family support, $1.4 million in room and board, $940,000 in fines and court fees, and $1.4 million in taxes. Offenders also performed community service worth more than $266,000. The annual cost per offender was $8249.[53]

✧ INTENSIVE SUPERVISION

In a compelling and sobering article entitled "When Probation Becomes More Dreaded Than Prison," Joan Petersilia, director of the criminal justice program for the Rand Corporation, questions whether or not community sanctions are punitive enough to convince the public that the "punishment fits the crime." Petersilia considers intensive supervision programs (ISPs) as offering some hope of relieving prison crowding without draining the public purse.[54]

Petersilia acknowledged that intensive supervision programs are "still on trial." However, in several states, *given the option of serving prison terms or participating in ISPs, many offenders have chosen prison* [emphasis hers].[55] For many offenders, it may seem preferable to get a short stay in prison over with than spend five times as long in an ISP. Consider the alternatives now facing offenders in Oregon:

◊ *ISP*. The offender will serve 2 years under this sanction. During that time, the offender will be visited by a probation officer two or three times per week, who will phone on the other days. The offender will be subject to unannounced searches of his home for drugs and have his urine tested regularly for alcohol and drugs. He must strictly abide by other conditions as set by the court—not carrying a weapon, not socializing with certain persons—and he will have to perform community service and be employed or participate in training or education. In addition, he will be strongly encouraged to attend counseling and/or other treatment, particularly if he is a drug offender.

or

◊ *Prison*. A sentence of 2 to 4 years will require that the offender serve about 3 to 6 months. During his term, he is not required to work nor will he be required to participate in any training or treatment, but may do so if he wishes. Once released, he will be placed on 2 years routine parole supervision, where he sees his parole officer about once a month.[56]

For these offenders, freedom is probably preferable to imprisonment. However, the ISP does not represent freedom. In fact, it may stress and isolate repeat offenders more than imprisonment does. Their homes can be searched and they must submit regularly to urine testing.

In sum, the views of this country's serious offenders must be taken into account when structuring sanctions. Obviously, it is illusory to believe that imprisonment represents a horrible punishment and should therefore punish and deter. If prison does not deter criminals, perhaps ISPs might provide a feasible means to this end. This country must get over its preoccupation with imprisonment as the only suitable sanction for serious offenses.[57]

The Bureau of Justice Statistics recently reported that over 55,000 probationers were under intensive supervision—about 2 percent of all adults on probation—at the beginning of 1991. Furthermore, a total of about 17,000 parolees were under intensive supervision.[58]

No common standard exists for deciding when a supervision program for probationers becomes intensive. An inspection of "intensive" supervised probation programs in 37 states disclosed a range from two contacts per month by probation officers with offenders in Texas to as many as 32 contacts per month in Idaho.[59]

For the purpose of clarification, intensive supervision probation (ISP) will consist of the following:

◊ Small client–officer caseloads, not more than a 10-to-1 ratio
◊ Weekly face-to-face contacts between officer and clients
◊ Regular field visits at an offender's workplace, perhaps monthly or bimonthly
◊ The inclusion of preventive conditions such as regular drug and alcohol testing
◊ Swift and certain administrative review and revocation procedures for violating one or more probation conditions.[60]

Although there has been a great deal of interest and research on the effects of intensive supervision,[61] some researchers have found it to have been of questionable value.[62] According to Edward Latessa and Gennaro Vito, the three major issues surrounding the use of intensive probation have been the effectiveness question, caseload size, and the classification question. The effectiveness question has largely gone unanswered; the findings concerning the impact of intensive supervision upon recidivism rates have been inconclusive.[63] There appears to be some success with "specially" selected offenders.[64] As far as caseload is concerned, intensive supervision projects have resulted in lower numbers of clients, with the average around 25 cases per officer. The crucial operational issue has been the dilemma of accurately selecting cases appropriate for higher levels of supervision, with the most widely used screening techniques involving either risk or needs assessment instruments.[65]

As expected, the numbers of contacts with clients have increased under intensive supervision; the average number has been about four contacts per month, compared to around one per month under "regular" supervision. This difference in contact levels has not invoked a sense of "intense" supervision. Recently, Georgia and New Jersey instituted programs that assigned two offices caseloads of 10, with contacts required on at least a daily basis. However, it appears, according to Latessa and Vito, that the primary purpose of these contacts was for surveillance, not treatment.[66]

Georgia's program is an interesting study as well as a look at what many have felt is a model intensive supervision program. Georgia, founded in 1733 by the British, was conceived as a prison alternative, a colony where those imprisoned for debt in England could get a new start. The state, which later acquired a reputation as the "chain-gang capital of the United States," seems an unlikely place for a progressive corrections idea. Indeed, Georgia still has one of the highest imprisonment rates in the country. However, Georgia officials have been forced to come to grips with correctional problems and the high costs of building enough prisons to house all of its criminals. When the intensive probation program began in earnest in the mid-1980s, Georgia was sentencing 13,000 criminals to prison each year, with a state prison capacity of 16,000 beds. The state obviously had to do something; it was assisted by the fact that federal courts threatened to take over the management of the corrections system because of overcrowding.[67]

Georgia listened to a Rand study, which recommended intensive probation supervision as the most realistic way to deal with this "serious threat to public safety."[68] The program, which had the mission of keeping people out of prison without creating a community crime wave, could accommodate about 1400 offenders annually. The program cost, with 33 trained two-person surveillance teams, was about one-fifth as much as caring for and feeding a prisoner and was paid entirely by the state's probationers. The state cited a 78 percent success rate.[69]

✦ ELECTRONIC MONITORING/HOUSE ARREST

Like intensive supervision, electronic monitoring began in the mid-1980s. It began when in the early 1980s, a judge in New Mexico named Jack Love saw a Spiderman comic in which evildoers placed an electronic monitor on Spiderman to track his whereabouts. Love persuaded a friend to develop the idea and the technology; the rest is history.[70] Electronic monitoring has become another form of intermediate sanction which is applied to offenders who are less serious than those requiring long-term incarceration but more serious than those deserving standard probation. At the beginning of 1991, nearly 7000 probationers were under electronic monitoring, about 13 percent of all those under intensive supervision. Furthermore, of the parolees who were under intensive supervision, about 1300 were under electronic monitoring.[71]

There are two basic types of electronic monitoring devices. *Continuously signaling devices* constantly monitor the presence of an offender at a particular location. They consist of a transmitter attached to the offender which sends out a continuous signal. A receiver–dialer apparatus is attached to the offender's telephone and detects signals from the transmitter. A central computer accepts reports from the receiver-dialer over telephone lines, compares them with the offender's curfew schedule, and alerts corrections officials to unauthorized absences.[72]

Programmed contact devices contact the offender periodically to verify his or her presence. Various manufacturing companies use different methods to assure that the offender is the person responding to the call and is in fact at the monitored location as required. One system uses voice verification technology. Another requires a "wristlet," a black plastic module that is strapped to the offender's arm. When the computer calls, the wristlet is inserted into a verifier box connected to the telephone, to verify that the telephone is answered by the monitored offender. A third system uses visual verification. Use of the telephone requires corrections officials to verify that certain technologies are not in use on the offender's telephone. For example, "call forwarding" and a portable telephone would make it easy for the offender to respond to calls while away from home, but "call waiting" might interfere with the equipment's efforts to call the central computer.[73]

Like intensive supervision, the use of electronic monitoring has generated controversy. There are those who feel that monitoring is improper. It has led to some debate concerning the purpose of correctional supervision in the community. Indeed, a recent conference of the American Probation and Parole Association stated the conflict in its title, "Supervision in the 1990s: Surveillance vs. Treatment."[74] The American Civil Liberties Union (ACLU) agrees with probation administrators that the system is an effective, inexpensive method of supervising probationers. However, the union is concerned that with these devices, the state can monitor its citizens in the last bastion of privacy: the home. And unlike old-fashioned probation, electronic monitoring empowers the government to control a population from *within* the halls of authority. That, they feel, is a qualitative increase in police power. They argue that the prospects for greater incursions into privacy are ominous. For example, video-cameras are already used to monitor drunk drivers in Maryland; the cameras are installed in offenders' homes, and a jailer calls the offender once or twice a day and asks him to step in front of the camera, take a self-administered breath alcohol test, and display the results before the camera.[75]

The ACLU also feels that the devices are not the answer to prison over-crowding, because the nation's penal institutions are overcrowded by the thousands, not by the hundreds. They assert that turning homes into jails is not the answer to overcrowding. They concur with federal judge Henry Bramwell, who wrote in the *Howard Law Journal* that "the poor and the minority defendant is usually one who has committed a violent crime, is without means, and has little or no recognition in his community. As a result, the middle-class defendant gets alternative sentencing or part-time imprisonment, usually without incarceration, and the poor and minority defendant gets a heavy jail term. This certainly is not justice. Alternative sentencing and part-time imprisonment have strong class overtones."[76]

Conversely, Rolando Del Carmen maintained that electronic monitoring provides a more structured environment, better supervision, and accomplished a curfew situation for the probationer. He contended that judges can be prevented from "widening the net," a term for sanctioning (in this case, putting someone on electronic monitoring) who would normally not have been sanctioned (or, in this situation, would have been placed on regular probation): "You identify certain offenses where defendants are currently sent to jail, such as burglary, or where the penal code provides mandatorily that the defendant would have gone to prison. You want to hit that middle cohort instead of dipping down."[77]

✦ SHOCK PROBATION

Originally adopted in 1964, shock probation is an early release program that grants the sentencing judge the discretionary authority to release an offender from prison and place that offender on probation.[78] It uniquely combines the elements of probation and parole, while attempting to impress offenders with the reality of prison life, provide greater protection to society, and make offenders appreciate the seriousness of their crimes without employing a long and possibly debilitating prison experience.[79] Shock probation is now used in 26 states and the Federal Bureau of Prisons; several other states have legislatively authorized programs but are not funded or have program proposals under review. The range is three to six months in prison, with most (10 of 26) states having programs three months in length.[80]

Shock probation also encompasses two basic theories: deterrence and reintegration. The judge, using the presentence investigation, has a number of options available: Place the offender on probation, sentence the offender to a stay in a community-based correctional facility, or sentence the offender to jail or prison. When the offender is sentenced to prison, a motion for release on shock probation may be initiated by the inmate, the trial lawyer, or through unilateral action by the court. The decision to grant shock probation lies with the judge; state and local probation departments cannot release offenders on shock probation through their own initiative.[81]

Two studies of shock probation have attempted to compare the performance of shock and regular probationers. In Ohio, Gennaro F. Vito and Harry E. Allen [82] discovered that regular probationers had a 42 percent lower probability of reincarceration than did shock probationers. Another study in 1985 reported that the shock cases had a higher rearrest rate than the regular probationers.[83] More recently, a study performed by Edward Latessa and Gennaro

Vito examined the effects of using intensive supervision on shock probationers; no significantly lower recidivism rates were found.[84]

On the basis of such studies it has been concluded that (1) shock probationers generally have a higher recidivism rate than regular probationers, (2) no evidence of a deterrent effect for shock probation has been documented, and (3) given the financial and human costs associated with incarceration, the diversionary aspects of the program should be emphasized in the future.[85] Put simply, shock probation should not be used with offenders who could be considered as candidates for regular probation.

Summary

This chapter demonstrated that changes in national ideological thought and problems with contemporary probation administration practices have combined to cause problems for the corrections field. It is clear that probation and parole agencies have borne, and are presently bearing, the brunt of the combined effects of increased crime, tougher mandatory sentencing laws, a "get tough" public and justice-system attitude toward crime that permeates the country, and tremendously overcrowded prisons. Given this situation, it is probably a credit to corrections administrators that they have managed to cope under such exigent circumstances, and have even implemented several alternative methods for addressing their problems, known as intermediate sanctions.

Hopefully, the call to look closely at the "punitive" nature of prisons will not fall on deaf ears. We must realize that for a large number of offenders, prison is not the ultimate form of punishment short of death. For those people, who view imprisonment as a "badge of courage," there must be a tougher alternative. Intensive supervision programs hold promise for being molded to serve this purpose. Correctional administrators seeking alternatives to imprisonment must be open to the concept.

Questions for Review

1. Delineate the various types of probation systems being administered in the United States.
2. Should probation services be placed within the judicial or executive branch of government? Defend your answer.
3. What are some of the major needs, problems, and concerns of probation administrators?
4. Describe the two basic models of parole administration.

5. Why are intermediate sanctions being used so widely in probation and parole? Explain what is meant by *intensive supervision* and *house arrest*.

6. How can shock probation further the goals of corrections? What problems have been found with this practice?

For Further Reading

HOWARD ABADINSKY, *Probation and Parole: Theory and Practice*. (5th ed.). Englewood Cliffs, N.J.: Prentice Hall, 1994.

HARRY E. ALLEN, CHRIS W. ESKRIDGE, EDWARD J. LATESSA, and GENNARO F. VITO, *Probation and Parole in America*. New York: Free Press, 1985.

DEAN J. CHAMPION, *Corrections in the United States: A Contemporary Perspective*. Englewood Cliffs, N.J.: Prentice Hall, 1990.

DEAN J. CHAMPION, *Probation and Parole in the United States*. New York: Macmillan, 1990.

CLAYTON A. HARTJEN and EDWARD E. RHINE, *Correctional Theory and Practice*. Chicago: Nelson-Hall, 1992.

BELINDA R. MCCARTHY, *Intermediate Punishments: Intensive Supervision, Home Confinement, and Electronic Surveillance*. Monsey, N.J.: Criminal Justice Press, 1987.

Notes

1. Todd R. Clear, "Punishment and Control in Community Supervision," in Clayton A. Hartjen and Edward E. Rhine (eds.), *Correctional Theory and Practice* (Chicago: Nelson-Hall, 1992), pp. 31–42.

2. See the President's Commission on Law Enforcement and Administration of Justice, *Task Force Report: Corrections*, (Washington, D.C.: U.S. Government Printing Office, 1967), p. 7.

3. Franklin E. Zimring and Gordon J. Hawkins, *Deterrence: The Legal Threat in Crime Control* (Chicago: University of Chicago Press, 1973).

4. Joan Petersilia, "When Probation Becomes More Dreaded Than Prison," *Federal Probation* 54 (March 1990):23.

5. *Ibid.*

6. *Ibid.*, p. 25.

7. Allen Beck, Susan Kline, and Lawrence Greenfield, *Survey of Youth in Custody: 1987* (U.S. Department of Justice, Bureau of Justice Statistics, 1988).

8. Joan Petersilia, "When Probation Becomes More Dreaded Than Prison," p. 24.

9. John Conrad, "The Pessimistic Reflections of a Chronic Optimist," *Federal Probation* 55 (June 1991):4–9.

10. Dean J. Champion, *Corrections in the United States: A Contemporary Perspective* (Englewood Cliffs, N.J.: Prentice Hall, 1990), p. 37.

11. American Correctional Association, *Directory* (College Park, Md.: Author, 1988).

12. Barry J. Nidorf, "Community Corrections: Turning the Crowding Crisis into Opportunities," *Corrections Today* (October 1989):82–88.

13. Howard Abadinsky, *Probation and Parole: Theory and Practice* (5th ed.) (Englewood Cliffs, N.J.: Prentice Hall, 1994), p. 32.

14. *Ibid.*

15. *Ibid.*, pp. 32–36.

16. See the *Task Force Report: Corrections*, pp. 35–37.

17. E. Kim Nelson, Howard Ohmart, and Nora Harlow, *Promising Strategies in Probation and Parole* (Washington, D.C.: U.S. Government Printing Office, 1978).

18. *Ibid.*

19. Howard Abadinsky, *Probation and Parole: Theory and Practice* (5th ed.), pp. 34–35.

20. E. Kim Nelson, Howard Ohmart, and Nora Harlow, *Promising Strategies in Probation and Parole.*

21. Howard Abadinsky, *Probation and Parole: Theory and Practice* (5th ed.), p. 35.

22. *Ibid.*

23. E. P. Volz, "Staff Supervision and Organization," in *Proceedings of the National Probation Association: 1924* (New York: National Probation Association, 1924), pp. 103–105.

24. Patricia L. Hardyman, "Management Styles in Probation: Policy Implications Derived from Systems Theory," in Clayton A. Hartjen and Edward E. Rhine (eds.), *Correctional Theory and Practice*, pp. 61–81.

25. David Duffee, "The Community Context of Probation," in Patrick McAnany, Doug Thompson, and David Fogel (eds.), *Probation and Justice: Reconsideration of Mission* (Cambridge, Mass.: Oelgeschlager, Gunn, and Hain, 1984).

26. Eric Trist, "On Socio-Technical Systems," in Kenneth Benne and Robert Chin (eds.), *The Planning of Change* (2d ed.) (New York: Holt, Rinehart and Winston, 1969), pp. 269–281.

27. Daniel Katz and Robert I. Kahn, *The Social Psychology of Organizations* (New York: Wiley, 1966).

28. Patricia L. Hardyman, "Management Styles in Probation: Policy Implications Derived from Systems Theory," p. 68.

29. *Ibid.*, p. 70.

30. *Ibid.*

31. *Ibid.*, p. 71.

32. *Ibid.*, pp. 74–75.

33. Howard Abadinsky, *Probation and Parole: Theory and Practice* (5th ed.), p. 32.

34. National Advisory Commission on Criminal Justice Standards and Goals, *Corrections* (Washington, D.C.: U.S. Government Printing Office, 1973), pp. 396–397.

35. *Task Force Report: Corrections*, p. 71.

36. *Ibid.*

37. National Advisory Commission, *Corrections*, pp. 396–397.

38. *Task Force Report: Corrections*, p. 65.

39. Patricia L. Hardyman, "Management Styles in Probation: Policy Implications Derived from Systems Theory," p. 76.

40. *Ibid.*, pp. 77–78.

41. Donald Cochran, "Corrections' Catch 22," *Corrections Today* (October 1989):16–18.

42. Barry J. Nidorf, "Community Corrections: Turning the Crowding Crisis into Opportunities," p. 82.

43. John P. Conrad, "The Redefinition of Probation: Drastic Proposals to Solve an Urgent Problem." Patrick D. McAnany, Doug Thomson, and David Fogel (eds.), *Probation and Justice: Reconsideration of Mission*, p. 258.

44. Peter J. Benekos, "Beyond Reintegration: Community Corrections in a Retributive Era," *Federal Probation* 54 (March 1990):53, p. 54.

45. *Ibid.*

46. *Ibid.*, p. 53.

47. Barry J. Nidorf, "Community Corrections: Turning the Crowding Crisis into Opportunities," p. 84.

48. Belinda R. McCarthy, *Intermediate Punishments: Intensive Supervision, Home Confinement, and Electronic Surveillance* (Monsey, N.J.: Criminal Justice Press, 1987), p. 3.

49. Barry J. Nidorf, "Community Corrections: Turning the Crowding Crisis into Opportunities," p. 85.

50. Peter J. Benekos, "Beyond Reintegration: Community Corrections in a Retributive Era," p. 54.

51. Belinda R. McCarthy, *Intermediate Punishments: Intensive Supervision, Home Confinement, and Electronic Surveillance*, p. 3.

52. *Ibid.*, pp. 85–86.

53. Charles Colson and Daniel W. Van Ness, "Alternatives to Incarceration," *The Journal of State Government* (March/April 1989):59–64.

54. Joan Petersilia, "When Probation Becomes More Dreaded Than Prison," pp. 23–27.

55. *Ibid.*, p. 23.

56. This information was compiled from ISP brochures and information from the Oregon Department of Correction, by Joan Petersilia.

57. Joan Petersilia, "When Probation Becomes More Dreaded Than Prison," p. 27.

58. U.S. Department of Justice, Bureau of Justice Statistics Bulletin, *Probation and Parole* (Washington, D.C.: U.S. Government Printing Office, 1991), p. 4.

59. James M. Byrne, "The Control Controversy: A Preliminary Examination of Intensive Probation Supervision Programs in the United States," *Federal Probation* 50 (1986):4–16.

60. Adapted from Vincent O'Leary and Todd R. Clear, *Directions for Community Corrections in the 1990s* (Washington, D.C.: National Institute of Corrections, 1984).

61. See, for example, Don Gottfredson and Marc Neithercutt, *Caseload Size Variation and Difference in Probation/Parole Performance* (Pittsburgh, Pa.: National Center for Juvenile Justice, 1974); J. Banks, A. L. Porter, R. L. Rardin, T. R. Silen, and V. E. Unger, *Issue Paper: Phase I Evaluation of Intensive Special Probation Project* (Atlanta, Ga.: School of Industrial and System Engineering, Georgia Institute of Technology, 1976); and D. Fallen, C. Apperson, J. Holt-Milligan, and J. Roe, *Intensive Parole Supervision* (Olympia, Wash.: Dept. of Social and Health Services, Analysis and Information Service Division, Office of Research, 1981).

62. R. Adams and H. J. Vetter, "Effectiveness of Probation Caseload Sizes: A Review of the Empirical Literature," *Criminology* 9 (1971):333–343; Edward J. Latessa, "Intensive Supervision: An Evaluation of the Effectiveness of an Intensive Diversion Unit," unpublished doctoral dissertation, Ohio State University, Columbus, Ohio: 1979.

63. Edward Latessa and Gennaro F. Vito, "The Effects of Intensive Supervision on Shock Probationers," *Journal of Criminal Justice* 16 (1988):319–330.

64. J. Banks, A. L. Porter, R. L. Rardin, T. R. Silen, and V. E. Unger, *Issue Paper: Phase I Evaluation of Intensive Special Probation Project*.

65. See C. Baird, "Probation and Parole Classification: The Wisconsin Model," in American Correctional Association (ed.), *Classification as a Management Tool: Theories and Models for Decisionmakers* (College Park, Md.: American Correctional Association, 1983).

66. Edward Latessa and Gennaro F. Vito, "The Effects of Intensive Supervision on Shock Probationers," pp. 320–321.

67. Kathy Sawyer, "The Alternative to Prison," *The Washington Post National Weekly Edition* (September 2, 1985):6–7.

68. *Ibid.*

69. *Ibid.*

70. Keenen Peck, "High-Tech House Arrest," *The Progressive* (July 1988):26–28.

71. U.S. Department of Justice, Bureau of Justice Statistics Bulletin, *Probation and Parole: 1990*, p. 4.

72. Annesley K. Schmidt, "Electronic Monitors: Realistically, What Can Be Expected?" *Federal Probation* 59 (June 1991):47–53.

73. *Ibid.*, p. 47.

74. *Ibid.*, p. 48.

75. Keenen Peck, "High-Tech House Arrest," p. 27.

76. Quoted in Keenen Peck, "High-Tech House Arrest," p. 27.

77. *Ibid.*

78. Edward Latessa and Gennaro F. Vito, "The Effects of Intensive Supervision on Shock Probationers," p. 320.

79. Gennaro F. Vito, "Developments in Shock Probation: A Review of Research Findings and Policy Implications," *Federal Probation* 48 (June 1984):22–27.

80. Timothy J. Flanagan and Kathleen Maguire (eds.), *Sourcebook of Criminal Justice Statistics: 1991* (Washington, D.C.: U.S. Department of Justice, Bureau of Justice Statistics, 1992), pp. 671–672.

81. *Ibid.*, pp. 22–23.

82. Gennaro F. Vito and Harry E. Allen, "Shock Probation in Ohio: A Comparison of Outcomes," *International Journal of Offender Therapy* 25 (1981):70–76.

83. Gennaro F. Vito, Ronald M. Holmes, and Deborah G. Wilson, "The Effect of Shock and Regular Probation upon Recidivism: A Comparative Analysis," *American Journal of Criminal Justice* 9 (1984):152–162.

84. Edward Latessa and Gennaro Vito, "The Effects of Intensive Supervision on Shock Probationers," p. 327.

85. Gennaro F. Vito, "Developments in Shock Probation: A Review of Research Findings and Policy Implications," p. 27.

13
Issues and Practices

I never saw a man who looked
With such a wistful eye
Upon that little tent of blue
Which prisoners call the sky.

—Oscar Wilde

✦ INTRODUCTION

In the preceding two chapters we addressed several administrative issues in corrections. In this chapter we expand on that theme, discussing more challenges for contemporary correctional administrators. We briefly continue our "what works" theme, looking at intermediate sanctions, coed prisons, and smoke-free jails. Next are examinations of several of the more pressing issues for corrections managers: sex and violence (including by and against staff and inmates), and drug use, interdiction, and treatment. Then we consider a growing trend: the surge of inmate civil litigation. Following a look at inmate gangs, we examine inmate classification, another important matter for correctional administrators.

We then turn to discussions of two relatively new issues and practices: corrections privatization and accreditation. Following those matters is an overview of the difficulties of calculating the actual costs of correctional services. We conclude with a review of stress and burnout among corrections personnel, including coping strategies.

◆ "WHAT WORKS": INSTITUTIONAL PROGRAMS

Like the police and courts subsystems, corrections has been engaged in developing new programs and practices, many of which are of such recent formation they are still in the initial stages of evaluation. Following are discussions of some of the more prominent experiments.

◇ INTERMEDIATE SANCTIONS

Although there are doubtless many Americans who still subscribe to the "nothing works" notion propounded by Robert Martinson in the mid-1970s (discussed in Chapter 10), corrections has not been standing still; a number of innovations have been attempted that seem to be enjoying success. Three alternatives to incarceration—intensive supervision, electronic monitoring, and shock probation—which come under the general heading of "intermediate sanctions," appear to have achieved positive outcomes and were discussed at length in Chapter 12. Also, some would consider privatization of prisons and jails to be a positive innovation (discussed in the present chapter). Additional innovations are discussed below.

◇ COED PRISONS

Segregation of prisoners according to their gender dates back several centuries to the Walnut Street Jail and, later, the Auburn Penitentiary in New York. Reasons given then included the improvement of inmate morality, a reduction in inmate promiscuity, and greater privacy for both sexes. In recent years, however, prisoners of both sexes have expressed interest in co-correctional or coed prisons.[1] These institutions include those where administrators and policymakers have allowed men and women prisoners to live together, supervised by male and female staff, and participate in all activities together (although, unlike Denmark and other countries, they may not share the same quarters or have sexual encounters).

The ratio of male to female inmates is recommended to be 50–50.[2] When women are in the minority, they feel conspicuous and tend to be treated as a minority group by their male counterparts.[3] Also, jealousies among the dominant sex may arise because of greater competition for social encounters and more intimate relationships.

A major public misconception about co-correctional prisons is that there is unchecked promiscuity, shared quarters by male and female inmates, and numerous illegitimate births.[4] This is not the case. Experiments have instead found several successful outcomes, including: greater staff enthusiasm, positive media coverage, privacy rights of both sexes being observed, and parolees finding employment more easily. Also, one institution realized a 40 percent reduction in the number of violent discipline charges, a 73 percent reduction in the number of general discipline charges, and a 42 percent reduction in the number of grievances filed by inmates.[5]

Some negative outcomes have also been anticipated, however. A superintendent of a women's prison in a western state offered several caveats to co-correctional institutions. The "look but don't touch" aspects of these institutions can aggravate sexual frustrations of both sexes and may actually encourage homosexual relationships. There is also the strong possibility that suspicion will arise in the minds of husbands or wives of the residents of a co-correctional institution. Finally, one must question whether the stresses and strains caused by sexual frustrations may well be detrimental to the programmatic planning designed for a given inmate; if an inmate finds himself or herself strongly attracted to a member of the opposite sex but can make no advances, will this not make the treatment process more difficult to accomplish?[6]

✦ SMOKE-FREE JAILS

Today, cigarette smoking is recognized as the single most preventable cause of death in our society; more than 300,000 premature deaths occur each year as a result of cigarette smoking. Smokers also put others around them at risk. Studies have indicated that involuntary smoke may be even more dangerous than mainstream smoke, due to the lower temperature compared to the temperature during a puff.[7] The Surgeon General has suggested that the simple separation of smokers and nonsmokers within the same airspace may significantly reduce this unnecessary risk.[8]

Largely as a result of these findings, smoking is becoming less socially acceptable, and Americans are fighting over where, when, and whether a smoker may smoke. Correctional institutions are not immune. The American Correctional Association conducted a survey in 1987 on implementing smoking restrictions in correctional institutions. The survey discovered that most correctional institution administrators had very serious reservations about the effect of such policies, with most believing that it would make their jobs more difficult and worsen the overall environment of their facilities.[9]

On the other hand, also hearing of studies concerning secondhand smoke, inmates have not been reluctant to file lawsuits for a smoke-free environment. Furthermore, a number of court decisions in the past few years have held that inmates have no constitutional right to smoke while incarcerated. Support for "no smoking" jails has thus been provided from the courts, health care agencies, and the Surgeon General. Once a few facilities made the decision to become smoke-free, others have followed the example.

Thus a growing trend by sheriffs and other correctional administrators is to outlaw smoking in detention facilities. When the decision is first announced, there is normally an outcry from all sectors, about workers' rights, prisoner rebellion, and so on. Administrators have had to hold their ground and refuse to capitulate on any point or relinquish any small area of their facilities for smokers. They have typically followed a certain "protocol" in implementing the plan: (1) requesting a legal opinion from the appropriate counsel's office concerning the constitutionality of the proposal and its chance for prevailing in the face of inmate challenges (it is more likely that a nonsmoking inmate would prevail who sued because of being forced to share a cell with a smoking companion); (2) discussing the plan openly with employees to assuage their concerns, explaining among other things that where smoke-free jails have been implemented, no extraordinary behavior by inmates occurs; (3) announcing the decision well in advance of the plan's taking affect, to allow time for people to adjust to the idea, smoke all their cigarettes, and perhaps most important, attend counseling and smoking cessation programs provided by the county health department.[10]

It has been found that following a few months of minor irritation and complaints, the policy has met with little resistance. Inmates eventually appreciate the benefits of the policy: easier breathing, cleaner walls and ceilings, and an overall healthier environment. The administration spends less on repainting walls and replacing cigarette-burned carpets and air filters.[11] Perhaps the greatest advantage of all is the elimination of a potential fire hazard.

✦ THE "PAINS" OF INCARCERATION: SEX AND VIOLENCE

✧ SEXUAL VICTIMIZATION

People sent to serve terms in correctional institutions do not leave their sexuality at the front gate. Paul Tappan maintained that homosexuality is a universal concomitant of sex-segregated living, a perennial problem in camps, boarding schools, one-sexed colleges, training schools, and, of course, correctional facilities. From a biological point of view, he argued, homosexuality is normal behavior in the latter institutions.[12]

Persons entering prisons and jails are not transformed into eunuchs, and their sexuality can be expressed in many forms, some of which are innocuous and others very violent. If placed on a continuum, this range might include solitary or mutual masturbation, or the manufacturing of a sexual object (using rolled-up magazines, towels, vaseline, and so on, sometimes referred to in prison jargon as a "Fifi bag") at one end, consensual homosexual behavior in the middle, and gang rapes on the other end. The most frequent form of sexual release is solitary masturbation: "Nobody—inmate, staff, or visitor—is in a prison very long before seeing an inmate masturbating in a toilet, shower, or cell."[13]

There are relatively few studies on the subject of homosexual behavior and rape among inmates. Estimates are that between 30 and 45 percent of inmates have experienced homosexual behavior, with the variations depending upon the degree of custodial surveillance, the nature of the inmate population, and the average length of confinement in a given prison.[14]

Like the free world, people in prison are often extremely dominant or submissive, and the latter can easily be exploited. Also like heterosexual rape in the free world, this exploitation is not due to sexual *need*, but rather is driven by hate and a desire to dominate, control, and conquer. This problem exists in women's institutions as well as in those for men. However, women rarely sexually assault other women prisoners; they tend to join groups similar to families, obtaining support and protection for individual members. But when such attacks do occur, they can be quite brutal and involve the use of such objects as broom handles. Among women, homosexuality appears to develop out of mutual interest. The nature of physical contact among women also tends to be different from that among males, who tend to use direct actions, such as oral and anal scx, and mutual masturbation. For women, there may be only a strong emotional relationship with some body contact, such as embracing or holding hands. Some women do, however, engage in serious sexual unions, such as deep kissing, oral-genital stimulation, and body contact that attempts to simulate heterosexual intercourse.[15]

Violent sexual incidents among inmates fall into two categories. In the first, the aggressor employs violence to coerce his target, and force is decided upon in advance. The primary cause of this violence is the need to uphold men's "rights" to use force to gain sexual access. The second category of incidents is that in which targets react violently to propositions perceived as threatening. This type often resembles free-world victim-precipitated homicide because words or gestures perceived as offensive provoke retaliatory insults, threats, or violence.[16]

A few authors have contended that the problem of homosexual rape is *the* major problem inside correctional institutions, while others (including many administrators) maintain that sexual violence is practically no problem at all. Indeed, while early studies of the prison [17] suggested a high rate of homosexual rapes, more recent studies [18] have suggested that the actual incidence of homosexual rape is far less than had been earlier reported. The latter researchers, however, do report widespread fear of sexual victimization among inmates. Norman Smith and Mary Ellen Batiuk argued that because the social setting of prisons is hostile, the fear of being sexually victimized permeates every social act (e.g., inmates are extremely conscious of the need to act macho, not to show emotion, be careful of what they wear—nothing which can be interpreted as a weakness or "signal" of homosexuality propensities).[19]

Inmate fear of sexual victimization is justified. In fact, many believe that homosexual attacks are quite common, even reaching epidemic proportions in some institutions: "Sexual assaults are epidemic in some prison systems. Virtually every slightly built young man committed by the courts is sexually approached within a day or two after his admission to prison. Many of these young men are overwhelmed and repeatedly 'raped' by gangs of inmate aggressors."[20]

It is clear that today's violent gang- and clique-dominated prison society fosters increased fears of rape and other unwanted sexual activity, particularly the role of "insertee" or "punk." The fear is greatest—and most justified—among young white prisoners. Most targets of rape and other aggressive sex are white, as many as 83 percent, in contrast to about 15 percent of blacks and 2 percent of Hispanics. Most aggressors are black (80 percent), some are Hispanic (14 percent), and only a few are white (6 percent). Several facts explain these proportions: Whites are perceived as weak and are objects of racial hatred; they are also poorly organized and less likely to band together for protection. Thus they are isolated and more vulnerable to attack. Blacks coming to prison usually know someone and join a clique or gang for protection.[21] "It's a way for the black man to get back at the white man. It's one way he can assert his manhood. Anything white, even a defenseless punk is part of what the black man hates. It's part of what he's had to fight all his life just to survive, just to have a hole to sleep in and some garbage to eat....It's a new ego thing. He can show he's a man by making a white guy into a girl."[22] Lee Bowker, in his study of prison victimization, commented that "like heterosexual rape on the streets, prison homosexual rape has effects that go beyond the immediate victims. Homosexual rape impacts all prisoners and fundamentally alters the social climate of correctional institutions.[23]

It is probably surprising that sexual aggression in correctional institutions is not more widespread. Even in men's prisons, estimates on the incidence of sexual assault run as low as 1 percent.[24] Still, it remains a serious problem for the weak and unprotected. Is there anything correctional administrators can do to reduce or eliminate the problem of homosexual rapes, given their biological nature and the violent tendencies of many? Programs that may reduce prison sexual violence are aimed at targets as well as aggressors. However, such a program faces difficulties. Aggressors with histories of violence ruthlessly exploit others, while targets often use force to protect themselves and to promote masculine images. Furthermore, threatened men are often reluctant to go to staff because existing official remedies can cause more problems than they solve.

Daniel Lockwood suggested that administrators consider human relations training, with the goals of increasing interpersonal skills, relieving interpersonal or intergroup tension, and developing individual and group problem-solving skills. Another possibility involves social literacy training, which has achieved some success in group settings but has not been attempted in prisons. Such training focuses on (1) a study of the group's thoughts, language, and action by an outsider; (2) definition of "central conflicts" by the outsider and leaders of the group; (3) analysis of the causes of the problem by group members; and (4) solving the problem by group members. Specific problem-solving techniques include creation by group members of a "survival guide" and addressing stress in a group role-play setting.[25]

✧ INSTITUTIONAL VIOLENCE

Violence by Inmates. Personal safety for prisoners and staff members is at best uncertain; there is always some risk of injury or material loss at the hands of aggressive or unbalanced fellow prisoners and prison gangs.[26] Violence by inmates includes homicides and very serious assaults that are inflicted with a variety of ingenious homemade weapons. As was shown in Chapter 11, when we discussed the four stages that penal institutions can proceed through, all institutions have the potential to become violent.

As with incidents of homosexual rape, the extent of violence against inmates in prisons is not known precisely; nor do we know whether or not institutional assaults occur with more or less frequency than in the community at large.[27] However, prisons are unquestionably violent settings, particularly so where penal institutions contain large proportions of young inmates, who account disproportionately for disruptive behavior.[28] The probabilities of violence are also enhanced with large numbers of "state-raised" youths, prisoners who have extensive experience in juvenile institutions, where a climate of exploitation and violence is usually prevalent.[29] In addition to inmate age, the amount of violence in an institution is normally influenced by its population density and factors tied to prisonization, such as deprivation and continuation of violent, aggressive, and unacceptable *previous* behavior patterns in the institutional setting.

Prison violence of conventional kinds is confined almost exclusively to male prisons. However, violence does occur in women's institutions, often comprised of angry outbursts in reactions to stressful situations. Former inmates have noted that whereas men may engage in short-term fights to prove their manhood and achieve a reputation, women inmates often like to leave permanent scars by tearing out earrings from pierced ears, or by trying to inflict lasting scars on the faces of other inmates by scratching them with their fingernails.[30]

Turmoil and prisoner violence frequently follows court efforts to improve prison conditions; this reaction has been referred to as the "paradox of reform," where attempts to make the prison better can make it a more dangerous place. Studies show that prisoners are often safer *before* the reforms and that high rates of violence and fear become a normal element of postreform prison life.[31]

Assaults are perpetrated against correctional officers with some frequency. In fact, from 1985 to 1990, 21 officers were killed in 10 states and the Federal Bureau of Prisons. Peter Kratcoski, examining assaults against correctional officers, determined that four factors were significantly related to these assaults: location (more than 70 percent of the assaults occurred in detention/ high-security areas); shift (the majority of all such assaults occurred during the day); work experience (inexperienced trainees received a disproportionate number of assaults); and age of the assaultant (most assaults against staff members were committed by inmates age 25 and younger). The type of situation was also examined. While only 3 percent of federal correctional officers were assaulted while attempting to break up inmate fights, 32 percent of the assaults on state correctional officers occurred in such situations. Generally, when an officer is required to break up a fight, he or she will request backup assistance. An inexperienced officer may try to handle such a situation alone and be assaulted. The sex of correctional officers was not found to have a relationship to assaults.[32]

Violence against Inmates. One response by guards when they perceive a loss of control over prisoners is to employ repressive tactics.[33] In these situations, guards become more custodial and punitive toward prisoners; in addition to using more insults and obscenities, the repression of the guards is rooted in their willingness to use physical violence. The guards' attempts to maintain control may create relatively unstable conditions and may even produce rebellious prisoners and an unsafe working environment for guards.[34]

✧ ADMINISTRATIVE APPROACHES TO VIOLENCE

What can be done by prison administration to improve the prison climate when violence reaches serious levels? Again, we might consider what approaches are available to correctional administrators to reducing the problem of nonsexual institutional violence. Any such undertaking should be done with four groups in mind: (1) the administration, which wants to regain control; (2) inmates, who want to live without fear; (3) the correctional officers, who desire a say in developing a safe working environment and control over inmates; and (4) noncustodial staff, who want equity with the custodial staff and information concerning the control and treatment of inmates. Indeed, two major administrative problems that can occur within an institution are (1) a lack of control over staff and inmates, and (2) polarization between custodial and noncustodial staff.[35]

One approach that has been attempted to curb violence is the *unit management* concept, which has been described as one of a number of small, self-contained "institutions" operating in semiautonomous fashion within the confines of a larger facility.[36] Unit management is operationalized by housing 50 to 100 inmates together in one physical area and keeping them together for as long as possible. These inmate groups (units) are supervised by a multidisciplinary management team normally composed of at least (1) a unit manager, (2) a caseworker, (3) a secretary, (4) a correctional counselor, (5) a correctional officer, (6) an educator, and (7) a psychologist or other mental health worker. These teams have discipline, classification, and programmatic authority and are guided by a set of common policies and procedures. Such a program implemented at the Massachusetts Correctional Institute at Walpole in 1980 all but eliminated the hostile conditions that had existed there for nearly a decade and had resulted in a violent death occurring every 39 days.[37]

There are other recommendations for dealing administratively with prison staff–inmate violence:

1. Understanding violence "hot spots" and low-violence subenvironments. Staff and inmates in violent settings should be interviewed for clues about the high or low level of violence; given everyone's stake in minimizing trouble, there is incentive for problem-centered information sharing that has no disciplinary consequence. Available statistics about types of inmates, schedule of activities, levels of interaction, population movements, and patterns of supervision can be collated and utilized.

2. Helping inmates and staff in high-violence settings to address their own violence problem. Staff and inmate groups can be run separately or together, charged with documenting the reasons for violence patterns, and asked to recommend policy changes to neutralize violence patterns.

3. Creating support systems for victims and potential victims. By segregating aggressors, they form enclaves in which levels of violence become quite high; victim-centered strategies also entail problems, such as stigmatizing inmates. Less drastic measures include the creation of new settings where violence-prone inmates are mixed with others for peer support.

4. Using violence-related data in staff training and inmate indoctrination. After collating relevant information about the setting, training should consist of more than human-relations training for staff and rule-centered, legalistic lectures for inmates. Statistics and illustrations should be used to sensitize staff and inmates to situations they are likely to encounter on the tier, on the job, in the classroom, and in recreation areas. "Canned" curricula should be avoided. These combined strategies have the single goal of reducing violence through the creation of a climate that begins to defuse occasions for violence.[38]

✦ DRUG INTERDICTION AND TREATMENT IN PRISONS

One of the major needs of prison inmates is treatment for drug abuse, a major problem for some prior to their incarceration. Survey data presented in Chapter 10 revealed that 35 percent of all male inmates were under the influence of drugs at the time of their current offense.

However, a companion dilemma for correctional administrators is that of trying to stop the entry and use of illegal drugs *after* a person is incarcerated. This is not an insignificant matter, according to a study of 957 state confinement facilities for adults. About seven of every eight U.S. prisons conducted urinary drug tests with about 565,500 inmates for one or more illegal drugs in 1990. Of those tests, 1.4 percent were positive for cocaine, 1 percent for heroin, 2.3 percent for methamphetamines, and 5.8 percent for marijuana.[39]

Methods of drug interdiction were found to vary, including physical checks, verbal questioning, patdowns, clothing exchanges, and body cavity searches. These checks were conducted among all persons entering prisons, random groups, or only those suspected of carrying drugs. About three-fourths (76 percent) of all federal and state confinement institutions tested inmates for drugs when use was suspected. The most intrusive interdiction technique was body cavity searches; facilities testing with body cavity search showed lower rates of drug use among inmates than did facilities using other methods of interdiction.

Questioning and search of belongings were also widely used for visitors to both state and federal facilities. Patting down new and returning inmates and requiring them to exchange clothes generally applied to all inmates. Over 80 percent of federal facilities patted down all inmates and required an exchange of clothing. Almost 78 percent of state confinement facilities frisked all inmates, and 57 percent substituted prison clothes. Table 13.1 shows the criteria for drug interdiction activity for prisoners in federal and state institutions.[40]

TABLE 13.3

Who was chosen for interdiction	Interdiction activity							
	Verbal questioning		Patdown		Clothing exchange		Body cavity search	
	Federal	State	Federal	State	Federal	State	Federal	State
Total	100%	100%	100%	100%	100%	100%	100%	100%
All inmates, inmates chosen randomly, and inmates suspected using drugs	6.3	9.7	13.8	9.7	6.3	4.2	2.5	2.3
All inmates and inmates chosen randomly	3.8	6.1	8.8	7.9	2.5	2.3	1.3	1.4
All inmates and inmates suspected of using drugs	3.8	9.4	2.5	8.3	1.3	8.4	6.3	3.2
All inmates but no other criteria	67.5	38.3	57.5	51.8	72.5	41.6	36.3	12.7
Inmates chosen randomly and inmates suspected of using drugs	1.3	4.6	1.3	3.3	0	3.0	1.3	2.1
Only inmates chosen randomly	3.8	3.7	5.0	3.3	3.8	3.3	2.5	1.7
Only inmates suspected of using drugs	0	9.9	0	5.5	1.3	5.3	15.0	31.1
No reported interdiction activity	13.8	18.3	11.3	10.0	12.5	31.9	35.0	45.5
Number of facilities	80	957	80	957	80	957	80	957

Note: Facilities indicated whether they performed an interdiction activity on all inmates, on suspected drug user/couriers, and on inmates at random. Criteria for selection of inmates are arranged in mutually exclusive categories.

(Source: U. S. Department of Justice, Bureau of Justice Statistics, Drug Enforcement and Treatment in Prisons: 1990 (Washington, D.C.: Author, 1992), p. 3,)

Aside from visitors, of course, another method by which inmates may acquire illegal drugs is by staff members. Because of this potential security breach, about half of all state confinement administrators had policies whereby staff are questioned or patted down upon reporting to work. About one-fourth of state facilities frisked staff members at random. Most interdiction activities involving staff were conducted on suspicion of smuggling drugs.[41]

Correctional administrators have responded to the growing numbers of drug-involved offenders by increasing the enrollment of inmates in prison programs. In 1979, about 4.4 percent of inmates in the United States were in drug treatment; by 1987, that number had increased to 11.1 percent. Despite this large increase, the number of drug-using inmates far exceeds the enrollment level. However, in addition to treatment benefits, administrators have found that these programs furnish other managerial benefits, including the following: they help provide good security, improve working conditions for staff, reduce staff conflict, and provide a resource for conflict resolution and the potential for positive publicity.[42]

✦ TRENDS IN INMATE CIVIL LITIGATION

✧ The Resurgence of the Hands-Off Doctrine

Although incarceration in jails and prisons entails stringent restrictions on freedom of movement and the loss of numerous privileges, inmates nonetheless enjoy several important constitutional rights. Legal circumstances of prison inmates have changed tremendously since the Virginia Supreme Court told murderous inmate Woody Ruffin in 1871 that he was a "slave of the state" with no rights that need be recognized.[43]

The demise of the *hands-off doctrine,* where courts deferred to the expertise of correctional administrators in the operation of their institutions, began in the mid-1960s; in *Cooper v. Pate* [44] the U.S. Supreme Court held that state inmates could bring lawsuits against prison authorities under Title 42, Section 1983 of the Civil Rights Act. This decision hailed a new era for inmates and fostered an explosion of inmate litigation. During the 1971–1972 Supreme Court term, following the deadly prison riot at Attica, New York, there were additional court decisions expanding prisoners' rights and remedies. One of the major decisions was *Wolff v. McDonnell* [45] (1974), in which the U.S. Supreme Court stated that "there is no Iron Curtain drawn between the Constitution and the prisons of this country."

The turning point in this barrage of inmate-oriented expansion of rights was the well-known case of *Bell v. Wolfish* [46] (1979), which considered among other issues, double-bunking in the Metropolitan Correctional Center in New York City. The Court seemed to revert to the original hands-off doctrine; in a 6-to-3 decision, it declared that jail management should be left to corrections personnel. In other words, the Court felt that deference should be extended to persons noted for their expertise in correctional matters, and administrative decisions should not be invalidated by the Court unless extreme circumstances required it. Chief Justice Rehnquist took the opportunity to address the critical tension between courts and administrators in the development of corrections law.

During the litigation explosion of the 1970s and 1980s, several other significant, positive events occurred as well. First, all state jurisdictions and the federal government undertook to revise their existing sentencing schemes. The most prominent sentencing reforms were the shift from indeterminate to determinate, presumptive, and mandatory sentencing schemes and greater restrictions on the autonomy of the judiciary and paroling authorities relating to sentencing and early releases. There was also increased reliance by correctional administrators on inmate classification and risk assessment instruments for deciding the appropriate level of inmate custody (discussed below). Finally, there was the large-scale establishment of alternative dispute resolution mechanisms for prisoner grievances (such as ombudsmen, mediation, inmate councils, legal assistance, and external review bodies). By 1982, all 50 states had created inmate grievance systems.[47]

✦ The Litigation Explosion Continues

Today, the results of past litigation, defending against current lawsuits, and attempting to avoid future liability consume tremendous amounts of time for most correctional administrators (as well as that of the states' central departments of corrections and the offices of many state attorneys general). The volume of inmate litigation has not abated. In 1980, 23,287 petitions were filed by inmates of state and federal correctional institutions alleging both civil and criminal violations and seeking compensatory damages, injunctions, and property claims.[48] By 1990 the number of petitions filed in federal district courts by state and federal prisoners had swollen to 42,630 (or an overall increase of 83.1 percent), of which 25,992, or 61 percent, alleged violations of civil rights, and 12,784, or 30 percent, were habeas corpus petitions.[49]

Prisoners sue primarily because they are either unwilling to accept their conviction or because they wish to hassle their keepers.[50] However, those who challenge conditions of confinement or policies seem to do so for a variety of reasons.[51] Today, there are basically two types of prisoner litigants. First are those who file a single suit during their entire period of incarceration (usually requiring the assistance of others to do it); one study found that 71 percent of all litigants filed only one action but accounted for about half of all litigation.[52] Second, there are inmates who make a prison career out of law: "jailhouse lawyers."[53]

Dean Champion, analyzing trends in inmate litigation from 1975 to 1987, found that the number of filings increased systematically. There were also significant increases in the proportion of Section 1983 suits in both state and federal jurisdictions (from 48 percent of the total to 69 percent). Meanwhile, the number of habeas corpus petitions decreased both in number and proportion during this period, as well as the number of suits against administrators alleging negligence and other liability. This may be due in part to the growth of administrative grievance procedures and internal policies mentioned above, and the fact that correctional officer unions and increased susceptibility to lawsuits has created a greater awareness of legal liabilities and responsibilities.[54]

A bit of irony is worth mentioning. While the litigious inmates described above have certainly been a thorn for correctional administrators, until the increased court intervention of the 1960s and 1970s, conditions in many prisons were almost insufferable. Staff members as well as inmates despaired because state and local governments were not willing to "loosen the pursestrings" and provide funding to improve those conditions. (It is a long-standing political adage that prison reform and the improvement of prison conditions seldom obtain votes for elected officials.) Keepers often had to battle the same vermin and insects and eat the same food (some of which was laced with lead peeling from the kitchen walls), and for at least eight hours per day, generally endure the same conditions as the kept. The irony here, of course, is that in order for working conditions to improve for penal administrators and staff, they had to hope to be sued by inmates for violating their Eighth Amendment rights, and lose.

✦ THE DUE DEFERENCE DOCTRINE

To trace the recent trends in corrections and prisoners' rights law, we must go back to the aforementioned Supreme Court decision in *Bell v. Wolfish* (1976), which is also the "cornerstone of the future edifice of correctional law."[55] From about that point in time to the present, the general trend has been for federal courts to defer to the expertise of prison administrators. This is the emergence of the *due deference doctrine*, of judicial noninterference in prison administration. However, this doctrine has not been developed sufficiently to determine for the courts when they should intervene and when they should not. Frequently, the result has been, as in *Bell*, that courts accept jurisdiction over prisoners' claims but fail to provide remedies. One concern with this narrowing of the scope of federal jurisdiction over inmate claims is that it will blunt the once powerful tools that prisoners used to complain of administrative abuses.[56]

According to Rutgers' law professor Charles Jones, although the Supreme Court decisions during the terms of court under Chief Justices Burger and Rehnquist purport to continue to reject the old hands off policy abandoned by the Court almost 50 years ago, recent decisions make clear that the federal doors to prison litigation have all but closed. Theoretically, the doctrine of due deference is distinguishable from hands off, where the federal courts claimed to lack power to supervise prison administration. Now, under due deference, they purport to distinguish substantive prisoner rights claims from frivolous complaints against prison administrators.[57] This "judicial retreat" or gradual return to the *Bell* decision troubles some observers, as it may reverse what has been termed "the most important development in the prisoner's environment,"[58] the substitution of the rule of law and rational/legal decision making for arbitrariness in prison administrative decision making. Although it is unlikely, given the current levels of education and attitudes of correctional administrators, they fear that the implications of deference for prisoner participation in prison governance are critical.[59]

✦ PRISON GANGS

It has been argued that because of weakened authority of correctional administration over inmates due to court intervention and the resulting prisoners' rights and remedies, an era has been created where inmate gangs have formed for the purpose of sharing and eventually dominating, through violent means, the power base once occupied by the "keepers."[60] For whatever reason, it is clear that gangs have gained a substantial foothold in the day-to-day activities and operation of prisons and even jails.

The formation of prison gangs began in 1950, at Washington Penitentiary in Walla Walla, when a group of prisoners organized themselves and became known as the Gypsy Jokers.[61] Then, in 1967, a tightly knit Chicano clique of youths from Los Angeles and a number of other prisoners began to take over

San Quentin. Known as the "Mexican Mafia," they quickly gained a reputation for toughness, enhanced by the rumor that to become a member, one had to kill another prisoner.[62] Soon a rival Chicano group formed, La Nuestra Familia; the rivalry between these two gangs became so deadly that the state segregated them into two prisons: San Quentin for the Mexican Mafia, and Soledad for La Nuestra Familia.[63]

Violent crimes by these two groups led to the development of black and white gangs. Whites formed the Aryan Brotherhood, and blacks organized the Black Guerilla Family. Amid escalating racial tension, the Aryan Brotherhood formed an alliance with the Mexican Mafia and the Black Guerillas allied with La Nuestra Familia.[64]

Recent figures show that prison gangs exist in the federal prison system and 32 state jurisdictions. In 29 of those jurisdictions, prison administrators have identified gangs by name. And of those 29 jurisdictions, 114 gangs exist, with an estimated membership of about 12,600 inmates. Overall, gang members comprise about 3 percent of the total federal and state prison populations.[65]

With the emergence of prison gangs, two serious conditions have developed: the increased difficulty of prison officials to maintain order and discipline [66] and a rapid increase in inmate violence, often related to increases in drug trafficking, extortion, prostitution, protection, gambling, and contract inmate murders.[67] One study of prison gangs reported that they account for half or more of all prison problems.[68]

Gang members have a belligerent attitude toward all authority and its institutions when they enter prison; members are preoccupied with status and gang rivalry. They plan boycotts, strikes, and even riots. Despite administrative attempts to accommodate gangs in some prisons, they continue to pursue "loot, sex, respect, revenge, [and] will attack any outsider."[69] The close confinement and limited space in prisons make it impossible to ignore gang threats. Prisoners who want to continue to circulate beyond their own cells often must join a clique or gang for protection.

Wardens and superintendents have been brought into gang-ridden prison systems specifically to "do something" with the gang problem; by transferring gang leaders and using other methods to segregate and isolate members, some have managed to greatly diminish the gangs' power. However, with the crowding problem—and the aforementioned court decisions, court orders, and consent decrees, and other contemporary administrative limitations that served to curtail the power of correctional administrators—their power to use such tactics today would seem to have waned in large measure.

✦ INMATE CLASSIFICATION

One of the most important and potentially far-reaching responsibilities for today's correctional administrators is inmate classification. The relating of human and environmental variables can improve prisoner adjustment and prison management.[70] As rehabilitation fell into disfavor and prison populations began to soar, traditional diagnostic techniques of classification were no longer appropriate or practical, and a shift in the function and structure of classification occurred.

The four major purposes of classification systems are management, treatment, understanding, and prediction.[71] More broadly, these four primary functions of classification are to assign inmates to appropriate security levels, to place prisoners in different living quarters, to designate inmates to particular custody levels, and to select program activities for prisoners. Classification forms the basis for assigning inmates to settings to minimize problems cost-effectively and to make policy decisions regarding the proper care and supervision of prisoners.[72]

The search for accurate and precise classification models has become a legal issue for correctional administrators. Courts have repeatedly found that traditional classification procedures and criteria were based on unfounded assumptions regarding inmate behavior and that criteria were not applied uniformly to all inmates.[73] In several cases,[74] courts have also held that classification methods cannot be "capricious, irrational, or discriminatory." For a classification model to be "coherent" and thus judicially acceptable, "placement and assignment must be clearly understandable, consistently applied and conceptually complete."[75]

The search for classification systems that meet these criteria has gone in several directions. Three of the most commonly used systems today are: *Megargee's MMPI typology*, which uses a psychology inventory to classify inmates into groups with particular characteristics related to their criminality and projected troubles in prison; *Toch's Prison Preference Inventory*, measuring inmates' concerns about eight environmental attributes to determine individual needs; and *risk assessment*, currently the most common form of classification, using demographic, criminal, and behavioral characteristics to distinguish inmates according to their chances of institutional misconduct.[76]

These three systems serve different purposes, use different variables to classify inmates into groups, and are operationalized in quite different ways. Each predicts some adjustment outcomes but not others. According to an analysis of the three methods by Kevin Wright, no system emerges as clearly superior. Risk assessment appears to predict aggressive disciplinary infractions, whereas neither of the other two was useful in this regard. However, risk assessment did not predict the probabilities of self-reported internal and physical problems, but the other two systems did. All three successfully predicted self-reports of external problems. Of the three, Toch's system predicted outcome least successfully.[77]

✧ Implications for Institutional Management

If for no other reason, classification would be justified on the grounds that it provides a security strategy. With offenders receiving longer prison sentences than ever before, and a national recidivism rate of more than 30 percent, the task of protecting the public must involve more than architectural design. Indeed, with the enactment of the 1987 federal sentencing guidelines and "life without parole" statutes in many states, classification of inmates has in effect become a continuous, lifelong process. Institutional managers must realize that the classification of offenders for security purposes is essential to the operation of an orderly and safe prison.

Classification eases the burden of a major consent decree regarding crowding and conditions of confinement, provides consistency and equity to inmates in placement and treatment, and enables cost-efficient management and planning of funds and human resources. Classification can also reduce institutional escapes and the need for protective custody; furthermore, it permits violent incidents to be limited to certain units of the institution.[78]

✦ CALCULATING CORRECTIONAL COSTS

Correctional administrators and several organizations report annual cost figures for housing prison inmates, including the U.S. Census Bureau, the American Correctional Association, and other agencies of government. At present, we are often given estimates that the cost to house an inmate in prison for a year is in the range $16,000 to 20,000; however, the actual cost was probably much higher than these figures would indicate. For jails, estimated costs are even more "shaky." One recent estimate was that it cost about $24 per day to house a prisoner in jail; another figure was closer to $38.[79] The bottom line is that none of the estimates of average jail costs seems strong enough to be relied upon with confidence.

Indeed, according to Douglas McDonald, senior social scientist for a Cambridge-based research organization: "The vast majority of estimates used to represent total costs are of questionable accuracy. Most are derived from agency expenditures—or worse, from budgets—and...ignore several important categories of costs. What is needed is better agreement and understanding about what should be counted as costs."[80]

The problem is that many correctional expenditures that should be counted as costs of providing a particular service are overlooked. The total cost of a particular correctional service should include both *direct* costs, expenditures made by an agency of government to provide the service in question, and *indirect* costs, those borne by government or nongovernmental parties to support a particular correctional activity. Although the latter costs are real, their calculation is often difficult, speculative, and controversial.[81]

The direct costs other agencies incur in serving a correctional agency's mission must also be counted as direct costs. For example, teachers in prisons and jails are sometimes paid not by the correctional agency but by the school district; the same holds true for doctors and other medical workers paid by local or state departments. In-hospital care is often charged to the public hospital, utility bills in correctional facilities are sometimes paid by departments of public works, and departments of transportation often provide the vehicles used to

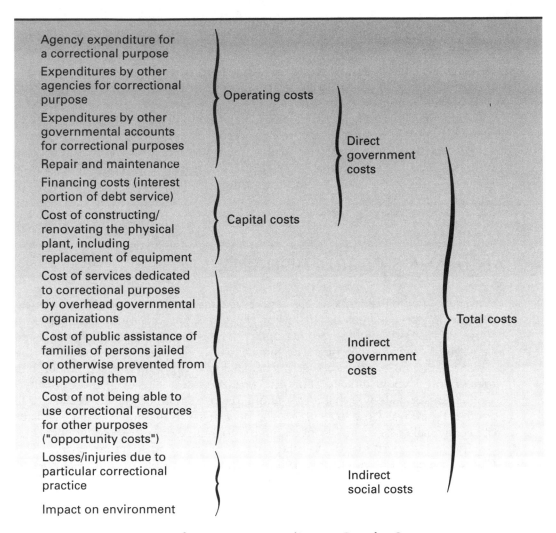

Figure 13.1 Components of corrections costs. (Source: Douglas C. McDonald, "The Cost of Corrections: In Search of the Bottom Line," in Research in Corrections, U.S. Department of Corrections, National Institute of Corrections, Vol. 2 (February 1989), p. 7.)

move prisoners. The failure to count these kinds of services provided by other agencies and levels of government will result in significantly underestimating the total direct cost of a correctional service.[82]

Other areas that are often undercounted in correctional costs are personnel fringe benefits and retirement pensions. In many jurisdictions, those costs are not assigned to corrections agency budgets; instead, they are transferred from the government's general fund into a separate account for all employees as a group. Obviously, the failure to count the added costs of benefits and pension plans results in the loss of a major expense item.

Correctional pension contributions can be quite costly. For example, in 1987–1988 in New York, contributions by state government to the retirement fund for prison employees equaled nearly 23 percent of all salary and wage payments; this was in addition to expenditures for other fringe benefits, which added additional costs of almost 12 percent. During the same year, pension contributions for city jail employees in New York City averaged about 35 percent of all salary and wage payments. According to the American Correctional Association, the average fringe and pension rate is about 24 percent of salary.[83] Figure 13.1 presents these and other components of corrections that enter into its total costs.

How much higher are the real costs of corrections likely to be? Studies indicate that the actual cost of operating public correctional programs is about 33 percent to 66 percent higher than is usually reported.[84] This obviously represents a significant amount of money, especially given the states' scramble from 1971 to 1985 to purchase, build, and rehabilitate facilities to handle their swelling inmate populations, and during which time they spent a total of $6.05 billion for capital outlays in corrections. Inflation has certainly not assisted the taxpayer in providing correctional services: sadly, *three-fourths* of the increase in correctional spending between 1971 and 1985 was due to inflation and the dollar's corresponding loss of purchasing power.[85] Not to be overlooked is inmate litigation, which has also brought a marked increase in corrections spending. One study of 14 state prison systems found that per-prisoner spending during the third and fifth years following court orders increased an average of 164 percent.[86]

Obviously, correctional administrators need good data and cost figures for reporting, planning, projecting, and general public accountability. To the extent possible, the shortcomings in determining the total direct cost of a correctional service noted above must be addressed.

✦ THE MOVE TOWARD PRIVATIZATION

✧ EMERGENCE OF THE CONCEPT

"Punishment for Profit," "The Corporate Warden," "Incarceration Unlimited": These headlines in business journals have proclaimed a new opportunity for venture capital—criminal punishment.[87] Attracted by the huge sums of money devoted each year to holding adult criminals behind bars (almost $13 billion in state institutions alone in 1992),[88] entrepreneurs have been trying to turn prisons into profit-making corporations. One commentator remarked: "There's a whole new industry developing, from the likely meeting of pinstripes and prison stripes."[89] These entrepreneurs are often cheered on by prison administrators, who think the government can stand the competition.[90]

This concept is not new in this country. Private vendors supply health care services, educational and vocational training, and an array of other services to public institutions.[91] The most prominent of the corporations attempting to operate correctional institutions privately are the Corrections Corporation of America (CCA), Behavioral Systems Southwest, Buckingham Security Limited, and American Corrections Corporation. CCA is the largest of the private operators, formed in 1983 by Thomas Beasley, a Tennessee entrepreneur involved in real estate and insurance. Two former and well-known state corrections officials, Don Hutto (former Commissioner of Corrections in Arkansas and Virginia) and Travis Snellings (former budget director for the Virginia Department of Corrections), have been affiliated with the company.[92]

All of these corporations pursue contracts for the construction and/or management of prisons and detention facilities. To date, most of the contracts awarded to these and other firms have been for small, low-security facilities for the Immigration and Naturalization Service, the Federal Bureau of Prisons, or county jails. A 1991 survey by Charles Thomas and Suzanna Foard found 49 such contractual arrangements in the country, the earliest of which was initiated in May 1984.[93] "The private jail market is ripe," says one source, "and it's the brokers, architects, builders and banks—not the taxpayers—who will make out like bandits."[94]

✦ ARGUMENTS PRO AND CON

Proponents for privatization of prisons and jails cite a number of advantages of the concept, including a greater diversity of programs and facilities and the ability to handle special inmate populations or offer special rehabilitative or training programs.[95] The strongest argument, however, is the belief that private industry can respond quickly and cost-efficiently to the current pressure for more prison space, and that they can act faster than government bureaucracies in doing so (they are not bound by state civil service rules or by employee unions). The state, they believe, can benefit in two ways. First, the private corporation makes the initial capital investment in facility construction, which enables the state to avoid debt ceilings and voter approval on bond issues. Second, the private prison charges the state less per day to hold each inmate than does the publicly operated facility. They maintain that these savings are realized through reduced building costs, reduced labor costs, and economies of scale. They finally argue that the profit motive creates an inherent efficiency.[96]

There are also arguments against the privatization of prisons. Concerns exist that the profit motive might restrict or eliminate services to underprivileged groups or those with special needs. And with regard to the argument that privatization will streamline operations by reducing bureaucratic red tape, opponents note that much of that red tape assures public participation and review of policy decisions;[97] they also feel that in a lot of cases, red tape exists to protect the public.[98] There is also concern that reduced costs will come at the expense of reduced salaries and training for staff members (indeed, one contracted site provided less than 50 hours of training, compared to the 320-hour program mandated for public employees).[99]

These pessimists are also apprehensive about the hidden costs of privately operated prisons, such as the administration of contracts. But, they argue, the biggest hidden cost would be with the necessary creation of a regulatory bureaucracy to oversee the private corporation's operations. Federal and state guidelines on the custody and care of inmates must be upheld, and to ensure compliance, the state must develop a system for monitoring private prisons.[100] Adversaries of the concept believe that private operators can (and will) work the crime trend both ways: any decrease will be touted as their work with prisons, and any increases will be used as fodder to obtain more prisons.[101]

Another problem, cited by eminent prison researcher Alexis Durham, is that although privatization will increasingly become an important force in corrections in the United States, adequate effort has not been committed to an evaluation of these programs: "Only through exacting monitoring and evaluation can a reasoned assessment of achievements of privatization be made. Furthermore, only with the information produced by such evaluations can sensible correctional policy be developed. Thus it is crucial that adequate effort be committed to evaluating the initiatives of the private sector."[102]

Finally, opponents believe that for the state to abdicate its power of punishment to the lowest bidder will seal off prisons more completely from constitutional and societal controls.[103] They point to the words of one inmate, that "Corrections is already too much of a business and needs to become less so. Look in the financial section of your daily newspaper to see how many points Prison Industries went up today. If there has been a prison riot and $50 million worth of machinery and plant are destroyed, the stockholders will sell out in droves."[104]

✦ CORRECTIONS ACCREDITATION

In Chapter 6 we discussed the growth of police accreditation. However, accreditation has been in existence longer and is far more advanced in the corrections field. In the 1970s a national system of corrections accreditation was developed to generally upgrade correctional institutions and programs. This movement was preceded by years of experience on an international level, not with accreditation as such, but with its most essential element: The formulation of agreed-upon standards. International committees had been working off and on for many decades to develop standards, especially with the old League of Nations.

This effort became more organized and effective through United Nations authorization of the U.N. Commission on the Prevention of Crime and the Treatment of Offenders.[105] By the spring of 1980, the commission had accredited 47 different correctional facilities or agencies in the United States and Canada, and nearly 400 more were in various stages of the process of qualifying.[106]

The development of corrections standards and the accreditation process in the United States was begun in 1974, when the Law Enforcement Assistance Administration (LEAA) funded a new organization, the Commission on

Accreditation for Corrections. The Commission was directed by a board of 19 persons from various aspects of the field. The American Correctional Association was chosen to be the sponsor of the new Commission. [107]

Although the Commission exists today, the American Corrections Association (ACA) has taken over the responsibility for day-to-day accreditation operations, through its Division of Standards and Accreditation. However, the ACA does not actually grant accreditation; that function is still performed by the Commission on Accreditation for Corrections.

Any agency wishing to be accredited makes application to the Commission and pays a fee for the services involved. Next the agency is aided in the conduct of a self-evaluation. For those items not in compliance, the agency must submit a plan for correcting the deficiency. The Commission will review the self-evaluation reports and audit the agency's evaluation by use of on-site visits from staff and a visiting committee of consultants.

This system of voluntary accreditation is felt to possess several benefits; in short, it provides (1) the best means for ensuring quality in correctional services, (2) the best means of mobilizing and capitalizing on professional talent, (3) the best means of infusing research findings into correctional practices, (4) support for elected and appointed state and federal officials committed to improving corrections, (5) correctional administrators with a sound rationale when appropriations for correctional services are requested, (6) interested citizens with factual measurements of the correctional services in their communities or states, and (7) overall professionalization of correctional services.[108]

◆ STRESS: CONSEQUENCES AND COPING STRATEGIES

◇ THE PROBLEM

There is a growing body of research establishing what correctional officers already knew: that correctional institutions are unpleasant and stressful places in which to work.[109] In fact, the correctional field is one in which the incidence of high blood pressure is especially high.[110] Tremendous interest in correctional officer job satisfaction began in the 1980s, possibly due to the growing recognition of chronic labor supply problems. The turnover rate for correctional officers in 1961 was 24.8 percent;[111] a 1976 study concluded that correctional officers had the highest turnover rate of any workers in the justice system,[112] and a 1981 national survey revealed that it was 24.5 percent.[113] More recently, attrition rates of correctional officers in a majority of the states have been found to be 25 percent or higher.[114] In the last several decades, a number of prominent panels and commissions have also been created to address the chronic labor supply problems in corrections.

It is not surprising that correctional officers report feelings of burnout, given the level of general dissatisfaction that has been reported with their jobs. Studies suggest that the nature of the correctional institution environment contributes more to officer burnout than do personal characteristics.[115] The more ineffective or powerless staff feel with inmates, the more emotionally and physically exhausted they feel.[116] Officers who engage in stimulating activities experience less burnout than those who have no control (e.g., patrolling the cell block) or engage in boring activities.[117] In general, stress is more closely tied to the nature of the working environment. But the most important contributor is the staffs' relationship with the inmates.[118]

Persons viewing a job as threatening have been found more likely to cope through the use of intrapsychic processes, such as avoidance (avoiding people in general), wishful thinking (e.g., hoping a miracle will happen), and/or minimization of threat (attempting to gain sympathy and understanding from someone). These mechanisms have been noted especially for workers in the correctional field.[119] Corrections officers experiencing higher diastolic blood pressure have been found to cope with greater reliance on all three of these mechanisms. However, officers who attempt to cope by partially withdrawing from the situation by using these mechanisms place their physical well-being and that of their co-workers at risk. Alternatively, they may quit their jobs [120] or be absent with greater frequency.[121]

The implications for correctional administrators appear rather straightforward. Ongoing correctional staff training and research are needed to fend off stress-related problems. Individualized institutional programs need to be designed to enhance the quality of the relationship between staff and inmates. Programs involving inmates and staff in cooperative recreational and maintenance activities would be beneficial, as would programs involving these groups in community outreach and, in some instances, prison reform.[122]

✦ PROBATION AND PAROLE OFFICERS

Stress and burnout among probation and parole officers has been linked with longevity; officers who experience stress and/or burnout are more likely to leave the position or try to avoid additional work.[123] Studies also suggest that officers under a democratic or laissez-faire management style tend to stay with the department longer, reducing staff turnover and producing more experienced officers. In turn, a stable, experienced staff is more able to handle the caseloads better, and officers do not have to handle excessive or multiple caseloads due to vacant positions caused by turnover. Thus the number of officers employed by a department, and the length of time an employee remains with it, are probably linked closely to management style. It is therefore the responsibility of the manager to monitor and minimize stress and thereby reduce officer burnout.[124]

Most important, probation and parole administrators need to maintain an "open door" with their line officers and communicate openly and directly with their staff. The type and amount of communication within a department often mirrors the administrators' management style. Laissez-faire probation and parole administrators tend to communicate solely through memos and written operations manuals, while authoritarian leaders hold formal staff meetings and scheduled appointments as well as issuing written and operations manuals. The democratic administrator prefers to meet informally with officers on an ad hoc basis, with formal decisions being announced via memos and operations manuals; generally, large staff meetings are considered a waste of time.[125]

Summary

Continuing the inventory of problems and issues plaguing corrections and its administrators in the two preceding chapters, this chapter has perhaps shown that our correctional institutions do indeed mirror society at large. There is significant violence and aggression, both sexual and physical in prison, and inmates can and do engage in drug abuse; furthermore, like their free-world counterparts, a veritable epidemic of "hair-trigger suing" has emanated from inside the walls for some time.

Can we anticipate the diminution of these issues in the near future? It would seem that society is gradually turning away from the vastly expensive "lock-em-up" notion for some offenders. However, the problems of sex and violence, drug abuse, and gangs are not so easy to overcome, given the nature of imprisonment, the gains of inmates in controlling the prisons, and the "pains" that inmates perceive in their lifestyle.

Questions for Review

1. What new and successful programs are at work in corrections?
2. Analyze some of the "pains" of imprisonment, including sexual victimization and violence. What can be done to reduce staff–inmate violence.
3. To what extent is drug abuse a problem in correctional institutions? How may administrators interdict and treat this problem?
4. How has inmate litigation changed correctional administration?
5. What can correctional administrators do to control gangs in prisons?
6. Why is inmate classification an important responsibility for correctional administrators?
7. What are some advantages and disadvantages of privatization?
8. What are some problems inherent in calculating the cost of correctional services? What actual costs tend to be ignored or undercounted? How might this problem be rectified?
9. What are some unique stressors for persons employed in corrections? Is it more difficult for these workers to manage job-related stress?

For Further Reading

HARRY E. ALLEN and CLIFFORD H E. SIMONSEN, *Corrections in America: An Introduction* (5th ed.). New York: Macmillan, 1989.

LYNN GOODSTEIN and DORIS LAYTON MacKENZIE (eds.) *The American Prison: Issues in Research and Policy.* New York: Plenum Press, 1989.

CLAYTON A. HARTJEN and EDWARD E. RHINE (eds.), *Correctional Theory and Practice.* Chicago: Nelson-Hall, 1992.

RICHARD HAWKINS and GEOFFREY P. ALPERT, *American Prison Systems: Punishment and Justice.* Englewood Cliffs, N.J.: Prentice Hall, 1989.

ROBERT JOHNSON and HANS TOCH, *The Pains of Imprisonment.* Prospect Heights, Ill.: Waveland Press, 1982.

Notes

1. Clarice Feinman, *Women in the Criminal Justice System* (2d ed.)(New York: Praeger, 1986), pp. 64–65.
2. Sue Mahan, "Co-corrections: Doing Time Together," *Corrections Today* 48 (1986):134–165.
3. *Ibid.*, p. 134.
4. Sally Chandler Halford, "Kansas Co-Correctional Concept," *Corrections Today* 46 (1984):44–54.
5. *Ibid.*, p. 54.
6. Jacqueline K. Crawford, "Two Losers Don't Make a Winner: The Case Against the Co-Correctional Institution," in John Ortiz Smykla (ed.), *Coed Prison* (New York: Human Sciences Press, 1980), pp. 262–268.
7. Brad L. Neiger, "Development of a Smoke-Free Jail Policy: A Case Study in Davis County, Utah," *American Jails* (Summer 1988):20–23.
8. U.S. Department of Health and Human Services, *The Health Consequences of Involuntary Smoking: A Report of the Surgeon General* (Rockville, Md.: Author, 1986).
9. American Correctional Association, *Corrections Today* 49 (August 1987):14.
10. Brad L. Neiger, "Development of a Smoke-Free Jail Policy: A Case Study in Davis County, Utah," p. 23.
11. *Ibid.*
12. Paul W. Tappan, *Crime, Justice, and Correction* (New York: McGraw-Hill, 1960), pp. 678–679.
13. Gene Kassebaum, "Sex in Prison," *Psychology Today* (January 1972):39.
14. Joseph Fishman, *Sex in Prison* (New York: National Library Press, 1934); Donald Clemmer, *The Prison Community* (New York: Rinehart, 1958), pp. 249–273; Gresham Sykes, *The Society of Captives: A Study of a Maximum Security Prison* (Princeton, N.J.: Princeton University Press, 1958); Peter C. Buffum, *Homosexuality in Prisons* (Washington, D.C.: U.S. Government Printing Office, 1972).

15. See Rose Giallombardo, *Society of Women: A Study of a Women's Prison* (New York: Wiley, 1966); David Ward and Gene Kassebaum, *Women's Prisons* (Chicago: Aldine, 1965), pp. 80–101; John H. Gagnon and William Simon, "The Social Meaning of Prison Homosexuality," *Federal Probation* 32 (March 1968): 23–29.

16. Daniel Lockwood, "Reducing Prison Sexual Violence," in Robert Johnson and Hans Toch, (eds.) *The Pains of Imprisonment* (Prospect Heights, Ill.: Waveland Press, 1982): 257–265.

17. Donald Clemmer, *The Prison Community* (New York: Rinehart and Company, 1940); Gresham M. Sykes, *The Society of Captives: A Study of a Maximum Security Prison*; Alan J. Davis, "Sexual Assaults in the Philadelphia Prison System and Sheriff's Vans," *Trans-Action* 6 (1968):8–16.

18. Clemens Bartollas, Stuart J. Miller, and Simon Dimitz, *Juvenile Victimization: The Institutional Paradox* (New York: Halsted, 1976); Lee Bowker, *Prison Victimization* (New York: Elsevier, 1980); Daniel Lockwood, *Prison Sexual Violence* (New York: Elsevier, 1980); Ulla Bondeson, *Prisoners in Prison Societies* (New Brunswick, N.J.: Transaction Publishers, 1989).

19. Norman E. Smith and Mary Ellen Batiuk, "Sexual Victimization and Inmate Social Interaction," *The Prison Journal* 69 (Fall/Winter 1989):29–38.

20. "Sexual Assaults in Prison," from *Report on Sexual Assaults in a Prison System and Sheriff's Vans* (1968), cited in Leon Radzinowicz and Marvin E. Wolfgang (eds.), *Crime and Justice: The Criminal under Restraint* (New York: Basic Books, 1977).

21. Daniel Lockwood, *Prison Sexual Violence*, p. 29.

22. Leo Carroll, "Humanitarian Reform and Biracial Sexual Assault in a Maximum Security Prison," *Urban Life* 5 (January 1977):422.

23. Lee Bowker, *Prison Victimization*, p. 1.

24. *Ibid.*, p. 30.

25. Daniel Lockwood, "Reducing Prison Sexual Violence," pp. 261–262.

26. Lee H. Bowker, "Victimizers and Victims in American Correctional Institutions," in Robert Johnson and Hans Toch (eds.), *The Pains of Imprisonment*, pp. 63–76.

27. D. Jones, *The Health Risks of Imprisonment* (Lexington, Mass.: D. C. Heath, 1976); Sawyer F. Sylvester, John H. Reed, and David O. Nelson, *Prison Homicide* (New York: Spectrum, 1977); and Lee H. Bowker, *Prison Victimization*.

28. Timothy J. Flanagan, "Correlates of Institutional Misconduct among State Prisoners," *Criminology* 21 (1983):29–39.

29. John Irwin, *The Felon* (Englewood Cliffs, N.J.: Prentice Hall, 1970; Clemens Bartollas, Stuart J. Miller, and Simon Dinitz, *Juvenile Victimization: The Institutional Paradox* (New York: Wiley, 1976).

30. Tom Howard, personal communication.

31. Ben M. Crouch and James W. Marquart, "Resolving the Paradox of Reform: Litigation, Prisoner Violence, and Perceptions of Risk," *Justice Quarterly* 7 (March 1990):103–123.

32. Peter C. Kratcoski, "The Implications of Research Explaining Prison Violence and Disruption," *Federal Probation* 52 (March 1988):27–32.

33. Lucien X. Lombardo, "Stress, Change and Collective Violence in Prison," in Robert Johnson and Hans Toch (eds.), *The Pains of Imprisonment*, pp. 77–93.

34. John R. Hepburn, "Prison Guards as Agents of Social Control," in Lynne Goodstein and Doris Layton MacKenzie (eds.), *The American Prison: Issues in Research and Policy* (New York: Plenum Press, 1989), pp. 191–206.

35. J. Forbes Farmer, "A Case Study in Regaining Control of a Violent State Prison," *Federal Probation* 52 (March 1988): 41–47.

36. Robert B. Levinson and Roy E. Gerard, "Functional Units: A Different Correctional Approach," *Federal Probation* 37 (December 1973):8–16.

37. J. Forbes Farmer, "A Case Study in Regaining Control of a Violent State Prison," p. 46.

38. Adapted from Hans Toch, "Social Climate and Prison Violence," in Michael Braswell, Steven Dillingham, and Reid Montgomery, Jr. (eds.), *Prison Violence in America* (Cincinnati, Ohio: Anderson, 1985), pp. 37–46.

39. U.S. Department of Justice, Bureau of Justice Statistics Special Report, *Drug Enforcement and Treatment in Prison: 1990* (Washington, D.C.: Author, 1992), p. 1.

40. *Ibid.*, pp. 1–2.

41. *Ibid.*, p. 2.

42. U.S. Department of Justice, Office of Justice Programs, National Institute of Justice, *Prison Programs for Drug-Involved Offenders* (Washington, D.C.: Author, 1989), pp. 1, 4.

43. *Ruffin v. Commonwealth*, 62 Va. 790, 796 (1871).

44. 378 U.S. 546 (1964).

45. 418 U.S. 539 (1974).

46. 441 U.S. 520 (1979).

47. Dean J. Champion, "Some Recent Trends in Civil Litigation by Federal and State Prison Inmates," *Federal Probation* 52 (September 1988):43–47.

48. Timothy J. Flanagan and Kathleen Maguire (eds.), *Sourcebook of Criminal Justice Statistics 1991*. U.S. Department of Justice, Bureau of Justice Statistics (Washington, D.C.: U.S. Government Printing Office, 1992), p. 555.

49. *Ibid.*

50. Jim Thomas, Kathy Harris, and Devin Keeler, "Issues and Misconceptions in Prisoner Litigation," *Criminology* 24 (1987):901–919.

51. Dragan Milovanovic and Jim Thomas, "Overcoming the Absurd: Prisoner Litigation as Primitive Rebellion," *Social Problems* 36 (February 1989):48–60.

52. Jim Thomas, "Repackaging the Data: The 'Reality' of Prisoner Litigation," *New England Journal of Criminal and Civil Confinement* 15 (1989).

53. *Ibid.*, p. 50.

54. Dean J. Champion, "Some Recent Trends in Civil Litigation by Federal and State Prison Inmates," p. 46.

55. Charles H. Jones, "Recent Trends in Corrections and Prisoners' Rights Law," in Clayton A. Hartjen and Edward E. Rhine (eds.), *Correctional Theory and Practice* (Chicago: Nelson-Hall, 1992), pp. 119–138.

56. *Ibid.*, p. 120.

57. *Ibid.*, pp. 121–122.

58. James Jacobs, *Stateville: The Penitentiary in Mass Society* (Chicago: University of Chicago Press, 1977).

59. Charles H. Jones, "Recent Trends in Corrections and Prisoners' Rights Law," p. 122.

60. James Jacobs, *Stateville: The Penitentiary in Mass Society.*

61. George M. Camp and Camille G. Camp, *Prison Gangs: Their Extent, Nature, and Impact on Prisons*, Grant 84–NI–AX–0001, U.S. Department of Justice, Office of Legal Policy (Washington, D.C.: U.S. Government Printing Office, 1985).

62. John Irwin, *Prisons in Turmoil* (Boston: Little Brown, 1980), pp. 189–190.

63. *Ibid.*, p. 190.

64. Joel Samaha, *Criminal Justice* (St. Paul, Minn.: West, 1988), p. 558.

65. *Ibid.*

66. James Jacobs, *Stateville: The Penitentiary in Mass Society.*

67. John Irwin, *Prisons in Turmoil.*

68. George M. Camp and Camille G. Camp, *The Correctional Year Book* (South Salem, N.Y.: Criminal Justice Institute, 1987).

69. John Irwin, *Prisons in Turmoil*, p. 192.

70. K. N. Wright, J. M. Harris, and Nancy Woika, *Improving Correctional Classification through a Study of the Placement of Inmates in Environmental Settings*, Final Report, NIJ Grant 83-IJ-CX-0011 (Washington, D.C.: U.S. Government Printing Office, 1985).

71. Doris Layton MacKenzie, C. Dale Posey, and Karen R. Rapaport, "A Theoretical Revolution in Corrections: Varied Purposes for Classification," *Criminal Justice and Behavior* 15 (March 1988):125–136.

72. Kevin N. Wright, "The Relationship of Risk, Needs, and Personality Classification Systems and Prison Adjustment," *Criminal Justice and Behavior* 15 (December 1988):454–471.

73. James Austin, "Assessing the New Generation of Prison Classification Models," *Crime and Delinquency* 29 (1983):561–576.

74. See *Holt v. Sarver*, 1971; *Morris v. Travisono*, 1970; *Pugh v. Locke*, 1976; *Laman v. Helgemoe*, 1977; *Palmigiano v. Garrahy*, 1977; *Ramos v. Lamm*, 1979.

75. J. Austin, "Assessing the New Generation of Prison Classification Models," pp. 562–563.

76. *Ibid*, pp. 455.

77. Kevin N. Wright, "The Relationship of Risk, Needs, and Personality Classification Systems and Prison Adjustment," p. 468.

78. Parker Evatt, Sammie Brown, and Lorraine T. Fowler, "Offender Classification: Don't Overlook This Important Security Strategy," *Corrections Today* (July 1989):34–37.

79. National Institute of Corrections, *Research in Corrections* 2 (February 1989), p. 4.

80. Douglas C. McDonald, "The Cost of Corrections: In Search of the Bottom Line," in National Institute of Corrections, *Research in Corrections* 2 (February 1989), p. 6.

81. *Ibid.*

82. *Ibid.*, p. 8.

83. *Ibid.*, p. 10.

84. *Ibid.*, p. 11.

85. *Ibid.*, p. 12.

86. Linda Harriman and Jeffrey D. Straussman, "Do Judges Determine Budget Decisions? Federal Court Decisions in Prison Reform and State Spending for Corrections," *Public Administration Review* 43 (1983).

87. Craig Becker and Mary Dru Stanley, "The Downside of Private Prisons," *The Nation* (June 15, 1985):728–730.

88. Kathleen Maguire, Ann L. Pastore, and Timothy J. Flanagan (eds.), *Sourcebook of Criminal Justice Statistics 1992*. U.S. Department of Justice, Bureau of Justice Statistics. (Washington, D.C.: U.S. Government Printing Office, 1993), p. 7.

89. Quoted in Craig Becker and Mary Dru Stanley, "The Downside of Private Prisons," p. 728.

90. Kerry Elizabeth Knobelsdorff, "The Move to Hand Prisons over to Private Businesses Draws Flak," *The Christian Science Monitor* (July 27, 1987):17–18.

91. Camille Camp and George Camp, "Correctional Privatization in Perspective," *The Prison Journal* 65 (1985):14–31.

92. Craig Becker and Mary Dru Stanley, "The Downside of Private Prisons," p. 729.

93. Charles W. Thomas and Suzanna L. Foard, *Private Correctional Facilities Census* (Gainesville, Fla.: University of Florida, Center for Studies in Criminology and Law, 1991).

94. Quoted in Craig Becker and Mary Dru Stanley, "The Downside of Private Prisons," p. 728.

95. Robert B. Levinson, "Okeechobee: An Evaluation of Privatization in Corrections," *The Prison Journal* 65 (1985):75–94; J. Mullen, "Corrections and the Private Sector," *The Prison Journal* 65 (1985):1–13.

96. Ted Gest, "Prisons for Profit: A Growing Business," *U.S. News and World Report* (July 2, 1984):45–46.

97. Christine Bowditch and Ronald S. Everett, "Private Prisons: Problems Within the Solution," *Justice Quarterly* 4 (September 1987):441–453.

98. T. Bivens, "Can Prisons for Profit Work?" *The Philadelphia Inquirer Magazine* (August 3, 1986):14–15.

99. Christine Bowditch and Ronald S. Everett, "Private Prisons: Problems within the Solution," p. 447.

100. *Ibid*, p. 448.

101. Craig Becker and Mary Dru Stanley, "The Downside of Private Prisons," p. 729.

102. Alexis M. Durham III, "Evaluating Privatized Correctional Institutions: Obstacles to Effective Assessment," *Federal Probation* 52 (June 1988):65–71.

103. Craig Becker and Mary Dru Stanley, "The Downside of Private Prisons," p. 730.

104. Quoted at *Ibid*.

105. Paul Keve, *Corrections* (New York: Wiley, 1981), p. 478.

106. *Ibid.*, p. 480.

107. *Ibid.*, p. 481.

108. Adapted from E. Preston Sharp, "Why Accreditation?" *Proceedings of the 104th Annual Congress of Correction,* Houston, Texas, August 18–22, 1974 (College Park, Md.: American Correctional Association, 1975), pp. 31–32.

109. See Carroll Brodsky, "Long-Term Stress in Teachers and Prison Guards," *Journal of Occupational Medicine* 19 (1977):133–138; Carroll Brodsky, "Work Stress in Correctional Institutions," *Journal of Prison and Jail Health* 2 (1982):74–102.

110. B. Sheppard, "Mortality and Stress Survey of San Francisco Juvenile Probation Officers," pamphlet published by Local No. 21 AFL-CIO (San Francisco: AFL-CIO, 1982).

111. Walter Lunden, *The Prison Warden and the Custodial Staff* (Springfield, Ill.: Charles C. Thomas, 1965).

112. National Planning Association, American Institutes for Research, and the Bureau of Social Science Research, A *Nationwide Survey of Law Enforcement Criminal Justice Needs and Resources* (Washington, D.C.: Author, 1976).

113. "Corrections Officers," *Corrections Compendium* 6 (1982):1–7.

114. S. Rogers, "Thy Brother's Keeper: A Review of the Literature on Correctional Officers."

115. Lawrence H. Gerstein, Charles G. Topp, and Gregory Correll, "The Role of the Environment and Person When Predicting Burnout among Correctional Personnel," *Criminal Justice and Behavior* 14 (September 1987):352–369.

116. See Cary Cherniss, *Staff Burnout: Job Stress in the Human Services* (Newbury Park, Calif.: Sage Publications, 1980); Lucien Lombardo, *Guards Imprisoned: Correctional Officers at Work* (New York: Elsevier/North Holland, 1981).

117. *Ibid.*

118. Lawrence H. Gerstein, Charles G. Topp, and Gregory Correll, "The Role of the Environment and Person When Predicting Burnout among Correctional Personnel," p. 362.

119. Frances Cheek and Marie Miller, "The Experience of Stress for Correction Officers: A Double-Bind Theory of Correctional Stress," *Journal of Criminal Justice* 11 (1983):105–120.

120. J. Foote, "Prison Guards Ever under Pressure, First to Be Attacked," *San Francisco Examiner* (August 27, 1981):A1.

121. J. Reiterman, "Ticking Bombs in Prisons: Conditions Set Stage for Huge Explosion," *San Francisco Examiner* (August 17, 1981):A1.

122. Lawrence H. Gerstein, Charles G. Topp, and Gregory Correll, "The Role of the Environment and Person When Predicting Burnout among Correctional Personnel," p. 363.

123. John T. Whitehead and Charles Lindquist, "Job Stress and Burnout among Probation/Parole Officers: Perceptions and Casual Factors," *International Journal of Offender Therapy and Comparative Criminology* 29 (1985):109–119.

124. Patricia L. Hardyman, "Management Style in Probation: Policy Implications Derived from Systems Theory," in Clayton Hartjen and Edward E. Rhine (eds.), *Correctional Theory and Practice* (Chicago: Nelson-Hall, 1992), pp. 61–81.

125. *Ibid.*, p. 73.

Case Studies

Prisons, Politics, Poverty, and the Rebellious Rurals*

It is time to prepare the annual budget for the Department of Prisons for the legislature. The entire country is suffering a recession, and your state is no different. Tax revenues are down. All state agencies, including the Department of Corrections, have suffered a blanket 10 percent cut in their budget during the current fiscal year. For the prison system, this meant the closure of a prison and the firing of over 100 staff members. Your state is overwhelmingly urban in distribution of population and political power.

The director of the prison system has just returned from the governor's cabinet meeting, where he has been told that the governor will recommend to the legislature an even lower budget amount for prisons next year. This is very troubling, given that the legislature will be considering a budget that will not even begin for another 18 months, and that the inmate population is sure to grow during that time.

Meetings within the prison system over the next several days result in a three-part proposal to live within the smaller budget:

1. The closure of all minimum-custody work camps in the rural areas of the state.
2. Operating the remaining institutions and facilities at the absolute limit of their capacity.
3. Proposing the enactment of an emergency release bill that would parole early (60 days) inmates who are closest to discharge, to keep from exceeding prison capacity.

The early-release proposal is approved by the governor and is now being presented to the legislature. At present, the state's prison system houses 12,000 inmates. According to population projections, it is estimated that 800 inmates would be eligible for release under this program: two-thirds from the minimum custody institutions, one-fourth from camps, and the remainder being medium- or maximum-custody inmates.

---

*Contributed by Ron Angelone, Director, Virginia Department of Corrections, and Glen Whorton, Classification and Planning Specialist, Nevada Department of Prisons.

Upon learning of this plan, a tremendous outcry is heard from the rural areas of the state over the closure of their work camps and, consequently, the ensuing layoffs of many workers and the negative impact on their local economy. Furthermore, some legislators complain to the governor and prison director about the early release program (exhibiting their traditional "tough on crime" posture). A sticky political situation has developed, because the "rurals" carry a lot of clout when they band together on an issue.

Legislative hearings are imminent on this issue, and the media have begun to clamor for responses to the concerns of rural interest groups and "tough on crime" advocates, who include the staff members at the camps who are at risk of being laid off. The attacks on the program generally relate to one or more of the following categories:

1. "Why doesn't the Department close prisons instead of camps, so that rural communities can continue to benefit from the economic influence of salaries and purchases, and the public works performed by the inmates?"

2. "Releasing inmates early into the community will place our citizens at risk."

3. "How does the Department justify the practice of not operating institutions at their emergency capacities at all times, during good economies as well as bad?"

You, the department's budget analyst, have been instructed by the director to prepare a response to these questions as well as a general position paper on the three-point plan.

Questions for Discussion

1. What is the rationale for the closure of the camps? Is it basically sound?
2. What would be the effect of closing prisons instead of camps, as desired by the rural people?
3. What is the risk to the community, and is the public's concern legitimate?
4. How can the department defend its practice of not operating prisons at their emergency capacity levels?
5. What, if any, action(s) should be taken by the director against the staff members in rural areas who appear to be engaging in political "mutiny"?
6. To what extent, if any, should the prison director play the political "game" and begin contacting state legislators to solicit their support of the foregoing proposal?

The Prison Director vs. the Irate Inmate*

The director of the state Department of Prisons has received a grievance from an inmate who indicates that the classification staff at the maximum prison have classified him incorrectly. Specifically, the inmate argues that he is serving a sentence for forgery and his offense has been treated (for purposes of classification) as if it were murder. He also maintains that the staff have begun to retaliate against him because of his grievances regarding his classification placement. The inmate states that if he does not receive satisfaction in regard to the classification, he is going to file suits based on the conditions of confinement at the prison. This is troubling to the director, given the overcrowding that already exists, the physical deficiencies of the maximum prison, and the type and extent of programs available there.

A review of the inmate's file indicates that he is incarcerated as a habitual offender with three life sentences. The root offenses for the habitual offender findings were indeed forgery. He has been incarcerated only 18 months on the first life sentence. He has four prior felonies for similar offenses in other states. The inmate is 56 years old and in poor health. The file is replete with complaints about other inmates and staff. He has sued the central records staff on one previous occasion claiming that staff misconduct resulted in the mishandling of a request for a speedy trial on a detainer that had been lodged against him. This suit was dismissed when it was discovered that the inmate had lied about having requested the trial. The file also includes numerous disciplinary violations related to refusing to work and possession of unauthorized property. There is no violence in the record or evidence of serious misconduct.

The file also discloses that the inmate is embroiled in a dispute with the chief of the prison medical division over his treatment for cancer. The inmate has recently claimed that staff physicians have completely ignored his medical condition and have refused to treat the cancer. The computerized inmate information system indicates that about four months ago the inmate was taken to a local hospital and remained there for approximately one week. A call to the institution doctor reveals that the inmate's cancer was surgically removed during that visit.

A review of classification documents reveals that the staff have correctly scored the inmate's offense on the objective classification instrument. The score for Murder II and Habitual Offender are the same. However, the instrument's computed score on the classification documents indicates that he is a medium custody inmate. He was assigned to a higher level of custody because of the

*Contributed by Ron Angelone, Director, Virginia Department of Corrections, and Glen Whorton, Classification and Planning Specialist, Nevada Department of Prisons.

extremely long sentence that he has to serve. This custody assignment, and the original transfer to the maximum prison, was approved by the central classification staff who review classification recommendations for the director.

You are the director's administrative aide, and enjoy the director's trust. She has asked that you prepare a position statement on this matter, representing all relevant viewpoints and possible pitfalls and developing recommendations. You are told, however, that "the bottom line is to do what's right for the inmate."

Questions for Discussion

1. What are the primary inmate-related issues that the director must deal with: classification or transfer? Were the classification staff technically correct is sending the inmate to a maximum-security institution in the first place?

2. Can the inmate be safely transferred to a lower-level institution? If so, to medium or minimum? (Bear in mind that while being infirm and a relatively old inmate, he is nevertheless serving a lengthy sentence.)

3. If the inmate is transferred, have the Director and staff lost any real power in the eyes of other inmates?

4. How does the director deal with these issues without giving an obviously litigious inmate more "ammunition" with which to harass staff or sue the department? Should the director ask the classification team to reconsider the case?

5. What are the staff-related issues the director has to deal with? What are the options in regard to dealing with those issues?

6. Are any broader policy issues presented in this situation? If so, what action do they suggest?

"Out of Town Brown" and the Besieged Probation Supervisor*

Joan Casey is a career probation officer. She majored in criminal justice as an undergraduate and plans to get her master's in criminology within the next few years. She holds memberships in several national correctional organizations, attends training conferences, and does a lot of reading on her own time to stay current in the field.

---

*Contributed by Catherine Lowe, Director, California Center for Judicial Education and Research, Emeryville, California.

Joan began working for the Collier County Probation Department soon after she graduated from college and was promoted to a supervisory position within five years, a remarkable accomplishment considering her relative lack of seniority in the organization. She supervises an adult probation unit consisting of eight seasoned probation officers, all of whom have been in the work force longer than she has. The unit is responsible for investigation and preparation of presentence investigation reports on approximately 80 offenders a month.

The Collier County Probation Department has made the front page of the local newspapers twice in the past year. Both times it was a nightmare for the chief probation officer, Jack Brown, and the entire agency. "Collier County Soft on Crime!" screamed the first headline—then, just a month later, "Northside Stalker Gets Probation!"

Brown called a management team meeting. It was short and to the point: "No more lousy publicity," he said, "or heads are gonna roll! Has everybody got it?" Everybody got it. However, there exists no written policy concerning media relations, nor is any particular person authorized to release agency information.

This week Brown is on annual leave, the assistant chief is out of state at an American Correctional Association meeting, and Joan Casey is the designated officer in charge. One of Joan's probation officers has recommended community-based treatment for a 16-year old boy who was prosecuted as an adult. The youth murdered his stepfather with an axe after submitting to many years of physical and mental abuse. He had been an incest victim since he was 5 years old, and is mentally retarded.

Joan is aware of the probation officer's recommendation and agrees with it. After all, she reasons, the boy is a low risk for recidivism, and he is as much a victim of this offense as was his stepfather.

It is 4:45 P.M. on Thursday. The phone rings at Joan's desk. Joan's secretary has put through a call from a reporter at a local newspaper. The reporter is a strong crusader in the local war against crime. He has his own byline weekly column at the paper. He knows that the "kiddie-killer" will be sentenced tomorrow.

Questions for Discussion

1. What should be Joan's response to the reporter (other than hanging up or telling him to call back)?
2. If she does elect to discuss her officer's recommendation, what should she say to justify it?
3. What should the chief probation officer do upon his return to work?
4. Was the probation officer's recommendation correct, based on these facts?
5. Should a policy be immediately drafted for this situation? Should any personnel actions be taken?

"Cheerless Chuck" and the Parole Officer's Orientation Day*

"So, you're the new parole officer with a criminal justice degree from the university? Well, I hope you last longer than the last recruit I had. She meant well, but I guess her idealistic ideas about the job of parole officer couldn't handle the realities of the work.

"In a way, I understand what she went through. Same thing happened to me 12 years ago when I started this job. There I was, fresh out of college with a brand new diploma with 'Social Work' written on it. I figured that piece of paper made me a social worker, and I better get right to work fixing society. It didn't take me long to realize that the real world was different from what I had learned in college. It was like I had been trained as a sailor, and I was about to set out on a voyage, but I couldn't take the time to steer the ship because I was so busy bailing water. The crises we deal with here make it darned difficult to do the work we all see needs to be done.

"Years ago, when I first started with the parole department, things were a lot better than they are now. Caseloads were lower, fewer people were getting parole who didn't deserve it, and the rest of the criminal justice system was in a lot better shape, which made our jobs a lot easier to do. Think about it. We vote in politicians who promise the public that they are going to 'get tough' on crime and the first thing they do is allot more money for law enforcement stuff: beat cops, car computers, helicopters, and so on. These things are great, but all they do is add more people into a system that is already overloaded. No one gets elected by promising to build more courts or add jail and prison space, or probation and parole officers. Eventually these added police officers arrest more people than the system can handle.

"The courts back up, which in turn messes up the prisons and the jails. The inmates stuck in these crowded places get tired of living like sardines, so they sue the prisons and jails. Remember, the Constitution prohibits cruel and unusual punishment. A lot of times inmates' complaints are legitimate, and they win. The judge orders the prison to lower its population to a reasonable level, which forces the parole board to consider more inmates for early release. They come knocking on our doors, hoping we can get them out of the mess that politics and budgets have created. Nobody mentions giving the parole department more officers, or a bigger budget for added administrative help. No, the bucks go to the flashy, visible things like cops and cars. Meanwhile, in the past 10 years our average caseload for a parole officer has increased 75 percent. We have more people who need supervision, and we are doing it on a budget that has not kept pace with the remainder of the criminal justice system.

"This wouldn't be so bad if the system was at least adding things to other areas, like the jail or the courts. The problem here is that we depend on the jail to hold our parolees who have violated their conditions. We catch some of

---

*Contributed by Matthew Leone, Assistant Professor of Criminal Justice, University of Nevada, Reno.

them using booze or drugs, and we are *supposed* to bring them in to the county jail to wait for a hearing to decide if they are going back to prison, or back on the street. But the jail has its own set of problems. A couple of years ago the U.S. District Court slapped a population cap on our jail. If it goes over that population, the jail will not accept our violators. So we send them home. If they get into more serious trouble, we call it a new crime, the police arrest them, and the jail has to take them. Then they have to sit and wait for the court to catch up, since the courts are not in much better shape than the jail.

"I guess the job would be easier if the prisons were doing their jobs, too. I can't really blame them, since the prisons are funded in much the same way that parole is. We are not 'glamorous' places to send your tax dollars, but if the prisons were getting more money, they might be able to improve the quality of inmate they send to us. Maybe a little more vocational training and substance abuse counseling, so they could stay off the booze and drugs. Maybe then fewer of these parolees would wind up back behind bars a few years later.

"The worst part about the job is the caseload. We presently have so many on parole that I am lucky if I can get a phone call to each of them once a week, and maybe a home visit once a month. You can't tell me that a phone call and a home visit is really keeping these guys from committing crimes. The sad part about it is that with the proper budget and staff, we could really make a difference. We spend so much time bailing water out of the boat, we don't realize that there is no one steering, and we are just drifting in circles.

"By the way, my name is Charlie Matthews, but everyone calls me Chuck. I'm a supervisor here as well as the designated new-employee orientation specialist and all-round public relations person. I hope I've not depressed you too much on your first day, but now is a good time to drop your idealism and get to work 'bailing.' What're *your* views and ideas?"

Questions for Discussion

1. How would changes in politics affect the parole system directly and indirectly? How does an old criminal justice planning adage that "You can't rock one end of the boat" seem to be applicable to what Chuck says about law enforcement getting so much new political funding?

2. What could you tell Chuck about existing means of dealing with bloated caseloads?

3. What kinds of administrative problems and practices might be responsible for this agency's situation?

4. Why do crowded jails and prisons make the job of parole officers more difficult?

5. How could practices of the jails and prisons change the success of the parole system?

6. Based on Chuck's assessment of the local situation, where do you believe the greatest misconceptions about courts and corrections exist?

7. Should Chuck be retained as orientation coordinator? Why or why not?

The Wright Way*

Randall Wright has been a shift supervisor at the Granite County Jail Facility for the past 10 years and has a total of 18 years in the jail. Wright enjoys taking visitors on tours of the facility and takes pride in the fact that he knows every aspect of the jail's operation.

This summer, Wright is providing some of the supervision for an intern the facility has accepted from the local university's criminal justice program. The intern, Tom Sharpe, finds Wright to be an interesting and outspoken person. In their conversations about work in the jail, Tom asks Wright how he deals emotionally with his job, because he has read about stress in university textbooks.

"I'm glad you asked that, young fella," the veteran responds. "I have some good advice for you if you are going into any kind of correctional work." He continues, "First, I never take this job home with me. My wife and kids used to ask about what I do at work, but I have made it a strict policy never to discuss what happens here. My family wouldn't understand what goes on here. They might be concerned about what I do, so I decided long ago that it was best to dummy up about it all.

"Second, I find that you have to be realistic about your chances for having any positive influence on these birds who come through here. Oh, I have seen lots of guys who thought they could change the world come in here, and they are the ones who will come down hard. Me? Well, I'm a realist. Let's face it. We get the people everyone else has given up on, so what can we be expected to do? I tell visitors that 'We get the cream of the crap here,' and I mean it. Don't set your expectations very high, and you won't be disappointed.

"The job tends to get you down if you let it. I have found that you have to find a relief from all the frustrations you experience and the problems created by some of the SOBs who come through here. About once a week, the gang and I hold 'choir practice.' Kelsey's Place down the street is where we go. After about five or six beers, this place and the world look a helluva lot better. People who don't work corrections don't understand the need to let off a little steam, but I can tell you that 'choir practice' keeps me going.

"One more bit of advice for you, Sharpe: Don't lose your sense of humor. I have always prided myself on my ability to laugh at almost any situation. Hell, the top brass around here and the politicians over at the courthouse are easy to laugh at. All you need to do when you're down is look at some of the orders these clowns put out and some of the things our glorious leaders tell the public about rehabilitation, efficiency, blah, blah, blah. I usually tell my staff to disregard new memos and such. Sometimes it's hard to stop laughing. It has all worked for me. Why, in just nine years, three months, and twenty days I will be able to retire and walk away from this place."

---

*Contributed by Ted Heim, Department of Criminal Justice, Washburn University, Topeka, Kansas.

Questions for Discussion

1. Assume that you are Wright's supervisor and, while standing in the hallway, overhear this conversation. What would be your *immediate* reaction to his speech about on-the-job actions? What *long-term* actions—disciplinary or otherwise—would you take with Wright?

2. If you were Wright's supervisor, would you feel compelled to look into, leave alone, or halt the "choir practices"?

3. Assume that you are the student intern who just listened to this delivery. Of all the points made by Wright, which do you agree with? Disagree with? Would you now feel more or less compelled to enter the field? Do you value such a person's candor?

4. In your estimation, is Wright the sort of employee who should be supervising others? Greeting interns? Will an employee of this nature last until retirement?

5. Do you believe such cynicism is common in corrections? In criminal justice, generally? In most other occupations? Is it healthy or debilitating?

Spanning The System: Administrative Problems and Practices

This part consists of three chapters, all of which focus on administrative problems spanning the entire justice system. In Chapter 14, we examine the rights of criminal justice employees; Chapter 15 covers shared issues and influences; and in Chapter 16 we discuss financial administration.

Rights of Criminal Justice Employees

Good orders make evil men good and bad orders make good men evil.

—James Harrington

✦ INTRODUCTION

Our society has rapidly transformed into one that is highly complex and dangerous. At the same time, the rights and obligations of criminal justice employees, like those of workers in the private sector, have changed dramatically. As Robert Chaires and Susan Lentz put it:

> Changes in values, demographics, law and technology have blurred the line dividing line and staff, manager and managed in enforcement, judicial, and correctional agencies. Employees once chosen for their size and skill with a nightstick and/or political connections, or because they were the only ones willing to take low paying and often brutal and dangerous work, have been substantially replaced by highly educated individuals expecting much more than just a job. The contemporary criminal justice employee is far more sophisticated about employee rights.[1]

And, of course, that sophistication is today reflected in the fact that many criminal justice employees are represented by some employee group, ranging from a local, primarily fraternal order or association to a national organization.

As a result of the combination of sophisticated employees, powerful employee groups, and a socially conscious criminal justice environment, contemporary criminal justice managers must be more aware of the law surrounding employee rights. Dramatically increasing participation by women in traditionally male-dominated fields brings increased problems with sexual harassment claims.[2] Drug testing and privacy issues have emerged, as well as major limitations on the hiring (including recruitment and selection), disciplining (rule relevance, investigation, consistency), and firing (due process, property rights) of criminal justice personnel. Criminal justice employees also want a safe workplace. In this chapter we look at the impact of the law and litigation on criminal justice employee rights in all of these areas. We also examine the rights and privileges that are retained by criminal justice *employers*. Specifically, we focus on the employers' right to maintain and enforce policies in the areas of sexual misconduct, residency requirements, moonlighting, and rights under the First, Fourth, and Fifth Amendments to the U.S. Constitution. A common theme throughout this chapter is that it is far better to learn one's rights and limitations "in house," through education and training of one's volition, than via the "courthouse" method, as a result of a lawsuit.

✦ AN OVERVIEW

Law and litigation affecting criminal justice employees can arise out of federal and state constitutions, statutes, administrative regulations, and judicial interpretations and rulings. Even poorly written employee handbooks or long-standing agency customs or practices may create vested rights. The ripple effect begun by improper or illegal hiring, training, discipline, or discharge can lead not only to poor agency performance and morale, but also to substantial legal and economic liability. It should become apparent in the following overview—and court decisions that follow—that utilizing good common sense as well as a sense of fairness will go a long way toward preventing legal problems in the employment relationship.[3]

It should also be noted that the Civil Rights Act of 1991 may result in significant changes in public- and private-sector employment; however, it will take several years for significant decisions to wind their way through the courts for a final determination of the intent and reach of the act by the Supreme Court. Therefore, in this section we focus on presenting the issues rather than on attempting to settle the law in these areas.

◊ *Fair Labor Standards Act* (at 29 U.S.C. 203 et seq.): This act provides minimum pay and overtime provisions covering both public- and private-sector employees. Part 7(a) contains special provisions for firefighters and police officers. We discuss the FLSA more fully below.

◊ *Title VII of the Civil Rights Act of 1964 and its Amendments* (42 U.S.C. 2000e): this broadly based act established a federal policy requiring fair employment practices in both the public and private sectors. It prohibited unlawful employment discrimination in areas such as the hiring process, discharge, discipline, working conditions, and the provision of benefits based on race, color, religion, sex, and national origin. Its provisions extend to "hostile work environment" claims based on sexual, racial, or religious harassment.

◊ *Equal Pay Act* [29 U.S.C. 206(d)]: this legislation provided an alternative remedy to Title VII for sex-based discrimination in wages and benefits, where people do similar work. It applies the simpler Fair Labor Standards Act procedures to claims. Note that the Equal Pay Act does not mean "comparable worth"—an area that attempts to determine wages by requiring equal pay for employees whose work is of comparable worth even if the job content is totally different.

◊ *The Pregnancy Discrimination Act of 1978* [42 U.S.C. Section 2000e(k)]: this act is an amendment to the scope of sexual discrimination under Title VII. It prohibits unequal treatment of women because of pregnancy or related medical conditions (e.g., nausea). The act requires that employers treat pregnant women like other temporarily disabled employees. The U.S. Supreme Court decided a major case in 1991 that limited employers' ability to exclude women who are pregnant or of childbearing years from certain jobs, under a fetal protection policy.[4]

◊ *Age Discrimination in Employment Act* (29 U.S.C. 623): this act generally prohibits the unequal treatment of applicants or employees based on their age, if they are age 40 or over, in regard to hiring, firing, receiving benefits, and other conditions of employment.

◊ *Americans with Disabilities Act of 1990* (42 U.S.C. 12112): the goal of this legislation is to remove barriers that might prevent otherwise qualified individuals with disabilities from enjoying the same employment opportunities available to persons without disabilities. Although this act has only recently been implemented, the Rehabilitation Act of 1973 (see 29 U.S.C. 701) and its amendments have long prevented similar disability discrimination among public agencies receiving federal funds.

◊ *42 U.S.C. 1983*: this major piece of legislation is the instrument by which an employee may sue an employer for civil rights violations based on the deprivation of constitutional rights. It is the most versatile civil rights action and is also the most often used against criminal justice agencies. (Section 1983 is discussed more thoroughly in Chapter 15.)

In addition to the foregoing legislative enactments and state statutes which prohibit various acts of discrimination in employment, there are additional remedies that have tremendous impact on public-sector employees. Civil tort claims may be brought by public-sector employees against their employer for a wide variety of claims, ranging from assault and battery to defamation. Contractual claims may grow out of collective bargaining agreements. Bargained agreements may include procedures for assignments, seniority, due process protections (such as in the "Police Officers' Bill of Rights"), and grievance procedures. Often, the source of the right defines the remedy and the procedure to obtain that remedy. For example, statutes or legal precedents often provide for an aggrieved employer to receive back pay, compensatory damages, injunctive relief, or punitive damages.

◆ THE EMPLOYMENT RELATIONSHIP

✧ RECRUITMENT AND HIRING

Numerous selection methods for hiring police officers have been tried over the years. Issues in recruitment, selection, and hiring also often involve internal promotions and assignments to special units, such as an "alert team" in a prison. Requirements concerning age (e.g., the FBI will hire no one older than 37 years of age), height, weight, vision, education, and possession of a valid driver's license have all been utilized over the years in criminal justice. In addition, tests are commonly used to determine intelligence, emotional suitability and stability (with psychological examinations and oral interviews), physical agility, and character (with polygraph examinations and extensive background checks).[5] More recently, drug tests have become frequently used as well (discussed more fully below).

The critical question for such tests is whether or not they validly test the types of skills needed for the job. A companion concern is whether or not the tests are used for discriminatory purposes or have unequal impact on protected groups. As a result of these considerations, a number of private companies have developed so-called "canned" examinations, providing valid, reliable test instruments for use by the public sector.

✧ DISPARATE TREATMENT

It should be emphasized that there is nothing in the law which states that an employer must hire or retain incompetent personnel. In effect, the law does not prohibit discrimination. Thus it is not unlawful to refuse to hire people who have a record of driving while intoxicated for positions that require driving. What *is* illegal is to treat people differently because of their age, gender, sex, or other protected status; that is *disparate treatment*. It is also illegal to deny equal employment opportunities to such persons; that is *disparate impact*.[6]

Federal equal opportunity law prohibits the use of selection procedures for hiring or promotion that have a discriminatory impact on the employment opportunities of women, Hispanics, blacks, or other protected classes. An example of overt discriminatory hiring is reflected in a court decision in 1987 arising out of a situation in a sparsely populated county in Virginia. Four women sued because they were denied positions as courtroom security officer, deputy, or civil process server because of their gender. Sheriffs had refused to hire the women, justifying their decision by contending that being male was a *bona fide occupational qualifier* (BFOQ) for the position and because the positions were within the "personal staff" of the sheriff, thus exempting such positions from the coverage of Title VII. The Fourth Circuit overturned a lower court decision, finding that the sheriff did not establish that gender was a BFOQ for the positions and that the positions were not part of the sheriff's personal staff (the positions were not high level, policymaking, or advisory in nature). Thus the refusal to hire the women violated Title VII.[7] There may, however, be a "business justification" for a hiring policy even though it has a disparate impact. For example, in one case an employer required airline attendants to cease flying immediately upon discovering they were pregnant. The court upheld the policy, on the ground that pregnancy could affect one's ability to perform routine duties in an aircraft, thereby jeopardizing the safety of passengers.[8]

A classic example of an apparent neutral employment requirement which actually had a disparate impact of gender, race, and ethnicity, was the once prevalent height requirement used by most public safety agencies. Minimum height requirements of "5 feet, 10 inches or above" were often advertised and effectively operated to exclude most women and many Asians and Hispanics from employment.[9] Such a requirement has gradually been superseded by "height in proportion to weight" requirement. Nonetheless, other existing physical agility tests serve to discriminate against the lesser upper-body strength of women and smaller men. One is forced to wonder how many pushups a police officer must do on the job, or be able to do, to perform the duties adequately, or how many six-foot walls, ditches, and attics officers must negotiate. (Occasionally, the situation of pre-employment physical abilities testing becomes ludicrous. For example, the author once allowed a recruiter from a major western city to recruit students in an upper-level criminal justice course. The recruiter said the city's physical test included a six-foot wall; however, he quickly pointed out that testing staff would boost all female applicants over it.)

Litigation is blossoming in these areas. For example, in another western city, a woman challenged the police department's physical abilities test as discriminatory and not job-related, prompting the agency to hire a Canadian consultant who developed a job-related pre-employment agility test (currently used by the Royal Canadian Mounted Police and other agencies across Canada), based on data provided by officers and later computer analyzed for incorporation into the test. In other words, recruits are now tested on the physical demands placed on police officers in that specific community (no pushups or six-foot walls are included).[10]

Discrimination may also exist in criminal justice positions in promotions and job assignments. As an example of the former, a Nebraska female correctional center worker brought suit alleging that her employer violated her Title VII and equal protection rights by denying her a promotion. The woman was qualified for the position she sought promotion to (assistant center manager for programming), and she also alleged that the center treated women inequitably and unprofessionally, that assertiveness in women was viewed negatively, and that women were assigned clerical duties not assigned to men. The court found that she was indeed denied a promotion because of her sex, in violation of Title VII and the equal protection clause of the Fourteenth Amendment; she was awarded back pay ($7500), front pay ($122 biweekly, until a comparable position became available), general damages, and court costs.[11]

With respect to litigation in the area of job assignments, four women matron/dispatchers who were refused assignments to correctional officer positions in Florida, even though they had been trained and certified as jail officers, were awarded damages. It was ruled that a state regulation prohibiting females in male areas of the jail was discriminatory without proof that gender was a BFOQ.[12] However, a particular assignment may validly exclude one sex. Thus an assignment to work as a decoy prostitute could validly demonstrate a "business necessity" for women.[13]

✧ How Old Is "Too Old" in Criminal Justice?

State and public agencies are not immune from age discrimination suits where arbitrary age restrictions have been found to violate the law. In Florida, a police lieutenant with the state highway patrol with 29 years of service was forced by statute to retire at age 62. The Equal Employment Opportunity Commission (EEOC) brought suit, alleging that Florida's statute violated the Age Discrimination in Employment Act (ADEA). The court held that age should not be a BFOQ, as youthfulness is not a guarantee of public safety. Rather, a physical fitness standard would better serve the purpose of ensuring the ability to perform the tasks of the position.[14]

Indeed, the U.S. Supreme Court rejected mandatory retirement plans for municipal firefighters and police officers.[15] Until 1985 the City of Baltimore had relied on a *federal* police officer and firefighter statute (5 U.S.C. 8335b), an exemption to the ADEA, to establish age limits for appointing and retiring its fire and police officers; the city also contended that age was a BFOQ for doing so. The U.S. Supreme Court said that while Congress had exempted federal employees from application of the ADEA, another agency cannot just "adopt" the same standards without showing an agency-specific need. Age is not a BFOQ for nonfederal firefighters (or, by extension, police officers). The Court also established a "reasonable federal standard" in its 1984 decision in *EEOC v. Wyoming*,[16] where it overturned a state statute providing for the mandatory retirement of state game wardens at age 55; it held that the ADEA did not require employers to retain unfit employees, only to make more individualized determinations about fitness.

✧ Criminal Justice and Affirmative Action

Probably no single employment practice has caused as much controversy as affirmative action. The very words bring to mind visions of quotas and of unqualified people being given preferential hiring treatment.[17] Indeed, quotas have been at the center of legal, social, scientific, and political controversy for more than two decades.[18] However, the reality of affirmation is substantially different from the myth; as a general rule, affirmative action plans give preferred treatment to affected groups only when all other criteria (e.g., education, skills, etc.) are equal.[19]

The legal question (and to many persons, a moral one) that arises from affirmative action is: When does preferential hiring become *reverse* discrimination? The leading case here is *Bakke v. Regents of the University of California*,[20] 1978, where Allan Bakke was passed over for medical school admission at the University of California, Davis, partly because of the school's setting aside a number of its 100 medical school admissions slots annually for "disadvantaged" applicants. The Supreme Court held, among other things, that race could be used as a criterion in selection decisions, but it could not be the only criterion.

In a series of cases beginning in 1986,[21] the Supreme Court considered the development and application of affirmative action plans, establishing a two-step inquiry that must be satisfied before an affirmative action plan can be put in place. A plan must have (1) a remedial purpose, to correct past inequities, and there must be (2) a manifest imbalance or significant disparity to justify the plan. (However, the Court emphasized that such plans cannot completely foreclose employment opportunities to nonminority or male candidates.)

Generally, however, the validity of such plans is determined on a case-by-case basis. For example, the District of Columbia Circuit held in 1987 that an affirmative action plan covering the promotion of blacks to management positions in the police department was justified, as only 174 of the 807 positions (22 percent) above the rank of sergeant were filled by blacks, in a city where 60 percent of the labor market was black.[22] There, 21 past and present detectives of the Metropolitan Police Department who were passed over for promotion challenged the department's voluntary affirmative actions plan, designed to place "special emphasis" on the hiring and advancement of females and minorities in those employment areas where there existed an "obvious imbalance" in their numbers.[23]

The plaintiffs felt their failure to be promoted was attributable to illegal preferential treatment of blacks and women—reverse discrimination—violating their rights under Title VII and the due process clause of the Fifth Amendment. The court held that the nonminority and male employees of the department failed to prove that the plan was invalid; there was a considerable body of evidence of racial and sexual imbalance at the time the plan was adopted, and the plan did not unnecessarily trammel any legitimate interests of the nonminority or male employees since it did not call for displacement or layoff and did not totally exclude them from promotion opportunities.[24]

In summary, then, whenever a criminal justice employer wishes to implement and maintain job requirements, they must be job related. Furthermore, whenever a job requirement discriminates against a protected class, it should have a strong legitimate purpose and be the least restrictive alternative. Finally, attempts to remedy past hiring inequities by such means as affirmative action programs need substantial justification to avoid becoming reverse discrimination.[25]

✧ PROPERTY RIGHTS IN EMPLOYMENT

The Fourteenth Amendment to the U.S. Constitution provides in part that "No state shall make or enforce any law which shall abridge the privileges or immunities of citizens of the United States; nor shall any State deprive any person of life, liberty, or property without due process of law; nor deny to any person within its jurisdiction the equal protection of the law." Furthermore, the Supreme Court has set forth four elements of a due process claim under Section 1983: A (1) person acting under color of state law (2) deprived an individual (3) of constitutionally protected property (4) without due process of law.[26]

A long line of court cases have established the legal view that public employees have a property interest in their employment. This flies in the face of the old view, that employees served "at will" or until their employer, for whatever reason, no longer had need of their services. The Supreme Court has provided some general guidance on how the question of a constitutionally protected "property interest" is to be resolved: "To have a property interest in a benefit, a person clearly must have more than an abstract need or desire for it. He must have more than a unilateral expectation of it. He must, instead, have a *legitimate claim of entitlement to it.* It is a purpose of the ancient institution of property to protect those claims *upon which people rely in their daily lives, reliance that must not be arbitrarily undermined*" [emphasis added].[27] The Court has also held that employees are entitled to both a pre-termination and post-termination notice,[28] and an opportunity to respond, and that state legislators are free to choose not to confer a property interest in public employment.

The development of a property interest in employment has an important ramification: it means that "due process" must be exercised by a public entity before terminating or interfering with an employee's property right. What has been established, however, is that a probationary employee has little or no property interest in employment. For example, in one case the Ninth Circuit held that a probationary civil service employee ordinarily has no property interest and could be discharged without a hearing or even "good cause." But in that same decision, the court held that a woman who had passed her six-month probationary period, and who had then been promoted to a new position for which there was a probationary period, had the legitimate expectation of continued employment.[29]

On the other hand, an Indiana police captain was deemed to have a property interest in his position even though a state statute allowed the city manager to demote without notice. There, a captain of detectives, a Democrat, was demoted by a newly elected Republican mayor. The court determined that the dismissal of even a "policymaking" public employee for politically motivated reasons is forbidden unless the employee's position is "policymaking" in a sense that the position inherently encompasses tasks that render political affiliation an appropriate prerequisite for effective performance.[30]

Normally, however, policymaking employees (often called exempt appointments) possess an automatic exception to the contemporary property interest view. Generally these personnel, often elected agency heads, are free to hire and fire those employees who are involved in the making of important decisions and policy. Examples of this area include new sheriffs who appoint undersheriffs and wardens who appoint deputy wardens. These employees currently have no property interest in their positions and may be asked at any time to leave the agency or revert back to an earlier rank.

This property interest in employment is, of course, generally implied. An example of this implication may be found in a Utah case, where a property interest was found to exist based on an implied contract founded on an employment manual. Due process standards were therefore violated when the police department fired an officer without showing good cause or giving him a chance to respond to the charges against him.[31] In a Pennsylvania case, where a patrol officer was suspended for 30 days without pay for alleged violations of personnel policies and was not given an opportunity to file a written response to the charges, the court held that the officer's suspension resulted in a deprivation of property.[32]

Also, the property right in one's employment does not have to involve discipline or discharge to afford an employee protections. For example, the claim of a parole officer that he was harassed, humiliated, and interfered with in a deliberate attempt to remove him from his position established a civil rights action for deprivation of property.[33] This decision, against the Illinois Department of Corrections, resulted from allegations that the department engaged in "a deliberate and calculated effort to remove the plaintiff from his position by forcing him to resign, thereby making the protections of the personnel code unavailable to him." As a result, the plaintiff suffered anxiety, stress, and eventually went on disability status at substantially reduced pay.[34]

The key questions, then, once a property right is established, are: (1) What constitutes adequate grounds for interference with that right? and (2) what is adequate process to sustain that interference?[35]

✦ DISCIPLINE AND DISCHARGE

There are well-established, minimum due process requirements for discharge of public employees. They must:

1. Be afforded a public hearing
2. Be present during the presentation of evidence against them and have an opportunity to cross-examine their superiors
3. Have an opportunity to present their own witnesses and other evidence concerning their side of the controversy
4. Be permitted to be represented by counsel
5. Have an impartial referee or hearing officer presiding
6. Have an eventual decision based on the weight of the evidence introduced during the hearing

Such protections apply to any disciplinary action that can significantly affect a criminal justice employee's reputation and/or future chances for special assignment or promotion. A disciplinary hearing that might result, say, in only a reprimand or short suspension may involve fewer procedural protections than one that could result in more severe sanctions.[36]

However, when a particular disciplinary action does not seek termination or suspension, it may still be subject to due process considerations. An example is a Chicago case involving a police officer who was transferred from the Neighborhood Relations Division to less desirable working conditions in the patrol division, with no loss in pay or benefits. The court found that the officer's First Amendment free speech rights were violated, as his de facto demotion was in retaliation for his political activities (inviting political opponents of the mayor to a civic function and in retaliation for a speech given there, criticizing the police department), and that he was thus entitled to civil damages. The court stated that "certainly a demotion can be as detrimental to an employee as denial of a promotion."[37]

On the other hand, no due process protection may be required when the property interest (one's job) was fraudulently obtained. Thus a deputy sheriff was not deprived of due process when he was summarily discharged for lying on his application about a juvenile felony charge, which would have barred him from employment in the first place.[38]

In sum, agency rules and policies should state what due process procedures will be utilized under certain disciplinary situations; the key questions regarding due process are whether or not the employer followed established agency guidelines, and if not, whether the employer has a compelling reason not to.

Occasionally, the criminal justice agency determines that an employee must be disciplined or should be "freed to pursue another career opportunity." What are adequate grounds for discipline or discharge? Grounds for discipline or discharge can vary widely from agency to agency. Certainly, the agency's formal policies and procedures should specify and control what constitutes proper and improper behavior. Normally, agency practice and custom enter into these decisions. Sometimes administrators will "wink" at the formal policies and procedures, overlooking or only occasionally enforcing certain provisions contained in them. But the failure of the agency to enforce a rule or policy for a long period of time may provide "implied consent" by the employer that such behavior, although officially prohibited, is permissible. (In other words, don't allow an employee to violate policy by smoking for three months in your dynamite factory, then decide one day it's time to fire him summarily.) Attempts to fire employees for behavior that has been ignored or enforced only infrequently at best may give rise to a defense by the employee.

The hiring of minority employees to meet state hiring goals, and later attempting to terminate them as quickly and often as possible, also violates the employee's Title VII rights. Such a situation occurred in a 1988 Indiana case where it was alleged that black prison correctional officers were hired to fulfill an affirmative action program, only to be fired for disciplinary reasons for which white officers were not discharged.[39] The court also held that the prison guard-plaintiff was entitled to present statistics to support his claims concerning the employee disciplinary procedures at the prison.

Generally, violations of an employee's rights occur in discharge and discipline where such actions are taken (1) in violation of a protected interest; (2) in retaliation for the exercise of protected conduct; (3) with a discriminatory motive; and (4) with malice.[40]

✧ PAY AND BENEFITS

The Fair Labor Standards Act (FLSA), described above, has had a major impact on criminal justice agencies. One observer referred to the FLSA as the criminal justice administrator's "worst nightmare come true."[41] Initiated in 1938 to establish minimum wages and to require overtime compensation in the private sector, amendments were added in 1974 extending its coverage to state and local government employees and special work period provisions for police and fire employees. However, in 1976 the U.S. Supreme Court ruled that the extension of the act into the area of traditional local and state government functions was unconstitutional.[42] Then, in 1985 the Court reversed itself, bringing local police employees under the coverage of the FLSA. In this major (and very costly) decision, *Garcia v. San Antonio Transit Authority*, [43] the Court held, 5 to 4, that Congress imposed the requirements of the FLSA on state and local governments.

Criminal justice operations, being 24 hours per day, seven days per week, often require overtime and participation in off-duty activities such as court appearances and training sessions. The FLSA comes into play when overtime salaries must be paid. It provides that an employer must generally pay employees time and a half for all hours worked over 40 per week. Overtime must also be paid to personnel for all work in excess of 43 hours in a seven-day cycle or 171 hours in a 28-day period. Public safety employees may accrue a maximum of 480 hours of "comp" time, which, if not utilized as leave, must be paid off upon separation from employment at the employee's final rate of pay or at the average pay over the last three years, whichever is greater.[44] Further, employers usually cannot require employees to take compensatory time in lieu of cash. The primary issue with FLSA is the rigidity of application of what is compensable work. The act prohibits an agency from taking "volunteered time" from employees.

Today, an officer who works the night shift must receive pay for attending training or testifying in court during the day. Further, officers who are ordered to remain at home in anticipation of emergency actions must be compensated. Notably, however, the FLSA's overtime provisions do not apply to persons employed in a bona fide executive, administrative, or professional capacity. In criminal justice, the act has generally been held to apply to detectives and sergeants but not to those of the rank of lieutenant and above.

A companion issue with respect to criminal justice pay and benefits is that of equal pay for equal work. Disparate treatment in pay and benefits can be litigated under Title VII or statutes such as the Equal Pay Act or the equal protection clause. An Ohio case involved matron/dispatchers who performed essentially the same job as jailers but were paid less. This was found to be in violation of the Equal Pay Act and, since discriminatory intent was found, Title VII.[45]

In a related case, a court ruled that a Section 1983 claim by 133 southern Virginia state troopers could be filed where the plaintiffs did not receive a salary differential as did troopers in the northern part of the state. The plaintiffs argued that the salary differential was arbitrary, without any rational relationship to legitimate state interests, and as such was an unconstitutional denial of their rights to due process and equal protection under the Fourteenth Amendment. Conversely, the State of Virginia argued that based on the results of a statewide study and the need for higher salaries to attract qualified applicants in the north and prevent in-service troopers to leave for positions in private security, the differential was necessary.[46]

Other criminal justice employee benefits are addressed in Title VII, the ADEA, and the Pregnancy Discrimination Act (PDA). For example, it is illegal to provide less insurance coverage for a female employee who is more likely to use maternity leave, or one who is older and more liable to use more coverage. Also, an older person or a woman could not be forced to pay higher pension contributions because (it is felt) they would be paying in for a shorter period of time or would be expected to live longer. Regarding pregnancy, the PDA does not require an employer to discriminate in favor of a pregnancy-related condition. It demands only that the employer not treat pregnancy differently from any other temporary medical condition. For example, if an agency has a six-month leave policy for officers who are injured ill from off-duty circumstances (on-duty circumstances would probably be covered by worker's compensation), that agency would have to provide six months' leave (if needed) for a pregnancy-related condition.[47]

✦ CRIMINAL JUSTICE AND A SAFE WORKPLACE

It is presently unclear what duties are owed by public employers to their employees in providing a safe workplace. Federal, state, and local governments are exempted from the coverage of the Occupational Safety and Health Act, in 29 U.S.C. 652. Nonetheless, criminal justice work is often dangerous, involving the use of force and often occurring in locations outside governmental control. Therefore, workplace safety issues in criminal justice are more likely to revolve around adequacy of training and supervision than physical plants.[48]

The Supreme Court has noted the unique nature and danger of public service employment. In one case, the Court specifically stated that an employee could not bring a Section 1983 civil rights action alleging a workplace so unsafe that it violated the Fourteenth Amendment's due process clause. In this matter, a sewer worker was asphyxiated while clearing a sewer line. The widow alleged that the city knew the sewer was dangerous and that the city had failed to train or supervise the decedent properly.[49]

However, other federal courts, especially the federal circuits, have ruled inconsistently on the safe workplace issue. One federal circuit held that a constitutional violation could be brought if it was proven that the city actively engaged in conduct which was "deliberately indifferent" to the employee's constitutional rights.[50]

But the Fifth Circuit held differently in a Louisiana case, based on a failure to comply with a court order to have three officers on duty at all times in a prison disciplinary unit.[51] Here, a prison correctional officer in Baton Rouge was the only guard on a dangerous cellblock. While attempting to transfer a handcuffed inmate, the guard got into a scuffle with the inmate and was injured, although not severely. However, he claimed that he received insufficient medical attention and that as a result, he became permanently disabled and that the Institute "consciously" and with wanton disregard for his personal safety conspired to have him work alone on the cellblock. He invoked 42 U.S.C. 1983 in his charges, claiming that the Institute acted in an indifferent, malicious, and reckless manner toward him, and that he suffered "class-based discrimination." The court held that the guard had no cause of action (no federal or constitutional grounds for litigation).

Liability for an employee's injury, disability, or death is a critical concern for criminal justice agencies. In particular, police and correctional officers often work under circumstances where violent actions occur. While state worker's compensation coverage, disability pensions, life insurance, and survivor pensions are designed to cover such tragedies, such coverage is typically limited and only intended to be remedial. On the other hand, civil tort actions in such cases can have a devastating impact on governmental budgets. Clearly, this is a difficult and costly problem to resolve. Certainly, it is also an area with moral dilemmas as well. Consider, for example, what should be done with a prison intelligence unit, having knowledge of an impending disturbance but failing to alert its officers (who are subsequently injured)? And might a police department, with knowledge that its new police vehicles have defective brakes, fail to take immediate action for fear that its officers will refuse to drive the vehicles, thus reducing the effective manpower?[52] These moral and legal dilemmas are not easily resolved in the criminal justice realm.

✦ CONSTITUTIONAL RIGHTS OF CRIMINAL JUSTICE EMPLOYEES

✧ FREE SPEECH

Most, if not all criminal justice employees—especially police officers, judges, and probation or parole officers—see and know much about other citizens; they observe people in their most embarrassing and vulnerable moments. Therefore, because of their position in our society, information criminal justice practitioners pass on by way of formal or informal conversation assumes a tremendous air of importance and gravity. A former midwestern police commissioner described the situation well, commenting that "I'm sorry to say that many police, without realizing they carry such authority, do pass on rumors. The average police officer does not stop to weigh what he or she says." That statement could probably be made about many other types of criminal justice employees as well. Given the delicate nature of their work, they must all guard against being indiscreet with the information they possess.

The 24-hour shift configuration found in criminal justice work serves to exacerbate the "grapevine." Even while on routine patrol, police officers witness many illegal or immoral acts—acts for which citizens would gladly pay the officer for his or her silence. Thus police officers are often in the limelight with respect to speech-related activities. Criminal justice personnel can also become chronic complainers. Normally, passive grumbling is not unhealthy, but it can take a serious turn when a grapevine is running rampant, incomplete or inaccurate information is being disseminated, or when personnel go public to air their views.

Many criminal justice executives have attempted to harness what their employees say to the public; executives develop and rely on policies and procedures designed to govern employee speech. As will be seen below, on occasion those restrictions will be challenged; a number of court decisions have attempted to define the limits of criminal-justice employees' exercise of free speech.

Although the right of freedom of speech is one of the most fundamental of all rights of Americans, the Supreme Court has indicated that "the State has interests as an employer in regulating the speech of its employees that differ significantly from those it possesses in connection with regulation of the speech of the citizenry in general."[53] Thus the state may impose restrictions on its employees that it would not be able to impose on the citizenry at large. However, these restrictions must be reasonable.[54]

There are two basic situations in which a police regulation may be found to be an unreasonable infringement on the free speech interests of officers.[55] The first is when the action is overly broad. A Chicago Police Department rule prohibiting "any activity, conversation, deliberation, or discussion which is derogatory to the Department" is a good example, as such a rule obviously prohibits all criticism of the agency by its officers, even in private conversation.[56] A similar situation arose in New Orleans, where the police department had a regulation that prohibited statements by a police officer that "unjustly criticize or ridicule, or express hatred or contempt toward, or...which may be detrimental to, or cast suspicion on the reputation of, or otherwise defame, any person."[57] The regulation was revised and later ruled constitutional.[58]

The second situation in which free speech limitations may be found to be unreasonable is in the way in which the governmental action is applied. Specifically, a police department may be unable to demonstrate that the statements by an officer being disciplined actually adversely affected the operation of the department. For example, a Baltimore regulation prohibiting public criticism of police department action was held to have been unconstitutionally applied to a police officer who was president of the police union and had stated in a television interview that the police commissioner was not leading the department effectively,[59] and that "the bottom is going to fall out of this city."[60]

A related area is that of political activity. As with free speech, government agencies may restrict the political behavior of their employees, the rationale being that without such restrictions, there is a danger that employees could be pressured by their superiors to support certain political candidates or engage in political activities, under threat of loss of employment or other adverse action. At the federal level, various types of political activity by federal employees are controlled by the Hatch Act; its constitutionality has been upheld by the U.S. Supreme Court.[61] Many states have similar statutes, often referred to as "little Hatch Acts."

Although it may appear that Supreme Court decisions have laid to rest all controversy in this area, that has not been the case. Two recent cases show lower courts opting to limit the authority of the state to restrict political activities of their employees. In Pawtucket, Rhode Island, two firefighters ran for public office (mayor and city council member), despite a city charter provision prohibiting all political activity by employees (except voting and privately expressing their opinions). The Rhode Island Supreme Court issued an injunction against enforcing the charter provision, on the ground that the provision applied only to partisan political activities.[62] In a similar Boston case, however, the court upheld the police department rule on the basis that whether the partisan–nonpartisan distinction was crucial was a matter for legislative or administrative determination.[63]

In a Michigan case, a court declared unconstitutional, for being too overbroad, two city charter provisions that prohibited contributions to or solicitations for any political purpose by city employees.[64] Clearly, although the Supreme Court seems to be supportive of governmental attempts to limit the political activities of their employees, lower courts seem just as intent to limit the Supreme Court decisions to the facts of those cases.

May a police officer be disciplined, even discharged, because of his or her political affiliations? The Supreme Court ruled on that question in a case arising out of the Sheriff's Department in Cook County, Illinois.[65] The newly elected sheriff, a Democrat, fired the chief deputy of the process division and a bailiff of the juvenile court, both of whom were nonmerit employees, because they were Republican. The Court ruled that it was a violation of the employees' First Amendment rights to discharge them from nonpolicymaking positions solely on the basis of their political party affiliation.[66]

Nonpolitical associations are also protected by the First Amendment; however, it is common for police departments to prohibit officers from associating with known felons or others of bad reputation, on the ground that "such associations may expose an officer to irresistible temptations to yield in his obligation to impartially enforce the law, and…may give the appearance that the police are not themselves honest and impartial enforcers of the law."[67]

However, rules against association, as with other First Amendment rights, must not be overbroad. A Detroit Police Department regulation prohibiting knowing and associating with known criminals or persons charged with crimes, except in connection with regular duties, was declared unconstitutional; the court held that it prohibited some associations that had no bearing on the officers' integrity or public confidence in the officer (e.g., an association with a fellow church member who had been arrested on one occasion years ago, and the befriending of a recently convicted person who wanted to become a productive citizen).[68]

Occasionally, a criminal justice employee will be disciplined for improper association even though it was not demonstrated that the association had a detrimental affect on the employee or the agency. For example, a Maryland court held that a fully qualified police officer who was a practicing nudist could not be fired simply on that basis.[69] On the other hand, a court upheld the discharge of an officer who had had sexual intercourse at a party with a woman he knew to be a nude model at a local "adult theater of known disrepute."[70]

The First Amendment's reach also includes means of expression other than verbal utterances. For example, the Supreme Court upheld the constitutionality of a regulation of the Suffolk County, New York, Police Department that established several grooming standards (regarding hair, sideburn, and moustache length) for its male officers.[71] In this case, *Kelley v. Johnson*, the court felt that to make officers readily recognizable to the public and to maintain the esprit de corps within the department, the agency justified the regulations and did not violate any right guaranteed by the Fourteenth Amendment.

✧ SEARCHES AND SEIZURES

The Fourth Amendment to the U.S. Constitution protects "the right of the people to be secure in their persons, houses, papers, and effects, against unreasonable searches and seizures." In an important case in 1967, the Supreme Court held that the amendment also protected individuals' reasonable expectations of privacy, not just property interests.[72]

The Fourth Amendment usually applies to police officers when they are at home or off duty in the same manner as it applies to all citizens. However, because of the nature of their work, police officers can be compelled to cooperate with investigations of their behavior where ordinary citizens would not. Examples would include equipment and lockers provided by the department to the officers. There, the officers have no expectation of privacy that affords or merits protection.[73] However, lower courts have established limitations where searches of employees themselves are concerned. The rights of prison authorities to search their employees arose in a 1985 Iowa case, where employees were forced to sign a consent form as a condition of hire; the court disagreed with such a broad policy, ruling that the consent form did not constitute a blanket waiver of all Fourth Amendment rights.[74]

Police officers may also be forced to appear in a lineup, a clear "seizure" of his or her person. Normally requiring probable cause, a federal appeals court upheld a police commissioner's ordering 62 officers to appear in a lineup during an investigation of police brutality, holding that "the governmental interest in the particular intrusion [should be weighed] against the offense to personal dignity and integrity." Again, the court cited the nature of the work, noting that police officers do "not have the full privacy and liberty from police officials that [they] would otherwise enjoy."[75]

❖ SELF-INCRIMINATION

The Supreme Court has also addressed questions concerning the Fifth Amendment as it applies to police officers who are under investigation. In *Garrity v. New Jersey*,[76] a police officer was ordered by the attorney general to answer questions or be discharged. The officer testified that information obtained as a result of his answers was later used to convict him of criminal charges. The Supreme Court held that the information obtained from the officers could not be used against him at his criminal trial, because the Fifth Amendment forbids the use of coerced confessions.

In *Gardner v. Broderick* [77], a police officer had refused to answer questions asked by a grand jury investigating police misconduct, as he felt his answers might tend to incriminate him. The officer was terminated from his position as a result. The Supreme Court ruled that the officer could not be fired for his refusal to waive his constitutional right to remain silent. However, the Court added that the grand jury could have forced the officer to answer or be terminated for his refusal, provided that the officer was informed that his answers would not be used against him later in a criminal case.

As a result of these decisions, it is proper to fire a police officer who refuses to answer questions that are related directly to the performance of his or her duties, provided that the officer has been informed that any answers may not be used later in a criminal proceeding. Although there is some diversity of opinion among lower courts on the question of whether or not an officer may be compelled to submit to a polygraph examination, the majority of courts that have considered the question have held that an officer can be required to take the examination.[78]

❖ RELIGIOUS PRACTICES

Criminal justice work often requires that personnel are available and on duty 24 hours per day, seven days a week. Although it is not always convenient or pleasant, such shift configurations require that many criminal justice employees work weekends, nights, and holidays. It is generally assumed that one who takes such a position agrees to work such hours and abide by other such conditions (i.e., carrying a weapon, as in a policing position); it is usually the personnel with the least seniority on the job who must work the most undesirable shifts.

However, there are occasions when one's religious beliefs are in direct conflict with the requirements of the job. For example, there may be conflicts between one's work assignments and attendance at religious services or periods of religious observance. In these situations, the employee may be forced to choose between his or her job and religion. (The author is acquainted with a midwestern state trooper whose religion posed another related cause of job–religion conflict—his religion banned the carrying or use of firearms. Here, the officer chose to give up his weapon, and thus his job.) However, there have been a number of people who chose to litigate the work-religion conflict rather than cave in to agency work demands.

Title VII of the Civil Rights Act of 1964, discussed above, prohibits religious discrimination in employment. The act defines religion as including "all aspects of religious...practice, as well as belief, unless an employer...is unable to reasonably accommodate to an employee's...religious...practice without undue hardship on the conduct of the employer's business."[79] Thus Title VII requires reasonable accommodation of religious beliefs, but not to the extent that the employee has complete freedom of religious expression.[80] For example, an Albuquerque firefighter was a Seventh Day Adventist and refused to work Friday or Saturday nights as they interrupted with his honoring the Sabbath. He refused to trade shifts or take leave with (as vacation) or without pay, even though existing policy permitted his doing so, saying the *department* should have to make such arrangements for coverage or simply excuse him from his shifts. The department refused to do either, discharging him. The court ruled that the department's accommodations were reasonable and that no further accommodation could be made without causing an undue hardship to the department. His firing was upheld. The court emphasized, however, that future decisions would depend on the facts of the individual case.[81]

Recently, a court also held that the termination of a Mormon police officer for practicing plural marriage (polygamy), in violation of state law, was not a violation of his right to freely exercise his religious beliefs.[82]

✦ OTHER JOB-RELATED PROBLEMS

✧ SEXUAL MISCONDUCT

To be blunt, there is ample opportunity for criminal justice employees to become engaged in affairs, incidents, trysts, dalliances, or other behavior that is clearly sexual in nature. History (and news accounts) have shown that wearing a uniform, occupying a high or extremely sensitive position, or being sworn to maintain an unblemished and unsullied lifestyle does not mean that all people will do so for all time. Some people are not bashful about their intentions: Several officers have told the author they aspired to police work because they assumed that wearing a uniform made them sexually irresistible. On the civilian side, there are definitely a number of police "groupies," who do in fact chase police officers and others in uniform.

Instances of sexual impropriety in criminal justice work can range from casual flirting while on the job to becoming romantically involved with a foreign agent whose principal aim is to learn delicate matters of national security.

And there have been all manner of incidents between those extremes, including the discipline of female police officers who posed nude in magazines. Major police departments have even been compelled to recruit officers for their sexual preference (i.e., homosexuality).

Clearly, this is a delicate area, one in which discipline can be and has been meted out as police managers attempt to maintain high standards of officer conduct. It has also resulted in litigation, as some officers feel that their right to privacy has been intruded upon.

Instances for which police officers may be disciplined for impropriety involving sexual conduct are generally cases involving adultery and homosexuality. Most court decisions of the 1960s and 1970s agreed that adultery, even when involving a off-duty police officer and in private, could result in disciplinary action,[83] as such behavior brought debilitating criticism upon the agency and undermined public confidence in the police. However, the views of the courts in this area seem to be moderating with the times. A case involving an Internal Revenue Service agent suggested that to uphold disciplinary action for adultery, the government would have to prove that the employing agency was actually discredited.[84] The U.S. Supreme Court more recently appeared to be divided on the issue of extramarital sexual activity in public employment, however. In 1984 the Sixth Circuit held that a Michigan police officer could not be fired simply because he was living with a woman to whom he was not married (a felony under Michigan law).[85]

The issue of homosexual activity as grounds for termination of public employees recently arose in an Oklahoma case, where a state law permitted the discharge of schoolteachers for engaging in "public homosexual activity."[86] A lower court held the law to be unconstitutionally restrictive, and the Supreme Court agreed.[87] Another federal court held that the firing of a bisexual guidance counselor did not deprive the counselor of her First or Fourteenth Amendment rights. The counselor's discussion of her sexual preferences with teachers was not protected by the First Amendment.[88]

✦ RESIDENCY REQUIREMENTS

Many government agencies specify that all or certain members in their employ must live within the geographical limits of their employing jurisdiction. In other words, employees must reside within the county or city of employment. Such residency requirements have been justified by employing agencies, particularly in criminal justice, on the grounds that employees should become familiar with and be visible in the jurisdiction of employment, or that they should reside where they are paid by the taxpayers to work. Perhaps the strongest rationale given by employing agencies is that criminal justice employees must live within a certain proximity of their work in order to respond quickly in the event of an emergency.

Prior to 1976 there were numerous challenges to residency requirements, even after the Michigan Supreme Court ruling that Detroit's residency requirement for police officers was not irrational.[89] Then, in 1976, when the U.S.

Supreme Court held that Philadelphia's requiring firefighters to live in the city did not violate the Constitution, the challenges subsided. The cases now seem to revolve around the question of what constitutes residency. Generally, the police officer must demonstrate that he or she spends a substantial amount of time at the in-city residence.[90] Strong arguments have been made, however, that in areas where housing is unavailable or is exceptionally expensive, a residency requirement is unreasonable.[91]

✧ MOONLIGHTING

The courts have traditionally supported criminal justice agencies placing limitations on the amount and kinds of outside work their employees can perform.[92] For example, police department restrictions on moonlighting range from a complete ban on outside employment to permission to engage in certain forms of work, such as investments, private security, teaching criminal justice courses, and so on. The rationale for agency limitations is that "outside employment seriously interferes with keeping the [police and fire] departments fit and ready for action at all times."[93]

However, in a Louisiana case, firefighters successfully provided evidence that moonlighting had been a common practice for 16 years before the city banned it, no firefighters had ever needed sick leave as a result of injuries acquired while moonlighting, there had never been a problem locating off-duty firefighters to respond to an emergency, and moonlighting had never caused a level of fatigue that was serious enough to impair a firefighter's work. With this evidence, the court invalidated the city ordinance which had sought to prohibit moonlighting.[94]

✧ MISUSE OF FIREARMS

Because of the need to defend themselves or others and be prepared for any exigency, police officers are empowered to use lethal force when justified. Although restricted in this use of force by the Supreme Court's 1985 decision in *Tennessee v. Garner* [95] (deeming the killing of unarmed, nondangerous suspects as unconstitutional), the possession of, and familiarity with, firearms remains a central aspect of the contemporary officer's role and function. Some officers take this responsibility to the extreme, however, becoming overly reliant on and consumed with their firepower.

Thus police agencies typically attempt to restrain the use of firearms through written policies and frequent training of a "Shoot/Don't Shoot" nature. Still, a broad range of potential and actual problems remain with respect to the use and possible misuse of firearms, as the following will show.

As mentioned above, in the face of extremely serious potential and real problems and the omnipresent specter of liability suits, police agencies generally have policies regulating the use of handguns and other firearms by their officers, both on and off duty. The courts have held that such regulations need only be reasonable and that the burden rests with the disciplined police officer to show that the regulation was arbitrary and unreasonable.[96] The courts also grant considerable latitude to administrators in determining when their firearms regulations have been violated.[97] Police firearms regulations tend to address three basic issues: (1) requirements for the safeguarding of the weapon; (2) guidelines for carrying the weapon while off duty; and (3) limitations on when the weapon may be fired.[98]

Courts and juries are increasingly becoming more harsh in dealing with police officers who misuse their firearms. The current tendency is to "look behind" police shootings to determine if the officer acted negligently or the employing agency negligently trained and supervised the officer/employee. In one case, a federal appeals court approved a $500,000 judgment against the District of Columbia when a police officer who was not in adequate physical shape shot a man in the course of an arrest. The court noted that the District officer had received no fitness training in four years and was physically incapable of subduing the victim; the court felt that had the officer been physically fit and adequately trained in disarmament techniques, a gun would not have been necessary. However, in his condition, the officer posed a "foreseeable risk of harm to others."[99]

Courts have awarded damages against police officers and/or their employers for other acts involving misuse of firearms, such as when an officer shot a person while intoxicated and off-duty in a bar;[100] an officer accidentally killed an arrestee with a shotgun while handcuffing him; [101] an unstable officer shot his wife five times and then committed suicide with an off-duty weapon the department required him to carry;[102] and when an officer accidentally shot and killed an innocent bystander while pursuing another man at nighttime (the officer had had no instruction on shooting at a moving target, night shooting, or shooting in residential areas).[103]

✦ ALCOHOL AND DRUGS IN THE WORKPLACE

Alcoholism and drug abuse problems have "taken on a life of their own" in contemporary criminal justice; employees must be increasingly wary of the tendency to succumb to these problems, while administrative personnel must be able to recognize (drug testing is discussed below) and attempt to counsel and treat these companion problems of the 1990s.

Indeed, in the aftermath of the November 1992 beating death of Malice Green by a group of Detroit police officers, it was reported that the Detroit Police Department had "high alcoholism rates and pervasive psychological problems connected with the stress of policing a city mired in poverty, drugs, and crime."[104] It was further revealed that while the Detroit police department had paid $850,000 to two drug-testing facilities, the department did not have the counseling programs many other cities offer their officers. A psychologist asserted that "there are many, many potential time bombs in that department."[105]

It is obvious, given the extant law of most jurisdictions and the nature of their work, that criminal justice employees must not be "walking time bombs," but be able to perform their work with a "clear head," unbefuddled by alcohol or drugs.[106] Police departments and prisons will often specify in their manual of policy and procedures that no alcoholic beverages will be consumed within a specified period prior to reporting for duty.

Such regulations have been upheld uniformly as rational because of the hazards of the work. A Louisiana court went further, upholding a regulation that prohibited police officers from consuming alcoholic beverages on or off duty to the extent that it caused the officer's behavior to become obnoxious, disruptive, or disorderly.[107] Enforcing such regulations will occasionally result in criminal justice employees to be ordered to submit to drug or alcohol tests. That issue—testing—is discussed next.

✧ DRUG TESTING

The courts have had several occasions to review criminal justice agency policies requiring employees to submit to urinalysis to determine the presence of drugs or alcohol. For example, it was held as early as 1969 that a firefighter could be ordered to submit to a blood test when the agency had reasonable grounds to believe he was intoxicated, and that it was appropriate for the firefighter to be terminated from employment when he refused to submit to the test.[108]

In March 1989, the U.S. Supreme Court issued two major decisions on drug testing of public employees in the workplace. *Skinner v. Railway Labor Executives Association* [109] and *National Treasury Employees Union v. Von Raab* [110] dealt with drug testing plans for railroad and U.S. Customs workers, respectively. Under the Fourth Amendment, government workers are protected from unreasonable search and seizure, including how drug testing can be conducted. The Fifth Amendment protects federal, state and local workers from illegal governmental conduct.

In 1983, the Federal Railway Administration promulgated regulations that required railroads to conduct urine and blood tests on their workers following major train accidents or incidents. The regulations were challenged, one theory arguing that since railroads were privately owned, government action, including applying the Fourth Amendment, could not legally be applied. The Supreme Court disagreed in *Skinner*, ruling that railroads must be viewed as an instrument or agent of the government.

Three of the most controversial drug testing issues have been whether testing should be permitted when there is no indication of a drug problem in the workplace, whether or not the testing methods are reliable, and whether a positive test proves there was on-the-job impairment.[111] The *Von Raab* case addressed all three issues. There, the U.S. Customs Service implemented a drug-screening program that required urinalysis for employees desiring transfer or promotion to positions that were directly involved in drug interdiction, where carrying a firearm was necessary, or where classified material was handled. Only five of 3600 employees tested positive. The Treasury Employees Union argued that such an insignificant number of positives created a "suspicionless search" argument; in other words, drug testing was unnecessary and unwarranted. The Supreme Court disagreed, ruling that although only a few employees tested positive, drug use is such a serious problem that the program could continue.

Further, the Court found nothing wrong with the testing protocol. (An independent contractor was used; succinctly, the worker, after discarding outer garments, produced a urine specimen while being observed by a member of the same sex; the sample was signed by the employee, labeled, placed in a plastic bag, sealed and delivered to a lab for testing.) The Court found no "grave potential for arbitrary and oppressive interference with the privacy and personal security of the individuals" in this method.

Proving the connection between drug testing and on-the-job impairment has been an ongoing issue. Urinalysis, for example, cannot prove when a person testing positive actually used the drug. Therefore, tests may punish and stigmatize a person for extracurricular drug usage that may have no effect on the worker's on-the-job performance.[112] In *Von Raab*, the Court indicated that this dilemma is still no impediment to testing. It stated that the Customs Service had a compelling interest in having a "physically fit" employee with "unimpeachable integrity and judgment."

Together, these two cases may set a new standard for determining the reasonableness of drug testing in the criminal justice workplace. They may legalize many testing programs that formerly would have been risky. *Von Raab* presented three compelling governmental interests that could be weighed against the employee's privacy expectations: the integrity of the work force, public safety, and protection of sensitive information. *Skinner* stated that railroad workers also had diminished expectations of privacy because they are in an industry that is widely regulated to ensure safety.[113]

Summary

Although this chapter has by no means exhausted the issues revolving around criminal justice employee rights, it has illuminated several that are very pressing for today's administrator. As stated in the introduction, it is far better to learn one's rights and limitations "in house," through education and training of one's volition, than via the "courthouse" method, as a result of a lawsuit imposed from without.

Perhaps more important, however, the rights and issues presented in this chapter have come into being simply because they represent, in most cases, a more humanitarian means of dealing with people. Far too many rights were won or expanded because of what Abraham Maslow termed the Theory X management style of the past—the authoritarian, unilateral, "Do as I say, not as I do," management by fear, "I'm the boss" style of leadership. That attitude of the past (although, of course, it still lingers among many managers) caused and is causing many problems and also served to foment the rapid spread of labor unions during the past two decades.

New issues and interpretations arise regularly. Often, new solutions create new problems as well. But the laws comprising employee rights are intended to bring about *fairness*. There are still glaring inequities that will someday be addressed by the courts; we may see further judicial activism in such areas as the "glass ceiling" (women doing the same work and having the same qualifications as men, yet receiving less pay and fewer promotions); demographic parity (with respect to hiring and promotions) in the workplace; and expanded rights for the elderly, the disabled, and the single parent. Criminal justice employees will also continue to be active in pursuing the "American Dream."

Questions for Review

1. Provide an overview of criminal justice employee rights at the workplace, under federal statutes.

2. Describe the general employee–employer relationship in criminal justice, regarding recruitment and hiring, affirmative action, and pay and benefits.

3. It has been stated that criminal justice employees have a "property interest" in their jobs as well as a right to a safe workplace. Explain.

4. What constitutional rights are implicated for criminal justice employees on the job? (In your response, address whether rights are held regarding freedom of speech, searches and seizures, self-incrimination, and religion.)

5. In what regard is a higher standard of conduct expected of criminal justice employees? (In your response, include discussions of sexual behavior, residency, moonlighting, use of firearms, and alcohol/drug abuse.)

For Further Reading

GEORGE F. COLE (ED.), *Criminal Justice: Law and Politics* (6th ed.). Belmont, Calif.: Wadsworth, 1992.

RICHARD HAWKINS and GEOFFREY P. ALPERT, *American Prison Systems: Punishment and Justice*. Englewood Cliffs, N.J.: Prentice Hall, 1989.

WILLIAM E. HEWITT, GEOFF GALLAS, and BARRY MAHONEY, *Courts That Succeed*. Williamsburg, Va.: National Center for State Courts, 1990.

CHARLES R. SWANSON and SUSETTE M. TALARICO (EDS.), *Court Administration: Issues and Responses*. Athens, Ga.: University of Georgia, 1987.

CHARLES R. SWANSON, LEONARD TERRITO, and ROBERT W. TAYLOR, *Police Administration* (3d ed.). New York: Macmillan, 1993.

Notes

1. Robert H. Chaires and Susan A. Lentz, "Criminal Justice Employee Rights: An Overview," *American Journal of Criminal Justice* 13 (April 1994):(in press).
2. *Ibid.*
3. *Ibid.*
4. See *United Autoworkers v. Johnson Controls*, 111 S.Ct. 1196 (1991).
5. See Kenneth J. Peak, *Policing America: Methods, Issues, Challenges* (Englewood Cliffs, N.J.: Regents/Prentice Hall, 1993), pp. 77–82.
6. Robert H. Chaires and Susan A. Lentz, "Criminal Justice Employee Rights: An Overview," (in press).
7. *U.S. v. Gregory*, 818 F.2d 114 (4th Cir. 1987)
8. *Harris v. Pan American*, 649 F.2d 670 (9th Cir. 1988).
9. Robert H. Chaires and Susan A. Lentz, "Criminal Justice Employee Rights: An Overview," (in press).
10. See Ken Peak, Douglas W. Farenholtz, and George Coxey, "Physical Abilities Testing for Police Officers: A Flexible, Job-Related Approach," *The Police Chief* 59 (January 1992): 52–56.
11. *Shaw v. Nebraska Department of Corrections*, 666 F.Supp. 1330 (N.D. Neb. 1987).
12. *Garrett v. Oskaloosa County*, 734 F.2d 621 (11th Cir. 1984)
13. Robert H. Chaires and Susan A. Lentz, "Criminal Justice Employee Rights: An Overview," (in press).
14. *EEOC v. State Department of Highway Safety*, 660 F.Supp. 1104 (N.D. Fla. 1986).
15. *Johnson v. Mayor and City Council of Baltimore* 105 S.Ct. 2717 (1985).
16. 460 U.S. 226, 103 S.Ct. 1054, 75 L.Ed.2d 18 (1983).
17. Robert H. Chaires and Susan A. Lentz, "Criminal Justice Employee Rights: An Overview," (in press).
18. Paul J. Spiegelman, "Court-Ordered Hiring Quotas After *Stotts*: A Narrative on the Role of the Moralities of the Web and the Ladder in Employment Discrimination Doctrine," 20 *Harvard Civil Rights Review* 339 (1985).
19. Robert H. Chaires and Susan A. Lentz, "Criminal Justice Employee Rights: An Overview," (in press).
20. *Regents of the University of California v. Bakke*, 98 S.Ct. 2733, 438 U.S. 265, 57 L.Ed.2d (1978).
21. See *Wygant v. Jackson Board of Education*, 106 S.Ct. 1842 (1986).
22. Robert H. Chaires and Susan A. Lentz, "Criminal Justice Employee Rights: An Overview," (in press).
23. *Ledoux v. District of Columbia*, 820 F.2d 1293 (D.C. Cir. 1987), at 1294.
24. *Ibid.*
25. Robert H. Chaires and Susan A. Lentz, "Criminal Justice Employee Rights: An Overview," (in press).
26. See *Parratt v. Taylor*, 451 U.S. 527, 536-37, 101 S.Ct. 1908, 1913-14, 68 L.Ed.2d 420 (1981).
27. *Board of Regents v. Roth*, 408 U.S. at 577, 92 S.Ct. at 2709.
28. *Cleveland Board of Education v. Loudermill*, 470 U.S. 532, 541 (1985).
29. *McGraw v. City of Huntington Beach*, 882 F.2d 384 (9th Cir. 1989).
30. *Lohorn v. Michael*, 913 F.2d 327 (7th Cir. 1990).
31. *Palmer v. City of Monticello* 731 F.Supp. 1503 (D. Utah 1990).
32. *Young v. Municipality of Bethel Park*, 646 F. Supp. 539 (W.D.Penn. 1986)

33. *McAdoo v. Lane*, 564 F.Supp. 1215 (D.C.Ill. 1983)

34. *Ibid.*, at 1217.

35. Robert H. Chaires and Susan A. Lentz, "Criminal Justice Employee Rights: An Overview," (in press).

36. *Ibid.*

37. *McNamara v. City of Chicago* 700 F.Supp. 917 (N.D. Ill. 1988), at 919.

38. *White v. Thomas*, 660 F.2d 680 (5th Cir. 1981).

39. *Yarber v. Indiana State Prison* (713 F. Supp. 271 (N.D. Ind. 1988).

40. Robert H. Chaires and Susan A. Lentz, "Criminal Justice Employee Rights: An Overview," (in press).

41. Lynn Lund, "The 'Ten Commandments' of Risk Management for Jail Administrators," *Detention Reporter* 4 (June 1991):4.

42. *National League of Cities v. Usery*, 426 U.S. 833 (1976).

43. 105 S.Ct. 1005 (1985).

44. Charles R. Swanson, Leonard Territo, and Robert W. Taylor, *Police Administration* (3d ed.) (New York: Macmillan, 1993), p. 439.

45. *Jurich v. Mahoning County* 31 Fair Emp. Prac. 1275 (BNA) (N.D. Ohio 1983).

46. *Eldridge v. Boulchard*, 620 F. Supp. 678 (D.C. Va.).

47. Robert H. Chaires and Susan A. Lentz, "Criminal Justice Employee Rights: An Overview," (in press).

48. *Ibid.*

49. *Collins v. City of Harker Heights*, 112 S.Ct. 1061 (1992).

50. See *Ruge v. City of Bellevue*, 892 F.2d 738 (1989).

51. *Galloway v. State of Louisiana*, 817 F.2d 1154 (5th Cir. 1987).

52. Robert H. Chaires and Susan A. Lentz, "Criminal Justice Employee Rights: An Overview," (in press).

53. *Pickering v. Board of Education*, 391 U.S. 563 (1968), at 568.

54. *Keyishian v. Board of Regents*, 385 U.S. 589 (1967).

55. Charles R. Swanson, Leonard Territo, and Robert W. Taylor, *Police Administration* (3d ed.), p. 419.

56. *Muller v. Conlisk*, 429 F.2d 901 (7th Cir. 1970).

57. *Flynn v. Giarusso*, 321 F.Supp. 1295 (E.D. La. 1971), at 1299.

58. *Magri v. Giarusso*, 379 F.Supp. 353 (E.D. La. 1974).

59. Charles R. Swanson, Leonard Territo, and Robert W. Taylor, *Police Administration* (3d ed.), p. 419.

60. *Brukiewa v. Police Commissioner of Baltimore*, 263 A.2d 210 (Md. 1970).

61. *United Public Workers v. Mitchell*, 330 U.S. 75 (1947); *U.S. Civil Service Commission v. National Association of Letter Carriers*, 413 U.S. 548 (1973).

62. *Magill v. Lynch*, 400 F.Supp. 84 (R.I. 1975).

63. *Boston Police Patrolmen's Association, Inc. v. City of Boston*, 326 N.E.2d 314 (Mass. 1975).

64. *Phillips v. City of Flint*, 225 N.W.2d 780 (Mich. 1975).

65. *Elrod v. Burns*, 427 U.S. 347 (1976); see also, *Ramey v. Harber*, 431 F.Supp 657 (W.D. Va. 1977); and *Branti v. Finkel*, 445 U.S. 507 (1980).

66. Connick v. Myers, 461 U.S. 138 (1983); *Jones v. Dodson*, 727 F.2d 1329 (4th Cir. 1984).

67. Charles R. Swanson, Leonard Territo, and Robert W. Taylor, *Police Administration* (3d ed.), p. 421.

68. *Sponick v. city of Detroit Police Department*, 211 N.W.2d 674 (Mich. 1973), p. 681; but see *Wilson v. Taylor*, 733 F.2d 1539 (11th Cir. 1984).

69. *Bruns v. Pomerleau*, 319 F.Supp. 58 (D. Md. 1970); see also *McMullen v. Carson*, 754 F.2d 936 (11th Cir. 1985), where it was held that a Ku Klux Klansman could not be fired from his position as a records clerk in the sheriff's department simply because he was a Klansman. The Court did uphold the dismissal because his active KKK participation threatened to negatively affect the agency's ability to perform its public duties.

70. *Civil Service Commission of Tucson v. Livingston*, 525 P.2d 949 (Ariz. 1974).

71. *425 U.S. 238* (1976).

72. *Katz v. United States*, 389 U.S. 347 (1967).

73. See *People v. Tidwell*, 266 N.E.2d 787 (Ill. 1971).

74. *McDonell v. Hunter*, 611 F.Supp. 1122 (S.D. Iowa, 1985), affd. as mod., 809 F.2d 1302 (8th Cir., 1987).

75. *Biehunik v. Felicetta*, 441 F.2d 228 (1971), at 230.

76. 385 U.S. 483 (1967).

77. 392 U.S. 273 (1968).

78. See *Gabrilowitz v. Newman*, 582 F.2d 100 (1st Cir. 1978). Cases upholding the department's authority to order a polygraph examination for police officers include: *Eshelman v. Blubaum*, 560 P.2d 1283 (Ariz. 1977); *Dolan v. Kelly*, 348 N.Y.S.2d 478 (1973); *Richardson v. City of Pasadena*, 500 S.W.2d 175 (Tex. 1973); *Seattle Police Officer's Guild v. City of Seattle*, 494 P.2d 485 (Wash. 1972); *Roux v. New Orleans Police Department*, 223 So.2d 905 (La. 1969); and *Farmer v. City of Fort Lauderdale*, 427 So.2d 187 (Fla. 1983), *cert. den.*, 104 S.Ct. 74 (1984).

79. 42 U.S.C. 200e(j).

80. *United States v. City of Albuquerque*, 12 EPD 11, 244 (10th Cir. 1976); see also *Trans World Airlines v. Hardison*, 97 S.Ct. 2264 (1977).

81. *United States v. Albuquerque*, 545 F.2d 110 (10th Cir. 1977).

82. *Potter v. Murray City*, 760 F.2d 1065 (10th Cir. 1985).

83. *Faust v. Police Civil Service Commission*, 347 A.2d 765 (Pa. 1975); *Stewart v. Leary*, 293 N.Y.S.2d 573 (1968); *Brewer v. City of Ashland*, 86 S.W.2d 669 (Ky. 1935); *Fabio v. Civil Service Commission of Philadelphia*, 373 A.2d 751 (Pa. 1977).

84. *Major v. Hampton*, 413 F.Supp. 66 (1976).

85. *Briggs v. City of North Muskegon Police Department*, 563 F.Supp. 585 (6th Cir. 1984).

86. *National Gay Task Force v. Bd. of Ed. of Oklahoma City*, 729 F.2d 1270 (10th Cir. 1984).

87. *Board of Education v. National Gay Task Force*, 53 U.S.L.W. 4408, No 83-2030 (1985).

88. *Rowland v. Mad River Sch. Dist.*, 730 F.2d 444 (6th Cir. 1984).

89. *Detroit Police Officers Association v. City of Detroit*, 190 N.W.2d 97 (1971), appeal denied, 405 U.S. 950 (1972).

90. *Miller v. Police Board of City of Chicago*, 349 N.E.2d 544 (Ill. 1976); *Williamson v. Village of Baskin*, 339 So.2d 474 (La. 1976); *Nigro v. Board of Trustees of Alden*, 395 N.Y.S.2d 544 (1977).

91. *State, County, and Municipal Employees Local 339 v. City of Highland Park*, 108 N.W.2d 898 (1961).

92. See, for example, *Cox v. McNamara*, 493 P.2d 54 (Ore. 1972); *Brenckle v. Township of Shaler*, 281 A.2d 920 (Pa. 1972); *Hopwood v. City of Paducah*, 424 S.W.2d 134 (Ky. 1968); *Flood v. Kennedy*, 239 N.Y.S.2d 665 (1963).

93. Richard N. Williams, *Legal Aspects of Discipline by Police Administrators*, Traffic Institute Publication 2705 (Evanston, Ill.: Northwestern University, 1975), p. 4.

94. *City of Crowley Firemen v. City of Crowley*, 264 So.2d 368 (La. 1972).

95. 471 U.S. 1, 105 S.Ct. 1694, 85 L.Ed.2d 1 (1985).

96. *See Lally v. Department of Police*, 306 So.2d 65 (La. 1974).

97. See, for example, *Peters v. Civil Service Commission of Tucson*, 539 P.2d 698 (Ariz. 1977); *Abeyta v. Town of Taos*, 499 F.2d 323 (10th Cir. 1974); *Baumgartner v. Leary*, 311 N.Y.S.2d 468 (1970); *City of Vancouver v. Jarvis*, 455 P.2d 591 (Wash. 1969).

98. Charles R. Swanson, Leonard Territo, and Robert W. Taylor, *Police Administration* (3d ed.), p. 433.

99. *Parker v. District of Columbia*, 850 F2d 708 (1988), at 713, 714.

100. *Marusa v. District of Columbia*, 484 F.2d 828 (1973).

101. *Sager v. City of Woodlawn Park*, 543 F.Supp. 282 (D. Colo. 1982).

102. *Bonsignore v. City of New York*, 521 F.Supp. 394 (1981).

103. *Popow v. City of Margate*, 476 F.Supp. 1237 (1979).

104. Eloise Salholz and Frank Washington, "Detroit's Brutal Lessons," *Newsweek* (November 30, 1992), p. 45.

105. *Ibid*.

106. See *Krolick v. Lowery*, 302 N.Y.S.2d 109 (1969), p. 115; *Hester v. Milledgeville*, 598 F.Supp. 1456, 1457 (M.D.Ga. 1984).

107. *McCracken v. Department of Police*, 337 So.2d 595 (La. 1976).

108. *Krolick v. Lowery*.

109. 489 U.S. 602 (1989).

110. 489 U.S. 656 (1989).

111. Robert J. Aalberts and Harvey W. Rubin, "Court's Rulings on Testing Crack Down on Drug Abuse," *Risk Management* 38 (March 1991):36–41.

112. *Ibid*., p. 38.

113. *Ibid*., p. 40.

Shared Issues and Influences

Uneasy lies the head that wears the crown.
—William Shakespeare

We have all enough strength to bear other people's troubles.
—Duc de la Rochefoucauld

✦ INTRODUCTION

This chapter is indeed about the "troubles" of those who "wear the crown." As will be seen, however, the kinds of troubles discussed are shared by all of society and the justice system. As we have seen from previous chapters, the topics included here are only some of the problems that span the justice system and pose unique challenges for justice administrators. These issues are not presented in any particular order or with any ranked or logical severity; each is onerous and challenging standing alone, and none is likely to dissipate soon.

The subjects discussed are: The long-standing charge that the processes and decision makers of the justice system are racist; the omnipresent dilemma of civil liability, due to one's own or a subordinate's negligence; the influence of politics over the justice system; and the ebb and flow of union power.

✦ IS THE JUSTICE SYSTEM RACIST?

Is the criminal justice system biased against blacks? Over the past four decades a number of eminent criminologists have studied the question. Many blacks are apparently convinced that it is. This has been and continues to be one of the most sensitive—and as will be seen, complex—charges against the criminal justice system throughout its history.

✧ STUDIES POINTING TO A NONRACIST SYSTEM

A number of researchers have concluded that the justice system does *not* engage in systematic racism. One of the more prominent works was by Gary Kleck, who reviewed 17 studies of the imposition of the death penalty and 40 studies of noncapital sentencing. His major conclusions were: (1) the death penalty had generally not been imposed for murder in a fashion discriminatory toward blacks, except in the south; (2) discrimination against black defendants who had raped white victims was substantial in the south but has disappeared as death sentences are no longer imposed for rape; (3) regarding noncapital sentencing, the evidence did not indicate a general or widespread overt discrimination against black defendants; (4) although black offender–white victim crimes are generally punished more severely than crimes involving other racial combinations, the evidence indicated that this is due to legally relevant factors related to such offenses, not the racial combination itself; and (5) there appeared to be a general pattern of less severe punishment of crimes with black victims than of those with white victims, especially in connection with imposition of the death penalty. In connection with capital sentencing, the evidence was too sparse to draw firm conclusions.[1]

Defenders of the existing justice system say that sentencing decisions are based on objective measures such as prior arrests, employment history, and stability of family background—factors commonly believed to predict whether an offender will err again (recidivate). Perhaps the most ardent opponent of the notion that the system is racist is William Wilbanks, author of *The Myth of a Racist Criminal Justice System*,[2] which "rapidly became the focus of attention and outrage...."[3] Wilbanks found little support for what he termed the "DT"—Discrimination Thesis—and does not believe that the system is characterized by racial discrimination or prejudice against blacks. While admitting that racism did permeate the system in earlier periods of American history, especially in the south, Wilbanks found today an *equal* tendency for criminal justice decision makers to favor blacks over whites, and felt that this "canceling-out effect" results in studies finding no *overall* racial effect.[4] Wilbanks maintained that there is no pervasive racial discrimination across the system. In his own study of more than 230,000 felony cases in California and Pennsylvania, Wilbanks did not find any "black/white gap" in treatment as defendants moved across the system.[5]

✦ RESEARCH INTIMATING A RACIST SYSTEM

A sizable body of literature has also developed in support of the position that the system *does* discriminate against minorities. In their widely used textbook, *Criminology*, Edwin Sutherland and Donald Cressey concluded the following in 1974: "Numerous studies have shown that African-Americans are more likely to be arrested, indicted, convicted, and committed to an institution than are whites who commit the same offenses, and many other studies have shown that blacks have a poorer chance than whites to receive probation, a suspended sentence, parole, commutation of a death sentence, or a pardon."[6] Over the course of several decades, a number of other studies have offered support for the discrimination thesis against both adults and juveniles in the minority.[7] For example, renowned criminologist Marvin Wolfgang, in a landmark 1972 study that tracked 10,000 Philadelphia boys, discovered that 77 percent of white juveniles were let go after an arrest with just a warning, compared with 56 percent of nonwhites. In a follow-up study in 1985, Wolfgang found that 49 percent of the white youngsters were released versus 40 percent of the nonwhites, an improvement he attributed to the increasing number of black police officers.[8]

The perception lingers that justice remains far from color-blind. "There is a view in this country that if you're poor and black or Hispanic or Native American, you won't get a fair deal. And the basic contentions that there are biases at every level of the system are well founded," said James B. Eaglin, chairman of the National Association of Blacks in Criminal Justice. A discriminatory nature has also been implied in the civil courts; a 1985 Rand Corporation study of 9000 civil cases in Cook County, Illinois, from 1959 to 1979, found that the median award to a white in a wrongful-death auto accident was $79,000; for a black it was $58,000.[9]

A forceful rebuttal to Wilbanks' "no DT" idea was recently leveled by Coramae Richey Mann, who wrote that "Wilbanks is mistaken…there *is* racial prejudice and discrimination in the criminal justice system…which is rooted in racism."[10] Richey challenged Wilbanks' work, stating that he took a simplistic and rather naive view of what occurs in the "real world" of criminal justice, and that his complete dependence on quantitative data for his "proof" resulted in his dismissal of much qualitative information. Mann also found what she felt were other methodological flaws and problems in interpretation of data. It should be pointed out that in attempting to counter and refute Wilbank's NDT, Mann relied heavily on research by Joan Petersilia of the Rand Corporation; Petersilia's study, discussed in more detail below, actually found no widespread and consistent racial prejudice in the system.

✦ RACE AND THE DEATH PENALTY

Blacks still make up a much larger share of death row inmates than of the nation's population. According to the Bureau of Justice Statistics, as of January 1, 1992, 982 blacks (39.6 percent of all death row inmates) were under sentence of death. The Bureau also reported that the U.S. population is 11.2 percent black and 85.6 percent white.[11] While Marvin Wolfgang and others began indicating a pattern of discrimination in the death penalty as early as 1962,[12] a number of recent studies have also supported the notion of discrimination in capital sentencing.[13] However, in 1987 the U.S. Supreme Court ruled that statistical evidence of discrimination is insufficient to render death-penalty statutes unconstitutional. That decision came in *McCleskey v. Kemp*,[14] in which the plaintiff, a black man, was executed in September 1991 for the killing of a white Atlanta police officer during a 1978 furniture store robbery. In McCleskey's appeal, evidence was introduced that those who killed white victims were four times more likely to get death sentences than those who killed black victims. However, that argument "wasn't enough to make it unconstitutional," according to the director of the American Civil Liberties Union's capital punishment project; "they're asking for the kind of absolute proof that doesn't exist—like prosecutors confessing discrimination."[15]

Death penalty studies purporting to show discrimination have been challenged on methodological grounds; even renowned criminologist James Q. Wilson was compelled to observe that "the great majority [of the studies] were methodologically defective in important ways. The most serious fault was the failure of the analysts to take into account the prior record of the offender. We would expect persons with more serious prior records to be more likely to receive the death penalty for a given offense than persons with no prior record or only a modest one."[16]

✧ RAND CORPORATION FINDINGS

One of the most respected studies of racial disparities in the justice system was a two-year effort by Joan Petersilia and the Rand Corporation. There were a number of major findings in the study. First, although case processing generally treated offenders similarly, racial differences were found at two key points. Minority suspects were more likely than whites to be released after arrest; however, after a felony conviction, minority offenders were more likely than whites to be given longer sentences and to be put in prison instead of jail. Because minorities were not found to have a higher probability of arrest, Petersilia concluded higher release rates might be explained by evidentiary problems. Research indicates that prosecutors do have greater problems making minority cases "stick" because victims often have difficulty identifying minority suspects. Moreover, minority victims and witnesses often refuse or fail to cooperate after an arrest is made. Second, there were no consistent, statistically significant racial differences in the probability of arrest, given that an offender had committed a crime.[17]

Minorities were also found to receive harsher sentences and serve longer terms in prison. Plea bargaining resolved a higher percentage of felony cases involving white defendants, and jury trials resolved a higher percentage of minorities. Conviction by jury usually results in more severe sentencing. Recidivism variables contained in the presentence investigation (PSI), concerning personal and social information, may also contribute to longer sentences.

Minorities often do not fare well in PSI indicators of recidivism, such as family stability and unemployment. As a result, judges and probation officers are often impelled to identify minorities as higher risks.[18] Significantly, Petersilia noted that "if recidivism indicators are valid and explain racial disparities in sentencing and time served, the system is not discriminating. It is simply reflecting the larger racial problems of society, and it can do little about the overrepresentation of minorities in prison."[19]

Regarding disparities in case processing, it found that at most major decision points, the criminal justice system does not discriminate against minorities; they are not overrepresented in the arrest population *relative to the number of crimes they actually commit* [emphasis hers], nor are they more likely than whites to be arrested for those crimes. However, researchers did find that police were apparently more hesitant to arrest white persons without a warrant. This finding suggested that the police operated on different assumptions about minorities than about whites when they made arrests (one possible assumption offered was that police may assume that minority suspects are less likely than white suspects to make false arrest charges or other kinds of trouble if a case is not filed).[20] It was also discovered that blacks and Hispanics were less likely to be given probation, more likely to receive prison sentences, and more likely to serve longer sentences. With respect to property crimes, the disparity between whites' and blacks' proportions of arrest and prison populations widened considerably. The same held true for Hispanics, who served even longer time than blacks.[21]

The Rand investigation is perhaps summarized best in its following statements:

> Although this study shows that minorities are treated differently at a few points in the criminal justice system, it has not found evidence that this results from widespread and consistent racial prejudice in the system. Instead, what racial disparities we found seem to be due to the system's adopting procedures without analyzing their possible effects on different racial groups. Criminal justice research and policy... need to focus on the key actors and their decision making: what information they use, how accurate it is, and whether its imposition affects particular racial groups unfairly.[22]

✧ CONCLUSIONS

In summary, there is certainly no dearth of arguments *for* and *against* the proposition that the individual actors, and therefore the entire criminal justice system, discriminate against blacks. No solid conclusion is evident. Perhaps one legitimate way to extricate ourselves from this confusion is to view this massive and conflicting body of research in different points in time. Certainly, the research of several decades ago, performed by several renowned criminologists, appears to strongly support the discrimination thesis. However, recent (primarily, 1980s) studies, also by very able researchers and no less an organization than the highly respected Rand Corporation, have determined that although there are some individuals and decision points where discrimination occurs, there is no widespread and pervasive racism in the justice system.

Clearly, future research should devote more attention on individual decision makers as well as the multiple decision points in the process. Finally, if, as Wilbanks indicated, the *belief* that the system is racist leads to criminality, research should attempt to learn why blacks and whites differ so sharply on the discrimination thesis, and the consequences in terms of behavior.[23]

✦ CIVIL LIABILITY IN JUSTICE ADMINISTRATION

No group of workers (with the exception of physicians) in the private or public sectors is more susceptible to litigation and liability as an outgrowth of their work than police and corrections officers. Frequently cast into confrontational situations, and given the complex nature of their work and its preceding training needs, they will from time to time act in a manner that evokes public scrutiny and complaints. Compounding this problem is the fact that some officers are overzealous in the pursuit of their work; they may, intentionally or not, violate the rights of the citizens they are sworn to protect or the clients they are to detain.

It should be noted that there are defenses and immunities against Section 1983 suits. The states themselves, for example, are granted absolute immunity from Section 1983 suits,[24] as well as judges, prosecutors legislators, and federal officials (they usually act under color of federal law, as opposed to state law specified in the act). Police officers are granted "qualified immunity," meaning that as long as they acted in "good faith" and their conduct was reasonable, they have a defense.[25] Overzealous conduct, however, not done in good faith and without regard for the rights of a citizen(s), will result in a finding of liability.

✧ Early Use of Section 1983 Legislation

Following the Civil War, Congress, in reaction to the activities of the Ku Klux Klan, enacted the Ku Klux Klan Act of 1871, later codified as Title 42, U.S. Code Section 1983. It states that "Every person who, under color of any statute, ordinance, regulation, custom, or usage of any State or Territory, subjects, or causes to be subjected, any citizen of the United States or any other person within the jurisdiction thereof to the deprivation of any rights, privileges, or immunities secured by the Constitution and laws, shall be liable to the party injured in an action at law, suit in equity, or other proper proceeding for redress...." This legislation was intended to provide civil rights protection to all "persons" protected under the act, where a defendant acted "under color of law" (misused power of office), and provided an avenue to the federal courts for relief of alleged civil rights violations.

The original intent of the law did not include police or corrections misconduct litigation. In fact, the law was virtually ignored for 90 years, until the U.S.

Supreme Court's decision in *Monroe v. Pape* in 1961.[26] There, 13 members of the Chicago Police Department broke into a home without a warrant, forced the family out of bed at gunpoint, and made them stand naked while the officers ransacked the house. Monroe was then taken to the police station, where he was held incommunicado and questioned for 10 hours before being released without charges. The U.S. Supreme Court held that the officers acted "under color of law" as set forth in Section 1983, violating their constitutional rights, but that the City of Chicago was immune from liability under the statute.

In the five-year period following *Monroe*, only a few police misconduct suits were filed in the federal courts where this federal statute was utilized. However, there was a virtual boom of Section 1983 suits from 1967 through 1976.[27] Then in 1978, the Supreme Court, in *Monell v. Department of Social Services* [28] also held that Section 1983 applies to municipalities, which can be sued for damages under Section 1983.

✦ LIABILITY OF POLICE SUPERVISORS

Section 1983 also allows for a finding of personal liability on the part of police supervisory personnel, when improper training is shown or it is proven that they knew, or should have known, of the misconduct of their officers, yet failed to take corrective action and prevent future harm.

Such a factual case was that of *McClelland v. Facteau*,[29] in which McClelland was stopped by Officer Facteau for speeding and taken to the city jail; there he was not allowed to make any phone calls, was questioned but not advised of his rights, and was beaten and injured by Facteau in the presence of two city police officers. McClelland sued, claiming that the two police chiefs were directly responsible for his treatment and injuries, due to their failure to train and supervise their subordinates properly. Evidence was also produced of prior misbehavior by Facteau. The court ruled that the chiefs could be held liable if they knew of prior misbehavior, yet did nothing about it.

A related case was that of *Brandon v. Allen*,[30] in which two teenagers parked in a "lovers' lane" were approached by an off-duty police officer, Allen, who showed his police identification and demanded that the male exit from the car. Allen struck the male with his fist and stabbed him with a knife, then attempted to break into the car where the female was seated. The young male was able to reenter the car and manage an escape. As the two teenagers sped off, Allen fired a shot at them with his revolver, the shattered windshield glass severely injuring the youths to the point that they required plastic surgery. Allen was convicted of criminal charges, and the police chief was also sued under Section 1983. The plaintiffs charged that the chief and others knew of Allen's reputation as a "mental case"; none of the other police officers wished to ride in a patrol car with him. At least two formal charges of misconduct had been filed previously, yet the chief failed to take any remedial action or even to review the disciplinary records of officers when he became chief. The court called this behavior "unjustified inaction," held the police department liable, and allowed the plaintiffs damages. The U.S. Supreme Court upheld this judgment.[31]

Police supervisors have also been found liable for injuries arising out of an official policy or custom of their department. Injuries resulting from a chief's verbal or written support of heavy-handed behavior resulting in excessive force by officers have resulted in such liability.[32]

✦ LIABILITY OF CORRECTIONS PERSONNEL

The liability of corrections workers often centers on their lack of due care for persons in their custody. This responsibility concerns primarily police officers and civilians responsible for inmates in local jails.

When an inmate commits suicide while in custody, police agencies are frequently—and often successfully—sued in state court under negligence and wrongful death claims. The standard used by the courts is whether the agency's act or failure to act created an unusual risk to an inmate. A "special duty" of care exists for police officers to protect inmates suffering mental disorders and those who are impaired by drugs or alcohol. Foreseeability—the reasonable anticipation that injury or damage may occur—may be found when inmates make statements of intent to commit suicide, have a history of mental illness, are in a poor emotional state, or are at a high level of intoxication or drug dependence.[33]

Suicides are not uncommon among jail inmates; in 1988, 284 jail inmates took their own lives, followed by 121 in 1989, and 148 in 1990.[34] As noted above, inmate suicide rates are higher in small jails and highest in small jails with lower population densities.[35] State courts generally recognize that police officials have a duty of care to persons in their custody.[36] Thus, jail administrators are ultimately responsible for taking reasonable precautions to ensure the health and safety of persons in their custody; they must protect inmates from harm, render medical assistance when necessary, and treat inmates humanely.[37]

Several court decisions help establish the expectations of jail administrators and their employees for the care of their charges. An intoxicated inmate in possession of cigarettes and matches started a fire that resulted in his death; the court stated that "the prisoner may have been voluntarily drunk, but he was not in the cell voluntarily... [he] was helpless and the officer knew there was a means of harm on his person...." The court concluded the police administration owed a greater duty of care to such an arrestee.[38] Emotionally disturbed arrestees can also create a greater duty for jail personnel. In an Alaskan case a woman had been arrested for intoxication in a hotel, and had trouble talking, standing, and walking; her blood-alcohol content was 0.26 percent. Two and a half hours after her incarceration, officers found her hanging by her sweater from mesh wiring in the cell. The Alaska Supreme Court said the officers knew she was depressed, and that in the past few months one of her sons had been burned to death, another son was stabbed to death, and her mother had died. Thus, the court felt officers should have anticipated her suicide.[39]

In New Mexico, a 17-year-old boy was arrested for armed robbery; later he told his mother he would kill himself before he would go to prison, and subsequently tried to cut his wrists with an aluminum can top. The assistant chief ordered the officers to keep watch over him, but he was found dead by hanging the following morning. The Supreme Court of New Mexico held that the knowledge officers possessed is an important factor to be considered in determining liability and negligence in such cases.[40] In a New Jersey case, where a young man arrested for intoxication was put in a holding cell but officers failed to remove his leather belt, which he used to take his own life, the court found the officers' conduct could have been a "substantial" factor in his death.[41]

Courts have also found the design of detention facilities as a source of negligence. A Detroit holding cell did not permit officers to observe inmates' movements unless the inmates were standing directly in front of the door, and no electronic monitoring devices were in use. A suicide in this case led the court to hold that these conditions, and the absence of a detoxification cell, were proximate causes and constituted a building defect.[42] In another incident, an intoxicated college student was placed in a holding cell at the public safety building. Forty minutes after being placed in the cell, officers found the man hanging from an overhead heating device by a noose fashioned from his socks and belt. The court found the university liable for operating a defective building and awarded the plaintiff $650,000.[43]

The behavior of jail personnel *after* a suicide or attempted suicide may also indicate a breach of duty. Officers are expected to give all possible aid to an inmate who is injured or has attempted suicide. Thus, when officers found an inmate slumped in a chair with his belt around his neck and left him in that position instead of trying to revive him or call for medical assistance, the court ruled this behavior established a causal link between the officer's inaction and the boy's death.[44]

It is clear that correctional administrators must ensure that their organizations are cognizant of their legal responsibility and expanded custodial role with their detainees.

✦ POLITICS AND JUSTICE

✧ CRIMINAL JUSTICE AND POLITICS, GENERALLY

Another long-standing influence over criminal justice and its administration is that of politics. The 1988 presidential campaign between George Bush and Michael Dukakis (from Massachusetts) also conjured up the image of a convicted murderer, Willie Horton, who had walked away from a Massachusetts prison furlough program and, in Maryland, raped a woman and assaulted her husband. This heinous event contributed in large measure to Dukakis's defeat, as Horton epitomized for many Americans the specter of violent crime, especially that committed by minorities; "liberal" politicians were to be feared as well.

Although many police chiefs, judges, and correctional administrators would prefer, and proclaim, to be "above" playing politics, the Horton case demonstrated the often close relationship between criminal justice and politics. In fact, there are a number of common "linkages": penal codes and justice system budgets are passed by legislators who are responsible to the voters; many criminal justice officials are elected; and decisions by police officers, prosecutors, judges, and corrections officials are influenced by community concerns. Candidates for public offices often use a "law and order" platform in their bid for election. City and county governing bodies increase and decrease justice system budgets as needs dictate. Congress appropriates millions in the war against drugs. Political considerations determine to a large extent who gets or does not get the "good" (justice) that is produced by a legal system.[45]

✧ POLITICAL EXPLOITATION OF THE POLICE

Historically, police departments in the United States have been political bodies, extensions of the municipal political authority.[46] Because of the close relationship between police departments and the political leadership of the community, and because the political systems developed at about the same time as the police agencies, abuse of political power has often occurred. From the beginning of this century, when journalist Lincoln Steffens exposed corruption in American cities, to more recent times, when scandals have rocked several major police departments, politics has been shown to be entwined in the relationships that often bind criminals and police officers. Partisan politics has often fostered police corruption.[47] Even in the nineteenth century police forces were not autonomous; political figures outside the departments began to make key decisions regarding promotions, assignments, and disciplinary matters.[48]

The chief executive in a police agency must become politically astute by becoming familiar with the governing board's priorities for the administration of law enforcement, learning of sensitive policy areas and communicating with the mayor so as not inadvertently to step out of line. Perhaps the most extensive area of collaboration and consultation occurs during the development of the budget, when the police administration must be especially attuned to the service and enforcement priorities set by the governing board.[49] Often, it is here that the police executive can be caught in the middle, between subordinate officers and citizens on the one side and the governing board on the other.

In sum, the prevailing policing style is not determined explicitly by the community. Police work is carried out under the influence of a political culture, which involves shared expectations as to how governmental objectives will be determined and met. James Q. Wilson felt, however, that in overall, day-to-day police work, a "zone of indifference" is created, within which the police are free to act as they see fit.[50]

✧ POLITICS AND THE JUDICIARY

Our courts, contrary to what many may believe, do not and have never operated independently. Our federal, state, and local court systems, as well as their rules and technical elements, were born out of political conflict. Political interest groups interact with the courts, because courts have considerable influence over the distribution of goods and services. Courts are also dependent on legislatures for staffing, equipment, facilities, and other resources, and depend on political connections for day-to-day operations, such as sending people to probation offices or mental health clinics.

Nor are judges independent. It *does* matter to the citizenry who sits on the bench, and whether theirs is a city with a "traditional" political system or one practicing "good government."[51] It will be seen below that our courts do not simply render passive decisions; rather, they are "the most terrifying governmental force in the United States," according to a justice of the West Virginia Supreme Court.[52]

Should judges be involved in politics? As indicated in the beginning of this chapter, politics and criminal justice are almost inseparable; and as a state supreme court justice put it, "In every state a judge needs to be some kind of politician."[53] Indeed, one study of federal and state supreme court justices found that political party affiliation was a better predictor of judicial decisions than was ethnic background.[54] For many years attorneys, their professional associations, many judges, and reform-minded laypersons have advocated taking the selection process of judges out of politics. One popular method of doing so is the Missouri Plan, discussed in Chapter 8.[55] Another selection method, which reformers feel is less ideal, is the use of truly nonpartisan elections.

To test whether urban politics had any significant effect on judicial behavior and, consequently, criminal defendants, Martin Levin examined two very different political climates, Pittsburgh and Minneapolis. Pittsburgh had a traditional political system, with a formally partisan city government. The Democratic Party dominated Pittsburgh politics during the study, and the public had little appetite for taking judges "out of" politics; indeed, positions on the courts were viewed as sources of rewards for political workers. Judges' career paths reflected the dominance of the party and the limited influence of the bar association in judicial selection. Minneapolis, conversely, had a formally nonpartisan and a structurally fragmented city government; political parties were loosely organized, undisciplined, and weak. The public had a negative feeling toward partisanship.[56]

On the whole, sentencing decisions of judges were more lenient in Pittsburgh than in Minneapolis. Both white and black defendants received probation more frequently and shorter prison terms in Pittsburgh. Minneapolis judges tended to be more oriented toward "society" and its needs and protection, with little feeling of "closeness" to the defendant. Most nonjury trials were formal and unabbreviated in Minneapolis, where prisons were used for punishment and deterrence. Succinctly, Pittsburgh judges differed from their counterpart in Minneapolis in all of these, and many other respects. The behavior of both cities' judges appears to be the indirect product of the political systems in which they work. These systems influenced judicial selection, which led to different patterns of socialization and recruitment that in turn influenced the judges' views and decision-making processes.[57]

✧ JURIES AND POLITICS

As Levin's comparative study of Pittsburgh and Minneapolis demonstrated, local political cultures, in addition to those at the state and federal levels, can exert tremendous influence over criminal justice operations. Another interesting area where politics is seemingly at work is in the jury room, because, as Alexis de Tocqueville observed in his probe of the United States in 1946, "the jury is, above all, a political institution and it must be regarded in this light in order to be duly appreciated."[58]

Attitudes toward crime and criminals are complex, but often they come down to the person sitting in the jury box and whether that person is ideologically liberal or conservative. What is at stake are the competing demands of two often-cited value systems: the due process model of justice, which supports protecting the innocent, and that of crime control, which is geared to maintain social order. Extreme liberals, committed to the presumption of innocence, need overwhelming proof in order to convict; they have tremendous compassion for the accused. Extreme conservatives, on the other hand, will convict without hesitation; they are angry about the breakdown in law and order, damage to victims, and the wickedness of offenders.[59]

Most people—and jurors—fall somewhere in between these two political or ideological extremes. However, there are real differences in the way jurors view the evidence and reach their conclusions. These differences are carried with them into the jury room. The Bronx in New York City is a good example of this and how local political culture affects verdicts. Bronx juries are as liberal as anywhere in the country; their verdicts say so.[60] The largesse of juries has led lawyers to refer routinely to the Bronx as "plaintiff city," and author Tom Wolfe wrote in *Bonfire of the Vanities* that "in a civil case a Bronx jury is a vehicle for redistributing the wealth."[61]

Although the nation has taken a conservative turn of late, there is still a balance between the liberal and conservative sentiment among juries from place to place. Florida is a good example, where counties and juries have been identified as very conservative, conservative, and moderate. In California, people in three adjacent counties vary: Los Angeles is moderate, San Diego is conservative, and Orange County is ultraconservative; jury verdicts match the prevailing ideology exactly.[62] Another correlation between cities and juries is possible: Large cities are almost always more liberal, and by and large the conviction rates in big cities is lower than that in less populated areas.[63]

The day after President Reagan was shot, a *New York Daily News* reporter, Earl Caldwell, was covering the courthouse beat. He sensed something was in the air, a feeling that jurors and prospective jurors were deeply affected by John Hinckley's actions. Caldwell sat in on a murder trial that day, later writing: "In the courtroom…it was different. The jurors make decisions. They have the power to act, and…the talk in the courtroom was that it was the worst possible time for a case involving killing and a gun to be put in the hands of the jury."[64]

In summary, as with judges, jurors are also affected by the political climate in which they operate. Local political cultures vary enormously, from somewhat liberal to conservative to very conservative. Jury behavior reflects these differences.[65]

✧ POLITICS IN CORRECTIONS

In the corrections chapters, we necessarily dealt at some length with politics, particularly how prisons and their administrators have historically been strongly influenced by legislators as well as the community; this is especially true in the long-standing treatment versus custody debate and other issues, such as programming for inmates, funding, new construction, and so on. However, corrections has additional political involvement at the state and local levels.

One might suspect that the controlling authority over the operations of a state prison system is the governor, and that governors might even take a "hands-on" approach to overseeing prisons from time to time. However, a national study learned that governors typically lack power and influence. Top administrators perceived legislators as having more impact and influence on their agencies than did their governors.[66] Other practitioners have agreed with that finding, concluding that governors do not run state bureaucracies; they simply are not administrators. In addition, one researcher found that governors in many states expect prisons to be administered by those like themselves, individuals having political, not professional, credentials.[67]

In addition, others have determined that state officials at the executive level traditionally avoid prison administration. David Rothman went so far as to state that a 200-year-old agreement exists between state executives and prison officials, whereby administrators enjoy autonomy as long as there is no adverse publicity due to riots, escapes, deaths, or other unpopular events.[68]

However, history aside, governors (as we saw with judges) occasionally become involved in prison administration. Sometimes this involvement is helpful, sometimes it is not. Governor James R. Thompson guided a major prison expansion in Illinois and formed his own task force on crowding to protect the future of the system under construction.[69] In contrast, Governor George Wallace's resistance to court-ordered prison reform was notorious. The federal courts, Wallace charged, were "making country clubs or hotels out of our prison."[70] Similarly, the governor of New Mexico hampered efforts by the state attorney general to settle an ACLU suit and thereby to improve prison conditions; two years later, the New Mexico State Penitentiary erupted in a horrible riot, resulting in 33 people dead and $20 million in damages.[71]

✦ UNIONIZATION AND JOB ACTIONS

One of the major issues in justice administration during the past two decades has been that of collective bargaining. The unionization of the rank and file has, in the minds of many, improved working conditions for criminal justice employees; for others, labor relations have suffered tremendously since the advent of collective bargaining, pitting the administration against the line officers and generally creating an atmosphere of distrust and enmity.

Probably as a result of their difficult working conditions, as well as traditionally low salary and benefits packages, police and corrections groups have elected to band together within their disciplines to fight for improvement. It is probably also accurate to say that a major force in the development of unionization of these two groups was the authoritarian, unilateral, and "do as I say, not as I do," management style that characterized many police and prison administrators of the past.

✧ THE MOVEMENT BEGINS: LAW ENFORCEMENT

The first campaign to organize the police started shortly after World War I, when the American Federation of Labor (AFL) reversed a long-standing policy and issued charters to police unions in Boston, Washington, D.C., and about 30 other cities. August Vollmer and many other police chiefs promptly condemned this move, insisting that police officers had no more right to unionize than did military personnel. However, many police officers were suffering from the rapid inflationary rate following the outbreak of the war and felt that if their chiefs could not get them long-overdue pay raises, then perhaps unions could. Capitalizing on their sentiments, the fledgling unions signed about 60 percent of all officers in Washington, 75 percent in Boston, and a similar proportion in other cities.[72]

The unions' success was short-lived, however. The Boston police commissioner refused to recognize the union, forbade officers to join it, and filed charges against several union officials. Shortly thereafter, on September 9, 1919, the Boston police initiated the famous strike of three days' duration, causing major riots and a furor against the police all across the nation; nine rioters were killed and 23 were seriously injured. During the strike, Massachusetts Governor Calvin Coolidge uttered his now-famous quote: "There is no right to strike against the public safety by anybody, anywhere, anytime."

During World War II, however, the effort was reignited. Unions issued charters to a few dozen locals all over the country and sent in organizers to help enlist the rank and file. Most police chiefs continued speaking out against unionization, but their subordinates were moved by the thousands to join, sensing the advantage in having unions press for higher wages and benefits.[73] But in a series of rulings the courts upheld the right of police authorities to ban police unions.

The unions were survived in the early 1950s by many benevolent and fraternal organizations of police. Some were patrolmen's benevolent associations (PBAs), like those formed in New York, Chicago, and Washington, while others were fraternal orders of police (FOPs). During the late 1950s and early 1960s a new group of rank-and-file association leaders came into power. They were more vocal in articulating their demands. Soon a majority of the rank-and-file vocally supported higher salaries and pensions, free legal aid, low-cost insurance, and other services. For the first time, rank-and-file organizations were legally able to insist that their administrators sit down at the bargaining table.[74]

During the past 15 years the unionization of the police has continued to flourish, becoming what Samuel Walker has called a "hidden revolution." Today nearly three-fourths of all American police officers hold membership in unions.[75] The International Conference of Police Associations (ICPA) is the largest organization, with more than 100 local and state units representing more than 200,000 officers.[76] George Cole attributed this dramatic rise in union membership to several factors: job dissatisfaction, the belief that the public is hostile to police needs, and an influx of younger officers who hold less traditional views on relations between officers and the department hierarchy.[77]

With some justification, administrators fear that their control over the organization will be concomitantly reduced as union power increases and that traditional matters within their scope, such as promotion and transfer of personnel, will become enmeshed in union negotiations. And, of course, there is always the specter of police job actions, including work slowdown, work stoppage (strikes or blue flu), work speedup, or votes of confidence. The threat of a police work stoppage is real, as there were a number of major strikes by police during the mid-1970s. Several guidelines exist to prevent police strikes: police and city administrators should work toward developing an atmosphere of trust and cooperation; an effective internal communications system must be developed in police agencies and between the police administrator, the city administration and the union leaders; training must be provided police management, city administration and union leaders in the area of negotiation; and "eleventh-hour" bargaining and negotiation must be eliminated.[78]

✧ CORRECTIONS FOLLOWS THE PRECEDENT

It is sometimes assumed that the movement to unionize correctional officers was a response to the increased power given inmates. While both occurred at about the same time, unionization grew out of a general impetus toward public employee organization (certainly fostered by the strong drive by the police, in the 1950s and 1960s). Correctional officers (COs) were probably the last group of public workers to organize. Currently, over half the states have correctional unions. Like the police, most CO unions are prohibited by law from striking; only seven states legally recognize the right to strike.[79]

The results of correctional unionization are mixed. On the positive side, unions have helped improve working conditions. And as opposed to the conventional union concern of salary and benefits, COs are more concerned with secure and safe working conditions—keeping inmates in their place and neutralizing gains made in the individual rights of inmates. COs see unions as a way to return to the paternalistic model of authority, displacing the competitive model. In most institutions, CO unions seek to limit the power of inmates at every turn. But inmates also want safe and secure living conditions; thus inmates often privately support the demands of the unions.[80] CO unions also exert pressure on administration concerning prison policy. For example, the union at Walla Walla, Washington, put pressure on the warden to close the workshop run by the Bikers Club, because they were making weapons there while repairing their motorcycles.[81]

The biggest problem facing CO unions is their potential lawlessness. As most such unions cannot legally strike, they are limited in their collective power against administrators. Most of the union's bargaining weapons are illegal. Unlawful strikes occur with some frequency, however. The most infamous strike action, on a plane with the Boston police strike of 1919, was in New York State in 1979, when 7000 correctional workers simultaneously struck the state's 33 prisons. The National Guard was called in to staff the prisons at a cost of $1 million per day. A court found the union in violation of the law, heavily fined the union for failing to return to work, and jailed union leaders for contempt of court.[82] The strike ended 17 days after it began; the guards gained very few concessions, and salary gains did not offset fines imposed on the strikers.[83]

Illegal strikes by COs have not been effective for several reasons. First, these workers are unlikely to obtain public sympathy. Furthermore, a strike does not actually strike down the industry; the presence of the National Guard greatly strengthens the bargaining position of the state. COs will also lose face if overseers are appointed by the court in the aftermath of a strike to prevent CO retaliation against nonsupportive inmates. Further tension is created when prison administrators impose disciplinary actions against COs who struck.[84] And because not all COs belong to the union, there will probably be conflict between co-workers prior to and following the strike.

As corrections unions push to become a major instrument of institutional policy, the warden's troubles will increase. Wardens today must worry about CO lawlessness as well as that of inmates. Many resign or seek early retirement as a result.[85]

✦ UNIONIZATION IN THE COURTS

The movement to exercise the right to bargain collectively, especially when compared with law enforcement and corrections, has been very rare in the courts, occurring on a random, localized basis (however, there are unified court systems where court personnel are organized statewide, as in Hawaii). Many states adhere generally to model legislation on public employee relation commissions, which provide mediation and fact-finding services and make determinations of unfair labor practices. On occasion, these commissions are called upon to make decisions that greatly affect the management authority of the judiciary over its personnel.

However, where a collective bargaining unit exists in a court system, the process has all of the basic elements found in any such circumstance: (1) recognition (the employing court recognizes that henceforth employees will be represented by their chosen agent); (2) negotiation (there are established methods for arriving at a collective bargaining agreement, breaking deadlocks, ratifying contracts, etc); and (3) contract administration (the day-to-day management of a court is accomplished within the framework of the labor contract).[86]

Summary

Working in a justice-oriented capacity has never been easy. However, the issues facing today's practitioners have probably never been more difficult, for many of the weighty issues and problems discussed in this and earlier chapters. These issues affect not only those "wearing the gold badge," but certainly filter down to the grass-roots workers as well.

These are difficult, litigious, and political times for the justice system, where one act of negligence can mean financial disaster for an individual, a supervisor, or even an entire community. And to a greater extent, at times the "tail is wagging the dog" in the area of labor relations, but that is largely an outgrowth of the authoritarian methods used by administrators of the past. Clearly, administrators must have the mettle to cope with such matters on a daily basis, for surely that mettle will often be tested.

Questions for Review

1. Is the justice system "racist"? (In formulating your response, highlight findings that indicate that it is, along with those demonstrating that it is not, as well as the Rand findings.)
2. Analyze the potential for civil liability for criminal justice employees, especially for police and corrections personnel.
3. How are the three justice system components affected by politics? Will they ever be wholly extricated from political influence? Defend your views.
4. Trace the development of unionism in criminal justice. Explain why this rapid development occurred and what appears to be the future of unionism in criminal justice.

For Further Reading

GEORGE F. COLE (ED.), *Criminal Justice: Law and Politics* (6th ed.). Belmont, Calif.: Wadsworth, 1993.

VICTOR E. KAPPELER, *Critical Issues in Police Civil Liability.* Prospect Heights, Ill.: Waveland Press, 1993.

VICTOR E. KAPPELER, MARK BLUMBERG, and GARY W. POTTER, *The Mythology of Crime and Criminal Justice.* Prospect Heights, Ill.: Waveland Press, 1993.

HARRY W. MORE, JR., *Critical Issues in Law Enforcement.* Cincinnati, Ohio: Anderson, 1985.

Richard Neely, *Why Courts Don't Work*. New York: McGraw-Hill, 1983.

William Wilbanks, *The Myth of a Racist Criminal Justice System*. Monterey, Calif.: Brooks/Cole, 1987.

James Q. Wilson, *Thinking About Crime* (rev. ed.). New York: Basic Books, 1985.

Notes

1. Gary Kleck, "Racial Discrimination in Criminal Sentencing: A Critical Evaluation of the Evidence with Additional Data on the Death Penalty," *American Sociological Review* 46 (1981):783–405.

2. William Wilbanks, *The Myth of a Racist Criminal Justice System* (Belmont, Calif.: Wadsworth, 1987).

3. Coramae Richey Mann, "Racism in the Criminal Justice System: Two Sides of a Controversy," *Criminal Justice Research Bulletin* (Huntsville, Tex.: Sam Houston State University) 3 (1987):1.

4. *Ibid.*, p. 6.

5. *Ibid.*, pp. 149–171.

6. Edwin H. Sutherland and Donald R. Cressey, *Criminology* (9th ed.) (Philadelphia: J. B. Lippincott, 1974), p. 133.

7. Edwin M. Lemert and Judy Rosebert, "The Administration of Justice to Minority Groups in Los Angeles County," *University of California Publications in Culture and Society* 2 (1948):1–28; Thorsten Sellin, "Race Prejudice in the Administration of Justice," *American Journal of Sociology* 41 (September 1935):212–217; Sidney Alexrad, "Negro and White Male Institutionalized Delinquents," *American Journal of Sociology* 57 (May 1952):569–574; Nathan Goldman, *The Differential Selection of Juvenile Offenders for Court Appearance* (New York: National Council on Crime and Delinquency, 1963); Irving Pilavin and Scott Briar, "Police Encounters with Juveniles," *American Journal of Sociology* 70 (September 1964):206–214; Robert M. Terry, "The Screening of Juvenile Offenders," *Journal of Criminal Law, Criminology, and Police Science* 58 (June 1967):173–181; see also Ramsey Clark, *Crime in America* (New York: Simon & Schuster, 1970), p. 51: "Negroes are arrested more frequently and on less evidence than whites and are more often victims of mass or sweep arrests"; and see Donald Taft, *Criminology* (3d ed.) (New York: Macmillan, 1956).

8. In Janice C. Simpson, "White Defendants, Black Defendants," *Time* (August 8, 1988):17.

9. *Ibid.*

10. Coramae Richey Mann, "Racism in the Criminal Justice System: Two Sides of a Controversy."

11. U.S. Department of Justice, Bureau of Justice Statistics Bulletin, *Capital Punishment, 1991* (Washington, D.C.: Author, October 1992), p. 1.

12. Marvin E. Wolfgang, Arlene Kelly, and Hans C. Nolde, "Comparisons of the Executed and the Commuted among Admissions to Death Row," *Journal of Criminal Law, Criminology, and Police Science* 53 (September 1962):301–311.

13. David Baldus, Charles Pulaski, and George Woodworth, "Comparative Review of Death Sentences: An Empirical Study of the Georgia Experience," *Journal of Criminal Law and Criminology* 74 (1983):661–725; Raymond Paternoster, "Race of Victim and Location of Crime: The Decision to Seek the Death Penalty in South Carolina," *Journal*

of *Criminal Law and Criminology* 74 (1983):754–788; Raymond Paternoster, "Prosecutorial Discretion in Requesting the Death Penalty: A Case of Victim-Based Racial Discrimination," *Law and Society Review* 18 (1984):437–478; Samuel Gross and Robert Mauro, "Patterns of Death: An Analysis of Racial Disparities in Capital Sentencing and Homicide Victimization," *Stanford Law Review* 37 (1984):27–120.

14. 107 S.Ct. 1756 (1987).

15. Quoted in *Gannett Suburban Newspapers* (September 30, 1991): A11.

16. James Q. Wilson, *Thinking about Crime* (New York: Vintage Books, 1983), p. 190.

17. Joan Petersilia, "Racial Disparities in the Criminal Justice System: Executive Summary of Rand Institute Study, 1983," in Daniel Georges-Abeyle (ed.), *The Criminal Justice System and Blacks* (New York: Clark Boardman Company, 1984), pp. 225–258.

18. *Ibid.*, p. 243.

19. *Ibid.*, p. 230.

20. *Ibid.*, pp. 240–241.

21. *Ibid.*, pp. 241–242.

22. *Ibid.*, pp. 231, 249.

23. William Wilbanks, *The Myth of a Racist Criminal Justice System*, pp. 147–148.

24. Per *Alabama v. Pugh*, 438 U.S. 781 (1978).

25. Charles R. Swanson, Leonard Territo, and Robert W. Taylor, *Police Administration* (3d ed.). (New York: Macmillan, 1993), p. 411.

26. *Monroe v. Pape*, 365 U.S. 167, 81 S.Ct. 473 (1961).

27. Wayne W. Schmidt, "Section 1983 and the Changing Face of Police Management," in William A. Geller (ed.), *Police Leadership in America: Crisis and Opportunity* (New York: Praeger, 1985), pp. 226–236.

28. 436 U.S. 658 7 (1978).

29. 610 F.2d 693 (10th Cir., 1979).

30. 516 F.Supp. 1355 (W.D. Tenn., 1981).

31. *Brandon v. Holt*, 469 U.S. 464, 105 S.Ct. 873 (1985).

32. See, for example, *Black v. Stephens*, 662 F.2d 181 (1991).

33. U.S. Department of Justice, Bureau of Justice Statistics Bulletin, *Jail Inmates, 1990* (Washington, D.C.: U.S. Government Printing Office, 1991), p. 4.

34. U.S. Department of Justice, Bureau of Justice Statistics Special Report, *Population Density in Local Jails, 1988*, (Washington, D.C.: U.S. Government Printing Office, 1989), p. 9.

35. *Thomas v. Williams*, 124 S.E.2d 409 (Ga. App. 1962).

36. Victor E. Kappeler and Rolando V. delCarmen, "Avoiding Police Liability for Negligent Failure to Prevent Suicide," *The Police Chief* (August 1991):53–59.

37. *Ibid.*, p. 53.

38. *Thomas v. Williams*.

39. *Kanayurak v. North Slope Borough*, 677 P.2d 892 (Alaska 1984).

40. *City of Belen v. Harrell*, 603 P.2d 711 (N.M. 1979).

41. *Hake v. Manchester Township*, 486 A.2d 836 (N.J. 1985).

42. *Davis v. City of Detroit*, 386 N.W.2d 169 (Mich. App. 1986).

43. *Hickey v. Zezulka*, 443 N.W.2d (180 (Mich. App. 1989).

44. *Hake v. Manchester Township*.

45. George F. Cole, *The American System of Criminal Justice* (6th ed.) (Pacific Grove, Calif.: Brooks/Cole, 1992), p. 34.

46. Richard Brzeczek, "Chief–Mayor Relations: The View from the Chief's Chair," in William A. Geller (ed.), *Police Leadership in America: Crisis and Opportunity*, pp. 48–55.

47. George Cole, *The American System of Criminal Justice* (5th ed.), p. 261.

48. James F. Richardson, *Urban Police in the United States* (Port Washington, N.Y.: Kennikat Press, 1974), pp. 55–58.

49. Donald M. Fraser, "Politics and Police Leadership: The View from City Hall," in William A. Geller (ed.), *Police Leadership in America: Crisis and Opportunity*, pp. 43–44.

50. James Q. Wilson, *Varieties of Police Behavior* (Cambridge, Mass.: Harvard University Press, 1968.

51. Martin A. Levin, "Urban Politics and Policy Outcomes: The Criminal Courts," in George F. Cole (ed.), *Criminal Justice: Law and Politics* (6th ed.) (Belmont, Calif.: Wadsworth, 1993), pp. 348–367.

52. Richard Neely, *Why Courts Don't Work* (New York: McGraw-Hill, 1983), p. 9.

53. *Ibid.*, p. 41.

54. See Robert A. Carp and C. K. Rowland, *Policymaking and Politics in the Federal District Courts* (Knoxville, Tenn.: University of Tennessee Press, 1983), p. 27.

55. See Kathleen Maguire, Ann L. Pastore, and Timothy J. Flanagan (eds.), *Sourcebook of Criminal Justice Statistics 1992*. U.S. Department of Justice, Bureau of Justice Statistics (Washington, D.C.: U.S. Government Printing Office, 1993), pp. 84, 87–88.

56. Martin A. Levin, "Urban Politics and Judicial Behavior," in Sheldon Goldman and Austin Sarat (eds.), *American Court Systems: Readings in Judicial Process and Behavior* (San Francisco: W. H. Freeman, 1978), pp. 338–347.

57. *Ibid.*, pp. 340–344.

58. In Henry Reeve (ed.), *Democracy in America*, Vol. I (New York: Alfred A. Knopf, 1946), p. 282.

59. James P. Levine, *Juries and Politics* (Pacific Grove, Calif.: Brooks/Cole, 1992), pp. 119–120.

60. Sam Roberts, "On Bronx Juries, Minority Groups Find Their Peers," *The New York Times* (April 19, 1988):B1; John Kifner, "Bronx Juries, a Defense Dream, a Prosecutor's Nightmare," *The New York Times* (December 5, 1988):B1.

61. Tom Wolfe, *Bonfire of the Vanities* (New York: Farrar, Strauss, 1987), p. 392.

62. James P. Levine, *Juries and Politics*, pp. 128–129.

63. James Levine, "Using Jury Verdict Forecasts in Criminal Defense Strategy," *Judicature* 66 (May 1983):460–461.

64. Earl Caldwell, "In Our Courtrooms, .22 Aims Bulletins at Minds of Jurors," *New York Daily News* (April 1, 1981):6.

65. James P. Levine, *Juries and Politics*, p. 127.

66. Glen Abney and Thomas P. Lauth, "The Governor as a Chief Administrator," *Public Administration Review* 43 (1983):40–48.

67. Richard McGee, *Prisons and Politics* (Lexington, Mass.: Lexington Books, 1981).

68. David Rothman, *Conscience and Convenience: The Asylum and Its Alternatives in Progressive America* (Boston: Little, Brown, 1980).

69. James R. Thompson, "Illinois' Response to the Problem of Prison Crowding," *University of Illinois Law Review* 2 (1984):203–206.

70. Charles Prigmore and R. T. Crow, "Is the Court Remaking the American Prison System?" *Federal Probation* 40 (June 1976):8–15.

71. Alvin Bronstein, "Prisoners and Their Endangered Rights," *Prison Journal* 65 (1985):3–17.

72. W. Clinton Terry III, *Policing Society: An Occupational View* (New York: Wiley, 1985), p. 168.

73. *Ibid.*, p. 168.

74. *Ibid.*, pp. 170–171.

75. Samuel Walker, *The Police in America: An Introduction* (2nd ed.) (New York: McGraw-Hill, 1993), p. 372.

76. George F. Cole, *The American System of Criminal Justice* (6th ed.) (Pacific Grove, Calif.: Brooks/Cole, 1992), p. 320.

77. *Ibid.*, p. 318.

78. Harry W. More, Jr. (ed.), *Critical Issues in Law Enforcement* (4th ed.) (Cincinnati, Ohio: Anderson, 1985), pp. 155–161.

79. Scott Christianson, "How Unions Affect Prison Administration," *Criminal Law Bulletin* 15 (1979):238–247.

80. Richard Hawkins and Geoffrey P. Alpert, *American Prison Systems: Punishment and Justice* (Englewood Cliffs, N.J.: Prentice Hall, 1989), p. 354.

81. *Ibid.*, p. 356.

82. James B. Jacobs, *New Perspectives on Prisons and Imprisonment* (Ithaca, N.Y.: Cornell University Press, 1983), p. 153.

83. *Ibid.*, pp. 154–155.

84. *Ibid.*, p. 156.

85. Richard Hawkins and Geoffrey P. Alpert, *American Prison Systems: Punishment and Justice*, p. 357.

86. U.S. Department of Justice, National Institute of Law Enforcement and Criminal Justice, Trial Court Management Series, *Personnel Management* (Washington, D.C.: U.S. Government Printing Office, 1979), pp. 42–47.

Financial Administration 16

How pleasant it is to have money, heigh ho!
How pleasant it is to have money.
> —Arthur H. Clough

Money is like muck, not good except it be
spread.
> —Francis Bacon

✦ INTRODUCTION

Another administrative practice—problematical to many—that spans the justice system is financial administration. The red-letter importance of financial administration for this country is unquestionable. Today's news stories note the arrest and indictment of an official for embezzling public funds, the defeat or passage of a bond referendum to construct a jail or prison, an auditor's report that describes the department's accounting procedures for handling funds for informants and narcotics purchases, or the closing of a school or precinct station because funds were no longer available for operation.[1]

Budgets make the administrative world go round; planning, organizing, directing, and all other administrative functions revolve around this activity. There would be no need for planning if unlimited funds were available. Indeed, the mark of a good manager is often the ability to obtain and expend necessary financial resources. As Frederick Mosher observed, "Not least among the qualifications of an administrator is [one's] ability as a tactician and gladiator in the budget process."[2] Unfortunately, many administrators (and others of us with personal checking accounts) loathe having to work with numbers, make projections, and keep track all year of the budget status. In a word, many of us detest math or even anything involving numbers. The educators' term for those people who are numerically illiterate is "innumeracy."

Earl Babbie [3] jokingly attributed this "congenital math deficiency syndrome" to our early exposure in high school to "Mathematical Marvin," the mathematical genius who was not very athletic, usually wore glasses, and was not the envy of the "cool" crowd. Babbie's point is that many of us have formed a subconscious association between mathematical proficiency and Marvin's unenviable characteristics. However, as one needs to be responsible in keeping a personal checking account balanced so as to avoid legal and personal difficulties, so must the agency administrator be a responsible steward with the public's funds. This is an indispensable part of administration.

Therefore, we must discuss this important management task. This chapter, what some might call "the basics of 'bean counting,'" covers some of the fundamental elements of knowing how to control fiscal resources. It is not intended to prepare the reader to be an expert on fiscal management; rather, it will provide an overview of some of the basic methods and issues surrounding financial administration. There are three component parts to financial administration discussed here: auditing, accounting, and budgeting. We focus most heavily on the latter. Specifically included are discussions of budget definitions and uses; the influence of politics and fiscal realities in budgeting, which often leads to constricted financial conditions for the organization; the several elements of the budget, including formulation, approval, execution, and audit; budget formats; and some strategies for augmenting criminal justice budgets in tight fiscal times.

✦ A WORKING DEFINITION OF BUDGET

The word *budget* is derived from the old French *bougette*, meaning a small leather bag or wallet. Initially, it referred to the leather bag in which the chancellor of the exchequer carried the documents to English Parliament stating the government's needs and resources.[4] Later, it came to mean the documents themselves. Currently, "budget" has been defined in many ways, including a plan stated in financial terms, an estimate of future expenditures, an asking price, a policy statement, the translation of financial resources into human purposes, and a contract between those who appropriate the funds and those who spend them.[5] To some extent, all of these uses of the term are true.

The budget is a management tool, a process, and a political instrument. It is a "comprehensive plan, expressed in financial terms, by which a program is operated for a given period. It includes (1) the services, activities, and projects comprising the program; (2) the resultant expenditure requirements; and (3) the resources usable for their support.[6] It is "a plan or schedule adjusting expenses during a certain period to the estimated income for that period."[7] Lester Bittel added that "a budget is, literally, a financial standard for a particular operation, activity, program, or department. Its data is presented in numerical form, mainly in dollars...to be spent for a particular purpose—over a specified period of time. Budgets are derived from planning goals and forecasts."[8]

Although that is certainly an apt definition, there are some writers who warn that budgets contain an inherently irrational process: "Budgets are based on little more than the past and some guesses. Yet they are treated with reverence by accountants and by incompetent chief executive officers. This can lead to all sorts of unseemly behavior...Accountants can be smarter than anybody else or more ambitious or both, but essentially they are bean counters. Their job is to serve the operations. They can't run the ship."[9]

Budgets may also be defined as operating and capital. An operating budget is usually for one year and is for items that have a short life expectancy, are consumed in the normal course of operations, or are reincurred each year. Included in operating budgets are batteries, paper, duplicating and telephone expenses, and salaries and fringe benefits.[10]

✦ A DIVERSION: EXIGENCY AND POLITICS

✧ "SLASHING TO THE BONE"

During the 1970s, financial assistance from the federal government increased the budgets of state and local units immensely. Federal agencies pumped billions of dollars into the criminal-justice coffers across the country, and much of the time the local matching funds amounted to a mere 5 percent of the total cost of a project. All justice administrators were required to do was complete an application for the funds.

This largesse was discontinued, however, in the 1980s, with the economic downturn and the frank realization that all of these monies had done little to reverse increases in crime. With the cessation of federal assistance, state and local governments had to make some very tough choices, some of which have involved job layoffs and reduced governmental services. The years 1991 and 1992 wrought even greater financial havoc with government revenues all across the country. Because of the deep national recession there were more actual and threatened layoffs of criminal justice personnel, including police officers, than in recent memory. Early 1992 provided another example of how an unplanned, nonbudgeted event can wreak chaos with an operating budget—the Los Angeles riots in the aftermath of the Rodney King verdict. Overtime costs were nearly $138 million.

Historically, few occupations afforded a level of job protection like that found in criminal justice organizations, but today that is not necessarily the case. For example, following are some budget-related dilemmas taken from news items during the country's deep recession:

◊ The New York mayor announced that he expected to lay off 3600 police officers in an attempt to close an expected budget gap of $2.6 billion over an 18-month period,[11] and Massachusetts froze hiring new state troopers, while existing troopers had to forego pay raises.[12]

Detroit planned to lay off 300 police officers,[13] and the Teterboro, New Jersey, city manager proposed eliminating the eight-member, half million dollar per year police department altogether.[14] A number of police unions across the country were opposing police layoffs as too dangerous for their communities.

◊ District of Columbia Metropolitan police reached an impasse in contract talks; over 1000 officers are eligible for retirement and the city risks losing more because of a three-year-old pay freeze. District officials cited a $400 million budget deficit as the main obstacle to reaching an agreement.[15]

◊ The Alabama corrections commissioner stated that the agency will lay off 468 employees and close two detention facilities unless legislators provide $13 million in funds. Lawyers seeking an injunction against lay-offs argue that the staff reductions may result in increased prison violence. This attempted layoff followed the furloughs of 300 correctional employees and the closing of a prison in 1991.[16]

◊ New Orleans, Louisiana, police officials said that unless $4 million was added to the police department's budget, 24 recruits would not be sworn in and the agency could lose up to 75 officers through attrition.[17]

◊ The thousands of officers who worked 12-hour shifts for two weeks during the Los Angeles riots were paid with $16.7 million in federal funds. One sergeant said the overtime funds will mean an extra $2500 in pay. But many officers said they suffered from burnout and would rather have time off. Los Angeles received an additional $4.7 million to be divided among the fire, water and power, and general services department.[18]

◊ Delmar is one of the few cities in the country that straddles the borders of Maryland and Delaware. What any police department does, Delmar has to do twice. Its seven officers are trained and certified in both states, squad cars carry two radios, and officers must learn two sets of "10-codes." Each side of town has separate state and county laws, public officials, and budgets.[19]

◊ Arkansas officials reported that the prison system's new regional unit was near completion but there was not enough money to open it because $2.7 million in general taxes to pay for guards and operating costs was cut.[20]

◊ Township trustees voted to disband the St. Clair Police Department in Ohio, after residents refused to approve a 3-mill, five-year levy. Only a part-time police chief remained after the vote. The defeated levy would have provided $168,000 in revenues each year and provided around-the-clock coverage for the 20-square-mile township.[21]

◊ The New Jersey governor vetoed a bill that would have barred him from laying off state police troopers and corrections officers to deal with budget cuts proposed by legislators.[22]

◊ The mayor of Baltimore said a court order forcing the city to pay $3.3 million to police officers and teachers furloughed for two days in early 1992 could force layoffs. A judge ruled that budget constraints do not allow the city to break the terms of union contracts.[23]

In addition, there is always the potential fiscal turmoil caused by such unforeseen, unbudgeted occurrences as civil judgments against the government jurisdiction through negligence, excessive force, sexual harassment, or embezzlement by administrators (as occurred in the Detroit Police Department recently).

✧ LAW ENFORCEMENT: CUTTING SERVICES, ALTERING PRIORITIES

Because of its relatively high cost and overall proportion of total justice system funding, the police component has probably suffered the greatest budget "hits," but it has also done much to address those fiscal straits. Police executives are reassessing many services formerly provided free of charge, restricting some nonemergency services, and charging the public for others. For example, because the vast majority of burglar alarms are false (set off by weather conditions or, often, an embarrassed store owner), many police agencies no longer treat all such alarms as "hot," responding quickly to the scene. Increasingly, as in the affluent Meridian Township outside Lansing, Michigan, the first false alarm now costs residents or business owners $25, followed by $50 for the second, and up to $100 per call for the rest of the year. With only 33 officers in a community of 38,000, township officials recognized that the more than 1000 false alarm runs by police per year threatened to stretch the police budget dangerously thin.[24]

Another chronic problem involves people who lock themselves out of their cars. In Detroit, the police send a patrol car only if one is available, and in nearby Lansing, the police limit their assistance in such matters to providing names of available locksmiths who charge a fee. Another area of cost-cutting concerns the business community. In Newport News, Virginia, a study confirmed that numerous calls involved gas station patrons who sped away without paying. Even when the police caught the absconders, station managers often refused to follow up by pressing charges; the police were in effect unpaid bill collectors. Consequently, the department adopted a policy whereby a patrol car is dispatched to the scene only if the caller first agrees to press charges. And in Aurora, Colorado, the police now refuse to handle obscene telephone call complaints unless the telephone company has identified a suspect. The rationale is that private corporations can more easily pass along the costs to the consumer than can the public police.[25]

Financial management is clearly a part of politics. Anything done through government entails the expenditure of public funds.[26] Thus the single most important political statement that any unit of government makes in a given year is its budget. Essentially, the budget process confronts decision makers with the gambler's adage, "Put your money where your mouth is."[27] However, when demands placed on government increase while funds are declining or stable at best, the competition for funds is keener than usual, forcing justice agencies to make the best case for their own budget. The heads of other departments, if they are doing their jobs well, are also putting forth the best case possible for necessary appropriations. Special-interest groups, media, and politicians with their own views and priorities often engage in "arm twisting" during the budgeting process, along with the public (as when hearings are being held concerning whether to build a shelter for homeless persons); the political orientation of the budgeting process is inescapable.

✧ User Fees in the Courts?

With court dockets full and waiting time extended in our litigious society, some people advocate a rethinking of the courts' funding mechanisms. They recognize that users of the courts pay only nominal fees and costs (with tremendous sums of money often going to private attorneys), and feel we should reconsider the long-standing view that society is obligated to provide public resources for the court system. Furthermore, they maintain that because the courts now cost users so little, people tend to overuse the service; thus there are no natural incentives for reducing costs within the system. Charging user fees, it is asserted, would provide adequate funds for running an efficient court and reduce unnecessary litigation.[28]

Under the "users-pay-what-they-cost-the-courts" point of view, fees would be determined by such factors as use of court time, processing of papers, salaries of clerks, and time spent on the case by all court personnel, including judges. Criminal cases would be more difficult than civil cases to "cost out," but it is increasingly recognized that crime has an important economic dimension (especially with white-collar criminals); while criminal defendants with financial means would pay, those who are unable to pay would be excused from this responsibility.[29]

The problem is that this proposed system of court users' fees smacks of "rationing justice" to many people, and represents what a democratic system of justice is not intended to do: compelling suspected criminals and tortfeasors to bear the costs of defending their actions. In this camp, the words of highly respected Judge Learned Hand are often quoted: "If we are to keep our democracy, there must be one commandment: Thou shalt not ration justice."[30] This system, they add, would lead to justice on the basis of ability to pay.

✦ ELEMENTS OF A BUDGET

✧ The Budget Cycle

Administrators must also think in terms of a budget cycle, which in government (and, therefore, all public criminal justice agencies) is typically on a fiscal-year basis. Some states have a biennial budget cycle—their legislatures, such as those in Kentucky and Nevada—budget for a two-year period. Normally, however, the fiscal year is a 12-month period that may coincide with a calendar year or, more commonly, will run from July 1 through June 30 of the following year. However, the federal government's fiscal year is October 1 through September

30. Obviously. the budget cycle is important because it drives the development of the budget and determines when new monies become available.

The budget cycle consists of four sequential steps, repeated every year at about the same point in time: (1) budget formulation, (2) budget approval, (3) budget execution, and (4) auditing.

✦ BUDGET FORMULATION

Depending on the size and complexity of the organization, and the financial condition of the jurisdiction, budget formulation can be a relatively simple or exceedingly difficult task. However, formulating the budget is by far the most complicated stage of the budgeting process. The administrator must operate as if he or she had a crystal ball, anticipating overtime costs, increased costs (such as with gasoline, postage, maintenance contracts, etc.), and any major incidents or events that might arise. Certain assumptions can be made while formulating the budget, based on the previous year's budget. However, those assumptions are not necessarily a shortcut to the final product. As one observer noted, "Every expense you budget should be fully supported with the proper and most logical assumptions you can develop. Avoid simply estimating, which is the least supportable form of budgeting."[31] Another criminal justice administrator, discussing budget formulation, added that

> the most important ingredient for any budgeting process is planning. [Administrators] should approach the budget process from the planning standpoint of "How can I best reconcile the [criminal justice] needs of the community with the ability of my jurisdiction to finance them, and then relate those plans in a convincing manner to my governing body for proper financing and execution of programs?" After all, as budget review occurs, the document is taken apart and scrutinized piece by piece or line by line. This fragmentation approach contributes significantly to our inability to defend interrelated programs in an overall budget package.[32]

For the purpose of illustration, we will assume that a police department budget is being prepared in a city having a manager form of government. (An example of a *state's* budget preparation process is also presented below.)

Long before a criminal justice agency (or any other unit of local government) begins the preparation of its annual budget, the city manager and/or the staff of the city has done considerable legwork, including making revenue forecasts, considering how much (if any) of the current operating budget will be carried over into the next fiscal year, analyzing how the population of the jurisdiction will grow or shift (affecting demands for public services), and examining other priorities for the coming year. The city manager may also appear before the governing board to get a view of their fiscal priorities, spending levels, pay raises, new positions, programs, and so on. The city manager may then send a budget preparation manual to all department heads, outlining in a memorandum the general fiscal guidelines to be followed in their budget preparations.

Upon receipt of the city's budget preparation manual and the city manager's fiscal recommendations in a memorandum, the chief of police will have the planning and research unit (assuming a city large enough to have this level of specialization) prepare the internal budget calendar and an internal fiscal policy memorandum. Input may then be received from the union as well as lower supervisory personnel. Each bureau is then given responsibility for preparing its individual budget request. Table 16.1 shows an internal budget calendar for a large municipal police department.

In small police departments with little or no functional specialization, the chief may prepare the budget alone or with input from the other officers or the city finance officer. (Or, in some small agencies, chiefs and sheriffs may not even see their budget or assist in its preparation; because of tradition, politics, or even laziness, the administrator has abdicated control over the budget. This puts the agency in a precarious position indeed; it will have difficulty engaging

TABLE 16.1   BUDGET PREPARATION CALENDAR FOR A LARGE POLICE DEPARTMENT

What should be done	By whom	On these dates
Issue budget instructions and applicable forms	City administrator	November 1
Prepare and issue budget message, with instructions and applicable forms, to unit commanders	Chief of police	November 15
Develop unit budgets with appropriate justification and forward recommended budgets to planning and research unit	Unit commanders	February 1
Review of unit budget	Planning and research staff with unit commanders	March 1
Consolidation of unit budgets for presentation to chief of police	Planning and research unit	March 15
Review of consolidated recommended budget	Chief of police, planning and research staff, and unit commanders	March 30
Department approval of budget	Chief of police	April 15
Recommended budget forwarded to city administrator	Chief of police	April 20
Administrative review of recommended budget	City administrator and chief of police	April 30
Revised budget approval	City administrator	May 5
Budget document forwarded to city council	City administrator	May 10
Review of budget	Budget officer of city council	May 20
Presentation to council	City administrator and chief of police	June 1
Reported back to city administrator	City council	June 5
Review and resubmission to city council	City administrator and chief of police	June 10
Final action on police budget	City council	June 20

(*Source:* National Advisory Commission on Criminal Justice Standards and Goals, *Police* (Washington, D.C.: U.S. Government Printing Office, 1973), p. 137.)

in long-term planning and spending money productively for personnel and programs when the executive has to get prior approval from the governing body to even buy pencils and paper clips for the office.)

The planning and research unit then reviews the bureau budget requests for compliance with the budgeting instructions and the chief's and city manager's priorities. Eventually, a consolidated budget is developed for the entire police department and submitted to the chief, who may, in turn, meet with the planning and research unit and bureau commanders to discuss the budget. Personalities, politics, priorities, personal agendas, and other issues may need to be addressed; the chief may have to mediate disagreements concerning these matters, while sometimes rewarding "the loyal" and taking money from "the disloyal."[33] Programs, equipment requests, travel, personnel requests, or anything else in the draft budget may be deleted, cut back, enhanced, or assigned new priorities.

The budget is then presented to the city manager. At this point, the chief executive's reputation as a budget framer comes into play. If the chief is known to "pad" the budget heavily, the city manager is far more likely to cut the police department request than if the chief is known to be reasonable in the budget request, engage in innovative planning, and have a flexible approach to budget negotiations.

The city manager consolidates the police budget request with those from other municipal department heads, then meets with them individually to discuss their requests further. The city manager directs the city finance officer to make any necessary additions or cuts and then prepare a budget proposal for presentation to the governing body.

Hal Rubin [34] described how the $550 million budget for the California Highway Patrol is typically developed. According to the budget section, "It's an all-year and year-on-year process" that begins at the level of the 99 area commands, where budget requests originate. The requests are dealt with in one of three ways: (1) funded within the department's base budget, (2) disapproved, or (3) carried forward for review by CHP personnel.

At the division level, managers review the area requests, make needed adjustments, and submit a consolidated request to the budget section at headquarters. This section passes input from the field to individual section management staff (e.g., planning and analysis, personnel, training, communications, etc.) for review. Budget section staff meet with individual section management staff. Within two or three months the budget section identifies proposals for new funding that have department-wide impact and passes them on to the executive level.

The commisioner and aides review the figures along with those from other state departments and agree on a budget to submit to the governor. The governor submits this budget to the legislature, which acts on it and returns it to the governor for signature.

The courts have a similar budgetary process. In a large court, there may be five major procedures in the process: (1) developing an internal budgetary policy, (2) reviewing budget submissions, (3) developing a financial strategy, (4) budgetary presentation, and (5) budgetary monitoring. Figure 16.1 shows these major procedures and the other various steps in the process that are employed.

✦ BUDGET APPROVAL

With the city manager's proposed budget requests in hand, the governing board begins its deliberations on the citywide budget. The city manager may appear before the board to answer questions concerning the budget; individual department heads may be asked to appear also. Hints for being successful in getting monies approved and appropriated include the following:

1. Have a budget that is carefully justified.
2. Anticipate the environment of the budget hearing by reading news reports and understanding the priorities of the council members. Know what types of questions elected officials are likely to ask.
3. Determine which "public" will be at the police department's budget hearing and prepare accordingly. Public issues change from time to time; citizens who were outraged over traffic problems one year may be incensed with downtown streetwalkers the next.
4. Make good use of graphics in the form of pie charts and histograms, but be selective and do not go overboard. Short case studies of police successes are normal and add to graphics.
5. Rehearse and critique the presentation many times.
6. Be a political realist.[35]

After everyone requested has been heard from, the city council will give directions to the city manager. These directions may include further cuts in the budget, where certain funds or programs cut earlier by the manager are to be reinstated, and so on. The budget is then approved. It is fair to say that at this stage, budgeting is largely a legislative function that requires some legal action, as a special ordinance or resolution approving the budget is passed each year by the governing board.

As shown in several figures below, the budget approval process is clearly shown on the final budget form; different column heads indicate (1) the budget amount requested by the chief of police, (2) the amount recommended by the city manager, and (3) the amount finally approved by the city council.

✦ BUDGET EXECUTION

The third stage, execution, has several objectives: (1) to provide for an orderly manner of carrying out the police department's accomplishment of its budgeted

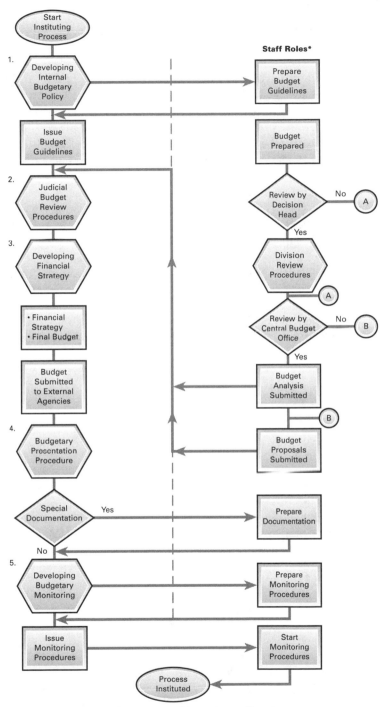

Figure 16.1 Steps in a judicial budgetary process.

* Particularly applicable in a large court, much less so in a small court.

objectives for the fiscal year, (2) to ensure that no financial obligations or commitments, other than those funded by the city council, are undertaken by the department, and (3) to provide a periodic accounting of the administrator's stewardship over the department's funds.[36]

The budget execution phase is an executive function and is a fairly detailed process of the establishment of some kind of fiscal control system, usually at the direction of the city or county manager. Periodic reports on accounts are an important element of budget control; they serve to reduce the likelihood of overspending and identify areas in which deficits are likely to occur due to such things as gasoline prices, extensive overtime, natural disasters, unplanned emergencies (such as riots), and so on. A periodic budget status report informs the administrator what percentage of the total budget has been expended to date (see Table 16.6).

The prudent administrator will normally attempt to be conservative with the budget until eight or nine months of the budget year are gone, "holding the line" on spending until most fiscal "crises" have hopefully passed. Then, after being frugal most of the fiscal year, he or she is able to expend monies more confidently; the rewards of being thrifty are now realized as the administrator and staff engage in legitimate "shopping sprees" for nonessential items. Again, unplanned incidents and natural disasters can wreak havoc with any budget, so this conservatism is normally the best course. However, during the fiscal year, fiscal officers may be keeping close watch on the manager's expenditure of funds.

✧ THE AUDIT

The word *audit* means the act of verifying something independently.[37] The basic rationale for the audit has been described by the Comptroller General of the United States as follows:

> Governments and agencies entrusted with public resources and the authority for applying them have a responsibility to render a full accounting of their activities. This accountability is inherent in the governmental process and is not always specifically identified by legislative provision. This governmental accountability should identify not only the object for which the public resources have been devoted but also the manner and effect of their application.[38]

The auditing function (also known as *postauditing*) is therefore also a legislative function whereby, after the close of each budget year, an audit is made of the year's expenditures to ensure that the agency is protected from accusations of misappropriation of funds. Succinctly, audits are concerned with three broad areas of accountability: *financial* (focusing on proper fiscal operations and reports of the justice agency), *management* (seeing if funds were utilized efficiently and economically), and *program* (determining whether the city council's goals and objectives were accomplished.)[39]

Also, the audit will determine whether or not funds were spent legally, the budgeted amount was exceeded, and the budgeting process proceeded in a legal manner. For example, auditors will look to see if there were any unauthorized transfers of funds between accounts, any grant funds were used improperly, computations were made accurately, disbursements were documented, and established competitive bidding procedures were followed.[40]

Justice administrators should welcome the auditors' helping hand, even though their final report may uncover weaknesses and embarrassing methods. The audit provides the opportunity to correct those weaknesses and deficiencies that might otherwise cause serious problems later.

✦ BUDGET FORMATS

There are three types of budgets in predominant use today: the line-item (or "object-of-expenditure") budget, the performance budget, and the program (or "results" or "outcomes") budget. Two additional types, the planning–programming–budgeting system (PPBS) and the zero-based budget (ZBB), are still discussed in the literature but are used to a lesser extent today. We review briefly these formats as well.

✧ THE LINE-ITEM BUDGET

The line-item or object budget is the most commonly used type of budget format and had its major expansion of use from about 1915 to just after World War II. It is the basic system on which all other systems rely because it affords control. It is so named because it breaks down the budget into about four or five major categories commonly used in government (e.g., personnel, equipment, contractual services, commodities, and capital outlay items); every amount of money requested, recommended, appropriated, and expended is associated with a particular item or class of items.[41] In addition, large budget categories will be broken down into smaller line-item budgets (in a police department, examples would include patrol, investigation, communications, or jail function). The line-item format fosters budgetary control because no item escapes scrutiny.[42] Tables 16.2 through 16.5 show line-items for actual budgets in police, courts, probation and parole, and state prison organizations, respectively. They each demonstrate the range of activities and funding needs of each agency. Note how the recent recession affected budgets and requests from year to year in many categories, resulting in severe cuts and even total elimination of items previously funded. Also note some of the ways in which administrators are deviating from the norm in order to save money (e.g., the police budget shows the department finding it cheaper to lease its patrol vehicles rather than buying a huge fleet of its own).

TABLE 16.2 POLICE OPERATING BUDGET IN A COMMUNITY OF 150,000 POPULATION

Description	FY 1992–93 Expenses	FY 1993–94 Expenses	FY 1994–95 Dept. Req.	City Manager	City Council
Salaries/wages					
Reg. salaries	14,315,764	14,392,639	16,221,148	16,221,148	16,221,148
Overtime	988,165	782,421	951,875	951,875	711,875
Severance pay	36,194	226,465	82,000	0	0
Holiday pay	395,952	591,158	698,958	698,958	698,958
Call-back pay	45,499	49,833	49,555	49,555	49,555
Subtotals	15,781,574	16,042,516	18,003,536	17,921,536	17,681,536
Employee benefits					
Retirement	3,345,566	3,485,888	4,069,521	4,069,521	4,069,521
Group ins.	1,256,663	1,467,406	1,752,718	1,752,718	1,752,718
Life ins.	43,797	53,164	117,590	117,396	117,396
Disability ins.	726,885	794,686	1,346,909	1,346,038	1,024,398
Uniform allowance	188,079	193,827	196,750	196,750	196,750
Medicare	77,730	80,868	100,058	99,739	99,739
Long-term dis.	11,583	21,974	48,517	48,517	48,517
Subtotals	5,650,303	6,097,813	7,583,546	7,630,679	7,309,039
Services and supplies					
Office supp.	62,357	49,292	51,485	51,485	51,485
Operating supp.	227,563	148,569	270,661	270,661	270,661
Repair/maint.	248,922	195,941	233,118	233,118	233,118
Small tools	49,508	788	12,175	12,175	12,175
Prof. serv.	337,263	290,359	334,765	334,765	334,765
Communication	287,757	223,200	392,906	392,906	392,906
Public utility	111,935	116,773	121,008	121,008	121,008
Rentals	81,840	96,294	113,071	113,071	113,071
Vehicle rental	834,416	1,193,926	1,363,278	1,363,278	1,169,278
Extradition	20,955	22,411	20,000	20,000	20,000
Other travel	4,649	5,123	23,500	23,500	23,500
Advertising	2,662	2,570	4,100	4,100	4,100
Insurance	328,360	595,257	942,921	942,921	942,921
Books/manuals	16,285	12,813	12,404	12,404	12,404
Employee training	47,029	30,851	0	0	0
Aircraft exp.	0	0	15,000	15,000	15,000
Special inv.	11,527	13,465	15,000	15,000	15,000

TABLE 16.2 (*CONTINUED*)

Description	FY 1992–93 Expenses	FY 1993–94 Expenses	FY 1994–95 Dept. Req.	City Manager	City Council
Services and supplies (*continued*)					
Other serv. & supplies	1,386,201	1,039,651	1,386,201	1,386,201	1,386,201
Subtotals	4,059,229	4,037,283	5,311,593	5311,593	5,117,593
Capital outlay					
Machinery and equipment	572,301	102,964	0	0	0
Totals	26,063,407	26,280,576	30,898,675	30,863,808	30,108,168

TABLE 16.3   OPERATING BUDGET FOR A DISTRICT COURT IN A COUNTY OF 300,000 POPULATION

Categories	Amounts
Salaries and wages	
Regular salaries	2,180,792
Part-time temporary	9,749
Incentive/longevity	50,850
Subtotal	2,241,391
Employee benefits	
Group insurance	170,100
Worker's comp.	8,470
Unemployment comp.	3,220
Retirement	412,211
Social security	605
Medicare	13,503
Subtotal	608,109
Services and supplies	
Computers and office equipment	22,865
Service contracts	2,000
Minor furniture/equipment	1,000
Computer supplies	10,000
Continuous forms	4,000
Office supplies	36,066
Advertising	50
Copy machine expense	40,000
Dues and registration	4,000

TABLE 16.3 (*CONTINUED*)

Categories	Amounts
Services and supplies (*continued*)	
Printing	24,000
Telephone	16,000
Training	2,000
Court reporter/transcript	235,000
Court reporter per diem	265,000
Law books/supplements	9,000
Jury trials	75,000
Medical examinations	80,000
Computerized legal research	20,000
Travel	1,500
Subtotal	847,481
Child support	
Attorneys and other personnel	66,480
Court-appointed attorneys	656,000
Grand juries	18,600
Family court services	762,841
Total	5,200,902

TABLE 16.4 PROBATION AND PAROLE BUDGET FOR A STATE SERVING 3,000,000 POPULATION

Description	FY 1993–94 Actual	FY 1994–95 Agency Req.	FY 1994–95 Gov. Recomm.	Legis. Approval
Personnel	13,741,104	14,290,523	13,620,991	13,540,222
Travel	412,588	412,588	412,588	401,689
Operating expenses	1,307,020	1,395,484	1,307,020	1,256,787
Equipment	10,569	4,379	4,379	4,379
Loans to parolees	4,500	4,500	4,500	4,500
Training	9,073	9,073	9,073	9,073
Extraditions	200,000	200,000	200,000	185,000
Client drug tests	112,962	112,962	112,962	112,962
Home arrest fees	114,005	114,005	114,005	114,005
Community programs	50,000	50,000	50,000	47,500
Residential confinement	496,709	500,709	496,709	487,663
Utilities (paid by building lessors)				
Totals	16,458,530	17,094,223	16,332,227	16,163,780

TABLE 16.5   OPERATING BUDGET FOR A STATE MEDIUM-SECURITY PRISON WITH 1000 INMATES

Description	FY 1993–94 Actual	FY 1994–95 Agency Req.	FY 1994–95 Gov. Recomm.	Legislature Approved
Personnel				
Salaries	5,051,095	5,370,979	5,186,421	5,105,533
Worker's comp.	184,362	143,462	201,198	198,016
Retirement	1,142,010	1,174,968	1,215,674	1,196,028
Recruit tests	49,447	51,528	45,692	44,972
Insurance	474,330	488,250	513,000	500,175
Retirement insurance	30,963	31,872	35,917	35,349
Unemployment comp.	6,003	6,383	6,162	6,065
Overtime	165,856	0	0	0
Holiday pay	150,519	158,500	154,643	151,936
Medicare	39,965	45,140	42,225	40,948
Shift Differential	95,925	101,011	98,553	96,828
Standby pay	6,465	6,807	6,641	6,526
Longevity pay	18,095	18,095	18,095	18,095
Subtotals	7,415,035	7,596,995	7,524,221	7,400,471
Services and supplies				
Operating supplies	180,672	277,495	180,647	214,859
Communications/freight	4,877	5,314	5,023	5,023
Printing/copying	20,900	47,222	19,016	21,527
Equipment repair	14,385	13,542	14,817	14,817
Vehicle operation	20,405	21,601	21,016	21,016
Uniforms—custody	118,122	105,976	103,237	113,856
Inmate clothing	72,436	184,790	72,430	86,167
Equipment issued	20,403	13,236	15,451	17,086
Inmate wages	36,645	52,815	35,572	42,309
Food	895,897	1,299,838	895,759	1,065,403
Postage	7,738	8,793	7,036	7,738
Telephone	24,808	23,802	22,130	24,808
Subscriptions	382	401	725	401
Hand tools	110	286	113	113
Subtotals	1,417,780	2,055,111	1,392,972	1,635,123
Special equipment	116,863	34,088	12,557	13,661
Grounds maint.	150,098	209,003	138,560	185,843
Inmate law library	18,564	20,115	16,419	21,836
Special projects	53,237	8,887	8,887	8,887
Gas and power	554,478	586,604	505,823	604,335
Water	60,390	69,377	52,266	67,171
Garbage	80,035	101,240	82,436	82,436
Canine unit	13,936	2,521	4,260	2,543
Grand totals	9,880,416	10,683,941	9,738,401	10,022,306

The line-item budget has several strengths and weaknesses. In addition to ease of control, strengths include ease of development, comprehension (especially by elected and other executive branch officials), and administration. Weaknesses are that long-range planning is neglected, and its limited ability to evaluate performance. Furthermore, the line-item budget tends to maintain the status quo; old and ongoing programs are seldom challenged. Line-item budgets are based on history: This year's allocation is based on last year's history. While that allows the inexperienced manager to prepare the budget more easily, it also often precludes the reform chief's careful deliberation and planning for the future.

To illustrate the ease of control afforded by this budget format, Table 16.6 demonstrates how the administrator can check the "health" or status of the budget as of the end of December, halfway into the fiscal year. When examining the budget status report, the administrator must also take into consideration how far the agency has proceeded into the fiscal year; the numbers in the "percent used" column mean something very different if they apply to the first three months of the fiscal year than for nine months.

Virtually all criminal justice agencies are automated in some manner, whether the financial officer prepares his or her budget figures using a spreadsheet on a personal computer or a clerk enters information onto a database, to be uploaded to a state-level mainframe computer. Some justice agencies go further than spreadsheets, however, and use an automated budgeting system

TABLE 16.6   A POLICE DEPARTMENT'S BUDGET STATUS REPORT

Line Item	Amount Budgeted	Expenses to Date	Amount Encumbered	Balance to Date	Percent Used
Salaries	16,221,148	8,427,062.00	0	7,794,086.00	52.0
Prof. services	334,765	187,219.61	8,014.22	139,531.17	58.3
Office supplies	51,485	16,942.22	3,476.19	31,066.59	39.7
Repair/maintenance	49,317	20,962.53	1,111.13	27,24334	44.8
Communication	392,906	212,099.11	1,560.03	179,246.86	54.4
Utilities	121,008	50,006.15	10,952.42	60,049.43	51.4
Vehicle rental	1,169,278	492,616.22	103,066.19	573,595.59	51.9
Travel	23,500	6,119.22	2,044.63	15,336.15	34.7
Extraditions	20,000	12,042.19	262.22	7,695.59	61.5
Printing/binding	36,765	15,114.14	2,662.67	18,988.19	48.4
Books/manuals	12,404	5,444.11	614.11	6,345.78	48.8
Training/education	35,695	19,661.54	119.14	15,914.32	55.4
Aircraft expense	15,000	8,112.15	579.22	6,308.63	57.9
Special investiagion	15,000	6,116.75	960.50	7,922.75	47.2
Machinery	1,000	275.27	27.50	697.23	30.3
Advertising	4,100	1,119.17	142.50	2,838.33	30.8

(ABS). This system can store budget figures, make all necessary calculations for generating a budget request, monitor expenditures from budgets (similar to that shown in Table 16.6), and even generate some reports.

✦ THE PERFORMANCE BUDGET

The key characteristic of a performance budget is that it relates the types of volume of work to be done to the amount of money spent.[43] The performance budget is input–output oriented, and it increases the responsibility and accountability of the manager for output as opposed to input.[44] This format specifies activities of the organization, using a format that is similar to that of the line-item budget. It normally measures activities that are easily quantified, such as numbers of traffic citations issued, crimes solved, property recovered, cases heard in the courtroom, and caseload of probation officers. These types of services are then compared by the unit that performs the most services, which attempts to allocate funds accordingly. Using a police department as an example, the commander of the traffic accident investigation unit requests an additional three investigators, which the chief approves. Later the chief might compare the unit's output and costs of the unit with the additional three investigators in relation to the previous unit structure (with three fewer investigators). The chief can make an informed decision about how productivity was affected by this change.[45] An example of the police performance budget is provided in Table 16.7.

The performance budget format could be used in other justice system components besides the police. For example, the courts could use such performance measures as case filing, opinions written, cases disposed, pending cases, and presentence investigations.

Advantages of the performance budget include a consideration of outputs, the establishment of the costs of various justice agency efforts, improved evaluation of programs and managers, an emphasis on efficiency, increased availability of information for decision making, and the enhancement of budget justification and explanation.[46] The performance budget works best for an "assembly line" or other organization where work is easily quantifiable, such as paving streets. However, there are several disadvantages as well, including its expense to develop, implement, and operate because of the extensive use of cost accounting techniques and the need for additional staff (Figure 16.2, page 425, demonstrates the complexity of using cost accounting to determine the cost of providing a criminal justice service); the controversy surrounding attempts to determine appropriate workload and unit cost measures (in criminal justice, while many functions are quantifiable, such reduction of duties to numbers often translates to "quotas," which is anathema to many people); its emphasis on efficiency rather than effectiveness; and the failure to lend itself to long-range planning.[47]

It is difficult in criminal justice to determine which functions are more important (and should therefore receive more financial support). Therefore, in terms of criminal justice agency budgets, the selection of meaningful work units is very difficult and irrational. How can a justice agency measure its successes? How can it count what does not happen?

TABLE 16.7 EXAMPLE OF A POLICE PERFORMANCE BUDGET

Total Budget		$
Units/activities		
Administration (Chief)	Subtotal	$
Strategic planning		$
Normative planning		$
Policies and procedures formulation		$
Etc.		
Patrol	Subtotal	$
Calls for service		$
Citizen contacts		$
Special details		$
Etc.		
Criminal Investigation	Subtotal	$
Suspect apprehension		$
Recovery of stolen property		$
Transportation of fugitives		$
Etc.		
Traffic Services	Subtotal	$
Accident investigation		$
Issuance of citations		$
Public safety speeches		$
Etc.		
Juvenile Services	Subtotal	$
Locate runaways/missing juveniles		$
Arrest of offenders		$
Referrals and liaison		$
Etc.		
Research and Development	Subtotal	$
Perform crime analysis		$
Prepare annual budget		$
Prepare annual reports		$
Etc.		

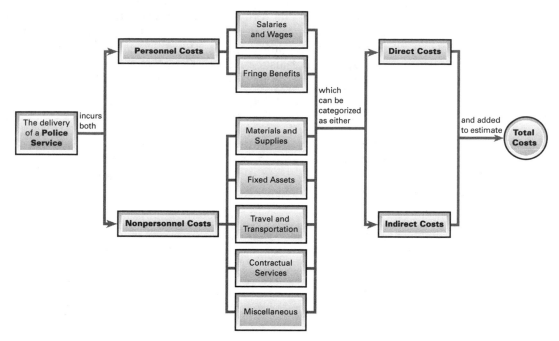

Figure 16.2 Elements of total costs for police services. (*Source:* U.S. Department of Justice, National Institute of Justice, *Measuring the Costs of Police Services.* (Washington, D.C.: Author, 1982, p. 20.)

✦ THE PROGRAM BUDGET

The best known management budget for monitoring the activities of the organization is the program budget, developed by the Rand Corporation for the U.S. Department of Defense. This format examines cost units as units of activity rather than as units and subunits within the organization. Here, the budget becomes a planning tool; it demands justification for expenditures for new programs and for deleting old ones that have not met their objectives.

A police agency probably has greater opportunities for creating new community-based programs than do the courts or corrections agencies. Some of these include crime prevention and investigation, drug abuse education, home security, selective enforcement (e.g., drunk driving) programs, and career development for personnel. Each of these endeavors requires instructional materials or special equipment, all of which must be budgeted. For example, traffic accident investigation (TAI) may be a "cost area." The program budget emphasizes output measures. Outputs for TAI include the numbers of accidents worked and enforcement measures taken (such as citations issued, DUI and other arrests made, public safety speeches given, etc.). If the budget for these programs were divided by the units of output, the administrator could determine the relative cost for each unit of output or productivity. The cost of TAI, however, entails more than just the TAI unit; patrol and other support units also engage in this program.

Thus this is an extremely difficult form of budget to execute and administer, because it requires tracking time of all personnel by activity as well as figuring in the cost of all support services and supplies. For this reason, the program budget is rarely used by criminal justice agencies.[48] Examples of police and court program budgets are presented in Tables 16.8 and 16.9.

TABLE 16.8   EXAMPLE OF A POLICE PROGRAM BUDGET

Total Budget		$
Program Area		
Crime prevention	Subtotal	$
Salaries and benefits		$
Operating expenses		$
Capital outlay		$
Miscellaneous		$
Traffic accident investigation	Subtotal	$
Salaries and benefits		$
Operating expenses		$
Capital outlay		$
Miscellaneous		$
Traffic accident prevention	Subtotal	$
Salaries and benefits		$
Operating expenses		$
Capital outlay		$
Miscellaneous		$
Criminal investigation	Subtotal	$
Salaries and benefits		$
Operating expenses		$
Capital outlay		$
Miscellaneous		$
Juvenile delinquency prevention	Subtotal	$
Salaries and benefits		$
Operating expenses		$
Capital outlay		$
Miscellaneous		$
Special investigations	Subtotal	$
Salaries and benefits		$
Operating expenses		$
Capital outlay		$
Miscellaneous		$
Etc.		

TABLE 16.9   EXAMPLE OF A COURT'S PROGRAM BUDGET

Total Budget		$
Program Area		
Adjudicate criminal cases	Subtotal	$
Adjudicate felony cases		$
Adjudicate misdemeanor appeals		$
Adjudicate civil cases	Subtotal	$
Adjudicate major civil cases		$
Adjudicate minor civil cases		$
Adjudicate domestic relations cases		$
Adjudicate juvenile cases	Subtotal	$
Adjudicate delinquency and dependent and neglect cases		$
Adjudicate crimes against juveniles		$
Provide alternatives to adjudication	Subtotal	$
Divert adult offenders		$
Divert juvenile offenders		$
Provide security	Subtotal	$
Handle prisoner transport		$
Provide courtroom security		$
Etc.		

Source: Adapted from U.S. Department of Justice, National Institute of Law Enforcement and Criminal Justice, *Financial Management* (Washington, D.C.: American University, 1979), p. 41.1.

Some advantages of the program budget include emphasis on the social utility of programs conducted by the agency; a clear relationship between policy objectives and expenditures; its ability to provide justification and explanation of the budget; its establishing a high degree of accountability; and its format and the wide involvement in formulating objectives, which leads employees at all levels of the organization to understand more thoroughly the importance of their roles and actions. Disadvantages, as indicated above, include its cost in terms of time and money to develop, implement, and administer. Also, there are difficulties in developing objectives and performance measures; data collection may be costly; and agency managers may not have, or want to develop, the skills necessary for directing large-scale, complex programs.[49]

✦ "PPBS" AND "ZERO-BASED" BUDGETING FORMATS

Actually, the planning-programming-budgeting system (PPBS) died in the federal government, and it never really caught fire at the state or local levels.

Although PPBS treated the three basic budget processes—planning, management, and control—as compatible, they were treated as co-equals; PPBS was predicated on the primacy of planning.[50] This "futures" orientation transformed budgeting from an "annual ritual" into "formulation of future goals and policies."[51] The PPBS budget featured a program structure; zero-based budgeting (discussed below); the use of cost-budget analysis to distinguish between alternatives; and a budgetary horizon, often five years.[52] General Motors was using PPBS as early as 1924,[53] and the Rand Corporation contributed to its development in a series of studies dating from 1949.[54] By the mid-1950s several states were using it, and Secretary Robert McNamara introduced PPBS into the Defense Department in the mid-1960s.[55] However, by 1971 a survey revealed that only 28 percent of cities and 21 percent of counties contacted had implemented PPBS or significant elements of it;[56] and in 1971 the federal government announced that it was discontinuing its use.

Associated with PPBS, the zero-based planning and budgeting process required managers to justify their entire budget request in detail rather than simply to refer to budget amounts established in previous years.[57] Following Peter Phyrr's example at Texas Instruments, Governor Jimmy Carter adopted ZBB in Georgia in the early 1970s, then as President implemented it in the federal government for fiscal year 1979. However, an analysis of this experience at the Department of Agriculture found that while $200,000 was saved in the department's budget, it cost at least 180,000 labor-hours of effort to develop the ZBB.[58]

It is important to note that few budgets are purely one format or another; because of time, tradition, and personal preferences, it is more likely that a combination of several is used.

✦ POTENTIAL PITFALLS IN BUDGETING

✧ FLEXIBILITY IN BUDGETING

Ancient Greek mythology tells of a highwayman named Procrustes who had an iron bedstead, and all who fell into his hands were measured on the bed. If they were too long, their legs were lopped off to fit the bed. If they were too short, they were stretched to fit the bed. Few are the criminal justice administrators who have not seen their monies and programs laid out on the Procrustesean bed of a state or municipal budget officer and "lopped off."

It therefore becomes imperative that one build as much flexibility into the planned program and budget as possible. One technique utilized is to make up three budgets: an optimistic one, reflecting the ideal level of service to the jurisdiction and organization; an expected one, giving the most likely level of service that will be funded; and finally, an optimistic budget plan that will provide a minimum level of service.[59]

To maximize the benefits of using budgets, managers must be able to avoid other potential pitfalls. Some of these major pitfalls, according to Samuel Certo,[60] are:

1. *Placing too much emphasis on relatively insignificant organizational expenses.* In preparing and implementing a budget, managers should allocate more time for dealing with significant organizational expenses and less time for relatively insignificant organizational expenses. For example, the amount of time spent on developing and implementing a budget for labor costs typically should be more than the amount of time managers spend on developing and implementing a budget for office supplies.

2. *Increasing budgeted expenses year after year without adequate information.* Perhaps the best-known method developed to overcome this potential pitfall was zero-based budgeting, discussed above.[61]

3. *Ignoring the fact that budgets must be changed periodically.* Administrators must recognize that such factors as costs of materials, newly developed technology, and demand for services are constantly changing and that budgets should reflect that fact by being reviewed and modified periodically in response to those changes. A special type of budget, the performance budget (discussed above), is designed to assist in determining how much resources should be allocated for each organizational activity.

✧ COMMON COST AND WASTE PROBLEMS

To manage costs, managers must be able to identify areas where waste and costs might be controlled. Louise Tagliaferri [62] identified 14 common cost factors that can be found in most organizations. Note that some costs are simply uncontrollable, but others are within the scope of the manager to reduce or at least maintain within a reasonable scope.

◊ Absenteeism and turnover	◊ Paperwork
◊ Accident loss	◊ Planning and scheduling
◊ Direct and indirect labor	◊ Productivity
◊ Energy	◊ Product quality
◊ Maintenance	◊ Tools and equipment
◊ Materials and supplies	◊ Transportation
◊ Overtime	◊ Waste

Tagliaferri also noted that "Literally billions of dollars are lost to industry (and criminal justice!) each year through carelessness, inattention, waste, inefficiency and other cost problems."[63]

✦ STRATEGIES FOR AUGMENTING
   CRIMINAL JUSTICE BUDGETS

In these difficult fiscal times, agencies of criminal justice would welcome any means by which they can increase their operating budgets. Unfortunately, there are limited opportunities for doing so, especially for courts and corrections agencies; however, the police have recently fared better in this regard, albeit some measures have been controversial. While prisons and jails have some income-producing inmate-labor programs (see Chapter 10), the police can presently draw supplemental funds from several sources.

Federal and general foundation grants are still available. Grants have been used for a variety of purposes, including vehicle and riot equipment purchases, communications centers, regional crime laboratories, alcohol safety–accident prevention, and programs for rape victims and the elderly. Potential grantors are located through such publications as the *Federal Directory of Domestic Aid Programs* and by preparing well-conceived grant proposals.

Agencies of criminal justice also receive donations. For example, the Erie County, New York, sheriff's office got $5000 from a local bank to renovate an old van for use in a crime-prevention program. On a bigger scale, since 1971 the New York City Police Foundation has raised money for such endeavors as scholarships, a police stress program, and establishing a bomb squad. In one recent year the foundation raised $1.3 million. Also, the Chicago Police Department raised $1.5 million recently to purchase bulletproof vests for officers.[64]

Forfeiture laws bring in huge supplemental revenues for police agencies, through apprehensions of cash and property involved with narcotics and contraband goods trafficking, racketeering, gambling, and other offenses. Upon seizing airplanes, cash, cars, boats, guns, or other property covered by the state's forfeiture law, the agency may initiate forfeiture proceedings by forwarding a formal request to the prosecutor or other such party. For example, between 1980 and 1983, during the initial stages of such laws, the Fort Lauderdale (Florida) Police Department accumulated forfeitures totaling $5,500,000.[65]

Another source of extra income is user fees. Some police departments are initiating controversial user fees for services formerly provided for free, such as unlocking vehicles and responding to false burglar alarms. Less controversial have been fees for hooking up burglar alarms to the police alarm board or computer-assisted dispatch system. In one year, Miami, Florida, collected $270,000 in alarm permit and false alarm fees.[66]

Finally, Internal Revenue Service rewards have been paid to police agencies that capture racketeers who have not properly reported their income taxes. The program began in Atlanta, Georgia, where the police department approached IRS about collecting the 10 percent informer's fee on unpaid taxes. Through a special city ordinance, the police department was awarded the informer's fee on behalf of the city. By 1988, the department had filed 31 such claims.[67]

Summary

Although surely not succeeding in making a budgetary expert of anyone, hopefully this chapter has served to remove much of the mystique often surrounding the budgetary process. An old axiom tells us that we "learn best by doing." It is surely so with respect to budgeting; the science of budgeting can be learned only through on-the-job experience.

It bears repeating that no single budgeting format is best; through tradition and personal preference, a "hybrid" format normally evolves in an organization. Nor should an administrator, under any normal circumstances, surrender control of the organization's budget to another individual or body; the budget is too integral to planning, organizing, and directing programs and operations. In these fiscally tight times, the justice administrator should attempt to become knowledgeable about opportunities for enhancing the budget through grants, donations, user fees, forfeitures, rewards, and other such means of "fattening" the budget. Uncommon times call for uncommon methods.

In sum, although revenues may be tight, and forecasting and budgeting difficult, administrators can only hope for better times and remember the words of Samuel Pepys: "But it is pretty to see what money will do."

Questions for Review

1. Define a budget and its uses.
2. Why is criminal justice no longer the sacred cow it has traditionally been with respect to job security? Provide examples.
3. Defend the growing practice of charging the public for criminal justice services that have traditionally been provided free of charge. Conversely, develop a rationale for keeping these services *gratis* in nature.
4. Describe the budget cycle and its importance in budgeting.
5. What is involved in formulating a budget? Its approval and execution?
6. List four types of budget formats used in the past. Which type is used most frequently today? What are its major advantages and component parts?
7. How are criminal justice agencies augmenting their budgets? Can additional means be used in this regard? Provide some examples.

For Further Reading

SAMUEL C. CERTO, *Principles of Modern Management: Functions and Systems* (4th ed.). Boston: Allyn and Bacon, 1989.

Larry K. Gaines, Mittie D. Southerland, and John E. Angell, *Police Administration*. New York: McGraw-Hill, 1991.

Charles R. Swanson and Susette M. Talarico, *Court Administration: Issues and Responses*. Athens, Ga.: University of Georgia, 1987.

Charles R. Swanson, Leonard Territo, and Robert W. Taylor, *Police Administration* (3d ed.). New York: Macmillan, 1993.

Notes

1. Examples taken from Felix A. Nigro and Lloyd G. Nigro, *Modern Public Administration* (5th ed.) (New York: Harper & Row, 1980), p. 337.
2. Charles R. Swanson, Leonard Territo, and Robert W. Taylor, *Police Administration* (3d ed.) (New York: Macmillan), 1993, p. 561.
3. Earl Babbie, *The Practice of Social Research* (6th ed.) (Belmont, Calif.: Wadsworth, 1992), pp. 430–431.
4. See James C. Snyder, "Financial Management and Planning in Local Government," *Atlanta Economic Review* (November/December 1973):43–47.
5. Aaron Wildavsky, *The Politics of the Budgetary Process* (2d ed.) (Boston: Little, Brown, 1974), pp. 1–4.
6. Orin K. Cope, "Operation Analysis: The Basis for Performance Budgeting," in *Performance Budgeting and Unit Cost Accounting for Governmental Units* (Chicago: Municipal Finance Officers Association, 1954), p. 8.
7. Lester R. Bittel, *The McGraw-Hill 36-Hour Management Course* (New York: McGraw-Hill, 1989).
8. *Ibid.*, p. 187.
9. Robert Townsend, *Further up the Organization: How to Stop Management from Stifling People and Strangling Productivity* (New York: Alfred A. Knopf, 1984), p. 2.
10. Charles R. Swanson, Leonard Territo, and Robert W. Taylor, *Police Administration* (3d ed.), p. 568.
11. Josh Barbanel, "Dinkins Is Expected to Lay Off 16,000 to Close Budget Gap," *The New York Times* (January 16, 1991):B14.
12. "Mass. SP Transfers Personnel to Offset Manpower Drain," *Law Enforcement News* 16 (1991):322.
13. Angel Cannon, "DPOA Sues to Bar 300 Police Layoffs," *Detroit Free Press* (March 29, 1991).
14. Robert Hanley, "Tax Haven in Jersey in Bind, Plans to Drop Police," *The New York Times* (February 12, 1991):A13.
15. *Law Enforcement News*, John Jay College of Criminal Justice (November 15, 1992):2.
16. *Ibid.* (September 15, 1992):2.
17. *Ibid.* (November 15, 1992):2.
18. *Ibid.* (June 30, 1992):2.
19. *Ibid.* (June 30, 1992):4.
20. *Ibid.* (September 15, 1992):2.
21. *Ibid.*, p. 4.
22. *Ibid.* (September 30, 1992):2.
23. *Ibid.* (October 15, 1992):2.

24. Robert Trojanowicz and Bonnie Bucqueroux, "Restructuring Police Priorities: Police Chiefs Must Take the Lead in Enlisting Support," *Footprints: The Community Policing Newsletter* (Michigan State University) 3 (Summer 1990):1–2.

25. *Ibid.*, p. 2.

26. Roland N. McKean, *Public Spending* (New York: McGraw-Hill, 1968), p. 1.

27. S. Kenneth Howard, *Changing State Budgeting* (Lexington, Ky.: Council of State Governments, 1973), p. 13.

28. David Bresnick, "User Fees for the Courts: An Old Approach to a New Problem," in Charles R. Swanson and Susette M. Talarico (eds.), *Court Administration: Issues and Responses* (Athens, Ga.: University of Georgia, 1987), pp. 43–66.

29. *Ibid.*, pp. 45–46.

30. Learned Hand, "Address before the Legal Aid Society," 9 *NLADA Briefcase* 5 (February 16, 1951).

31. Michael C. Thomsett, *The Little Black Book of Budgets and Forecasts* (New York: AMA-COM, a division of the American Management Association, 1988), p. 38.

32. Quoted in V. A. Leonard and Harry W. More, *Police Organization and Management* (7th ed.) (Mineola, N.Y.: Foundation Press, 1987), p. 212.

33. Charles R. Swanson, Leonard Territo, and Robert W. Taylor, *Police Administration* (3d ed.), p. 573.

34. Hal Rubin, "Working Out a Budget," *Law and Order* (May 1989):27–28.

35. Adapted, with some changes, from Aaron Wildavsky, *The Politics of the Budgetary Process* (2d ed.), pp. 63–123.

36. Lennox L. Moak and Kathryn W. Killian, *A Manual of Techniques for the Preparation, Consideration, Adoption, and Administration of Operating Budgets* (Chicago: Municipal Finance Officers Association, 1973), p. 5, with changes.

37. Lennis M. Knighton, "Four Keys to Audit Effectiveness," *Governmental Finance* 8 (September 1979):3.

38. The Comptroller General of the United States, *Standards for Audit of Governmental Organizations, Programs, Activities, and Functions* (Washington, D.C.: General Accounting Office, 1972), p. 1.

39. *Ibid.*

40. Peter F. Rousmaniere (ed.), *Local Government Auditing* (New York: Council on Municipal Performance, 1979), Tables 1 and 2, pp. 10, 14.

41. Charles R. Swanson, Leonard Territo, and Robert W. Taylor, *Police Administration* (3d ed.), p. 586.

42. Allen Schick, *Budget Innovation in the States* (Washington, D.C.: Brookings Institution, 1971), p. 14–15. Schick offered 10 ways in which the line-item budget fosters control.

43. Malchus L. Watlington and Susan G. Dankel, "New Approaches to Budgeting: Are They Worth the Cost?" *Popular Government* 43 (Spring 1978):1.

44. Jesse Burkhead, *Government Budgeting* (New York: Wiley, 1956):11.

45. Larry K. Gaines, Mittie D. Southerland, and John E. Angell, *Police Administration* (New York: McGraw-Hill, 1991), p. 398.

46. Charles R. Swanson, Leonard Territo, and Robert W. Taylor, *Police Administration* (3d ed.), p. 591.

47. *Ibid.*

48. Larry K. Gaines, Mittie D. Southerland, and John E. Angell, *Police Administration*, pp. 396, 398.

49. *Ibid.*, p. 600.

50. Allen Schick, "The Road to PPBS: The Stages of Budget Reform," *Public Administration Review* 26 (December 1966):244.

51. *Ibid.*

52. Charles R. Swanson, Leonard Territo, and Robert W. Taylor, *Police Administration* (3d ed.), p. 593.

53. David Novick (ed.), *Program Budgeting* (New York: Holt, Rinehart and Winston, 1969), p. xxvi.

54. *Ibid.*, p. xxiv.

55. See Council of State Governments, *State Reports on Five-Five-Five* (Chicago: Council of State Governments, 1968).

56. International City Management Association, *Local Government Budgeting, Program Planning and Evaluation* (Urban Data Service Report, 1972):7.

57. Peter A. Phyrr, "Zero-Base Budgeting," *Harvard Business Review* (November/December 1970):111–121; see also E.A. Kurbis, "The Case for Zero-Base Budgeting," *CA Magazine* (April 1986):104–105.

58. Joseph S. Wholey, *Zero-Base Budgeting and Program Evaluation* (Lexington, Mass.: Lexington Books, 1978), p. 8.

59. Donald F. Facteau and Joseph E. Gillespie, *Modern Police Administration* (Englewood Cliffs, N.J.: Prentice Hall, 1978), p. 204.

60. Samuel C. Certo, *Principles of Modern Management: Functions and Systems* (4th ed.) (Boston: Allyn and Bacon, 1989):484–485.

61. George S. Minmier, "Zero-Base Budgeting: A New Budgeting Technique for Discretionary Costs," *Mid-South Quarterly Business Review* 14 (October 1976):2–8.

62. Louise E. Tagliaferri, *Creative Cost Improvement for Managers* (New York: Wiley, 1981), p. 7.

63. *Ibid.*, p. 8.

64. Charles R. Swanson, Leonard Territo, and Robert W. Taylor, *Police Administration* (3d ed.), p. 605.

65. *Ibid.*, pp. 605–606.

66. *Ibid.*, p. 606.

67. *Ibid.*, p. 613–614.

Part VI

Challenges of the Future

In the sole chapter of this part of the book, Chapter 17, we review challenges of the future. Specific chapter content is provided in the introductory section of the chapter.

"Peeking Over the Rim": What Lies Ahead

I like the dreams of the future better than the history of the past.

—Patrick Henry

The trouble with our times is that the future is not what it used to be.

—Paul Valery

✦ INTRODUCTION

What will the future bring? In attempting to answer that impossible question, we all have probably wished at some time that we could gaze into a crystal ball and have what former President George Bush referred to as "the vision thing." It is important that today's criminal justice students listen to what the prognosticators tell us about the future and understand their methods; they could well be the administrators of justice in a mere decade. They, like current justice administrators, must take the time today to "peek over the rim" to anticipate and plan for the future.

This final chapter opens by examining several methods by which futurists attempt to determine what the future holds—in short, tools for prediction. Using those best-guess methods, we then look at what appears imminent with respect to demographics and crime in the United States. We then view what the experts portend in terms of police technology to cope with crime, as well as forecasted changes in both courts (including possibilities for reform) and corrections (population growth and the need to build more prisons). We close with discussions of how computers have changed (and will continue to change) justice administration, and how AIDS has affected personnel, policy, and litigation, and clients of the justice system.

✦ HOW TO PREDICT THE FUTURE

Many variables can affect predictions and trends, one of the most important being money. If you have unlimited funds, you do not need to be concerned with futures. Over the next 14 to 20 years, the driving force for major changes in law enforcement agencies will be the economy. In a phrase, "there is a lot of crime prevention in a T-bone steak." Unfortunately, with the volatile nature of the world's oil supplies, the value of the dollar, and many other related matters, our economy is in a delicate balance and our future is uncertain.

Contemporary futures research has two major aspects: environmental scanning and scenario writing. Environmental scanning is an effort to put a social problem under a microscope, with an eye toward the future. We may consult experts on their opinions, such as demographers, social scientists, technologists, and economists. A Delphi process may also assist, gathering experts, looking at all possible factors, and getting an idea of what will happen in the future. Thus environmental scanning permits us to identify, track, and assess changes in the environment.[1]

Through scanning, we can examine the factors that seem likely to "drive" the environment. "Drivers" are factors or variables—economic conditions, demographic shifts, governmental policies, social attitudes, technological advances, and so on—that will have a bearing on future conditions. Three categories of drivers will serve to identify possible trends and impacts on the American criminal justice system by and beyond the year 2000: (1) social and economic conditions (e.g., size and age of the population, immigration patterns, nature of employment, and lifestyle characteristics); (2) shifts in the amounts and types of crimes (including the potential for new types of criminality and for technological advances that might be used for illegal behavior); and (3) possible developments in the criminal justice system itself (e.g., changes in the way the police, courts and corrections subsystems operate; important innovations).[2]

Scenario writing is simply the application of drivers to three primary situations or elements: public tolerance for crime, amount of crime, and the capacity of the criminal justice system to deal with crime. An important consideration is whether each will occur in high or low degrees. For example, drivers may be analyzed in a scenario of *low* public tolerance for crime, a *high* amount of crime, and a *high* capacity of the criminal justice system to deal with crime. Conversely, a scenario may include a view of the future where there is a *high* tolerance for crime, a *low* amount of crime, and a *low* capacity for the system to cope with crime; and so on.

✦ THE CHANGING FACE OF AMERICA

In 1996 the first wave of "baby boomers" will turn 50; by 2010 one in every four Americans will be 55 or older. By the year 2000, an estimated 34.9 million elderly people will constitute 13 percent of the population. The minority population is increasing rapidly; by the year 2000 an estimated 34 percent of American children will be Hispanic, black, or Asian. More than 25 million women headed their own households in 1990, 28 percent of the nation's 91 million households. Two-thirds of black and Hispanic households are headed by women. And if present trends continue, one-half of all marriages occurring today will end in divorce within a decade.[3]

In our "postindustrial" society, there are fewer blue-collar jobs and more white-collar jobs. Jobs that are declining in number are those that could be filled by those with fewer skills. The fastest-growing jobs are those requiring more language, math, and reasoning skills. For the next decade, 90 percent of all new jobs will be in the service sector—fields that often require high levels of education and skill. Ten years ago, 77 percent of all jobs required some type of generating, processing, retrieving, or distribution of information; by the year 2000, heavily computerized information processing will be involved in 95 percent of all jobs. Statistics indicate that America is becoming a bifurcated society with more wealth, poverty, and a shrinking middle class. The gap between the "haves" and "have nots" is widening. An underclass of people—those who are chronically poor and live outside of society's rules—is growing. Between 1970 and 1980 the underclass tripled.[4]

The influence of immigration to America, and the growth of minority-group populations in general, cannot be overstated. America now accepts nearly a million newcomers per year, which equates to about 10 million new residents each decade (excluding their offspring) even if immigration rates do not rise. Shortly after the turn of the twenty-first century, Asians are expected to reach 10 million; today's 18 million legal and illegal Hispanics may well double by then. In less than 100 years we can expect white dominance of the United States to end, as the growing number of blacks, Hispanics, and Asians together become the new majority. History has shown that where newcomers cluster together in poor neighborhoods with high crime rates, the police are soon involved. And when these various minority groups are forced to compete for increasingly scarce, low-paying service jobs, intergroup relations sour and can even become combative, as has occurred recently in Los Angeles, Miami, and other cities.[5]

In sum, today's economy is based on knowledge. Whereas employers in the past mostly wanted muscle, today more and more jobs presuppose skills, training, and education. Fewer jobs remain for those on the bottom rung; the results are clear in our inner cities.

✦ A CHANGING NATURE OF CRIME

Three important drivers contribute to the changing nature of crime in the West: (1) the advent of high technology in our society; (2) the distribution and use of narcotics; and (3) a declining population in the 15 to 24 age bracket.[6]

The nature of crime is rapidly changing. The new crimes of data manipulation, software piracy, industrial espionage, bank card counterfeiting, and embezzlement by computer are here to stay. What will probably tend to decrease will be the traditionally illegal means of obtaining funds: robbery and burglary. These new crimes will require the development of new investigative techniques, specialized training for law enforcement investigators, and the employment of people with specialized, highly technological backgrounds.

The abuse of narcotics is spreading in numbers and throughout various social classes, continuing to demand an ever-increasing amount of law enforcement time and resources. The real solution to the drug problem is for people to stop demanding a supply. However, that is probably an impossible goal at this time.

The decline in the size of the 15 to 24 cohort, the crime-prone youth of our society, has significantly affected crime rates. We are witnessing a decline in several types of crime, although crimes of violence are increasing. As we see the increase in the "graying of America," however, the young criminals will increasingly prey on the elderly and flourish. The growing numbers of crime-prone youths in our metropolitan areas virtually ensures that high crime rates will continue in the inner city.

Future criminal justice recruiting efforts are implicated by the nation's shift in demographic makeup. A change toward older workers, fewer entry-level workers, and more women, minorities, and immigrants in the population will force criminal justice and private industry to become more flexible to compete for qualified applicants. With the aging of America, justice agencies that only recruit recent high school graduates will probably face a shortage of qualified workers. Agencies must devise new strategies to attract 21- to 35-year-olds. This age group will be at a premium over the next 10 years, and the trend will continue well into the middle of the next century. Criminal justice will also need to offer better wage and benefits packages to compete with private businesses, such as day care, flexible hours, and paid maternity leave.[7]

By the year 2000 an estimated 75 percent of the labor force will need retraining; justice agencies will have to train existing personnel, both professional and clerical, and a major thrust will be toward communication with non-English-speaking communities.

✦ POLICING AND TECHNOLOGY IN THE FUTURE

The high-speed technological revolution, which has barely begun, will introduce new weapons for criminals and the police alike. Some futurists feel that the old methods and equipment for doing police work will soon fall by the wayside, replaced, for example, by electric and methane-fueled scooters and bubble-topped tricycles for densely populated areas; steamwagons and diesel superchargers for police in the rural and suburban areas; and methane-filled helium dirigibles, equipped with infrared night goggles and sophisticated communications and lighting devices, for patrol and assistance in planning barricades to trap high-speed drivers and search and rescue operations.[8]

Patrol officers in this scenario will be able to type in an analysis of how a crime was committed and receive a list of suspects. With a bit more analysis and data, the computer will also give a probability of various suspects committing that particular crime at that particular place. All homes and businesses will be linked to a central dispatch system in a police-approved, computer-based remote linkage system that will combine burglar and fire alarms. Community policing teams will be assigned by zone, the officers wearing blazers instead of paramilitary uniforms. Basic police training will last a minimum of 10 months and will be geared so that the lower one-third of the class will flunk out.[9]

Others see the future of policing differently. The twenty-first-century cop may patrol by means of jet backpack flight equipment, and officers will be able to tie in to "language banks" of translators via their wrist radios. Holographic, or three-dimensional, photography may be used for mug photos, and satellite photography will probably be used to assist in criminal investigations. Police vehicles will have all electronic equipment built in, and private vehicles will have a factory-installed "kill switch" that can be activated by depressing a button in a nearby patrol vehicle, thus preventing high-speed pursuits. Police officers may spend no time in court, instead transmitting their testimony by home computer/video systems.[10]

Obviously, law enforcement needs to assign some of its best thinkers to the task of probing the future. What should be the agency's budget? How should police personnel be trained? What skills will be needed? What new technologies will the police face? How should forces be deployed?

An area of concern among futurists is law enforcement's organizational structure. Increasing numbers of law enforcement executives are beginning to question whether or not the "pyramid"-shaped police bureaucracy will be effective in the future. Communications within the pyramid structure are often broken down and frustrated by the levels of bureaucracy; perhaps the organizational structure, the argument goes, could be changed to a more horizontal design to facilitate the flow of information and ideas.

Personnel and labor/management problems will continue to loom large in the future. Opportunities for graft and corruption will not decline, so police administrators must be sure to develop personnel policies that will protect the integrity of the profession. Debate is currently underway regarding mandatory drug testing and the use of the polygraph to safeguard the organizations. Traditional police personnel problems are not anticipated to decline, either. Such matters as age discrimination, employment misconduct, sexism, new employee attitudes, and poor work habits will not be resolved in the near future.

✦ FUTURE ADAPTATIONS BY THE COURTS

✧ MAJOR MODIFICATION ON THE HORIZON

Notwithstanding the several court innovations described in the "what works" section of Chapter 9, many people still believe that the inability to think systematically about the future is particularly apparent in the court community. In 1990 the chairman of the board of directors of the State Justice Institute and former Chief Justice of the Supreme Court of Alabama noted with regret that "The common picture of an American court is that of an institution rooted in the past, resistant to change, and resigned to inefficiency."[11] And in the early 1980s a futurist working with the Hawaii judiciary asked what were the most important long-term issues facing the courts; one reply was "how the parking spaces are allocated." The reasons for this short-term focus in the courts are several: the urgent pressure to attend to the present; judicial priorities set in annual or biannual legislative sessions; legal personnel being trained to apply the past (precedent-guiding decisions made in the present); the common law assumes the future will take care of itself; and judges, in particular, having an inherent preference for sensing the facts before them, not intuiting probable or possible future possibilities.

Looking at current trends, however, futurist Clement Bezold offered some court-related speculation for the early twenty-first century:

1. Rise of courts as a business: Efficiency and cost/benefit focuses will become more important. Private judging, arbitration, and mediation will increasingly compete with public-run courts for faster and fairer dispute resolution.

2. Death of the adversary system: The adversary system is slow, costly, and fraught with "unfairness." New, less confrontational, more humanistic ways to resolve disputes will arise, buttressed by the increase in technology.

3. The vast majority of judicial decision making (in such grass-roots areas as small claims, traffic, and status offenses) will be by nonlawyer, citizen pro-tempore judges. The need for quick decisions will lead more and more to this system for cases requiring little legal knowledge or training.

4. Courts will be depoliticized. Appointed professional managers will become the norm, and merit selection of judges will become more commonplace.

5. Technology will allow quick, easy synthesis of information and data for judicial decision making. This will provide a "quicker path to decision" and greater efficiency.

6. Courts will increasingly be called upon to resolve social problems involving drugs, poverty, and domestic violence—with little success.

7. Court programs will become increasingly decentralized. As courts become more service oriented, court programs will move closer to client groups.

8. Court organization structures will become more informal, with less reliance on hierarchical, bureaucratic structures, and shared leadership.[12]

✧ SUGGESTIONS FOR REFORM

Suggestions for reform in the federal courts include adding additional judges to handle the increasing federal calendars, geographic alignment to balance the court caseloads, delegating court management to professional managers, and diverting certain cases for arbitration. However, a major problem that permeates all of these reforms is the decentralized nature of the federal judiciary.[13]

At the state court level, three major administrative reforms have been recommended by such groups as the American Bar Association and the American Judicature Society, all of which come under the heading of "court unification": structural unification, administrative centralization, and unified budgeting. *Structural unification* involves consolidating and simplifying existing trial courts and forming a single superior court on a countywide basis; lower courts cease to exist. *Administrative centralization* would place statewide authority for court policy and administration in the supreme court or judicial council, with overall governance placed with the chief justice of the highest court or a chief administrative judge. Such an organization "provides the state's highest court with the power to make rules, appoint managerial personnel, assign judges nonjudicial staff, and prepare and execute a centralized, state-financed yearly budget."[14] Under this system, a high degree of uniformity is achieved; judges can also be moved across counties on temporary assignments to reduce case backlogs.

Opponents of unification and centralization argue that such changes would lead to a large central bureaucracy which would be insensitive to local concerns; rigidity would be substituted for individual justice.[15] *Unified budgeting* "means that the budget for the court system is prepared at the state level, regardless of the source of funds, and that the executive branch does not have the authority to modify the budget request" since this would encroach upon the separation of powers.[16]

✧ HOW TO APPROACH REFORM

In an excellent book entitled *Court Reform on Trial*,[17] in which he examined reform with bail, pretrial diversion, sentence reform, and speedy trial rules, Malcolm Feeley provided several stages in the planned-change process for the courts; succinctly, they are: (1) diagnosis or conception (identifying problems and solutions); (2) initiation (new functions added or practices significantly altered); (3) implementation (staffing, clarifying goals, adapting to a new environment); (4) routinization (commitment to supply funding and a physical base of operations); and (5) evaluation (assessment should take place during the first three stages).[18]

The courts, Feeley wrote, while staffed with trained professionals, are also enmeshed in a web of rules that can often be inimical to change. Because of rigid segmentation, broad perspectives and systemwide thinking are discouraged and innovation is stifled.[19] Segmentation in the adversary process inhibits communication, feeds distrust, and breeds antagonism. Finally, because of the large numbers of cases that courts must handle, courts are forced to emphasize efficiency; the greater this emphasis, the more likely that program change will be discouraged. When change *is* initiated, it often cannot be implemented. Because attempts to change encounter at least some of these problems, the successes are few and far between.[20] Feeley concluded that "The courts do face real problems—and problems that have not been taken seriously enough. The question is: Can proponents of planned change adequately identify these problems, diagnose them accurately, and make improvements?"[21]

◆ THE FUTURE AND CORRECTIONS

✧ CONTINUING THE "BOOM INDUSTRY"

Probably nowhere in the justice system is forecasting for the future more difficult and dismal than in corrections. The most ominous problems for the future of corrections will continue to be those we have concentrated upon already and which are the most difficult to predict—crowding and its related costs.

Attempts were made in the mid-1980s to estimate future state prison populations, using a mathematical model that extrapolated crime, incarceration, and demographic patterns to the year 2020. The conclusion was that prison populations would continue to rise into the early 1990s, and then that the "birth dearth" that followed World War II would begin to affect prison admissions, and the number of persons behind bars would decline slightly for about a decade. Around the turn of the century, levels were predicted to rise again and continue upward through 2020.[22]

However, reality has a way of outstripping forecasts and mathematical models, especially in corrections. One estimate was that by 2020, prison populations would grow between 20 and 25 percent over 1983 levels. But between 1983 and 1986 alone, those populations grew 30 percent.[23] The projections fell short partly because the forecasters could not anticipate changes in sentencing policy and partly because they did not capture adequately the subtle and possibly changing interactions among age, race, crime, and criminal justice processing. For example, the baby boom never really stopped in the black and Hispanic communities, and these groups will constitute an increasingly large proportion of the young male cohort in the coming decades. Because young black and Hispanic men have higher arrest and incarceration rates than whites, and because there is some evidence that those rates are increasing, the slowdown in prison populations that has been forecast may not come to pass.[24]

Even more ominous is the prediction by corrections author and futurist Douglas McDonald that the U.S. prison population might double again in the next 10 years. The current rates of growth are pointing in that direction. If the prison population doubles, governments will rapidly have to construct as many cells as now exist to handle the demand, as well as replacing currently substandard facilities. The cost of this construction, based on a projected average of $51,000 per bed, will be approximately $26 billion in constant 1986 dollars. Jail populations have also been rising quickly and could also double in the next 10 years if past trends continue. Assuming an average construction cost of nearly $49,000 per bed, doubling the size of America's jail capacity would cost approximately $12 billion.[25]

Pains will be more severe in those states having high incarceration rates, few alternative-to-incarceration programming planned, and higher levels of poverty (with, by extension, weaker tax bases). Most states in the south are so characterized. Local governments maintaining jails will fare even worse than state governments, because their revenue bases are narrower.[26]

Another concern today is with correctional administrators being able to "find their way." As one corrections worker observed, "Correctional administrators...tend to face inward toward their organizations...and are little in touch with the outside world...and seem to be isolated from organized efforts to advance and refine general understanding of administration, especially public administration."[27] And as Alvin Cohn noted:

> Unfortunately, many correctional managers have learned that [their bosses have] as a motto, "Let sleeping dogs lie." More unfortunately, they have learned that "barking" or "attacking" dogs generally will not survive. This is not to argue that there cannot be change; we know that change is inevitable. The question is whether an executive chooses to be reactive or proactive...will simply ride the currents of change...or deliberately attempt to harness and control change. The former is crisis management, the latter is the kind of manager we should be training to assume mantles of leadership.[28]

✦ PRISONS: TO REFORM OR NOT TO REFORM

Given the extent of corrections' responsibility and problems throughout its history, it is not surprising that many people have called for its reform. The story of penal reform in the United States is an old and discouraging one. From the development of the penitentiary in the late eighteenth and early nineteenth centuries, to the determinate sentencing movement of the last two decades, penal "reforms" in this country have led to few real improvements in the practice of punishment. Even if the reforms alleviated old problems, in so doing they often created new ones, requiring new reforms, which led to further problems, and so on.[29] However, now that we are ending the current reform cycle, that of determinate sentencing, it is timely and perhaps even necessary to consider why reforms fail, and whether or not anything will work. According to Samuel Pillsbury, "Reform begins with the proposal of a scheme for penal improvement. In most instances it is suggested by an idealist who links the proposed penal reform to a view of the ideal society prominent at the time. The idealist promotes a penal ideology which emphasizes the rightness or goodness of the proposed change in terms of society's relation to the offender."[30]

George Bernard Shaw warned against penal reform more than a half century ago. He urged the following upon persons interested in pursuing penal reform for benevolent purposes: "To put it down and go about some other business. It is just such reformers who have in the past made the neglect, oppression, corruption, and physical torture of the common gaol the pretext for transforming it into that diabolical den of torment, mischief, and damnation, the modern prison.[31]

There are many who have sought, both from within the system as well as from without, to make prisons better places. Internally initiated reform has from time to time involved inmate rioting; although this method is not the most effective tool for the expression of inmate grievances, it has focused attention on prison problems and helped pave the way for inmate councils, grievance procedures, conflict resolution, and the position of ombudsman. Changing the internal administration is another means of attempting internal reform. An example was Arkansas Governor Winthrop Rockefeller's hiring in the 1960s of Tom Murton to administer a prison system that had become corrupted and even lethal (Murton unearthed a number of scandals and even human skeletons at the prison). This attempt at reform was made famous by the 1980 movie "Brubaker," starring Robert Redford.

Murton was quite critical during his tenure, referring to the "facade of reform" and saying that the "reform of penal practices has often appeared to follow the motto, 'Do something, even if it proves to be wrong'."[32] He added that "the reformer long ago came to realize that chief executives, prison boards, prison staffs, and most inmates are not willing to risk the consequences of seeking real reform."[33]

Normally, internally initiated reform by the staff is short-lived; either the old routine returns or the reforms settle into a new but equally sterile routine. Unless real reform occurs at all levels, there is little incentive for initiating new programs. The most lasting reforms appear to be those that have been initiated by external sources or with the knowledge and support of the outside community and public leaders.[34]

At the state level, externally induced reform is usually brought by legislative or executive action. A state's criminal code may be revised, allowing such benefits as educational and home furloughs. The executive branch of government can enact executive orders. At the federal level, the most active reformer has been the U.S. Supreme Court. A number of major court decisions have affected prisoners' rights. External pressure is also brought to bear by private organizations, such as the John Howard Association, the American Correctional Association, and the National Council on Crime and Delinquency. All seek reform through prison certification visits and suggestions to correctional administrators. Organizations of ex-offenders who work with prisoners, such as the Seventh Step Foundation, Man-to-Man, and the Fortune Society, also seek correctional reform.[35]

An official of the California school system provided some food for thought for simple prison reform, saying:

> You want to know where prison reform starts? I'll tell you. It's the third grade. We know the high risk groups who will drop out of school. We know individuals from these groups make up a disproportionate share of prison inmates. Give me part of the $20,000 a year we now spend on these kids as adults [in prison], give it to me now, and we can make sure they won't wind up in prison, costing the state money not only to lock them up, but for the crimes they've committed, and for the welfare payments if they have a family.[36]

According to prison expert John DiIulio, Jr., three steps could be taken by prison officials to help create better prisons in the short and long terms:

1. Provide continuity in the commissioner's office (and, it should be added, in the warden's office; both have an average tenure that is often less than five years). The current situation of high turnover for the past 15 years fosters a power vacuum at many levels of management.
2. Adopt the practice of unit management (the concept described earlier in this chapter) as a means of reducing prison violence. In addition to its potential for calming the institution and its residents, there are fewer staff rotations, allowing management to measure performance better. Officers are given more authority, act more as professionals, and morale is boosted.
3. Allow products manufactured by inmates in state prisons to be sold to the federal government. This would eliminate the presently endless hours of idleness for inmates. The federal system has a large and ready market for its products.[37]

✦ BUILDING MORE PRISONS: LARGE, SMALL, OR NONE AT ALL?

No issue has brought criminal justice more to the forefront of public policy—and into the living rooms of America—than that of corrections cost. In fact, state spending for corrections throughout the nation grew by more than 50 percent during the 1980s—the greatest increase of any state-funded service.[38] Furthermore, from 1975 to 1985, the cost of operating corrections in the country rose by nearly 240 percent.[39] Americans now spend $13 billion each year to confine adult offenders.

Legal reforms have expanded the use of determinate and mandatory sentences and thus enlarged the correctional population. With the current annual cost of incarceration running as high as $50,000 per inmate, there is increasing concern over the cost of incarcerating such large numbers of offenders and crowding in general. As a result, a variety of proposals have surfaced to cope with the problem of population and save money. One purported cost-saving mechanism is privatization, discussed earlier in this chapter. Others include marginally credible ideas ranging from that of a New York City mayor, to make use of old tugboats to hold prisoners,[40] to politically volatile solutions such as early-release programs,[41] to electronic surveillance home-detention programs.

Although it is clear that the concern among legislators, correctional administrators, and the public over the cost of corrections is justified, the public is sending mixed messages. For example, legislative changes to penal codes in the late 1980s, in the form of mandatory prison terms for drunk drivers and for those who commit gun crimes, as well as calls for the abolition of parole boards, seemed to indicate a popular sentiment for more prison space. More recently, however, the public seems to be gradually reversing itself, balking at the prospect of spending $30 to 50 million every few years to construct a new prison for housing offenders (especially when schools, highways, health care, and social services are suffering). Thus we now see a movement beginning toward early release and other types of programs designed to reduce the overload and divert offenders away from incarceration.

Douglas McDonald determined that larger prisons were less expensive on a per-prisoner basis than smaller ones. In addition, the average per-capita cost of operating maximum-security prisons was lower than the cost of minimum-security camps, which in turn were less expensive than medium-security facilities. These cost differences resulted largely from variations in the way each type of facility was staffed. Maximum-security prisons were larger, on average, and had fewer staff persons per inmate than other facilities. "*As the staff/inmate ratio increased, so did cost.*" [emphasis his].[42]

All is not gloom and doom in the area of corrections costs, however. Construction and financing costs can make building prisons seem overwhelmingly expensive. However, according to the National Institute of Justice (NIJ), when these charges are amortized over the useful life of a facility, they become quite modest. But the NIJ also noted that there are other unintended costs of imprisonment for a community. Imprisonment of breadwinners may force their families into welfare dependency. There are other variables as well. For example, if an inmate was unemployed at the time of imprisonment, the state would actually gain by paying less unemployment compensation.[43]

One estimate is that society lost an average of $408 in taxes and $84 in welfare payments per year of imprisonment. Assuming a total social loss of $5000 per year, the NIJ concluded that a year in prison implies confinement costs of roughly $20,000, for a total social cost of about $25,000. Carrying this analysis a bit further and adding new twist, by combining crime costs and offense rates, NIJ found that a typical inmate (found in a survey to commit 187 crimes per year) is responsible for $430,000 in crime costs. Sentencing 1000 more offenders to prison would obligate correctional systems to an additional $25 million per year, but about 187,000 felonies would be averted in the process of incapacitation. *These crimes represent about $430 million in social costs* [emphasis theirs].[44]

In addition to being sensitive to the high cost of imprisonment and the political sensitivity of this issue, correctional administrators must be adept at determining the best approach to keeping abreast with the structural needs of their criminal population. Timing can be a hidden, yet important variable, as the public is not always amenable to new, normally expensive construction proposals. Also, legislative enactments (such as those concerning mandatory sentencing or early-release proposals) also weigh into the prison construction decision. Alternatives to imprisonment (such as those discussed in Chapter 12) must also be considered.

✦ CAN ADMINISTRATORS "REINVENT" CRIMINAL JUSTICE?

✧ CASTING OFF OLD WAYS

Reinventing Government, the book that recently swept the country and was on the bookshelves of many governors, city managers, and criminal justice administrators, provided ideas about how government can and should work as efficiently and productively as the best-run private businesses. It uses myriad examples of government agencies that have slashed red tape, begun focusing on the "customer," cut costs tremendously, revamped the budget-expenditure process to provide incentives for saving money, abandoned archaic civil-service systems, decentralized authority, and empowered their employees. It showed how these agencies can become more entrepreneurial and "steer" rather than "row," be driven by missions rather than by rules, encourage competition over monopoly, and invest in prevention rather than cure. Generally —and the reason for the book's widespread popularity—it demonstrated what can be accomplished when government leaders decided to "break the mold" and try new methods.

The authors of *Reinventing Government,* David Osborne and Ted Gaebler, went beyond the five principles of total quality management, espoused by W. Edwards Deming in 1950, which focused on results, customers, decentralization, prevention, and a market (or systems) approach. Osborne and Gaebler found that most entrepreneurial governments focused on promoting *competition* between service providers; they *empower* citizens by pushing control out of the bureaucracy and into the community; and they measure the performance of their agencies, focusing not on inputs but on *outcomes*. They are driven by their goals—their *missions*—rather than by rules and regulations. They redefine their clients as *customers* and offer them choices—between levels of involvement, training programs, and so on. They *prevent* problems before they emerge, rather than simply offering services afterward. They *decentralize* authority, embracing participatory management. They prefer *market* mechanisms to bureaucratic mechanisms. And they focus not simply on providing public services, but on *catalyzing* all sectors—public, private, and voluntary— into action to solve their community's problems.[45]

✧ SOME SUCCESS STORIES

Can some or all of these principles be applied in criminal justice agencies? Indeed, several principles are at the very heart of community-oriented policing problem solving, discussed in Chapter 4. Perhaps a closer look at some justice-related examples will demonstrate how many of the Osborne and Gaebler principles can be implemented when administrators become determined to "reinvent" their organizations.

◊ The Visalia, California, Police Department pioneered a lease-purchase program for squad cars which allowed the city to cut its energy consumption by 30 percent. In a few years, the department had saved $20 million in cash, almost its entire operating budget.[46]

◊ In Tulsa, Oklahoma, police studied arrest trends, school dropout statistics, drug treatment data, and the problems of the city's public housing developments. They concluded that teenagers from one section of town were creating most of the city's drug problems, so they began working with the community to attack the problem. They organized residents and together prosecuted and evicted residents who were dealing, they created an antidrug education program in the projects and established job placement and mentoring programs, they set up a youth camp for teenagers, and they worked with the schools to develop an antitruancy program.[47]

◊ Sunnyvale, California, developed performance measures for all municipal departments, defining the results it wanted. In each program area, the city articulated a set of "goals," a set of "community condition indicators," a set of "objectives," and a set of "performance indicators." Objectives set the specific targets for each unit of city government. For example, in public safety, one objective was to keep the city "within the lowest 25 percent of Part I crimes for cities of comparable size, at a cost of $74.37 per capita."[48]

◊ Many police agencies now survey their communities—victims, witnesses, even offenders—regarding agency performance and ways to generate revenue. The Madison, Wisconsin, Police Department mailed surveys to every thirty-fifth person it encountered. It asked citizens to rate the police on seven factors: concern, helpfulness, fairness, knowledge, quality of service, professional conduct, how well they solved the problem, and whether they put the person at ease.[49]

◊ The St. Louis County Police Department developed a system that allows officers to call in their reports; the department licensed the software to a private company and earns $25,000 each time the package is sold to another department.[50]

◊ Paulding County, Georgia, built a 244-bed jail when it needed only 60 extra beds, so that it could charge other jurisdictions $35 a night to handle their overflow. In the first year of business, the jail brought in $1.4 million, $200,000 more than its operating costs.[51]

◊ Some enterprising police departments in California are earning money renting out motel rooms as weekend jails. They reserve blocks of rooms at cheap motels, pay someone to sit outside to ensure that inmates stay in their rooms, and rent the rooms to convicted drunk drivers at $75 a night.[52]

✧ A Shift in Governance

These examples clearly demonstrate what can happen when administrators begin thinking like entrepreneurs rather than strict bureaucrats. Unfortunately, the great majority of our federal, state, and local government agencies do not so operate. They reward failure and enhance bureaucracies rather than creating incentives to save money or serve customers. When the crime rates increase, justice agencies are given more money; if they continue to fail, they are given even more. As police departments professionalized, they began focusing on chasing crooks, not on solving community problems. This approach encourages agencies to ignore the root causes of crime, simply continue chasing criminals, and not consider possible solutions to problems.

What Osborne and Gaebler call for is nothing less than a shift in the basic model of governance used in America—a shift that is already under way, doubtless largely because of the recent recession and demands on government agencies to "do more with less." It is now essential that justice administrators engage in strategic planning, looking beyond tomorrow and anticipating the future. Some police administrators began coping with recent revenue shortfalls in some new and unique—if not always popular—ways: charging fees for traditionally free public services, such as accident investigations, unlocking vehicles, and response to false alarms.

It will become increasingly important for justice administrators to think of such revenue-enhancing possibilities and ways to save money. They must also listen more to one of their greatest resources—the rank and file—although a revamped or "inverted" pyramidal organization structure may be necessary for accomplishing this goal. Greater collaboration with the public is also needed; the police must insist that private citizens, institutions, and organizations within their communities shoulder greater responsibility for assisting in crime control. Some examples of excellent collaborative efforts are D.A.R.E., M.A.D.D., Neighborhood Watch, and Court Watch.

In sum, justice administrators and society must rethink its approach to crime. They must play a catalytic role, not just reduce services or, as in the past, throw more money and personnel at ongoing problems. They must steer rather than row, with a clear map in hand. In short, they need a new vision of government.

✦ COMPUTER APPLICATIONS IN CRIMINAL JUSTICE

✧ An Information Technology Revolution

Advances in computer technology have revolutionized many concepts of organizational management, altered the value of information, and affected the flow of information within organizations. Computer technology has changed our society, the processes of government, and the disposition of justice itself. We are witnessing an "information technology revolution."[53]

When a police officer investigates a crime, a probation officer prepares a presentence report, a court schedules a case for trial, a victim calls the district attorney's office to learn the status of his case, or a parole board tracks an inmate's parole eligibility date, information is collected, analyzed, and stored for future use. Criminal justice agencies use many different types of files, including those of criminal information, case investigation, budgets, and personnel.

Computers also allow justice administrators to engage in *planning* at a level never before possible. As shown earlier in this chapter, strategic planning and forecasting are essential for developing and implementing policy within the limitations of present knowledge and decision making within political and economic realities.[54] Data bases that contain information specifically used by management in decision making (planning, budgeting, fiscal, personnel management, or inventory control information) are called *management information systems* (MISs). Data bases that are used in agency operations (investigations, crime trend analysis, social history information, and arrest information) are called *operations data bases* (ODB).[55]

Mainframe computer systems are designed to store, retrieve, manipulate, and analyze massive amounts of information. There are three mainframe data bases in criminal justice: (1) the National Criminal Justice Information Center (NCIC), which contains detailed arrest and intelligence information on known and wanted offenders; (2) the *Uniform Crime Reports* (UCR), published annually by the FBI, which compiles, summarizes, and reports national crime data on a quarterly and annual basis; and (3) the *Sourcebook of Criminal Justice Statistics*, published by the federal Bureau of Justice Statistics, U.S. Department of Justice, which publishes a comprehensive summary of justice activities across the country. Mainframe data-based management systems are also used extensively in criminal justice at all levels of government in functions ranging from psychological profiles of terrorists and kidnappers to automobile registration and construct descriptions and sketches of criminal subjects. Computers are also used as investigative tools in crime laboratories across the country.[56]

✧ HARNESSING COMPUTERS IN JUSTICE AGENCIES

Courts use computers not only to schedule cases but also to monitor jail populations and ensure that prisoners scheduled for court appearances are brought to court on time. In San Diego, police use computers as memory banks for storing nicknames, scars and marks, and field investigations. In Dallas, the court uses a mainframe computer to issue subpoenas and summonses. Patrol cars in many jurisdictions come equipped with computers, linking officers with NCIC and other crime bases and allowing them to do reports in the field. Corrections agencies are able to use computers to manage inmate records, conduct presentence investigation, supervise offenders in the community, provide instruction to inmates, and train correctional personnel. Jail administrators, with computer assistance, receive daily reports on court schedules, inmate rosters, time served, statistical reports, maintenance costs, and other data.[57]

The fiscal savings and overall accomplishments provided by microcomputers and mainframes is considerable. The St. Louis, Missouri, Police Department experienced a 53 percent reduction in time spent by investigators in writing and typing reports. San Diego's computerized investigations systems resulted in over 3000 arrests. In St. Petersburg, all emergency dispatching is computerized. In Chicago, computers coordinate field command communications. In Baton Rouge, drug investigators search out abusers and unethical doctors from among mountains of pharmaceutical prescriptions. Many police agencies use computer-aided instruction to train police officers. In Dallas, courts use computers to transmit subpoenas via electronic mail.[58]

Clearly, criminal justice students as well as in-service practitioners need to become knowledgeable in basic computer operation. As strongly indicated earlier in this chapter, the future holds far greater growth and development in our information-processing society. Several questions and issues attend this development, however. Will justice agencies become overly dependent on computers? Will personnel forget how to write reports? Does efficiency and productivity mean a fairer justice system? Does computerization actually save time and eliminate unnecessary paperwork?

Administrators must be certain that the advent of high technology does not become a bane to their mission. Nonetheless, it is certain that "the future is now" in this regard.

✦ AIDS AND RELATED PROBLEMS

Doomsayers predicted that the effect of AIDS on criminal justice would be calamitous, that the system's "clients" infected with the virus would be innumerable, and that those who deal directly most closely with them—police, correctional, and probation and parole officers—would become infected. They predicted that prison hospitals would overflow with junkies, homosexual rapists, and cellblock "queens."[59] Fortunately, this grievous scenario has not yet not come to pass. In fact, in 1987 it was recently reported that "there is no evidence of police officers, paramedics, correctional officers, or firefighter contracting HIV-infection through performance of their duties.[60] Unfortunately, however, that is not the case today.

The offender population contains a substantial number of people at high risk for contracting the disease, primarily drug abusers. In addition, offenders are most prevalent in the 20 to 39 age category. Hence there is a strong likelihood that police and corrections personnel will interact professionally with persons who are HIV antibody positive or with AIDS.[61] Table 17.1 presents AIDS training information that is being provided by the U.S. Department of Justice to all criminal justice personnel.

TABLE 17.1 EDUCATIONAL AND ACTION MESSAGES FOR AIDS-RELATED TRAINING OF LAW ENFORCEMENT AND CRIMINAL JUSTICE PERSONNEL

Issue/Concern	Educational and Action Messages
Human bites	◊ The person who bites is typically exposed to the victim's blood rather than the reverse; therefore, the victim is at extremely low risk for HIV infection.
	◊ HIV transmission through saliva is highly unlikely because the virus has been isolated only in extremely low concentrations in saliva.
	◊ If bitten by a person who has tested seropositive, one should allow the wound to bleed, wash the area thoroughly, and seek medical attention.
Spitting	◊ Viral transmission through saliva is highly unlikely.
	◊ CDC no longer recommends "universal precautions" for saliva.
Urine/feces	◊ HIV has been isolated only in very low concentrations in urine and not at all in feces.
	◊ There have been no cases of AIDS or HIV infection associated with either urine or feces.
	◊ CDC no longer recommends "universal precautions" for urine or feces.
Cuts/puncture wounds	◊ Use caution in handling sharp objects and searching areas hidden from view.
	◊ Needle-stick studies show that the risk of infection is very low.
CPR/first aid	◊ Use masks/airways to eliminate the minimal risk of HIV transmission associated with CPR.
	◊ Avoid blood-to-blood contact by keeping wounds covered and wearing gloves when in contact with bleeding wounds.
Body removal	◊ Observe the crime scene rule: Do not touch anything.
	◊ Those who must come into contact with blood or other body fluids contaminated with visible blood should wear gloves in accordance with official policy and CDC guidelines.
Casual contact	◊ No cases of AIDS or HIV infection are attributed to casual contact.
Contact with blood or body fluids	◊ Wear gloves if contact with blood, semen, or body fluids containing visible blood is likely.
	◊ If contact occurs, wash thoroughly with soap and water; clean spills with 1:10 solution of household bleach and water.
Contact with dried blood	◊ The drying process inactivates the virus. Laboratory studies showing persistence of AIDS virus for 3 days in dried samples used viral preparation 100,000 more concentrated than that found in normal blood samples.

Source: U.S. Department of Justice, National Institute of Justice, *AIDS and HIV Training and Education in Criminal Justice Agencies* (Washington, D.C.: Author, 1989), p. 3.

✦ THE POLICE: HANDLING INFECTED PERSONS AND EVIDENCE

Today's investigators and crime scene technicians are more likely than ever before to encounter crimes of violence involving blood and other body fluids of persons with infectious diseases. Police officers and laboratory personnel are cautioned to protect their hands against infection at crime and accident scenes, keeping them clean and away from the eyes, mouth, and nose. They should wear disposable gloves, and any person with a cut or other break on the skin should not handle blood or other body fluids.

Police officers deal with a variety of body fluids; they often come in contact with blood, saliva, and urine. Today, giving cardiopulmonary resuscitation can have lethal consequences. Even the mouthpieces used on breath alcohol instruments can be contaminated with the saliva of a person with a communicable disease. Searching suspected drug users can result in lethal puncture wounds from hidden hypodermic needles.[62]

✦ AIDS IN CORRECTIONS

Medical and legal issues surrounding AIDS have become more acute in the corrections field. Since the first AIDS-related litigation reached the federal courts in 1984, the pace of litigation has increased markedly. By 1990, there were more than 20 AIDS-related opinions rendered by federal courts, primarily involving inmates in state prisons using Section 1983. The success rate has been low, and almost all cases have been disposed of with a hearing and without a full trial.

To this point there have been (1) actions by infected inmates challenging confinement in isolated or segregated facilities, (2) actions by general population inmates seeking testing and isolation of infected inmates, and (3) actions by seriously ill prisoners (or their families) seeking damages from inadequate care by institutional medical personnel.[63]

Regarding cases challenging the confinement or segregation of infected inmates, almost every lawsuit has been decided in favor of the prison systems and their administrators (and without a full trial). Courts have not found any rights that are infringed by their isolation, as long as the decision to isolate is made in good faith and is rationally related to the goals of disease diagnosis, treatment, and control. With respect to litigation out of administration's failure to segregate infected prisoners, the courts have generally held that inmates failed to show that the absence of segregation created a risk of contracting AIDS so great as to implicate constitutional rights. Interestingly, one successful case in Alabama involved inmates joining forces with the prison administration to defend the testing and segregation of infected inmates.

In the final area, lawsuits by infected inmates alleging inadequate medical care, the inmates have received no satisfaction. The courts have not found "deliberate indifference" or violation of constitutional rights in denying access to private physicians and experimental drugs. However, where the disease has been misdiagnosed or mistreated, the courts have upheld claims against the state.[64]

Challenges of mandatory AIDS testing policies and legislation have also not met with success in federal courts. Courts have felt that no First or Fourteenth Amendment rights are violated, and that the goal of preventing the spread of the disease outweighed expectations of prisoner privacy. Federal courts have also tended to uphold institutional policies or actions limiting participation in work and rehabilitation programs by HIV-positive inmates. The one area where the courts have tended to side with inmates involves the casual disclosure of HIV-positive status to persons not in a medical "need-to-know" position. Such disclosure, carrying negative connotations as to deviancy, is not within the discretionary function of prison administration or staff.[65]

Some infected inmates have attempted to infect others through biting attacks. In a Minnesota case, the federal court held that an inmate's deliberate infliction of deep bite wounds on two federal correctional officers could give rise to criminal liability for "assault with a deadly weapon or dangerous weapon."[66] Understandably, a recent survey of probation personnel found a considerable amount of alarm among those workers, with 93 percent of the respondents rating AIDS as a "somewhat" or "very important" issue for their occupation. Another 83 percent reported that they would feel "somewhat uncomfortable" supervising a confirmed or suspected HIV-positive offender, and 20 percent stated they would be "very uncomfortable."[67]

In summary, correctional administrators face difficult decisions concerning prevention, housing, and the provision of medical care. They must formulate policies allowing them to manage their organizations effectively while dealing with a serious health problem that may cause fears among staff and clients. Major policy areas include education and training; antibody testing; and medical, legal, and correctional management issues.[68]

Summary

Can anyone now believe that the years ahead are likely to be tranquil? Does anyone think we can afford to "hurtle into the future with our eyes fixed firmly on the rear-view mirror?"[69] In truth, we are moving into some of the most turbulent years in the history of this nation. This turbulence will put enormous strains on our criminal justice system. We are witnessing the "overhaul" of America and can no longer afford to wait until there are problems and new challenges to take action. Administrators must anticipate what is coming down the road and plan for it.

In addition to problems involving the economy, personnel, demographics, narcotics and high-tech crimes, AIDS, and others mentioned above, we now face the growing specter of terrorism (witness the World Trade Center explosion in March 1993). An often overlooked element of society—the Supreme Court—could also change the way in which law enforcement operates. A more liberal Supreme Court could change the rights of employees and criminals alike.

In closing, not all innovation is simple. The strongest obstacles to change for any organization is probably that which is within—its own resistance. For criminal justice organizations to implement innovation successfully, administrators and their staffs must have an abiding commitment to change and must motivate personnel for supporting innovations. Many people will prefer to cling to the old methods and must be brought along with the new methods of thinking and operation. Criminal justice agencies, often reactive in nature, must become more proactive. The administrator who neglects the real, and the opportunity to "peer over the rim," may awaken one day in the future to find that time has passed by the organization, and in a cruel fashion indeed.

Americans—customers—who want the best criminal justice service that is humanly possible must challenge their justice system to do all that is possible to assess what the future will bring in *local* terms, and then determine what they are going to do about it. Americans deserve the best analytical efforts, the most imaginative solutions, and the sincerest problem-solving abilities that justice administrators can provide as we head into the turbulent twenty-first century.

Questions for Review

1. Discuss the primary methods for justice administrators to use for predicting the future.
2. What are some of the country's major demographic changes on the horizon? Which of them is/are most significant for criminal justice?
3. What does the future hold concerning crime? What criminal justice technology will be developed? How must justice agencies adapt to change?
4. What are some reasons put forth to justify future court and corrections reform? How might such reform be accomplished, and what are some obstacles and approaches to reform?
5. Is new construction of correctional institutions cost-effective? Why or why not? Provide political, economic, and social perspectives in your response.
6. Discuss specific means by which government—and justice administrators in particular—can "reinvent" their operations, and reasons why many people feel they must do so.
7. How has computer technology changed criminal justice? In what ways will it continue to change justice administration in the future?
8. What are some of the ways that AIDS has changed criminal justice and its operations? What must criminal justice administrators do to assist their employees to avoid contamination?

For Further Reading

GEORGE F. COLE, *The American System of Criminal Justice* (6th ed.). Pacific Grove, Calif.: Brooks/Cole, 1992.

JOHN NAIBSITT, *Megatrends.* New York: Warner Books, 1982.

R. M. STEERS, *Organizational Effectiveness: A Behavioral View.* Santa Monica, Calif.: Goodyear, 1977.

GENE STEPHENS, *The Future of Criminal Justice.* Cincinnati, Ohio: Anderson, 1982.

Notes

1. Kenneth J. Peak, *Policing America: Methods, Issues, Challenges* (Englewood Cliffs, N.J.: Regents/Prentice Hall, 1993), p. 419.
2. *Ibid.*
3. *Ibid.*, p. 423.
4. *Ibid.*
5. *Ibid.*
6. *Ibid.*, pp. 424–425.
7. Rob McCord and Elaine Wicker, "Tomorrow's America: Law Enforcement's Coming Challenge," *FBI Law Enforcement Bulletin* 59 (January 1990):31.
8. Edward A. Thibault, "Proactive Police Futures," in Gene Stephens (ed.), *The Future of Criminal Justice* (Cincinnati, Ohio: Anderson, 1982), pp. 67–85.
9. Ibid., pp. 73–77.
10. Clyde L. Cronkhite, "21st Century Cop," *The National Centurion* (April 1984):26–29, 47–48.
11. Quoted in James A. Dator and Sharon J. Rodgers, *Alternatives for the State Courts of 2020* (Chicago: American Judicature Society, 1991), p. ix.
12. Clement Bezold, "On Futures Thinking and the Courts," *The Court Manager* 6 (Summer 1991):4–11.
13. J. Woolford Howard, Jr., *Courts of Appeal: A Study of the Second, Fifth, and District of Columbia Circuits* (Princeton, N.J.: Princeton University Press, 1981).
14. Ronald Stout, "Planning for Unified Court Budgeting," *Judicature* 69 (December/January 1986):206.
15. Thomas A. Henderson, Cornelius M. Kerwin, Randall Guynes, Carl Baar, Neal Miller, Hildy Saizow, and Robert Grieser, *The Significance of Judicial Structure: The Effect of Unification on Trial Court Operations* (Washington, D.C.: U.S. Government Printing Office, 1984), p. 5.
16. Ronald Stout, "Planning for Unified Court Budgeting," p. 206.
17. Malcolm Feeley, *Court Reform on Trial* (New York: Basic Books, 1983).
18. *Ibid.*, pp. 35–37.
19. For a thorough discussion of this subject, see Jerald Hage and Michael Aiken, *Social Change in Complex Organizations* (New York: Random House, 1970).
20. Malcolm Feeley, *Court Reform on Trial*, pp. 38–39.
21. *Ibid.*, p. 32.

22. Thomas F. Rich and Arnold I. Barnett, "Model-Based U.S. Prison Population Projections," *Public Administration Review* 45 (November 1985):780–789.

23. U.S. Department of Justice, Bureau of Justice Statistics Bulletin, *Prisoners in 1985* (Washington, D.C.: Author, 1986), p. 1.

24. Douglas C. McDonald, "The Cost of Corrections: In Search of the Bottom Line," in Joan Petersilia (ed.), *Research in Corrections* (U.S. Department of Justice, National Institute of Corrections) 2 (February 1989):1–25.

25. *Ibid.*, p. 23.

26. *Ibid.*, pp. 23–24.

27. R. Sanfilippo, *Management Development: Key to Increased Correctional Effectiveness* (Washington, D.C.: Joint Commission on Correctional Manpower and Training, n.d.):5.

28. Alvin W. Cohn, "The Failure of Correctional Management Reviewed: Present and Future Dimensions," *Federal Probation* 56 (June 1991):12–16.

29. Samuel H. Pillsbury, "Understanding Penal Reform: The Dynamic of Change," *The Journal of Criminal Law and Criminology* 80 (1989):726–780.

30. Ibid., pp. 726–727.

31. George Bernard Shaw, *The Crime of Imprisonment* 13 (1922).

32. Tom Murton and Joe Hyans, *Accomplices to the Crime: The Arkansas Prison Scandal* (New York: Grove Press, 1967); Thomas O. Murton, *The Dilemma of Prison Reform* (New York: Holt, Rinehart and Winston, 1976), p. xii.

33. *Ibid.*, p. 89.

34. Harry E. Allen and Clifford E. Simonsen, *Corrections in America: An Introduction* (5th ed.) (New York: Macmillan, 1989), p. 66.

35. *Ibid.*, p. 71.

36. Quoted in Jim Bencivenga, "State Prisons: Crucibles for Justice," *The Christian Science Monitor* (July 28, 1988):14–15.

37. Quoted in *Ibid.*

38. National Institute of Corrections, *Research in Corrections* 2 (February 1989), Editor's Note.

39. *Ibid.*, p. 1.

40. *New York Times* (October 14, 1986).

41. *Gainesville Sun* (June 16, 1987):3B, (April 21, 1988):3B.

42. Douglas C. McDonald, "The Cost of Corrections: In Search of the Bottom Line," p. 19.

43. U.S. Department of Justice, National Institute of Justice Research in Brief, *Making Confinement Decisions* (Washington, D.C.: Author, 1987), pp. 2–3.

44. *Ibid.*, p. 4.

45. David Osborne and Ted Gaebler, *Reinventing Government: How the Entrepreneurial Spirit Is Transforming the Public Sector* (Reading, Mass.: Addison-Wesley, 1992), pp. 19–20.

46. *Ibid.*, p. 4.

47. *Ibid.*, p. 50.

48. *Ibid.*, pp. 143–144.

49. *Ibid.*, p. 173.

50. *Ibid.*, p. 197.

51. *Ibid.*, p. 197.

52. *Ibid.*, p. 197.

53. William G. Archambeault and Betty J. Archambeault, *Computers in Criminal Justice Administration and Management: Introduction to Emerging Issues and Applications* (2nd ed.) (Cincinnati, Ohio: Anderson, 1989), pp. 1, 3.

54. William G. Archambeault and Betty J. Archambeault, *Correctional Supervisory Management: Principles of Organization, Policy, and Law* (Englewood Cliffs, N.J.: Prentice Hall), p. 10.

55. William G. Archambeault and Betty J. Archambeault, *Computers in Criminal Justice Administration and Management: Introduction to Emerging Issues and Applications* (2nd ed.), p. 61.

56. *Ibid.*, p. 63.

57. *Ibid.*, pp. 63–70.

58. *Ibid.*, pp. 192–193.

59. James N. Baker, "Learning to Live with AIDS in Prison," *Newsweek* (February 13, 1989):27–28.

60. Thomas M. Hammett, Harold Jaffe, and Bruce A. Johnson, "The Cause, Transmission, and Incidence of AIDS" (Washington, D.C.: U.S. Department of Justice, National Institute of Justice, 1987), p. 2.

61. Dana Hunt, "AIDS in Probation and Parole Services: Issues and Options" (Rockville, Md.: U.S. Department of Justice, National Institute of Justice, 1988).

62. Paul D. Bigbee, "Collecting and Handling Evidence Infected with Human Disease-Causing Organisms," *FBI Law Enforcement Bulletin* 56 (July 1987):1–5.

63. Daniel L. Skoler and Richard L. Dargan, "AIDS in Prisons: Administrator Policies, Inmate Protests, and Reactions from the Federal Bench," *Federal Probation* 54 (June 1990):28.

64. *Ibid.*, pp. 28–29.

65. *Ibid.*, p. 30.

66. *United States v. Moore*, 846 F.2d 1163 (8th Cir. 1988), affirming, 669 F. Supp. 289 (D. Minn. 1987).

67. Arthur J. Lurigio, "Practitioners' Views on AIDS in Probation and Detention," *Federal Probation* 53 (December 1989):19–21.

68. U.S. Department of Justice, National Institute of Justice Research in Brief, *AIDS in Prisons and Jails: Issues and Options* (Washington, D.C.: Author, 1986), p. 1.

69. Quoted in David Osborne and Ted Gaebler, *Reinventing Government: How the Entrepreneurial Spirit Is Transforming the Public Sector*, p. 19.

Index

Traffic Records Imaging System (Los
    Angeles Municipal Court), 210
Training, 153–54
    AIDS-related, educational/action mes-
        sages for
    court administrators, 192–93
    field training officers (FTOs), 154
    jail administrators, 285
    liability/negligence, 153
    parole/probation administrators,
        302–3
    recruit academy, 154
Trait theory, 34–35
Trial delay, 213–15
    consequences of, 214–15
    courts, 213–15
    practical effects of, 228–29
    speedy trial laws, 215
Twain, Mark, 30

U

U.N. Commission on the Prevention of
    Crime and the Treatment of
    Offenders, 335
Unified budgeting, 442
Uniform Crime Reports (UCR), 451
Unionization, 125, 269, 396–99
    and corrections personnel, 398–99
    and court personnel, 399
    and the police, 397–98
Unity of command, 144–45
Upward communication, 31
U.S. Sentencing Commission, 302

V

Vanderbilt, Arthur T., 61–63
Videotape, 146–48
    use by police, 148
    use by public, 146–48
Violence and the Police (Westley), 138
Vollmer, August, 57–58

W

Walnut Street Jail (Philadelphia), 67
Wardens/superintendents, 245, 269
    and new federal sentencing guidelines,
        302
    and prison gang problem, 329
Warning shots, 139, 140
Weber, Max, 22–23
"When Probation Becomes More
    Dreaded Than Prison" (Petersilia),
    306
Why Courts Don't Work, 229
Wilbanks, William, 385, 386
Wilson, O. W., 59–60
Wolff v. McDonnell, 138, 257
Workload approach, to patrol deploy-
    ment, 129

Z

Zero-based budgeting (ZBB), 428
    as management fad, 42